THE SAILING YACHT

Plate 1: A starcut spinnaker sets well even with the wind abeam. ALYSINA *was designed as a Half Tonner, but she is also a comfortable cruising yacht. She is built in series as a Nicholson 30 by Camper & Nicholson, Gosport. Her dimensions are LOA 28 ft 10 in, beam 9 ft 9 in.*

Juan Baader

The Sailing Yacht

Translated from the German by
Inge Moore

W · W · Norton & Co · Inc

NEW YORK

First published in Spanish in Buenos Aires in 1962
under the title of *El Deporte de la Vela*
© Juan Baader 1962

German translation revised and augmented by the author
published by Verlag Delius, Klasing & Co, 1963
under the title *Segelsport-Segeltechnik-Segelyachten*
Second edition 1974
© Juan Baader 1963 and 1974

Copyright © Adlard Coles Limited 1965 and 1979
First American Edition 1979
ISBN 0 393–03220–5

Printed in Great Britain by
Fletcher & Son Ltd, Norwich

Contents

Foreword

Since the time when the first lines of the original manuscript of this book were written, fifteen years have passed. In these years the sport of yachting has undergone a rapid, even revolutionary development, from which have emerged super racing machines like the Laser dinghy, the Tempest and Soling keelboats, the Olympic Tornado catamaran and the current type of thoroughbred ocean racer.

Ocean racing has expanded tremendously, initially under RORC and CCA Rules and for some years now under the International Offshore Rule, IOR for short. The tonnage classes, which had begun to evolve earlier in a gradual way, are now dominating the ocean racing scene and have introduced an additional element of challenge to it.

Amongst the highlights of international ocean racing are the Admiral's Cup Races including the Fastnet Race, the Onion Patch Trophy with the Bermuda Race, and the Southern Cross Cup with the Sydney–Hobart Race. The Admiral's Cup Races in particular, as well as the championships in the various tonnage classes, draw world-wide participation.

Besides increasing in number and popularity, ocean races have become longer and longer – the Cape Town–Rio Race being one example – and are now extending virtually all the way round the world. As these lines are being written, the first yacht race 'round the world' is about to finish.

The Single-Handed Transatlantic Race has become a regular, highly competitive event with spectacular international support. Anyone who said that 50 to 60 feet was about the maximum length of sailing yacht that anyone could cope with single-handed had to eat his words. In the 1972 race one of the participating, and successful, yachts was over 128 feet long!

There has, of course, been rapid progress in the development of self-steering devices, which make such single-handed feats possible, and a separate chapter has been given to them in this book.

The shape of ocean racing yachts has changed dramatically. They have become more functional, with shorter overhangs, wider beam, more efficient rig and radically changed underwater profile with narrow keel and completely detached rudder aft.

Multihulls, i.e. catamarans and trimarans, have gained a following for themselves and, although capsizable, a number of them have sailed round the world and rounded Cape Horn – members of a veritable fleet of small cruising yachts circumnavigating the globe along proven routes, exploring the Polynesian Islands, sportsmen and vagabonds at one and the same time.

Another aspect of modern yachting is the constant striving towards higher speeds under sail. The astounding record for a sailing yacht – not a land or ice yacht – now stands at 54 km/h, which is almost 30 knots, logged over a distance of 500 metres.

Cotton sails have so irrevocably disappeared from the yachting scene that the younger generation is almost ignorant of them. Terylene and nylon have totally monopolized sail-making and result in extremely efficient sails. Boat hulls, as a matter of interest, are made of basically the same material as synthetic sailcloth fibre, namely polyester resin, but in the case of boats it is reinforced with glass-fibre.

During my six years in New Zealand I gained an insight into yachting in that country and found that it is more orientated towards amateur construction than anywhere else in the world. Glueing techniques, plywood construction and glass-fibre sheathing have been developed in a way which makes them accessible to everyone. Even the reinforced concrete hull, by no means new but nearly forgotten, has been raised from oblivion and given a new lease of life.

We have tried our best to include all these things in the new edition of this book without appreciably increasing its size, keeping it light and free from unnecessary ballast and hoping that a favourable planing breeze will speed it on its way . . .

Juan Baader

Written in the Yacht Club Argentino Darsena Norte, Buenos Aires, September 1974

From the First Sail to the Fast Clipper

Many thousands of years ago someone had the ingenious idea of letting the wind drive a boat. Whether it really was a boat, or perhaps a raft or a dugout, is left to historical speculation. There are no records of the early beginnings of naval architecture, or let us more modestly call it the building of vessels that would float and carry loads, because man's ability to build primitive vessels goes considerably further back in time than the art of recording human knowledge and experience.

There is a definite possibility that the first real ship which was propelled with the help of sails was built in China, but there is no proof of this. More accurate information is available about early navigation on the Nile. As early as *circa* 3000 BC the Egyptians were navigating the Nile in strong, serviceable sailing boats.

Considerably earlier, maybe around 4000 BC, an Egyptian artist painted a vessel which clearly shows a square sail set on one mast. From the raised fo'c'sle the conclusion can be drawn that the vessel thus depicted was by no means a dugout but a real, properly *built*

Fig. 1: Even today the small-boat traffic on the Nile uses the picturesque Lateen sail.

ship. There is, furthermore, in existence a clay model found in 1929, which clearly represents a vessel with mast and sail and whose age would put the beginnings of sail back by a further few thousand years.

In some parts of the world vessels are still in use today which bear such close similarity to prehistoric boats that time might have stood still. In northern Brazil, following an ancient tradition, fishermen still use the so-called *jangadas*, which are rafts made of tree-trunks. To our modern way of thinking they are incredibly primitive, having no shelter or accommodation of any kind. The fishermen, who take them far out into the Atlantic Ocean, have actually to stand in the water for most of the time. Some years ago one of these Brazilian *jangadas* sailed as far as Buenos Aires, which is all the more remarkable when one considers that the waters further south are both rougher and colder than those near the equator.

In present-day Vietnam sailing vessels are still in use whose strange shape and construction are reminiscent of boats built in biblical Babylon. Because of the shortage of home-grown timber, the hull is made of light bamboo wicker-work, covered inside and out with a glutinous mixture of powdered resin, lime and manure. Only the deck is made of wood and consequently outlives several hulls, which are renewed from time to time without much trouble or cost.

On Lake Titicaca which, at a height of 12,500 ft (4000 m) in the South American Andes between Peru and Bolivia, is the highest navigable stretch of water in the world, the Bolivian Indians still use fishing boats made of bundles of reeds. They are so like the reed rafts used on the Nile ten thousand years ago that Thor Heyerdahl had his replica built on African shores by Bolivian Indians.

The wind was only useful to the primitive sailor as long as it blew moderately and from the direction opposite to the one in which he wanted to steer his boat. Head winds, or even beam winds, were no good to him: his boat stayed anchored inshore while he waited for a favourable shift. If the wind increased to gale force, the mast was unshipped. This was easily done, since masts were frequently bi-pod (two-legged) to give them better support. It never occurred to the primitive sailor to sail in any direction except before the wind, and this is how things remained until shortly before the Christian era.

Fig. 2: Meeting of two worlds: a Hanseatic brig and a Chinese junk. When the astonished Europeans saw the junk rig for the first time, they did not by any means recognize its advantages.

With it, the Chinese had invented a true fore-and-aft rig long before anyone had made the first attempts at windward sailing with the awkward Northern square rig or the Arab lateen sail.

There are sea coasts, however, where the winds blow from the same direction for months on end and where one cannot very well wait for a wind shift. Even in those slow-moving times that would have been asking too much. A way had to be found to make use of side winds, and about 2000 years ago the lateen sail made its appearance in the Arab world. This was an innovation of astounding boldness and an important step forward in navigation. For the first time it was possible to sail to a chosen destination without being entirely dependent on the wind direction. Cautiously at first, but with growing determination, longer and longer yards were used, until they were longer than the supporting mast. The sail, which was more or less triangular, could be set at any angle to the wind. In fact, the lateen sail was an early, intuitive experiment in *aerodynamics*. If hulls had been equally highly developed, the art of sailing to windward, and even of tacking, would probably have been discovered then.

The lateen sail is characteristic of Arab vessels and the Arab sphere of influence, and as such it appeared in the Mediterranean in the seventh century. Not unexpectedly, the lateen sail was soon added to the existing square rig to make mixed rigs. When Christopher Columbus set out in 1492 to discover the sea passage to India, the two larger of his three ships, the SANTA MARIA and the PINTA, had square sails set on the

fore and main masts, and lateen sails on the mizzen. The smallest of the three, the NIÑA, even had lateen sails set on all three masts but was later re-rigged.

Cathay, the legendary land now known as China, lived its prosperous, industrious life in complete isolation, protected from the intrusion of foreigners by a great wall. For thousands of years it had kept itself aloof from the rest of the world and when, at last, it opened its seas to sailors from the Western World, the historic development of the Chinese junk had long been forgotten. The junk's hull was relatively heavy and not unlike that of European ships of that time. The amazing, miraculous junk sail, however, was beyond the understanding of European sailors. And because it was not understood, it was not copied and did not spread outside the Chinese sphere of influence. This sail by far surpassed anything known in Europe and the Near East, since it enabled the ship to make use of the wind from practically any direction. The junk sail is a true fore-and-aft sail, comparable to our modern lugsail. Moreover, it was fitted with *full-length battens*, which made it even more closely related to the modern racing rig. Each batten had its own sheet, which was led on deck either directly or by a purchase. Thus the sail could be trimmed over its entire height. It can be seen that the sail as such had, indeed, reached a high degree of perfection, and if the industrious Chinese had found a

9

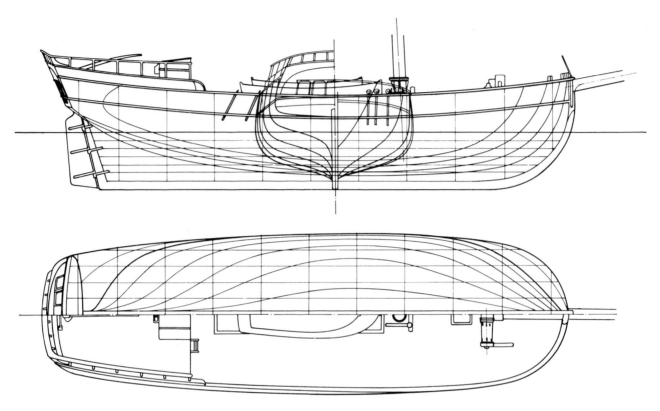

Fig. 3: Merchant sloop EXPERIMENT *built in 1780 in the United States. At that time Dutch shipbuilding was predominant, and its influence is clearly shown here.*

way to check the leeway made by their hulls, they would doubtlessly have discovered close-hauled sailing and even tacking, and been the first to *sail to windward.*

No less important for the evolution of sailing was the invention of the fixed stern rudder. The Chinese invented this independently of the Europeans and apparently much earlier. To us it is inconceivable that a pivoting rudder fixed permanently to the stern should only have appeared as late as the twelfth century and not have found general application until the fourteenth century. The late adoption of the fixed rudder is all the more incredible, when one contemplates how difficult sailing must have been for thousands of years while steering was done by means of a board held over the side by hand.

Meanwhile, in the extreme north of Europe, the most sophisticated ship yet conceived by the human mind was built: the Viking ship. It far surpassed in refinement all the heavy, crude hull constructions hitherto known. Its creators, experienced warriors, craftsmen and artists, were the first to succeed in an effort to get close to the wind by building a hull of perfect shape and weight. The fine underwater lines of the Viking ship can compete even with modern hull design, and the ability of these craft to sail to windward surpassed anything previously known.

Only in the Pacific Ocean had one other people succeeded in developing a highly original type of fast sailing craft: the Polynesian *flying proa.* Magellan's chronicler, Pigafetta, wrote about these twin-hulled craft: 'The islanders took pleasure in going to sea in their small, narrow boats, which looked like dolphins shooting from wave to wave, exchanging bow for stern at will.' The Polynesians with their twin-hulls and the Vikings with their light, fine-lined clinker boats had each managed to get a bit closer to the wind. Both used the system of interchanging bow and stern, although this was only really necessary with the Polynesian outrigger boats, where the small outrigger has always to remain on the windward side.

10

For many thousands of years sailing ships were rigged with one mast only. Shortly before the birth of Christ a tentative attempt was made by the Phoenicians to rig two masts. This was done to ease steering and reduce weather helm, rather than to carry more sail in order to improve the ship's speed. Two-masted rigs did not become popular until the fourteenth century, and very soon three masts became the rule, since, in the meantime, the dimensions of ships had increased. The size of these vessels must not be overestimated, though. Fifteenth-century ships, nearly all of them three-masted, were of relatively modest size. Columbus' largest, the SANTA MARIA, measured only 85 ft (26 m) overall and had a beam of 26 ft (8 m). She had a capacity of about 200 registered tons, and her crew numbered 45. The PINTA and NIÑA, which accompanied her on her voyage of discovery, were still smaller, but equally rigged as three-masters.

As sea trade increased, the desire for profit brought a new impetus to ship-building. Ships became bigger and faster, and the beginnings of something like naval architecture began to take shape. After the caravels came the galleons, then the frigates and finally the 'ships' proper, which the Spaniards called *naos* or *navios*.

As vessels increased in size and bulk a new problem arose: how to stop the hull, built of relatively short lengths of timber, from falling apart in a seaway and when fully laden. A seventeenth-century merchant sailing vessel must be looked upon as a real miracle. The high, ornamental poop aroused admiration far and wide, and demonstrated at the same time that labour costs were only of minor importance in those days. Later, purely economic reasons led to the final refinement of the sailing ship. The opium traffic on the one hand and the trade in tea and oriental silk on the other, created the necessary financial conditions which were soon afterwards boosted by the Californian Gold Rush. From this trade was born, around 1830, the fastest, most admirable and most efficient type of sailing vessel, the clipper. For the first time the desire for speed overshadowed all other considerations. What counted was not maximum capacity but passage time, and it is greatly to the credit of designers at that time that seaworthiness kept pace with growing speed.

One of the most famous of all clippers, the ARIEL, had a length of 197 ft (60 m), a beam of 34 ft (10·3 m)

Plate 2: *The 76 ft brig* ROYALIST *was designed by Colin Mudie for the English Sea Cadets. This design of a rarely built type received Lloyds' award for the best design and construction of 1971. Even if the rig does not attain the efficiency of the modern yacht, it is quite incomparable for teaching seamanship.*

and a tonnage of 852 tons. 100 tons of ballast were permanently stowed in her bilges, and another 20 tons could be shifted for trimming purposes. The sail area was a little over 32,000 sq ft (3000 m²) and was split into 37 separate sails, not counting light-weather canvas.

Now that ships could go close to the wind, the high-towering stern castles had to go. Instead, their outward

11

Clipper Rainbow

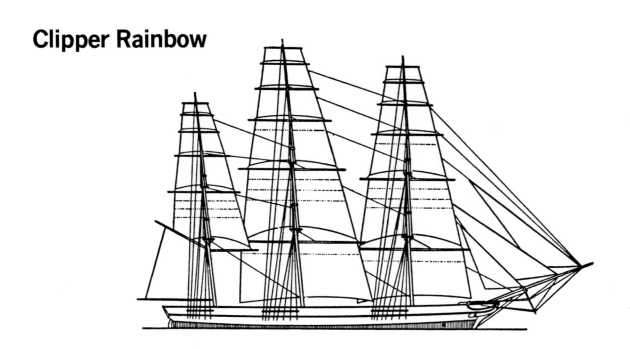

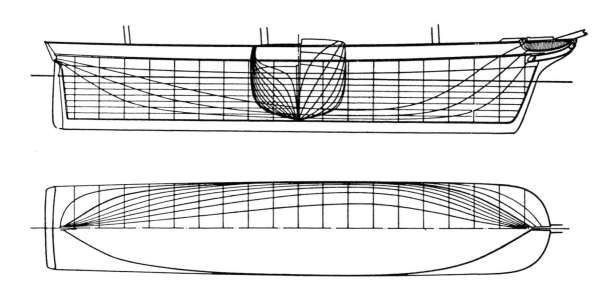

Fig. 4: RAINBOW *is frequently referred to as the first clipper.*
Built in 1845 she had a low, drawn-out stern and particularly
slim lines in comparison with ships of that period.

appearance was characterized by their *skyscraper* rigs. It was a lucky coincidence that, shortly after the building of the first clipper, steel wire rope was invented, which gave these fantastically high rigs a certain measure of safety. The modern yachtsman who gets the opportunity to study the sail plan of one of the few remaining square-rigged ships cannot hide his admiration for so much artistry and technical ingenuity.

THE DEVELOPMENT OF MERCHANT SHIPS UNDER SAIL

Year	Ship	Average Speed	Displacement	Closeness to wind
1000 BC	Greek	1 knot	50 tons	14 points (155°)
AD 1000	Viking	3 knots	60 tons	8 points (90°)
AD 1492	*Santa Maria*	3½ knots	80 tons	12 points (135°)
AD 1850	Clipper	7 knots	2500 tons	7 points (80°)

The Early History of Yachting

Even the Pharaohs practised boating for pleasure and navigated the peaceful waters of the Nile in sailing vessels, although they did not turn it into a sport. Similarly, the Vikings might have kept their private ships for pleasure purposes. History books tell us that as early as 1326 King Robert of Scotland amused himself by sailing his own yacht. But yachting as a sport evolved much later.

In the fourteenth century the Dutch began to use small, fast ships to pursue smugglers and pirates. They called them *jaght*, from the Dutch word *jagen* = to hunt. Soon the wealthy Amsterdam shipowners discovered that these so-called *jaghtschippen* were handy for going out to meet their large merchant ships when they returned from their voyages to the East Indies. Eventu-

ally it even became fashionable to offer one's friends a pleasure trip in one of these small sailing craft. It is not surprising, therefore, that in 1660 a *jaght* was chosen when the Dutch citizens wanted to make a present to the young King of England on the occasion of his restoration to the throne. There is no doubt that yachting originated in Holland, which is, after all, only natural, since this nation possessed a particularly flourishing merchant fleet at that time and a correspondingly highly developed shipbuilding technique.

The Dutch present to Charles II meant the introduction of sailing as a sport in England. The MARY, this first English yacht of Dutch origin, had a length of 52 ft (16 m) a beam of 19 ft (5·8 m) and a burden of 100 tons. According to Dutch custom she was rigged as a 'sloop', but today one would probably call her a cutter. The rig consisted of a gaff-rigged mainsail, staysail, jib and square topsail. It was the first time such a rig had been seen in England. Two wide leeboards emphasized the Dutch appearance of this first royal yacht, but they also enabled it to get closer to the wind. As was customary then, a permanent crew of 20 men went with the little ship and, what is more, it had a number of small cannons on deck. The young king was so enthusiastic about this new sport that, in a very short space of time, he had acquired a considerable amount of knowledge of navigation and seamanship as well as the technical aspects of shipbuilding. It is said that he himself designed the JAMIE, which was built two years later. But his outstanding achievement was, in 1675, the building of the Greenwich Observatory, which became of great and lasting importance to the whole seafaring world. As is well known, the meridian passing through Greenwich marks 0° longitude.

Although the Dutch practised sailing for pleasure, their attitude towards it was in no way comparable to modern racing. Their sport consisted of a procession of ships in orderly lines, decorated with flags and with small cannons on board. The tradition of parade-sailing, which originated in the fifteenth century, is still practised in Holland today. In 1958 one hundred traditional Dutch yachts took part in the procession, all of them with the typically round, full bow and stern, bent gaff and leeboards. This display took place on the occasion of the 600th anniversary celebrations of the town of Hoorn which is, incidentally, the birthplace of the Dutch sailors Schouten and Le Maire, who

Fig. 5: A Dutch jaght *in an informative print of the year 1642. The leeboards and the noticeably high schooner rig are both features aimed at improving performance*

14

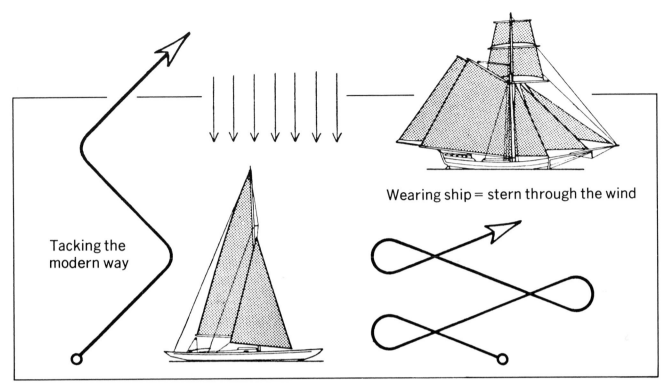

Tacking the
modern way

Wearing ship = stern through the wind

Fig. 6: Modern boats possess the ability to sail close to the wind and also to tack *through the eye of the wind. Never before in history has a sailing vessel reached a comparable speed 'into the wind'. Earlier sailing ships not only pointed less high but had to* wear ship, *i.e. turn the stern through the wind, in order to come onto the other tack. How this affects progress to windward is illustrated on the right.*

discovered Cape Horn and thereby established that South America could be rounded.

Shortly after the arrival of the MARY in England the Dutch spelling of *jaght* was changed into *yacht*. Strangely enough the word *Jacht* had already been used for centuries in Germany and Denmark to describe a type of small freighter, sailing in the coastal waters of the North Sea and Baltic. In 1797 there were as many as 412 of these *jachts* registered in Schleswig-Holstein, with a capacity of 25 to 100 tons each, which were mainly used as freighters in the Baltic.

The appearance of the royal yacht MARY aroused a lively interest in sailing in England. During the following twelve years no less than twelve yachts with keel lengths between 28 ft (8·5 m) and 74 ft (22·5 m) were built. In 1662 the first two of these, the CATHERINE built for the King, and the ANNE belonging to the Duke of York, sailed the first race of which we know.

Leeboards had become universal in Holland at least 200 years before the centreboard was invented. However, a peculiar version of the centreboard was used by the natives of South America long before that continent was discovered. When the Spanish conquerors approached the coast of what is now Ecuador they watched with amazement the strange manoeuvres of a number of sailing rafts. Thanks to the studies of Thor Heyerdahl and Emilio Estrada we know now that these rafts made of balsa wood used several centreboards which were inserted between the logs. By changing the arrangement of these centreboards the South American Indians could make the rafts change direction in relation to the wind. These comparatively shapeless craft, which were really unsuitable for sailing, are reported to have sailed very well with the wind on the beam and to have been surprisingly manoeuvrable.

The first sailing or yacht club was started in Ireland and not, as one might have expected, in England; it was the Cork Water Club, founded in 1720. It was followed much later, in 1773 and 1775 to be exact, by the first two English yacht clubs, the Star Cross Yacht Club and the Cumberland Fleet in that order. The latter eventually became the Royal Thames Yacht Club. The first American yacht club was not founded until 1844; its club house was the schooner GIMCRACK anchored in New York Harbour. Seven years later this, the New York Yacht Club, laid the foundations for the most important periodically recurring yachting event: The America's Cup Race. When the schooner AMERICA

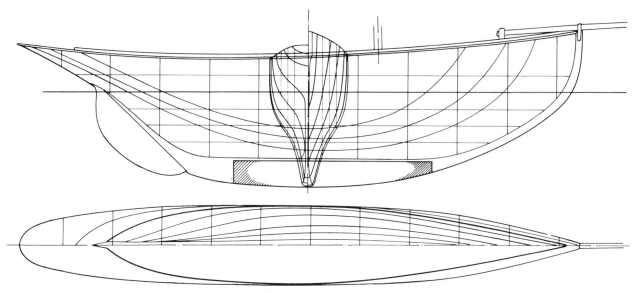

Fig. 7: English cutter of the end of the last century. Because of their extremely narrow beam, these yachts were called 'plank on edge' or 'six-beamers', i.e. six times as long as broad.

sailed to England in 1851 under the NYYC pennant, this was, at the same time, the inauguration of international yacht racing. It was probably around the middle of last century that sailing boats were, for the first time, designed purely as yachts. This created a new, specialized profession, that of yacht designer. The AMERICA was designed by George Steers, a dynamic young man dedicated wholly to the design of keel and centreboard yachts.

Large vessels of different types and dimensions raced against each other, usually helmed by professional skippers and manned by large crews. But small craft also increased in popularity, and they were sailed by amateur skippers with the help of crews made up of amateurs and paid hands. Soon the handicap system was introduced by which differences in type and dimensions are compensated for by adding or subtracting time. And, of course, it did not take long for designers to come up with extreme designs which took advantage of loop-holes in the formulae.

In 1855, for example, the so-called 'sandbaggers' appeared on the scene, which aimed at high speed but a low handicap by using movable internal ballast. These dinghy-like vessels were between 18 ft (5·5 m) and 28 ft (8·5 m) long, with a flat bottom and without any keel or

fixed ballast. Instead, they used a large centreboard, which enabled them to point very high. The comparatively small and light hulls carried enormous rigs with absurdly large sail areas. The necessary stability was ensured in the following way: a 'sandbagger' carried 25 to 28 sandbags on board, each weighing 52 lb (24 kg). There was a large crew, between 8 and 17, depending on the wind strength, whose task it was not only to shift their own weight to windward but also to take the sandbags with them. Thirty years later the use of movable ballast was prohibited and, around 1885, these interesting 'sandbaggers' vanished from the scene.

At the beginning of the last century, around 1815, the centreboard first appeared in the United States, and soon the other elements of the modern, fast sailing boat followed: efficient fore-and-aft rig, fixed stern rudder and retractable centreboard. Only one important part

Plate 3: An authentic classic cutter still sailing today, PASTIME was built in New Zealand in 1886 and launched in 1887. The hull is constructed in top grade kauri and is 45 ft long. The original timber still remains, only the deck having been renewed in 1938. The rig is that of a classic cutter. In spite of being an astonishing 88 years old the yacht has a long life expectancy, since no repairs are either planned or necessary at the moment. PASTIME must be one of the oldest yachts in the world which is regularly sailed. The secrets: good wood, good craftsmanship, good maintenance. Photo: N.Z. Sea Spray, Don Buick

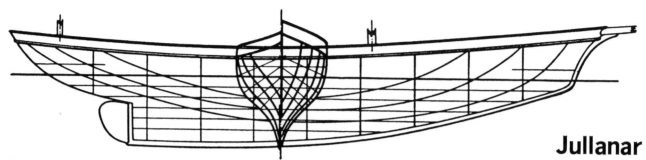

Jullanar

Fig. 8: Lines of JULLANAR, *which achieved fame on account of her unconventional underwater profile and the position of the stern post rather far forward. Her designer and owner, E H Bentall, had the courage to cut the forefoot away rather drastically. To the astonishment of his contemporaries this did not impair her performance on the wind but considerably improved her speed and manoeuvrability.*

was still missing: the deep ballast keel.

The advantages and disadvantages of ballast were not clearly understood at that time. The most extraordinary ideas about its nature, effect and the way it should be installed were current. It was alleged, for instance, that the pigs of ballast in the bilges had to be rested on steel springs in order that they might follow the frequent violent movements of the yacht elastically. The idea that in ocean-going cruising vessels only part of the total ballast weight should be fixed externally under the keel was upheld until comparatively recently. It was said that an essential part of the ballast must be placed in the bilges to avoid excessive stability, which would lead to violent movement in a seaway and could loosen the ship's fastenings.

Two unfortunate incidents eventually accelerated the introduction of external ballast. In 1873 the schooner MOHAWK with an overall length of over 132 ft (40 m) and a beam of 33 ft (10 m) capsized while lying at anchor in New York Harbour. Ten years later, in 1883, the yacht GRAYLING capsized under sail in a stiff quartering breeze. She, too, was of respectable size, 82 ft (25 m) in length with a beam of 23 ft (7 m). In both cases the considerable quantity of internal ballast was found to be the cause. When the yachts heeled over, the ballast slid to leeward, thus increasing the angle of heel and eventually reducing stability beyond the limits of safety.

Towards the end of the last century the Americans preferred beamy, shallow-draught hulls, frequently fitted with a centreboard and almost always with internal ballast. In England, on the other hand, the newly introduced external ballast and an age-old

tonnage formula led to exceptionally narrow, deep-draught hulls with almost straight stems and long, over-hanging counters. Since their beam was normally one-sixth of their length, the name 'six-beamers' was coined for them.

The fact that stability in the classical English hull was largely ensured by its weight meant that it had a low initial stability. As the angle of heel increased, however, stability improved proportionally and made the vessel practically uncapsizable. In the typical American boat, on the other hand, stability was essentially determined by hull shape, i.e. by its broad beam. This gave much greater initial stiffness but made the overall range of stability insufficient. The American yachts appeared stable but were in constant danger of capsizing.

Most boat builders in those days worked without proper plans by simply using carved half-models. It was doubtlessly very pleasing to carve the shape of a prospective yacht patiently out of a block of wood. The boat builder's eye could judge the design from a familiar three-dimensional shape, and his hands could trace the hull form. He would work on the model until its shape finally pleased him visually and convinced the customer. It was then cut up into layers and sections, and their lines were copied on paper by running a pencil round them. Calculations of weight were usually dispensed with, the displacement of the immersed body was only estimated or, rather, the waterline was guessed. Yachts were frequently altered on the basis of empiric observation after a short time afloat.

In the light of such primitive ideas one amateur's efforts in the furtherance of yacht design have to be

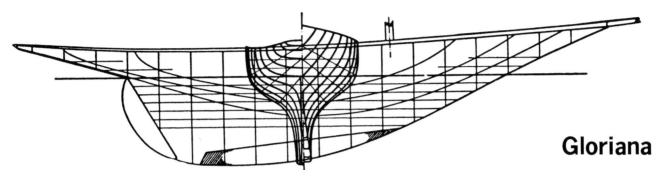

Gloriana

Fig. 9: The yacht GLORIANA *was designed by Herreshoff in 1891. With her the concept of the modern yacht was born. It is characterized by the disappearance of the forefoot and the disposition of* *the total ballast in an external lead keel. The sail plan of* GLORIANA *is reproduced in Fig. 110.*

rated all the more highly. This was E H Bentall, maker of agricultural machinery, who was the first boldly to cut down the forefoot. He designed the famous JULLANAR built in 1875. When, despite the absence of a forefoot, she showed no signs of drifting to leeward but sailed very well, she caused a sensation in British yacht design. She not only had excellent windward qualities but also proved extremely fast on all points of sailing. Of course, JULLANAR was the most famous 'tonnage cheater' of her time for, thanks to an ingenious design feature of Bentall's, she was given a low rating when purely by her LWL she should have had a much higher one. The old Thames Measurement formula rates length not on the actual waterline but from stem to stern post. Exploiting this fact, Bentall placed JULLANAR's stern post well forward of the end of the waterline thus obtaining a shorter rated length.

Since Bentall was not a draughtsman himself, he enlisted the services of a talented designer, John Harvey, who had gathered valuable experience on an international scale during ten years' work in the United States of America. Amongst the work he did was that of yacht construction expert for Lloyds, where he drew up tables of scantlings which are still in use today. Harvey was a unique case in that he was the only designer who, due to his work both in England and the United States, designed a challenger as well as a defender for the America's Cup Race.

After the spell of tradition had been broken, a period of feverish activity began in yacht building. In 1891 the most gifted of all designers, Nathaniel Herreshoff, built the cutter GLORIANA on entirely new principles. Everyone who saw the vessel on the stocks, boat builders and

spectators alike, prophesied that she would be a dismal failure. Her long drawn-out bow was utterly devoid of any trace of forefoot. But however much ridicule was heaped on this 'peculiar ship', when she was launched, the critics were soon silenced.

GLORIANA was a spectacular success. She was unexpectedly fast, close-winded and stable, while her manners were nothing but confidence-inspiring. So this 'peculiar ship' became the prototype of the modern yacht. Her long bow was subsequently copied blindly and also applied to conversions, even if it was inconsistent with the existing lines. GLORIANA's elegant sail plan still appeals to even the most critical of modern yachtsmen.

The reputation of Herreshoff, whose ancestors had emigrated from the Rhineland, was enhanced from year to year by the success of his designs. His keen mind was ever ready to break away from convention without losing itself in unrealistic fantasies. With his wide-reaching technical knowledge combined with a touch of real genius he turned every new design into an instant success. From 1893 to 1920 all defenders of the America's Cup were designed by Herreshoff and built in his yard. His unquestionable brilliance earned him the title of 'Wizard of Bristol'. But, of course, we must not forget Edward Burgess and William Gardner. Edward Burgess' son W Starling Burgess designed the victorious Cup-defenders of 1930 and 1935. England produced men like George Watson, William Fife and Charles E Nicholson, apart from those already mentioned.

In other countries, too, there were men of unusual talent, who gave their energies to the development of yacht design. In Germany there were first Max Oertz and later Henry Rasmussen and Henry Gruber specializing in keel yachts. Reinhard Drewitz became the master of racing dinghy design, and his influence spread far beyond the national boundaries. Sweden's Gustav A Estlander must not remain unmentioned, either, since it was his influence that was decisive in the development of the Skerry cruiser right up to its maximum dimensions.

When, in 1851, the schooner AMERICA won the race round the Isle of Wight, she amazed the world. Not only did her fine waterlines attract attention, but so did her particularly flat-cut cotton sails. British sails at that time were cut very full and made of heavy, hand-woven flax. Another innovation was that the AMERICA had her mainsail laced to the boom, whereas all the defenders carried a loose-footed mainsail.

When all is said and done the question arises whether, after so much progress and improvement, any signifi-cant tasks remain to be done in the present and near future. Evolution never stands still, of course. After 1920 the Bermudan rig began its triumphant march. Sailmaking has become a veritable science, all the more so since the arrival of synthetic fibres. Hull-shapes continue to be improved. Hulls are now lighter, livelier, faster, more easily handled and point higher. The exciting possibility of planing in keelboats opens up new fields of research.

The great merit of modern yachting lies in the refinement of the sailing and handling qualities of yachts, the astounding growth of their numbers and the fact that they are sailed almost entirely by amateurs.

Plate 4: The 30 sq m Skerry Cruiser has an elegant, slim hull and excellent sailing qualities. The built-in curve in the upper part of the mast assists in the optimum set of the mainsail when sailing to windward, but was only used up till 1930. Such a glued, wooden mast, hollow with a large degree of curvature is a real gem of the sparmaker's craft.
Photo: Hohmann

EVOLUTION STAGES OF THE SAILING SHIP

4000 B.C.	The first sailing ships on the Nile.
100 B.C.	A second mast appears on the foredeck.
A.D. 100	The lateen sail appears in Arab countries.
A.D. 1300	The introduction of the fixed rudder at the stern.
A.D. 1400	Three-masted sailing ships with mixed rig.
A.D. 1600	The gaff-rig and leeboards improve windward efficiency.
A.D. 1820	The introduction of retractable centreboard.
A.D. 1875	The first appearance of the Bermudan rig.
A.D. 1880	External ballast begins to be universally accepted.
A.D. 1946	Nylon first used for sailcloth.
A.D. 1954	First successful windward sails made from polyester.
A.D. 1956	First large fibreglass yachts built.

Keelboats and Centreboarders, Round Bilge and Hard Chine

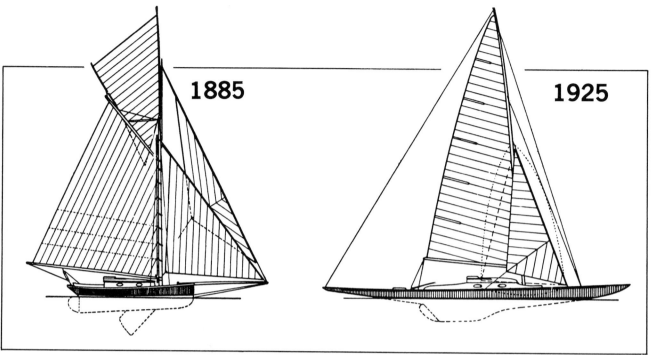

Figs. 10 & 11: In the space of only forty years the short, over-canvassed boats changed into the extremely long and virtually under-canvassed type of the Skerry cruiser. Despite its consider- *ably reduced sail area, the modern boat is faster on all points, except in very light airs. It is also safer, more seaworthy, livelier and simpler to handle.*

In the early days of sailing, hulls were heavy and needed no ballast, or only a small amount. Evolution then led through all stages of ballast ratio, in extreme cases as much as 72 per cent of the total weight. Speed and safety are in constant contradiction in this process. The speed of a boat under sail is limited by its weight but also by its stability, i.e. its ability to carry sail. Added to this there is the peculiar dependence of speed on wind strength and the vessel's course relative to wind direction. With a following wind, for example, the attainable wind propulsion decreases in proportion to the increase in the yacht's speed, for only the *difference* between true wind and the yacht's speed remains effective as forward thrust.

The special characteristics of wind propulsion bring about an equally peculiar conflict when the boat is sailing to windward. The higher the vessel's speed the less close it can go to the true wind, because its own speed makes the *apparent wind* draw further and further ahead.

In a race sailed between similar boats the absolute speed attained is of secondary importance. The course is normally set in such a way that it can be sailed in about 2 hours. If it were desired to shorten this time by some 10 minutes, then this could be achieved by shortening the course rather than by increased speed. Only in the case of trading vessels was absolute speed of real significance, because it influenced the commercial aspects of using the wind. The growing number of followers of the relatively slow sport of sailing are not interested in speed as such, but derive satisfaction and relaxation from all sailing activity. The existence of a vast, world-wide fleet of yachts and dinghies proves that with steadily increasing prosperity more and more people are attracted to this delightful sport.

Every sailing boat has its own inherent speed or speed limit, which is essentially dependent on the length of the hull, in the same way as it has its own specific stability and comfort. The boat's overall size has a bearing on all three factors, but cost and upkeep are often opposed to individual wishes.

In principle, all sailing boats fall into one of three basic categories: there are the *keel yachts*, in which stability and safety are ensured by a deep ballast keel; then there are the *unballasted dinghies*, whose stability and safety depend on their beam and the stabilizing influence of their crew; and finally there are the *multihulls*, i.e. catamarans and trimarans, in which stability

22

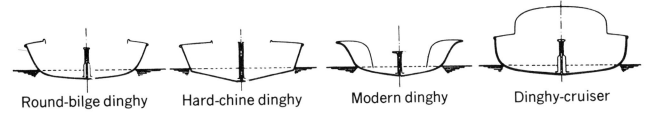

Round-bilge dinghy   Hard-chine dinghy   Modern dinghy   Dinghy-cruiser

Fig. 12: Four different mid-sections of dinghies. The normal dinghy has a retractable centreplate and no ballast. Stability depends partly on the hull shape but in stronger winds relies increasingly on the crew as 'live ballast'.

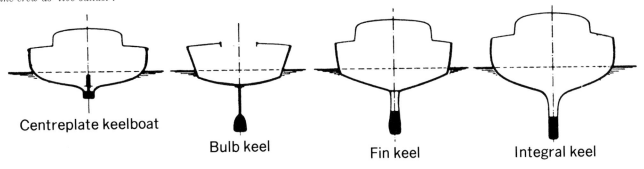

Centreplate keelboat   Bulb keel   Fin keel   Integral keel

Fig. 13: Four different mid-sections of keelboats. There are several accepted types of ballast-keel design. On the far left is a boat with a drop keel or ballasted centreboard, which is characterized by its shallow draft but has slightly less stability.

and safety is provided by the lateral distance between two or three hulls.

Unfortunately stability cannot be defined by a simple figure like size or weight. To simplify matters it has become accepted to use the ballast ratio, i.e. the relation between ballast weight and ready-to-sail total weight (displacement) as an approximate stability factor for keelboats. The ready-to-sail weight includes all the gear but not the weight of the crew. Two schooner yachts designed by John Alden, although no longer typical, exemplify the interim period, in which trends were changing:

1921: MALABAR I 24% internal ballast } Total 33%
9% external ballast

1930: MALABAR X 14% internal ballast } Total 44%
30% external ballast

Around 1930 it became generally accepted for ocean-going cruising vessels to have the total ballast in the keel, i.e. externally. Racing yachts had for some time exploited the advantages of ballast placed as low as possible. For modern boats the following ballast ratios are considered normal:

Cruising boats with ample beam .... 26 to 45%
Offshore racing yachts .... 42 to 55%

Inshore class racing yachts .... 50 to 70%

The lighter a yacht's hull is constructed, the greater her ballast ratio can be and the greater, therefore, her stability. It is perfectly possible to build a vessel whose ballast ratio is 75 to 80 per cent of the total weight.

The number of sailing keelboats is easily surpassed by that of unballasted *dinghies*. Despite their simple shape and frequently simple method of construction, they have outstanding sailing qualities and this, together with their modest cost, has led to their enormous popularity throughout the world. There must be about 25,000 boats of the 15 ft 6 in (4·73 m) Snipe-class in existence today, roughly 25,000 of the 420 class, and as many as 50,000 of the 10 ft 6 in (3·35 m) Mirror dinghy. Numerous other types and classes have reached very high numbers. Although most dinghies are capsizable, or maybe because of it, their helmsmen and crews are usually so skilled at handling them that capsizes occur comparatively rarely. If the worst does happen it is considered a challenge to right the boat as quickly as possible without outside help and sail on.

Without a centreplate a dinghy could not go to windward, because the light, shallow hull as such offers no lateral resistance. It is only the centreplate that resists

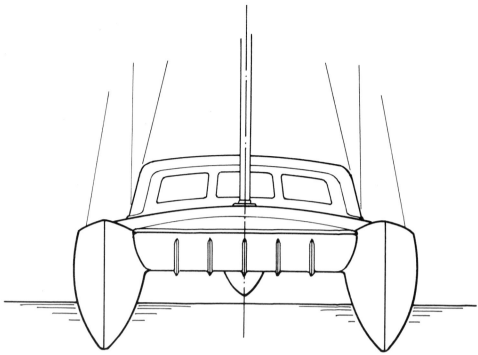

Fig. 14: Mid-section of a catamaran. In this cruising multi-hull the accommodation is in the central section, above the water. Racing catamarans without such accommodation reach high speeds.

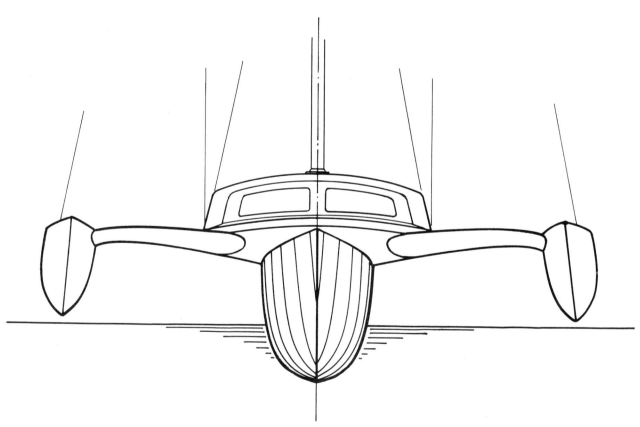

Fig. 15: Mid-section of modern cruising trimaran. A large part of the accommodation is in the central hull, which means that it lies considerably lower than in the catamaran. Depending on the individual design, the floats are either above the water or just in it.

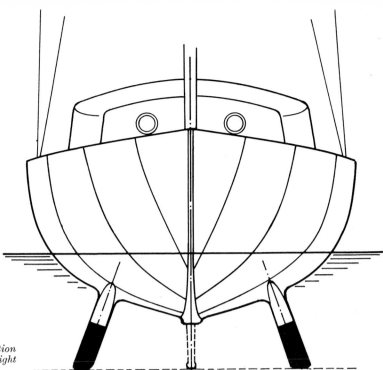

Fig. 16: Mid-section of a twin bilge keeler. This configuration comes into its own in tidal waters where the boat remains upright as she dries out.

leeway and enables the dinghy to point as high as a slim keelboat, or even higher. The use of a centreplate is by no means limited to unballasted dinghies. Any keel-yacht could have a centreplate as well, which would be all the more effective the shallower the vessel's draught. A shallow-draught keelboat with a comparatively large plate would be called a centreplate keelboat. Many big racing keelboats, on the other hand, as well as a number of ocean racers have used additional centreplates without being named thus. There are any number of intermediate stages from the completely unballasted dinghy to the pure keelboat.

In the last 15 years *multihulls* in all their different versions have gained increased popularity. The two main types are the *catamaran* with two completely symmetrical hulls, and the *trimaran* with a main central hull and two smaller outside hulls or outriggers. There are racing catamarans and trimarans, which are very lightly constructed and have no accommodation at all, and there are cruising types, which are larger and heavier to provide ample accommodation and stowage space for gear. It should be mentioned that the Tornado, a small, light racing catamaran, has been recognized as a class by the IYRU (International Yacht Racing Union) and, what is more, was chosen for the 1976 Olympic Games.

Light racing catamarans normally have two centreplates, one in each hull, while heavier cruising catamarans frequently have no centreplates at all. Trimarans often have a small fin under each outrigger. An unusual version of small catamaran has been developed in Spain

under the name of *patin a vela* (= sail sledge). This robust little boat has no rudder or steering gear, and changes in course are effected solely by altering the trim of the sails and by the crew shifting their weight rather like a sailboard or windsurfer.

Finally the *twin-keel* type of hull ought to be mentioned, in which the deep ballast-keel is replaced by two shallower bilge-keels, each carrying half the total ballast weight. These boats are particularly useful in tidal waters on drying moorings, because they will sit upright on the bottom. Frequently the rudder skeg comes down to the same level as the two bilge-keels, which gives the boat a very firm stand on three points. Quite erroneously, a special stabilizing effect is frequently attributed to bilge-keels, because the lee-keel moves down slightly lower as the boat begins to heel. This is a fallacy, but the type certainly has its advantages in tidal waters, and although its sailing qualities cannot quite match those of the true keelboat, they are perfectly satisfactory.

The following pages show three columns of hull profiles, which represent the most common types of keelboats and centreplate boats: the first shows ocean-going keel yachts, the second inshore keelboats and the third centreplate boats. The last group shows the various stages from the unballasted dinghy to the proper racing keel-yacht with small auxiliary plate.

All these various types can be *round-bilge* or *hard-chine*. In the latter, the floor and sides of the hull are nearly or completely straight, which makes this construction method particularly suitable for the amateur

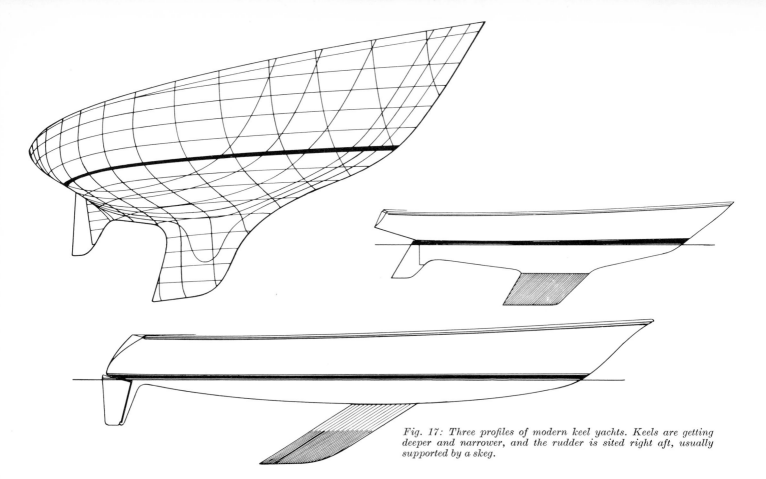

Fig. 17: Three profiles of modern keel yachts. Keels are getting deeper and narrower, and the rudder is sited right aft, usually supported by a skeg.

who wants to build in plywood. On the whole, a hard-chine boat is not quite as fast as a round-bilge boat, but the difference is minimal. Under certain circumstances, when sailing 'on the chine' and thus increasing the waterline length, a hard-chine boat can even be the faster of the two.

The majority of ocean-going yachts are of round-bilge section, but this does not mean that a hard-chine type would not be adequately seaworthy. On the contrary, the first yacht to sail *twice round the world single-handed* was a hard-chine type, and her seaworthiness was irrefutable.

SECTIONS AND PROFILES OF MODERN OCEAN RACERS

In a design competition for modern aspiring one-tonners in 1965 each of the three winning designs had the rudder immediately aft of the keel. One-ton yachts in those days were still rated under the RORC (Royal Ocean Racing Club) formula, but in the following year some of the One-Ton Cup contenders already had rudders hung freely on the stern.

The practice of hanging the rudder at the stern quite separate from the keel had begun to emerge long before the turn of the century. The fact that it did not meet with more response was probably due to the rudder often being too small to prevent the boat from coming up into the wind. It was not until 1966 that the modern skeg and fin idea was generally adopted.

Although the position of the rudder at the extreme after end did not make boats measurably faster, it improved their steering qualities quite considerably.

The illustrations in Figure 17 show (top left) the lines of an S & S 34 by Sparkmen & Stephens. This design is a typical example of the modern ocean racer with a clearly subdivided underwater profile, narrow, deep ballast-keel and a relatively large rudder right aft, with a vestigial bridge between rudder skeg and keel.

The second illustration (middle) shows a boat which is not very much dissimilar: GAMBLING designed by Jan Linge. The third illustration (bottom) shows an ocean racer with an extreme underwater profile: SALTY GOOSE designed by Robert Derecktor, an American Admiral's Cup contender of 1973. Every detail of this design is unusual, from the narrow skeg with its unusually large rudder blade to the abruptly emerging keel, which looks more like a narrow centreplate. In a sense this is what it is because, despite its weight of 6 tons (6000 kg), it is retractable.

On the following pages the development of older types of yachts, from around 1880 until the present, has been briefly outlined.

Plate 5: The Hunter Sonata 7, rating as a Mini Tonner (16 feet IOR) represents a new breed: the small one design offshore racer, offering both highly competitive boat-for-boat racing and proper accommodation on a budget.
LOA .... 22 ft 7 in   Draft .... 4 ft 6 in
Beam .... 8 ft 6 in   Sail area .... 250 sq ft.
Builders: Hunter Boats, England   Photo: Janet Harber

PROFILES AND MAIN SECTIONS OF OCEAN-GOING KEEL BOATS: the following six *classical* profiles are, from top to bottom (Fig. 18):

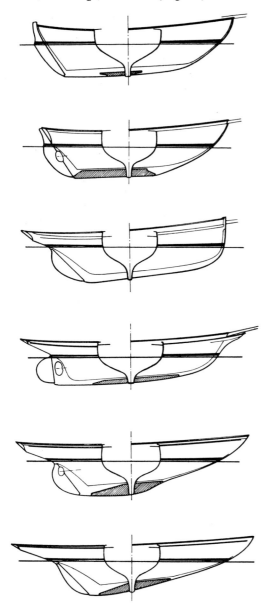

The long underwater profile of all these types makes for exceptional steadiness on course and ensures safe heaving-to in a storm. At the same time, the large wetted surface means increased friction, which counteracts speed.

DOUBLE-ENDER: Ocean-going rescue and pilot boat designed for the Norwegian coast by Colin Archer. Its stern is almost as pointed as the bow. The remarkably small ballast keel is compensated by massive construction and the use of internal ballast.

TRANSOM YACHT: With this type of flat stern a considerable area of after-deck is gained over the previous type without the sea-going qualities of the boat being diminished in any way. True transom vessels have their rudder hung on the stern, and many have a long underwater profile, which ensures steadiness on course. Innumerable small craft of this type have made remarkably long ocean voyages and even circumnavigated the world.

PILOT CUTTER: The straight stem and long, straight keel clearly show the origin of JOLIE BRISE. She was originally built for the French pilot service but looked very much like a yacht. These boats did not normally have a ballast keel but carried internal ballast only.

YACHT WITH CLIPPER BOW: This type is characterized by the long keel, which leads to a clipper bow and terminates aft in a fine, drawn-out yacht stern. Great beam and shallow draught combine with excellent sea-going qualities to arouse nostalgia for the romantic side of ocean sailing. To be true to type, this boat should be rigged to include some square sails.

CLASSIC OCEAN-GOING CRUISER: The last but one profile illustrates the fast offshore cruiser for long ocean passages. A somewhat shorter underwater profile, ample external ballast, reasonable beam and good freeboard are typical. Such a vessel is fast and very close-winded yet retains adequate steadiness on course.

FAST OFFSHORE CRUISER/RACER: This type represents the stage before the out-and-out modern ocean racer. The underwater profile is further reduced, the long overhanging counter serves primarily for the staying of the mizzen mast. Larger yachts of this type are most commonly rigged as yawl or ketch, partly because this gave them a favourable rating under previous rating rules.

KEELBOATS FOR INSHORE RACING AND WEEKEND SAILING. The following types of sailing boat are characterized by their considerably shorter underwater profile, which is appropriate to their different purpose (Fig. 19).

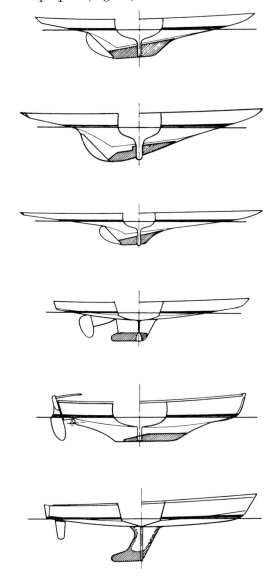

The shorter the underwater profile of a hull, the livelier will be its response to the rudder. Against this must be counted the disadvantage that safe heaving-to in a storm is not possible. On the other hand, a much smaller sail area is needed to achieve higher speeds, since the frictional resistance is reduced to a minimum.

DRAGON CLASS: This widely known international keelboat is characterized by its strikingly moderate lines without any extremes. It still enjoys considerable popularity, although it was designed as long ago as 1925.

IYRU CLASSES: A relatively large displacement is typical of these vessels built to the rules of the International Yacht Racing Union. Only the 5·5-metre and 6-metre classes are still active today, while the 12-metres compete for the America's Cup at irregular intervals of several years.

SKERRY CRUISER: As the name suggests, this type was designed for use among the skerries (= rocky islets) of the Swedish archipelago. It is probably the purest type of fast racing keelboat, with long overhangs, narrow beam and short underwater profile. A very high, narrow rig emphasized the style of this thoroughbred, which was first designed around 1920 and was still popular until comparatively recently.

STAR CLASS: This is characterized by three features in which it differs from the previous types: it has a bulb keel, it has a hard-chine section, and the rudder is hung on a skeg separate from the keel. Although designed in 1911 and by no means particularly fast, hard-fought national and international championships are still competed for in this class by top helmsmen.

SMALL LIGHT - DISPLACEMENT KEEL CRUISER: This type of keelboat has a typical dinghy shape but, instead of a centreplate, is fitted with a keel of moderate ballast weight. It was designed many years ago by the author for his own use and is particularly suited for use in areas like the River Plate and the extensive rivers of the Parana Delta.

EXTREMELY REDUCED UNDERWATER PROFILE: This design by Van de Stadt can be considered a successful predecessor of the modern racing yacht concept. The drastically reduced underwater profile has proved itself, but it is now realized that the rudder is more effective if hung on a skeg. The hull has a hard-chine section, which makes it suitable for light, plywood construction.

DINGHIES AND YACHTS WITH CENTREBOARDS:

The typical centreboarder, the dinghy, is characterized by its outstanding windward efficiency but is capsizable due to its low inherent stability. The windward performance of keelboats, on the other hand, can be improved by the addition of a supplementary centreplate, the effect of which will be all the more noticeable the shallower the boat's draught is (Fig. 20).

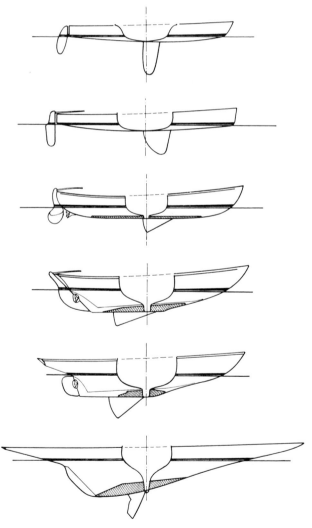

All centreplates have been shown in the fully lowered position used for beating to windward. The position of the plate can alter the rudder pressure to some extent so that it can have considerable influence on the balance.

THE MODERN RACING DINGHY: This type has practically no overhangs. Leeway is prevented solely by the narrow, deep plate, which is hydrodynamically more efficient than a wide, shallow one. Due to minimum weight, low friction and flat, drawn-out stern sections, these boats plane easily. The mid-section shows the flared shape favoured today.

THE DINGHY-CRUISER: Compared with the open dinghy, these boats have much more roomy hulls with surprisingly spacious accommodation, but no ballast whatever. Although they are as capsizable as any dinghy, they are popular on sheltered waters.

THE WHALEBOAT AS YACHT: The characteristics of the whaleboat are its pointed stern, shallow draught and small ballast ratio, which in many cases amounts to only 15 per cent of the total weight. The sail area, which takes into account the low inherent stability, is of low-aspect ratio, but due to low frictional resistance the whaleboat is still remarkably fast. It finds adherents in shallow rivers and coastal waters and cannot be relied upon to be non-capsizable.

KEELBOAT WITH CENTREPLATE: Although the whaleboat, strictly speaking, belongs in this category, the following profile shows a much more popular type. It has more ballast in the keel, a more substantial hull and a wide transom on which the rudder is hung (not necessarily, but usually). Even with the plate up and correspondingly reduced draught, these boats will still tack satisfactorily. They are uncapsizable.

OFFSHORE CRUISER WITH CENTREPLATE: Yachts of this type, which have a broad beam and moderate draught, have found considerable popularity in ocean sailing. Once again, the large centreplate improves windward performance.

RACING YACHT WITH SMALL AUXILIARY PLATE: The large J-class yachts, which competed for the last time for the America's Cup in 1937, had small auxiliary plates of this type to get the ultimate out of windward performance and also to compensate for possible rudder pressure. ENTERPRISE even used two small plates one behind the other.

One- and Two-Masted Rigs of Modern Yachts

Before the fast clippers made their appearance in the first third of the last century, it was usual for sailing ships to wait for favourable winds before setting out on a voyage. The modern yacht with its advanced rig is expected *to sail in all winds and on any desired course.*

Sailing close to windward is of predominant importance compared to all other points of sailing. The higher a yacht can point whilst maintaining good speed, the greater the effective distance made good when working to windward. Thus, the modern rig was developed with optimum close-hauled performance in mind. The Vikings may have been capable of building excellent hulls which would have been well suited to windward work but, since they knew of no other rig than the shapeless square sail, this prevented them from pointing any closer.

The medieval lateen sail offered better possibilities, but the hulls used in the Mediterranean in those days were much too clumsy. The idea of outsmarting the wind simply did not occur to the medieval sailor. Only the modern yacht during the last hundred years has managed to combine a fast, slim hull of great lateral resistance with a type of efficient rig, which enables the boat to *eat* its way to windward. No sailor of past centuries would ever have dreamt of what the youngest dinghy sailor now takes for granted: to sail virtually into the eye of the wind by tacking.

Of course, the square rig was inherently unsuited to any such refinement, which is why a description of square-riggers, from the brig to the fully-rigged ship, is not given here. Modern sailing vessels use the fore-and-aft rig almost exclusively. Only in exceptional cases is a square sail or a wing sail still used on long ocean passages in zones of constant trade winds. Even the spinnaker, which has now reached a very advanced stage of development, cannot be considered a descendant of the square sail, since it is not set on a yard and is of triangular rather than square shape. Its amazing development during the past few years is a result of the only weakness from which the fore-and-aft rig suffers: low efficiency before the wind.

In practice every sailing boat has one principal sail, sometimes the only sail, the *mainsail.* In most cases this is accompanied by a number of smaller foresails set before the mast. The following six illustrations show different types of mainsail, starting with the square sail and ending with the Bermudan mainsail (pp. 32–3).

THE LATEEN SAIL: This was hardly ever set on yachts but is still in popular use on trading vessels, fishing boats and other coastal vessels in the Mediterranean and in Arab countries. The essentially triangular sail is bent to a long yard suspended at its centre of gravity from the top of a short, sturdy mast. The picturesque appearance of this rig never fails to delight the sailor who chances to come across it. Its major drawback lies in the complicated process involved in going about. Both yard and sail have to be swung round in front of the mast (which accounts for the absence of a forestay) for, if it is left, it will be pressed against the mast on the new tack and rendered partly ineffective. To facilitate this business of going about, the mast of the lateen rig is frequently raked forward.

THE LUGSAIL: It is particularly suited for smaller boats like tenders and lifeboats. It is of unequalled simplicity and needs hardly any fittings, no boom and only one single halliard. Frequently the length of mast and yard are made to fit into the boat's length. Even staying can be dispensed with if the mast is strong and accommodated in a sturdy step. Children learn to handle these boats at a very early age, which is why boats for youngsters, often under the age of eight, are often rigged with lugsails.

The illustrations show that a sail is characterized by its position relative to the mast. In the normal square sail one half of the sail is before the mast and one half behind it. In the lateen sail only a small part of the sail is left before the mast, and in the lugsail this proportion is even smaller. At the same time the yard, which starts off in a horizontal position for the square sail, takes on a steeper and steeper angle until it reaches a vertical position in the Bermudan rig.

In the following three types of mainsail the entire sail area is aft of the mast. Thus the mast serves not only as *support* for the sail but also becomes the *leading edge*, and as such has an aerodynamic significance over and above its structural significance.

THE GAFF SAIL: Its efficiency by far surpasses any former sail. Its superiority to windward became obvious as soon as suitably shaped hulls could be built. Its upper part is laced to a yard called a gaff which is hoisted into position by two halliards. In this way the

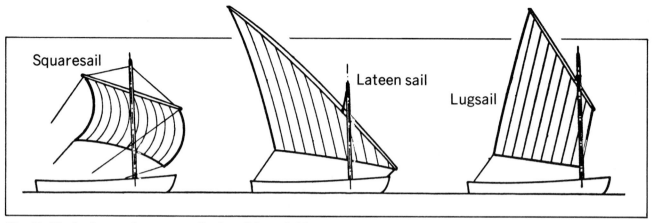

Fig. 21: The development from squaresail to lugsail is marked by the position of the yard and the ratios of sail area before and after the mast.

set of the sail can be considerably influenced. The gaff need not be like the one shown, but can be short or long, straight or curved, steep or nearly horizontal. The Dutch, who are assumed to have invented it, still prefer the short, curved gaff. Many racing dinghies in the twenties carried long gaffs, which were curved and hollow and set nearly vertically.

THE GUNTER RIG: A relatively insignificant variation of the gaff rig was given a separate name: the sliding gunter. It is distinguished by its almost vertical gaff, which makes for a higher aspect ratio without the need to lengthen the mast.

THE BERMUDAN MAINSAIL: This simple looking sail with its high aspect ratio first showed its superiority at the 1920 Olympic Games in Amsterdam, when competitors in international classes included both gaff-rigged and Bermudan-rigged boats. The straight, high leading edge of the Bermudan sail was so much more efficient, especially to windward, that it proved itself undeniably superior to any rig hitherto known.

To bring out the full advantages of the Bermudan rig it was necessary to develop a special technique for building masts. No mast made of solid timber could be

Plate 6: The American designer, John Atkin, enjoys designing very substantial, sea-going sailing cruisers. But he has a happy knack with so-called ships of character, as for example the fine small schooner-brig ANNA MARIA. She is only 32 ft long with a beam of 12 ft 4 in and carries 463 sq ft of sail, in seven sails. She is intended for day sailing. But the owner says she is easier to handle than you think. All sails are set and stowed without anyone having to climb the foremast. Photo: John Atkin, Darien

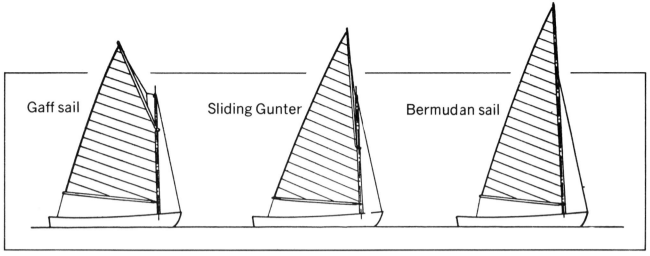

Gaff sail   Sliding Gunter   Bermudan sail

Fig. 22: In the modern fore-and-aft mainsail the total sail area is abaft the mast, and this enables it to go much closer to the wind than any previous type of sail.

light in weight and stand straight at the same time. Only with the arrival of hollow, glued masts did the Bermudan rig show its true advantages. This is why it did not become popular until after the discovery of weather-resistant glues.

The origin of the Bermudan rig probably lies in the Bermudas, where sailing boats called 'dinghies' used it long before the end of the last century. In their case the sail was not set with slides in a mast track but was simply laced to the mast.

Whereas a gaff sail normally stays bent to its gaff and boom and is protected from the elements merely by a sail cover, the Bermudan mainsail can very easily be lowered and stowed below decks where it is protected from damp and dirt, which would otherwise shorten its life. A further advantage of the Bermudan rig is the ability to have a permanent backstay, which considerably improves the safety of the mast before the wind, especially when gybing.

THE WISHBONE RIG: Occasionally one still comes across a variation of the Bermudan rig in which the mainsail is extended by a twin gaff called a wishbone. The wishbone supports the sail about two-thirds up, where the sail is at its widest (see Fig. 115). It can really only be used with a ketch rig, because the sheet lead

Plate 7: The ketch ROLAND, *which is a familiar sight on Lake Constance, uses a wishbone spar on the mainsail, the sheets of which are led to the mizzen masthead. As can be seen, the mainsail sets very well. A similar wishbone can be seen on the mizzen, in this case it replaces the boom.*   *Photo: Risch-Lau, Bregenz*

from the wishbone goes via the top of the mizzen or jigger mast. However, a wishbone can be used at the foot of the sail, instead of a boom. In both cases it greatly improves the set of the sail because it enables the curvature over the entire height to be regulated accurately.

FORESAILS: On older yachts it was usual to set three foresails, whose names, beginning at the mast, were staysail, inner jib and outer jib. The latter, if set slightly higher, was also called a jib-topsail. With a normal sloop rig with only one foresail this is called the jib.

In many classes it is customary to measure not the foresail itself but the so-called foretriangle, within the limits of which shape and size of foresail are either completely optional or, just recently, subject to certain not very serious restrictions. These were only introduced because the leniency of the measurement rules led to the use of enormous overlapping foresails with their leech far aft of the mast, the handling of which, especially when tacking, became correspondingly difficult.

The large, overlapping foresail was first seen during the 1927 International Regatta in Genoa on the 6-metre yacht LILIAN belonging to the well-known Swedish yachtsman Sven Salen; it was subsequently named a

genoa by the Americans. A similar but fuller foresail known as a 'balloon' jib was already known then, but could not be used to windward, because its fullness caused it to lift.

The use of very large foresails and speculation about the nature of the gap between fore and mainsail gave rise to the *slot-effect* theory. According to this, the airflow from the jib, if carefully directed smoothly over the lee side of the mainsail, will increase the total thrust of the rig.

The truth of this theory has never been convincingly proved, but the interesting case of the Bembridge Redwing gives food for thought. This British keelboat class with an overall length of 28 ft (8·5 m) was allowed a sail area of 200 sq ft (18·6 m²). Only the actual sail area was regulated, the shape, height and subdivision of the sail was completely optional. Over a number of years innumerable variations were tried in races, some of them extreme (including a windmill driving a water propeller), but *all without exception were inferior to the normal rig*, which was a Bermudan sloop rig of average height. One thing surprised everybody, though: there was *no overlap*. The rig did not use a genoa but a normal, comparatively small jib set completely free from and even slightly forward of the mast, with its tack kept well away from the mast. From this it can be deduced that:

Fig. 23: A simplified explanation of the combined working of the mainsail and jib to windward. The diversion of the air flow by the sail causes an area of high pressure on the windward side and an area of low pressure on the leeward side of the sail. Together they produce a force in the direction of the arrow. The air on the windward side of the jib is diverted onto the leeward side of the mainsail, where it contributes to the lowering of pressure through acceleration.

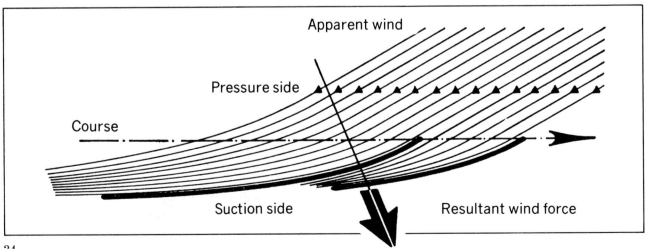

(a) overlap and slot effect are only of advantage if the overlapping sail area is not rated,

(b) the overlapping part, i.e. the slot, produces less thrust per unit sail area than the non-overlapping part of the jib.

Should the rating rules for sail areas ever be changed, yacht rigs could alter in an unforeseen way.

THE SPINNAKER: In order to make the most of the least favourable of all courses, i.e. before the wind, the modern racing yacht uses a *wind bag* of enormous dimensions called a *spinnaker*. This sail, in its turn, gives rise to so many problems that it is dealt with in a separate chapter. It should be said here, however, that the modern spinnaker enables the Bermudan rig to beat the gaff rig on all points of sailing, including courses dead before the wind.

RIGS: The various types of mainsail and foresail can be combined in a wide variety. Three types of rig use one mast only, a further three use two. The simplest form of one-masted rig with only one mainsail on the mast and no foresail is the 'cat boat'. Various junior and one-man racing dinghies use this rig, as does the occasional small cruising yacht. If a single foresail is added we get the 'sloop'. Two or three foresails make the 'cutter'. The classic gaff cutter rig is made up of

mainsail, staysail, jib, jib-topsail and main-topsail. It is by no means easy to set and take in a topsail, but it is very efficient in light airs and delights the eye of sailor and non-sailor alike. Large yachts with big professional crews always used to hoist a topsail if wind conditions permitted. But as large, expensive yachts gave way to smaller ones sailed by amateurs, the topsail became rarer and rarer and finally disappeared altogether as the Bermudan rig took over.

Larger boats are two-masted for preference, because this splits up the total area into smaller sails, which are easier to handle. The name given to two-masted rigs depends on the height and position of the after mast, called the mizzen or jigger. If it is comparatively small and placed aft of the rudder, i.e. aft of the end of the waterline, we have a 'yawl'. If the mizzen mast is rather taller and stands forward of the end of the waterline, we have a 'ketch'. If, however, the after mast is taller than the foremast (and is then called the mainmast), the boat is a 'schooner'. Schooners can also be three-masted, in which case the after mast need not be the tallest. There are numerous variations besides, of which the wishbone ketch has already been mentioned. Schooners frequently do not set a Bermudan or gaff sail on the foremast, but a triangular staysail and above it a large, quadrilateral fore-topsail or 'fisherman'. This type is called a 'staysail schooner' and used to be par-

Fig. 24: Four rigs of modern single-masted boats. Although the classic cutter rig included three foresails and a topsail, a Bermudan rig without topsail and only two foresails is often described as a cutter rig today.

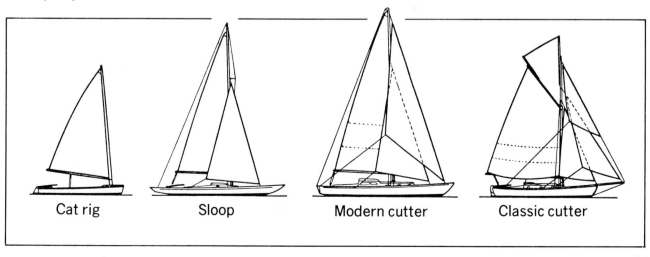

Cat rig   Sloop   Modern cutter   Classic cutter

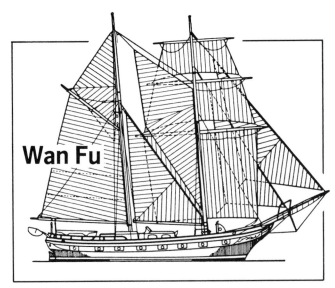

Fig. 25: A highly unusual rig designed by William Garden and built in 1959. This rig, which might be described as schooner brig, or brigantine, admirably suits the equally unusual hull.

ticularly popular in the United States of America.

None of these two-masted arrangements is superior to a one-masted rig. If one considers the effective forward thrust per unit sail area, the one-masted rig is clearly superior to any two masts. It is the practical advantages of the two-masted rig which make it desirable for larger vessels. Not only is the handling of the sails made easier by splitting up the area, but stability is increased on account of the lower centre of effort. In strong winds canvas can easily be reduced by

taking in individual sails, and this dispenses with the laborious job of reefing.

The lower efficiency of two-masted rigs is made up in races by a system of allowances, which has undergone frequent changes over the years. The difference in the efficiency of different rigs is best seen from the rig allowance table used by the RORC in 1955 (see page 37).

The first column gives the percentage of the sail area of which the *square root* was entered in the rating formula. The second column shows the actual percentage of sail area rated, and the third shows how much more sail area each of the two-masted rigs could carry before it was rated the same as the one-masted rig. Thus, in the case of the gaff-rigged ketch, 90 per cent of the square root of the sail area was entered in the rating formula, which meant that only 81 per cent of the sail area was effectively rated. Consequently, she could carry 23·3 per cent more sail area than a Bermudan sloop or cutter to get the same handicap.

This very simplified method of rig allowances has now been replaced by a rating system under the IOR (International Offshore Rule), which may do greater justice to the advantages and drawbacks of different rigs but is not nearly so simple.

For the cruising man, speeds attainable under racing conditions are of no interest. Long passages with a small crew call primarily for safety and simplicity in handling the boat. These requirements are particularly well met by the ketch, since single sails can be handed altogether, instead of being reefed, without giving the

Fig. 26: Four modern rigs of two-masted boats. There are still other possibilities, but nowadays most two-masted boats are ketch or yawl rigged.

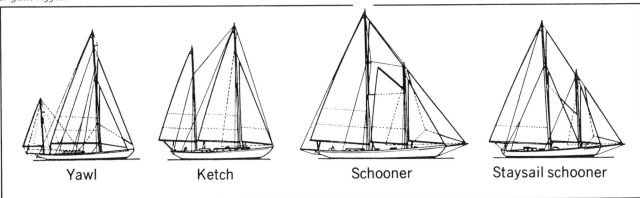

Yawl Ketch Schooner Staysail schooner

yacht increased lee or weather helm. A yawl rig offers roughly the same advantages as long as the mizzen or jigger mast can be adequately stayed. Schooners have largely lost their following, because their poor performance to windward is not outweighed by their good reaching abilities. Besides, the handling and especially the reefing of the enormous mainsail is difficult and requires great strength.

	√Sail area	Handicap	Additional sail area
Bermudan sloop or cutter	100%	100%	0%
Bermudan yawl	98%	96%	4%
Bermudan schooner or gaff schooner	96%	92%	8·5%
Bermudan ketch or gaff yawl	94%	88%	13·5%
Wishbone ketch or wishbone schooner	94%	88%	13·5%
Gaff schooner	92%	85%	17·5%
Gaff ketch	90%	81%	23·3%

Wind and Speed,
the Problem of their Inter-Dependence

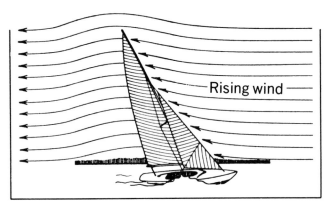

Fig. 27: As the airflow approaches the sail it is deflected from its course before it meets the sail. This deflection is at an oblique angle upwards, roughly parallel to the panels of the mainsail. The locally upward-moving airflow can actually be observed and measured.

Fig. 28: Illustration of the principal courses sailed relative to the wind. 'Points off the wind' are marked on a circle in the middle. Compass degrees are not easily usable when determining a direction relative to the wind.

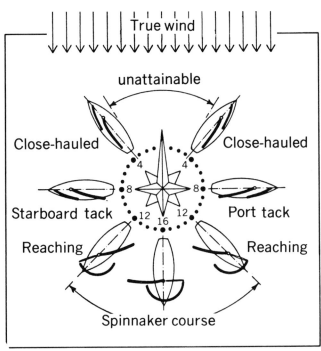

A sailing vessel moves through the water under the influence of a number of forces, a description of which will be given here as an introduction to the following chapters. The difficulty of assessing them exactly lies in their number and complexity: the constantly changing wind, the dissimilarity of sails and hulls, the *fluidity* of the water in which the hull moves, the personal influence of helmsman and crew, and finally the effect all these factors have on each other.

THE WIND: Its character changes in every imaginable way, from a dead calm to a hurricane, from one direction to another and from one minute to the next. The wind increases in strength with increasing height above the surface of the water, so that the upper parts of the sail are subject to greater wind pressure than the lower ones. Besides which, the wind stream is deflected before it meets the sail. Finally, the humidity and density of the air have a certain effect, and rain may spoil all calculations.

THE SAILS: Although the shape of a sail can be exactly defined on the drawing board, it is impossible to follow this in every detail in the actual making of the sail, quite apart from the change the sail shape

undergoes under the influence of the wind. In addition, the sail sets with a vertical twist, so that each part of the area works under a different angle of incidence, the angle being greater at the foot than at the top. Full-length battens improve the set of a sail, but for practical reasons they are often forbidden under class rules. From the aerodynamic point of view, the triangular shape of most sails is by no means favourable, because it results in areas of different effectiveness, including those which are completely ineffective but cannot be avoided, such as the head and clew of a mainsail. The optimum driving force derived from the sails depends to an inordinately large degree on the ability and intuition of the crew. Not surprisingly, it is frequently professional sail makers who win important races.

Sheet leads can hardly ever be adjusted far enough and with sufficient speed to meet changes in course and wind conditions. A boat is rarely equipped with a sufficient number of sails of different cut, size and weight of cloth to get the optimum performance under all conditions. Besides, the generally adopted limitation of sail areas makes most boats under-canvassed in light airs, whereas in strong winds the same sail areas have to be reduced by inefficient means.

38

THE HULL: Only very rarely can a boat be designed with a view to the best possible sailing characteristics. The hull is nearly always a compromise to satisfy the various demands for seaworthiness, stability, accommodation, speed and windward ability. Even boats in the same class may differ when it comes to rudder, plate, keel, weight, freeboard and even the weight of the crew. Modern rating rules lead to the identical rating of greatly dissimilar hulls, so that some vessels are specifically built as *ghosters*, whereas others perform best in moderate winds or heavy weather.

PERSONAL INFLUENCE OF THE CREW: No other craft not propelled by man-power is as sensitive to personal influence as the sailing yacht. This influence is not mainly dependent on physical strength but is a product of experience, training, quick reaction and intuition. All these qualities are needed in minute-by-minute decisions as well as in foreseeing possible tactics, changes of wind and sea conditions.

THE WATER: Although it is the sailor's favourite element, the sea has a number of traits which can only be described as a nuisance. Its surface is highly irregular, its liquid condition permits leeway and violent, undesirable motion of the hull in a seaway. Constant or temporary currents can upset a plotted course, and tides increase or reduce the depth of water. The water attacks the hull under the waterline and causes roughness, the growth of barnacles and weeds, rot, rust and electrolytic corrosion.

COURSES: The direction in which a boat sails is usually determined by the destination it wishes to reach, be it in a race or on a cruise. All courses are easily defined in relation to the earth's surface with the help of a compass. If, however, one wants to define a course in relation to the wind direction, which is particularly important to a sailing yacht, the compass card is of no use.

Far too few modern skippers define direction by points, although this is the only method which permits orientation in relation to wind and boat, independent of the earth's surface. Not so long ago compass courses were still defined in points. They are arrived at by dividing the compass into quarters, eighths, sixteenths and thirty-seconds, one 'point' being $\frac{1}{32}$ of the compass,

i.e. $\frac{1}{32}$ of 360°, which is $11\frac{1}{4}°$.

Figure 28 shows that a course of less than 3 points to the true wind is 'unattainable'. When sailing hard on the wind, a boat can be made to go as close as $3\frac{1}{2}$ to 4 points off the wind, less favourable hull shapes only reach 5 points. It is obvious that this is a useful way of defining a course. For example, during a race a helmsman wants to know where the next mark is and asks his forward hand to locate it. The latter might answer: 'The mark is 2 points on the port bow; the nearest rival boat is 12 points to starboard.' The influence of aviation, however, where compass degrees rather than points are used, has caused this practice to be widely adopted in sailing these days.

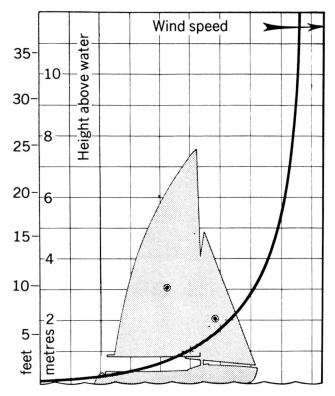

Fig. 29: The strength of the wind is least near the surface of the water and increases rapidly the higher up it is measured until, at about 30 ft, it can be considered normal and consistent. This difference in wind strength at different heights should be taken into account in the design of the sails and the way the sheets are led, since it can have a noticeable influence on the angle at which the sail sets.

The Effect of the Wind on the Sails and Boat

Plate 8: Solings racing. This fast, modern 3-man keelboat has Olympic status and is raced all over the world. The photo was taken at an important international series just at the start of a race.
Photo: P A Rostad, Oslo

During the whole of the Middle Ages ships of the western world could sail no closer than approximately at right angles to the wind. In fact, the usual point of sailing was with a quartering wind. If a ship wanted to alter course it had to 'wear ship', i.e. tack the *stern* through the wind. Neither sails nor hulls were capable of tacking *into* the wind and, indeed, no one would have thought of attempting it. It was only at the start of the last century that the bold design of the clipper opened up the possibility of sailing close enough to the wind to 'make up to windward' by tacking. This started the race to *cheat the wind*, which has found its triumphant conclusion in the concept of the modern racing yacht.

The speed of medieval ships was so modest and their angle to the wind so great that their captains never appreciated the difference between *true wind* and *apparent wind*.

An observer on land or on board a moored vessel can only feel the so-called *true wind*. As soon as the observer moves, his own movement causes an *apparent* change in the wind direction, and the *resultant force* of the two movements is the *apparent wind*. This apparent wind changes with the direction in which the observer moves and also depends on the speed with which he moves. The moving observer feels *only* the apparent wind, he can no longer determine the true wind, at least not empirically. He can do so approximately if he has access to 'outside' information such as the smoke from a chimney or a flag flying ashore. Wind-streaks on the water are another source of information.

Nobody can sail a modern yacht without constantly taking into account the apparent wind. Only the

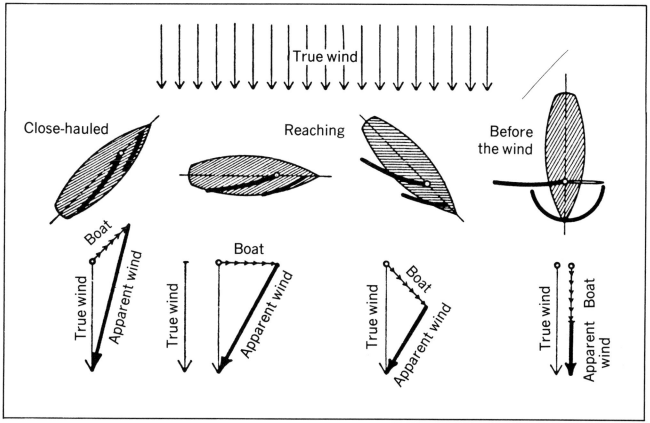

Fig. 30: Illustration of 'apparent wind'. Its direction and speed is indicated by the angles and lengths of the thick arrows. The apparent wind changes according to the point of sailing, although the true wind represented by the thin vertical arrows, remains unchanged.

apparent wind drives and affects a boat under sail, it is the only wind that matters to boat and crew.

Of course, in scientific terms, the boat's propulsion depends on both the true and the apparent wind. This is explained in Fig. 30, where the true wind is presented as coming from the top of the diagram. In any of the four courses shown the thick arrow represents the direction and speed of the apparent wind, being the result of true wind (thin arrow) and the direction and speed of the boat (multi-arrowed line) working together. When a boat sails close-hauled, the apparent wind comes from further ahead than the true wind, and its speed is greater. Thus, in the diagram, the thick arrow of the apparent wind comes from further to the right than the thin arrow of the true wind and is longer than the latter. When the boat sails with the wind on the

beam as in the second drawing, the direction of the apparent wind differs even more, but its speed is only a little greater than that of the true wind. In a quartering wind, the difference between the two directions is still considerable, but the apparent wind is now slower than the true wind. On courses dead before the wind, the two wind directions coincide, and the apparent wind is much *slower* than the true wind, because its speed is only the difference between the boat's speed and the speed of the true wind.

INFLUENCE OF THE APPARENT WIND
On the wind it is detrimental, because it strikes the sail at a more acute angle than the true wind. The higher the speed sailed, the more unfavourable the direction of the apparent wind becomes.

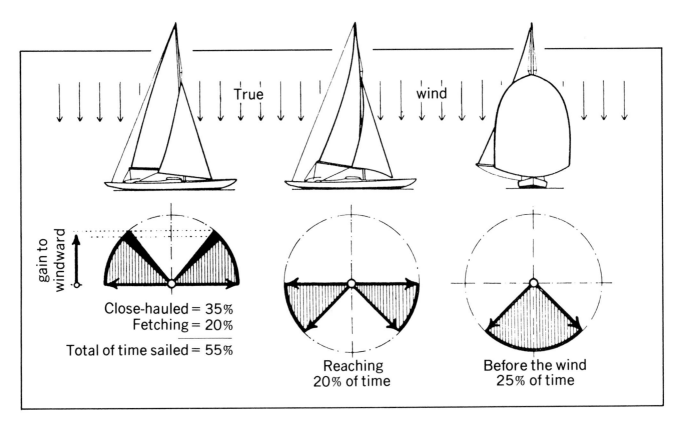

gain to windward

Close-hauled = 35%
Fetching = 20%
Total of time sailed = 55%

Reaching
20% of time

Before the wind
25% of time

Fig. 31: In this diagram the different points of sailing are considered in relation to time spent on each. The overwhelming importance of windward courses is evident. Of the total time spent on all points of sailing, about 55 per cent is to windward, 20 per cent reaching and 25 per cent running. This knowledge is of the greatest importance in the design and construction of the hull as well as the cut of the sails.

On a reach, its influence is beneficial, because its angle of incidence is then particularly favourable and its increased speed nearly always desirable.

On a run its influence is detrimental, because its speed decreases the faster the boat sails.

A hull can be shaped and sails cut to favour one particular point of sailing. Boats with outstanding windward abilities will not normally excel on reaching courses, and similarly boats that perform well off the wind are not particularly good on the wind. It would, therefore, be interesting to investigate the frequency and importance of the different points of sailing. It is assumed, for this purpose, that on average over an appreciable period of time, whether racing or cruising, a yacht covers equally long distances on all possible points of sailing.

In Fig. 31 an attempt has been made to determine how much time a yacht spends on each of the three most important points of sailing. Again, the true wind is

shown as coming from the top of the diagram. A yacht sailing at right angles to the true wind causes the apparent wind to draw ahead and is therefore, in practice, still sailing *on the wind*. All courses covered by the diagram on the left can therefore be counted as windward courses. Since it covers half of all possible courses, we can say that half of all courses sailed are on-the-wind courses. But this does not mean that half of a boat's sailing time is spent on the wind, because, firstly, the boat sails a zig-zag course when tacking and, secondly, the boat's speed on the wind is slower than it is when reaching. With this in mind it can be assumed that not less than 55 per cent of the time is spent sailing on the wind.

This leaves 45 per cent of the total sailing time for all other courses. Since reaching is the fastest point of sailing, it can be assumed that it takes up 20 per cent of the time, with 25 per cent left for the slightly slower courses before the wind. Since these figures are of great

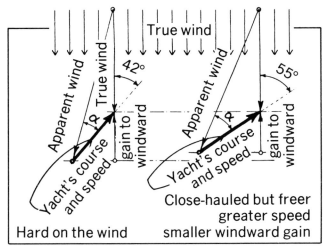

True wind

42°

Apparent wind

True wind

Apparent wind

gain to windward

Yacht's course and speed

Hard on the wind

55°

Apparent wind

gain to windward

Yacht's course and speed

Close-hauled but freer
greater speed
smaller windward gain

Gain to windward when Close-hauled

*Fig. 32: When sailing to windward it is important to aim at
the best possible speed made good and to decide whether it pays to
'pinch' or to sail fast and free. In the conditions in the diagram the
yacht on the left, which points higher, reaches the mark sooner,
although the speed of the boat sailing free is higher by 15 per cent.
However, pointing as high as possible is only profitable for yachts
which do not accelerate much when the sheets are eased.*

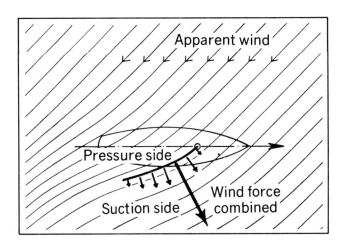

Apparent wind

Pressure side

Suction side

Wind force
combined

*Fig.T 33: he apparent wind is diverted by the sail, which is
slightly angled to the airflow. The resulting wind forces work on
the whole sail area and produce an area of high pressure on the
windward side and low pressure on the leeward side of the sail,
the magnitude of which is indicated by the many small arrows.
These can be combined in one large arrow, which illustrates the
total wind force and direction.*

importance for further investigations, we will summarize them below:

Average Time Spent on Each Point of Sailing

On the wind . . . . 55% of the total time sailed
Reaching . . . . 20% of the total time sailed
Running . . . . 25% of the total time sailed

Not so long ago it was generally recommended to sail
slightly *free* when on the wind, because the hull shapes
and rigs of older yachts were not suitable for sailing
very close. Even now on long cruises, especially on
ocean voyages, one would never force a boat to point
extremely high but would rather free the sheets a bit
and give her more speed. In any case, on long passages
there usually comes a wind change before long, so that
'pinching' nearly always proves a mistake in the end.

In a race, however, and especially with modern
yachts, it often pays to force the boat to point as high
as possible, even if speed is lost. Figure 32 explains the
situation, assuming that a boat could sail at either 42°
or 55° to the true wind, in the latter case gaining a
15 per cent speed increase. What has to be established
here is the *distance made good*, or rather the *speed made
good* to windward, for this alone matters in a race. As

can be seen from the diagram, a 15 per cent speed
increase is not sufficient to compensate for the freer
course of 55° to the wind. The boat on the left, sailing
at 42° and sheeted hard in, gains considerably in speed
made good and arrives at the mark sooner, although its
speed through the water is less and the angle of incidence of the apparent wind is more acute.

The ability to sail close to windward is undoubtedly
the most amazing achievement of the modern yacht.
A lot has been said and written about it, for it seems, at
first sight, incredible that forces can be extracted from
the air which will drive a boat practically *into* that very
wind.

If a sail is inclined at an angle to the wind, it diverts
the air stream from its original course. This diversion
produces a number of small forces, neither equally
strong nor having the same direction, which are spread
over the entire surface of the sail. These various individual forces could be shown as a single force, as has been
done in Fig. 33. In the diagram this force, indicated by
the bold arrow, has been called 'wind force', and it has
the same effect and direction as the sum of all the
individual forces taken together. In theory, the boat
should move in the direction of that arrow, but . . . and

43

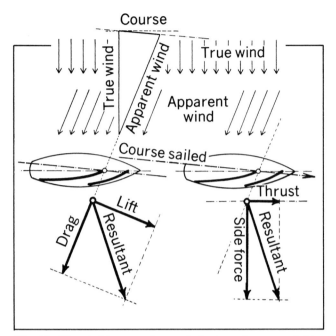

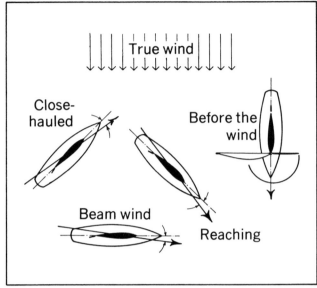

Fig. 34: The wind forces acting on the boat can be represented by the arrow marked 'resultant'. In aerodynamics this is resolved into two forces called 'lift' and 'drag', as shown in the parallelogram of forces on the left. The parallelogram on the right shows how the hull converts lift and drag into 'thrust', which is useful, and 'side force', which is detrimental but unavoidable.

Fig. 35: Leeway is made on nearly all points of sailing. This means that the boat does not actually sail on a course parallel to her centreline but at an angle to leeward. The amount of leeway made is indicated by the angle of leeway. In the diagram the rudder is slightly to leeward, which is the most favourable position for minimum resistance.

this is the crux of the whole science of sailing to windward: the highly developed hulls of modern yachts offer enormous resistance to this leeward drift and thereby convert part of the wind force into forward thrust.

The procedure employed in aerodynamic tests is not to measure the wind force and then divide it into drag and lift, but usually the reverse, namely to measure drag and lift and calculate from them the 'resultant' wind force. *Drag* is the force acting in the same direction as the wind, *lift* is the force acting at right angles to the wind direction. The term *lift* is one connected with aircraft and aeronautics but is used for our purpose, because lift must under no circumstances be confused with propulsion or forward thrust. Once the drag and lift of a profile have been determined, it is an easy matter to determine the resultant wind force by a parallelogram of forces, as shown in Fig. 34.

In fact, Fig. 34 is of basic significance, since it illustrates the whole phenomenon of the wind's propulsive influence on the sail. Along the upper edge of the diagram we see the true wind and immediately under-

neath the resultant apparent wind. The arrows indicate the direction and, by their length, the strength of the wind. When the apparent wind is diverted by the sail, numerous small forces are produced, the sum of which is shown by the long, bold arrow marked 'resultant' (calculated in this case with the help of lift and drag).

The right half of the diagram shows how the wind's 'action' is followed by the boat's 'reaction'. The 'resultant', as taken from the figure on the left, is now related to the boat as a whole, including the hull in the water. As it meets the resistance of the water, it is split into two new forces: *thrust* and *side force*. Since the direction of the resultant is almost at right angles to the hull, it is not surprising that the parallelogram of forces yields a *very considerable side force* and only *very little forward thrust*.

The conclusion drawn from this simple investigation is surprising. The only force which is really desirable in sailing on the wind, namely forward thrust, is the smallest of all, whereas the side force, which causes the boat to heel over and make leeway, is several times larger. If one considers that each works on the boat

44

simultaneously, it is surprising to see how modern yachts convert this small thrust force into spectacular speeds and at the same time suffer very little leeway despite the enormous side force. Since it is not possible to avoid leeway altogether, a yacht will never sail exactly in the direction of her centre-line, which is her *apparent course*, but on a *true course* which is determined by leeway (see centre of Fig. 34).

Without leeway, sailing on the wind is impossible. The amount of leeway made is measured by the so-called angle of leeway, which is the angle between the boat's centreline and the direction in which she actually moves. The angle of leeway in modern racing yachts is between 3° and 5°, in cruisers a little more than 5°.

The wind's side force has yet another effect on the boat: it makes it heel over. A sailing boat, therefore, reacts to the influence of the wind in three ways: by moving forward, by making leeway and by heeling.

What has been said so far is true for all courses from hard on the wind to broad reaching. It does not apply before the wind. Only when running before the wind does the sail cease to behave like an aerofoil and instead becomes a body of resistance. To sum up the characteristics of the two basic ways of sailing we can say that:

On the wind the sail works like an aerodynamic profile, inducing lift and drag by virtue of its cut and the angle at which it is set.

Before the wind the sail acts simply as a body of resistance and no longer has any of the characteristics of an aerodynamic profile.

If we refer once again to Fig. 31 we can see that for 25 per cent of the time sailed the sail acts as a body of resistance, while for 75 per cent of the time it acts as an aerodynamic profile, inducing lift which the hull converts into forward thrust and side force.

In order to offer the maximum resistance before the wind, a sail should be cut very full. For its function as an aerodynamic profile it should be cut rather flat. It has been proved, however, that if a sail is cut with the best possible aerodynamic profile for optimum performance on the wind, this will result in a superior average performance which is not outweighed by any advantages on other courses. No mainsail can be cut to give maximum performance both on and off the wind, and changing mainsails is not allowed on racing yachts and not desirable on cruising yachts, either.

If a yacht wants to reach a destination dead to windward she must get there by *tacking*. The clippers were probably the first to tack into the wind with reasonable reliability, but going about was not exactly easy for them. The ship usually lost speed as it came up into the wind and hung there until the foresail was backed to help to push the bow round, usually after the ship had started to make sternway. Then the rudder was brought into reverse action to bring her finally round on the new tack.

Every time a boat tacks she loses time. It is, therefore, advisable to make *long* boards. A modern yacht will hardly ever get caught in stays when tacking, but should this ever happen, the turn can usually be completed by backing the foresail. This was quite usual and normal during the first quarter of this century. Older sailors will still remember the deafening noise in the rigging of larger yachts when they got caught in stays and all sails, blocks, sheets and loose ends joined in a hellish dance.

Investigation into Sailing on theWind

A yacht sailing close-hauled virtually *eats* its way into the wind. The fact that on this point of sailing any forward thrust can be extracted from the wind amounts almost to a miracle. However, only a small part of the total wind forces is accounted for by forward thrust. The greater part, on average three times as much, is converted into side force, which causes leeway and heeling. Heeling, in its turn, reduces the projected sail area.

Sails cannot be set without the necessary rigging consisting of mast, boom, halliards and sheets. The mast again needs to be stayed by shrouds, stays, spreaders, jumpers etc. to help it take the wind pressure on the sail. All parts of the rigging are struck by the wind from almost ahead and thus cause a considerable part of the total wind resistance. Besides, the mast has an unfavourable influence on the sail by disturbing the air stream in exactly the place where it ought to strike the sail freely. All parts of the rigging, therefore, reduce the potential forward thrust of the sail and increase the heeling effect of the wind.

Every sail suffers a certain loss of efficiency when close-hauled, even if its cut is of the greatest perfection. The unavoidable twist in the upper part of the sail makes it necessary to sheet the sail in harder than is good for the lower part of the sail, so that *on average* the sail sets at the most efficient angle to the wind. To determine this angle, which has a decisive influence on the attainable speed, is largely a matter of the crew's skill.

As soon as the boat starts to heel, the centre of effort of all forward driving forces is no longer vertically over the boat's centreline but shifts to leeward. The thrust then acts on a lever arm outside the ship's centreline and therefore has a powerful luffing effect.

Despite these many disturbing influences, the boat makes its way through the water with astounding sureness and precision. It cannot even derive much benefit from the designed symmetrical shape of its hull, because a heeled hull is no longer symmetrical, and the water has to travel different distances to pass to windward and to leeward. Heeling always means increased resistance, but this is often compensated by an increase in the waterline length.

The side force of the wind causes *true* leeway. Boats with excessive lee or weather helm also make *false* leeway, which occurs as a result of the continued exaggerated angle of the rudder which is needed to hold a

Fig. 36: A ketch-rigged Arab dhow with lateen sails. Similar craft are still used in coastal traffic in the Near and Middle East.

badly balanced boat on course. The angle of leeway in modern yachts is between 3° and 5°, but considerably larger angles may occur. Shallow-draught boats with a poor underwater profile and badly setting sails may have an angle of leeway of 10° or more when sailing to windward. Whilst heeling increases the resistance due to the hull shape becoming asymmetrical, leeway causes a further significant increase in resistance which is called 'induced drag' and will be explained in a later chapter.

The lateral resistance of the hull, which counteracts leeway, can be imagined as being concentrated in the geometric centre of the hull. This, the centre of lateral resistance (CLR for short) is always marked in the line drawings of a boat. In practice, however, the actual pressure centre, the dynamic CLR, lies forward of the geometric CLR. This is so because the fore body of the hull cuts through undisturbed water, which resists leeward drift more than the disturbed water through which the after body moves.

Similarly complicated rules apply to the sails. Here, too, the dynamic centre of effort does not coincide with the geometric CE, because the forward parts of the sail are subject to greater wind pressure than the after parts. Thus, both centres, the CLR of the hull and the

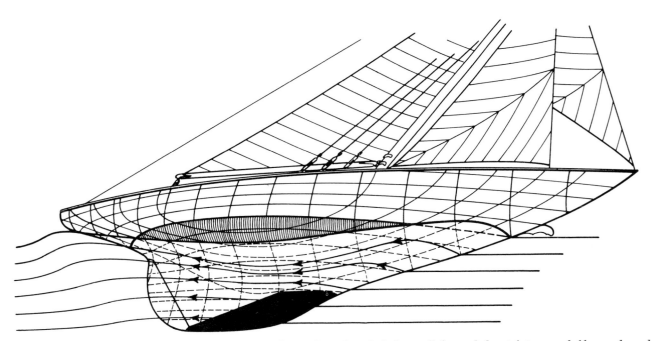

Fig. 37: The effect of the wind on a boat sailing to windward produces a threefold reaction in the hull: forward motion, heeling and leeway. Modern hull shapes are very efficient in converting the relatively small forward thrust into remarkable speeds and reducing leeway to a minimum, despite the fact that the side force is many times greater than the forward thrust.

CE of the sail area, lie forward of the geometric centres. It would seem, then, that to result in a balanced boat the CE should lie vertically above the CLR. Unfortunately, though, even if the two centres were to lie in the same vertical plane (and, as yet, no way has been found to calculate their position accurately), a balance of forces cannot be achieved because, due to heeling, the thrust acts from a point *far outboard* and has a considerable luffing effect. One might imagine that the boat was not being pulled along by the bow, but by a tow line attached to a boom sticking out over the side. It is obvious that this method of towing can only be compensated for by angling the rudder. The luffing effect of the thrust lever becomes stronger as the boat heels over. If the centre of effort of the sail area is moved forward some appreciable distance, an opposite falling-off moment can be obtained, which counterbalances the luffing moment at an average angle of heel. It is, of course, not possible to consider and counterbalance all angles of heel when determining the position of the centre of effort, merely an average angle.

In conclusion it must be added that the part of the hull which is above the water is also exposed to the wind and therefore causes air friction, which is most detrimental on the wind.

In Fig. 38 some of the things which occur in sailing to windward have been shown in diagrammatic form. It is assumed that the yacht sails at an angle of 45° to the true wind, which is well within the abilities of any modern sailing keelboat or dinghy. Under ideal racing conditions, some boats can get as close as 39° to the true wind. In the case of Fig. 38 average conditions have been assumed, with a wind speed of approximately 10 knots, in which non-planing types of boats already reach 90 per cent of their maximum speed. The apparent wind, shown by the arrow on the left, is much stronger than the true wind, indicated by the arrow on the right. At 45° to the true wind (which cannot be established from on board) the course sailed in relation to the apparent wind is 27°. If the mark lies dead to windward, which means the yacht will be tacking, 70 per cent of her speed through the water will be *speed made good*, which means speed, or way, into the wind.

In 1936 a scientifically measured series of experiments was conducted by the then head of the Stevens Institute of Technology, K S M Davidson. The yacht used in the experiment was GIMCRACK, a newly designed type of racing yacht similar to a 6-metre. An experienced and particularly skilled helmsman sailed her close-hauled in all winds, while all measurable values

47

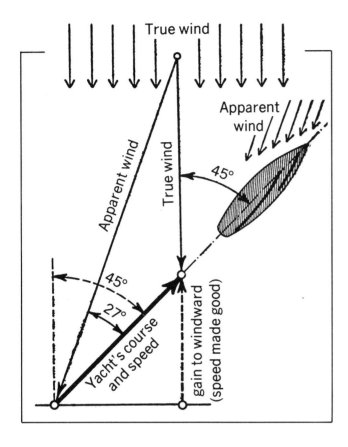

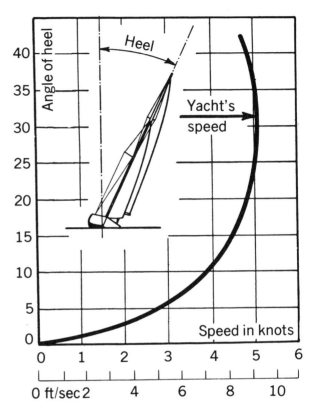

Fig. 38: Most modern boats can sail as close as 45° to the true wind. In this case the distance made good to windward is 70 per cent of the actual distance sailed.

Fig. 39: This graph, which shows the speed and angles of heel of a Dragon, was drawn up with reference to the experimental runs of the yacht GIMCRACK. *It can be seen that the greatest speed is reached at 32° of heel. As the wind force and the angle of heel increase further, the speed drops.*

were recorded. The results were used in comparison with test data obtained with models, which were just then assuming increased importance in yacht tests. The results of these test runs became known as the 'Gimcrack-coefficients'. Since GIMCRACK is not a widely known type, the figures have been adapted by the author to fit the internationally known Dragon class and are presented in diagrammatic form in Figs. 39 to 43.

The first of these graphs, Fig. 39, explains the relationship between speed and angle of heel, sailing on the wind. Even light winds, which cause the boat to heel only very slightly, give it an appreciable turn of speed. With an angle of heel of only 5° the boat already reaches half its maximum speed. At 11° of heel a speed of 4 knots is reached. As the wind increases so does the angle of heel, but the speed only increases by a very

small amount after this and reaches its maximum, 5·1 knots, at 30° of heel. If the wind increases further, the boat will continue to heel further, but the speed will then *decrease* rather than increase.

The next graph, Fig. 40, illustrates the total resistance at these speeds, at the same time showing the corresponding angles of heel. The dotted line shows what would happen if the boat was sailing upright and making no leeway. It can again be seen that at 11° of heel a speed of 4 knots is reached, and at the same time the total resistance can be read off: 30 lb (14 kg). At 30° of heel and a speed of 5·1 knots the total resistance is considerably greater: 82 lb (37 kg). As the angle of heel increases, so does the resistance. At an angle of heel of 40° the resistance rises to 110 lb (50 kg), but the thrust obtained from the sails does not increase at the same rate so that the speed actually *decreases*. The

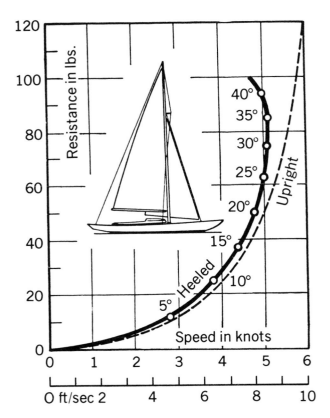

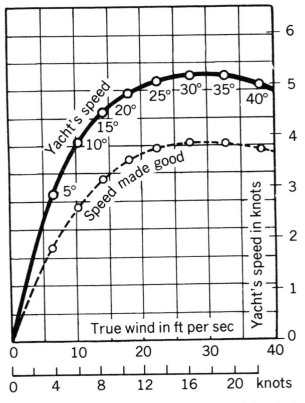

Fig. 40: Resistance to forward motion in a Dragon in relation to speed and angle of heel. The broken curve shows the resistance of an upright hull. The difference between the two curves shows the detrimental influence of heeling and leeway.

Fig. 41: The speed and distance made good to windward of a Dragon in relation to the true wind. Angles of heel are given as parameters.

difference between the dotted line for the boat sailing upright and the bold line for the boat sailing heeled illustrates the important effect of heeling (which upsets the symmetry of the hull) and leeway (which causes induced drag).

In the two first graphs wind speed is not indicated. Figure 41 shows all the previous figures in relation to wind speeds. In a 10-knot wind, for example, a Dragon will sail at an angle of heel of 20° and reach a speed of 4·8 knots. Once again it can be seen that the maximum speed is reached at an angle of heel of approximately 30°, which is related to a wind speed of 14·5 knots. With increasing wind speeds, the boat's speed does not increase any more and eventually decreases. The lower, dotted curve shows the speed made good, i.e. the actual way gained directly into the wind. The fact that this speed is as high as it is amounts virtually to a miracle

and is due only to the excellent windward qualities of hull and rig.

The fourth in this series of graphs, Fig. 42, illustrates the effect of the wind most clearly. The bold curve shows that the apparent wind is always much faster than the true wind. A true wind of 16 ft/sec (nearly 10 knots), for example, is turned by the speed of the boat itself into an apparent wind of 21·5 ft/sec (nearly 13 knots).

The upper, dotted curve is of special interest. It indicates the angle between course and true wind and shows that the exceptionally narrow angle of 39°, which we mentioned earlier, was never reached in this case. The smallest angle attained by the boat was 42° at a wind speed of over 14·5 knots. At first sight it seems illogical that the boat cannot get as close to the true wind in light airs, but this is a logical consequence of the

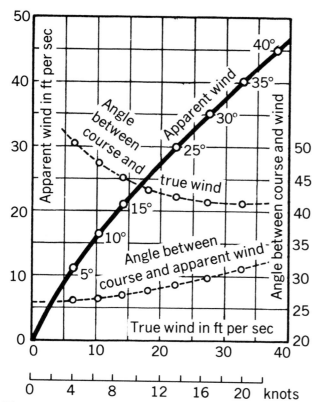

Fig. 42: Three curves pertaining to a Dragon sailing on the wind, indicating the speed of the apparent wind in relation to the true wind and the angles between course sailed and true and apparent wind respectively.

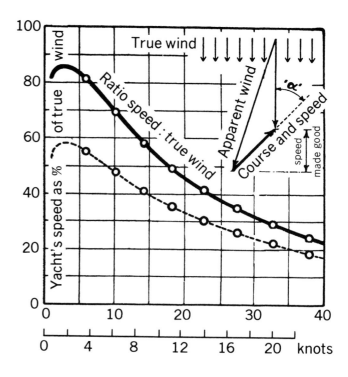

Fig. 43: The bold curve indicates the speed of a Dragon on the wind in relation to the true wind. In light winds the boat reaches speeds of over 80 per cent of the true wind speed. In strong winds the speed sailed drops to about 20 per cent of the true wind speed. The broken line represents the speed made good to windward in relation to the true wind.

fact that in light winds the boat already reaches a relatively high speed in comparison to the true wind and thereby makes the apparent wind *draw ahead* quite considerably.

The last diagram, Fig. 43, illustrates both the boat's speed through the water and the speed made good in relation to the true wind. The bold curve on top shows that even in the lightest of winds the boat never reaches the speed of the wind itself, which is hardly surprising. But it comes close to it. In a light breeze of about 2 knots the Dragon reaches 85 per cent of the true wind speed.

In a pleasant sailing breeze of about 10 knots the boat sails at just half the wind speed. The dotted line shows the *speed made good* to windward in relation to the true wind speed. At the same wind speed of 10 knots the Dragon's speed made good is 36 per cent of the speed of the true wind.

These Gimcrack-coefficients illustrate convincingly the wonderful ability of the modern yacht to cheat the wind into propelling it at remarkable speeds into the very wind itself.

Cause and Correction of Weather Helm and Lee Helm

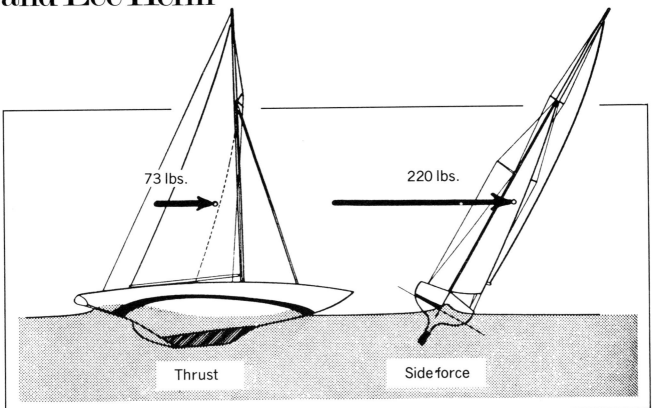

73 lbs.

220 lbs.

Thrust

Side force

Fig. 44: On the wind, the side force of the wind is three times as great as the forward thrust. The diagram is for a Dragon sailing in a wind of 13 knots.

A boat driven by the wind and sailing on a straight course is always in a state of equilibrium. One speaks of 'natural balance' if all forces, i.e. those of thrust and resistance, lie on one common axis. 'Forced balance' is the state in which these forces try to push the boat off course and this is prevented by the counter-balancing effect of the rudder.

There is a third kind of balance, so-called 'composite balance', in which two inequalities in balance counteract and cancel each other. Although the forces in this case act on different axes, no counter-balancing rudder action is needed. Sailing in a state of composite balance comes close to the ideal state of natural balance, but has the advantage of *actually* occurring on boats in practice, ideally by design.

In order to sail in a state of *natural balance* a boat would have to sail permanently on an even keel, and the thrust would have to act along the centreline. This can only be achieved in running dead before the wind, provided that mainsail and spinnaker produce equal forces at equal distances from the boat's centreline.

Forced balance is the most frequent state for a boat to find herself in on all courses. *Composite balance*, on the other hand, is the aim of all drawings and calcu-

lations. Every designer tries to create this ideal situation by calculating the positions of centre of effort and centre of lateral resistance. The racing man pursues the same aim by trimming his sails. The state of composite balance can actually be attained when sailing to windward and occurs fairly frequently, if only over a limited range of wind speeds.

It would be relatively easy to reach a state of natural balance before the wind, if class rules had not introduced certain restriction which, strangely enough, are also adhered to by pure cruising yachts. A modern spinnaker is as large as, or even larger than, the mainsail. Despite this, a state of balance before the wind is rarely achieved, because the spinnaker boom has to be very short to comply with class rules. It is always much shorter than the main boom, and consequently the centre of effort of the mainsail is further removed from the boat's centreline than the centre of effort of the spinnaker. The total thrust will only act along a common axis if the shorter lever of the spinnaker thrust is compensated for by *more* thrust from the spinnaker, so that the *moments* are equal on both sides.

During ocean passages in constant trade winds it is usual to set two identical, triangular sails before the

51

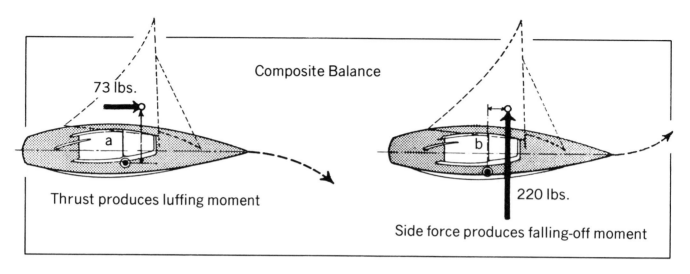

Composite Balance

73 lbs.

a

Thrust produces luffing moment

220 lbs.

Side force produces falling-off moment

Fig. 45: Perfect balance in a boat can be achieved by applying the principle of 'composite balance'. To this end, the luffing moment produced by the thrust has to be equal to the bearing-off moment produced by the side force.

mast, so-called twin runnings sails or twin spinnakers. If no mainsail is set, which is normally the case, a state of *natural balance* occurs automatically, and the yacht can sail for long distances without any rudder action whatever. Unfortunately, this state is often disturbed by wave motion, and then rudder action does become necessary.

For courses to windward it is extremely difficult to measure the forces which determine the desired balance. The thrust acts at a point far to leeward and outside the boat's centreline, while the resistance is concentrated at a point slightly to windward. Resistance itself, as a result of induced drag and lack of hull symmetry, becomes almost impossible to determine. Finally, there is the considerable side force, which causes heeling and leeway and which decisively affects lee or weather helm.

To examine these forces more closely we shall choose a Dragon, whose sail area, in a wind speed of 13 knots, gives it a thrust of 73 lb (33 kg) and a side force of 220 lb (100 kg). Due to the boat's angle of heel, the thrust acts far to leeward, and this produces a luffing moment, which seeks to turn the boat's bow up into the wind. In other words, *forward thrust causes weather helm*. The side force, on the other hand, need not in principle create any turning moment, because it could coincide with the centre of lateral resistance. However, a trick commonly employed by yacht designers places

the side force at a point where it is actually beneficial: by moving its centre slightly *forward*, a *falling-off* moment is produced, which is intentional. It partially cancels out the luffing moment produced by the thrust and sometimes even completely eliminates it. To sum up: the thrust produces a *luffing moment*, the shifting forward of the side force produces a *falling-off moment*.

Figure 45 shows an example of *equal moments* which make up *composite balance*. On the left, we see a thrust of 73 lb (33 kg) exert its force on a lever 'a' outside the centre of lateral resistance (not the boat's centreline). On the right, the side force is illustrated, which acts with 220 lb (100 kg) on the short lever 'b' *forward* of the centre of lateral resistance. The dotted arrow extending from the bow shows that the thrust seeks to push the boat up into the wind, while the side force seeks to push it off the wind. If the force multiplied by the length of the lever results in equal moments on either side, the boat sails in a state of composite balance.

It would be mathematically easy to bring about this balance. The levers 'a' and 'b' need only be inversely proportional to thrust and side force to give equal moments. If we assume that lever 'a', on which a thrust of 73 lb acts, has a length of 84 in, then the side force of 220 lb, would have to act on a lever 'b' of $\frac{73 \times 84}{220} = 28$ in. In other words, if the point at which

52

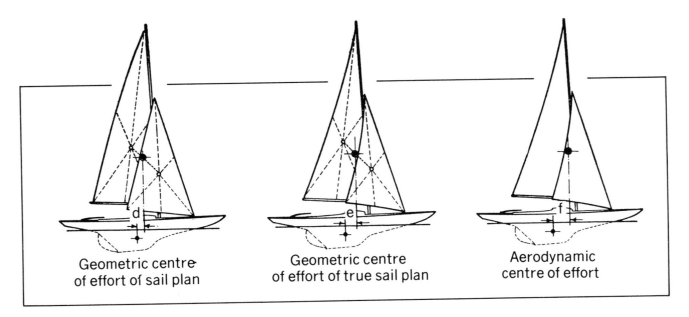

| Geometric centre | Geometric centre | Aerodynamic |
| of effort of sail plan | of effort of true sail plan | centre of effort |

Fig. 46: Three methods of locating the centre of effort of sail in a Dragon in relation to the centre of lateral resistance. On the left the conventional drawing-board method, in the middle as based on the true sail plan on the wind, and on the right the true aerodynamic centre.

the side force is exerted lies approximately 28 in forward of the centre of lateral resistance, its falling-off moment is equal to the luffing moment of the thrust and the yacht, in the example studied, will sail in a state of composite balance.

In practice, unfortunately, it is not as easy as that. The exact location of the dynamic centre of effort of the sail area can neither be determined mathematically nor by generally applicable experiments. In practice, therefore, the geometric centre of effort is used for calculations, although it is known that it definitely does not coincide with the dynamic centre of effort.

That this is so is shown in Fig. 46. The drawing on the left shows the conventional drawing-board method, by which the geometric centre of effort is established as lying forward of the centre of lateral resistance by the *lead* 'd'. However, when the boat is sailing, the sails do not remain in the centreplane and their side view looks like the drawing in the middle, where the geometric CE is further forward by the lead 'e'. The aerodynamic behaviour of the sails moves the true dynamic centre of effort even further forward, as is shown on the right by the lead 'f'. This happens for widely known reasons: the wind is deflected by the sail, starting at the luff. This makes the sail more effective in the forward part than in the after part, where turbulence is stronger. This and the twist of the sail complicate any attempt

to make even approximate calculations.

Similar complications apply to the centre of lateral resistance of the hull. Again, the dynamic centre lies forward of the geometric centre, and only model tests or experiments with real boats would make it possible to locate the actual position of the dynamic CLR. The practical designer, however, has no time for lengthy speculations and instead applies concrete values, which have been proven in practice. The final, corrective touches are left to the dedicated yachtsman, who spends much time and effort on tuning and trimming his rig. He may eventually come very close to the ideal state of balance but, of course, he will not be able to analyse it mathematically.

The following table gives various 'leads', i.e. horizontal distances between CE and CLR, which have proved satisfactory in practice. They are based on the geometric CE of the actual shape of the mainsail plus the fore triangle (before the mast), without considering the various possible shapes and sizes of foresail.

The CLR is based only on the fixed portion of the underwater profile, i.e. the rudder is excluded. It seems logical to consider the rudder as steering gear only and not as taking up part of the side force. The following table, then, gives the leads, expressed as a percentage of the LWL, by which the geometric CE should lie forward of the geometric CLR in various types of boat.

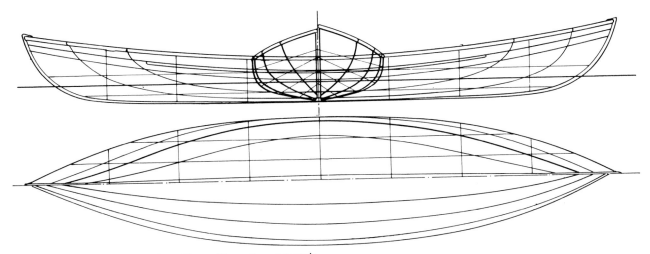

Fig. 47: Lines of a whaleboat. According to Turner's metacentric shelf theory, by which a number of boats were designed in England in the 1930's, the symmetry of lines would indicate a perfectly balanced hull.

LEAD OF CENTRE OF EFFORT BEFORE CENTRE OF LATERAL RESISTANCE

Bermudan Sloops

Racing keel-yachts with fine lines, 'Skerry' cruisers	3 to 4%
Dragon and International metre-classes ..	4 to 6%
Racing dinghies	4 to 6%
Offshore racing yachts to IOR	5 to 8%
Offshore cruisers with ample beam and long underwater profile	7 to 10%

Yawls and Ketches

Offshore racing yachts to IOR	3 to 5%
Offshore cruisers, beamy with long underwater profile	4 to 6%

Schooners

Offshore cruisers, beamy with long underwater profile	3 to 4%

In the following cases the shorter lead is applicable:
>   Yachts with a short, deep keel
>   Low aspect ratio rigs, two-masted rigs
>   Hulls with very fine water-lines, narrow beam
>   Yachts with very great stability

A longer lead is applicable in the following cases:
>   Yachts with very full waterlines
>   Short hulls with broad beam
>   High aspect ratio rigs
>   Yachts with shallow draft, long keel
>   Yachts with low stability

In sailing on the wind, the position of the rudder should by no means coincide with the boat's fore-and-aft centreline. The underwater profile, which has to resist the pressure of the side force, cannot be made like an aeroplane wing – concave on one side and convex on the other – because windward and leeward side alternate constantly. If the tiller is pulled up slightly to windward, this improves the profile, as has been proved by model tests at Wageningen, Holland, and at the Technical University in Istanbul, Turkey. An angle of between 3° and 4° is considered to produce the best windward performance. This means that the boat should carry slight weather helm and it should be necessary, when sailing to windward, to angle the rudder blade by 3° to 4° to leeward in order to hold the boat on a straight course. This slight inclination of the rudder evidently reduces the leeway and thus also reduces the total resistance. To achieve this condition, there must be a certain amount of pressure on the rudder. This pressure also makes it easier for the helmsman to *feel his way close to the wind* and makes steering much more pleasant. The angled rudder creates an asymmetrical underwater profile, in which the leeward

Plate 9: A modern ocean racer. The very narrow, deep keel carries the lead ballast and has the smallest area commensurate with the requirements of lateral resistance. In this case the rudder is free-standing, but in many cases there is a streamlined skeg which adds to the strength. BONAVENTURE V *is 54 ft long and was designed by Cuthbertson & Cassian, the Canadian firm.*

Photo: C & C Yachts, Ontario

or pressure side is slightly concave, as is the case in aircraft wings.

In recent years attempts have been made to improve the underwater profile in this way by fitting *trim tabs*, rather like large rudders, on the after edge of the keel of hulls which have their rudder far aft hung on a separate rudder skeg. In spite of numerous tests the effectiveness of trim tabs has never actually been confirmed in practice, nor has it been possible to establish the best angle, i.e. the one at which resistance is reduced to an optimum value. It is probably around 3°, but no improvement of speed under racing conditions has been observed. When, under the IOR, trim tabs were given a penalty of 0·75 per cent on the rating, they ceased to be of interest.

The more a yacht heels when sailing on the wind, the further the pressure point of the thrust shifts to leeward, i.e. to one side of the centreline. It follows that the boat will only sail in a state of balance in moderate to stronger winds if some lee helm is accepted in light winds. It also follows that if the boat heels a lot, i.e. in strong winds, there must be some weather helm. At best, a yacht will sail in a perfect state of *composite balance* in medium wind strengths, while in light winds a certain amount of lee helm is as unavoidable as some weather helm is in stronger winds. Unless, of course, sails are changed to give the right balance every time the wind increases or decreases, which may be tiresome but very worth while in racing.

A keelboat with auxiliary centreplate offers the additional remedy of employing the plate to alter the underwater profile. This was probably the reason why some of the very large J-class racing yachts had a plate in addition to their deep draught. Just recently more and more boats have been designed with two plates in line, with the help of which, according to wind strength,

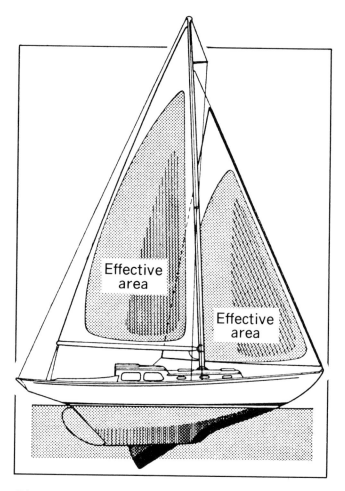

Fig. 48: The 'effective' zones of the sail plan are shaded. The white zones are ineffective but cannot be avoided. The darkest shading indicates those areas which do most of the work. Similarly, in the hull the shaded areas are responsible, to a greater or lesser degree according to shading, for counteracting leeway.

lee or weather helm can be reduced. When carefully adjusted, these twin plates even provide the ideal means of facilitating self-steering.

Introduction to the Aerodynamics of Sailing

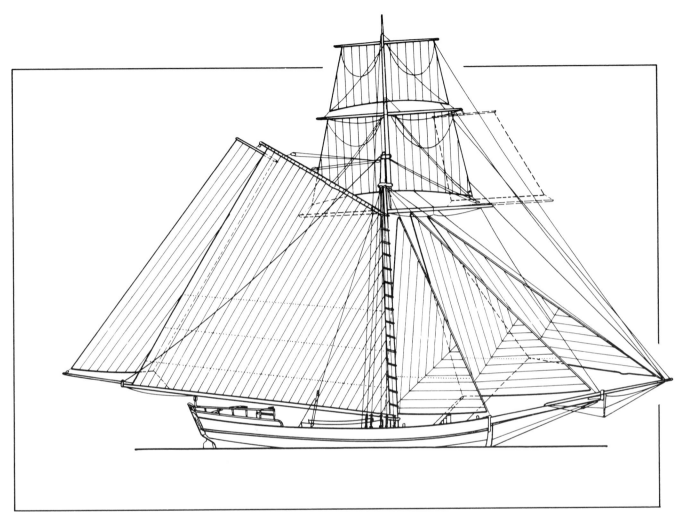

Fig. 49: This sail plan belongs to the hull of the merchant sloop reproduced in Fig. 3. When this rig was in use more than 200 years ago it was very efficient by contemporary standards, despite the fact that its designers had not the slightest knowledge of aerodynamics.

The word *aerodynamics* means 'science of the forces of the air'. Since a sailing boat both receives its forward thrust and suffers its resistance due to the forces of the air, it is useful to a yachtsman to have some knowledge of all the factors involved.

The majority of aerodynamic tests examine these forces in the shape of *drag* and *lift*, usually at small angles of attack. In applying the results to the propulsion of a sailing yacht, the fact that small angles only occur when a boat is close-hauled has to be taken into account. For courses off the wind and before the wind other conditions apply, which have been investigated only in very few tests.

The object of experimental aerodynamics is to study wing profiles, to investigate the effect of aircraft propellers and to measure the resistance of the fuselage and its attachments, with the aim of producing aircraft capable of high speeds using minimum engine power. Many of the findings made in these tests can be applied to sailing yachts, although there are considerable differences in the nature of their propulsion and dynamics. For example, the aeroplane *always* moves directly into the wind (even despite the apparent influence of side wind), the sailing yacht *never* does so.

When a boat sails before the wind, the force propelling it is equal to the resistance which the sails, rigging and hull present to the wind. For conditions on the wind, however, it has been established by aero-

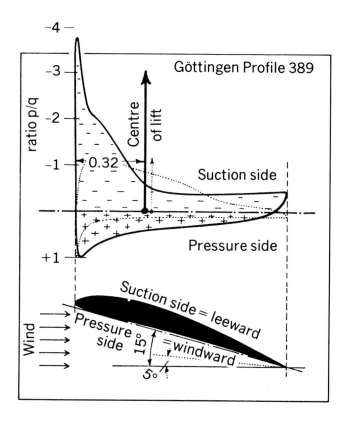

Fig. 50: Every aerodynamic profile produces a zone of low pressure on its leeward side, and this behaviour is also characteristic of a sail on the wind, where the negative pressure to leeward has a greater effect than the positive pressure to windward. Both forces work in the same direction and supplement each other.

dynamic tests that certain profiles and aspect ratios produce greater lift and less drag than others.

In the case of an aeroplane, the entire lift imparted by the wings serves to hold the plane balanced in the air. Too much lift forces it to rise, too little to sink. In sailing, on the other hand, we want *forward thrust* from the wind, which cannot be directly determined from aerodynamic profile measurements. Another difference is that the aircraft always receives the wind from one and the same direction, whereas the sailing yacht gets its wind from all points. Besides, its own speed causes a *false* wind (i.e. the apparent wind). Despite these numerous complications, it is not difficult to take all the facts into consideration and express them fairly accurately in mathematical terms. A short examination of a profile will serve to explain the theory in broad terms.

Figure 50 illustrates the 'Göttingen Profile No. 389' at an angle of inclination of 15°, based on experiments made at the aerodynamic test laboratory at Göttingen, Germany. This profile, chosen from many profiles tested, is of special value for our purposes, because it corresponds to a normal wing and was tested at *all* possible angles of inclination. The graph in the upper part of Fig. 50 shows two curves, the one marked (+) representing wind pressures on the under or high pressure side of the profile, the one marked (−) showing the negative pressure on the upper or low pressure side of the profile. Both act in the same direction and together produce lift. A sail angled at 15° to the wind would quite similarly produce positive pressure on the windward side and negative pressure on the leeward side, both combining to make the lift indicated by the bold vertical arrow. This force is the useful part of the wind forces. Drag, which is the detrimental part, has been ignored here.

The ratio values ρ/q, which vary between +1 and −4, represent the positive and negative pressures in relation to the so-called impact pressure or *dynamic* pressure. This dynamic pressure occurs at the leading edge of an aerofoil or of any other body exposed to an airflow and is arrived at by the following formula

$$\text{Dynamic pressure } q = \frac{\rho}{2} v^2$$

in which ρ is the density of air in slugs per cubic foot (1 sl. = 32·2 lb), v is the speed of air in ft/sec, and the result is in lb/sq ft. If $\rho = 0·0024$ is taken as the mean value for density of air, the figure 0·0012 can be substituted for $\frac{\rho}{2}$ in all future calculations. By comparison, water has an average density of 1·94, which explains why the dynamic forces of water are 810 times greater than those of air, given equal bodies and equal speeds. A breeze of nearly 10 knots = 16 ft/sec produces a dynamic force of $q = 0·0012 \times 16^2 = 0·307$ lb/ft². A current of water flowing with the same speed of 16 ft/sec would produce a dynamic pressure of

$$q = 0·97 \times 16^2 = 248 \text{ lb/ft}^2.$$

Both curves in the diagram show the highest values for negative and positive pressure near the leading edge.

It follows that the centre of effort cannot lie in the centre of the wing but must be rather further forward, as we have already established when considering the dynamic centre of effort of the sail. At the chosen angle of attack of 15° the centre of effort indicated by the arrow lies at a point 0·32 or approximately one third of the distance from the leading edge.

The dotted curve in the diagram illustrates a second angle of attack, this time of 5°. In this case, too, the negative pressure is greater than the positive pressure, but the centre of effort lies slightly further aft, indicated by the dotted arrow.

In comparing this wing profile with a sail, the first difference to be noticed is that a sail has no thickness. Amongst the numerous Göttingen tests are some made with flat and curved metal plates, which bear a closer resemblance to sails. The results of these very interesting tests are summarized in the polar diagram of Fig. 51. One of the plates is flat while three others have curvatures of between 1:20 and 1:6·66 of their chord lengths. The height of each of the plates is five times its width, so that such a 'plate sail' would look like the sketch in the upper right-hand corner of the diagram.

The left-hand portion of the polar diagram corresponds to sailing close-hauled. The vertical scale gives the coefficients of lift. While the flat plate only reaches a value of under 1, the curved plates reach values as high as 1·7. Coefficients of drag are indicated along the horizontal scale. They show that all plates, both the flat one and the curved ones, reach a value of about 1·2 *before the wind*, i.e. at an angle of attack of 90°; but even then the curved plates reach slightly higher values. As we have established earlier, increased drag when sailing before the wind is desirable, because on this point of sailing it equals forward thrust.

Inclined to the airflow at 15° like a sail when sailing to windward, the following values are obtained for the four plates:

	Coefficient of Lift
Flat plate	0·78
Slightly curved = 1:20	1·08
Moderately curved = 1:10	1·50
Strongly curved = 1:6·66	1·60

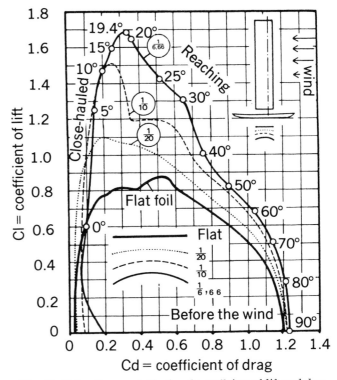

Fig. 51: Polar diagram indicating the coefficient of lift and drag for aerofoils of different curvatures. Their height in every case is five times the width. The plate with the strongest curvature attains the greatest lift on nearly all points of sailing, but of course lift is not equal to forward thrust.

If these coefficients are multiplied by 0·0012 (the dynamic pressure) and the square of the wind speed we get the lift in lb/ft². In the next table (p. 60) the coefficients for the four plates have been converted into lift per ft² for wind speeds of 16 ft/sec and 32 ft/sec (nearly 10 and 20 knots respectively). The former would be a pleasant breeze, the latter a fairly strong wind in which most small boats would be forced to reef.

It is immediately apparent that the curved plates have a considerable advantage over the flat plate. The plate with the strongest curvature produces more than *twice* the lift compared with the flat plate and 50 per cent more than the slightly curved plate. The diagram shows that this superiority holds good for all courses including the one before the wind, when the angle of attack is 90°. Only at very small angles do the other plates show better values.

		Lift per ft²	
	Wind =	16 ft/sec	32 ft/sec
Flat plate		0·240 lb	0·960 lb
Slightly curved = 1:20		0·332 lb	1·330 lb
Moderately curved = 1:10		0·461 lb	1·845 lb
Strongly curved = 1:6·66		0·492 lb	1·966 lb

	Coeff. of lift	Lift per ft²	
		16 ft/sec	32 ft/sec
Square plate	0·48	0·147 lb	0·590 lb
Height = 2 × width	0·72	0·221 lb	0·886 lb
Height = 3 × width	0·86	0·264 lb	1·058 lb
Height = 4 × width	0·96	0·295 lb	1·180 lb
Height = 5 × width	1·01	0·310 lb	1·243 lb
Height = 6 × width	1·07	0·328 lb	1·315 lb
Height = 7 × width	1·09	0·335 lb	1·340 lb

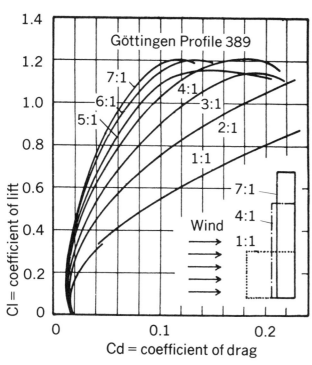

Fig. 52: If the profile in Fig. 50 is investigated for aspect ratios between 1:1 and 7:1, the value for lift and drag are different in every case.

It should be remembered that 55 per cent of the total time sailed is spent on the wind, added to which another 20 per cent is reaching, when the sail also produces lift in the aerodynamic sense. Only during 25 per cent of the time, namely when running, does the sail act purely as a body of resistance and produces no lift.

All the coefficients we have investigated so far refer to profiles with a height–width ratio of 5:1, a ratio which hardly ever occurs in sails. If other aspect ratios are chosen, the attainable lift changes, as can be seen in the diagram in Fig. 52. This examines the same Göttingen Profile No. 389 with aspect ratios ranging from 1:1 to 7:1.

It immediately becomes obvious that the highest, narrowest profile has the highest coefficient of lift and the lowest coefficient of drag. Conversely, the square profile with an aspect ratio 1:1 produces least lift and most drag *on the wind*. It might be compared to an old-fashioned, low-cut gaff sail, which would be much inferior on the wind to a modern, high-aspect ratio Bermudan sail. The higher and narrower the profile the greater the lift. This applies to small angles of attack only, i.e. on the wind. The second table above gives both the coefficients of lift and the actual lift per ft² surface for the same two wind speeds as before, i.e. 16 ft/sec and 32 ft/sec (nearly 10 and 20 knots respectively).

The superiority of a high-aspect ratio has been proved experimentally in the same way as the superiority of the curved plate over the flat one. The following conclusions, which can be usefully applied to sailing yachts, can be drawn from these aerodynamic experiments:

In order to obtain maximum thrust on the wind, a sail's height should not be less than five times its width. Its curvature should be no less than one-tenth of its chord width at any point of its height.

All the profiles investigated so far differ from actual sails by the absence of a mast, which causes a disturbing turbulence at the leading edge of the sail. To analyse the importance of this disturbance, Croseck investi-

gated a number of curved plates which had round spars fitted to their leading edge. Their trailing edge was thinned down to make them resemble an actual sail as closely as possible. The results of his experiments are set out in Fig. 53, which is all the more interesting for being the only graph to date which provides figures that can be applied to actual sails. Croseck, too, used plates with an aspect of ratio of 5:1, which is usual in aerodynamic tests, so that a direct comparison is possible between his observations and the Göttingen Profile.

All the plates tested by Croseck had a curvature of one-tenth of their chord width. Plate A had no spar, plate B had a small spar of a diameter comparable to a normal mast, its diameter being $7\frac{1}{2}$ per cent of the

Fig. 53: Important experiments were carried out by Croseck, who fitted round-section spars to the leading edge of curved plates to study the influence of the mast on the airflow round the sail. The drag in the case of curves B, C and D is greater and the lift smaller than in the case of profile A, which has no spar.

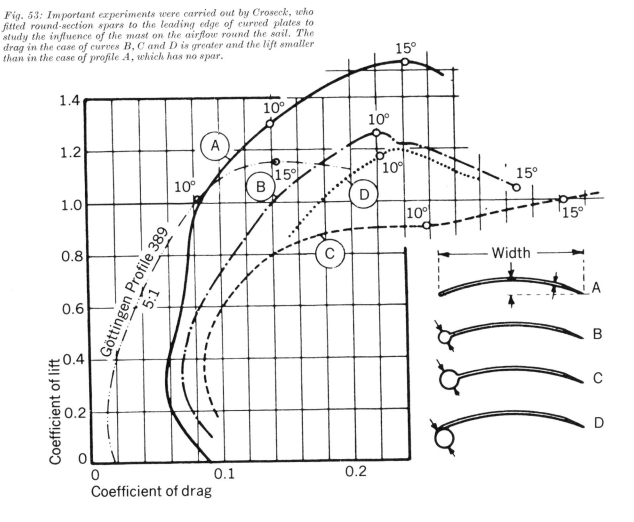

Plate 10: A modern ocean racer, LOA 43 ft 8 in, romps along under a large genoa. This is a Nicholson 45 with a waterline length of 32 ft 2 in, a beam of 12 ft 4 in and a displacement of 11·2 tons. Built in plastics by Camper & Nicholson.

Photo: John Etches, Bournemouth

width of the profile. C and D had thicker spars with a diameter of 10 per cent of their width, and in D the spar was attached asymmetrically. The Göttingen Profile 389 has been added to the graph for comparison.

As expected, A obtained by far the best figures for lift. Between 10° and 15° of attack it even surpassed the Göttingen Profile. Profile B comes closest to a normal sail. At an angle of attack of 10° it reaches a coefficient of lift of 1·25 as compared with 1·3 for profile A. Its coefficient of drag of 0·22, however, is much higher than that of 0·14 for profile A. *This means that its resistance to the wind is 57 per cent greater as a result of the presence of the mast!*

Profile C performs worst, whereas profile D with its mast to one side shows an improvement as a result of the undisturbed airflow on the leeward side.

Why does a high-aspect ratio sail produce better lift to windward than a low-aspect ratio sail? Quite intuitively a yachtsman would say that this is so because a high sail catches larger quantities of undisturbed wind. Although this explanation comes close to the truth, aerodynamic theory has found a more precise explanation.

Any profile inclined towards an airflow at a small angle gets its lift by diverting the air from its original course. Above the height of the sail the airflow continues undisturbed, and between these two zones, that of diverted air and that of undisturbed air, a boundary line of eddies forms. It can easily be seen that this line of eddies must be longer in a wide sail. A similar area of turbulence forms along the lower edge of the sail underneath the boom, and together they account for the so-called *induced drag*.

This induced drag only exists while the sail derives its thrust from aerodynamic lift. This is not the case in running before the wind, and since there is, consequently, no induced drag on that point of sailing, a high-aspect ratio sail loses its advantages before the wind.

The Aerodynamics of Sailing

Plate 11: Mass start of a race in the Korsar Class on the Sorpesee in 1973. The crews are not fully stretched out on the trapezes since the moderate wind does not call for their full use.

Photo: Karl Schwinn

The aeroplane moves in the very same air by which it is supported. It always moves directly into the direction from which the wind comes, since it receives its propulsion from mechanical means: the propeller or the jet. The sailing yacht moves in a medium – the water – which has nothing directly to do with its propulsion. Its weight is supported by the water, but its propulsion comes from the wind. It can never move directly into the wind. What it wants from the wind is not the thrust produced by the sails but another component called forward thrust. On the wind, it is not maximum speed as such which counts but maximum *speed made good to windward.*

The modern yacht's remarkable ability to make headway into the wind is to a large degree due to the modern rig, but the hull shape, too, has a large share in it. It is the hull's lateral resistance which enables the boat to make effective use of the close-winded qualities of the sails at small angles of attack. One degree gained on the angle of leeway and one degree gained on the angle of attack may mean a course of 3° closer to the wind. A yacht sailing at 42° to the true wind instead of 45° increases its speed made good to windward by 5 per cent.

The greater a sail's height in relation to its width, the smaller its induced drag and the better, consequently, its thrust to windward. If a yacht's stability were unlimited, rigs would, no doubt, be much higher than those currently in use.

In order to define the advantages of a high rig it is, first of all, necessary to define accurately the term 'aspect ratio'. This, however, is made difficult by the infinite diversity of rigs. Taking the Bermudan mainsail, it would be easy to say that in a sail of low aspect ratio the luff is twice the length of the foot, in a sail of medium aspect ratio the luff is $2\frac{1}{2}$ to 3 times the length of the foot, and in a high aspect ratio sail it is 4 times the length of the foot or more. As a technical definition this is not precise enough when dealing with a shape which is basically triangular. In aerodynamics, therefore, the aspect ratio is the luff related to the mean chord and is described by the formula

$$\text{Aspect ratio} = \frac{\text{Height}^2}{\text{Sail area}}$$

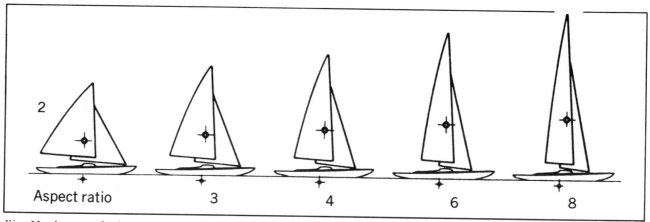

Fig. 55: Aspect ratio 4 corresponds to the actual sail plan of a Dragon. The four others between 2 and 8 have equally large sail areas but vary in efficiency on the wind. If the practical problems could be overcome, aspect ratio 8 would be the most efficient on the wind.

Figure 55 illustrates a number of aspect ratios between 2 and 8, 4 being the profile of an actual Dragon rig. If the only consideration were sailing to windward in light airs, aspect ratio 8 would probably give the best thrust. But this is by no means certain, for a number of practical arguments speak against it. To start with, the increased length of stays and shrouds causes increased resistance. The mast diameter would probably have to be greater and this again, especially with so narrow a sail, would cause considerable disturbance. To keep the long foresail luff under tension may cause great difficulties. Since the centre of effort of the sail lies 30 per cent higher, the boat's stability will be adversely affected. All this illustrates how practical considerations oppose the application of aerodynamic findings.

Let us now try to establish the actual thrust produced by a sail in easily understood figures. We use for this purpose the coefficients of lift (1·25) and drag (0·22) established for Profile B in Fig. 53. The modern expression of Newton's formula says that *a force produced by a flow is equal to the coefficient, multiplied by half the density of the medium, times the square of the speed, times the presented surface*, thus, in the case of air:

$$\text{Wind force P} = \text{coefficient} \times 0\cdot0012 \times v^2 \times S$$

where S is the sail area in ft². The wind force P can be the lift, by inserting the coefficient of lift, or any other wind force, by inserting the corresponding coefficient.

In a sail like Profile B each square foot of area sub-

jected to winds of 16 ft/sec (10 knots) and 32 ft/sec (20 knots) produces the following forces:

	Wind = 16 ft/sec	*32 ft/sec*
Lift $= 1\cdot26 \times 0\cdot0012 \times v^2 =$	0·387 lb	1·55 lb
Drag $= 0\cdot22 \times 0\cdot0012 \times v^2 =$	0·068 lb	0·27 lb

For a Dragon with a sail area of 286 ft² we obtain the following values:

	Wind = 16 ft/sec	*32 ft/sec*
Lift	111·5 lb	446 lb
Drag	19·4 lb	77·4 lb

It has already been explained that these two data are not sufficient to determine the forward thrust of a sailing yacht, since lift and drag are purely aerodynamic terms invented for wind-tunnel tests. Both these forces act on the boat's hull, but as a result of its great resistance to sideways drift it moves in a completely different direction to the one indicated by the resultant of lift and drag. But this resultant can be converted into thrust and side force, if the speed sailed and the angle between course and wind are known.

An example will demonstrate that practical results can be obtained without difficulty. For this purpose we will assume a wind speed of 16 ft/sec = 10 knots, in which a Dragon sails at an angle of 45° to the true wind and reaches a speed of rather more than 3 ft/sec or 4·3 knots. As can be seen from Fig. 56, the true wind is converted into an apparent wind which strikes the boat at an angle of 27° and has a speed of 21·5 ft/sec = 12·7 knots.

64

It is assumed that the yacht sails at an angle of 45° to the true wind, which is normal in practice. Furthermore, an angle of leeway of 4° has been assumed, which means that the boat's fore-and-aft centreline really points at an angle of only 41° to the true wind. But the actual course sailed is at 45° to the true wind, and the *speed made good* to windward is 70 per cent of the speed actually sailed through the water.

While lift and drag are direct consequences of the wind, thrust and side force result from the reaction of the hull. This is shown in Fig. 57 using slightly modified coefficients for Croseck's Profile B. The diagram in the middle uses a coefficient of lift of 1·30 and a coefficient of drag of 0·20, and a parallelogram of forces reveals the direction and magnitude of the resultant, which has a coefficient of 1·32. The term 'resultant' should not be misinterpreted. The resultant force is, in fact, the only force actually produced by the wind. It is not a consequence of lift and drag, but lift and drag emerge if the resultant force is resolved into two directions chosen almost at random.

In the diagram on the right the resultant has again been marked, but now the *reaction of the hull*, i.e. its forward motion and its resistance to leeway, resolves it into the two forces of thrust and side force. The coefficient of thrust, as obtained by this graphical

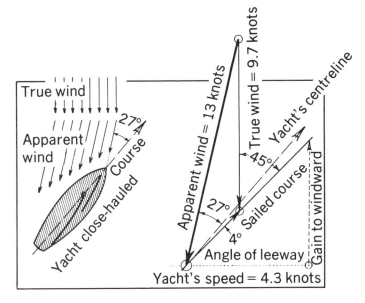

Fig. 56: Diagram of angles valid for a Dragon on the wind. At an angle of 45° between true wind and the course sailed, the angle between apparent wind and the boat's centreline is 27°, the angle of leeway being 4°.

Fig. 57: The diagram in the middle shows the action of the wind on the sails. The drag is very small in comparison with lift and resultant force. The diagram on the right shows how the reaction of the hull converts the same resultant force into forward thrust, which amounts to about one third, and side force, which is almost as great as the resultant and is responsible for heeling and leeway.

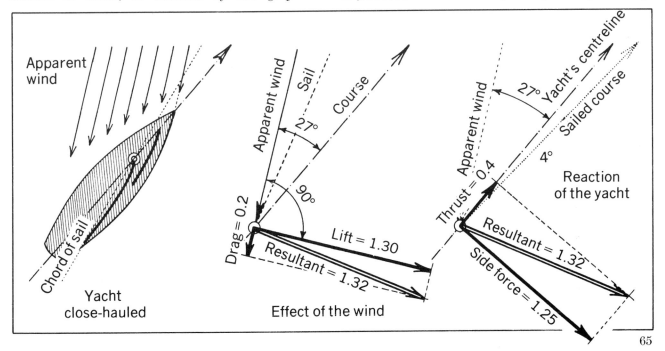

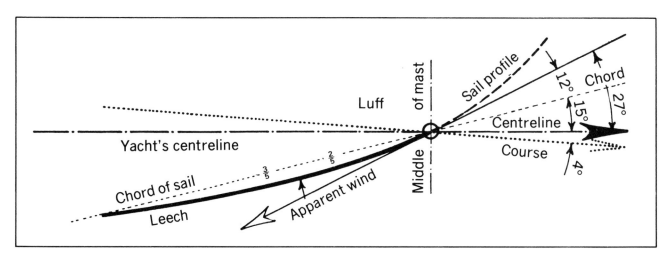

Fig. 58: Diagram showing the curvature of a sail and all pertaining angles on the wind. The chord of the sail makes an angle of 12° with the apparent wind and of 15° with the boat's centreline. These angles vary according to the type of boat, sail plan and wind speed.

method, is 0·40, the coefficient of side force is 1·25. Thus, the side force, which causes heeling and leeway, is three times as great as the thrust.

It must be stressed again that the wind produces one force only, the resultant. Only the remarkable qualities of the modern hull enable the boat to extract from this resultant, which is at a fairly adverse angle, sufficient thrust to sail at surprisingly high speeds and so relatively close to the wind. At the same time the hull shape effectively resists leeway despite the considerable side force.

After having established the necessary coefficients of thrust and side force it is now possible to calculate the actual thrust and side force acting on a Dragon:

Coefficient of thrust .... 0·40
Coefficient of side force . 1·25
True wind speed ...... 16 ft/sec (10 knots)
Apparent wind speed .. 21·5 ft/sec (12·7 knots)
Sail area .... 286 ft² (26·6 m²)
Half density of air .... 0·0012 (0·063)

This results in the following actual forces:

Thrust = 0·40 × 0·0012 × 21·5² × 286
63·4 lb (30·1 kg)
Side force = 1·25 × 0·0012 × 21·5² × 286
198·3 lb (94·1 kg)

The understanding of all the important angles of attack provides the basis for the study of the curvature of the sail. The choice of the most suitable curvature is of the greatest importance, because on it depends the ability of the sail to produce the maximum thrust with the minimum side force.

The curvature of the sail has to induce a uniform and progressive diversion of the wind flow over the entire width of the sail. This has to start at the mast imperceptibly, i.e. tangentially, and increase gradually until it reaches its maximum at the leech. The curvature of the sail in the leech area must never be allowed to become parallel to the boat's centreline.

Figure 58 is an attempt to reproduce this condition, with all the necessary angles, in diagrammatic form. The apparent wind strikes at an angle of 27° to the boat's centreline. The optimum angle of attack of the sail to the wind is measured from the *chord* of the sail – dotted line – and should be approximately half of the angle between the centreline and the apparent wind. Allowing for the fact that the sail twists in its upper part an angle of only 12° has been allowed.

If the leech zone of the sail was parallel to the boat's centreline it would no longer contribute any thrust. The luff zone, on the other hand, should be struck by the wind at a tangent. Within these narrow limits the curvature of the sail is practically determined, with the maximum depth of curvature being at a point approximately two-fifths of the chord length from the luff.

The diagram shows what might be called the ideal sail section. One must, however, take into account the unavoidable twist in the upper part of the sail. Since the boom is normally sheeted in too hard in order to give the best angle of attack to the middle region of the sail, the curvature near the boom can safely be greater than in the ideal section. In the uppermost part of the sail, where the twist is most pronounced, the curvature should be practically non-existent to improve the angle of attack.

Plate 12: The Neptun 22, which has been built in large numbers, is a centreboarder equally at home in inland waters and at sea in kindly weather. She is a recognized class of the German Sailing Association so that she can be raced as well as cruised. LOA 22 ft 4 in, beam 7 ft 10 in, draft, plate up, 1 ft 10 in, plate down 3 ft 5 in. Sail area 194 sq ft.
Builders: Neptun Boote GmbH, Lage/Lippe

Plate 13: A classic 42 ft deep sea boat for ocean cruising, constructed in fibreglass. The long distance sailor will know the advantages of the ketch rig, which is particularly suitable for a small crew. The hull is shapely with a generous beam, plenty of deck space and a clipper bow with a bowsprit, which has a guard rail.
Builder: Cheoy Lee, Hong Kong

Wind Forces on the Reach

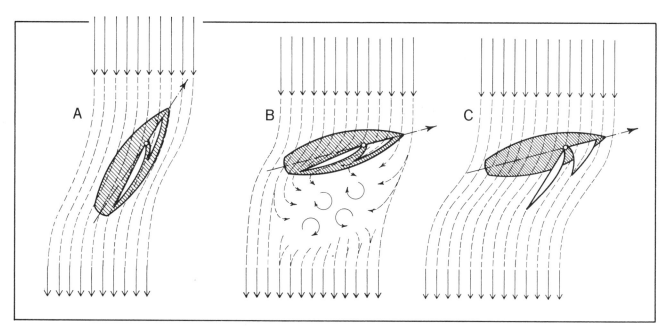

Fig. 59: If the sails are close-hauled on a reach, the airflow on the leeside of the sail is interrupted and replaced by disturbing eddies as in figure B. The important zone of low pressure is thereby destroyed and the thrust considerably diminished.

When a boat is sailing on the wind with the sails sheeted in hard and then starts to pay off to sail more free, the crew will obviously ease the sheets. It can happen, however, that the helmsman pays off without easing the sheets, for example if he wants to lose time before the start of a race; for if a boat is sailed close-hauled on a reach she will be considerably slowed down. This is so because the airflow past the sail is interrupted. To windward the diversion is too abrupt, to leeward the flow is completely broken off and a whirl of eddies is formed.

Figure 59 A shows the airflow round a boat sailing on the wind with sheets close-hauled. If she pays off on a reach without easing sheets the airflow will be disturbed as in B. The sail no longer functions as an aerodynamic profile but becomes an obstacle, which violently disrupts the airflow. *Any sudden disruption of the airflow causes disturbing turbulence.* In the present example, the negative pressure on the lee side of the sail has been destroyed almost completely and replaced by turbulence. Since the negative pressure on the lee side contributes much more to the total driving force of the

sails than the positive pressure on the windward side, this accounts for the noticeable reduction of the boat's speed. Once the sheets are eased as in C, the smooth airflow is re-established, negative and positive pressures are restored to normal and the correspondingly increased driving power gives the boat back its normal speed.

Few complete sailing yacht models have been tested in wind tunnels at all possible angles of attack. In experimental aerodynamics preference is given to the study of small angles of attack. Croseck, however, did test a completely rigged gaff sail in a wind tunnel and measured the forces on all possible courses. His results have been drawn up in a highly interesting graph, reproduced in Fig. 60, which gives *the coefficients of thrust for all rigs on all possible courses.*

The gaff mainsail chosen by Croseck was just about the most inefficient of any of the sails found on sailing yachts in the past; this accounts for the low coefficients indicated by the bottom curve. It can be seen that the gaff sail reaches its highest coefficient of thrust of slightly over 1·2 on a course of 10 points (112°) to the

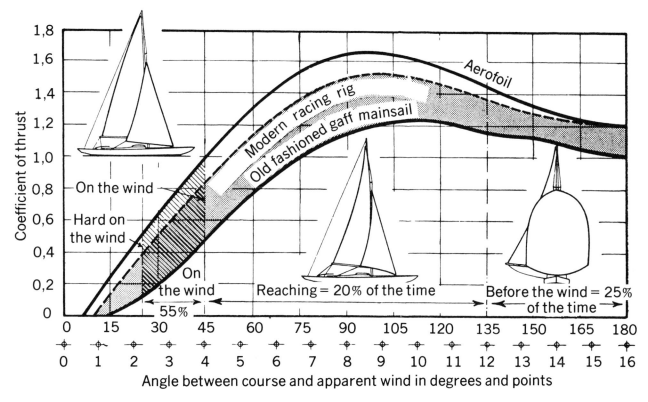

Fig. 60: A particularly interesting graph, which shows coefficients of thrust for a range of rigs on all points of sailing. The shaded zone between two curves encompasses all practical rigs, the zone above it refers to purely aerodynamic profiles. The darkly shaded area on the left covers the time spent on the wind, which is 55 per cent of the total time on all courses. All coefficients and courses are in relation to the apparent wind.

apparent wind, i.e. with the wind just aft of abeam. The top curve, which belongs to an aircraft wing, shows the best possible coefficients, which can probably never be reached by a conventional cloth sail. Its maximum coefficient of thrust is well above 1·6 and is reached with the apparent wind on the beam. In between those two curves lies a dotted line, which is the most important for us, because it represents the coefficients for a modern, expertly handled Bermudan racing rig. The shaded area between the two lower curves, therefore, contains all coefficients for all cloth sails on all possible courses.

Since the graph is based on the apparent wind, the spread of the points of sailing over the width of the graph is distorted. The horizontal scale has, therefore, been divided into the three basic courses sailed and their share of the total time sailed: 55 per cent on the wind, 20 per cent reaching and 25 per cent before the wind. For practical purposes, the figures can be found in the following tables:

COEFFICIENTS OF THRUST *Course*	*High-performance racing sail*	*Modern Ocean Cruiser*	*Inefficient sail*
Hard on the wind	0·4	0·3	0·2
Normally close-hauled	0·6	0·5	0·35
Free on the wind	0·8	0·7	0·5
Reaching	1·5	1·4	1·2
Before the wind	1·2	1·2	1·1

An example will show how the coefficient of thrust is applied to calculate the actual thrust of a boat. A Dragon with a very efficient racing rig, sailing on a reach, may attain a coefficient of 1·5. Given a sail area of 286 ft² (26·6 m²) and an apparent wind of 16 ft/sec (10 knots) the thrust can be calculated as follows:

$$\text{Thrust} = 1·5 \times 0·0012 \times 16^2 \times 286 = 132 \text{ lb (60 kg)}$$

The following table gives the thrust obtained on all courses for a Dragon sailing in an apparent wind of 16 ft/sec:

Course	Coefficient	Thrust
Hard on the wind	0·4	35 lb (16 kg)
Normally close-hauled	0·6	53 lb (24 kg)
Free on the wind	0·8	70 lb (32 kg)
Reaching	1·5	132 lb (60 kg)
Before the wind	1·2	115 lb (52 kg)

Our findings so far can, of course, be applied to all types and sizes of yachts and sail areas. The following easily comprehensible table gives the thrust per ft² of sail area for three apparent wind speeds and, as an additional line, the wind resistance per ft² of area. This wind resistance acts on all parts of the rigging except the sails, as well as on the hull above the water and the

Fig. 61. In this case it is based on a rigid sail with an area identical to a Dragon sail, which made it possible to draw on model tests with curved metal sheets. This rigid sail has an aspect ratio of 5:1, a curvature of 1:10 of its chord, and the true wind speed is assumed at 16 ft/sec or 10 knots.

The sailed speed of the boat on all courses had to be calculated very carefully beforehand, for only then was it possible to calculate the relating wind forces.

The result are three curves, the upper one representing the resultant, the middle one the side force and the bottom one the thrust. It may be surprising to find that the greatest total resultant force – nearly 200 lb in a 10-knot true wind – is attained in sailing normally close-hauled, i.e. at 45° to the true wind. A very large part of this, namely 180 lb, is converted into side force, but a thrust of 75 lb remains. This may sound confusing, but the figures for thrust and side force are

THRUST PER FT² OF SAIL AREA		Wind Speeds		
	Coefficient	16 ft/sec	32 ft/sec	64 ft/sec
Hard on the wind	0·4	0·123 lb	0·492 lb	1·97 lb
Normally close-hauled	0·6	0·184 lb	0·736 lb	2·95 lb
Free on the wind	0·8	0·246 lb	0·984 lb	3·94 lb
Reaching	1·5	0·460 lb	1·845 lb	7·38 lb
Before the wind	1·2	0·368 lb	1·475 lb	5·91 lb
WIND RESISTANCE PER FT² AREA				
Resistance	1·2	0·368 lb	1·475 lb	5·91 lb

crew, if exposed to the wind. Logically, therefore, it refers to area rather than sail area.

In the case of less efficient sails, the thrust coefficient has to be reduced according to the figures given in the first table 'Coefficients of Thrust'.

Once the sailed speeds are known, a graph which is based on the true wind can be prepared, as the one in

components of a parallelogram of forces and as such cannot be added up arithmetically.

This subject is particularly prone to a number of common misconceptions. Only recently someone wrote that on the wind 50 per cent of the resultant force was converted into thrust, 15 per cent into side force, 20 per cent into resistance and 15 per cent was lost due to the

70

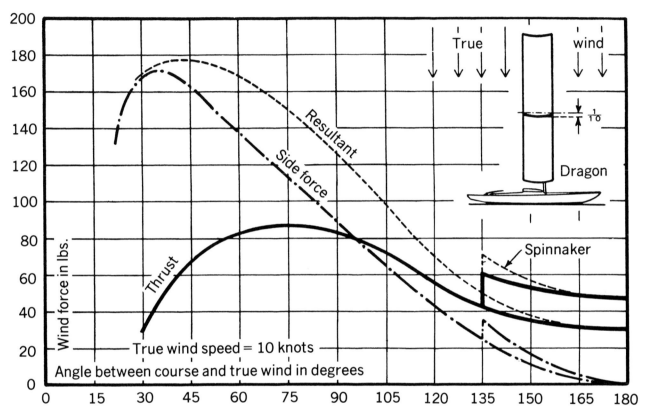

Fig. 61: This graph refers to a curved metal plate rigged on a Dragon and having the same area as a normal Dragon rig. The three curves indicate the total force of the wind (the resultant), the side force, which causes heeling and leeway, and lastly the actual forward thrust, all for a wind speed of about 10 knots and in relation to the true wind.

fact that the sail lifts immediately behind the mast. Quite apart from the fact that these figures are pro-portionally wrong, it must be stressed again that the individual forces cannot be added up in this way because the components act in different directions.

In returning to Fig. 61 it can be seen that as the course approaches dead before the wind (right margin), the side force disappears altogether and the resultant then equals the thrust, which is approximately 35 lb.

From 135° onwards the graph includes the use of a spinnaker, which produces some considerable side force, as experience proves. Dead before the wind this side force disappears completely, while the thrust is in-creased from 45 lb to 65 lb (20–30 kg).

The last of our graphs, Fig. 62, gives the values for thrust per unit sail area for application to any other type of boat. A true wind speed of 16 ft/sec (10 knots) has been assumed. It can be seen that the maximum

thrust of 0·72 lb/ft² (3·5 kg/m²) is obtained on a reach. On the wind, the average is 0·4 lb/ft² (2 kg/m²). Before the wind, the thrust is only 0·2 lb/ft² (1 kg/m²), because the apparent wind, which is the only wind that affects the yacht, has become much slower as a result of the yacht's own speed running away from it.

The question arises whether the attainable thrust could be expressed in a horse power rating. In an average wind speed of 16 ft/sec a Dragon on a reach can attain a speed of 4·2 knots at a thrust of 0·60 lb/ft². The total sail area of 286 ft² consequently produces a thrust of 172 lb. This thrust of 172 lb acting on a boat sailing at a speed of 4·2 knots (or 7·05 ft/sec) can be converted into horse power by the following equation:

$$\text{hp} = \frac{\text{thrust} \times \text{speed}}{550}$$

where the speed has to be in ft/sec. The result is

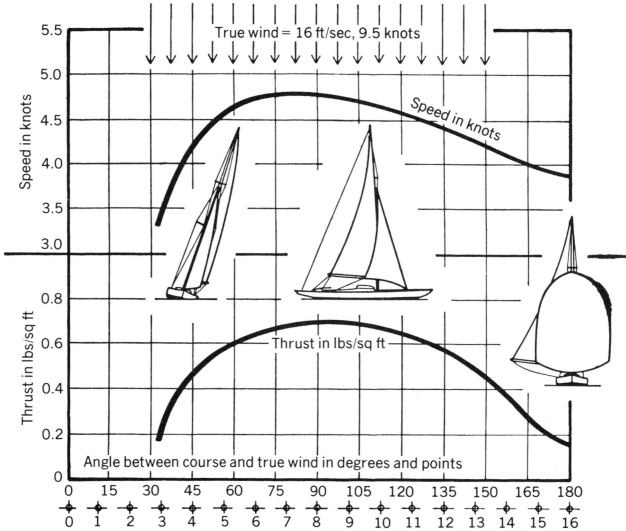

Fig. 62: This diagram is also for a Dragon but gives only the so-called specific values. It can therefore be applied to any other boat as long as its speed coincides approximately with the upper curve. The specific values are in lb/sq ft and apply to a true wind speed of about 10 knots.

$\dfrac{172 \times 7 \cdot 05}{550} = 2 \cdot 2$ hp. The wind plus the large Dragon sail thus only produce a thrust of 2·2 hp, and with this the yacht reaches the remarkable speed of 4·2 knots. *That is less than one-hundredth hp per ft² of sail area!*

It must be pointed out that the power of an auxiliary engine is not directly comparable with the power obtained from the wind. The wind force has been previously resolved into its components and only the thrust has been used for our calculations. Similar conditions apply to the auxiliary engine: it has to generate a greater power than 2·2 hp in order to produce a thrust

of 2·2 hp. To start with, as much as 50 per cent of its energy on average is wasted by the propeller, frequently even more. Added to this, the engine output suffers losses in the installation and as a result of resistance from the drive shaft and exhaust, so that an engine of about 5 to 6 hp would normally be needed to produce an actual thrust of 2·2 hp.

It is, nevertheless, interesting to know that in a breeze of 10 knots a sail, on average, can produce a thrust of one-hundredth hp per ft² of sail area.

Model Tests

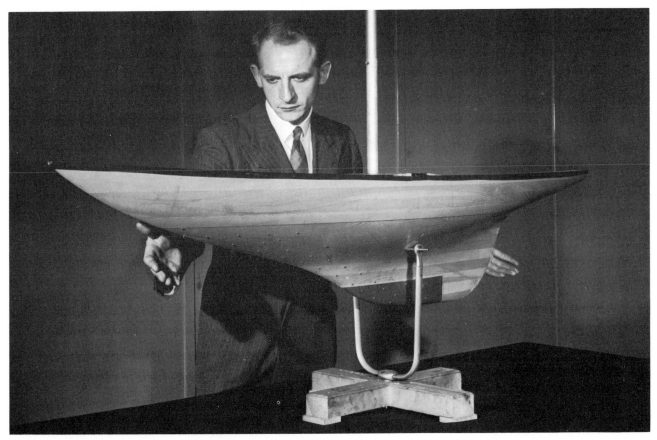

Plate 14: Model tank tests have to be conducted under conditions of turbulent water flow to ensure similarity between the experiment and the actual conditions in which a life-size craft performs. This model is fitted with buttons along the leading edge which create turbulence by breaking up the laminar flow. Note the classical keel profile by contrast with the pared down keel in Plate 9.

Photo: Saunders-Roe

For the past 125 years or so the America's Cup races have had a marked influence on the entire development of yacht design by creating unique conditions for international competition. The battle for the America's Cup is not just between two boats and their crews but very often between the entire technical resources and ingenuity of the two nations involved. Great ends demand great means, and so it is not surprising that every possible research is employed in order to perfect these large racing machines down to the last detail. Model tests were used quite early on, for every designer, every owners' syndicate, every country involved was ceaselessly seeking opportunities for improvement.

Model tests on a small scale are much less expensive than tests with full sized craft, possibly followed by a series of alterations. But can a model have the exact characteristics of the real thing? Can resistance, balance, in short all the racing qualities of the vessel under study be accurately copied in a model? Or is the comparison between the scaled-down model and the real thing dubious?

The most obvious way in which to conduct such a test might seem to build small, completely rigged model boats and let them compete against each other on some pool. This method, however, is the least reliable of all, not only because it is difficult to measure anything under those conditions, but above all because of a peculiar property of water called *viscosity*. Because of it the surface friction of the water on the model hull is disproportionate compared to the real yacht. The model

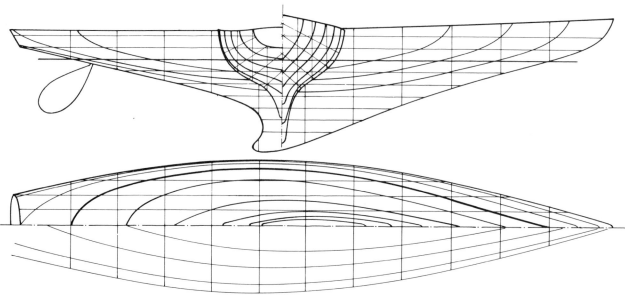

Fig. 63: Lines of the small keelboat KITTEN designed in 1892. Even then, as Uffa Fox confirms in his book Thoughts on Yachts and Yachting, certain boats showed all the characteristics of modern design, such as drastically reduced underwater profile and separate rudder aft. The boat was designed and built by Charles Sibbick and was termed a One Rater, i.e. its rating was one ton.

LOA .... 26 ft   Draft .... 4 ft 3 in
LWL .... 21 ft   Displacement ... 1·65 ton
Beam .... 5 ft 3 in   Sail area .... 284 sq ft

finds itself in a so-called instable zone of frictional resistance in which the resistance can fluctuate either above or below what would be true to scale.

There are other factors which increase the unreliability of this method:

1. It is impossible to make any actual measurements; only impressions, not figures are recorded.

2. The wind speed would have to be reduced in proportion to the square root of the scale chosen. For example, if a boat with a length of 64 ft is represented by a model 4 ft in length, the square roots are in a ratio of 4:1. The speed of the wind acting on the model would therefore have to be one-quarter of the wind speed expected in real life.

3. It is extremely difficult to cut and sew small sails true to scale, since both shape and weight of cloth have to be accurately reduced, and even the stitches have to be to scale.

4. The balancing of small model boats, which has to be done by the person conducting the test, is of indeterminate but great individual importance and further falsifies the impression which, as it is, is based on comparative observation rather than scientific measurements.

As early as 1901 model tests were carried out in Scotland by G L Watson before he designed the America's Cup challenger SHAMROCK II. Watson had his model towed in the Denny Tank at Dunbarton and measured the resistance at different angles of leeway. He relied on these model tests for the final design, but the new yacht was easily beaten by Herreshoff's COLUMBIA. Herreshoff had not made any model tests whatsoever, and Watson is said to have exclaimed in his disappointment: 'I wish Herreshoff had consulted model test!'

Despite initial disappointments, the problems of model tests and their application to life-size craft were in time understood and mastered.

Today, many countries have institutes of naval technology where models of ships and boats can be tested in so-called towing tanks. In order to overcome the effect of instable frictional resistance, the models tested are usually fairly large and the testing tanks are accordingly big and expensive. As long as tests are carried out for big ships, the experimental costs remain within reasonable limits in relation to the project, but the cost of testing individual model yachts would be far too high proportionately. With this in mind the

Stevens Institute of Technology, USA, built a test tank in 1931 which was designed to give good results with smaller models.

Thus the Stevens Tank on the Hudson River facing New York became popular in particular for testing sailing yacht models, although it had by no means been exclusively planned for this purpose. Under the directorship of K S M Davidson, methods of turbulence-making around the model were studied and improved in order to provide the model with conditions similar to those in which the real yacht finds itself. Shortly afterwards the challenge for the America's Cup offered a splendid opportunity for putting this new, relatively inexpensive installation to the test. But success was not immediate. It did not come until several years later with the victory of RANGER, winner of the 1938 race. RANGER's superiority was so convincing that since then the validity of model tests of sailing yachts in general and of small models in particular has generally been recognized.

The dramatic conflict between the designer's ingenuity and pure experimental science reached its climax in 1934, when ENDEAVOUR I designed by Charles E Nicholson, England, and RAINBOW designed by W Starling Burgess, USA, competed for the America's Cup. Their superimposed sections in Fig. 64 show that the difference in the shape of the two hulls was negligible. The lines of RAINBOW were the result of extensive models tests, whereas Nicholson relied solely on his experience, intuition and aesthetic sense in designing ENDEAVOUR I. On this occasion the designer's genius gained a victory over science, for ENDEAVOUR I was not only faster but pointed higher than her American opponent. Only an extraordinary helmsman like Sherman Hoyt could have saved the American defender at the last minute, so that the English yacht, despite her superior speed, had to return home without the coveted trophy.

For some time afterwards the reliability of model tests was seriously questioned. But when, four years later, a new challenge went out and the Cup had to be defended again, a team of leading experts was formed in the USA: W Starling Burgess and Olin Stephens, the two great designers, got together with the model test expert K S M Davidson in an effort to combine science and intuition in the design of the fastest yacht possible under the Cup regulations. Together they carried out the most extensive model test series ever applied to the

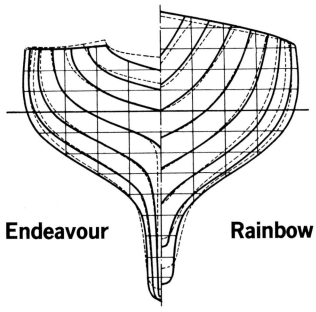

Endeavour   Rainbow

Fig. 64: In 1934 the two yachts ENDEAVOUR I *and* RAINBOW *competed for the America's Cup. Although* RAINBOW *was built after extensive model tests she proved inferior to* ENDEAVOUR I, *which was designed by Charles Nicholson relying entirely on intuition and experience. For complete lines see Fig. 239.*

specialized field of yacht racing, the results of which secured an irrefutable position of predominance for American yacht design.

It must be added, though, that these tests had an unusual basis from which to develop. In a rare and noble gesture, Nicholson had given Burgess the lines of his remarkable ENDEAVOUR I (Fig. 239). Models of the most successful yachts of the day, ENDEAVOUR I, RAINBOW and WEETAMOE, were then built and tested at the Stevens Institute. The three models were submitted to exhaustive tests, which measured their resistance at various speeds, angles of heel and angles of leeway. On the basis of these comparative data several new models were made and tested, and finally a 'family' of models was made from the best of these. The term 'model family' means that the various models belonging to it are all based on the same 'parental' lines but are of different dimensions, particularly length, beam and displacement. Four of these 'model children' led to the final design of the new yacht, which became famous under the name of RANGER.

RANGER was neither a product of man's genious alone nor of science alone, but was the combined work of both. The superiority of RANGER over Nicholson's

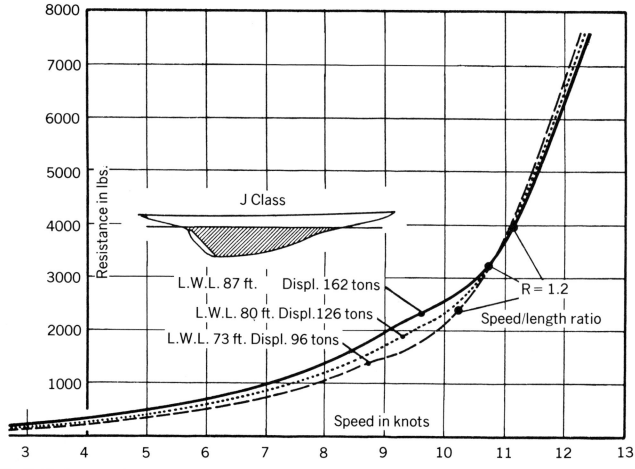

Fig. 65: The three curves shown here were drawn up for models of three J-class yachts of 73 ft, 80 ft and 87 ft LWL. They belong to the same model family, which means that although they are different in length their lines are identical. At slow to moderate speeds the smallest model produces the least resistance, at high speeds the most.

ENDEAVOUR II led to the final recognition of model tests for sailing yachts.

A testing tank cannot design a yacht, it cannot even show up with certainty any faults or merits in design. Model tests produce figures and curves, nothing else. If one submits a boat's lines drawing or a model to an experimental institute for testing, one gets back a lot of accurate figures, but they in themselves do not say anything about the merits of the design. The results of any test series are summarized in a number of resistance curves, which are of no immediate practical use. Such a curve could even be prepared with fair accuracy without the help of model tests, simply by calculation.

The value of tank testing lies chiefly in comparison.

By testing a number of different hull forms a number of different resistance curves are obtained, from the comparison of which valuable conclusions can be drawn. These curves can be worked out firstly for the model on an even keel, then at various angles of heel and finally with different angles of leeway. To go even further, the hull could be tested under various conditions of trim, and finally the whole process could be repeated in an artificially induced seaway.

It is by no means easy to choose, from a number of designs tested, the one with the least resistance. This is illustrated by the curves in Fig. 65, all three of which are of one 'model family' and are part of the RANGER test series. At a speed of just under 11 knots all three

Plate 15: Solings going downwind at San Francisco. The plans of this modern Olympic three-man keelboat are to be found in Fig. 167.
Photo: Diane Beeston

models record the same resistance, i.e. the smallest and lightest boat is equal in resistance to the largest and heaviest. At slower speeds the smallest is the most efficient of all, but at higher speeds it becomes the least efficient.

The investigation becomes more complicated if the rating rules allow the bigger boat a larger sail area. Only meticulous calculations together with extensive model tests would provide results of acceptable reliability.

When a model is towed in a testing tank, the resulting resistance is low. The conversion of the data thus obtained into resistance suffered by the real yacht cannot be made by simple magnification to scale (which

would have to be in the ratio of the displacements of model and full-sized hull). The two main parts of resistance, i.e. dynamic or form resistance and surface friction, cannot be measured separately in the tests although they follow completely different laws of physics. A complicated procedure involving a great deal of mathematical calculation is necessary for resolving the test result into its two parts, converting them to their true size and adding them up again. In the process a certain degree of speculation is unavoidable. Although the method has been perfected it is still unreliable in cases of extreme shape or dimensions. Another problem is how to establish the necessary similarity between the frictional resistance of the model and the real yacht.

77

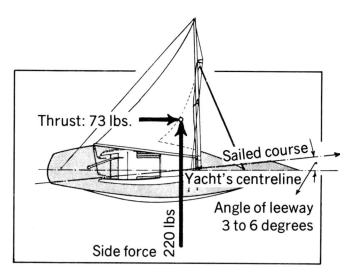

Thrust: 73 lbs.

Sailed course

Yacht's centreline

Angle of leeway
3 to 6 degrees

Side force 220 lbs

Fig. 66: A complete model test measures not only the behaviour of the boat on an even keel, but also investigates the effect of the side force, which causes heeling and leeway and alters the basic resistance. This diagram shows the magnitude of the side force compared with the thrust.

Fig. 67: This wind tunnel, which was designed by the Amateur Yacht Research Society, can take a complete boat up to about 215 sq ft sail area. The tunnel has proved itself in practice but not without highlighting a number of unforeseen problems, which were inevitable in an amateur installation of this kind.

It is essential to eliminate *laminar flow* round the model because, for all practical purposes, the real boat is surrounded only by *turbulent flow*. To achieve this, the bow of the model is either supplied with a roughened surface, fitted with *spoilers* or a series of *buttons* along the leading edge.

Apart from individual model tests for any particular design, institutes of naval technology carry out systematic independent tests of a general nature. Unfortunately, the financing of such tests is always a problem, but most institutes have at some time or other had an opportunity to carry out some research on fundamental problems. In writing this book, the author has consulted experiments made in the USA, Germany, England, Holland and even Turkey, whose test institute at Istanbul has carried out many basic investigations in the field of sailing yachts and published its findings.

It is much easier in practice to experiment with rigs than with hull shapes, and this is the reason why sails have been perfected to a remarkable degree purely by empirical observation without any great help from model tests.

Of course, some model sails have been tested in *wind*

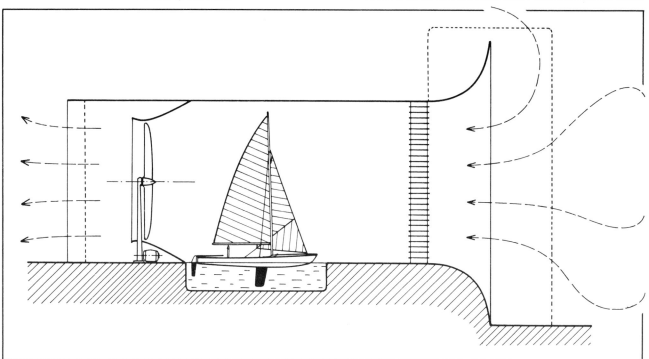

tunnels. Croseck's experiments with curved metal plates and a gaff mainsail have already been mentioned. Manfred Curry, too, tested a metal sail in a wind tunnel in 1925. In the same year, Warner and Ober submitted an exhaustive work, based on model tests conducted between 1915 and 1921, to the American Society of Naval Architects. The most thorough tests were made by K S M Davidson at the Stevens Institute in 1933 in connection with the rig of GIMCRACK, mentioned before. Since this yacht was to serve as a basis for the application of model tests, Davidson had her sailed on the wind by an experienced racing helmsman, while all data capable of measurement were being recorded. The hull model was then tested in the tank and the rig model in the wind tunnel. These comparisons provided the so-called *Gimcrack Coefficients* which, to this day, are used as a basis for the study of the sailing yacht on the wind. They were, for example, used in the preparation of the Dragon graphs in Figs. 39–43.

It is interesting to note that wind-tunnel tests of sails have not established themselves as a standard method for research. Apparently it is less costly to experiment with real, life-size sails than it is with real life-size hulls. The British Amateur Yacht Research Society built a very carefully designed wind tunnel large enough to take complete racing dinghies with a sail area up to 215 sq ft; Ratsey & Lapthorn, the sail makers, installed a wind tunnel for experiments with models. But in both cases the tunnels have not been used nearly as much as one might have expected.

When we hear the word model we are accustomed to think of it as a scaled-down edition of the real thing. But this need by no means be so, for in principle any boat can be used as a model for any other technically similar boat, be it bigger or smaller. Valuable data can be recorded from craft actually sailing, as the GIMCRACK tests have already illustrated. Similar test runs were made in England with the International 5·5-metre YEOMAN and the International 12-metre NORSAGA. In both cases the subjects were equipped with a multitude of instruments which recorded all available data such as the speed and direction of the apparent wind, speed through the water, leeway and angle of heel. Only the thrust produced by the sails and the resistance of the boat cannot be measured by this direct method. The effect of any change or improvement in sail or hull trim can only be observed in the increase or decrease of the speed sailed.

As this book is written many test tanks are kept exceedingly busy, for a number of countries are preparing for an America's Cup challenge and, of course, the USA are preparing for a defence. It would not be surprising if the result of all this research was another great step forward, especially since it is undertaken by the most notable experts in yacht design and experimental research, who have but one aim: to produce the fastest yet 12-metre yacht.

Stability as a Factor of Propulsion

Fig. 68: A Log Canoe from Cheaspeake Bay, USA. An original craft with an equally original rig.

A sailing boat driven by the wind is a unique thing. In contrast to a bird or a fish, an automobile or an aeroplane, the sailing vessel has its weight supported by *one* medium and its propulsion provided by *another*. A car stands with its wheels on the ground and is also driven by the same wheels. The aeroplane is supported by the flow of air along its wings, and the same air is used by the propeller for propulsion. A motorboat is carried by the water, and its propellers operate in the same water. Only the sailing boat finds itself in a position of rare duality: its weight is supported by the water, while its propulsion is derived from the air.

A sailing boat in motion has to overcome the resistance which the water offers to it, and in this respect it is like a motorboat. But the sailing boat receives its driving force at a point which lies at a considerable distance above the water supporting it, which means that the force acts on a long lever arm and has to overcome a resistance far below it.

A car can be turned over in an accident but never as a direct result of its propulsion. An aeroplane can crash due to a defect but never as a consequence of its propulsion. A sailing boat, however, can capsize, fill up and sink as a direct consequence of its propulsion. This is why stability in a sailing boat has a twofold significance:

80

(a) to counteract the heeling moment of the wind's driving force,

(b) as a safety factor against capsizing.

The attainable speed of a sailing boat depends to a large degree on its stability. If a boat could be designed with infinite stability, it could carry an unlimited sail area and reach undreamt-of speeds.

As it is, a sailing yacht's stability is only modest, sometimes scarcely adequate, and it can, therefore, only carry a sail area within the limits of this stability.

Lateral stability is dependent both on the beam and the weight of the hull. The two together determine the inherent stability of the boat. Beyond this, the crew, suitably positioned, can contribute an additional righting moment, especially in the type of boat which possesses a naturally low inherent stability. The stabilizing influence of the crew can be considerably increased by the use of artificial devices such as a trapeze or sliding seat. But maximum speed is not the only objective in the design of a sailing yacht, and this complicates the problem of stability.

At different times the efforts to improve the poor stability of light hulls has led to curious extremes. The previously mentioned 'sandbaggers' carried spectacularly large sail areas, because their stability was increased by the use of movable sacks of sand inside the hull. Their stability thus depended on the initiative of the crew, who had to carry the sacks from one side to the other.

The Chesapeake Bay log canoe, which has the typically narrow beam of a dugout canoe, carries an exceptionally large sail area, because its inherently low stability is improved by the crew as 'live' ballast (Fig. 68). Four to eight crew members sitting out to windward on sliding seats provide a powerful righting moment.

Stability could be defined as a boat's ability to *support the side force of the wind*, i.e. to resist it as much as possible. Can stability, that is a boat's power to

Plate 16: The Westerly Warwick, a bilge keeler, is an excellent cruising boat for coastal waters. She stands up on her keels if the tide leaves her high and dry. The comfortable four berth layout is accommodated in a length of 21 ft 6 in and a beam of 7 ft 8 in. The sail area is 172 sq ft. Westerly Marine, at Portsmouth, builds several sizes of bilge and fin keelers, all designed by Laurent Giles & Partners.   *Photo: Eileen Ramsay*

Plate 17: This shot of the Westerly Warwick on a trailer shows the bilge keel arrangement, which allows the boat to sit securely upright. The bilge keel is particularly popular in British tidal waters.
Photo: J A Hewes

carry sail, be expressed in mathematical terms? Figure 69 answers the question. It shows the mid-section of a keelboat at different angles of heel. The white arrow pointing upwards represents the upward force of buoyancy. The black arrow pointing downwards represents the downward force of gravity, concentrated at the centre of gravity. As the boat heels, the two arrows move horizontally apart, the horizontal distance being called the *lever of static stability*. The *righting moment* is obtained by multiplying the total weight of the boat by the length of the lever.

For the better understanding of Fig. 69 it is necessary to explain a number of 'centres' as shown in the section on the left. The highest point is the centre of gravity of the complete boat *without* ballast. This includes the hull, spars, rigging and all gear. The lowest point is the centre of gravity of the ballast. Both together give the centre of gravity (CG) of the complete vessel, the lower point without crew, the higher one including the crew. This latter centre is the actual CG for the purpose

of stability calculations and the one which is used in all the following diagrams. It lies in the upper part of the bilge, approximately at the height of the floorboards or slightly lower.

The submerged part of the hull displaces an amount of water, the weight of which is equal to the weight of the boat complete and ready to sail. The volume of this displaced water, too, has a centre, and this is the centre of buoyancy, marked CB. In designs with a deep ballast keel, the CG lies slightly lower than the CB. But there are numerous keel-yachts with a small ballast ratio or with shallow draft, in which the CG and CB coincide, or in which the CG is *above* the CB. This does not, in itself, indicate low stability or constitute a danger.

A vessel on an even keel has an *initial stability* which can be determined by the *metacentric height*. This is of little practical interest in connection with sailing boats, but constitutes an accepted ratio of stability for motor-boats. The so-called metacentre, which has not been indicated in our diagram, coincides roughly with the

82

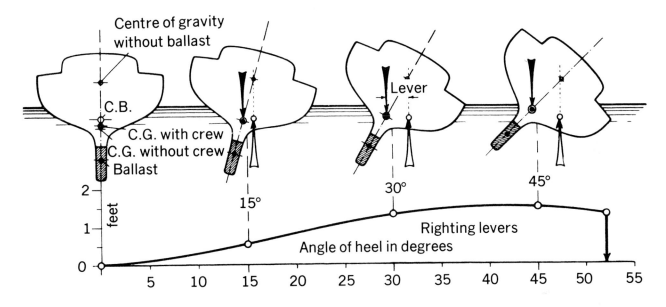

Fig. 69: Diagram illustrating the static stability in a keelboat. The curve indicates righting levers. Its sudden drop at 52° of heel is due to the fact that at this point the Dragon, which was chosen for the example, fills up and sinks.

CG without ballast, i.e. the highest point marked in the section on the left. The vertical distance between metacentre and CG of the complete boat is the *metacentric height*, which characterizes initial stability. Under the IOR (International Offshore Rule) an inclination test is prescribed for ocean racing yachts, which establishes initial stability, which is then inserted in the rating formula. This is not done to test stability as such but with the object of eliminating or at least handicapping light hulls with a high ballast ratio. (The inclination test is generally applied in shipbuilding as an *accurate* method of establishing the centre of gravity.)

As soon as a hull is heeled, the centre of buoyancy (CB) moves out to leeward, as illustrated in the second section of Fig. 69. This results in a horizontal distance between buoyancy (white arrow) and gravity (black arrow), both of which try to pull the hull back onto an even keel, thus creating a righting moment. The next section, at an angle of heel of 30°, illustrates that as the

angle of heel increases the righting lever (the horizontal distance) becomes longer, and the righting moment thus becomes greater. From the *curve of righting levers* drawn underneath the heeled sections the static stability for any angle of heel can be read off. It starts at zero on the left, when the boat is on an even keel, and reaches its maximum at an angle of heel of about 40°. It then decreases gradually until, at about 52°, it drops abruptly to zero. At this point the boat, a Dragon here, fills up through water getting over the cockpit coaming and sinks.

A sailing dinghy with centreplate presents an altogether different case. Figure 70 shows the mid-section of a modern dinghy, in this case an International 5-0-5. In the section on the left the CG and the CB have been marked. In spite of the CB being lower than the CG, the dinghy possesses some initial stability thanks to its metacentric height, which has not been marked in the drawing. The next section, which is heeled at an angle of 15°, shows that the crew sitting to windward con-

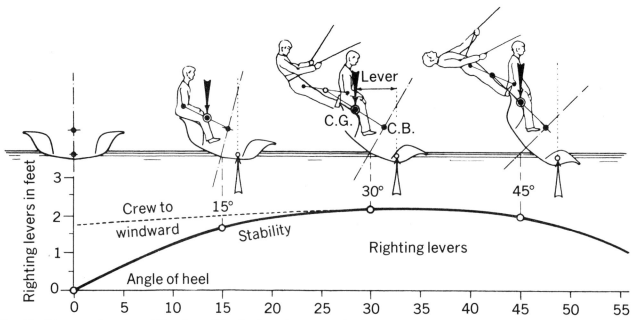

Fig. 70: Diagram of static stability in a light dinghy, whose stability depends essentially on its 'live ballast'. An International 5-0-5 serves as example, and it can be seen that even with the boat on an even keel there is a considerable righting moment if the crew is in the trapeze, see dotted line, This means that the boat can withstand considerable wind pressure without heeling at all. The trapeze was first introduced by Peter Scott in 1938.

tribute greatly to stability, because the CG is now at the tip of the black arrow. The CB, on the other hand, moves out to leeward, and between them they produce a powerful lever of static stability and an important righting moment.

As the boat heels over further, a trapeze is employed to obtain a further increase in the righting lever. As can be seen from the curve, the maximum righting lever is produced at an angle of heel of around 32°. At angles over 50° the crew has difficulties staying in position, and at an angle of 60° stability disappears altogether and the boat capsizes.

In contrast to a keelboat, the dinghy possesses an unusual quality as a result of its *live ballast*: a powerful righting moment can be produced with the boat on an even keel, especially if a trapeze is used. A dinghy can be sailed entirely upright under considerable lateral wind pressure, something which a keelboat with *dead ballast* could never do. The dotted extension of the curve of righting levers shows that with the hull on an even keel and the crew sitting to windward a righting lever of 2 ft (60 cm) can be produced, which is almost as much as the maximum at 30° of heel.

The stability created by the live ballast (i.e. the crew) can also be termed *stability out of the water*, as against the stability produced by low-lying dead ballast, which is *stability in the water*.

What side force can a dinghy, say a 5-0-5 or Flying Dutchman, take without heeling over? Both have an average weight of about 330 lb (150 kg) without crew. If one adds 285 lb (130 kg) for two crewmen, the total weight in a race would be 615 lb (280 kg). Assuming a righting lever of 2 ft (60 cm), the righting moment is $2 \times 615 = 1230$ ft lb ($0.60 \times 280 = 168$ m kg). The centre of effort of the average sail area of 150 ft² (14 m²) can be said to be at a point 8·8 ft (2·7 m) above the centre of buoyancy. Since heeling moment and righting moment have to be equal for sailing in a state of equilibrium, the lateral wind force acting on the lever of 8·8 ft (2·7 m) also has to produce a moment of 1230 ft lb (168 m kg). By dividing the moment of 1230 ft lb by the lever of 8·8 ft we are left with the side force of 140 lb (62 kg), which is $140 \div 150 = 0.93$ lb/ft² (4·4 kg/m²) of sail area.

The behaviour of a modern catamaran is, to a certain extent, similar to that of a dinghy because, like a dinghy, it is without ballast. Certain characteristic differences must be expected on account of its twin hulls. On an even keel the catamaran has *two* centres of buoyancy instead of just *one*, both marked by white

84

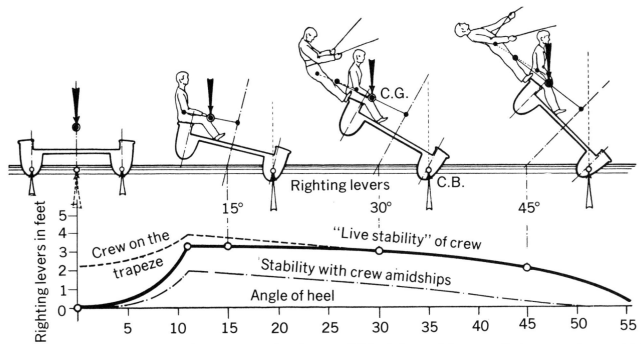

Fig. 71: The curve of static stability in a catamaran is quite different. The catamaran reaches its maximum stability at the moment the windward hull is just lifting out of the water. The stabilizing influence of the crew on the trapeze can be appreciated by comparing the lower, broken curve with the two curves above it.

arrows pointing upwards in the section on the left of Fig. 71. The initial stability, due to the great beam and ensuing great metacentric height, is quite considerable. Once the catamaran starts to heel it very quickly reaches its point of maximum stability. This happens at the exact moment when the windward hull starts to lift clear of the water which, in our example, is at an angle of heel of 11°.

With both crew members out to windward but not on the trapeze the exceedingly long righting lever of 4 ft (1·2 m) is produced. If one crew gets into the trapeze, the righting lever increases to 4·6 ft (1·4 m). If one assumes a weight of 310 lb (140 kg) for the complete boat and 285 lb (130 kg) for two crew, the total weight is 595 lb (270 kg). At an angle of 11° of heel and with a righting lever of 4·6 ft this produces a righting moment of 595 lb × 4·6 ft = 2737 ft lb (378 m kg).

By comparison, the dinghy reaches a maximum righting moment of 615 lb (280 kg) × 2·5 ft (80 cm) = 1537 ft lb (224 m kg). The Dragon, being our keelboat example, differs, to start with, by its much greater total weight, i.e. 4268 lb (1940 kg), including a three-man crew. At the same angle of heel of 11°, at which the catamaran produces its maximum righting moment, the Dragon would have a righting moment of only little

over half. Only at 17° to 18° of heel does the Dragon produce the same righting moment, i.e. the same power to carry sail, as the catamaran at 11° of heel. It must not be forgotten, in this connection, that the Dragon carries a sail area of 286 ft² (26·6 m²), which is considerably greater than the catamaran's 160 ft² (14·9 m²).

It is obvious that the catamaran with its exceptionally great stability has only a very small sail area, in other words, it is under-canvassed. The reason for this is characteristic of the type of hull: from the moment at which the windward hull lifts out of the water, which is at 11° of heel, the boat's stability *decreases* progressively until, at 57°, it reaches the critical point at which the boat capsizes.

Both catamarans and dinghies frequently come very close to capsizing without actually doing so. One must not forget that the sail area presented to the wind decreases as the angle of heel increases. This, of course, applies to all types of boat, keelboats as well as centreboarders.

The modern catamaran is an excellent example of how high-speed potential can be built into a boat. This high speed owes more to the boat's great stability combined with very low weight rather than the narrow beam and slender shape of the two hulls.

It should be added that catamarans do not usually
capsize along their fore-and-aft axis but diagonally over
the lee bow. This strange behaviour is not found in any
other type of boat, because only the catamaran combines great lateral stability with a relatively low
longitudinal stability. The latter is a direct consequence
of the fine bow-lines of its hulls. At high speeds they
undercut the water, which can lead to a split-second
capsize diagonally over the bow.

On the other hand, catamarans and dinghies can
avoid, at the last second, a capsize that seems unavoidable by quickly releasing the sheets or luffing up.
Either action will take the wind pressure out of the
sails.

There have been cases in which catamarans have
capsized on their mooring without any sails up and
without anyone on board. They capsized under bare
poles because, due to their extreme low hull weight,
their inherent stability was too low. What is more,
there are exceptional cases of dinghies with *negative
initial stability*, which are unable to stay upright even
when there is no wind. A certain French version of the
Moth class has such low initial stability (without crew)
that it is in constant danger of capsizing without
provocation. To avoid this, it has become customary to
drop a piece of ballast into the boat as soon as it is
moored and the crew ready to go ashore.

Plate 20: It is not only unballasted dinghies which use the crew's weight to increase stability, as is evident from this shot of a Dyas Class keelboat. Whilst previously the crew lay along the side as in the Star Class, the trapeze is used today.

Photo: Fritzmeier KG

Stability as a Safety Factor

In 1876 the large schooner MOHAWK capsized in a sudden violent squall when lying at anchor in New York harbour with her sails set and the owner and his guests on board. She sank immediately, drowning six people in all. Nobody could believe that a yacht of this size, 140 ft (40 m) overall and with a beam of 34 ft (10 m), could have insufficient stability. An ample beam makes for high initial stability and this gives a false impression of security.

The case of the Dragon, which can capsize and sink at an angle of heel of 52°, is different. The reason here is not inadequate stability but openings in the deck, through which water enters to fill up the boat. Any open or partly decked keelboat like, for instance, the Star, the Dragon, the Tempest and to a certain extent even the Folkboat can fill up and sink at large angles of heel. The Soling, a rather more modern concept of keelboat, can fill up but not sink, because it has built-in buoyancy compartments fore and aft. If a dinghy capsizes, it usually means no more than a wetting for the crew. The boat is neither damaged nor sinks. The most up-to-date dinghies have built-in buoyancy compartments running fore-and-aft on either side, so that hardly any water gets into the boat during a capsize. A skilful crew will waste no time in righting the boat and sailing on.

When one looks at dinghies and keelboats with the safety angle in mind, one cannot help but feel that any boat which can capsize or even fill up should be absolutely unsinkable. Modern materials like plastic foam, which is extremely light, enable nearly every boat to be made unsinkable. Some dinghies use inflatable buoyancy bags made of rubber or plastic, which are stowed under the side decks or the fore and after deck.

Open or semi-open keelboats, which are sinkable, must be sailed with extreme skill to avoid excessive heeling in strong winds.

On inland waters, capsizing and even sinking does not constitute as great a danger as in the open sea. Ocean-going yachts must, therefore, comply with much more stringent safety precautions. The following classification illustrates the different steps from safe ocean racer to dangerous boat:

Very Safe Seagoing Yachts
> Uncapsizable due to adequate deep ballast.
> Unsinkable due to watertight decks and superstructure.

> Example: the modern Ocean Racer.

Racing Keelboats
> Uncapsizable thanks to adequate deep ballast.
> Sinkable because water can enter through openings in the deck.
> Example: Dragon, Star.

Unballasted Boats, Dinghies
> Capsizable but unsinkable due to light weight and positive buoyancy.
> Example: modern racing dinghies of nearly all classes, most catamarans and many dinghy-cruisers (not all!).

The Dangerous Boat
> Capsizable because of insufficient stability.
> Sinkable due to openings in the deck and excessive hull weight.

Many merchant sailing vessels of all nationalities have crossed the Seven Seas in what could be described as the *dangerous* condition. For hundreds, even thousands of years, man was content to build ships which were sufficiently strong to withstand the ravages of the sea without falling to pieces. Shipbuilders in those times never dreamt of the possibility of an unsinkable or even uncapsizable ship. The caravels, the naval frigates, the fast clippers and the few merchant sailing ships still in existence today – all of them sailed the oceans and all of them were dangerous. Men entrusted their lives and their merchandise to them, not in ignorance of the danger, but possibly underestimating it, impressed by the ships' size and enormous weight. They had no choice but to trust in the skill and experience of the skippers and crews who sailed them. Right up to recent times, large merchant sailing vessels were not only capsizable but also ran the very real risk of sinking by filling their holds, which were only covered by wooden hatches with sail cloth stretched over the top.

In 1956 a replica was built of the MAYFLOWER, the ship in which the pilgrims sailed from England to America in 1620, and this replica nearly capsized during her launching! Such moments of danger were frequent enough in former times, one only has to think of the Swedish VASA which heeled excessively after her launching in 1628, filled through the lower gunports and sank. Naval architecture then lacked the necessary scientific foundations to complement the traditional empiric methods.

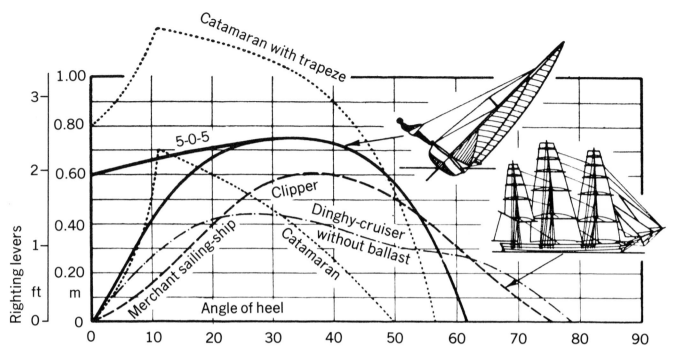

Fig. 72: Various curves of static stability for capsizable sailing craft. All without exception, from the catamaran to the clipper, capsize at angles of heel between 50° and 80°.

It is satisfying to know that a great number of sail training ships still sail the oceans and uphold the tradition of the square rig. In most cases these training ships are much safer than earlier merchant sailing vessels. The more modern ones, most of them built by German shipyards, have decks and superstructures that can be considered virtually watertight and they therefore run very little risk of sinking by filling up. The most recent training ships have been built with internal ballast amounting to as much as 20 per cent of their displacement, which even makes them uncapsizable. Amongst these are the EAGLE of the American Coast Guard, the GUANABARA of the Brazilian Navy, the TOVARISTSCH of the Soviet Navy and the latest, the GORCH FOCK of the post-war German Navy, all of which were built in Germany.

For the purposes of determining capsizability and stability, so-called *graphs of levers of static stability* are drawn up. Figures 72 and 73 illustrate two such graphs, one for capsizable and one for uncapsizable boats. The horizontal scale indicates angles of heel from 0° to 90°, and the vertical scale indicates righting levers up to 1 metre (3 ft 3 in) in length. If the length of the righting lever is known, the righting moment of the boat can be calculated by multiplying the righting lever by the total weight of the boat.

90

The bold curve marked 5-0-5 in Fig. 72 shows the values for a modern light racing dinghy sailed with the crew on a trapeze. It reaches its maximum stability at 35° of heel and capsizes at 62°. The second branch of the curve accounts for the effect of the crew on the trapeze.

In the group of capsizable craft the catamaran has the longest righting levers, especially if it is sailed with a trapeze. As long as the crew remains inboard, stability drops rapidly after reaching its maximum at 11° of heel. When the trapeze comes into use, the maximum righting lever increases from 70 cm (2·3 ft) to 1·2 m (just under 4 ft) and the point of capsize from 50° to 57°.

Surprisingly, the lever arms for the clipper are shorter than those for the small, light catamaran or the dinghy. Its maximum stability lies at approximately 37° of heel, but the relatively small lever of 2 ft produces a powerful righting moment together with the boat's massive displacement.

The least favourable of the curves in this graph belongs to a rather unusual boat: the dinghy with a cabin, or dinghy cruiser. This type of boat originated in Germany and has also spread to France but is hardly known in countries outside Europe, except Brazil. Its comparatively large hull and ample beam permit comfortable cabin accommodation, while its big centre-plate gives it a good windward performance. The boat

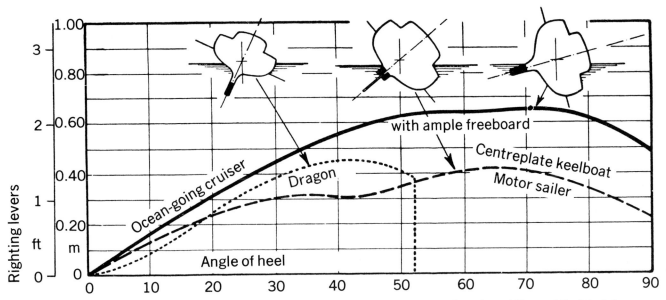

Fig. 73: These are the curves of righting levers for various self-righting types of boat. Their initial stability is relatively low, but there is still adequate static stability at angles of heel in excess of 90°. Only the Dragon loses its stability at 52° of heel, because, being an open boat, it fills up. The other two types reach their maximum stability at angles of heel between 65° and 72°.

is much cheaper to build than a keelboat with comparable accommodation but it is, normally, completely unballasted, and the large plate does little to increase stability. Under normal conditions, however, stability is more than adequate, particularly since dinghy cruisers usually carry a small sail area and are under-canvassed compared with racing dinghies. The dinghy cruiser examined in our graph, thanks to its ample beam, does not capsize until the angle of heel has reached 78°.

Figure 73 illustrates righting lever curves for non-capsizable sailing craft. Compared with the curves for capsizable boats, these curves show a considerably lower initial stability and relatively short righting levers. None of them reach more than a little over 2 ft. It must be pointed out, though, that these are only a few typical curves and that some longer yachts with greater beam and deeper draught can have considerably longer righting levers.

All yachts in this graph have low external ballast and a considerable displacement. The term *non-capsizable* implies that the boat still possesses a positive righting moment at an angle of heel of 90°. Only two of the three curves comply with this condition. The third, belonging to a Dragon, drops suddenly to zero at 52° of heel, because at this point the boat fills with water and

sinks.

The modern ocean-going cruiser or ocean racer has the most favourable curve of righting levers. Even at small angles of heel it has greater stability due to its ample beam. This superiority, brought about by favourable ratios between beam, draught, freeboard and ballast, extends over the whole of the curve. Of course, the boat has a watertight superstructure and self-draining cockpit. At an angle of heel of 55° the curve dips slightly and then rises again. This is the point at which the deck is immersed. In the curve for the shoal-draught keelboat with centreplate, this dip occurs as early as 40° because its deck, due to the lower freeboard, comes into contact with the water sooner.

A modern motor sailer can have the same curve as the centreplate keelboat, and for this reason both are covered by the same curve in our graph. In practice, of course, there can be marked differences between these as between any other types. It must be said here that the working out of a curve of righting levers, which looks so simple, is an involved and time-consuming business, which is why, quite frequently, curves are merely estimated.

So far, stability has only been mentioned as something of which boats can never have enough. But there is also the opposite case of excessive stability. It rarely occurs in sailing vessels but is occasionally encountered in fishing boats. It results in extremely hard movements in a seaway and makes life aboard almost unendurable for the crew. Excessive stability is not established with the help of a curve of righting levers, since this is meaningless at small angles of heel, but by the *metacentric height*. If a fishing boat has a metacentric height of more than 4 ft 6 in (1·4 m), the boat is excessively stable and unsuitable for fishing. If the metacentric height is less than 2 ft (60 cm), this is insufficient and the boat is tender.

Any sea-going yacht should, as far as possible, comply with the conditions of being both *non-capsizable* and *unsinkable*. The former poses no problem, but the latter is extremely difficult to achieve. The degree to which it can be achieved is marked by three stages:

1. *Generally unsinkable:* this type of boat needs careful preparation before putting to sea, such as sealing the hatches, fitting a canvas cover over the superstructure and protecting the forward part of an open cockpit with a dodger.

2. *Almost unsinkable:* watertight cockpit and strong, water-resistant superstructure are part of the basic design, so that the boat can only sink if it springs a leak.

3. *Absolutely unsinkable:* even if completely filled with water, the boat is still lighter than the displaced water. Light construction combined with buoyancy tanks and watertight compartments (less desirable) or spaces filled with light synthetic foam (highly recommended) make this the ideal boat.

It is by no means impossible to design uncapsizable yachts which have no ballast at all. Normal ocean-going yachts, however, should have fixed external ballast in a ratio of at least 20 per cent of their total displacement to be considered reasonably uncapsizable. Loose, internal ballast is dangerous and should definitely be avoided. If the boat should ever heel violently, the ballast might shift to leeward and in-

Plate 21: A small schooner on a fetch. Here you can see clearly how the gaff sail sags away at the leach as compared to the Bermudan sail, so that a boat so rigged cannot sail as closely to the wind. FLORENCE OAKLAND *has a long bowsprit and you can see the rows of reef points in all three sails. Designed by John Atken of Darien she is 22 ft 4 in long and is intended for day sailing, hence the extra large cockpit.* Photo: John Atkin, Darien

crease the angle of heel even further. This is what happened in the case of MOHAWK, which we mentioned earlier. We know of a number of cases in which boats rolled through 360°, and the loose ballast being flung around inside the cabin left marks on the deckhead before coming to rest somewhere along the cabin sides.

Determining the Sail Area

Plate 22: In the unsheltered and frequently stormy waters off Australia young sailors can learn their sport the hard way. This 16 ft skiff gets the necessary stability from a four-man crew, so that she can carry a quite excessive sail area in the prevailing conditions. The Australians, however, are very keen on this wild sailing. This splendid picture was taken by Neville E Bowler in Port Philip Bay, Melbourne.

The power of a boat to carry sail depends mainly on her stability. But even if precise stability figures were available in a particular case, which is rare, it would soon be found that on their own they are hardly sufficient to determine the optimum sail area for that boat. To start with, it would have to be suitable for all wind strengths from a dead calm to a hurricane. Then it has to suit the purpose for which the boat is to be used. Obviously, an inshore race and a single-handed transatlantic voyage impose different requirements. If one adds to this the enormous diversity of boat types, sizes, rigs and foresails one can easily appreciate that the *best* or *most useful* sail area cannot be mathematically calculated, but depends on a number of individual conditions.

Another consideration is the number of different courses sailed in relation to the wind. For example, even a simple change of course from close-hauled to running, with boat and wind strength remaining the same, requires a change in sail area.

An attempt is made in the following pages to give some idea of how to determine a so-called basic or

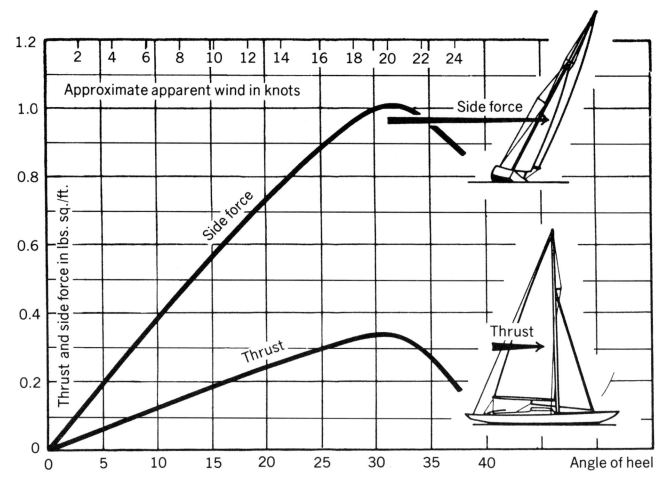

Fig. 74: This graph provides useful information for determining the power to carry sail. The curves for thrust and side force have been drawn up for a Dragon, but since the values are expressed in force per unit sail area they can easily be applied to other boats. Angles of heel are marked along the lower edge of the graph, corresponding apparent wind speeds along the upper edge.

normal sail area without difficult and exhaustive mathematical calculations. By 'normal sail area' we mean that amount of sail which gives good driving power but puts little strain on the rigging in a moderate wind of say 13 knots.

One sometimes reads statements, in complete contradiction to empiric reality, to the effect that a boat 'can carry so many square feet of sail area per ton displacement'. Area is a square measure whereas displacement, being a volume, is cubic. Therefore, displacement and sail area cannot be directly related.

When a boat sails in a state of static equilibrium, the heeling moment equals the righting moment. Expressed by a formula, it looks like this:

Sail area × specific pressure
(pressure per unit sail area)
× heeling lever × cos ε
= displacement × righting lever

Since the sail area presented to the wind becomes less as the boat heels over, the cosine of the angle of heel ε is included in the formula to make up for the reduction of sail area. At an angle of heel of 20° the sail area is reduced by 6 per cent, at 25° by 10 per cent and at 30° by as much as 14 per cent.

Once the course sailed, angle of heel and wind speed are known, the basic sail area required can be worked out with the help of the formula. But the procedure is laborious and in practice not very satisfactory. It is easier to work with coefficients which have proved themselves over years of practical experience. Every naval architect uses his own set of coefficients, and his choice of the suitable coefficient will depend on his assessment of the conditions under which the yacht will be sailing.

Any formula based on experience must, of course, be in accordance with the physical laws of similarity, for only then can it be applied to boats of all dimensions. The most common method is to divide the square root of the sail area by the cube root of the displacement:

$$\text{Coefficient} = \frac{\sqrt{\text{Sail area in square feet}}}{\sqrt[3]{\text{Displacement in cubic feet}}}$$

It must be admitted, though, that displacement alone is an inadequate criterion for stability, which is obvious when one thinks of the enormous difference between keelboat and dinghy. With this in mind another formula is given below, in which the sail area is related to the so-called 'waterline plane', which is the product of waterline length and waterline beam. This formula is expressed in this simple form:

$$\text{Sail area} = \text{coefficient} \times \text{LWL} \times \text{BWL}$$

On the basis of this it is possible to say that a yacht carries so many feet of sail area per square foot of waterline plane.

This sort of simplification gives only guide lines, of course, and not an absolute figure. The two most important factors, sail area on the wind and BWL, can be interpreted in totally different ways. Are we talking, for example, about the area of the biggest headsail or that of the foretriangle? Should the implications of a hull shape in which the beam increases notably between waterline and deck level be taken into account? Despite such ambiguities the progression of figures in the following table appears convincingly logical:

SPECIFIC SAIL AREA PER FT² OR M² OF WATERLINE PLANE

	Keelboats	
Class Racing Boats	Star	4·18 ft² or m²
	Tempest	2·80 ft² or m²
	Soling	2·32 ft² or m²
	Dragon	2·47 ft² or m²
	International 12-metre	3·67 ft² or m²
	J-class	4·50 ft² or m²
Ocean-going Cruiser/Racers	Folkboat	2·16 ft² or m²
	Yacht FINISTERRE	2·53 ft² or m²
	Modern Ocean Cruiser/Racer	2·50–2·80 ft² or m²
	One-Tonners to IOR	1·90–2·30 ft² or m²
Sail Training Ship GORCH FOCK		2·34 ft² or m²
	Dinghies	
Class Racing Dinghies	Olympic Monotype 1936	1·88 ft² or m²
	Flying Dutchman	2·09 ft² or m²
	International 5-0-5	2·45 ft² or m²
	Snipe and Lightning	1·94 ft² or m²
	International Contender	2·24 ft² or m²
Catamarans	Shearwater III	1·43 ft² or m²
	International Tornado	1·25 ft² or m²

When one compares the figures in this list one finds, surprisingly, that weight is of minor importance, with the noticeable exception of catamarans, which have a particularly small specific sail area. The reason for this lies in the great *waterline beam* and the fact that the boat is capsizable. Besides, the very light hull allows

Carina

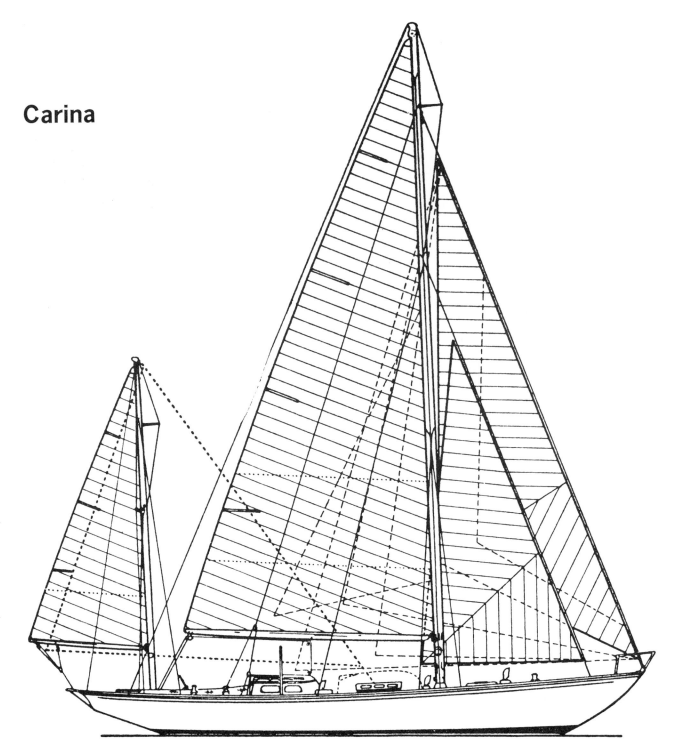

*Fig. 75: Sail plan of the successful, yawl-rigged ocean racer
CARINA designed by Phil Rhodes. Her hull and sail plan are perfectly matched, and this factor, no doubt, contributed greatly to her
many successes.*

LOA	*53 ft 7 in*	*Draft, plate down .*	*10 ft 2 in*
LWL	*36 ft 5 in*	*Displacement*	
Beam	*13 ft*	*approx.*	*19 ton*
Draft, plate up ...	*6 ft*	*Sail area*	*1194 sq ft*

high speeds to be reached with only a modest sail area. Amongst all the un-ballasted boats the 5-0-5 has the largest specific sail area, which is roughly twice that of the Tornado. Perhaps this contributes to the fact that the 5-0-5 is particularly easy to right after a capsize, contrary to the catamaran, which is extremely difficult and can hardly ever be righted without outside help.

The above figures are not applicable to extreme designs; in such cases an individual analysis of stability and propulsion has to be made to determine the suitable sail area. Detailed stability calculations should be made far more often for every type of boat, since both safety at sea and power to carry sail, i.e. speed, could benefit greatly by it. When the 'ocean racer' type of boat first appeared on the scene some forty years ago, it normally had a very narrow beam. The famous DORADE, for example, had a specific sail area of 3·56, and equally famous NIÑA of 3. Nowadays the normal specific sail area for ocean racers is 2·5 to 2·8.

Eric Hiscock, who circumnavigated the world in his small cruiser WANDERER III, set a specific sail area of 3·5 in light winds. Vito Dumas, who sailed his ketch LEGH II round the world by way of the Roaring Forties, carried a basic sail area of only 1·6 per unit waterline plane, allowing for the prevalent gale force winds in these latitudes. If he set a masthead genoa and a staysail between deck and mizzen masthead, the specific sail area increased to a normal value of 2·73.

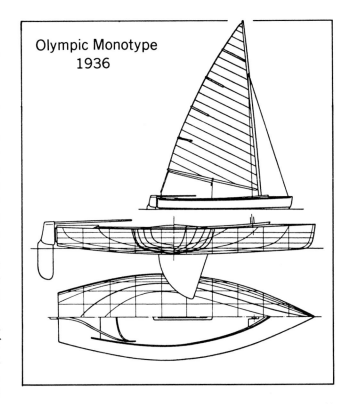

Fig. 76: The Olympic Monotype carries a relatively modest sail area for its power to carry sail. Its dimensions are:

LOA	16 ft 5 in	Draft, plate up	4 in
LWL	14 ft 9 in	Draft, plate down	3 ft 6 in
Beam	5 ft 5 in	Sail area	118 sq ft

The Mast - Main Problem of the Sailing Yacht

The question of whether a mast should be rigid or bendy, of light or heavy construction and a number of related topics frequently lead to heated arguments when experts discuss the intricacies of sail trim. One thing is certain though: mast and sail have to be matched to one another. A sail which has been cut for a rigid, straight mast has to be set on such a mast, which has very little give by which the sail can be adjusted to different wind strengths. On the other hand, a sail which has been cut for a bendy and/or initially curved mast, will set very badly on a straight, rigid mast.

Until hollow, glued masts were introduced around 1920, which had been dependent on the invention of waterproof glues, masts were simply built strong enough to carry the sails. In the days of the big merchant sailing ships it was quite normal to support enormous sail areas by very primitive means. Masts in three sections were made as early as the sixteenth century, because ships had reached dimensions where naturally grown tree-trunks were too short. Some clipper masts were even made in five sections.

The sole purpose of mast stays was to give the mast added strength in bad weather without, however, interfering with the yards. When galvanized steel wire came into use around 1850, rigs of greater height could be stayed much more reliably, but until then countless very complicated rigs relied solely on hemp and manila rope.

Without steel wire and water-resistant marine glues there would be no efficient modern rig, for even light alloy masts were only developed after hollow, glued wooden masts had already reached a high degree of perfection.

The effect of the mast on the driving power of the sails is always detrimental. Even in the most favourable circumstances, i.e. when the mast diameter is small, the loss of driving power is 20 per cent, as we can see from the graph in Fig. 53. The combined effect of reduced driving power and increased resistance is an appreciable loss of speed made good, as well as speed to windward. Anyone who has ever tried to put up a mast on a windy day will appreciate its surprisingly large wind resistance.

The large J-class yachts, about 130 ft (40 m) long, contributed in no small measure to a close study of the whole problem of masts. When W Starling Burgess designed his ENTERPRISE in 1930, he boldly decided to rig her with a metal mast. It was 164 ft (50 m) long

and had a maximum diameter of only 18 in (46 cm). It was made of two thin skins of duralumin riveted together with no less than 80,000 duralumin rivets.

ENTERPRISE easily won the series in 1930 against the British challenger SHAMROCK V, and her thin and very light mast was a complete success, although it turned out to be excessively flexible fore-and-aft and was considered downright dangerous. W Starling Burgess, who had originally planned to function as navigator during the 1930 series, had to relinquish this post and become 'nursemaid to the mast'. Everyone thought it was a miracle for ENTERPRISE to finish each race with her colossal metal spar still in one piece.

Only recently the problematic role of the mast was highlighted once again when PEN DUICK IV, hot favourite in the Round the World Race, broke her mast twice.

Is it possible to calculate the diameter which will give a mast adequate strength? The answer is yes, but calculations of the stresses which the mast has to carry must never be based on wind pressure, because the wind can never produce a greater heeling moment than is equalled by the righting moment of stability. Therefore, any calculations of mast and rigging have to be based on the yacht's stability rather than the estimated wind pressures.

A detailed calculation of the loads carried by the mast and rigging is a laborious procedure and is hardly ever undertaken. The following formula shows a simple and adequately accurate method of determining the diameter of solid and hollow wooden masts, together with correction values for all types of yachts. A subsequent paragraph deals with the application of these figures to light alloy masts.

Diameter of Solid Wooden Masts

Bermudan rig: D in inches $= 0.06 \, L + 0.12\sqrt{S}$

Gaff rig: D in inches $= 0.08 \, L + 0.12\sqrt{S}$

where L = length of mast in feet from deck to where upper shrouds are attached,

and S = basic sail area in sq ft (main and foresail).

The Dragon will serve as an example to explain the formula. In it, L = 32.8 ft and S = 286 sq ft hence

$$\text{Mast diameter D} = 0.06 \times 32.8 + 0.12 \times \sqrt{286}$$
$$= 1.97 + 2.03$$
$$= 4 \text{ inches}$$

This is an empirically determined, so-called normal

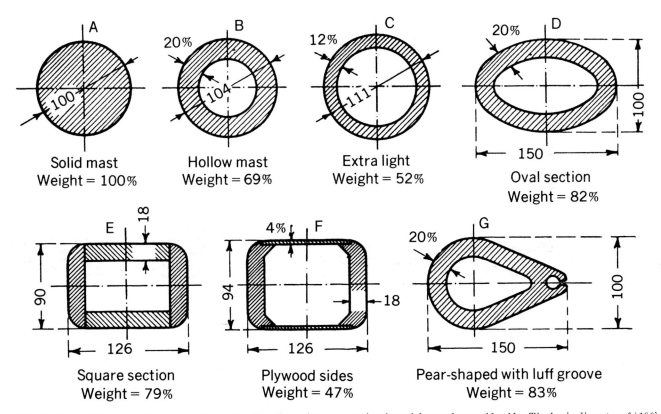

Fig. 77: Seven different sections of wooden masts. The dimensions of the six hollow sections are those at which they will be approximately comparable in strength with the solid, round mast. The saving in weight can be considerable. The basic diameter of '100' for the solid mast corresponds to the formula for the calculation of mast diameters as given in the text.

mast diameter. Differences in various types from the light racing boat to the heavy ocean racer are covered by the following corrections:

Type	Correction of Diameter
Light racing yacht with low stability	minus 10%
Normal racing yacht	minus 5%
Light inshore cruiser	as formula
Cruiser of moderate weight	plus 10%
Heavy cruiser	plus 15%
Modern ocean racer	plus 20%
Very heavy ocean racer	plus 30%

This explains why the actual diameter of a Dragon mast is 5 per cent smaller than the 4 inches we calculated.

TAPERING OF MAST: Normally, a mast tapers at both ends, to 85 per cent of its maximum diameter at the foot and to 50 to 60 per cent at the top. If a mast-head foresail is set, the masthead diameter is reduced to only 70 to 75 per cent. The maximum mast diameter should be approximately mid-way between the deck and the point where the lower shrouds are attached, or roughly one-third of the total mast height above the deck.

HOLLOW MASTS: If a hollow mast is used instead of a solid one, the saving in weight is considerable, but the diameter has to be correspondingly increased. Also, where the shrouds are attached, the mast has to be reinforced on the inside. In wooden masts the thickness of the mast wall is normally 20 per cent of the mast diameter, but this can vary for the sake of greater strength or reduced weight. In principle, though, the same strength is sought in a hollow mast as in a solid one, and the following table of dimensions is based on this assumption:

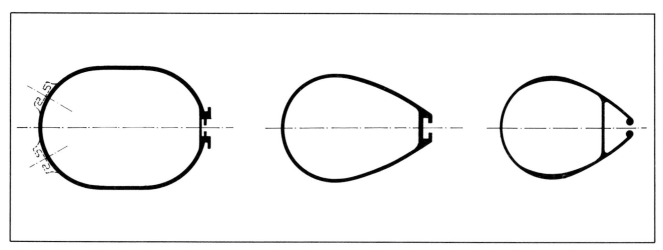

Fig. 78: Three different sections of aluminium masts. The mainsail track is different in each one. The largest section on the left also indicates two tracks for the spinnaker boom. The pear-shaped section on the right, in which the wall thickness is not uniform, is mainly used on racing dinghies. If the mast is strengthened by inside ribs, the outside diameter can be very much smaller. This results in considerable aerodynamic advantages, even if the mast is then heavier.

Diameter of Wall	Diameter of Mast	Weight in % of Solid Mast
Normal wall = 20% D	increased by 4%	69%
Thick wall = 25% D	increased by 2%	76%
Thin wall = 12% D	increased by 11%	52%

A thin wall of only 12 per cent D should only be chosen after very careful consideration. Not only is there an increased risk of breakage at the points where the shrouds are attached, even if the mast is reinforced at those points on the inside, but the surfaces of the glued seams become very narrow indeed.

Mast sections are not always round. Figure 77 shows various other sections and indicates their weight and scantlings as a percentage of the weight and diameter of a solid mast of the same strength. Thus, a mast of pear-shaped section, bottom right, weighs only 83 per cent of the solid round mast, the athwartship measurement of 100 is equal to the diameter of the solid mast, the fore-and-aft scantling of 150 is 50 per cent greater than the diameter of the solid mast. Although such a mast is very strong fore-and-aft, it is aerodynamically unfavourable on the wind, as can be seen in Fig. 79.

More and more masts are now made of aluminium alloys. The choice of available sections is so great that it is possible to find a suitable metal mast for almost any type and size of sailing vessel. Some common sections are shown in Fig. 78.

DIAMETERS OF ALUMINIUM MASTS: Diameters of aluminium masts are normally determined by the manufacturers as a result of long experience. It can be said, though, that such masts for racing dinghies may have a diameter roughly 15 per cent less than that of a corresponding wooden mast. In light racing keelboats the diameter reduction may be 5 to 10 per cent, whereas in ocean racers, which prefer a rather stronger mast, the diameter of an aluminium mast may be equal to that of a wooden mast. Much depends on the thickness of the mast walls and the interior reinforcements, of course.

An aluminium mast is not as perfectly proportioned as a good wooden mast, because it is difficult to achieve a gradual taper towards the ends. Usually, the mast is of uniform diameter over most of its length. Towards the masthead a wedge is cut out and the edges welded together.

A number of other materials have been used for masts: thin-walled steel tubing, fibreglass, carbon fibre and even titanium, which is very expensive.

Stress comes on the mast not only through the shrouds but also through the halliards. In boats of the Star class, which have a particularly thin mast, as well as on some large ocean-racing yachts, it is customary to hook the mainsail into a special masthead device which eliminates the pull of the running part of the halliard.

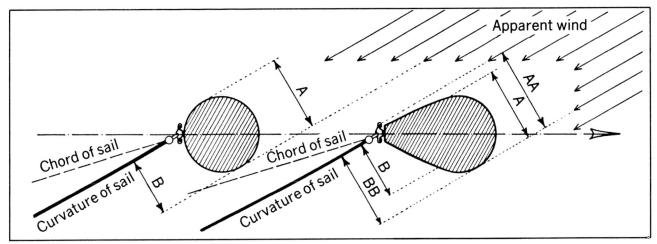

Fig. 79: Contrary to popular opinion, a pear-shaped mast section is aerodynamically unfavourable, as can be seen by comparing its width AA with the width A of the round mast. Particularly detrimental is its projection BB to leeward, because it interferes with the smooth airflow in the luff zone of the sail. A rotating mast would only be of value if it could be rotated past the angle of the boom.

STRAIGHT OR BENDY MASTS: At one time straight masts were the general rule, and only small racing dinghies like the Finn and the Star were conceded curved or bendy masts. This attitude changed mainly due to the introduction of synthetic sail cloths. It was realized that the set of a Terylene or Dacron mainsail can be appreciably influenced by an adjustable mast curvature, i.e. the sail can be flattened in strong winds and given more belly in light winds. At about the same time there was a certain following for an elastic, swinging mast, which was supposed to suffer less stress from the boat's motion and also minimize the disruption of the air-flow. This idea has long been abandoned, but some boats of very low stability still use a mast which bends at the top and thereby reduces the heeling moment in strong winds.

From an aerodynamic point of view, a mast which is to have the least detrimental effect should meet the following conditions:

(a) minimum diameter for minimum disruption of airflow at the leading edge,

(b) minimum weight for minimum adverse effect on the boat's stability,

(c) minimum number of stays, shrouds, spreaders and cross-trees,

(d) spreaders of minimum length for minimum interference with large headsails.

MAST RAKE: Looking about us, we see masts which stand vertically, some which lean slightly aft and a few which lean forward. Aerodynamically, the vertical mast is doubtlessly the most efficient. If there is any rake, it should be slightly *forward*, definitely not aft! Raking the mast aft has an added disadvantage in that it gives the mainsail and boom a tendency to want to fall back to the centreline in light winds for the simple reason that at that angle their weight pulls them back. So one should not be afraid of giving one's mast a slight rake forward, however strange this may appear to the eye at first.

MASTS FOR ONE-DESIGN CLASSES: In many one-design classes the mast measurements are rigidly controlled by the class rules. Since such boats only race against each other, their speed in comparison with other boats is of no importance. Excessively thin masts are, therefore, not justified, but they are nevertheless used by certain classes. This often leads to situations where boats prefer not to race in strong winds, because they do not want to expose their masts to costly risks. It would seem particularly important for one-design racing classes to have a strong mast of reasonable diameter.

AERODYNAMICALLY SHAPED MASTS: It is apparent from Fig. 79 that a pear-shaped mast section is by no means aerodynamically favourable. Its width 'BB' to leeward is considerably in excess of the width 'B' of a round mast. Only if such a mast could be made to rotate, i.e. rotate freely to any position including one considerably *past the boom* would it have a small aerodynamic advantage over a mast with a round section.

An extreme type of aerodynamic mast, in which this has been achieved, is the wing mast. This is, however, not normally used on class boats, because the rules preclude it, nor on cruising boats, because its problems outnumber its advantages. It has mainly proved itself with the C-class catamarans, which compete for the Little America's Cup. Since the wide wing mast would obviously add appreciably to the sail area, the whole of the mast width is counted in the measured sail area. These masts have undoubtedly proved successful and have gradually grown wider and wider to the point where in some cases the mast profile accounts for nearly half the sail area.

In general, aerodynamic masts of this type are not practicable, even for boats where the rules do not forbid them. The fact that the whole of the wing mast has to be able to rotate complicates the staying quite considerably. Stepping and lowering is a difficult undertaking, and if it were left standing on a light catamaran on her mooring, it could easily lead to her capsize. It cannot, of course, be reefed.

Plate 23: Wing masts are common on fast racing catamarans. Here is an A Class Typhoon catamaran, designed by the Australian, Lock Crowther, which has a sandwich construction wing mast (hulls and masts built by Canadian Multihull Services). The angle of attack of the mast must be greater than that of the boom, which can be seen at the foot of the mast.   Photo: Lock Crowther

Yardstick and Speed

What is known as the *Portsmouth Yardstick Scheme* is actually a British invention worked out in 1951 by S Zillwood Milledge. Its purpose is to allot handicap numbers to various current racing classes to enable them to compete against each other on equal terms.

The Portsmouth Yardstick Numbers, as they are known, are compiled in extensive tables. They are based on the mean time taken by boats in good racing trim to sail a common but unspecified distance. S Z Milledge became closely acquainted with the problems of handicapping before 1951, when he acted for several years as handicapper for one of the yacht clubs in the Portsmouth area. Most of the handicaps given to yachts for racing purposes at the time were pure guesswork and plainly unscientific. Milledge applied his conclusions to working out a system on a mathematically sound basis. The results proved him right, and meanwhile the system has been adopted by over 50 countries.

It must be stressed that the time for each class is based on a *distance of unknown length*, which means that the Portsmouth Yardstick Numbers are not meant to be an indication of speed. Nevertheless, they can easily be used to calculate individual speeds once a base-speed has been established. When it comes to organizing races between boats of different classes, however, it is unnecessary to know true speeds as long as comparative speeds are known. The system is particularly useful in organizing races in clubs that have a great number of different racing classes. Instead of having innumerable starts of only a few boats each, all classes can start together, and the results can be corrected on the basis of the Langstone Tables.

The Portsmouth Yardsticks for 1976 as published by the RYA cover Primary Yardsticks for 33 class boats, Secondary Yardsticks for 137 class boats and, in addition, 190 Provisional Portsmouth Numbers, which are constantly subject to adjustment in the light of practical experience. They cover centreboarders, keelboats, multihulls and cruisers. The author has added a column indicating mean speed, the significance of which will be explained afterwards.

Fig. 81: The bold curve defines the speed of a non-planing sailing boat on all points of sailing, measured from the centre of the circle. Between 5 and 12 points off the true wind the boat's speed is fairly constant, but before the wind it drops perceptibly. The top sector is unattainable, because the wind is too far forward.

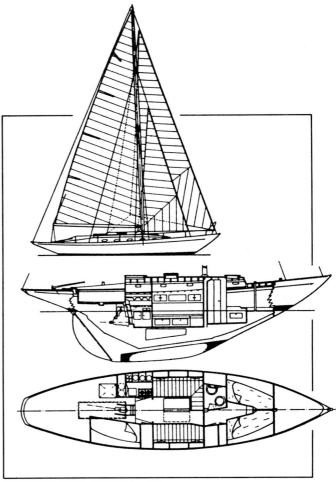

Fig. 80: This cruiser designed to the German KR Formula by Karl Vertens still rates as a fast, seaworthy type, even if by up-to-date standards the overhangs and the keel profile are excessive.

LOA	42 ft	Draft	6 ft 7 in
LWL	27 ft 4 in	Displacement	8·3 ton
Beam	9 ft 2 in	Sail area	710 sq ft

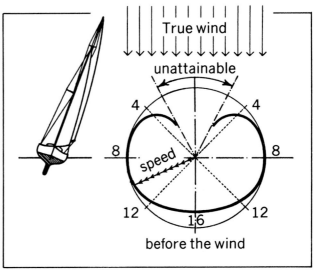

SELECTION FROM PORTSMOUTH YARDSTICKS 1978

Primary Yardsticks		Speed in knots
5-0-5	97	4·3
Dragon	107	4·0
Laser	114	3·7
Enterprise	118	3·6
OK	118	3·6
Mirror	146	2·8

Secondary Yardsticks		
Tornado Catamaran	75	5·5
Unicorn Catamaran	84	5·0
Flying Dutchman	94	4·5
Soling	98	4·3
Star	98	4·3
Tempest	98	4·2
Fireball	103	4·0
470	103	4·0
14 ft International	106	3·9
Finn	110	3·8

Primary Yardsticks		Speed in knots
Contessa 26	114	3·6
Achilles	114	3·6
Hunter 701	114	3·6
420	115	3·6
International Moth	120	3·5
Vivacity 24	126	3·3
Hurley 22	127	3·3
Cadet	154	2·7
Optimist	178	2·4

Provisional Portsmouth Numbers		
Arpège Mk I	109	3·8
Ecume de Mer	112	3·7
Folkboat	115	3·6
Alacrity	120	3·5
Hurley 27	121	3·4
Flying Junior	124	3·4
Minisail	130	3·2

Figure 81 illustrates the *normal speed* of a keel-yacht on all courses to the wind. The diagram has been prepared for a Dragon but is valid in general for all other non-planing sailing yachts. The outer circle indicates the maximum speed attainable, which is reached on a course 8 points (90°) off the wind, i.e. with the true wind on the beam. Over a large range of courses between 4 and 12 points (45° to 135°) off the true wind, the speed remains almost unchanged and never drops by more than 10 per cent of the maximum speed. Only when 'pinching', i.e. sailing at less than 4 points to the true wind, and when running dead before the wind, i.e. at 16 points off the wind, does the reduction in speed amount to approximately 20 per cent.

This speed curve is characteristic of all displacement hulls in moderate winds. If it is converted to actual figures for a Dragon sailing in a true wind of 12 knots, we get the following speed scale:

Course	Off True Wind		Speed Loss	Boat's Speed
Pinching	3½ points	(40°)	20%	3·6 knots
Normally close-hauled	4 points	(45°)	14%	3·9 knots
Wind on the beam	8 points	(90°)	0%	4·6 knots
Quartering wind	12 points	(135°)	8%	4·2 knots
Before the wind	16 points	(180°)	20%	3·6 knots
			Average speed	4·0 knots

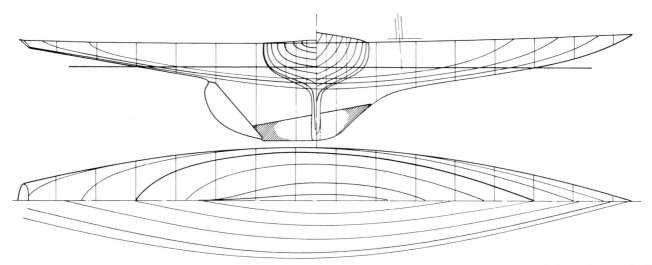

Fig. 82: The striking perfection of the lines of a 30-square-metre Skerry Cruiser could hardly be improved on even by extensive model tests. Although the class rules allowed great freedom of hull dimensions, these beautiful boats were hardly faster than restricted or one-design classes. The explanation for this rather surprising fact lies in surface friction.

The speed of 4 knots represents the normal speed of a Dragon. It can never reach twice that speed, even if the wind could impart ten times the driving force. The Dragon is not even able to surpass this speed by 50 per cent except in very unusual circumstances and for short periods only. On the other hand, it can reach half, probably almost three-quarters, of its normal speed in nothing more than a light breeze.

If we cast a look back at the Portsmouth Yardstick Table, we find that it does, indeed, list 4 knots as the normal speed of a Dragon, together with a Yardstick Number of 107. The normal speeds for all other classes were worked out with reference to their Yardstick Number as a ratio of the Dragon figures.

It is tempting to use the Portsmouth Yardstick to compare the normal speeds of different classes. It shows that by far the fastest boat of all is the Tornado catamaran. The immortal Star is exactly as fast as the Soling and the 5-0-5, while the Tempest, which is a very much lighter keelboat than the Soling, is slightly slower. The Dragon, on the other hand, is quite a bit slower. It must not be forgotten, however, that Secondary Yardstick Numbers are subject to modification, and Provisional Numbers 'are based on limited information and should be used only as a guide'.

Strange as it may appear, the knowledge of absolute speed sailed is unimportant to the racing yachtsman. He is purely interested in any advantage in speed, however small, which he can gain over his competitors. It is different for the cruising yachtsman: his plans, his time-table, depend entirely on the absolute speed sailed, and to him the knowledge of his yacht's average speed at any time is of great importance.

When comparing the speeds of sailing yachts with those of other means of transport, say the motor car or the aeroplane, it must be admitted that the sailing yacht is very slow. If, however, one considers the un-mechanized and unpredictable nature of its driving power, it is undeniably one of the most interesting and efficient craft in the world. Many aircraft pilots are sailing men in their free time, not only because they appreciate the absence of mechanical noise on the water, but also because they are fascinated by the constantly changing game of extracting driving power from the wind without burning a drop of fuel.

Every sailor has to decide for himself whether attainable speed as such is of importance to him. If it is and he is prepared to make the necessary sacrifices, he can achieve near-miracles in unexpected ways. It can happen that a big, expensive boat is beaten in speed by a smaller sister that has cost not even a hundredth to build. On the other hand, the experience of an ocean race on board a large yacht is totally different from the exhilaration of planing in a catamaran or light racing dinghy.

Absolute and Relative Speeds
of Displacement Yachts

How can a small, cheap boat occasionally go as fast as or even faster than a large racing yacht? The explanation lies in the fact that the keelboat, or more accurately the *heavy displacement yacht*, is *trapped* by its self-induced wave system. The small, unballasted dinghy, on the other hand, can *run away* from its wave system and enter the state of *planing*. Exciting as this may be, most of the vessels navigating the oceans of the world are displacement craft. Only the displacement hull can continue to make headway in heavy seas. Small, light planing hulls cease to be able to perform as soon as there is a moderate sea. *Every boat has its own, inherent mean speed under sail, which can be calculated.*

The driving power of the sailing boat, i.e. the wind, is constantly changing through all the stages from total calm to gale force. Its angle of incidence, too, changes from acute, when sailing close-hauled, to a right angle (to the sail chord) when sailing before the wind. Besides, there is a significant difference between true wind and apparent wind, which further complicates an investigation into normal speeds under sail. Nevertheless, every boat can be attributed a certain speed which is its own, inherent mean speed. It will reach it in no more than a moderate wind and exceed it only by little even in a gale.

The question is, why is it impossible to exceed these mean speeds by very much? One explanation lies in the unstable nature of the wind, but the main reason is in the water: wave formation.

Any wave, be it formed by the wind passing over the surface of the water or by a vessel moving through the water, has a speed of its own, which is strictly related to its length, i.e. the distance from crest to crest. The speed of advance of any wave equals $1.35 \times \sqrt{\text{wave length}}$, where the wave length is in feet and the speed will be in knots. A wave with a length of 9 ft from crest to crest will always move at a speed of
$$V = 1.35 \times \sqrt{9} = 4.05 \text{ knots}$$
Another wave of 49 ft in length, as is frequent in a smaller expanse of sea like the Baltic, for example, will have the following speed:
$$V = 1.35 \times \sqrt{49} = 9.45 \text{ knots}$$
Any displacement boat creates a wave at the bow and, except at very slow speeds, a second wave at the stern. A keelboat cannot, normally, create a wave longer than its own effective waterline length. Conse-

quently, a displacement boat cannot naturally sail faster than $1.35 \times \sqrt{\text{waterline length}}$ in knots. A Dragon, for example, with a waterline length of 19.68 ft, can reach a maximum speed of $1.35 \times \sqrt{19.68} = 6$ knots. Since, however, the wave resistance increases quite appreciably before this maximum is reached, it is attainable only under very exceptional circumstances.

The same principle applies to all normal displacement yachts. The figure of 1.35 represents a *relative* speed or, as it is more frequently termed, a *speed/length ratio* (1.35 being the maximum relative speed attainable by displacement craft). The mathematical formula for speed/length ratio is $R = \dfrac{V}{\sqrt{L}}$ where R is the speed/length ratio. By applying this speed/length ratio, the maximum attainable speed can be defined as follows:
A displacement boat can, under optimum conditions, reach a maximum relative speed of $R = 1.35$, with the waterline length measured in feet and the speed in knots. This maximum relative speed is only reached in exceptional cases.

A normal speed which is frequently reached corresponds to a speed/length ratio of 0.9, or approximately $\frac{2}{3}$ of the maximum attainable speed. For example, a boat with a waterline length of 25 ft will frequently reach a normal speed of
$$V \text{ normal} = 0.9 \times \sqrt{25} = 4.5 \text{ knots}$$
The transverse wave formation along the hull in relation to various speeds is shown in Fig. 83. The two boats on the left marked $R = 0.9$ and $R = 1.05$ illustrate normal speeds. On the right, wave formations are shown as they occur at *exceptionally high speeds*. We can see that at a speed/length ratio of $R = 0.9$ the vessel is supported by two wave lengths, at $R = 1.05$ only by one and a half. At $R = 1.2$ the vessel rides on one wave length only, which is a little shorter than its own waterline length. Wave resistance is now a strong and disturbing influence. $R = 1.35$ shows the maximum speed reached solely by wind propulsion, and then only in *exceptional cases*, since wave resistance is now very strong. $R = 1.5$ is no longer attainable by mere wind propulsion. It can only be reached in tow by a powerful motor vessel, which can overcome the enormous wave resistance. The boat enters the unnatural state where its bow rises on the crest of the bow wave and the stern sinks into the trough, while she drags a huge wave behind her.

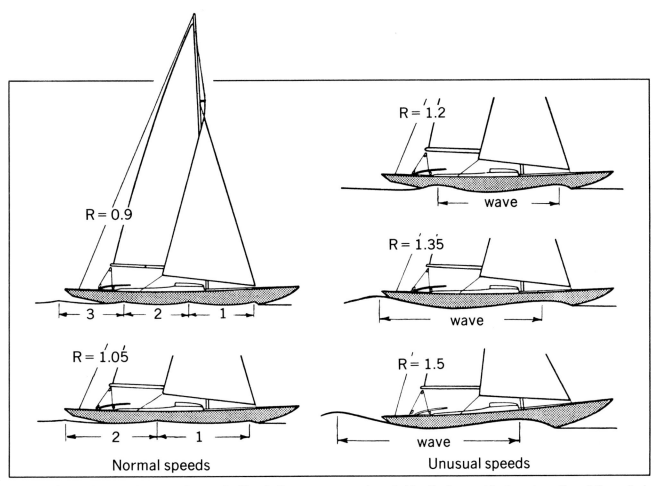

Normal speeds   Unusual speeds

Fig. 83: All displacement boats are characterized by similar wave formations at comparable speed/length ratios. Speed/length ratios of between 0·89 and 1·04 are most frequent. The highest relative speed reached by displacement boats under sail, and then only in exceptional circumstances, lies around 1·34.

It happens not infrequently that a yacht is dismasted at sea. In such a case the skipper should resist the temptation of accepting a tow by a passing ship, however well-meaning and persuasive the offer may be. Even the slowest freighter today has a speed of 12 knots, which is much too high for a relatively small yacht. If, say, an ocean racer with a waterline length of 36 ft is towed at a speed of 12 knots, the speed/length ratio will be $R = 12/\sqrt{36} = 2$! This is far in excess of the vessel's inherent maximum speed/length ratio of 1·35. The total wave resistance which she will have to contend with, and which will not bother the towing vessel, is so tremendous that after a short time she will spring a leak and sink.

A large yacht is nearly always faster than a small one, but due to the peculiar nature of wind propulsion, the larger boat has a *lower relative speed*. The larger yacht will much less frequently reach the high relative speed of $R = 1·2$. The table at the top of p. 108 gives comparative values for three types of sailing boats, valid for a wind speed of 16 knots.

It can be seen that in the same wind conditions the J-boat reaches the higher absolute speed, but its relative speed, i.e. its speed/length ratio, is only 1·07, which is 10 per cent lower than that of the much smaller Dragon. There is another factor which works against the larger vessel. Due to its higher absolute speed its apparent wind draws further ahead, which means *that*

	Dragon	Int. 12-metre	J-class
LWL	18·7 ft	45 ft	81 ft
Speed on a reach	5·2 knots	7·6 knots	9·7 knots
Speed/length ratio	1·2	1·1	1·07

she cannot point as high (to the true wind) as the smaller craft. To put all three boats on an equal footing, the wind, while being 16 knots for the Dragon, would have to be 24·4 knots for the International 12-metre and as much as 32·8 knots for the J-class yacht. But then stability would become a problem, so such a test would not be realistic.

The skipper of a *cruising boat on holiday* must equally base his plans on attainable average speeds, which he can ascertain with the help of speed/length ratios. Although $R = 0.9$ can be considered a normal speed, it must not be assumed as an average on a holiday cruise. A realistic average cruising speed, assuming that no calms are met with, is $R = 0.75$. For a yacht with a waterline length of 25 ft this would result in a cruising speed of $0.75 \times \sqrt{25} = 3.5$ knots.

EXTENDED OCEAN CRUISES: The small yacht WANDERER III, in which the experienced yachtsman Eric Hiscock sailed round the world, reached an average of $R = 0.54$ only over the longest of her distances at sea. Over one ten-day stretch of favourable winds, on the other hand, she attained the remarkably high average of $R = 0.97$. The maximum relative speed reached over one 24-hour period was even as high as $R = 1.27$, which was with the help of a favour-able current. A well-known ocean-racing yacht, STORMY WEATHER, recorded a relative speed of $R = 1.2$ for two 24-hour periods in the North Atlantic with a following wind and current.

INFLUENCE OF WAVE MOTION: The detrimental influence of ocean waves is one of the main reasons for low average speeds at sea. Their braking effect on the hull depends on their magnitude and the course sailed. Close-hauled and sailing into a choppy sea a boat's speed may drop to half the normal. If the seas are very heavy she may cease to make any headway whatever on that course. A following sea has scarcely any negative effect on headway; it sometimes has a positive effect, which comes about like this:

A boat sailing at sea with a strong following wind may encounter waves of enormous lengths, which move at considerable speed. A wave 81 ft long, which is frequently met with on all oceans of the world, must move at a speed of $1.35 \times \sqrt{81} = 12$ knots. If a boat runs dead before the crest of such a wave, she will receive two powerful impulses from it: one from the downward sloping face of the wave and the other from the particles of water, which, at this point, are moving in a forward direction in their elliptical orbit. For several seconds the hull will exceed the speed/length ratio of $R = 1.35$

SUMMARY
Relative Cruising Speeds

Strong wind and very favourable conditions	$1.2 \times \sqrt{L}$
Average in strong winds	$1.07 \times \sqrt{L}$
Normal wind strength	$0.9 \times \sqrt{L}$
Changing winds, light to moderate	$0.7 \times \sqrt{L}$
Average on ocean voyages, maximum	$0.75 \times \sqrt{L}$

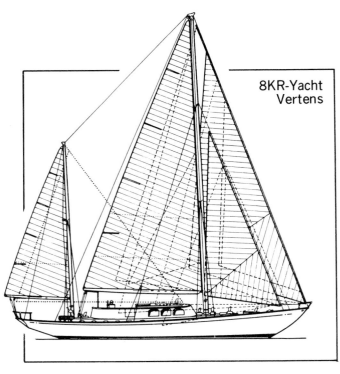

8KR-Yacht
Vertens

Fig. 84: Boats like the yawl BARLOVENTO II *are ideal for long ocean passages. She has a centre cockpit and two centreplates in tandem in the keel.*

LOA	71 ft 6 in	Draft, plates up	5 ft 6 in
LWL	50 ft	Draft, plates down	12 ft 6 in
Beam	18 ft	Sail area	2051 sq ft

without being subjected to excessive stress. Since this will happen again and again, the average speed attained will be very high.

The proud clippers, most beautiful of all vessels ever to sail the Seven Seas, may occasionally have reached maximum speeds of 20 knots. The famous clipper LIGHTNING, known for her spectacular performances, once logged a 24-hour run of 436 nautical miles, while the CHAMPION OF THE SEAS is reported to have logged 465 miles. This is not far short of 480 miles, which would equal an average speed of 20 knots, and leads to the assumption that 20 knots were certainly reached over short distances.

Nevertheless, the relative speed of the clippers was modest. Even if a maximum speed of 20 knots was occasionally reached under especially favourable conditions, this amounts to a quite moderate speed/length ratio of $R = 1.2$ only. For an entire passage the clippers never even reached an average relative speed of $R = 0.6$.

An important deduction which can be drawn from these considerations on speed/length ratio is that it is of value to have a great *effective length* in a hull. Effective length, however, is never synonymous with waterline length. The various rating rules for ocean racers attempt by all sorts of methods imaginable to arrive at the true effective length which is to be entered in the formula, while yacht designers apply all their cunning to achieve the maximum possible effective length with the minimum possible rated length. In this way, modern rating rules have led to the abandonment of long counter sterns, which have been replaced by short overhangs and a relatively large transom.

SPEED/LENGTH RATIOS FOR DISPLACEMENT YACHTS

$R = V/\sqrt{L}$ where V is in knots and L in feet.

R below 0·9   Comfortable sailing, small angle of heel, low wave resistance. Easily reached in a light breeze.

$R = 0.9$ Average speed under sail, producing moderate heel. The most pleasant speed, for which most yachts are designed.

$R = 1.05$ Increased speed, greater angle of heel, stronger wave formation. Frequently reached, a delightful sail and ideal for racing and cruising.

$R = 1.2$ Attainable under ideal conditions in strong winds. The angle of heel is considerable, so is the wave formation. Sailing at this speed is an experience!

$R = 1.35$ Maximum attainable speed under sail for displacement yachts, which can be reached in strong winds on a reach. A breathtaking experience. Strong wave formation prevents a further increase in speed, the hull is trapped between its own waves, so to speak.

$R = 1.5$ No longer attainable under sail, except by planing hulls. If reached in tow, the wave resistance places excessive strain on the towed vessel's structure.

R over 1·5   Only attainable in tow from a powerful motor vessel. Serious risk of the boat disintegrating and sinking.

Maximum Speeds under Sail

A displacement hull remains forever trapped in its own wave system, i.e. between its self-created bow and stern waves, whereas a light dinghy or catamaran, which does not rely on built-in ballast for stability, can literally run away from its wave system and leave its stern wave far behind.

The sailing boat which reaches the highest speed can be defined as the one which is characterized by maximum *stability out of the water*. The ballast keel of the displacement boat represents *stability in the water*. The dinghy, on the other hand, gets most of its stability out of the water by the crew sitting out to windward. The catamaran, at the moment the windward hull lifts out of the water, illustrates stability out of the water most clearly. If, besides, the crew is out on the trapeze, we have a virtually ideal case. By applying this principle of stability without ballast, it is easily possible to exceed the conventional speed limits and escape from the wave resistance, which would normally increase rapidly. The boat now enters the fascinating state of planing. Of course, the apparent wind draws further and further ahead as boat speed increases, and therefore really spectacular performance can only be expected on a reach. Before the wind, too, the apparent decrease in wind caused by the boat's speed has a detrimental effect.

Figure 85 shows the spectacular increase in speed attainable by a planing hull. Close-hauled and running, the boat does not reach planing speeds but behaves like a displacement craft. When sailing between 8 and 12 points (90°–135°) off the wind, however, a light dinghy begins to plane and can easily double its speed.

A boat will only plane if three conditions are met:

(a) A light hull with a flat bottom suitable for planing.

(b) Stability out of the water without the use of ballast.

(c) A suitable course in relation to the wind in order to gain the maximum driving force without the apparent wind drawing too far ahead.

If a light hull possesses a suitable planing shape, a small increase in thrust will free it from the critical and unfavourable condition of $R = 1.35$, see Fig. 86, and enable it to *run away from its wave*. At this moment the boat starts to *mount its bow wave*, see Fig. 87. If the wind force increases further, the boat will leave its stern wave far behind and enter the exciting state of planing at high speed.

It goes without saying that lightness is the first pre-

Plate 24: The crew of a Korsar use their weight to good effect. The crew has his arm outstretched and the helmsman has most of his body outboard. In this way the Korsar has reached a high planing speed as the clean wake shows. The boat is 16 ft 5 in long with a beam of 5 ft 7 in and a sail area of 158 sq ft.

Photo: Brigitte Reich

requisite for a planing hull. The shape of the bottom of the hull is also of great importance. If the shape is such that it traps the hull in its wave system, planing is impossible. The smooth flow of water off the afterbody, which is desirable for normal sailing, must be avoided in a planing hull, since there is no longer a stern wave, the smooth flow of which has to be furthered. The second condition, therefore, is a flat run in the after-

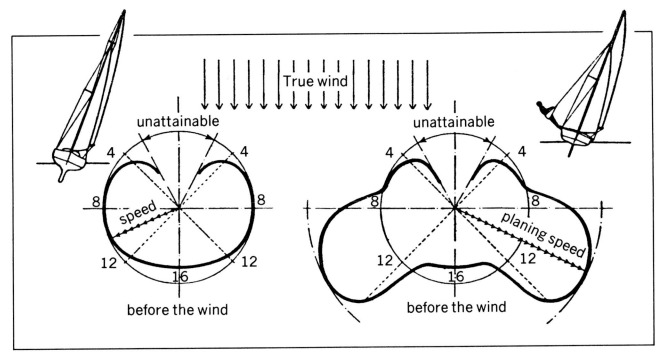

Fig. 85: Planing hulls reach their highest speeds on courses between 8 and 12 points off the true wind, as can be seen in the right half of the diagram. In strong winds a planing hull can even plane before the wind.

part of the hull, a transom which is in contact with the water and has a sharp trailing edge to encourage the detachment of the flow of water rather than dragging it behind.

The boat on the right in Fig. 87 illustrates a speed of $R = 3.6$, which is very fast planing, and in a 5-0-5 corresponds to a speed of 14 knots. The boat now *rides on its bow wave*. The bow wave is the only wave to have any contact with the hull, the stern wave having been left *seven boat-lengths* behind. The achievement of such high planing speeds depends no longer on resistance and wind speed but on the stability of the boat and the willingness of her crew to perform acrobatics and, if necessary, capsize.

Light keelboats with the necessary flat-bottomed after-sections can also plane, and boats of this type can reach speeds of up to $R = 2.4$ under favourable conditions. Even a number of modern ocean racers fall into this category. With their dinghy-shaped hulls and narrow, centreboard-like keels they have given rise to a new term: the *ocean-racing dinghy*.

A hull designed specifically with a view to facilitating planing is given a flat after-section. This theory is new and at the same time old-established. New, because it is only since 1950 that specific planing hulls have been designed. Old-established, because it was noticed long before then that some one-design classes could reach higher speeds if the original design was altered to make the after-body flatter. This led to completely new lines, within the permissible limits, being drawn up for some class-boats, in particular the Star. Inevitably the question arises: Why were these boats designed with an excessively rockered keel in the first place?

A genuine planing hull must be designed 'on the wave', as illustrated in Fig. 88. At the most frequently reached planing speed the wave length is about twice the waterline length of the boat. The design of a record-breaking hull, on the other hand, would be based on a wave length of 8 to 10 times the waterline length or even more. In the initial stages of a design it is difficult to forecast the exact shape of the wave graphically. The designer has to rely largely on comparisons with exist-

111

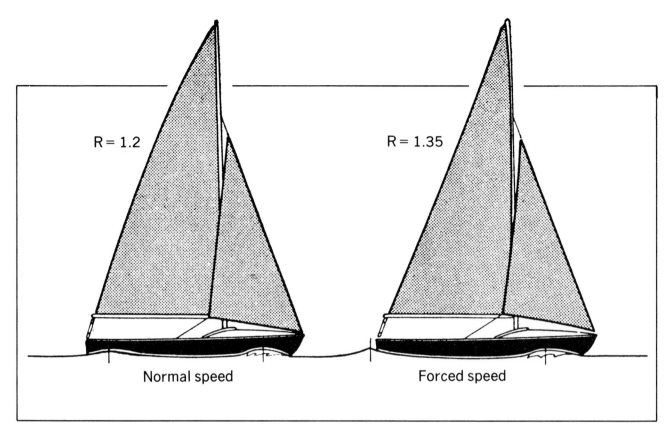

R = 1.2   R = 1.35

Normal speed   Forced speed

Fig. 86: The behaviour of a dinghy at normal, non-planing speeds is comparable to that of a displacement boat. At the same relative speed of R = 1·34 the dinghy enters a critical phase where resistance increases and planing is not possible.

ing hulls and refer to drawings like the one in Fig. 88. He designs the hull to fit the assumed wave pattern. He must also take into account that in planing the hull receives *partial dynamic lift*, which means that its displacement is less than the compound weight of boat and crew. The planing boat displaces less water than is equal to its own weight.

Definition of Planing

Planing is a state of sailing with partial dynamic lift in which the weight of water displaced is *less* than the weight of the hull. Furthermore, the hull detaches itself from its wave system, *leaving its stern wave far behind* and beginning to ride on its bow wave.

The partial dynamic lift and the resultant reduction in displacement produce a direct decrease in resistance. This can be clearly seen, because the planing hull leaves an insignificant, scarcely developed wake behind it. A further decrease in resistance is brought about by the reduced wetted surface as the hull lifts partially out of the water and skin friction decreases.

112

Light boats have even been made to sail with total dynamic lift by having hydrofoils fitted under the hull. Once the boat has overcome the critical speed, which requires greater propulsion because of the additional resistance of the hydrofoils, it begins to rise out of the water and a moment later it takes off at an amazing speed with total dynamic lift, supported only by its small foils.

The crowning achievement of modern racing dinghy design lies in the unexpected possibility of getting a boat to plane on the wind. To achieve this, both hull and rigging had to be drastically reduced in weight, and the sails had to be perfected to optimum aerodynamic efficiency, so that they would yield the considerable thrust needed.

Every profile, every sail, needs to be inclined to the airflow at a minimum angle in order to produce lift, which the boat converts into forward thrust. The higher the speed sailed, the more the apparent wind draws ahead. This explains why a very fast yacht cannot go as close to the true wind as a slower one. In

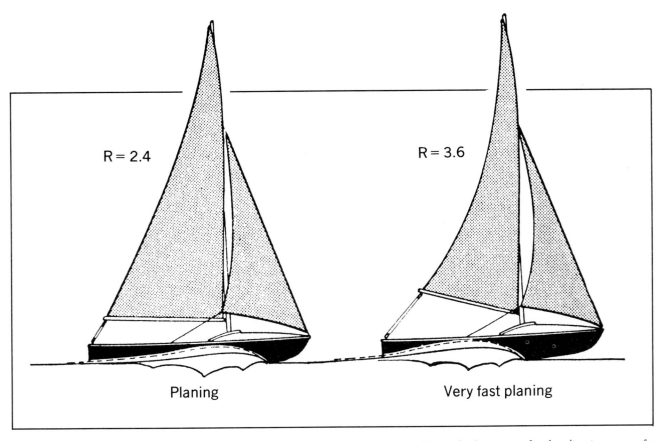

R = 2.4

R = 3.6

Planing

Very fast planing

Fig. 87: Once the critical phase is overcome, which happens at a speed/length ratio in excess of R = 1·78, a dinghy with a suitably shaped bottom begins to plane. If the wind increases further, the boat starts to ride on its bow wave, leaving its stern wave far behind.

other words, the conventional, slow sailing yacht points higher than the fast modern planing dinghy.

Figure 89 illustrates three characteristic types of boat. Top left is the conventional sailing yacht, which sails at a speed equal to half the true wind speed on a course 8 points off the true wind, i.e. with the true wind on the beam. The apparent wind is then increased by 12 per cent and its angle of incidence is 63° instead of 90°.

If a planing dinghy or catamaran sails on the same course of 8 points to the true wind, as shown in the illustration top right, it might move at a speed equal to that of the true wind, in which case the angle of incidence of the apparent wind is 45° and its speed is increased by 42 per cent. An ice-yacht, shown at the bottom of Fig. 86, can go as fast as three times the true wind speed. With the true wind still on the beam, as before, the angle of incidence of the apparent wind is now only 18° and the apparent wind speed is over three times that of the true wind.

Such very high speeds are rarely reached in actual practice, because the necessary conditions only prevail

Fig. 88: The underwater shape of a planing hull is of critical importance. It has to fit the wave it makes at planing speeds, in other words, it has to be designed 'on the wave'.

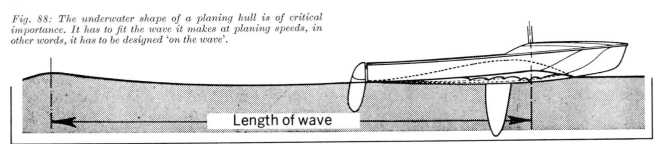

Length of wave

Maximum attainable speeds

Displacement Boats

Dragon	5·8 knots
International 12-metre yacht	9 knots
America's Cup J-class yacht	12·1 knots
Three-masted schooner ATLANTIC	15 knots
Clipper with cargo	18 knots

Planing Boats

International 5-0-5	16 knots
International Flying Dutchman	17 knots
Shearwater Catamaran	18 knots
Tornado Catamaran	20 knots
Catamarans AIKANE and MANU KAI	20 knots
Proa CROSSBOW	31·09 knots

Fig. 89: Depending on the speed of the boat, the speed and direction of the apparent wind, indicated by the bold arrows, change drastically even if the true wind remains the same. The conventional sailing boat, upper left, sails at half the true wind speed, the planing dinghy or catamaran, upper right, sails at a speed equal to the true wind speed, while the ice or sand yacht in the lower half of the diagram sails three times as fast as the true wind speed.

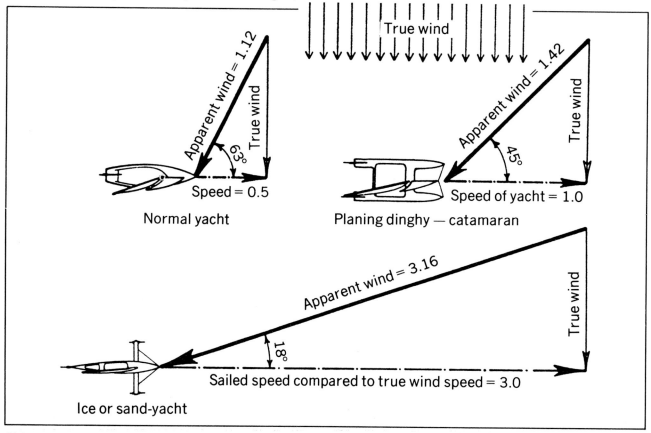

Plate 25: *Breathtaking performance of a large, modern ocean racer. In the prevailing wind and with a large sail area set, this 53 ft Brazilian IOR yacht reaches the limits of her speed potential.*

WA WA TOO *was designed by the Argentinian designer German Frers for the Admiral's Cup Series and built in light alloy.*
Photo: Beken, Cowes

on rare occasions. Besides, there is the problem of measuring them accurately. The momentary indication of a speedometer is not reliable, and a reliable measurement by radar or over a measured mile is hardly ever feasible. Nevertheless, the table opposite of attained maximum speeds can be taken to be fairly true, even if these speeds have been reached only very exceptionally.

Up to 1976, by far the highest speed, and this was accurately measured, was reached by a proa named CROSSBOW. A proa is a genuine outrigger boat, i.e. a boat with a main hull, which is usually very narrow, and an outrigger which adds stability. CROSSBOW was designed by Rod Macalpine-Downie the distinguished British catamaran designer, and he designed her specifically for a series of sailing speed trials held in British waters. The main hull had a length of 60 ft (18 m) and a beam of only 1 ft 10 in (56 cm) and had to carry the incredible sail area of 968 sq ft (90 m²). This was made possible by the outrigger to windward and the willingness of the five-man crew to perform acrobatics.

All of them, including the helmsman, could find room on the narrow outrigger which was nearly 20 ft (6 m) distant from the main hull and connected with it by ladder-like girders, on which the crew moved deftly out to windward and back again as the wind pressure required. In subsequent trials the crew remained permanently on the outrigger.

This extraordinary craft was a pure racing machine and unsuitable for any other purpose. It could neither tack nor gybe and required the constant stand-by of a motor launch without whose help sails could neither be set nor lowered. Once, when a strong gust of wind heeled CROSSBOW by 30°, the whole crew on the outrigger found themselves more than 15 ft (5 m) above the surface of the water. CROSSBOW could hardly be called a sailing yacht, nor would most sailing men say that she has contributed anything positive to the sport, but she does represent a brilliant effort to convert the wind into the highest possible speed on the water.

The Resistance of the Yacht under Sail

Few realize just how little thrust is needed to drive a boat at its normal speed. A Flying Dutchman, for example, reaches its normal speed of 5 knots with a thrust of just 27 lb (12·5 kg) before the wind and of 44 lb (20 kg) on the wind. The considerably heavier Dragon reaches its normal speed of 4 knots with a thrust of 44 lb (20 kg) before the wind and 66 lb (30 kg) on the wind.

The total resistance of a boat progressing under sail is made up of three virtually unrelated parts, two of them dependent on the water, one on the wind:

(a) *Form resistance*, also known as *dynamic resistance*. Its visible effects are the waves made by the hull and the turbulence in its wake.

(b) *Surface friction*. This is caused by the friction of water on the wetted surface of the hull.

(c) *Wind resistance*. This is created by the pressure of the wind on hull and rigging. It does not exist on courses before the wind, because all wind forces including those on the hull, mast and rigging, coincide with the direction of the ship's movement and as such act as forward thrust.

Dynamic or Form Resistance

Any boat-like body moving on the surface of the water causes form resistance, which is made up chiefly of wave formation. If a pear-shaped body moves along at a sufficient depth *below* the surface of the water, no waves are formed, and consequently there is no wave resistance. An example is the cigar-shaped lead ballast at the bottom of the modern fin keel. The collective term of dynamic resistance comprises, apart from wave-making resistance, the resistance caused by eddies at the bow, stern, keel, rudder and chine.

At slow speeds form resistance is small. As the speed increases, the resistance increases rapidly at more than a square ratio; this can be seen from the steepness of the curve in the left half of the diagram Fig. 90. This curve can be applied to all types of craft, keelboats and light planing dinghies alike, at any speed. Form resistance for any boat can be determined by means of the relative speed, or speed/length ratio $R = V/\sqrt{L}$, which is plotted along the horizontal scale of the graph, and the *specific form resistance* plotted along the vertical scale. The specific form resistance is given in lb per lb displacement for a speed unit of 1 ft/sec.

For most boats the specific form resistance lies between 0·0015 and 0·003 lb per lb displacement, but it reaches as much as 0·0045 at the vertex. Up to this point, which lies at $R = 1·5$, the resistance increases steeply. Displacement boats of conventional shape cannot reach this speed/length ratio under sail, as we have shown previously. If they are forced to unnatural speeds while in tow, the increase in resistance becomes enormous, as shown by the branch of the curve which shoots vertically upwards.

This explains why $R = 1·35$ is the maximum speed/length ratio attainable by conventional displacement hulls under sail. Beyond this, the boat is held back by the enormous increase in form resistance.

The part of the curve going off to the right applies to planing hulls. It has its apex at $R = 1·6$, and from thereon the increase in form resistance is less than in a square ratio to the speed. A look at the descending curve might lead to the erroneous assumption that in a planing boat *no* further increase in resistance occurs after a speed/length ratio of $R = 1·6$ has been reached. This is not so. The increase is still quite considerable, because in the formula for form resistance speed (V) is squared.

Newton found that the resistance of a body is proportional to the density of the medium in which it moves, to the sectional surface it presents to that medium and to the square of its speed. Modern research on resistance still acknowledges this basic theory, allowing for considerable variants which occur by applying coefficients. In order to find the actual form resistance from the curve of specific resistance the following formula has to be applied:

Form resistance = specific resistance ×

$$V^2 \times \frac{\text{Displacement (in lb)}}{\text{Length (in ft)}}$$

The ratio Displacement/Length represents the *mean weight* of a boat. A fully equipped Dragon with a waterline length of 18·7 ft has a displacement of 4480 lb, which makes its mean weight

$$4480 \div 18·7 = 240 \text{ lb}$$

If a Dragon sails at a speed of 4 knots, its relative speed is $R = \dfrac{4}{\sqrt{18·7}} = 0·9$. The speed/length ratio of 0·9, according to the graph in Fig. 90, corresponds to a specific form resistance of 0·0013. The total form resistance is found by multiplying this by the mean

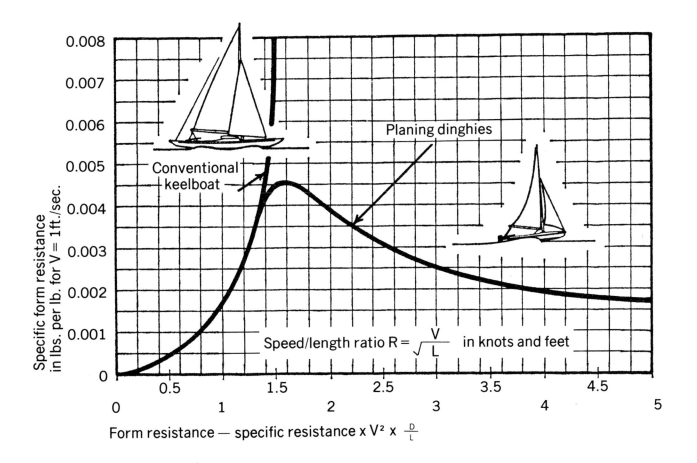

Fig. 90: Basic graph for the study of form resistance, approximately applicable to all types of craft under sail at all speeds. The specific form resistance is given in lb per lb of displacement for a basic speed of 1 ft/sec. The curve covers all possibilities from ghosting to planing.

Fig. 91: Every normally shaped hull loses its symmetry when heeled. This illustration shows the asymmetrical shape of the heeled waterlines of a Dragon. The broken line indicates that part of the stern overhang which comes into contact with the water at high speeds.

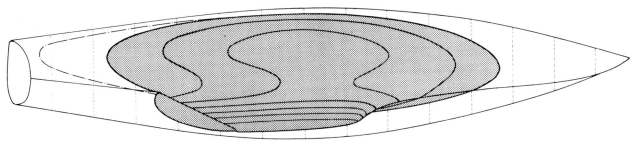

117

weight, i.e. 240 lb, and the square of the speed in ft/sec (4 knots = 6·75 ft/sec), which brings the total form resistance of a Dragon to

$$0·0013 \times 240 \times 6·75^2 = 14·2 \text{ lb}$$

Similarly, the form resistance of a modern planing dinghy like the Flying Dutchman can be calculated. If, in this case, we assume a speed/length ratio of $R = 3·6$ we can extract from the graph in Fig. 90 a corresponding specific resistance of 0·0021. If the boat's total weight, inclusive of crew and gear, is 660 lb and its LWL 18 ft, this gives a mean weight of 36·6 lb. The absolute speed is $V = 3·6\sqrt{18} = 15·3$ knots = 25·8 ft/sec. Now the total form resistance can be calculated as follows:

$$0·0021 \times 36·6 \times 25·8^2 = 51·16 \text{ lb}$$

The effect of speed on form resistance is immediately obvious. This very light boat produces four times the form resistance of a Dragon, which is much heavier but sails much more slowly.

So far, all calculations have been based on the assumption that the boat sails upright and without leeway, which is only possible on courses dead before the wind. As soon as the boat is heeled, the underwater lines of the hull are no longer symmetrical, see Fig. 91. The following table of mean values for the increase in resistance due to heeling is valid for most modern types of displacement yacht:

Mean Increase in Resistance Due to Heeling	
Heeled 5°, increase less than	1%
Heeled 10°, increase less than	2%
Heeled 15°, increase less than	4%
Heeled 20°, increase less than	7%
Heeled 25°, increase less than	13%
Heeled 30°, increase less than	25%

While the added resistance due to heeling is a result of a lack of symmetry, the resistance caused by leeway is of a different nature altogether. The boat reacts to the side force of the wind by going sideways, the angle of sideways drift being called leeway. The entire volume of water in contact with the keel or centreplate is

118

diverted, and this diversion constitutes the resistance against the sideways component of the wind force. Below the keel or centreplate, however, the water is not diverted. The flow is disrupted, and this disruption causes the so-called *induced drag*. A similar thing happens at the wing-tips of an aeroplane, where the air not in contact with the wing detaches itself from that diverted by the wing, thus producing a *vortex trail*. Figure 92 attempts to illustrate this phenomenon.

The induced drag increases as the angle of leeway, at which the yacht has to sail in order to resist the wind's side force, becomes bigger. The following figures may be considered approximate for normal yachts at mean speeds:

Induced Drag in Addition to mere *Form Resistance*	
Angle of leeway 2°, increase	14%
Angle of leeway 4°, increase	34%
Angle of leeway 6°, increase	56%
Angle of leeway 8°, increase	80%
Angle of leeway 10°, increase	106%

These figures show at a glance that the effect of induced drag is considerably greater than that of resistance due to heeling. Yet few skippers know of its existence, and even fewer realize its magnitude. A small angle of leeway of 4°, which cannot usually be achieved by a conventional cruising boat, means an increase of 34 per cent over the total form resistance calculated for the boat sailing on an even keel, while an angle of heel of 20° only produces an increase of 6 per cent. If we relate this figure to the Dragon used in previous examples, we can calculate the total form resistance as follows:

Form resistance on even keel	13·00 lb
6% increase at 20° heel	0·78 lb
34% increase at 4° leeway	4·42 lb
	———
Total	18·20 lb

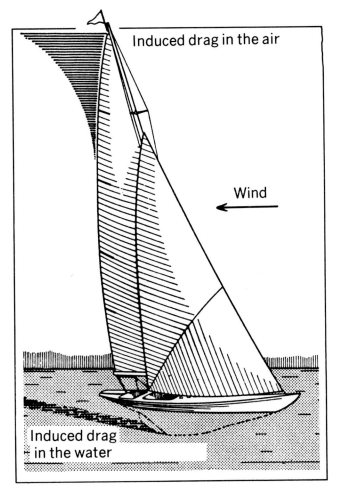

Induced drag in the air

Wind

Induced drag in the water

The angle of leeway of 4° is purely an assumed one. Most helmsmen don't even know the angle of leeway of their particular boat. Only a well-designed and skilfully handled modern boat would sail with an angle of leeway of 4°. The following table of mean angles of leeway for various types of boat will give a fair idea of what can be expected. However, strict accuracy must not be expected from any of the many figures in this chapter. Although successfully applied to individual cases, the critical mathematical and experimental analysis of the sailing yacht is still in its infancy when it comes to general application.

The modern, close-winded yacht compares favourably with any type of sailing craft of the past. Its superiority is due not only to its advanced hull shape but also to the perfection of its rig. But even the most advanced keelboat cannot compete with the modern thoroughbred dinghy. A centreplate is exceptionally efficient, especially if it is deep and narrow, because it resembles most closely the modern aircraft wing.

Fig. 92: The friction between the wind deflected by the sail and the undisturbed wind above the masthead causes the so-called 'induced drag'. A similar condition develops in the water underneath the keel.

NORMAL ANGLES OF LEEWAY

| Type of Yacht | Angle of Heel | |
	Less than 20°	Over 20°
Pointing exceptionally high	3°	3½°
Modern Racing Yacht	4°	4½°
Modern Ocean Racer	4°	5°
Modern Offshore Cruising Boat	5°	6½°
Cruising boat of inefficient shape	8°	12°
Square-rigged Training Ship, approx.	12°	16°
Sixteenth-century Caravel	45°	—

Surface Friction

Plate 26: Light weather trim in a Soling. Note the sails eased slightly to carry the boat through the sloppy waves. The helmsman is Crown Prince Harald of Norway, on his way to winning the Kiel Week Soling class in 1972.   Photo: François Richard

When a vessel moves through the water, the particles of water flow along the submerged surface of the hull, called the *wetted surface*. The flow may be smooth and undisturbed, when it is called *laminar flow*, or it can be disturbed and erratic, when it is known as *turbulent flow*. No surface is sufficiently smooth or water-repellent for water not to adhere to it to some extent. Increasing friction and increasing speed cause turbulence, which is why laminar flow is, in any case, only possible at slow speeds. In practice, every sailing vessel has to reckon with a turbulent flow along its wetted surface. Only small model sailing boats can expect a smooth laminar flow along the frictional boundary layer.

This boundary layer, which is the body of water set in motion as a result of friction between hull and water, accompanies every moving vessel. It is very thin in the bow region but increases in thickness towards the stern. It has the following characteristics:

(a) *laminar flow* is only possible at slow speeds and along an exceptionally smooth surface.

(b) *turbulent flow* is experienced at normal and high speeds along the entire length of the underwater body.

(c) the boundary layer is thin forward.

(d) its thickness increases considerably aft.

Towards the end of the last century, William Froude made a thorough study of the phenomena of friction. He made the surprising discovery that a long metal plate towed through the water caused considerably less resistance per unit surface area than a short one, and also that an area of roughness on a short plate caused much more resistance per unit surface area than the same roughness on a long plate. Only much later the explanation for this phenomenon was found in the frictional boundary layer. Since this layer is very thin in the forward region, the roughness often protrudes through it into the unmoved water, which causes increased resistance. The boundary layer becomes progressively thicker going aft along the length of the

120

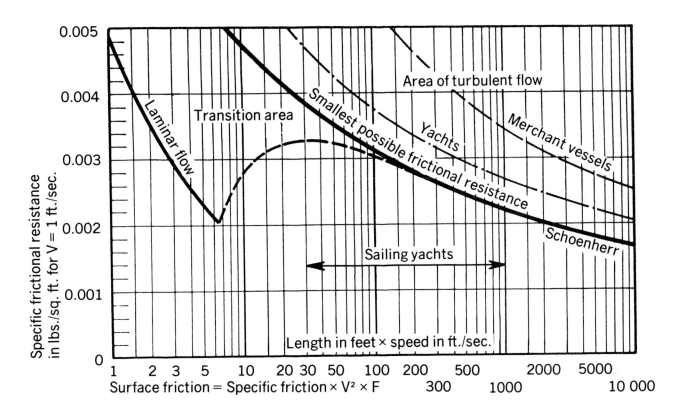

Fig. 93: Graph giving basic values for surface friction valid for any hull shape and speed. They are related to a simplified version of 'Reynold's Number', i.e. the product of length and speed. In tests with model boats the formation of laminar flow, which causes very low resistance (see curve in left quarter of graph) must be avoided in order to preserve the similarity with real conditions.

object and covers the roughness. For this reason the surface friction in the after-part of a long plate is much less per unit surface area than in the fore-part.

Much later, the British physicist Reynolds discovered the principle on which the behaviour of surface friction is based. He established that surface friction is equal if the product of length and speed is equal, provided the medium is the same. To enable his discovery to be applied to any liquid, Reynolds introduced into his formula the value of 'kinematic viscosity'. In the case of water this is practically invariable and can be expressed by the mean value of 0·0000125. The so-called *Reynold's Number* is expressed by the formula $V \times L \times 0.0000125$ (for water), where $V =$ speed of flow in ft/sec, and $L =$ wetted length in ft.

The graph in Fig. 93 is based on Reynold's principle. The figure for kinematic viscosity has been omitted, because it is constant for water. If all factors are known, the surface friction of any yacht at any speed, and even allowing for any degree of roughness, can be calculated with considerable accuracy with the help of this graph. For example:

If we once again take the Dragon, we initially have to calculate the product of length and speed, i.e. waterline length 19·6 ft × sailing speed 6·75 ft/sec (4 knots) = 132. The number 132 is found in the graph on the horizontal scale immediately to the right of 100 (due to the logarithmic scaling of the graph).

The first of the curves, leading obliquely downwards from the top left-hand corner of the graph, applies to laminar flow only, which can occur in a model but not on a life-size hull, except in an almost dead calm. The thick curve is the so-called Schoenherr line, applicable only to ideally smooth surfaces. Above it is the curve

121

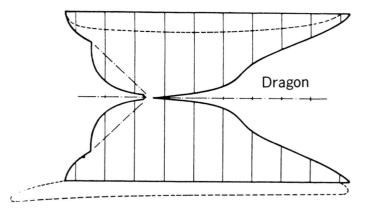

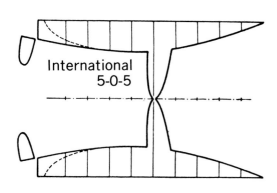

Fig. 94: The wetted surface of a Dragon and an International 5-0-5 determined by half-section girths. The dotted lines in the Dragon apply to the heeled position.

for yachts, but this again applies only to the perfectly smooth bottoms of highly competitive racing yachts. Any yacht less meticulously cared for would approach the curve for merchant vessels.

To get back to our Dragon where $V \times L = 132$, we find that in the graph this corresponds to a specific resistance of 0·0035 (vertical scale) along the curve labelled 'yachts'. Since the total wetted surface of a Dragon is 150 sq ft, the surface friction at a speed of 6·75 ft/sec (4 knots) can be calculated as follows:

Surface friction $= 0\cdot0035 \times 6\cdot75^2 \times 150 = 23\cdot9$ lb

The Dragon sailing on an even keel has a form resistance of only 13 lb (6 kg), the additional resistance due to heeling and leeway making a total of 18·2 lb (8·25 kg). This proves that, contrary to popular belief, the surface friction in our example, at the very common speed of 4 knots, is considerably *larger* than form resistance.

The calculated surface friction is, of course, dependent on the exact condition of the yacht's bottom. A highly polished finish, such as can be achieved by using a buffing disc or the careful use of wet and dry sandpaper (not the application of graphite), may produce an improvement of 10 per cent. If the bottom is simply painted in the normal way and neither smoothed nor

Plate 28: Lasers round a mark during a race. The design and class rules aim at a strict one-design. Consequently this cunningly designed single-hander has found great popularity all over the world. Plans are shown in Fig. 156.

Photo: Performance Sailcraft, Banbury

polished, an increase of around 5 per cent over the specific resistance for 'yachts' can be expected. Badly built and maintained hulls with planking seams visible, or even caulking protruding, can reach values as high as those for 'merchant vessels'.

The important thing when it comes to hull finish is the technical smoothness of the surface, not the material used or the type of paint applied. A well-painted bottom is neither better nor worse than a fibreglass or metal bottom. A greased bottom is deciedly unfavourable, because of the inevitable roughness of whatever sort of grease is used. For the same reason the application of graphite, once fashionable, is useless.

Figure 94 shows the wetted surfaces of a Dragon, representing the typical keelboat, and of an International 5-0-5, representing the fast planing dinghy. The wetted surface logically includes both sides of the hull, the centreplate and the rudder. For the Dragon the wetted surface at a moderate angle of heel has been indicated by the dotted lines, and it can be seen how the effective length increases aft.

It is obvious from both plans that only very few of the water particles run along the full waterline length of the hull. In the case of a Dragon with a waterline length of 19·6 ft (6 m) they only cover an average distance of 10 ft (3 m) in the keel region. The centreplate of a 5-0-5 is only 16 in (40 cm) wide. Surface friction should, therefore, not be calculated as a whole but in bands corresponding to the varying effective length of the hull at different points. This would invariably *increase* the specific resistance and hence the total value for surface friction.

The following summary sets out the findings of our investigation into the resistance of a Dragon sailing at a speed of 4 knots with an angle of heel of 15° and making 4° of leeway:

Form resistance, basic	13·00 lb	
Additional 4% for 15° heeling	0·52 lb	
Additional 34% for 4° leeway	4·42 lb	
Total form resistance		17·94 lb
Surface friction, normal	23·90 lb	
Less 10% for highly polished finish		21·50 lb
Total resistance in the water		39·44 lb

Wind Resistance

For centuries rivers and oceans were navigated by sailing vessels without any sailor ever being aware of wind resistance other than empirically. Probably, nobody even gave it a thought. Sailing craft can be navigated over vast expanses of sea without any knowledge of resistance. Aeroplanes, on the other hand, have not been a familiar sight until comparatively recently. The first primitive and short-lived flight of the Wright brothers would not have been possible without a fairly intimate knowledge of aerodynamics.

A sailing yacht gets both its forward thrust and part of its resistance from the wind. Only the sailing yacht finds itself in the unique situation, i.e. dead before the wind, when the entire wind resistance is converted into forward thrust. In this case, and in this case only, there is no wind resistance, because everything on the boat – hull, superstructure, mast, boom, rigging and even the crew in the cockpit – contribute towards forward thrust. When the apparent wind is on the beam, that part of it which strikes the sails produces excellent thrust, whereas that part which strikes the rest of the boat produces heeling and leeway, but no resistance.

It can be said with fair accuracy that during two-thirds of the time sailed, the angle of incidence of the wind is forward of the beam and only during one-third of the time is it more than 90° off the bow. It is only in this latter case that the wind produces no resistance to forward motion.

All dynamic forces produced by currents of wind or water can be calculated with a universal formula based on the modern development of Newton's theory:

$$P = C \times \frac{\rho}{2} \times V^2 \times S$$

where C is the coefficient of the force in question, ρ the density of the air (0·0024), V the velocity in ft/sec, and S the surface projected to the wind. One need only know the coefficient C to be able to calculate any force, e.g. resistance, lift, forward thrust or side force, at any wind speed on any surface.

It is also possible to calculate these forces for bodies submerged in any liquid by substituting the density of the particular liquid for that of air.

The coefficient of air resistance for any normal body of non-aerodynamic shape is $C_a = 1·2$ in most cases. In special cases this can rise to 1·3, for a hemisphere open on the windward side even to 1·42. An open hemisphere like this is used, for example, in driving

124

wind indicators, and its shape is also used in the modern parachute spinnaker. For aerodynamically shaped bodies, on the other hand, the coefficient can assume a very low value, because their form resistance is practically non-existent. Only the friction produced by the airflow remains as resistance.

If 1·2 is assumed as the normal coefficient for most bodies such as masts, buildings and also sails angled at 90° to the wind, 1 sq ft of surface creates the following resistance in a breeze of 8 ft/sec (4·75 knots):

$$P = 1·2 \times 0·0012 \times 64 \times 1 = 0·092 \text{ lb/sq ft}$$

At ten times the wind speed, i.e. in a strong gale of 47 knots = 80 ft/sec, the same surface of 1 sq ft produces a resistance of:

$$P = 1·2 \times 0·0012 \times 6400 \times 1 = 9·2 \text{ lb/sq ft}$$

Ten times the wind speed thus produces one hundred times the force, true to Newton's law that flow forces vary proportionally as the *square of the speed*.

The coefficients for some common shapes of bodies are given in Fig. 95. The first is the cylinder with a coefficient of 1·2. Many parts of a yacht's rigging are of cylindrical shape: mast, boom, stays, shrouds, halliards, sheets and spinnaker boom. Strictly speaking, the coefficient would not always be exactly 1·2, but for our purposes it is good enough. Flat plates differ a little from this value, the coefficient being 1·15 for a square plate and 1·16 for a disc. A sphere has the low value of 0·5. A hemisphere open on the windward side has the highest coefficient of 1·42.

So far, the air resistance of the body of a sailing boat can only be estimated, since no conclusive results of any test series have yet been published. Figure 96 compares the body of a boat with an estimated sectional coefficient of 0·7 with an aerodynamically shaped body of equal length and section area and with a known coefficient of 0·05. This is *less than one-tenth* the coefficient for a normal sailing hull. In motorboat racing this fact is frequently put to use when superstructures are given aerodynamic shapes. Nothing has become known about the application of the principle to the boat as a whole, but the rounded corners of modern cabin mouldings reflect an effort which may at least pay off in a small way.

A sailing vessel never moves right into the eye of the wind except when under power. Hence, under sail, the

Mast, surface offered to the wind	9·7 sq ft
Boom, projected surface	1·0 sq ft
Shrouds, stays, cross-trees, jumpers	2·8 sq ft
Sheets, halliards, blocks, bottle screws, etc.	2·5 sq ft
Total surface of all cylinders	16 sq ft

Total wind resistance of rigging: $1·2 \times 0·0012 \times 24^2 \times 16 = 13·2$ lb

wind strikes the boat at an angle, and the resistance is reduced proportional to the cosine of the angle.

The hull of a Dragon might offer an area of 22 sq ft to the wind. If it sails with a true wind of 17 ft/sec and an apparent wind of 24 ft/sec, we can calculate the wind resistance of the hull as follows:

$$W = 0·7 \times 0·0012 \times 24^2 \times 22 = 10·6 \text{ lb}$$

Mast and rigging consist of a great number of cylinders, for which a coefficient of 1·2 can be assumed. The calculation above shows that the resistance of the rigging is greater in this case than the resistance of the hull.

Hull and rigging together give the total resistance of $10·6 + 13·2 = 23·8$ lb. This figure is not final, however, because the incidence of the wind is not exactly from ahead but makes an angle of say 27° to the heading. The corresponding cosine value is 0·89, and the corrected total wind resistance is $0·89 \times 23·8 = 21·2$ lb.

It is obvious that *wind resistance is of very real importance.* Like surface friction on the underwater body, it is often underestimated by skippers. Paradoxically, in the case of the Dragon which we examined, both are greater than the form resistance, which is the subject of such intensive study, as can be seen from the summary below:

Form resistance including heeling and leeway	17·94 lb
Surface friction on highly polished bottom	21·5 lb
Wind resistance on hull and rigging	21·2 lb
Total resistance to windward	60·64 lb

Wind resistance in the present example accounts for a little more than one-third of the total resistance. If a member of the crew sat out to windward and exposed to the wind an additional area of 3 sq ft, the additional wind resistance, calculated with a coefficient of $C_a = 1·2$, would be 2·5 lb. The helmsman must judge whether the gain in stability compensates for the added wind resistance.

Wind resistance diminishes as the yacht sails freer.

When the wind is at right angles to the heading, the cosine value drops to zero, i.e. there is no wind resistance. The wind then produces only heeling and leeway. As the wind moves further aft, it produces a progressively increasing thrust, which is again a function of the cosine of the angle of incidence, except that this angle is now measured from the stern. If the wind strikes the boat at an angle of 45° from aft, i.e. a quartering wind, the cosine is 0·707, but now 0·707 of the wind force acting

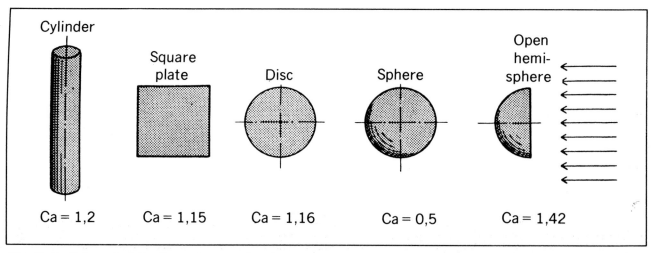

Fig. 95: Coefficients of wind resistance for a number of common shapes. The cylindrical shape appears in the masts and the staying of sailing boats. The highest resistance is caused by the open hemisphere, a shape which we find in the modern spinnaker.

on the hull and rigging are converted into forward thrust. Dead before the wind, the angle of incidence is zero and the cosine value 1·0, which means that the entire wind force on hull and rigging is converted into forward thrust.

This course is thus favoured by three factors: no wind resistance, no heeling, no leeway. Unfortunately, however, the speed of the boat itself becomes an adverse influence, because it reduces the apparent wind speed. The faster a boat sails, the more it takes the wind out of its own sails.

Anyone with a knowledge of wind resistance can also calculate the minimum output required of an auxiliary engine to enable it to drive a yacht against a strong wind. Furthermore, wind resistance is one factor which determines the holding power required of an anchor or mooring ground tackle, another being resistance due to current, which can also be calculated.

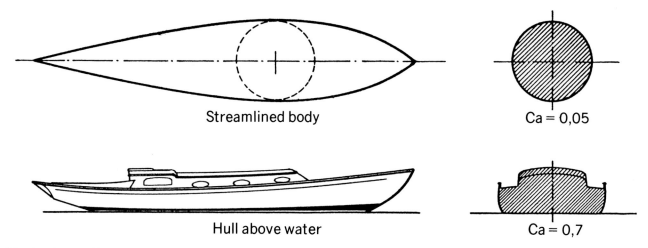

Fig. 96: A streamlined body of equal length and mid-section area as the hull illustrated is aerodynamically much more favourable. It assumes a coefficient of wind resistance of only 0·05. The coefficient for the hull is 0·7, which means that it produces 14 times the wind resistance.

Plate 29: The trapeze is an aid to stability. The body of the crew is completely outside the hull and acts as a large righting moment. Peter Scott was the first man to use the trapeze in 1938. It is being used here on a Jeton. This dinghy is built in GRP by Klepper and is 16 ft 3 in long with a beam of 6 ft.   Photo: Klepper-Werke

Wind Balance

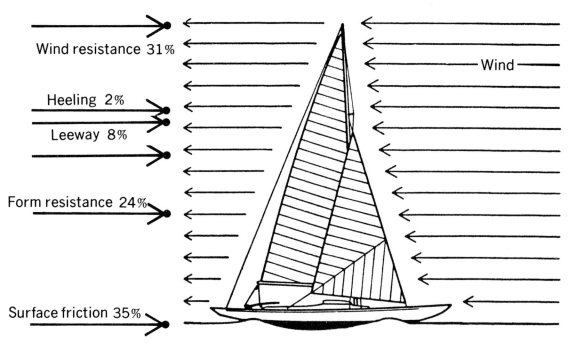

Fig. 97: The wind forces acting on the sails are used by the boat to overcome five kinds of resistance: surface friction, form resistance, leeway, heeling and wind resistance. Their respective magnitudes are indicated by the spaces between the arrows, the figures being valid for a Dragon on the wind in a moderate wind.

Any machine can be analysed to establish its efficiency. A steam engine converts a small part of the energy contained in the fuel it burns into the power, the rest is lost up the chimney. A diesel engine is much more efficient. Similarly, the efficiency of a car, a locomotive, a ship or an aeroplane can be determined by drawing up a *caloric balance*. It is tempting to analyse a sailing yacht in this way, i.e. by drawing up a *wind balance*. Since the wind costs nothing, the working out of a wind balance can have no commercial purpose. Nevertheless, every sailor ought to know what happens to the energy contained in the wind, what part of it is converted into useful thrust and how much of it is lost. We will investigate this for two points of sailing, illustrated in Figs. 97 and 98: close-hauled and before the wind.

Figure 97 illustrates a yacht sailing close-hauled, with the wind direction indicated by thin arrows from right to left. The thick arrows in the opposite direction indicate the various forces of resistance which act against the wind force. The distance between the

arrows shows the magnitude of each particular type of resistance.

The total resistance can be divided into the three familiar categories. In our example the wind resistance accounts for 31 per cent, the surface friction for 35 per cent; the remaining 34 per cent, made up of form resistance, heeling and leeway, goes under the heading of dynamic resistance. If one considers that the side force of the wind is, on average, three times as great as the forward thrust, one can only marvel at the low percentages for heeling and leeway.

The wind resistance could be substantially reduced, if sails could be set without the help of supporting rigging. Sails as such produce no resistance, only forward thrust and side force. The side force, however, is converted into resistance by the hull. In other words, the entire wind resistance of 31 per cent is caused solely by mast, rigging and hull, but not by the sails.

As is to be expected, the picture is a different one if the same yacht is examined running before the wind.

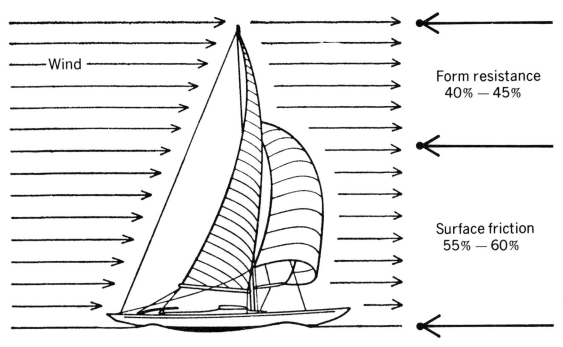

Wind

Form resistance
40% — 45%

Surface friction
55% — 60%

Fig. 98: If the same Dragon is sailing before the wind and symmetry of wind pressure can be accomplished by setting the spinnaker, only two kinds of resistance remain: form resistance and surface friction. The wind itself causes no resistance on this point of sailing.

The example assumes that a spinnaker is set in such a way as to compensate completely for the one-sided pull of the mainsail, in which case no leeway occurs. In Fig. 98 only two forms of resistance remain: form resistance and surface friction. All the parts of hull and rigging, which would otherwise cause resistance, now contribute to forward thrust, so that there is no wind resistance. The remaining resistance is made up as follows: 55 to 60 per cent of the wind force is used to overcome surface friction on the underwater part of the hull, 40 to 45 per cent is absorbed by form resistance through wave-making and turbulence.

If, of course, the spinnaker were not set when sailing before the wind, the thrust would not be along the boat's axis, and the boat would have a tendency to go off course, which in turn is counteracted by rudder pressure. In this case leeway would once again occur and with it induced drag.

Resistance on all Points of Sailing

In this chapter we shall investigate the complete pattern of resistance for all speeds attainable and on all points of sailing. This is a somewhat daring undertaking, but we can draw on adequate research for usable data.

Figure 99 illustrates, for a Dragon, the pattern of all categories of resistance over the full range of speeds attainable. The wedge-shaped, shaded zone at the bottom of the graph represents the surface friction, expressed in lb along the vertical scale. The thick curve to the left of surface friction indicates form resistance, which also represents the total resistance when sailing before the wind without heeling and leeway. At increased speeds the form resistance of the Dragon, which is a non-planing keelboat, rises so steeply that all the curves above it are affected. At increased speeds the sum of surface friction and form resistance together rises enormously, as can be seen by these figures:

Dragon sailing before the wind

Speed	3	4	5	6	7 knots
Resistance ...	13	31	64	134	440 lb

This steep increase in resistance must be considered natural and inherent in the very shape of a keelboat, and cannot be attributed to a fault in hull design. In a hull capable of planing this sharp increase would not occur, but its performance at normal speeds would, by comparison, be inferior.

Three more curves are shown in the diagram, which refer to the Dragon sailing on the wind, and they represent leeway, heeling and wind resistance. The uppermost curve thus delimits the total resistance of a Dragon sailing close-hauled. Since it is not possible close-hauled to get a thrust of more than 220 lb, the steep continuance of the group of curves beyond the edge of the graph need not be considered.

The diagram for a planing dinghy, Fig. 100, shows a completely different pattern. The Flying Dutchman in the example has been investigated up to the very high speed/length ratio of $R = 5$, which a Dragon could never reach.

Once a dinghy has reached planing speed, the increase in form resistance is negligible. Surface friction,

Plate 30: The Soling, an international three-man keelboat, is sailed widely throughout the world since it offers outstanding sport and is comparatively cheap to buy and maintain. Here we see the spinnaker set on a reach, while the jib is in too tight and is acting partly as a brake. Photo: Diane Beeston

on the other hand, is greatly increased and, in fact, accounts for the greatest part of the total resistance over the whole range of speeds. In the graph, starting from the bottom, we find recorded surface friction, form resistance, induced drag through leeway, heeling (very small here) and finally wind resistance.

The same diagram allows an interesting observation

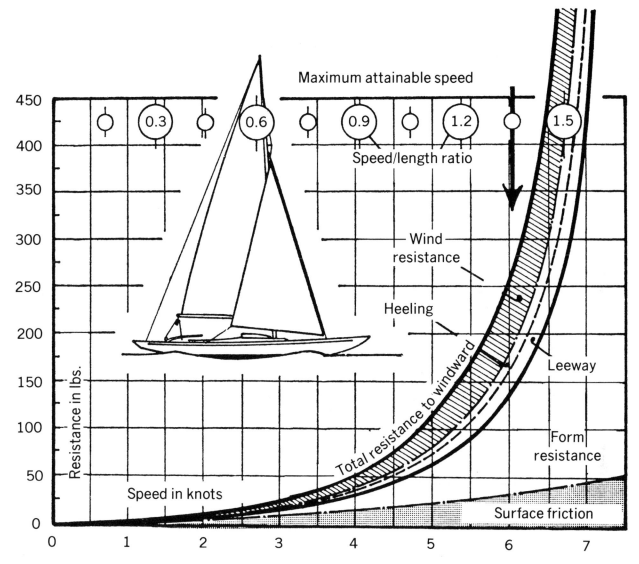

Fig. 99: This graph summarizes all types of resistance at all attainable speeds, once again for a Dragon. It can be seen that surface friction at high speeds does not increase as steeply as form resistance, which imposes its character on the curves above it. The sum of surface friction and form resistance is the total resistance before the wind, while the uppermost curve indicates the total resistance on the wind.

to be made, which is in full agreement with the behaviour of such types of boat in practice. There is always a transitional stage between *normal sailing* and *planing*, which occurs at the approximate speed/length ratio of 1·5 = 6 knots. At about 5 knots the boat seems to fight against mounting the wave and 'taking off'. This strange behaviour is caused by the stern wave, which is still clinging to the boat, unwilling to detach itself, until the increased thrust forces it to. At about 6 knots we can clearly see the hump in the curve of 'total resistance', which indicates the sudden increase

in resistance. One would, of course, have to be very observant to notice this actual moment in practice. Keelboats, i.e. displacement hulls, under sail can never reach this hump of maximum relative resistance, since the stern wave, in a true keelboat, cannot detach itself. In a planing hull, once this critical stage is overcome, the *specific* form resistance decreases again. That the actual increase in resistance is still considerable can be seen from the graph and from the figures in the following table:

131

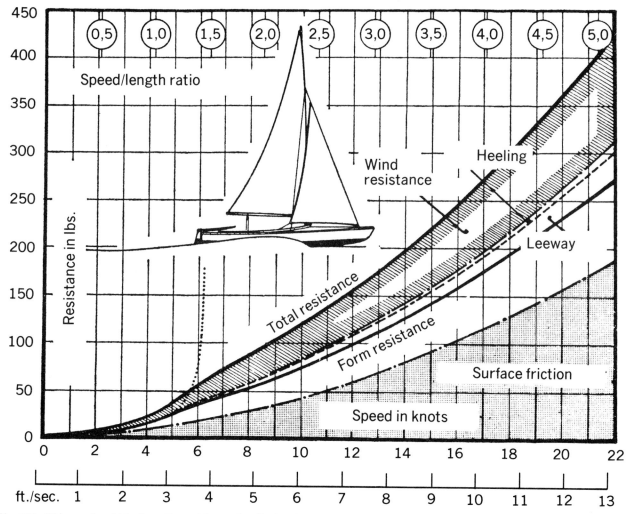

Fig. 100: This graph, which shows the resistance of a dinghy, in this case a Flying Dutchman, is extended into fast planing speeds. Friction accounts for the greater part of resistance at all speeds. Form resistance is much reduced at planing speeds.

Speed	4	7	10	13	16	19	22 knots
Total resistance	26	70	120	174	246	330	426 lb
Total resistance minus wind resistance	18	49	82	125	178	240	317 lb

For a specific reason the total resistance has been indicated minus wind resistance. These figures are valid for high planing speeds which can only be reached with the wind aft of the beam, in which case there is no wind resistance.

The last graph, Fig. 101, illustrates the difference

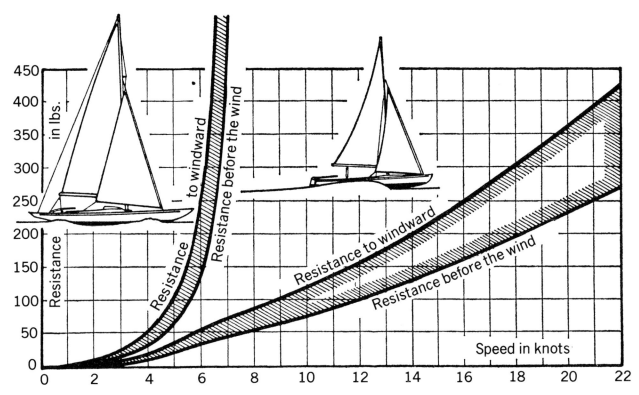

Fig. 101: Graph of total resistances for both keelboat and planing dinghy, based on the two preceding graphs. The Dragon can never be as fast as the planing dinghy because of its enormous increase in resistance at speeds beyond 6 knots. In the planing dinghy the increase in resistance is slight even at high speeds.

between the displacement hull and the planing dinghy. Since the two have different waterline lengths, the comparison has to be based on true rather than relative speeds. It can be seen that the Dragon, due to enormously increasing resistance, is held back before it even reaches 6 knots. The planing dinghy, too, notices the 'hump' at around 6 knots, but once it is over it it reaches very high speeds without more than a normal increase in resistance.

On the basis of what has been said one must not come to the erroneous conclusion that displacement boats are 'bad' and planing dinghies are 'good'. A planing dinghy has to be of extremely light construction, it has no comforts and it is capsizable. It only reaches really high speeds in a strong wind, on the right course and with the help of an athletic crew.

Speeds on Ocean Voyages

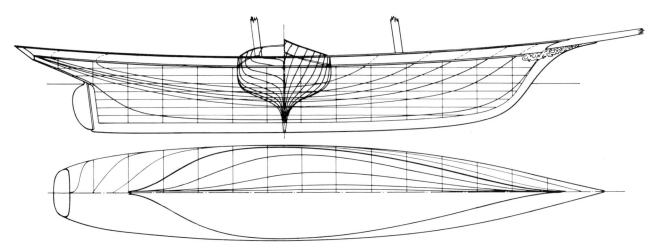

Fig. 102: Lines and sections of ENCHANTRESS, a large sailing yacht with a clipper bow designed by Robert Fisch, USA, in 1870. Note the long, straight keel and the absence of exterior ballast, as was usual with yachts of that time. The very fine water-lines forward must have made her very fast in a seaway.

Everything which has so far been said about resistance in sailing yachts refers to sailing in calm waters, i.e. without the detrimental effect of wave motion. Wave motion, as is well known, results in a considerable increase in resistance on most courses and hence a decrease in speed.

A cruising boat at sea, sailing with a following wind, will from time to time receive a powerful push forwards which is not imparted by the wind. This happens every time that a wave, which normally travels faster than a boat, comes up from astern. The yacht is then temporarily on an inclined plane, pointing downwards in the direction of its motion. Furthermore, the water particles, at this point in their orbital movement, travel in the same direction as the yacht, contributing to the spectacular acceleration. This only lasts a few seconds, though, until the wave crest has overtaken the yacht, which now finds itself inclined backwards and further slowed down by the water particles, which, at this point in their orbit, travel backwards. In this way any previous gain in speed is usually cancelled out.

On all other courses, wave motion causes an important increase in resistance, which rises as the wave motion increases. It is impossible to produce figures on the influence of wave motion, and research is made difficult by the fact that course, magnitude of waves and size of vessel vary infinitely. It can merely be said with certainty that the braking effect of a rough sea can be such that it stops a small boat from making any headway whatsoever.

For several reasons a boat suffers the maximum hindrance to forward motion when sailing close-hauled, not only because the braking effect of the waves is greatest then but also because the thrust imparted by the wind is least on this point of sailing due to the narrow angle of incidence.

With the wind and sea on the beam the boat is slowed down less, and possibly not at all with a following wind. The modern type of ocean racer with its extremely fine lines forward can negotiate heavy seas much more easily than the traditional, full-bowed cruiser. The latter will be drier and suffer less from pitching, but she will frequently be stopped dead by a heavy sea. The modern type of ocean racer is far superior in a seaway to any other type of ocean-going yacht. Even when close-hauled in heavy seas it will still make satisfactory headway, though the crew, of course, will be continually drenched in spray.

The speeds made good on long sea voyages depend not only on the state of the sea but also on strength and direction of the wind. The following table has been compiled on the basis of speeds actually experienced by boats of different sizes. It can be seen that speed/length ratios are higher for smaller vessels, but that larger craft achieve higher *actual* speeds (though not exactly proportionally to the square root of their LWL).

SPEED/LENGTH RATIOS AND ACTUAL SPEEDS
ON OCEAN VOYAGES

	Small	Medium	Large
LWL	20 ft	33 ft	52 ft
Maximum speed maintainable	1·25	1·2	1·1
Cruising speed under favourable conditions	0·96	0·93	0·89
Average cruising speed at sea	0·6	0·57	0·53
Normal 24-hour run	62 miles	78 miles	94 miles
Good 24-hour run	80 miles	100 miles	120 miles
Exceptional 24-hour run	120 miles	150 miles	180 miles

Any owner can calculate the attainable speeds of his particular boat by multiplying the speed/length ratio, as taken from the table above, by the square root of his waterline length. If we take a boat with a LWL of 25 ft, the square root would be 5. Her cruising speed might give a speed/length ratio of 0·95, which would mean an actual cruising speed of $5 \times 0·95 = 4·75$ knots.

The distances that can be covered in 24 hours, of course, are not absolute. Competing in an ocean race with an experienced, tough crew one might occasionally expect to exceed the figures for 'maximum speed maintainable' and cover a record distance. If we take, on the other hand, a boat on a holiday cruise with a small crew who want to take it fairly easy, who want to get their regular sleep to be fit for emergencies and who would normally sail under reduced canvas at night, we can expect, on average, to cover a 'normal' distance in 24 hours.

Changing conditions over different sea areas at different times of the year have an important influence on the average speed, of course. There is a world of difference between the stormy North Atlantic and the Doldrums. Anyone planning a long ocean passage would, therefore, study a Pilot Chart and be prepared for different wind strengths and directions in different parts before coming to any conclusions on average speeds to be expected. Those navigators in particular, who are planning a long ocean crossing for the first time, should give this point their careful attention in order to avoid optimistic estimates and possibly finishing up short of food and water.

The 1972 Single-handed Transatlantic Race from Plymouth England, to Newport USA illustrated particularly clearly how distance covered is dramatically affected by wind strength, sea, type of boat and, above all, personal effort. The winning yacht, MANUREVA, a long trimaran of light-weight construction, took 20 days and $13\frac{1}{4}$ hours. The majority of conventional craft took between 30 and 40 days to finish, whereas the slowest of them, the old lady GOLDEN VANITY, took all of 88 days. She was by no means particularly small, with a LOA of 38 ft (11·6 m) and a LWL of almost 36 ft (10·95 m). One of the smaller competitors, BINKIE, with a waterline length of only 25 ft 6 in (7·8 m), finished the race in only 31 days and 18 hours and proved that size is not everything in a single-handed race.

Following the race, the British Amateur Yacht Research Society published an analysis of the results. The following are some of their findings, and in evaluating them one must always remember that they refer to yachts with only a one-man crew:

(1) Catamarans and trimarans are no faster, length for length, than conventional yachts.
(2) The largest of all competing yachts, VENDREDI TREIZE, with a LWL of no less than 116 ft 6 in (35·5 m), was second to finish but, in relation to her waterline, was extraordinarily slow.
(3) All small, one-masted boats proved relatively fast. Similarly, sloop rigs were superior to two-masted rigs, at least among the small competitors.
(4) Among the larger craft the ketch rig justified itself.

Prior to the race, VENDREDI TREIZE had been hailed as a wonder boat, but it was generally feared that she

Vendredi Treize

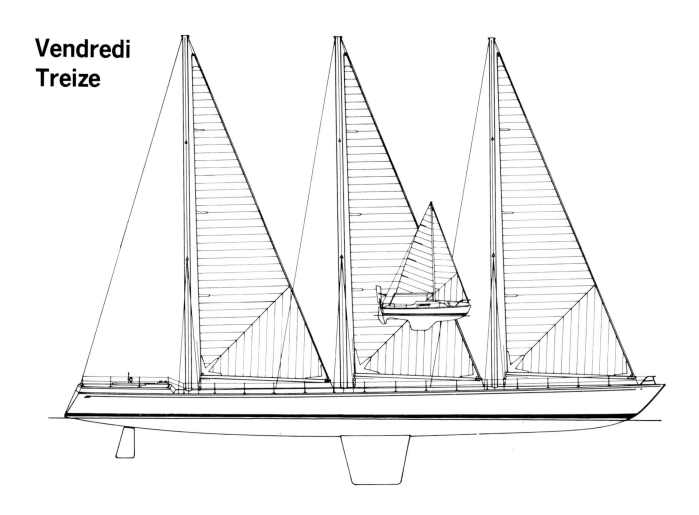

Fig. 103: The largest and the smallest competitor in the 1972 Single-Handed Transatlantic Race. VENDREDI TREIZE *proved that boats of such enormous dimensions can indeed be successfully sailed and handled by one man. She was designed by Dick Carter and sailed by Jean-Yves Terlain and came second in this race. Not so long ago it was thought that 40 to 50 ft was about the maximum which anyone could cope with single-handed.*

LOA	128 ft 4 in	Ballast	14 ton
LWL	116 ft 6 in	3 equal masts each 82 ft high	
Beam	19 ft 4 in	3 boomed staysails with a sail	
Draft	11 ft 6 in	area of 958 sq ft each	
Displacement . . .	35 ton	Total sail area . . .	2874 sq ft

Superimposed to scale on VENDREDI TREIZE'S *sail plan is the smallest of the entries,* WILLING GRIFFIN, *who came 37th.*

LOA	19 ft	Draft	3 ft 3 in
LWL	17 ft 3 in	Displacement . . .	1·5 ton
Beam	6 ft 6 in	Sail area approx. .	172 sq ft

would be too strenuous to handle for a single man. In practice, however, it proved that despite her enormous length and towering masts she was far easier and simpler to handle than many a vessel half her size. Of course, everything in her design had been aimed at ease of handling and minimum physical effort.

She did not set mainsails on her three masts, but boomed staysails reaching to the mastheads. The sail area of each was 958 sq ft (89 m²), which made a total of 2874 sq ft (267 m²). In light winds three big genoas could be set. The normal sail area could be carried until about Force 7 without reefing. If the wind increased to gale force the sail in the middle was taken down. To shorten sail even further, the two sails fore and aft were handed and only the middle one left up.

This enormous vessel, sailed by a single man, reached the finish 16 hours after the winning trimaran, much to the surprise of the experts, who had considered VENDREDI TREIZE the fastest of all competitors. The difference was much too great to be attributable to a small, built-in 'brake'. The yacht was equipped with electro-automatic steering, which constituted a fairly heavy drain on the batteries. Provision for battery charging had therefore been made by coupling the freely rotating propeller to a dynamo. This would increase the resistance caused by the prop in the water.

Before any more is said about this particular race in a later chapter it should, perhaps, be kept in mind that success in such events depends rather more on the effort of the crew than on the size of boat.

Chance 37

Plan I

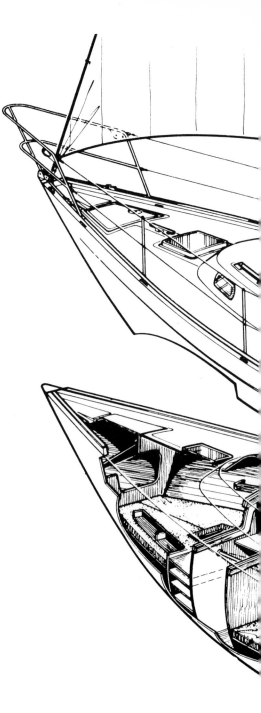

Plan I: One tonner 'Chance 37' illustrates all the features of the modern ocean-racer. Designed by the young American designer Britton Chance, she is series-built at the yard of Henri Wauquiez at Mouvaux in France. Both deck layout and accommodation are clearly presented in this perspective drawing.

Just forward of the companionway we can see the instrument panel with five dials. Both the backstay and babystay tension can be adjusted by wheel-operated turnbuckles and the mast bend thus controlled within certain limits. The actual navigation instruments are installed above the chart-table to port. The spacious galley faces the navigator's corner to starboard. The rudder is deep and narrow and hung on a skeg.

Hull		Sail plan	
LOA	37 ft	Mainsail	243 sq ft
LWL	30 ft	No. 1 genoa	550 sq ft
Beam	10 ft 6 in	No. 2 genoa	457 sq ft
Draft	5 ft 10 in	Working jib	285 sq ft
Displacement	14,500 lb	Storm jib	78 sq ft
Ballast	7700 lb	Spinnaker	1175 sq ft
Ballast ratio	53%		Drawing: L Mathieu

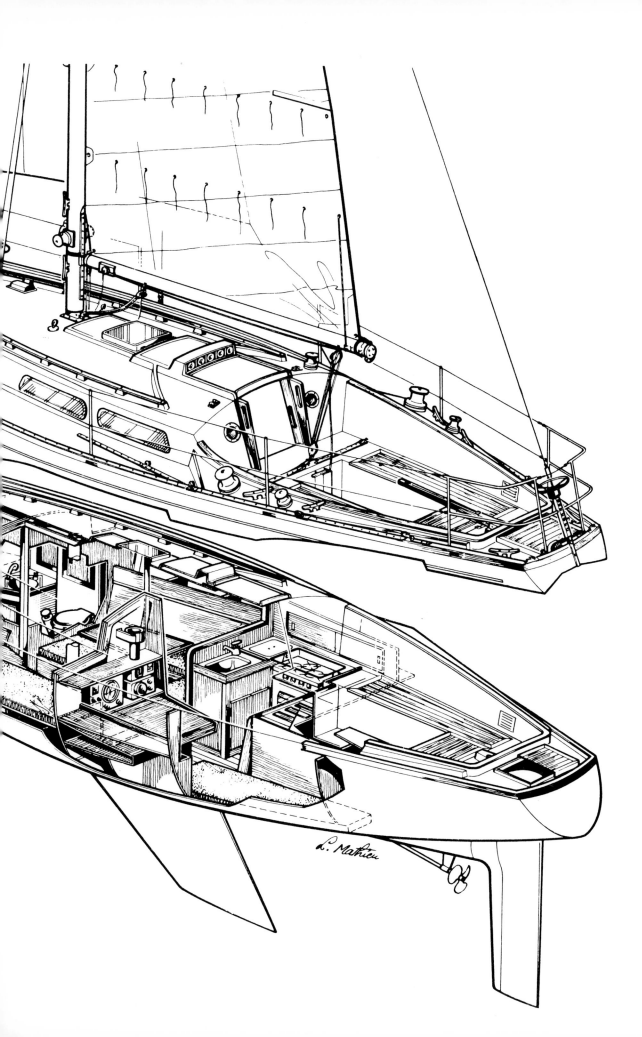

The Shape of Modern Yachts

The great majority of sailing yachts, whether of displacement or planing type, are characterized by curved shapes which do not conform to geometrical figures such as circles, ellipses or parabolas. To make the practical construction and calculation of such indefinable shapes possible, a yacht's lines are drawn up in sections, waterlines, bow-and-buttock lines and sometimes heeled waterlines. In their entirety these lines provide the basis for construction and calculation as well as the prediction of the yacht's characteristics.

The drawing up of a boat's lines is, undoubtedly, one of the most subtle jobs of a naval architect. It has to be based on meticulous calculation to ensure that, for example, weight and displacement agree and that centre of gravity and centre of buoyancy are in the right places. Very often rating rules have to be taken into consideration, and frequently financial limitations, too. On the other hand, the naval architect aims at speed, good windward characteristics, power to carry sail and good behaviour in a seaway.

It must not be assumed that harmony of lines is necessarily a guarantee for success. It is not apparent from a lines plan whether the hull shape makes for good weight distribution, whether hull and sail plan are well matched and whether other aspects, e.g. the disposition of the ballast, might not result in a disappointing performance in the end.

It quite frequently happens that the lines of a successful vessel are not particularly beautiful. Sound length, beam and weight ratios are as important as the careful design of lines.

It has been demonstrated in previous chapters that the total resistance of a boat is composed of three main elements, i.e. form resistance, surface friction and wind resistance. It was also shown that the three are of similar magnitude. The lines plan, on the other hand, is drawn up mainly with regard to form resistance, and only slowly is it becoming accepted that more consideration should be given at the design stage to both surface friction and induced drag.

Figure 105 shows a perspective lines drawing of a conventionally shaped yacht heeled on the wind. In it various zones have been indicated which determine different aspects of the boat's behaviour, without any zone being solely responsible for any one of the desired overall characteristics, which are stability, speed and seaworthiness.

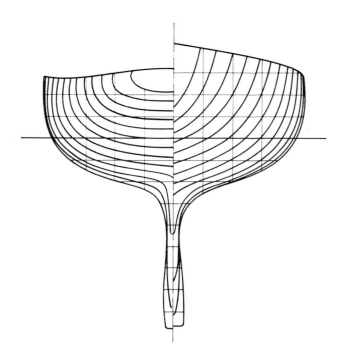

Fig. 104: Sections of a 30-square-metre Skerry Cruiser. These keelboats distinguish themselves by the beauty and perfection of their lines and contributed a great deal to the refinement of modern yacht design.

For example, in the drawing the area of maximum beam has been marked as the key-zone for stability, but it is really a combination of beam, draught, ballast and weight that constitute the criterion of stability. It would be easy enough to give a yacht all the stability in the world by increasing the beam freely, but by doing so one would end up with a considerable increase in resistance and ensuing loss of speed. The loss of speed could be made good by enlarging the sail area, but this, in turn, would have an adverse influence on stability. It takes a good deal of experience on the part of the designer, coupled with painstaking calculations, to arrive at the ideal combination.

Important aspects of a vessel's behaviour are governed by the shape of the bow and the stern. Full bow lines make for plenty of buoyancy forward, which means a dry ship but also a slower one. The lines at the stern determine the *run*, which has a marked effect on attainable speeds at the top end.

The detrimental effects of lateral drift could be reduced by giving the underwater profile a large lateral resistance, but the underwater profile cannot be increased *ad lib*, because this would, in turn, increase the surface friction.

140

The importance of windward efficiency cannot be overstressed. If one of two yachts sails close-hauled with an angle of leeway of 3° and the other with an angle of leeway of 6°, the first has to overcome an increase in resistance of 23 per cent, the latter of as much as 56 per cent. Besides, the second vessel's gain to windward will be less, due to the greater angle of leeway. Thus, leeway affects performance in two ways.

The size and shape of the rudder are not the only factors responsible for good steering qualities. The ideal size of rudder depends not so much on the size of the underwater profile as on the directional balance on the wind. The modern practice of positioning rudders rather further aft has improved steering efficiency.

In summing up it can be said that the lines of a yacht have to satisfy two major aims:

(a) The boat should be able to point exceedingly high and at the same time make very little leeway so as to combine minimum resistance with maximum gain to windward.

(b) She should have a favourable run towards the stern which must not be affected adversely by heeling.

Fig. 105: Perspective drawing of a displacement hull, in which various zones are shaded which are responsible for the primary characteristics of a sailing boat. These are: behaviour in a seaway, windward efficiency, resistance to leeway, stability, run at the stern and steering qualities. The demarcation of each zone is only approximate.

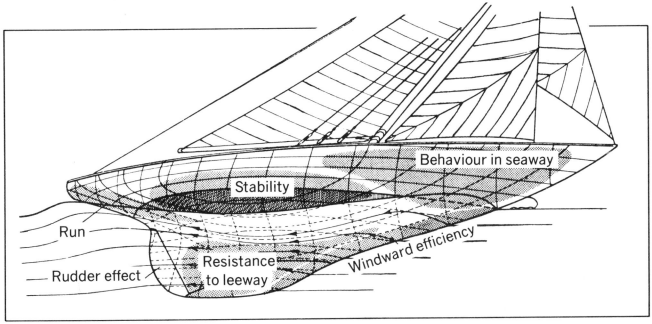

Single-Masted Rigs and their Headsails

The sailing yacht's remarkable 'engine', which is her rig, consists basically of a certain area of sail cloth, which catches the wind and deflects it from its course. The skipper knows, either from observation or by intuition, how to trim the sails in order to achieve the maximum propulsion in the desired direction.

The thrust achieved is in direct ratio to the available sail area and in the square ratio to the wind speed. Twice the sail area means twice the thrust, whereas twice the wind speed means four times the thrust. A normal sailing boat cannot carry any desired sail area, since her *power to carry sail* depends on her stability. A further restriction is imposed by the physical strength of the crew. If there are many hands, even a slightly excessive sail area can still be managed. The single-handed sailor, on the other hand, or a short-handed crew will only set those sails which can be handled safely and without undue exertion. It has been shown in recent years that, with the help of relatively simple mechanical aids, the ambitious single-handed yachtsman can cope with what would normally be considered excessive sail areas.

Aerodynamic tests have shown the advantages of narrow, high-aspect ratio sail plans. An aspect ratio of 5:1, at the critical small angles of incidence, results in much greater thrust than does a low rig with a 1:1 ratio. A high, narrow sail suffers, technically speaking, smaller losses as a result of *less induced drag*, since the vortex trail at the upper edge is narrower. Why, one asks, are so many other rigs used in practice, which ignore this known fact?

In a modern sail training ship like, for example, the GORCH FOCK, the rig is chosen with a view to crew efficiency rather than sail efficiency. The GORCH FOCK has three masts on which she sets a total of 23 normal sails. Full-rigged ships in the past had as many as five masts with the sail area split up into no less than 50 sails, without counting light-weather sails, purely for reasons of ease of handling.

A sub-divided sail area is easier to set and equally easier to reduce by lowering individual sails. The sloop rig is generally considered the most efficient rig, but aerodynamic tests by no means support this belief. They have proved that it is the cat rig which gives maximum efficiency per unit sail area. In practice, however, the sloop rig is superior, if only due to the generally accepted practice of measuring the fore-

142

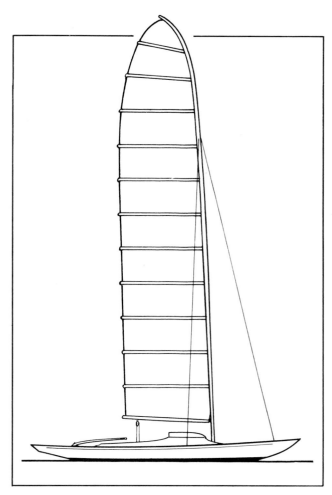

Fig. 106: Experimental cat rig on a Dragon. The size of the sail area corresponds to that of the Dragon's normal sloop rig. The mast pivots; the sail is fully battened.

triangle for rating purposes, which makes it possible to set various foresails of different size and cut to suit changing conditions, without these being rated.

All two-masted rigs result in lower efficiency than one-masted rigs, but they can have other advantages. Above all, the sail areas are smaller and easier to handle. Since the rig is lower, the yacht heels less and has fewer demands made on her stability. In the following pages we shall examine briefly the characteristics of the most widely used rigs.

THE CAT RIG

The mainsail which stands alone produces an unusually high degree of thrust per unit sail area. In addition, it is incomparably simple to handle. A number of racing dinghy classes, including Olympic and junior classes, use this rig. So does the majority of racing catamarans because of the cat-rig's outstanding aerodynamic efficiency on the wind.

Since no foresail is set on a cat-rigged boat, the possibility of improving efficiency by setting different foresails to suit varying conditions does not exist. On courses before the wind the high-aspect ratio offers no advantages, and the asymmetrical setting of the mainsail, which causes increased resistance, cannot be offset by the use of a spinnaker.

THE SLOOP RIG

If we add a foresail to a cat rig, we get the sloop rig, which is by far the most popular of all fore-and-aft rigs (the fore-and-aft rig being designed specifically for sailing on the wind, as opposed to the square rig, which was designed for sailing off the wind). Even the smallest of all international classes, the Cadet, is sloop-rigged, and so were the enormously long J-class yachts which competed for the America's Cup up until 1937. Almost all racing and knockabout dinghies and practically all keelboat classes are sloop-rigged, and so are all the popular one-design classes – except for racing catamarans – such as the 5-0-5, Flying Dutchman, Snipe, Lightning, Star, Soling, Tempest and Dragon.

Many class rules favour the sloop rig in that they do not rate the actual area of the foresails but the so-called *foretriangle*. Within this triangle formed by the forestay, mast and deck, almost any desired sail may be set. Certain restrictions had to be introduced when the overlap of enormous genoas threatened to go beyond reasonable limits. In some cases the clew of the genoa even reached aft of the boom end, as illustrated in Fig. 111.

It has already been explained that the overlapping part of a foresail is less efficient than the sail area lying directly in the path of the wind. But since the overlapping part is not rated, any thrust obtained from it is pure profit. It is, so-to-speak, 'something for nothing'.

A simple but complete sloop rig might comprise the following sails:

Working mainsail, Trysail, Working jib, Storm jib, Genoa, Spinnaker.

With these sails the sloop-rigged cruising yacht can cope in any weather. When it comes to competitive racing, of course, this simple sail wardrobe is hardly

Plate 32: This unusual pram is an American C-Class Scow. It is cat-rigged and instead of a centreplate has twin bilge plates. These boats are very fast because, due to the particular hull shape, the wetted surface can be reduced by heeling the boat to 15° or so.
Photo: Rosenfeld

adequate. Racing yachtsmen invest in a bewildering number of different headsails of different size and curvature, made of different weights of cloth, to be certain of getting the best performance in all winds and on all courses.

Changing foresails during the race is not only permitted but considered sporting. Changing mainsails during a race is not usually permitted. It is, however, common practice to have a number of mainsails of different cut and weight handy before the start of the race and to choose the one most suited to the prevailing conditions at the last minute. A complete wardrobe of sails for top-class racing could be almost unlimited, so restrictions on the number of sails allowed are often

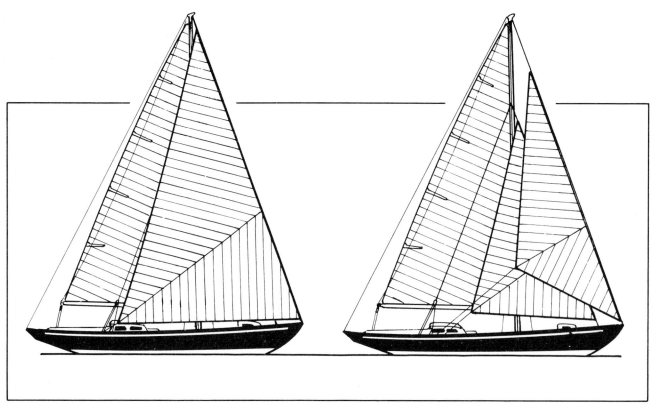

Fig. 107: Different headsails on a sloop-rigged ocean racer. On the left the large genoa used in light winds, on the right two jibs for moderate winds. The latter could be called a cutter rig.

Fig. 108: The same boat with a greatly reduced sail area: reefed on the left, with trysail and storm jib set on the right. In both cases she is balanced.

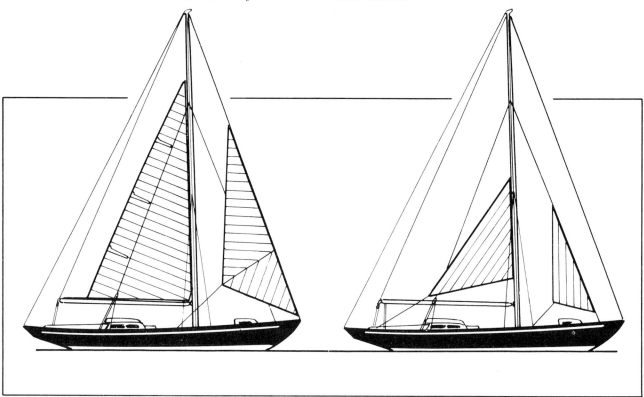

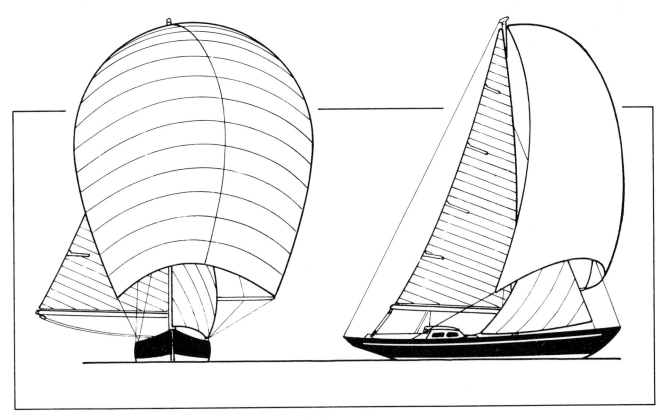

Fig. 109: Modern broad-shouldered spinnaker set before the wind. The space under the spinnaker is filled with a spinnaker staysail, the most up-to-date version of which would be narrower and higher.

included in the rules. The following sails might be considered a minimum for a racing keelboat, but would make a very complete set for a sloop for general purposes:

    Light weather mainsail
    Working mainsail
    Heavy weather mainsail
    Trysail (= storm mainsail)
    Large light-weight genoa
    Large working genoa
    Working jib
    Storm jib
    Especially large spinnaker of super light-weight cloth
    Large, full spinnaker for average winds
    Large, flat-cut spinnaker
    Small spinnaker for strong winds
    One or two spinnaker staysails

Figures 107 to 109 illustrate the surprising number of sail combinations which a sloop – with only one mast – can make use of. It is obvious that the sloop rig provides much greater adaptability to wind strength and course

than the cat rig. The particular sloop shown here can set one or two jibs. In very light winds a large, light-weight genoa is set. If the wind increases this is replaced by two smaller foresails, jib and staysail, whose small overlap causes no problems when going about. If the wind increases further, one or two reefs are taken in the mainsail and the staysail taken down, which balances the boat. Should the wind increase to gale force, the reefed mainsail and jib are replaced by trysail and storm jib. Under reduced sail the yacht still makes adequate progress and remains balanced. She also rolls less than she would under bare poles. Of course, the amount of way the yacht will be able to make will be severely curtailed, since the wind resistance of mast and rigging will be very great in relation to the drastically reduced sail area. Besides, storm sails are inherently less efficient per unit sail area, and then there will be heavy seas to contend with. Instead of a trysail and storm jib a jib of normal proportions but made of very heavy cloth can be set by itself.

In order to achieve a balanced boat under severely reduced canvas the centre of effort of the sails has to be

145

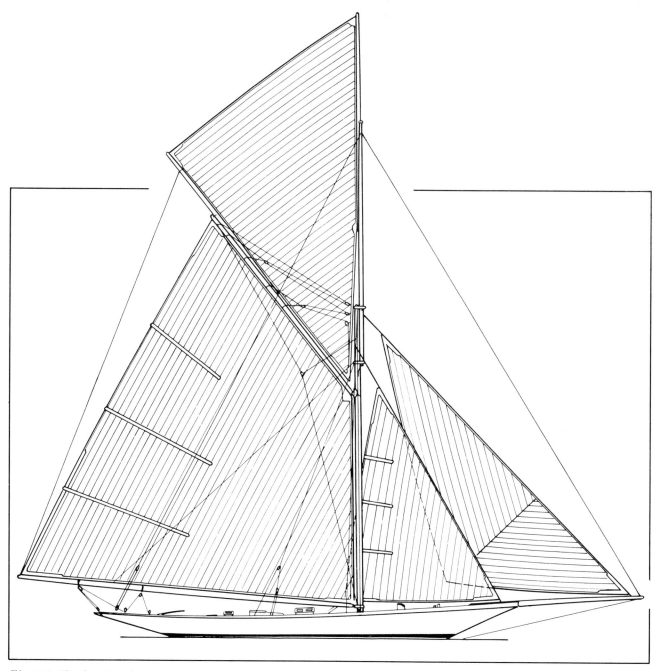

Fig. 110: Classic cutter rig on the famous GLORIANA designed by Herreshoff in 1891. A large professional crew was needed to handle these enormous sail areas. The hull lines are reproduced in Fig. 9.

moved further forward the more the yacht heels over. For this reason the mainsail should always be reefed first before the jib is changed for a smaller one.

At the other end of the scale, a sloop can set much larger sail areas when sailing on a reach. Since the apparent wind is then much reduced, an increase in sail area must result in a considerable increase in forward thrust. A large, symmetrical spinnaker complements the reduced effectiveness of the sail area due to the diminished apparent wind and also offsets the one-sided thrust of the mainsail.

146

THE CUTTER RIG

Anyone wanting to set the greatest possible number of sails on a single mast all at one time would choose the classic cutter rig. In the early days of yachting, before the perfection of laminated masts, many vessels were cutter-rigged to make up for the lack of mast height by numbers of sails. In any case, the advantages of a high-aspect ratio sail were not yet recognized at that time. A classic gaff cutter had a not very steep gaff and a long bowsprit, which favoured the setting of a number of foresails. A complete cutter rig would have comprised

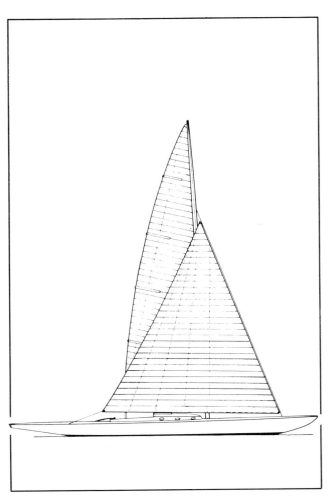

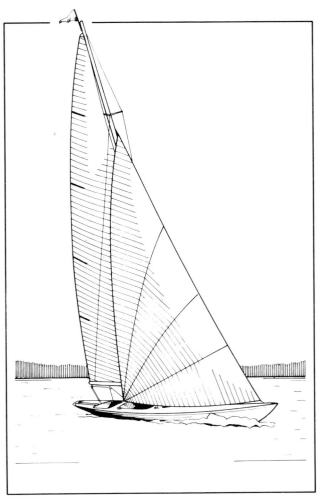

Fig. 111: In the unrestricted 30-square-metre Skerry Cruiser class the overlapping genoas assumed enormous dimensions. Their clews frequently overlapped the end of the boom. Five foresails of different size are indicated in the sail plan.

Fig. 112: The 1958 America's Cup challenger SCEPTRE *was probably the first to use a tri-mitre genoa. This cut aims at distributing the sheet pull evenly over the whole sail area.*

the following sails as a minimum:

Gaff mainsail, Topsail, Staysail, Jib, Flying Jib.

The first sail to be sacrificed to progress was the picturesque topsail, which was by no means easy to set and not very effective, either. As gaffs got steeper, there was no room for a three- or four-cornered topsail, and when the Bermudan rig took over the topsail finally had to go. Since the classic cutter rig was low and wide, it was not particularly efficient, and when it was realized that the same performance could be got from a considerably smaller but taller rig, the fate of

the classic cutter was sealed.

By a kind of tacit agreement all single-masted rigs without a bowsprit are called sloop, even if they have two jibs. There is no unanimity over this description, though. A rig with two foresails which is defined as a cutter in Britain is called a sloop in America. The genuine cutter with three foresails and a topsail is now only found in museums. It is illustrated in Fig. 110, although the flying jib is not set.

SAILS FOR RACING

The racing owner can never have enough sails. Ideally, he would like to have a different weight of cloth and a different cut or curvature for every wind strength and every new course. Frequently the class rules impose restrictions, and finance also enforces moderation. If there are no limitations, though, the sail wardrobe even for a simple sloop can be practically unlimited. The 12-metre yacht COLUMBIA, when defending the America's Cup in 1958, had the following sails on board during the races:

4 mainsails of different curvature and cloth

14 foresails of different size and cut

7 different spinnakers

2 spinnaker staysails

—

27 different sails in all

By today's standards this would not be considered excessive for an important race. Indeed, there might be some additions, like two tall spinnaker staysails (currently known as tallboys) or big boys.

The necessity to stow so many sails in a way that makes them all readily accessible presents a very real problem. It can only be solved with the help of a sail list which contains the precise cut of each sail together with its location on board, the sheets that are to be used with it and the position of sheet leads on deck. The optimum position of sheet leads for each sail is something which has to be experimented with during numerous sail trials. Once established, the positions are marked by numbers along the track.

The use of colours for different items, not only sheets but also sail bags, facilitates immediate location without the need for deciphering labels.

If the number of sails is limited either by class rules or financial considerations, they must be all the more carefully chosen. The working mainsail, which is most frequently used, should only have a moderate curvature. If there is more than one mainsail, the second should be made of light-weight cloth and cut much fuller to make a light-weather sail. A third mainsail should be a heavy-weather sail, made of heavy cloth and cut very flat.

Similar considerations apply to the choice of headsails. A particularly important point is the cut of the large genoa. Since it overlaps a considerable portion of the mainsail, its curvature is critical. The fullness should decrease gradually towards the leech and eventually flatten out completely. A leech which has a tendency to curl inwards or set at an angle to the adjoining sail area will disturb the airflow and act as a brake. It is essential that the airflow off the genoa leech be *parallel* to the mainsail. Under no circumstances must it be directed inwards towards the mainsail.

SAILS FOR CRUISING

There is nothing to prevent the owner of a cruising yacht from carrying as many sails as he likes, as long as he has the necessary stowage space. By contrast with the racing owner he will be primarily concerned with safety and the need not to overtax his crew. We note from the list of sails for the 12-metre yacht that no storm sails are mentioned. In a cruiser planning a prolonged passage these would be indispensable, indeed would be one of the most important safety factors. The following sails should be considered the absolute minimum for a sloop-rigged boat cruising offshore:

Heavy-weight mainsail

Heavy-weight working jib

Medium-weight genoa

Trysail

Storm jib

The size of a storm sail lies between one-third and one-quarter of the area of the corresponding normal sail which it replaces. It is not advisable to continue to carry a heavily reefed normal mainsail in a gale, since it is subjected to stress for which it was not designed and eventually will suffer permanent damage. Even synthetic cloths are not indestructible. One must consider that a reefed mainsail has to suffer not only the whole weight of the boom but also the pull from the sheets, which in heavy winds is very powerful. The least that should be done is to take the weight on the topping lift.

By comparison it is not unusual when blue-water sailing to come across days of light winds or complete calm, when the normal sail area is much too small and all possible headsails are set to get some way on the ship and also to damp down rolling in a swell.

If a cruising boat is under-canvassed in light airs, the owner should give his imagination free reign. He can refer back to the days of the square-riggers and consider the possibility of studding sails and 'Jimmie Greens' — more to keep himself and his crew busy than to add very

148

noticeably to the progress of the yacht. The unusual three- and four-cornered topsails of the Chesapeake log canoe in Fig. 68 are examples of such additional sails. The 200-year-old sloop in Fig. 49 has a studding sail attached to the mainsail, and a further studding sail is indicated for the topsail.

The enormous topsails of the classic cutter-rig really fulfilled the same purpose. The sail plan of GLORIANA in Fig. 110 shows a particularly large, triangular topsail. It may not have been easy to set or stow such a sail, but its effectiveness in light winds justified the trouble. It also contributed in no small measure to the attractive appearance of yachts of that period. A well-setting topsail, usually handled by a professional crew, enhanced the owner's pride.

For long voyages with a following wind, to enable the boat to steer herself quietly and without fuss for days on end, the so-called twin running sails and twin-spinnakers have been developed. More will be said about them in a later chapter.

Plate 33: Here we see the slot effect in action. The wind, passing through the slot between the genoa and the mainsail at an accelerated speed, increases the lift on the leeward side of the mainsail. The picture shows a modern IOR yacht, a Columbia 30, in the Bay of San Francisco.
Photo: Columbia Yachts, Costa Mesa, California

Modern Two-Masted Rigs

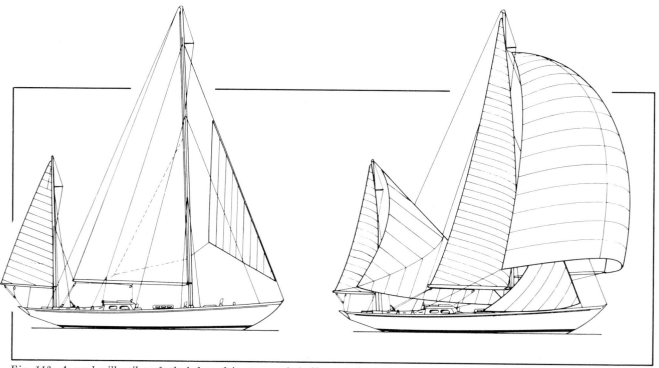

Fig. 113: A yawl will sail perfectly balanced in strong winds if only the mizzen and storm jib are set. In light winds and on a reach the advantages of the two-masted rig become particularly obvious, since a great number of sails can be set very efficiently, see figure on the right. The total sail area on a reach can be more than twice the working sail area.

No two-masted rig possesses the same aerodynamic efficiency as the simple sloop rig. Nevertheless, larger cruising boats are frequently fitted with two masts, because a number of other considerations may make such a rig preferable. One obvious advantage for long passages is the subdivision of the sail area, which makes the individual sails smaller and easier to set, reef and lower. To compensate for the lower efficiency, rating rules make allowances for two-masted rigs, i.e. they are allowed a larger sail area without the increase being rated. We give an example below of the additional sail areas, compared with the Bermudan sloop rig, allowed under the RORC Rule of 1955:

Rig	Additional Sail Area Allowed
Bermudan Yawl	4%
Bermudan Schooner or Gaff Cutter	8·5%
Bermudan Ketch or Gaff Yawl ..	13·5%
Wishbone Ketch or Schooner ...	13·5%
Gaff Schooner	17·5%
Gaff Ketch	23·5%

In a previous chapter these allowances have been explained in detail. Although they no longer apply today they give a useful idea of the aerodynamic efficiency of the different types of two-masted rig.

THE YAWL RIG

The various types of two-masted rig are distinguished by the relative size of the two masts and the two sails set on them. The one with the smallest after mast is the yawl rig. Until a few years ago, when the CCA and RORC Rules gave a 4 per cent allowance to yawls, which just about compensated for the lower efficiency, ocean racers were frequently yawl rigged. The yawl rig offers an attractive possibility, which is denied the sloop, in that a staysail can be set between the masts, which was not rated then, i.e. it was 'free' sail area. In the currently applied IOR formula the staysail is fully measured, but calculated with reference to mizzen sail area and a total sail area correction, so that the advantages or drawbacks of a yawl rig, when sailing under the IOR, are no longer immediately apparent.

In a two-masted rig there are many possibilities of subdividing the sail area to suit the wind or to increase it with additional sails. Figure 113 illustrates the two extremes: on the left an unreefed, drastically reduced heavy-weather rig, on the right the same yacht reaching with all sail crowded on, which means that apart from the mainsail and mizzen she sets a large staysail, a spinnaker and a spinnaker staysail.

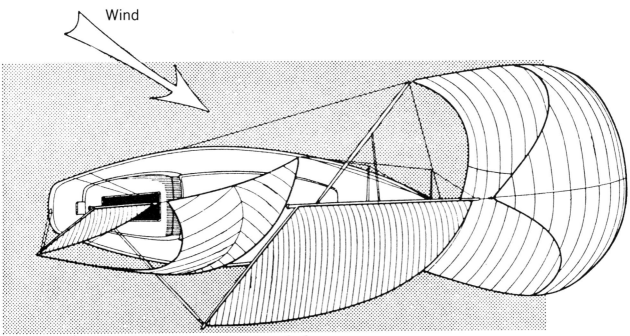

Wind

Fig. 114: Bird's eye view of the yawl in Fig. 113. It shows clearly the large area of the additional sails set on a reach.

It is obvious that on a reach in a stiff breeze the yawl rig offers its most exciting possibilities, since the sail area can be increased to more than twice its rated value. The bird's-eye view in Fig. 114 illustrates this ideal situation. Thanks to the jigger mast the yawl can set a mizzen staysail, which is much larger than the mizzen itself. Its tack is not set up amidships but to windward, because it catches more wind that way. Under the IOR there is now a penalty for this large staysail, though. The spinnaker, too, whose points of attachment depend on the size of the foretriangle, offers the wind a sail area which is *much more than twice* the rated area of the foretriangle.

Sailing close-hauled, the mizzen staysail could be left up, but its effect would be negligible, since the angle of the luff produces upward lift rather than forward thrust. Besides, the mizzen staysail makes tacking impossible, because it is in the way of the main boom. For the same reason an involuntary gybe when reaching must be avoided at all cost, as the risk of a broken boom or mizzen mast is considerable.

The disadvantage of the yawl rig lies mainly in the difficulty of staying the mizzen or jigger mast. The main boom prevents the use of a normal forestay, the mizzen boom the use of a permanent backstay. Thus it is left to running backstays to take the pressure of the mizzen and mizzen staysail on courses off the wind.

THE KETCH RIG

This is distinguished from the yawl rig by a relatively larger mizzen sail. Originally, the position of the jigger mast either before or aft of the rudder shaft was the distinguishing feature. In a ketch the tiller or wheel had to be aft of the mizzen mast; in a yawl it was before the mizzen mast. Another distinguishing feature was the position of the mizzen mast in relation to the after end of the waterline. Since, however, the different hull forms and stern shapes do not always allow a clear definition, it has recently become customary to base rating allowances on the proportions of sail areas. In any case, a true ketch carries a relatively large mizzen sail which, however, is not as large as the mainsail. A yawl, by comparison, sets a considerably smaller mizzen.

Much of what has been said about the yawl also applies to the ketch. The efficiency of a ketch rig is even less than that of a yawl, and accordingly it gets a bigger allowance. Under the now superseded RORC Rule a yawl was given an allowance of 4 per cent, a ketch of 13·5 per cent. The larger the area of the mizzen sail, the lower the aspect ratio of the whole rig and, consequently, the lower its efficiency.

While under the RORC Rule a yawl used to be rated rather favourably, the current rating under the IOR is so sophisticated that allowances for different rigs do no more than reflect its true efficiency.

151

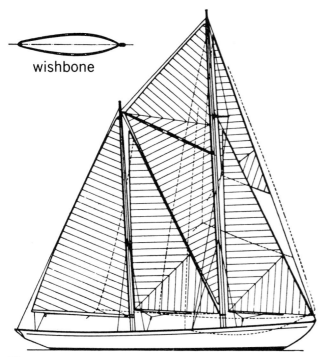

wishbone

Fig. 115: VAMARIE *aroused great interest in 1933, when she was the first to carry a wishbone rig. This rig, which is a variation of the ketch rig, makes use of the empty space between the masts. The section of a wishbone spar is shown top left.*

THE WISHBONE KETCH

The wishbone rig stands out among two-masted sail-plans by its relatively good aerodynamic efficiency. On the other hand, the rather complicated wishbone is a potential danger, and the rig is not very popular. On one occasion, on board a large yacht by the name of WISH-BONE, the wishbone sheet parted in a gale, although the sail itself had already been stowed. The wishbone now began a wild, uncontrollable dance, flung about by the violently rolling vessel. It was impossible to send someone up the mast to reeve a new sheet. After some time the flailing wishbone broke the mizzen mast, and some hours later, the weather not having moderated, the mainmast also went overboard. Thus, for the lack of a sheet, both masts were lost.

The wishbone obviously takes its name from the breastbone of a bird, whose shape it resembles. It not only allows the sail to be angled accurately to the wind, but also allows for the curvature of the sail to be altered at will by means of an outhaul. Since there is no main boom, the mizzen or jigger mast can be positioned further forward and adequately stayed. A wishbone

152

ketch with its sails completely filling the whole area from stem head across both mastheads down to the stern undoubtedly makes an impressive sight.

THE SCHOONER RIG

As the development of the modern, efficient windward rig progressed, so the lack of efficiency of the schooner rig became more and more apparent. In the same way that the newly emerged findings of aerodynamic research showed up the advantages of the wishbone rig, so they showed up the drawbacks of the schooner rig. On the wind it was undoubtedly inferior to higher aspect ratio rigs.

Figure 116 shows one of the most handsome classic schooners, MALABAR X, whose owner and designer was the well-known naval architect John G Alden. She illustrates the gaff schooner in its most perfect form. On the wind up to seven sails could be set, but their efficiency came nowhere near that of modern sails. The main mast was stepped at roughly the point of maximum beam, so that it could be stayed effectively athwartships. The lack of a permanent backstay should not be held against this rig, since it can never be used with a gaff rig anyway. The rather awkwardly sheeted staysail high up between the mastheads was called a 'fisherman', which reflects its origin on the Grand Banks fishing schooners.

THE STAYSAIL SCHOONER

In the search for an improved schooner rig an interesting solution was found at that time, namely the so-called staysail schooner. The most famous, possibly even the first representative was NIÑA, which won the Transatlantic Race as well as the Fastnet in 1928. Her design was the result of the combined efforts of W Starling Burgess and Henry Gruber. She introduced a new rig of improved efficiency, which was at the same time easy to handle.

As can be seen in Fig. 117 the mainsail provides the greater part of the thrust. The foremast does not carry its own mainsail but a whole range of staysails, including a fisherman between the mastheads. This sail uses an otherwise empty area between the mastheads, yet it cannot be made to set efficiently, since the sheet-leads have to be on the centreline.

Sailing has become increasingly popular in the course of the last few decades. Really large yachts are

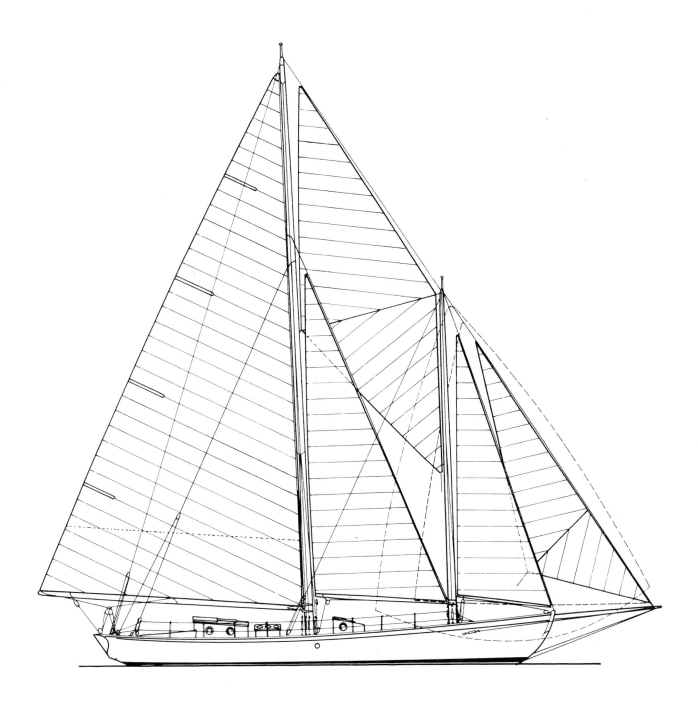

Fig. 116: Sail plan of the schooner MALABAR X *designed and owned by John Alden. It is the most perfect example of a typical schooner rig, which was popular on large yachts until around 1930.*

153

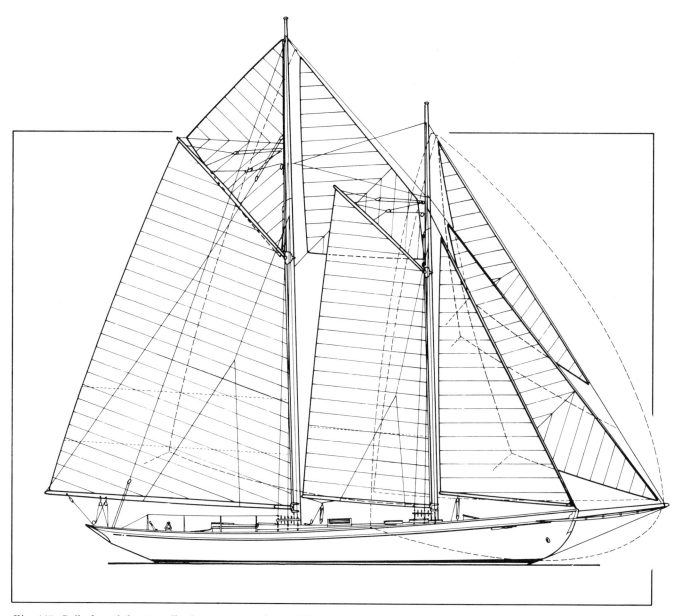

Fig. 117: Sail plan of the staysail schooner NINA, *winner of the 1928 Transatlantic Race. The perfectly balanced rig contributed in no small measure to this victory.*

built much less frequently now which is, no doubt, one of the reasons why the schooner is hardly ever used these days.

The largest yacht built since the war, CARITA, is shown in Fig. 186; she is 171 ft (52 m) overall. With such unusually large dimensions aerodynamic efficiency takes second place, since even with a relatively small, aerodynamically inefficient sail area a yacht of this size would reach considerable speeds. The primary consideration in her case had to be ease of handling. Large individual sail areas had to be avoided so that mechanical devices for handling, setting and stowing of sails could be kept to a minimum. CARITA would be

called a three-masted schooner, even though the aftermost mast does not carry the largest mainsail.

It is interesting to note that just recently large schooners seem to be making a come-back. In the 1973/74 Round The World Race the only competing schooner GRAND LOUIS finished third overall, which was a surprisingly good result. She was designed and built in France and skippered by a Frenchman.

Eric Tabarly, one of the most experienced offshore racing helmsmen of recent times, said once: 'The summary of my extensive ocean racing experience is the view that the schooner is the best of all rigs for ocean racing, including single-handed racing.'

The Art of Cutting Sails

When Herreshoff built his cup defender RELIANCE in 1905, a giant with a bronze hull of over 144 ft (44 m) LOA, he met with an unexpected problem. It was planned that she should carry the largest sail area ever set on one mast, but it was found that the heaviest sail cloth then made for commercial sailing ships and marked No. 0 was totally inadequate. A specially strong sail cloth had to be made, which had not been on the market till then. This was $\frac{1}{8}$ in (3 mm) thick and known as No. 000. Sails of this dimension have now disappeared from the scene, whereas the number of boats sailing on our waters has increased tremendously. The much-praised Egyptian cotton sails, which were unmatched for half a century, have been replaced by synthetic sails. The totally different characteristics of synthetic cloths made the traditional sailmaker's specialized knowledge null and void. Since polyester cloth has practically no stretch, the whole art of sail cutting had to be re-thought. A sail made from synthetic cloth may not be quite as inflexible as a metal foil, but it retains the shape given to it by the sailmaker forever. It cannot be influenced during the stretching period in the way that cotton sails could. The *fluid* shape of the classic cotton sail has been replaced by the *rigid* shape of modern synthetic sails.

One way of determining accurately the different sections of a sail is to prepare a lines plan of the sail. The study of a single sail section for a windward course has been explained in Fig. 58. In the example an angle of 12° between the apparent wind and the chord of the sail has been assumed. Two conditions must be met: the incidence of the apparent wind has to be tangential to the luff zone of the sail, and the leech zone must not be parallel to the boat's heading except at the very leech, where it would then cease to produce any thrust. Within these limits a curvature has to develop which produces a *gradual acceleration* of the airflow. It has been established that the most favourable curvature is one in which the maximum depth is at about two-fifths of the chord length from the luff.

The lines plan of the Dragon sail in Fig. 118 has been drawn up on the basis of this concept. The lower part of the sail is shaped for an angle of incidence of 12° to the chord. The decreasing angle towards the masthead takes into account both the twist of the sail and the increase in wind strength. At the masthead the angle of incidence is only 6°.

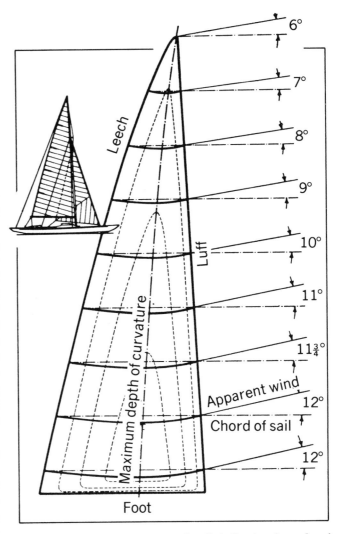

Fig. 118: 'Lines' of a Dragon mainsail, indicating the angles of attack to the apparent wind for sailing close-hauled. The bold lines mark the curvature, or draft, of the sail, which decreases towards the top.

The sailmaker is forced to adapt his technique to the relative rigidity of the cloth. His cutting techniques must be so perfect that any desired curvature can be produced accurately and exactly according to the lines plan. In cotton sails the panels were cut straight and joined by parallel seams, the desired fullness being achieved by adding a roach along the luff and foot. As soon as the sail was bent to mast and boom, this fullness shifted quite naturally towards the middle of the sail, because there was give in the cloth.

Synthetic cloth has no such give, and therefore each panel has to be shaped individually with mathematical

155

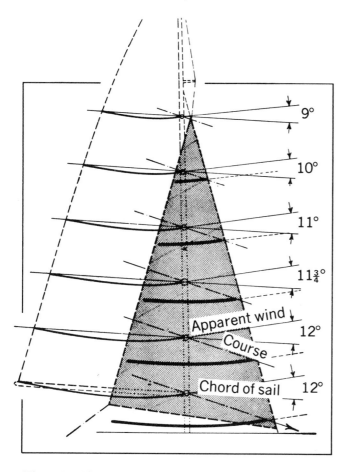

9°

10°

11°

11¾°

Apparent wind

Course

12°

Chord of sail 12°

Fig. 119: This figure illustrates the interaction between mainsail and jib at the same angles of attack as in Fig. 118. The angle is measured between the direction of the apparent wind and the chord of the sail. The direction of the course is also indicated. It can be seen that the curvature of the jib is flatter than that of the mainsail.

accuracy to ensure that the curvature is exactly as and where it should be according to the lines plan or other specification. The maximum width of each panel is at the point of maximum curvature, and it tapers gradually towards the leech to ensure a flat exit. Towards the luff the width of the panel is reduced in a curve to make it coincide with the wind angle. Additional fullness is added immediately above the boom to enable the sail to adopt its curvature as low down as possible.

What has just been said about the mainsail applies equally to all other sails used on the wind. Figure 119 shows the lines plan of a genoa used in conjunction with the mainsail which we examined just now. The concept is similar to that of the mainsail: the angle of incidence begins with 12° at the foot and decreases this time not to 6° but to 9° at the head, since the genoa is not led to the masthead. To enable the interaction of the two sails to be judged, the mainsail has been indicated in the drawing. This method of constructing a sail on the basis of a lines drawing which assesses mathematically the presumed airflow is still in its infancy and needs to be perfected in many ways, but even at this stage it can supplement empiric observation with greater technical accuracy. If the sailmaker supports every new piece of knowledge he gathers during his work with a technically accurate drawing, there will soon be a vast store of documentation which will help the further perfection of modern sails.

The Cut and Use of the Spinnaker

In 1865 a yacht by the name of NIOBE caused some stir by setting a very full, triangular masthead foresail aimed at making better use of quartering and following winds than the conventional headsails. The controversail sail was christened a 'niobe'. A year later the yacht SPHINX used a similar sail, with various improvements. Instead of being set loose it was made fast to a boom. In this way the tack could be moved further out to windward, which made the sail set better. The crew christened this sail a 'spinxer', and this name was gradually changed to 'spinnaker', as we know it today.

It is interesting to observe how successive rating rules have produced faster and faster boats with ever diminishing sail areas. The long bowsprits and enormous booms overlapping the stern have disappeared. Only one sail has not followed this tendency: the spinnaker. Since it first appeared over a hundred years ago it has steadily increased in size and has now reached shapes and dimensions which were thought impossible even some 30 years ago. The predecessor of the current extreme shape was a spinnaker designed by the Frenchman Herbulot about 20 years ago. But even as early as 1937 the spinnaker set on the yacht RANGER had the incredible sail area of 18,030 sq ft (1675 m²) and undoubtedly helped the defender to retain the America's Cup. It was about that time that the spinnaker first acquired its reputation: The devil invented it, and only the devil can handle it!

In most class rules only two dimensions of the spinnaker are fixed, except in one-design classes, where size and shape are strictly controlled. These two dimensions are height, i.e. the point of attachment of the spinnaker halliard, which must not exceed the height of the foretriangle, and length of the spinnaker boom, which must not exceed the length of the foot of the foretriangle. Under the IOR formula, which governs ocean racing, the rules are rather more detailed, without resulting in a substantially different shape of sail.

The true surface of the spinnaker within these limitations has increased to enormous proportions,

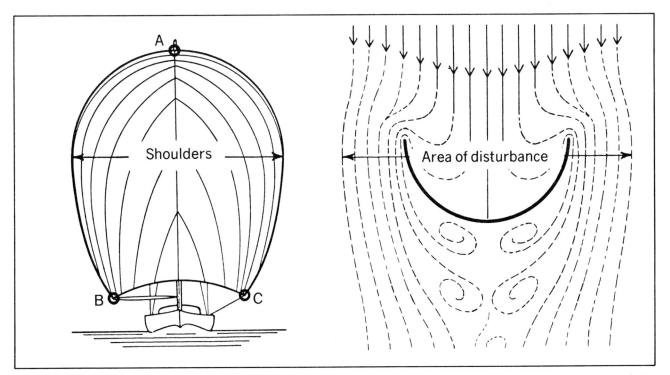

Fig. 120: The great efficiency of the modern, broad-shouldered spinnaker before the wind relies on the fact that the area of disturbance it produces far exceeds the actual dimensions of the sail.

If points A, B and C only are fixed by the rules, the shoulders should be cut as wide as possible.

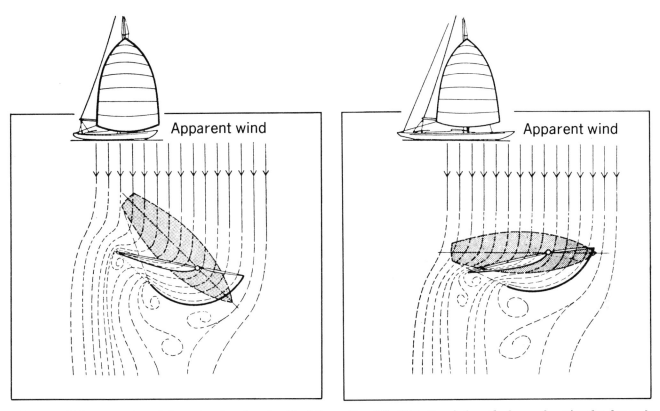

Fig. 121: With a quartering wind a spinnaker of moderately full cut is more efficient than a semi-spherical running spinnaker.

Fig. 122: With the wind on the beam, the spinnaker has to be even flatter in order to produce thrust over the whole of its area.

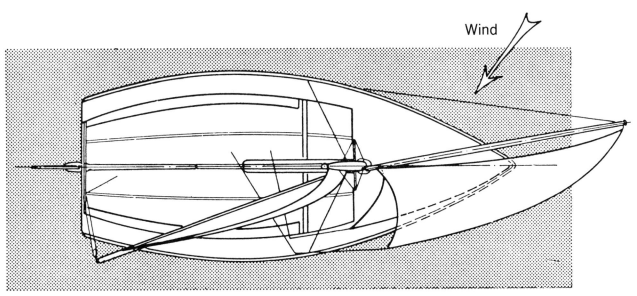

Plate 34: The modern starcut spinnaker of a large ocean racer. This one is specially designed by Hard Sails, USA, and is at its best on a beam reach. Since many of the panels are tapered, there is much seaming involved, and a lot of cloth has to be cut to waste, making this an expensive sail.   *Photo: Stanley Rosenfeld*

Fig. 123: Bird's eye view of an Australian spinnaker on the wind, where it is far more effective than the usual full-cut spinnaker. However, the excessively long boom it requires does not fit into the normal rules.

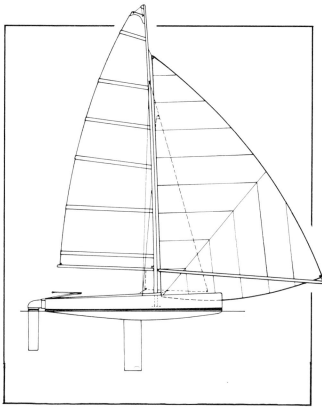

Fig. 124: A typical Australian spinnaker, which is cut asymmetrical and very flat. It uses a spinnaker boom of startling length. Its functions are those of a spinnaker and genoa combined.

mainly because of the adoption of a *hemispheric shape with broad shoulders*, as can be seen in Fig. 120.

If the spinnaker were used exclusively with a following wind, the design of its optimum cut would be relatively simple. Before the wind, forward thrust equals resistance, and hence the greater the surface presented to the wind and the wider the shoulders of the spinnaker the greater will be the thrust achieved. Ideally, the curvature of the spinnaker should be hemispherical everywhere, because its effectiveness before the wind consists in producing the maximum possible *disturbed section* in the airflow. It was shown earlier that an open hemisphere produces the maximum resistance, much greater than a flat disc of the same diameter. A completely flat spinnaker would have a resistance coefficient of say 1·16, whereas the open hemisphere has a coefficient of 1·42, which means an increase in thrust of 22 per cent.

All this applies only to a course dead before the wind.

But spinnakers are also set with a quartering wind and, depending on the cut, with a beam wind or even closer. It becomes immediately obvious that there can be no such thing as the ideal spinnaker. The parachute spinnaker, which is particularly efficient before the wind, becomes totally ineffective and unmanageable on a reach. Even in a quartering wind a spinnaker of hemispherical cut is no longer efficient, because the airflow is no longer symmetrical but directed quite obviously from luff to leech. What is needed now is a spinnaker of asymmetrical, or at least flatter, cut.

Many experienced helmsmen are fooled into thinking that a spinnaker is one hundred per cent efficient when it is full. On any course except dead before the wind this is not so. In a parachute spinnaker the trailing edge, i.e. the leech, is now excessively curved and does not allow a smooth exit of the airflow. It acts, in fact, as a brake. Its performance can be estimated to be approximately as follows:

$\frac{1}{2}$ of the spinnaker produces thrust

$\frac{1}{4}$ in the centre is indifferent

$\frac{1}{4}$ in the after part acts as a brake

It is obvious from what has been said that the parachute spinnaker is totally effective only dead before the wind, when *the airflow out of the spinnaker is completely symmetrical past luff and leech*. As soon as the boat goes closer to the wind the airflow resembles that in a fore-and-aft headsail, i.e. the air flows from the leading edge, or luff, to the trailing edge, or leech. Aerodynamic considerations now call for a spinnaker whose cut and curvature becomes more and more asymmetrical the closer the boat goes on the wind. Such a spinnaker gives excellent thrust but causes obvious problems when going about. For this reason almost all class rules forbid asymmetrical spinnakers. As an alternative the reaching spinnaker is cut very much flatter than the running spinnaker.

Figures 121 and 122 clearly illustrate the airflow in a quartering wind and a beam wind. With a beam wind resistance no longer produces any thrust, only heeling.

There can be no universal cut for a spinnaker simply because it is used on so many different points of sailing. To obtain the best propulsion on all spinnaker courses, at least three spinnakers of different cut are necessary: a hemispherical running spinnaker, a flatter spinnaker for quartering winds, possibly asymmetrical, and an even flatter one for winds on the beam or ahead of the

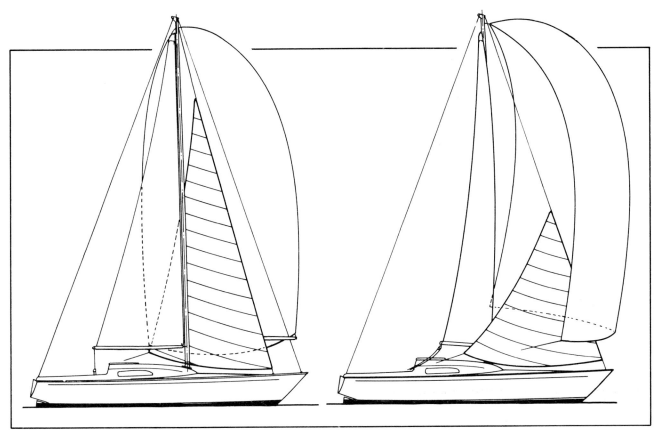

Fig. 125: On a reach a staysail like the one on the left is often set in conjunction with the spinnaker. Before the wind a similar staysail but much lower is often used.

beam. If the wind is ahead of the beam a genoa would set rather better, but it is tempting to leave the spinnaker up as long as possible because of its considerably larger sail area. To summarize, we can draw up the following list of spinnakers which a racing yacht might carry:

Course	Cut
Dead before the wind	Hemispherical with broad shoulders
Quartering wind	Flatter, possibly asymmetrical
Beam wind	Rather flat

The way the panels run has some considerable effect on the way the spinnaker sets, especially since it is made of very light cloth with a good deal of stretch in it. Over the years many different ways of arranging the panels

have been fashionable. At the time of writing it is probably the star-cut (also referred to as tri-radial), with seams radiating to all three corners, which is the most popular.

There is a limit to the degree with which a close-winded spinnaker can be cut flat. On cruising boats, of course, any variation from the pure spinnaker to the pure genoa can be set. It is different for rated racing yachts. Normally, not only a symmetrical outline but also the extent of roach on the luff and leech is stipulated. But no sail with a curved luff will set well on the wind, and cutting it flat would not help.

An interesting variation on the spinnaker is found in Australia and New Zealand where, contrary to international practice, some racing dinghy classes use asymmetrical spinnakers. Besides, the length of the spinnaker boom is not limited and may exceed the foot of the foretriangle. Figure 124 shows, using the example of a Cherub dinghy, how the large, flat-cut sail is set on an immensely long boom. It is still called a spinnaker, although set on the wind and used rather more like a genoa. Due to its flat cut, its resistance before the wind

161

comes nowhere near that of a hemispherical spinnaker, but this is compensated for to some extent by the long boom, which allows the sail to be boomed out far to windward so that its area resembles that of the mainsail. With the wind on the beam or ahead of the beam this flat, asymmetrical spinnaker is far superior to any full-cut spinnaker.

The advantages of a spinnaker become more obvious the slower the boat is in itself. Very fast craft like sand-yachts and ice-yachts cannot use a spinnaker, because it would *slow them down*. This extraordinary statement becomes plausible when one considers that these extremely fast machines never use the sail for resistance when sailing with a following wind but rather *tack downwind*. This is possible at speeds in excess of the wind speed. Racing catamarans are not quite comparable with sand and ice-yachts in this respect but they, too, do not normally use spinnakers.

It is almost impossible to describe all the different types of spinnaker used today. It is to be hoped that the revised IOR Rules bring some order to this complicated and expensive game of competing for the ultimate headsail. All we can do is give a brief survey of the types that are commonly set on different points of sailing, i.e. from running to close-reaching:

Floater: made of extremely light cloth
Light-air running Spinnaker: made of light cloth, for very light winds
No. 1 Spinnaker: made of fairly light cloth for moderate winds
Flanker: cut flatter, for reaching
Spanker: cut flatter still, for close-reaching
Reacher: almost as flat as a genoa
Genoa: normal headsail for sailing on the wind.

Every possible cross between running spinnaker and genoa has at some time or other been introduced or at least experimented with. Many fancy names have been coined, some of them fairly descriptive, like 'spinoa' and 'genniker', others purely imaginary.

STAYSAILS USED WITH THE SPINNAKER
For quite some time now it has been a widespread practice to fill the empty space below a normal spinnaker with a low, wide staysail. More recently, fierce competition for the One-Ton, Half-Ton and Quarter-Ton Cups has driven owners to renewed efforts to find ways of getting additional sail area which would remain un-

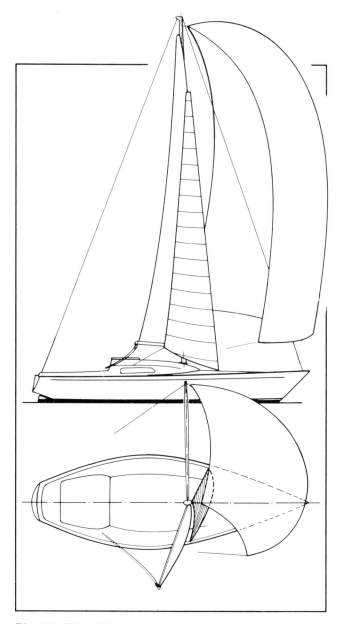

Fig. 126: This tallboy is another sail which is set in conjunction with the spinnaker. It is set on a stay which goes from the masthead to a point forward of the spinnaker boom on the windward rail.

rated. The aim is either to fill usefully any remaining empty spaces, or to improve and smooth the airflow over the whole rig. Developments are completely fluid in this respect at the moment, but we shall at least give a brief idea of the types of sails that are commonly set in conjunction with a spinnaker in an effort to improve the boat's performance.

In Fig. 125, on the right, we can see the *classic spinnaker staysail*. Its very long foot and modest height clearly suggest its role as space-filler underneath the spinnaker. It is usually tacked down to windward, i.e. on the side opposite the main boom, but is also used to leeward if the boat sails closer than running.

This low staysail has meanwhile been superseded as the standard staysail by the bigger genoa staysail, which is illustrated on the left in Fig. 125. It is usually set in a quartering to a beam wind and is less of a space-filler than a close-winded sail in its own right, which can be very effective on a reach. A rather more specialized form of staysail is the tallboy, which is illustrated in Fig. 126 and stands out not only by its extremely narrow, high cut but by the way it is sheeted. Its function is to smooth the airflow on the leeward side of the mainsail. When running, in order to catch any wind at all, its tack is made fast not on the centre-line but on the windward gunwale. In Fig. 126 this is just forward of the spinnaker boom. As the wind comes from further ahead the tack of the tallboy has to be shifted as the spinnaker boom moves forward. With the wind on the beam, and the spinnaker boom against the forestay, the tallboy tack is on the centreline. In other words, the tallboy tack follows the spinnaker boom.

There is still a lot of room for experimenting with specialized auxiliary staysails, not so much for the cruising man as for the racing skipper, to whom even a fractional improvement in performance may be critical. A much debated sail, at the moment, is the Big Boy, or Blooper, which is a lightweight, very full genoa tacked near the bow and trimmed opposite the spinnaker on the leeward side behind the main. Both sailmakers and racing skippers are bound to follow tendencies and changing rules very closely. The cruising man, on the other hand, can take his pick from this large crop of auxiliary sails and incorporate in his sail inventory only those which he considers justified in relation to usefulness versus cost and stowage space.

Plate 35: The tri-radial spinnaker is a good all purpose spinnaker on courses off the wind from a run to a broad reach. The Carter 33 shown here, designed by Dick Carter, has many of the features of the modern ocean racer including the very short overhang aft and the high aspect ratio mainsail. With an IOR rating of 22·5 ft this boat is only a little bigger than a Half Tonner.
Photo: Carter Offshore Inc

Plate 36: (overleaf) A combination of spinnaker and spinnaker staysail on a Swedish offshore boat, the Norlin 34. The acceptance of this latter sail was hotly contended. The Norlin 34 is designed by Peter Norlin and built by Solna Marin, Sweden. With a IOR rating of 26 ft she is between a Three- Quarter Tonner and a One Tonner. This fast, handy yacht is 33 ft 6 in long with a beam of 11 ft and a working sail area of 538 sq ft.
Photo: Solna Mar in AB, Sweden

The Tuning of Hull, Sails and Rigging

If a yard has built a new hull to a first-class design, and the sailmaker has produced for it a set of exquisitely cut sails, then it is a fair guess that the two together will make a very good boat. But this in itself is not yet a guarantee for outstanding racing results, for something important is still lacking: the vessel has not been tuned. By this is meant the adjustment of all parts of the hull and rig to each other so that they work together towards maximum speed and perfect balance.

This job of tuning cannot be done by the yard. Only a talented racing helmsman can do it really well. It requires experience, intuition, a keen eye and, preferably, a good deal of technical knowledge.

The hull offers comparatively few opportunities for

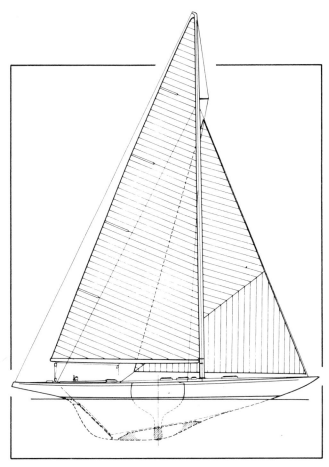

Fig. 127: Sail plan of a classic 12-metre boat. In these very large yachts the size and location of the mast posed a difficult problem. Masts of even this size are rigged with bend control devices, by which the set of the mainsail can be controlled.

tuning. Its thorough examination out of the water will reveal possible structural faults, such as lack of symmetry of hull shape, ballast keel or rudder, insufficient streamlining, especially between stern post and rudder, and similar points. The underside of the keel, which is frequently neglected, should be inspected to make sure that it is smooth. Once in the water, the trim effect of the crew is examined, and it is decided whether weight has to be shifted aft or, more frequently, forward.

Most of the work connected with tuning has to be done to the rigging and the sails. All adjustable rigging screws, all halliards, sheets and outhauls have to be positioned and checked against each other in such a way that optimum speed is the end result. Wind resistance must be reduced to a minimum and a balance must be achieved between luffing and falling-off moments. Of course, a yacht should be tuned in this way not only on all points of sailing but also over the full range of wind strengths, which is a daunting, not to say impossible task.

In his book *Successful Yacht Racing* Stanley Ogilvy publishes a table of factors which, in his opinion, account for a boat's racing success. The values for the same factors relating to the America's Cup races, which are given alongside, provide an interesting comparison:

	Ogilvy	America's Cup
Design	10%	50%
Smoothness of bottom .	10%	3%
Mast and rigging	5–10%	5%
Tuning	15%	7%
Sails	25%	15%
Racing technique and tactics	30–33%	20%

It is virtually impossible to prove mathematically or by experiment which of the two scales comes closer to the truth. On the whole, the racing helmsman will attach more importance to sails, tuning and racing tactics, whereas the designer or research man will attribute more importance to the quality of the design.

165

Fig. 128: Originally the 30-square-metre Skerry Cruisers carried a mast with built-in bend. This largely prevented the twist in the upper part of the mainsail on the wind. But there were dis-advantages before the wind and when the sail had to be reefed. These curved masts had their heyday between 1925 and 1930.

It is certain, however, that consistent success in top-class racing can only be expected if *all* the factors listed are given painstaking attention. This includes tuning, about which we will say a few words on the following pages.

THE MAST

From the point of view of optimum propulsion only, the mast should stand absolutely vertical. Any amount of rake reduces the sail area presented to the wind, by however little. There are, however, reasons why the raking of a mast might be beneficial. If a yacht suffers from excessive lee helm, the centre of effort must be moved aft. This can initially be achieved by raking the mast aft. If, on the other hand, the boat suffers from too much weather helm, the mast might possibly have to be raked forward. Lee or weather helm are not, of course, permanent characteristics of a yacht. A yacht which is completely balanced on the rudder in moderate winds will always carry lee helm in light winds and weather helm in strong winds. Strictly speaking, the position or rake of the mast should be altered for every change in wind strength. In light winds the mast should be raked aft, in strong winds forward.

When sailing in very light airs and with the mast raked aft, the boom and mainsail have an irritating tendency to fall back on the centreline. On the wind this can be avoided by heeling the boat, but before the wind there is very little one can do about it, which is why a forward rake of the mast is to be recommended for downwind courses.

It is preferable, however, when balancing a yacht, to move the mast as a whole rather than rake it and leave the rake purely as a consideration of optimum propulsion. For many years the Dragons had their masts in the position stipulated by their designer. Later it was discovered that the boat was much better balanced with the mast approximately ten inches further forward. The class rules were changed accordingly, and the result was a better balanced and faster boat. This proves that, in tuning, every possibility has to be examined to find the mast position which is conducive to both optimum balance and optimum speed.

A perfectly tuned boat does not by any means imply that there should be no pressure on the rudder at all. As was explained in previous chapters, a yacht can only sail close to the wind if its underwater profile offers effective resistance against leeway. It has been proved that slight weather helm, with the rudder angled about 4° to leeward, gives the underwater profile the desired asymmetry which allows the boat to point exceptionally high.

There is no question that the mast should be straight in an athwartships direction. When it comes to its fore-and-aft disposition, there are four possibilities: 1. straight; 2. with a permanent, built-in bend; 3. adjustable, i.e. capable of being bent to suit conditions; 4. 'swinging'. The permanent bend, as it was used on a number of older classes, notably the German Skerry-cruisers, is completely outmoded. The permanently straight mast is steadily losing ground except for larger cruising yachts. The 'swinging' mast, which is to counterbalance motion in a seaway, is no longer seriously considered. Racing helmsmen now concentrate on the adjustable mast in which bend can be regulated.

The main argument in favour of the adjustable mast is the possibility it offers of influencing the curvature of the mainsail to suit the wind strength. If the mainsail is cut to fit a slightly bent mast and the mast is left straight, this will increase the fullness of the sail and make it suitable for light airs. If, on the other hand, the mast is bent more than would be appropriate for the built-in curvature of the sail, this will flatten the sail and make it better for heavy weather. In light racing dinghies it is also common to have an elastic masthead which bends under pressure and allows the wind to be spilled from the upper part of the sail.

It must not be forgotten that the mast has to support the foresail, too. In racing dinghies it is often possible to give the mast a surprising amount of bend and still keep the foresail luff taut. As the size of boat and with it the size of sail area increases, these points have to be even more carefully considered.

THE MAINSAIL

During the races for the Prince of Wales' Cup in 1958 observers were fascinated by the way in which the New Zealander Geoffrey Smale, who emerged as the ultimate winner, attended to his mainsail. He had brought with him a small portable sewing machine. During each race he would watch his sail attentively for flaws and after the race undo seams where he thought he could improve the curvature. He would then re-stitch them on his

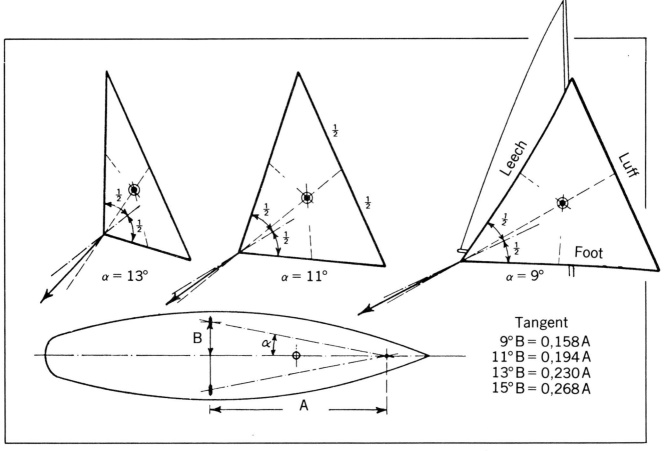

Fig. 129: The sheet pull of a triangular headsail should be on a line halfway between the bisector of the clew angle and the line which passes from the clew through the centre of gravity. This takes account of the forces on the sail and allows an even distri-bution of the curvature. The diagram also shows the angles between sheet lead and the boat's centreline, which decrease as the clew shifts aft.

sewing machine and proceed in this way until he felt that he had got the sail to set perfectly. Not many racing helmsmen will want to go to such lengths, but with cotton sails and modest sail areas the effort used to be well worth while. No sailmaker can watch a sail as closely as the helmsman himself during a race. Of course, synthetic sails can be improved in this way to a certain extent, but this is more difficult and also more risky and should best be left to an experienced sail-maker.

While one aspect of tuning the mainsail is the adjust-ment of the mast curvature to suit the cut of the sail, another is the placing of the sheet leads, which also influences the set of the sail. On the wind in strong winds the sheet leads are set up to leeward to flatten the mainsail, whereas in a light breeze they are moved

168

in amidships or even to windward to give the sail fullness.

The fit of the battens may have to be given some attention. If they are too long or too heavy there will be a fold all the way up the sail just aft of the battens. The luff of the mainsail should not be set up too tight for the prevailing wind conditions because this, again, flattens the sail. Nor must the clew be forced out to the end of the boom. In very light winds hardly any tension should be put on it.

If it is contemplated to have a sail altered, the sail-maker will need precise instructions. Curvature figures can best be obtained by offering a long batten up to the sail between luff and leech, and measuring the distances between this and the sail, preferably over the entire height of the sail. The sailmaker can then be given accurate instructions on where and by how much the sail needs to be altered.

HEADSAILS

The efficiency of any headsail depends firstly on the correct angle of attack to the wind and secondly on its aerodynamic interaction with the mainsail. The luff of a foresail must be absolutely straight, which presupposes adequate staying of the mast. In many cases this will have to be improved before the foresail luff can be set up taut. A straight luff is so important to the efficiency of the foresail that no effort should be spared to achieve it, without, of course, impairing the attitude of the mast.

The position of the foresheet leads must be infinitely adjustable so that the sail can be set at an optimum angle to the wind on every point of sailing. This angle will be greater in light airs than in a strong breeze. In general, it can be said that the position of the sheet leads should be between 9° and 15° to the boat's centre-line. This is illustrated in Fig. 129. The following table will serve as a rough guide. The angle is measured from the point where the tack of the sail is made fast on deck.

Position of Foresheet Leads	Strong Winds	Light Winds
Normal working jib	13°	15°
Large jib	11°	13°
Large genoa	9°	11°
Extreme cases	7°	9°

On modern cruising yachts these angles should be increased by one or two degrees; on heavy, beamy boats by three to four degrees. Figure 129 explains how the angle can be measured by using its tangent.

The direction of the sheet pull on the sail depends largely on the cut of the foresail in question. It should certainly not coincide with the bisector of the angle between the foot and the leech, because then the sheet pull would come in equal parts on the shorter foot and the longer leech. Experience has shown that the pull should come half-way between the angle bisector and the line to the centre of area of the sail, as illustrated in Fig. 129.

During tuning, not only the foresail as such is ob-

Plate: 37 The Shark 24 is built in Austria. It is a fast cruising boat which is built with bilge keel, fin keel or centreplate, as well as racing or cruising variations. The good racing performance is happily combined with comfortable cruising accommodation. Length 24 ft, beam 6 ft 10 in, sail area 215 sq ft.
Builder: Korneuburg AG

served but also its interaction with the mainsail. What has to be avoided at all cost is that dirty wind off the foresail is directed onto the mainsail. The leech area of the foresail must be parallel to the mainsail to ensure an effective slot.

Once the sheet lead positions have been found for courses on the wind, this is not the end. Now they have to be established for reaching. They will be different because the sail has to be fuller and set further outboard. Usually, for reasons of simplicity, the sheet leads are not constantly shifted. For racing dinghies, however, a very quick and simple jib adjustment system has become popular: the Barber hauler. This consists of a control line with a block at the end idling on the jib sheet near the clew and leading through a hole in the deck near the rail to the cockpit. As the boat pays off, the jib sheet is eased and the Barber haul control line hauled in. The sheet then goes from the jib clew to the Barber hauler, which is further outboard than the permanent sheet lead and gives the sail the desired fullness. The previous position can be instantly recovered by releasing the Barber hauler.

MISCELLANEOUS

The tuning of sails and rigging is never finished. Many helmsmen can get used to sailing a perfectly balanced boat very competently, but most prefer slight weather helm, which not only results in a favourable asymmetrical rudder position (4° to leeward) but also gives a better 'feel' of the boat on the wind.

Every possible source of resistance has to be minimized when sailing on the wind. All parts of the standing and running rigging should only have the minimum diameter required for safety. The same goes for rigging screws, shackles, blocks and spreaders.

When it comes to the fore-and-aft trim of the boat it is a smooth exit of the water-flow which has to be aimed at. In general, it is good practice for the crew to keep their weight away from either end, especially the stern. Only when planing at high speeds or running in strong winds should the crew shift their weight aft to counterbalance the wind pressure from aft.

Racing Technique - Racing Tactics

Racing technique consists in sailing a course with the greatest possible speed. Racing tactics are used to prevent an opponent, with all permissible means, from doing the same.

The formula which leads to optimum speed under sail is made up of many different factors. The battle does not start as the gun is fired, or even on the morning of the race, but many days or weeks before. Every imperfect manoeuvre, every ounce of excess weight, every missed opportunity to improve the rigging, mean the loss of valuable seconds which add up unmercifully in the course of the race.

PREPARATION OF THE HULL: There is a distinct difference between a *wet boat* and a *dry boat*. A hull kept in the water all the time is at a noticeable disadvantage compared with one which is normally kept on dry land and put in the water only prior to a race. Frequently a clause in the class rules or race regulations makes an appropriate allowance. A wet, wooden boat is heavier than the same boat in a dry condition. But even if the hull is made of a material other than wood, the surface below the waterline suffers under the constant effect of the water. It may get rough, even blistered, and have barnacles and algae growing on it. To be quite fair, wet boats and dry boats should not compete against each other.

The importance of a perfectly smooth surface below the waterline cannot be overstressed. There must be no rough patches on it, no blisters or rust, and certainly no marine growth. The underside of the keel is often neglected, because the yacht may stand on it when laid up ashore. The rudder and centreplate, if there is one, should be given attention, and there must be a smooth transition between centreplate and rudder.

Not so long ago it was believed that water-repellent substances, such as graphite, applied to the hull could reduce surface friction. This argument is supported by scientific facts. What matters is that the hull is *mechanically* smooth, and it is irrelevant how this smoothness is achieved, or what this surface is made of: be it paint or fibreglass or anything else. The best results are achieved by careful rubbing-down with wet-and-dry glasspaper. Subsequently the surface can be minimally improved by being polished to a high shine with a buffing disc, but the initial wet-and-dry process is much more important. It is smoothness which counts, not

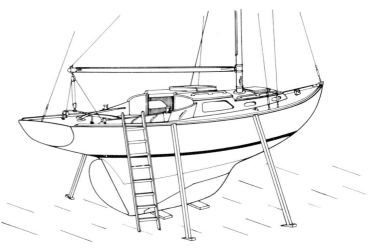

Fig. 130: While a boat is laid up ashore a thorough examination should be made of the hull below the waterline, the rudder, and, above all, the underside of the keel. Even the slightest roughness must be removed before the boat is put into the water and tuned for racing.

gloss since, in any case, there will be a thin layer of water – the boundary layer – which clings to the hull and gets dragged along. All leading edges deserve special attention: the stern post, the forward edges of keel, centreplate and rudder, and the transition from stern post to rudder. The meeting edge of bottom and transom must *not* be rounded off.

Some time ago someone discovered the ability to reduce the frictional properties of water by adding a chemical substance. Polymers released either by a coating applied to the hull below the waterline or from inside the hull through nozzles in the forepart encourage a laminar water flow along the hull and reduce skin friction by an average of 30 per cent. After the first successful trials, the use of such friction-reducing substances was, however, banned as being unsportsmanlike.

The state of physical fitness of the crew seems to have become an increasingly important factor over the years, for small racing dinghies and big ocean racers alike. The days are long past when one could win races 'by the seat of one's pants'. Athletic effort and dexterity are as much part of racing success as technique and tactics.

THE START: A good starting technique begins with accurately estimating, or better still timing, the time required from the last tack to crossing the starting line

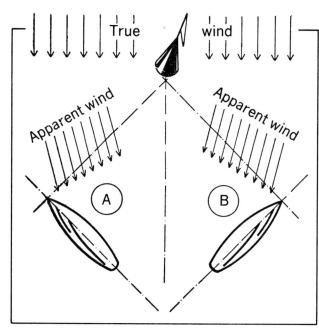

Fig. 131: When two boats approach the same mark on opposite tacks, they produce different apparent winds. The helmsman must realize this and not be misled by his opponent's apparent wind and go about too soon.

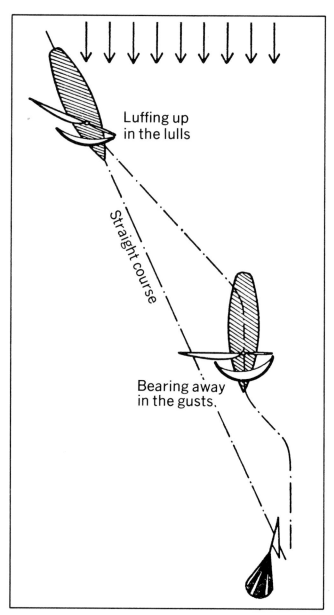

Fig. 132: When sailing with the apparent wind over the quarter it is advisable to luff up during temporary lulls and bear away in the squalls. This is exactly opposite to the technique used when sailing on the wind.

at full speed at the very moment the gun is fired. This manoeuvre has to be practised over and over again so that it can be adapted to the constantly changing conditions of wind, tide, starting line and landmarks. By landmark we mean a fixed reference point ashore which allows the helmsman to start the run for the starting line at a pre-determined spot. Only in this way can he hope to make a perfect start.

The best starting technique is frequently spoilt by the tactics of opponents. Right of way and blanketing are factors which can ruin the most carefully practised and technically perfect start. A well-thought-out starting technique begins with detecting any possible fault in the alignment of the starting line in relation to the next mark. The best starting point is the one from which one can hope to reach the first mark in the shortest time, possibly favoured by wind or tide, or by a wind change or the turning of the tide.

Since such considerations are not exclusive, nearly all competitors in a race will want to start at pretty much the same spot. There results a fight for time, for right of way or safe leeward position, the outcome of which cannot be foretold. If, in addition, the wind suddenly

drops or shifts, a good start will depend more on luck than judgement.

For this reason experienced helmsmen often stay in the lee of a massed start, hoping to use the safe leeward

172

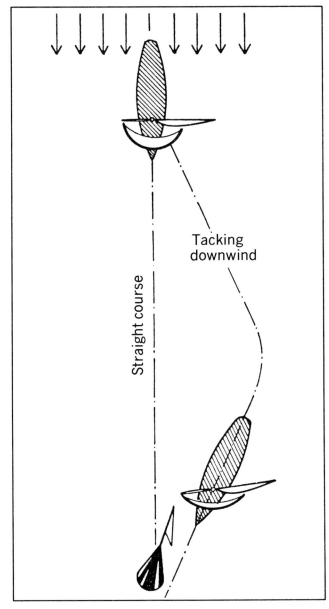

Fig. 133: When running dead before the wind in a race, many helmsmen are tempted to try tacking downwind. For keelboats and non-planing dinghies this is, on the whole, not profitable. It pays handsomely, though, if a planing dinghy can be made to plane by this technique.

position and right of way on the starboard tack to get to the point on the starting line from where they want to start.

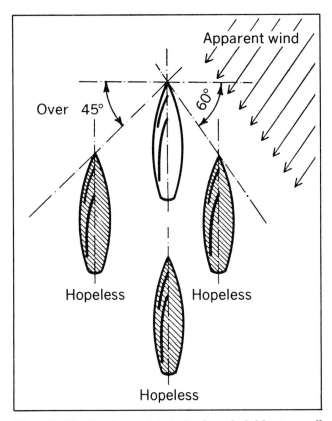

Fig. 134: The 'hopeless position': the three shaded boats are all in the 'hopeless position'. They should tack or change course immediately, because they have no hope of overtaking the white boat while they remain in this position.

RACING TECHNIQUE: The correct planning of a manoeuvre is as important as its quick and precise execution. The crew must be trained to work together smoothly and at speed. A good training system consists in laying two buoys about 100 yards apart, exactly in line with the wind direction, and in sailing this same course over and over again until every movement is executed with complete accuracy and confidence. Especially the repeated handling of the spinnaker will eventually lead to complete confidence in the use of this most difficult of all sails.

Another useful tuning procedure is to have two boats of the same class sail side by side over a complete range of courses. While one of them never alters the trim of the sail on a particular leg, the other experiments with trim, sheet leads, longitudinal trim and various angles

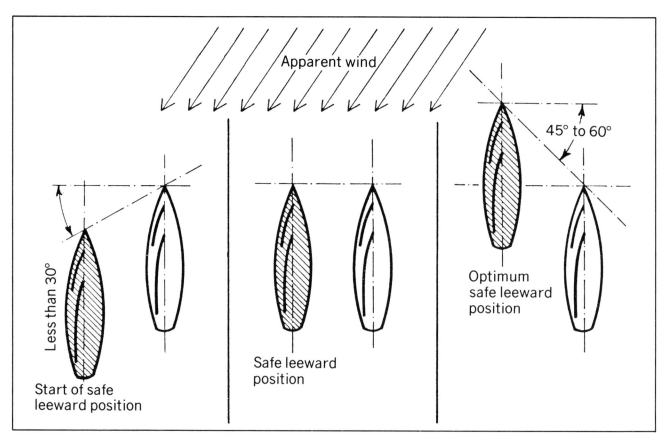

Fig. 135: In this diagram the shaded boat, in all three cases, is in the 'safe leeward position', and will gradually overtake the white boat. A thorough study of the interaction of boats when racing was made by the distinguished helmsman and theoretician Manfred Curry.

of heel, to study the effect of these on her speed as compared with her sister.

During the whole of a race an experienced helmsman will be intent on taking advantage of any wind change in order to gain distance to windward. He will make his boat 'eat its way into the wind' as soon as a puff gives him extra drive. With light, lively boats it is possible to luff up hard for several seconds. If this is done repeatedly the wake will resemble a slalom course. It is even advisable occasionally to luff up so hard that the forward part of the mainsail starts to lift, because the gain to windward is more important than a temporary loss of speed. It has been proved that this type of 'slalom sailing' gives a boat a spectacular advantage over one sailed on the wind in the conventional fashion,

always assuming that the boat in question is of the type that reacts quickly: any of the light planing dinghies, for example, or even the Soling.

When sailing before the wind the same procedure is followed, but the other way about: the boat bears away in the puffs and luffs up in the lulls. Even if bearing away means a diversion from the course to the buoy, subsequent luffing will once again result in increased speed. The pros and cons of tacking downwind are a frequently discussed subject. Normally, the gain in speed is cancelled out by the longer distance sailed and results in neither gain nor loss. But if a light planing dinghy can be got up to planing speeds by sailing that bit closer, then tacking downwind can mean a decided advantage.

RACING TACTICS: Whereas racing technique concerns each yacht individually, racing tactics affect the relationship of all competing yachts to each other. Its object is not to finish the course in the shortest possible time but to finish *before everybody else.*

Manfred Curry was probably the first to make a thorough study of racing tactics. He defined two positions, which have gained a classic importance in the interaction of two or more yachts: the *hopeless position* and the *safe leeward position.*

Figure 134 shows three cases of *hopeless position.* The white boat is in a safe position, whereas the three shaded boats are in hopeless positions. White, being ahead of the others, gets clean undisturbed wind and at the same time creates a zone of disturbance, both to leeward and to windward. All three of the shaded competitors are affected by this disturbed wind and will eventually drop back unless they change course. In that case the helmsman of the white boat, if he is smart, will immediately follow his opponent on the other tack to keep him in the hopeless position.

The *safe leeward position* is illustrated in Fig. 135. The shaded boat is now in the safe position, which starts when she is at an angle of less than 30° astern of the windward boat. Undoubtedly, at this point both vessels have a disturbing influence on one another, but the harm done by the one to leeward to her windward rival is greater than vice versa, because its dirty wind considerably disturbs the lee side of the windward boat's sails. The position of the shaded boat becomes safer as it draws alongside White, and the optimum safe position is reached when it is ahead by 45° to 60°. The shaded boat now gets clean wind, while White gets all the dirty wind on its lee side. The angles quoted must not be taken as strictly accurate, since they depend, after all, on the lateral distance of the vessels from one another.

On downwind courses a boat can easily blanket one in front, which will fall back and repeat the procedure in turn. As long as both are a long way from the mark this is more of a game than a battle, since no positive advantage can be gained from it. The same goes for luffing, which a right-of-way boat may do to another as often as she likes; it usually only benefits a third party. When nearing the mark the helmsman should aim to approach it in such a way that he has right of way and can force boats on the opposite tack to gybe. It is also profitable to round the mark on the inside of all the other boats.

TEAM RACING: In team racing several boats from one country or club get together to form a team, which races against teams from other countries or clubs. The important thing now is not the performance of an individual but that of the whole team, and consequently boats in one team must avoid competing against each other. On the other hand, every effort must be made to hinder any boat of an opposing team as often as possible, even if this results in a temporary loss of one's own position.

Rating Rules for Yachts

Yachting differs from many other sports in that the equipment used, i.e. the sailing boat, offers unlimited scope for variation. There are those who hold that yachting is at its most exciting when only identical vessels compete against each other. There are so many dinghy and keelboat classes that anyone who feels that way, whatever his age, his temperament and the waters he sails in, can find a class to race in. Strictly speaking, of course, boats within a class can only remain identical as long as no improvements whatsoever are made to any individual vessel. Many one-design classes have fallen victim to this temptation, which only shows the natural human tendency towards improvement. However, new efforts to remain strictly one-design are currently being made in the Laser class.

The urge for improvement within a class is met by the restricted classes, in which the basic measurements are laid down and the arrangement of certain details is optional. One example is the Flying Dutchman.

Finally, there is the vast armada of cruisers, day sailers and even racing yachts, which have been built to the specifications of one owner and do not fit into any rules. They used to be subsequently fitted into a handicap system by being rated under CCA or RORC Rules or whatever rating rule the particular country had adopted. This inevitably led to new boats being built with the rating rules in mind.

Others were specifically built as formula yachts for racing. Among these were the international metre-classes, like the 12-metre, built to the rule of the International Yacht Racing Union, and the large J-class yachts built before World War II to the American Universal Formula.

When boats were first rated it was done with the aim of establishing the capacity of cargo vessels so that they could be charged the appropriate tax or dues. The formulas used were extremely simple, like the one introduced by the British Admiralty in the fourteenth century:

$$\text{Tonnage} = \text{length} \times \text{beam} \times \text{depth of hull} \div 100$$

in which all measurements are in feet. It gives a vessel's carrying capacity of 'tuns' or casks of wine, and shows the origin of the modern words 'ton' and 'tonnage'.

A similar formula, the Thames Measurement Rule, which originated in 1854, is still in use in Britain today. It is a simplification of the fourteenth-century formula,

using only length and beam and abandoning the rather difficult-to-measure depth:

$$\text{Thames Tonnage} = \frac{(L - B) \times B \times \frac{1}{2}B}{94}$$

The tonnage as expressed by these two formulas is a volume measurement, which must not be confused with displacement. An approximate idea of the LWL of a medium-sized sailing boat can be obtained by multiplying the square root of the Thames Tonnage by 8·2. A yacht of 16 tons Thames Tonnage might have the following LWL:

$$\text{LWL} = 8\cdot2 \times \sqrt{16} = 32\cdot8 \text{ ft}$$

With small boats the square root should be multiplied by 9·8, with large yachts by 6·5. With progressive metrication in Britain it is unlikely that Thames Measurement will survive for much longer.

As soon as the driving force, i.e. the sail area, is combined in one formula with length, area or volume measurements of the hull, we get a speed rating. The oldest rating formula of this kind is the Seawanhaka Yacht Club Formula of 1883, which is ingenious as well as simple:

$$\text{RL} = \frac{\text{Length} + \sqrt{\text{Sail area}}}{2}$$

This formula is still used today in one-of-a-kind races, with the modification that 'length' entered in the formula is not simply LWL but the mean between LWL and LOA.

The Bermuda Rule, once much used, was of similar concept:

$$\text{R} = \frac{L \times \sqrt{\text{Sail area}}}{\sqrt{B \times D}} \times 0\cdot02$$

In the 1928 version L was not identical with LWL but was measured 4 per cent of LWL above the waterline. B and D stand for beam and depth respectively, and 0·02 was chosen as a coefficient because the end result thus approximated the length of the boat in question. The allowance for yawl rigs consisted in entering only 93 per cent of this value as rated length; for ketch and schooner rigs the figure was 90 per cent.

It is interesting to note that the first part of the now current IOR (International Offshore Rule), if stripped down to its essentials, looks surprisingly like the old Bermuda Formula:

$$R = \frac{L \times \sqrt{\text{Sail area}}}{\sqrt{B \times D}}$$

although, as a whole, there is much more to it, of course. The now superseded RORC Rule was built up in a similar way, whereas the German KR Rule has used the Seawanhaka formula, with certain additions.

Ideally, a rating formula should add all speed-promoting factors, such as length and sail area, and subtract all speed-reducing factors, such as beam and displacement. If, however, the formula is based on multiplication and division, as were the Bermuda Rule

and the even older Universal Rating Rule initiated by Herreshoff (1902 version: $R = L \times \sqrt{S} \div \sqrt{D}$) then this allows for widely divergent measurement values, and it becomes necessary to curb extremes by introducing limits.

Since the different design factors, such as effective length, beam, draft, weight of ballast, sail area, stability, propeller factor and draft can only be established by numerous measurements and converted into a rating by a string of formulation, the IOR procedure is not only very complicated but surprisingly fair. Measurement under the IOR is time-consuming and correspondingly costly, and justified mainly for international racing.

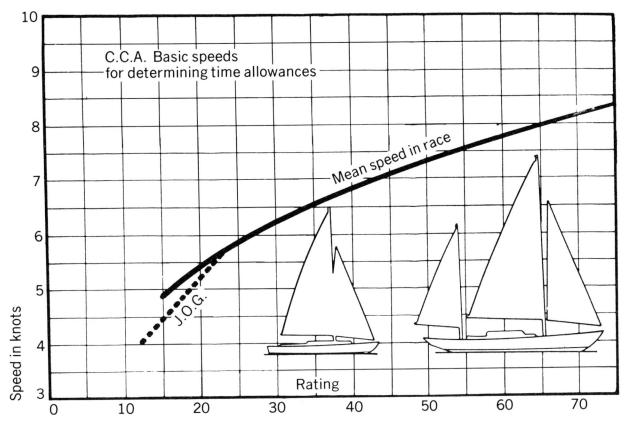

Fig. 136: Any system of time allowance is based on the mean speed of yachts. This is a graph of mean speeds of CCA-rated boats. According to it, a boat rating 20 ft should have a mean speed of 5·4 knots, one rating 40 ft should have a mean speed of 6·8 knots, *and one rating 60 ft should average 7·75 knots. The decreasing steepness of the bold curve coincides roughly with real conditions, whereas the steep ascent of the dotted JOG curve favours the smallest boats and would benefit from being revised.*

Partly for this reason the Scandinavians decided to formulate a much simpler yet workable cruiser rating, which has become known under the name of Scandicap. The 1973 improved version looks like this:

$$R = \frac{(L - B + \frac{2}{3}G + 0\cdot75AR \times \sqrt{S} \times SAF) \times PF}{2}$$

The effective length L is measured directly on the hull, 3 per cent (B + G) above the waterline. B is the mean of greatest beam and waterline beam; G is the greatest girth from sheer line to sheer line. AR stands for the rig factor, with the following ratings: yawl = 0·95, ketch = 0·90, gaff rig = 0·80, spritsail = 0·75. The other factors are S = sail area, SAF = spinnaker correction and PF = propeller factor (between 0·99 and 0·94, as specified in a detailed correction value table). The Scandicap rule is noticeably similar to the original IYRU Rule of 1906.

The basic aim in working out this formula, which was to simplify the measurement procedure as far as possible, has doubtlessly been achieved. It is doubtful, though, whether boats which diverge from average shapes and dimensions will be rated absolutely fairly.

No formula can be altogether fair which sets off greater length by smaller sail area and vice versa. Yacht races are sailed in *any* wind strength, there is no way as yet to compensate for wind effect. Take a vessel with a shorter waterline length and a larger sail area, and another with a longer waterline length and a smaller sail area. If both are given the same rating they may, indeed, be equally fast in average wind strengths. In a light breeze, however, the shorter boat with the larger sail area will have a decided advantage, whereas in strong winds she will lose by a margin. This lies in the nature of resistance and propulsion. Perhaps the results would be fairer if a measurement rule laid down a uniform *effective* length, and admitted only differences in beam, draft, displacement and sail area. It must be said, though, that the results of races sailed under the IOR have proved this rule to be fair beyond all expectations.

In principle, the aim of a measurement rule is to enable all boats rated under it, of whatever size, to race against each other. They are all given *different* time allowances according to their rating which, in fact, makes it possible for the smallest vessel to beat the largest on *corrected* time, if not on elapsed time.

The whole system of time allowances is currently under review to bring it in line with the internationally adopted IOR. Basically, there have been two classic methods of time allowance:

Time allowance on distance, which is usual in the United States. Each boat, according to its rating, gets a time allowance in seconds per sea mile covered, based on the following formula:

$$\text{Time in secs} = \frac{2160}{\sqrt{R}} + 183\cdot64$$

Time allowance on elapsed time, which is the accepted British procedure. It is based on a Time Correction Factor, TCF, according to the following formula:

$$\text{TFC} = \frac{\sqrt{R} + 3}{10}$$

Elapsed Time is multiplied by the TCF to give Corrected Time, which is always less.

Both methods have their advantages and disadvantages. The American method has the edge, because time allowances can be calculated *before* the race. Thus each skipper knows how many hours, minutes and seconds he is allowed against any of the other competitors. Under the allowance-on-elapsed-time system the results cannot be calculated until the last boat has finished.

On the other hand, the time-on-distance system accounts in no way for differences in weather conditions. The time allowance is always the same whether the race is a long one in light winds or a very short affair in half a gale. To eliminate some of the drawbacks, the RORC experimented for one year with the PF System (PF = Performance Factor), which combined time-on-time and time-on-distance. Naturally, it made calculations more complicated. It was found that it did not work satisfactorily, and so was abandoned after that year.

All so-called 'Ton' boats sail against each other without time allowance, since all boats in one class have the same rating. The same goes for the International metre-classes: 5·5-metre, 6-metre and 12-metre. But whenever vessels with different ratings race against each other, be it in the Admiral's Cup series or in the Round The World Race, it is essential to apply a fair time allowance system. The search for a perfect rating and time allowance system will obviously continue.

Plate 38: YDRA, *winner of the One Ton Cup in 1973 displays in this picture a typical wave formation. The bow wave builds up just behind the stem, the stern wave just inside the waterline length of the boat. The boat is achieving about 80 per cent of its maximum hull speed.* YDRA *was designed by the American, Dick Carter.*
Photo: Beken, Cowes

The International Offshore Rule for Ocean Racing Yachts (IOR)

For many years now certain offshore races have drawn large international competition, above all the Fastnet Race, which is held every other year, and the Bermuda Race, which is also biennial but held in the years between Fastnet Races. In particular the vessels competing in the Bermuda Race were initially genuine cruising boats, designed and built entirely to the individual specifications of their owners. In order to give all competitors equal chances of winning, a handicap system was needed, and for this purpose the Bermuda Rule was evolved.

Of course, it did not take long for capable designers to succeed in turning out fast cruising boats which were designed specially to rate favourably under the Bermuda Formula. This is when the Cruising Club of America stepped in and drew up a comprehensive and very much more complicated measurement system, which became known as the CCA Rule. A similar thing happened in Britain, where the Royal Ocean Racing Club rated cruising yachts under regulations drawn up for the purpose, the RORC Rule. This was based on entirely different mathematical principles, but the type of boat in which it resulted was not basically different from that built under the CCA Rule.

It must be remembered that cruiser ratings were originally aimed merely at handicapping existing yachts fairly, rather than serving as a blueprint for new designs. The CCA and RORC Rules did, however, come to be used as design formulas, similar to those which had for long been the basis of racing yachts like the international metre-classes or the J-class.

The situation was similar in other countries, which all had their own rating rules, some of them purely for local use. If a German KR-rated yacht wanted to compete in the Fastnet Race, or a British yacht in the Bermuda Race, she had to be re-rated under the measurement rule current in the country organizing the race. As long as this only applied to isolated cases, the owner just put up with the additional cost and bother. But when offshore racing became more and more popular, and the Admiral's Cup Races in Britain, as well as the Onion Patch Trophy in the United States of America, started to draw considerable international competition, the call for a common international rule became more and more urgent. Eventually a technical committee was set up which, under the chairmanship of the successful designer Olin Stephens and with the collaboration of many experts, examined the whole problem of yacht measurement from scratch. The results of their painstaking deliberations were presented to the public in 1968. This first draft of an internationally applicable measurement formula for ocean racers was no more than a working proposal, which was laid open to discussion. Thus it took another two years until, in 1970, the first official formulation appeared, which was named the International Offshore Rule Mark II. The term 'Mark II' is misleading, for this was not the second version actually *in use* but the first. It remained in that form for about two years.

The introduction to this impressive mathematical feat stated that the formula would be subject to modification as necessitated by new insight and experience. And indeed, since then a number of alterations and amendments have been made, so that the version in use at the time of going to press is by now the Mark III, which looks like this:

$$R = \left(0{\cdot}13\,\frac{L \times \sqrt{S}}{\sqrt{B \times D}} + 0{\cdot}25\,L + 0{\cdot}20\sqrt{S} + DC + FC \right) \times EPF \times CGF \times MAF \times SMF$$

The technical committee was aware that every designer, every owner and every sailmaker would be looking for loopholes, in order to build into a new boat every permitted advantage, or rather every advantage not actually forbidden by the rule. In order to thwart such efforts and to discourage all extreme shapes and dimensions, the IOR is very carefully thought out and tightly controlled down to the last detail. The text of the current version goes to 58 pages, including some 60 explanatory diagrams. It is, indeed, the most comprehensive and most complicated measurement rule for sailing yachts ever in existence. If one looks at the formula rather more closely, its mathematical composition turns out to be really quite simple. The few symbols used in it have the following meanings:

L = rated length

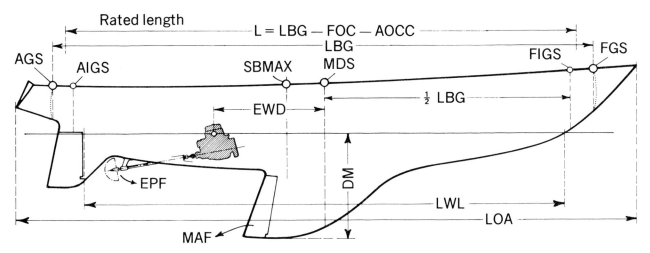

Fig. 137: The important rated length 'L' is not measured any-where on the actual hull but is based on the location of two girth stations. The actual LWL does not appear anywhere in the IOR rating system and, indeed, would be difficult to determine with today's rudder arrangements.

S = total rated sail area
B = rated beam
D = rated depth
DC = draft correction
FC = freeboard correction
EPF = engine and propeller factor
CGF = centre of gravity factor
MAF = movable appendage factor
SMF = spar material factor

The formulas used to determine these factors are too complicated to explain here in detail. To gain an idea of how involved the procedure is, let us merely look at how L = rated length is arrived at.

To start with, it must be pointed out that the actual length L is not measured anywhere on the hull. It is neither the LOA nor the LWL, nor the mean between the two. L is, actually, the *effective length when sailing* and is determined by the formula

$$L = LBG - FOC - AOCC$$

This means that initially the values for LBG, FOC and AOCC have to be established. As is well known, the overhangs fore and aft have a not negligible effect on a boat's performance, and this has been incorporated in determining the rated length, FOC being the forward overhang component and AOCC the after overhang component. Two whole pages of text and several diagrams explain how they are arrived at.

Nor can LBG (the length between girth stations) be found without an auxiliary formula. It is determined by the distance between the so-called forward and after girth stations, FGS and AGS. To establish the forward girth station a girth wire is stretched taut round the bow from the sheer line on one side to the sheer line on the other side. The girth station is at the point where a great circle course between the two sheer points, measured in chain girth, is equal to 0·5 B, B being the rated beam. The after girth station is estab-lished in a similar way, being the point where the girth length is equal to 0·75 B. There is an added complication in that B is at the point of maximum beam (BMAX) but is measured at $\frac{1}{6}$ BMAX below the sheer line.

LBG is deliberately greater than the effective length, so that the effects of bow and stern shape can be accounted for by deduction. Without going into detail it might be of interest to mention that occasionally a negative overhang component occurs aft, which has to be added to LBG, so that the rated length L projects beyond the transom.

Since the measurement procedure to determine the hull rating is such a complicated affair, the sailing man hardly ever concerns himself with it in practice. If he plans any modification of hull measurements, either by increasing the beam or changing the shape of bow, stern or keel, he will call on expert help. The interaction and combined effect of various factors is so difficult to

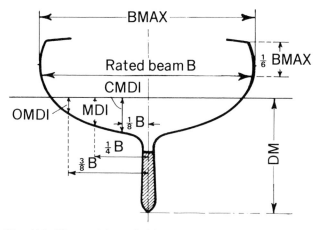

Fig. 138: The rated beam 'B' is probably the most easily determined part of the formula. Notice also the hull depth measurements at $\frac{1}{8}B$, $\frac{1}{4}B$ and $\frac{3}{8}B$ measured from the centre plane.

predict that frequently the data are fed into a computer.

Things are not quite so daunting when it comes to rating the sail area, where the foretriangle and the measurement LP = longest perpendicular luff to clew are current concepts. But here, too, there are all sorts of corrections to be made and penalties to beware of, which can be confusing to anyone who is new to the game.

Fundamentally, the area of a modern jib-headed mainsail is determined by the two most important measurements: length of hoist P and length of foot E. These measurements are not, however, taken on the sail itself but on the mast and boom. The actual rated sail area (not the true sail area) is somewhat more complicated, though, and is worked out by the following formula:

$$\text{RSAM} = 0.35\,(\text{EC} \times \text{PC}) + 0.2\,\text{EC}\,(\text{PC} - 2\text{E})$$

EC and PC stand for 'foot of mainsail corrected' and 'hoist of mainsail corrected', the corrections being determined by certain penalties incurred for sheeting limits, boom above deck, boom depth, battens, etc. It is interesting to note that the main part of the formula is not 0·5 hoist × foot, but only 0·35. The addition of 0·2 EC (PC — 2E) takes into account the aspect ratio of the mainsail. In all modern mainsails the hoist is longer than 2 × foot E. It is quite common for it to be over 3 × foot E. If the hoist P was exactly three times the length of the foot E, the mainsail area,

182

calculated with the factor 0·35, would be bigger by almost 20 per cent but still remain *below* the true sail area.

If anyone were to think of rigging his yacht with no mainsail at all, or only a very small mainsail and correspondingly larger foresails, he would find himself heavily penalized by a provision which is aimed at discouraging such undesirable rigs: a minimum mainsail area, dependent on the height of foretriangle I, is always rated, even if it is not actually there.

When it comes to measuring the foresails, one can summarize the procedure as follows. Once the size of the foretriangle, determined by the height I and the base J, is established, the longest perpendicular LP between luff and clew is found. This is measured on the sail itself and can be up to 1·5 JC (foretriangle base corrected) without being penalized. A very large genoa, whose clew reaches further aft, means a penalty in the rating of the foretriangle. In spite of this, an LP of 1·6 or 1·8 JC is often applied and considered worth the penalty. Once the LP line has been determined, any triangular foresail may be set within the foretriangle, as long as its clew is within the LP line.

The measurement formula for the foretriangle is fairly complicated and made up of three groups of figures representing the actual size of the triangle, the overlap and an additional penalty if the foretriangle is very high in relation to its base J.

The spinnaker dimensions, too, depend on the size of the foretriangle. In principle, an IOR spinnaker is symmetrical, and the luff limitation is $0.95\sqrt{I^2 + JC^2}$. Above this, the penalty is so severe that it is not worth incurring. The length of the spinnaker boom can be equal to the base J, after that it is penalized. A further limitation states that the maximum width of the spinnaker must not exceed 1·8 J or 1·8 SPL (spinnaker pole length). If it does, JC and hence the foretriangle rating will be increased.

The rule also includes instructions as to the limitations of sail setting and sheeting, and in the paragraph on 'Owner's Responsibility', it states that 'the owner is responsible that all members of his crew fully understand and comply with the limitations on sail setting and sheeting contained in the rule'.

Not infrequently the view is expressed that rating under IOR favours a sail plan with a large foretriangle and very small mainsail. This view is not only mistaken but, actually, the opposite could be proved. As we explained earlier, the rated mainsail area is frequently smaller than the true area. The fact that, in spite of this, designers are not tempted to give mainsails rather larger dimensions, is explained by the aerodynamic usefulness of the foretriangle on the different points of sailing. For every wind strength and on every point of sailing a different sail can be set for optimum performance, whereas a mainsail has only limited adaptability.

After reading this long yet drastically summarized explanation of the IOR measuring procedure, the question inevitably arises: have the time and trouble which have gone into working out this comprehensive rule been worth it and does it lead to a fair rating?

After all the practical experience gathered so far, one can only say that the International Offshore Rule may one day be hailed as the greatest achievement in its field. It is enormously thorough and contains an unprecedented measure of thought and research contributed by experienced and gifted men, among them Olin Stephens and Dick Carter, both successful designers of modern ocean racers. They gave a great deal of time quite selflessly, as did the other members of the committee, to find a *fair* way of assessing all the influences which are conducive to speed or speed-reducing. They drew on the staff of their design offices who, with the help of their vast experience and archives of technical drawings, could analyse every point in detail before the final formulation was decided on.

Meanwhile, many races have demonstrated that yachts of equal rating, but very different dimensions and sail areas, do genuinely compete against each other over short triangular courses as well as in long ocean races. The winning boat is nearly always the one which is sailed better or tuned better or favoured by a wind shift. But then the rating rule is not meant to equalize such influences . . .

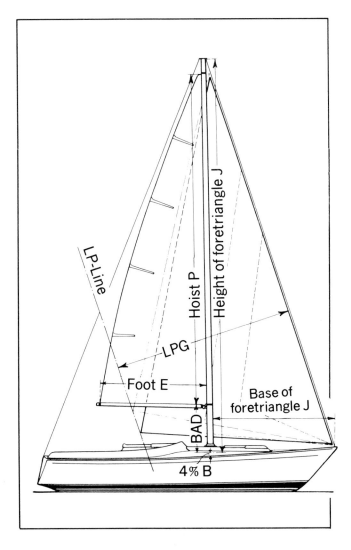

Fig. 139: Every racing man should be familiar with the details of sail rating procedure. The mainsail area is not simply determined by the hoist 'P' and the foot 'E' but undergoes a correction which depends on the height ratio. In this way most mainsails rate less than their true area. Other important measurements are 'LPG' as well as the height 'I' and the base 'J' of the foretriangle.

The Significance of Rating 'R'

If we take another look at the mathematical formulation of the IOR we find that it consists of a main part, in brackets, and an appendage of minimal corrections. The main part begins with the figure 0·13, which has been chosen more or less at random, purely in order to arrive at a 'convenient' figure for R. This is a trick used with rating rules in the past and it results in R being somewhere close to LWL. It is much more acceptable to speak in terms of a rating of 26 foot or 8 metres, which does give a fair idea of the yacht's size, than of '60' or '200', which would mean very little. Similarly, the terms 'foot' and 'metre' are added to the figures 26 and 8 respectively purely for convenience, because it is acceptable to yachtsmen. They could just as easily stand by themselves.

If the rated length of a yacht is combined with the square root of its sail area in a formula, the sail area can get larger as the length becomes smaller. Thus, if a boat has a LWL of 18 ft and a sail area of 256 sq ft, the formula $L \times \sqrt{S}$ gives a value of 288. If the LWL were reduced to 15 ft, the sail area could be increased to 368·6 sq ft to give a product of 288. As can be seen, a formula as simple as this can produce the ideal light-weather boat, which starts to fall behind as soon as the wind strength increases even moderately, because the short waterline acts as a brake.

To design an offshore racer specifically for light weather would be utter folly. On the contrary, most designs aim at the maximum possible waterline length or, in the case of IOR boats, the maximum effective length, without sacrificing very much in the way of sail area. At the same time, however, the countless correlations between the different factors have to be taken into consideration, as was already explained in the previous chapter. It is by no means enough to balance length against sail area, for beam and depth, draft and freeboard also affect the ultimate rating. At the moment there is a tendency to build boats with ample beam and in this way gain some additional sail area.

So much for the main part of the formula. What is the meaning of the four correction factors? EPF is the engine and propeller factor, and accounts for the weight and centre of gravity of an auxiliary engine in relation to the mid-point of LBG. If a heavy motor is installed far forward or far aft, which might be detrimental to the racing performance of the yacht in question, she may gain by this a small advantage on her

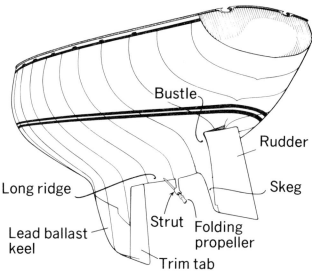

Fig. 140: *Perspective drawing of the hull of an ocean racer with trim tab on the keel. The rudder is a displacement rudder, i.e. it is not flat but has a volume. The rudder skeg, too, widens out towards the top into the so-called 'bustle'; a fairing piece connects it with the keel. Trim tabs have not improved performance in the way that was expected, neither by making the boat faster nor by making it more close-winded, and recently they have been generally abandoned.*

rating. It is conditional that engine performance and propeller dimensions are thus that the boat reaches a minimum speed of $\sqrt{L}$ in knots in calm water. For a half-tonner this means approximately $3\frac{1}{2}$ knots.

The propeller factor covers mainly the propeller drag under sail. The implications and formulations are complex, and take into account not only the diameter and blade width of the propeller but also whether it is solid, feathering or folding. Thickness of propeller shaft and shaft strut further influence the outcome. The maximum EPF is 0·96, which means that the rating can be influenced by it by no more than 4 per cent and no one can hope to gain an excessive allowance by resorting to tricks like installing an abnormally large propeller.

CGF means centre of gravity factor. It is determined by means of an inclining test with the yacht fully equipped and afloat, which establishes the righting moment at a very small angle of heel, in other words, her initial stability. In shipbuilding, an inclining test is the normal procedure for establishing the centre of gravity, but with yachts the accurate execution of such a test can cause the measurer a considerable headache.

184

A very stable yacht may get a CGF of more than '1', which means that her rating will be slightly increased by it. At the lower end of the scale the CGF may not be lower than 0·968, so that a very tender boat can never get more than a 3·2 per cent allowance. For the measurer the inclining test is a laborious and time-consuming affair. For the designer the CGF is an almost incalculable risk, unless he can draw on considerable experience gained from precedents. One must admire the courage of the committee in incorporating this troublesome yet fair stability control in the IOR.

MAF means movable appendage factor. A 'movable appendage' is defined as any underwater surface capable of inducing asymmetry. Up until recently, and certainly between 1968 and 1970, practically all ocean racers were designed with a trim tab on the trailing edge of the keel. It has never been proved conclusively that this really helps a yacht to point higher or go faster. The author once took part in a discussion among yachtsmen which followed a lecture by Olin Stephens on modern yacht design. One participant put the question: 'We have an ocean racer designed by you, one with a trim tab. We have conducted countless tests to establish the optimum angle of trim, but have come to no conclusion. Can you help us?' Olin Stephen's answer was non-committal: 'Up until now we have been unable to prove a measurable advantage of trim tabs. It seems, though, that racing yachtsmen insist on their new yachts being fitted with them, because they want them to be up to date. As far as the optimum angle of trim is concerned, I cannot help you either.'

When Dick Carter designed his one-tonner WAI ANIWA he suspended the whole keel on a 140 mm thick bolt, so that instead of a trim tab he had a fully pivoting ballast keel. This led to the introduction of the MAF. It is the least complicated part of the whole formula, for it simply imposes a penalty of 1·0075 on any yacht having a 'movable appendage', which means an 0·75 per cent increase on the rating. The true value of movable appendages is so doubtful that this penalty sufficed to make them unacceptable. The rudder, of course, is excluded, as are centreboards and drop keels, which are covered by a special provision.

The last factor in the formula is SMF, which means spar material factor. It imposes a penalty of 1·030 for spars built wholly or partially of any material other than wood, aluminium alloys, fibreglass or steel alloys.

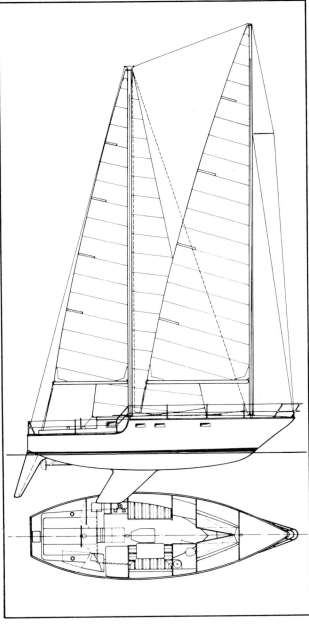

Fig. 141: Professor Jerome Milgram's CASCADE *has been the most controversial of IOR yachts, the rule makers' enfant terrible. The unusual cat-ketch rig slipped through a loop-hole in the rule, which resulted in the actual sail area of the yacht, including the huge mizzen staysail, being 80 per cent greater than the rated sail area. The keel and rudder arrangement of this ugly duckling are also highly unusual.*

LOA	37 ft 6 in	Rated sail area	325 sq ft
LWL	30 ft	Displacement	7·72 ton
Beam	12 ft 3 in	Ballast	4 ton
Draft	6 ft 9 in	Original IOR rating	22·8 ft

Displacement has always been an important factor in any previous rating rule, and it must have cost the IOR committee considerable heartsearching before they decided to leave it out of the formula altogether, probably to do away with the costly and sometimes impossible weighing of yachts. Displacement is merely represented by immersed depth stations (MDIA being midship depth immersed adjusted) and expressed by the formula

$$DSPL = \frac{L \times MDIA \times B}{2} \times 64 \cdot 0$$

which is used only for calculating gravity in certain cases.

The IOR suffers from an insignificant yet curious omission in that it fails to specify the measurement of yachts in salt water or the correction of a slightly advantageous measurement in fresh water. Probably it never occurred to anyone that ocean racing yachts might be anywhere other than in sea water.

A number of extreme designs have already tried to exploit loopholes in the rule. At the time of writing only one has so far been successful, the now-famous CASCADE, designed by Jerome Milgram, professor for aerodynamics at the Massachusetts Institute of Technology. He found that a cat-rigged ketch with high freeboard and no foresail whatsoever would rate very well under the rule. A ketch may set a large mizzen staysail, which in this case acted as an enormous foresail to the mizzen without being rated as such. The high freeboard was a further advantage so that CAS-CADE, of almost one-ton size, was found to rate little more than a half-tonner. After she had repeatedly finished first and second in several New York Yacht Club races, the controlling body of the IOR, the Offshore Racing Council, imposed on her a 10 per cent penalty. The IOR provides for such action, which is to prevent vessels of questionable design from gaining unjust advantages. The penalty was subsequently increased, which brought CASCADE's rating from 22·8 feet up to 27·2 feet, but still this did not stop her from scoring many successes.

Nobody objects to the rating figure being so adjusted by a simple correction coefficient that the result resembles a yacht's LWL. The fact that it is usually a bit smaller than the LWL tends to be interpreted as an advantage. In fact, it is the rated length L which indicates speed potential. It would be possible to work out values for R which indicate speed rather than length. Under the English system, where rating is in feet, one need only draw the square root of R to get the mean speed in knots. But this would result in inconvenient figures, and so it suffices, in practice, for the sailor to know that $\sqrt{R}$ expresses the speed potential.

The current IOR classification with ratings in feet and metres looks like this:

Class	Ratings, IOR Mk III	
I	33–70 ft	10·05–21·34 m
II	29–32·9 ft	8·84–10·02 m
III	25·5–28·9 ft	7·77– 8·81 m
IV	23–25·4 ft	7·01– 7·74 m
V	21–22·9 ft	6·40– 6·98 m
VI	19·0–20·9 ft	5·94– 6·37 m
VII	17·5–18·9 ft	5·31– 5·91 m
VIII	16–17·4 ft	4·80– 5·28 m

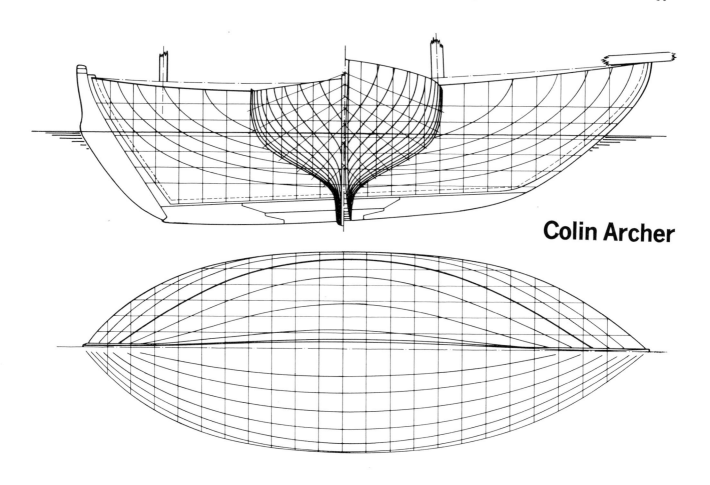

Plan II: Plans of three quite different keelboats:
Norwegian lifeboat designed by Colin Archer in 1909. Many
yachts have been built as double-enders and proved very seaworthy.

LOA	46 ft 9 in	Draft	7 ft 6 in
LWL	40 ft 8 in	Displacement	1137 cu ft
Beam	15 ft 10 in	Sail area	1273 sq ft

Colin Archer

Modern IOR One tonner. Lines drawn up by the author following
current tendencies.

LOA	37 ft 6 in	Draft	6 ft 3 in
LWL	28 ft 9 in	Displacement	240 cu ft
Beam	11 ft 2 in	Sail area	626 sq ft

International three-man keelboat of the Soling class. Designed by
Jan Herman Linge in 1964 it became an Olympic class in 1972.

LOA	26 ft 9 in	Draft	4 ft 3 in
LWL	20 ft	Displacement	35·3 cu ft
Beam	6 ft 3 in	Sail area	234 sq ft

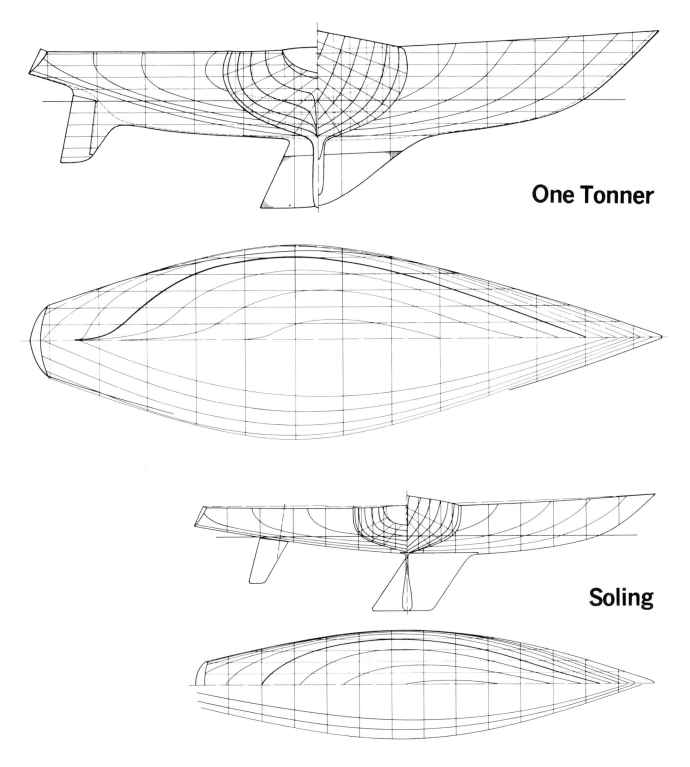

One Tonner

Soling

What are 'Ton-Yachts'?

In 1898 some members of the French *Cercle de la Voile de Paris* donated a silver cup, 220 lb in weight, which was to be competed for in international amateur yacht racing. This was the first international trophy of significance which could be competed for by *small* boats, and it was received with great enthusiasm. It was not usual in those days for the size of boats to be determined by limits or one-design rules, but it could vary within a formula. Just then a new handicap system had been worked out during a French yachting congress:

$$T = \frac{\left(L - \dfrac{P}{4}\right) \times P \times S}{1000 \times \sqrt{M}}$$

T = rating in tons
L = waterline length
P = girth of mid-section
S = sail area
M = area of mid-section

The three smallest classes, up to 1 ton, up to 2 tons and up to 5 tons respectively, competed among each other without handicap, as is usual with ton-yachts today. Only the larger classes, up to 40 tons, were given a handicap according to their rating. Even the smallest class could not have been all that small, since the number of amateur crew prescribed was three or more.

From 1899 onwards the cup, which went by the long name of *Coupé International du Cercle de la Voile de Paris*, was competed for in the 1-ton class on the Seine at Meulan near Paris and in the Solent off Cowes. Up until 1906 it was won twice by Britain and four times by France. Soon the British, who had difficulty pronouncing the long and (to them) foreign name, started calling it the One Ton Cup, and it has retained this name to the present day.

The cup itself was too valuable to be simply abandoned when the original one-ton class died. Instead, it was taken over by the newly introduced International 6-metre Class. The first race on the River Seine in 1907 was won by the German yacht ONKEL ADOLPH. In subsequent races winners came from Britain, Holland, France, Germany, Sweden, Norway and Switzerland. The American yacht LLANORIA even won on two occasions, off Stockholm and off Oslo. The last race in

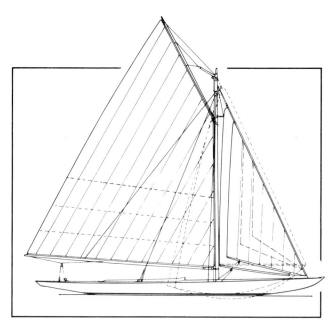

Fig. 142: The first so-called One Raters looked something like this. They were open keelboats with a large cockpit, low freeboard and a low aspect-ratio gaff rig. The name One Rater does not mean that these boats had a displacement of one ton but that they had a rating of 1. This meant originally a volume of 1 ton or tun, which was a large wine cask. Compare the lines of KITTEN, *Fig. 63.*

1962 was won by France off Palma de Mallorca. By then the term 'One Ton Cup' had become commonly accepted even though the 6-metre yachts were by no means called 'one-ton yachts'. Gradually, though, the 6-metres lost their popularity, and the cup remained unused for several years. It was the chairman of the Cercle de la Voile de Paris, Jean Peytel, who energetically campaigned for its reinstatement. In talks with influential British yachtsmen he suggested that the traditional One Ton Cup might be given a place in ocean racing, the most suitable class being the size rated 22 foot under the RORC Rule. The suggestion was accepted and immediately put into action, and it has turned out to be a real shot-in-the-arm for international ocean racing.

The first international offshore races for the One Ton Cup were held in 1965 off Le Havre, when fourteen yachts from eight nations, all with a 22-foot RORC rating, competed for victory. Almost automatically these boats started to be called 'one-tonners'. The first series was won by the Sparkman & Stephens-designed DIANA III from Denmark. In the following year, when the series was held off Copenhagen, there were already twenty-four yachts from nine countries. The winner was the Carter-design TINA. One-tonners on average have a waterline of 29·5 ft (or 9 m). Measured under the RORC Rule they rated only 22 feet. When in 1970 the new IOR-formula superseded all previous rating rules, it turned out that the same yachts now rated 27·5 ft which corresponded rather more realistically to their true size. Since, just then, the next One Ton Cup series was imminent, a new IOR rating of 27·5 feet was, perhaps rashly, agreed on, so that existing yachts could take part as before. This changed the rating of one-tonners, but not their real size.

This short sketch of the history of the One Ton Cup explains to the reader why some yachts are called one-tonners, half-tonners or quarter-tonners without having anything to do, neither by weight nor by volume, with these denominations.

The idea of class ocean racing kindled so much enthusiasm that in short succession several smaller ton-classes and one bigger one sprang into being. Under the then current RORC Rule half-tonners had a rating of 18 feet, quarter-tonners of 15 feet and two-tonners of 26 feet. The waterline length of all boats was then greater than their rating suggested, and the correction of this discrepancy under the IOR had its logical justification.

At present ton-boats are classified as follows:

TON CLASSES

	IOR Rating	No. of crew
Mini Ton	16·0 ft (4·9 m)	3
Quarter Ton	18·0 ft (5·50 m)	3–4
Half Ton	21·7 ft (6·60 m)	4–5
Three-Quarter Ton	24·5 ft (7·47 m)	5–6
One Ton	27·5 ft (8·38 m)	6–7
Two Ton	32·0 ft (9·75 m)	undefined

There are two attractive aspects to ton-racing which have contributed greatly to the growth of these classes: the first is the fact that seaworthy cruising yachts race against each other without handicap, i.e. boat for boat. The second is that many races are organized in series, which include short triangular courses as well as medium-long coastal courses and long offshore courses. In the Admiral's Cup Races, which are similarly organized, yachts of different IOR ratings compete. The same goes for the American Onion Patch Trophy and the Australian Southern Cross Cup.

If one compares the classic shape of racing yacht with the modern type of ocean racer, one notices some very distinct differences. To start with, the modern ocean racer is strictly functional. Gone are the long overhangs fore and aft, freeboard is reasonable and beam ample. One could describe the modern IOR yacht as the product of a healthy development. The sail plan is characterized by the short boom and the optimal use of the large foretriangle, all of which combine to a most efficient rig.

No less noticeable are the differences in the shape of the underwater body. In a design competition for One-Ton yachts run in 1965 by the magazine *Yachting World*, all three winning designs still showed a fairly pronounced yacht stern, a moderately long keel with a narrow, high rudder immediately attached to it. But already in the same year designers started to detach the rudder from the keel and moved it aft to arrive at the sort of underwater profile which is accepted as normal now. Keels became shorter and shorter, but steering characteristics improved as the most favourable size ratios of skeg and rudder were established.

One result of the success and international acceptance of the IOR has been the unceremonial disappearance of the International Cruiser/Racer classes, which were never too popular. They had been introduced in 1950 by the International Yacht Racing Union with the aim of enabling cruising yachts to race against each other without handicap, boat for boat. The five classes were rated 7-metre, 8-metre, 9-metre, 10·5-metre and 12-metre.

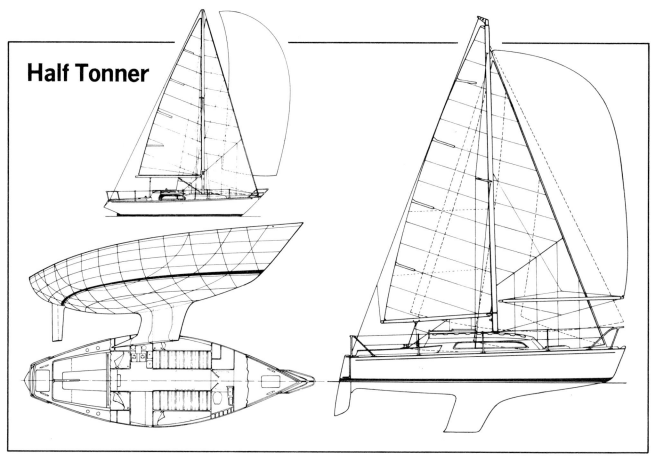

Half Tonner

Fig. 143: Arpège is one of the most successful and popular series-built ocean racer in the half-ton class. She was designed by Michel Dufour and is built at his yard. The perspective drawing shows her lines very well, also the bulb on the keel and the deep, narrow rudder on a skeg.

LOA	30 ft 3 in	Displacement	3·6 ton
LWL	22 ft	Ballast	1·5 ton
Beam	9 ft 10 in	Ballast ratio	42%
Normal draft	4 ft 5 in	Sail area	367 sq ft

Fig. 144: Half-ton boats can also be designed along dinghy-hull lines like TITUS CANBY designed by Bruce Farr. It is interesting to compare her dimensions with those of Arpege, Fig. 143, and of Scampi, Fig. 172.

LOA	26 ft 7 in	Displacement	2·1 ton
LWL	23 ft 8 in	Ballast	0·79 ton
Beam	9 ft	Ballast ratio	38%
Draft	4 ft 10 in	Sail area	298 sq ft

In conclusion a word might be said about the term 'offshore'. Strictly speaking it means 'a short way out to sea'. This is a modest description in our context, for the major offshore races like the Fastnet, the Bermuda, the Buenos Aires–Rio, etc. are genuine ocean races, no less demanding than a Transatlantic or a round-the-world race.

But the cruising man must not allow himself to be intimidated by the tremendous spread and popularity of the IOR yachts. A cruising yacht may still be built entirely according to her owner's specification. She need not be rated, and her season's sailing schedule is dependent only on the enterprise and seamanship of her skipper and crew. Of course, the designer can profitably draw on the experience gained in the IOR design field and give her a detached rudder hung on the stern, short overhangs, short boom and large foretriangle, but this is left entirely to his own fancy and judgement. Even a yacht with a conventional long keel remains, as ever, a good cruising yacht.

APPROXIMATE DIMENSIONS OF IOR YACHTS

	IOR Rating						
	Foot	*Meters*	*LOA*	*LWL*	*Beam*	*Displ.*	*Sail Area*
	16·0	4·80	21 ft 4 in	16 ft 5 in	7 ft 6 in	1·2 t	195 sq ft
Quarter Ton	18·0	5·50	25 ft	19 ft	8 ft 6 in	1·8 t	260 sq ft
Half Ton	21·7	6·60	30 ft 2 in	22 ft 7 in	9 ft 6 in	3·3 t	375 sq ft
Three-Quarter Ton	24·5	7·47	34 ft 2 in	25 ft 7 in	10 ft 6 in	4·8 t	485 sq ft
One Ton	27·5	8·38	37 ft 5 in	28 ft 6 in	11 ft 6 in	6·8 t	625 sq ft
Two Ton	32·0	9·75	42 ft	33 ft 6 in	12 ft 6 in	9·5 t	785 sq ft
	40·0	12·20	51 ft 10 in	42 ft	13 ft 9 in	16 t	1130 sq ft
	50·0	15·24	61 ft	50 ft 10 in	15 ft 9 in	24 t	1615 sq ft
	70·0	21·34	78 ft 9 in	69 ft	19 ft 8 in	36 t	2475 sq ft

This table was compiled with the help of Peter Johnson's book *Ocean Racing and Offshore Yachts*, but the figures have been completely revised by the author.

Classes of Sailing Yachts

The basic aim of racing is to master all the technical and tactical aspects of this wonderful and fascinating sport. In its purest form, yacht racing calls for *identical* boats, identical not only in size and weight but also in shape, equipment, gear, sails and rigging. In this context it is quite irrelevant whether the competing yachts are fast and modern and equipped with sophisticated fittings.

But it is part of human nature to strive towards improvement, and this compulsion is found also in the sailing field. Almost every racing man *invents* something, be it a sheet lead or a fitting, a better method of smoothing the bottom or a tapered batten. In short, these efforts naturally lead to the state of affairs in which boats of one class are no longer identical. This has given rise to a complex system of class rules, some of which are very restrictive, while others allow considerable freedom. Some classes are aimed purely at furthering *sailing expertise* by specifying every part of the boat down to the smallest detail. Others give considerable scope when it comes to dimensions, hull shape and rig so that competition is not merely between boats afloat but begins at the design stage. On the whole, all yachts fall into one of the following categories:

ONE-DESIGN CLASSES: All boats are governed by strict rules regarding shape, weight, equipment and sail area. The hull must be built precisely according to plans, down to the smallest detail. At the moment, this principle of absolute sameness is vigorously pursued in the Laser class.

RESTRICTED CLASSES: A large number of modern classes fall into this category. Generally speaking, hull dimensions, shape and weight as well as sail area are controlled, while details such as size and arrangement of the cockpit, centreplate, rudder and mast stays are optional. One of the best known restricted classes is the Flying Dutchman.

FORMULA RACING CLASSES: With this system of class rules the dimensions are not rigidly laid down. Boats belonging to one and the same class are different in length, beam, displacement and even sail area, although they compete boat for boat, i.e. without handicap. The differences in the dimensions are taken

194

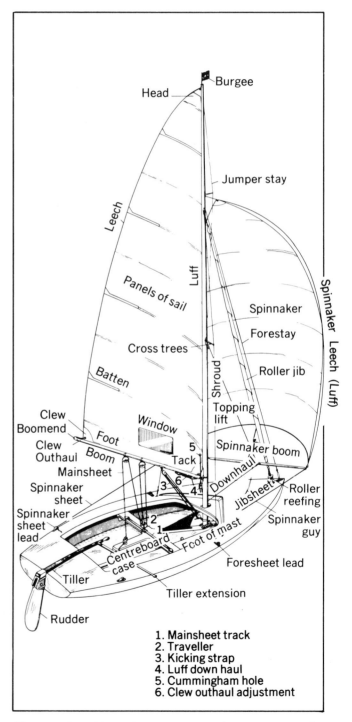

Fig. 145: This illustration names all the important parts of a modern racing dinghy. While this may be called a 'standard boat', every class, of course, has its own special features and fittings.

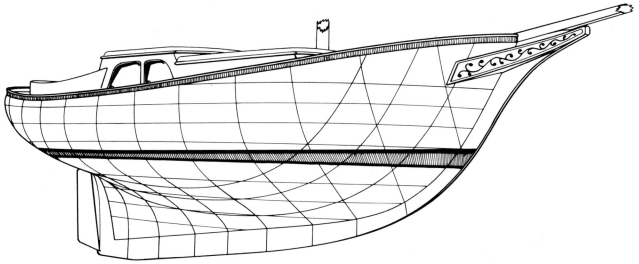

Fig. 146: This newly designed version of the traditional Friend-
ship Sloop, from the board of A. Mason, belongs to the large group
of classless and one-off boats. She is a comfortable cruising yacht
of character, though not very fast, and has the following dimensions:

LOA	29 ft 6 in	Displacement ...	4·7 ton
LWL	23 ft 4 in	Ballast	1·63 ton
Beam	9 ft 2 in	Sail area	678 sq ft
Draft	4 ft 6 in	Aux. engine	30 hp

into account at the design stage by a measurement
formula by which, for example, greater length is offset
by a smaller sail area or larger displacement. The international metre-classes belong to this group, among
which the 5·5-metre and 6-metre classes are still
reasonably active today, while yachts of the 12-metre
class compete for the most important of all trophies,
the America's Cup.

FORMULA CRUISING CLASSES: Not everybody
wants a pure racing boat, which is unsuitable for
extended cruising. To enable yachts designed primarily
for cruising to be organized into races, special cruiser
handicap rules were worked out. In time, of course,
boats started to be built specially with the aim of
rating favourable under a particular rule. The common
characteristic of all such craft is that they neither aim
at identical size nor identical speed. Each boat's rating
determines her handicap, i.e. time allowance. In this
way a smaller and slower vessel can win over a larger,
faster rival even if it finishes much later. There have
always been a number of different rating rules in
different parts of the world, the most important of
which, as mentioned before, were the CCA Rule
(Cruising Club of America), the RORC Rule (Royal
Ocean Racing Club) and the KR Rule of the German
Sailing Association. They have now all been super-

seded by the internationally accepted IOR Formula.

UNCLASSIFIED YACHTS: Obviously a large number of sailing boats are designed and built without
regard to any class or rating rules, purely for cruising
for pleasure, be it on inland waters or on the high seas.
An ocean-going yacht, in which the owner wants to
cruise the Seven Seas, must be built with regard to
many factors which do not fit into any measurement
rules. This category also comprises vessels with a
comparatively small sail area but a powerful engine,
the so-called motor sailer.

During the last two centuries sailing has experienced
a spectacular, world-wide growth. Previous editions of
this book still quoted the Snipe, Lightning and Star as
examples of large and popular classes. Meanwhile, so
many new classes, especially dinghies, have come into
being that it is difficult to keep track of them. On the
following pages a large number of class boats have been
illustrated, each of them being representative of a
characteristic idea. There has been no other reason for
the choice of examples. Features such as speed, price,
popularity or nationality have neither been deliberately
selected nor deliberately neglected. The boats have
been selected with a view to greatest variety and with
consideration to practically every tendency which is to
be found in the extensive field of modern sailing.

Since the size of this book had to be kept within certain limits, some of the examples illustrated in previous editions have had to be omitted, much to the author's regret, especially since most of them are important to the history of yachting. But the reader will, no doubt, be recompensed by the inclusion of all the new material.

An attempt has been made in every case to give dimensions with the greatest accuracy. Weights are for the boat complete with all equipment including the sails, but without the crew. Occasionally, therefore, weight figures differ from those listed in the class rules, which frequently refer to the hull without gear.

The LWL has generally been taken from the plans, but no great importance should be attached to this particular measurement, since the trim of the boat and the actual conditions of sailing often alter the waterline compared with what it would be in calm water. Similarly, the true sail area can be calculated in different ways, since the foresails, or the foretriangle, are not calculated uniformly in all classes.

Plate 40: This is the keel version of the Zugvogel showing typical layout with classic construction. You can see the slot for the retractable keel between the foot of the mast and the boom crutch. The centreboard version simply has a conventional centreplate case. Photo: Joachim Laabs, Essen

Racing Dinghy Classes

The more widespread sailing has become throughout the world, the more numerous have become the classes of small boats either for racing or day sailing. The modern sailing dinghy has been developed to a high degree of perfection and, in its value as a piece of 'sports equipment', is in no way inferior to a large yacht. The universal spread of the modern, unballasted dinghy began in about 1920. To start with, the boats were rather heavy, but soon lighter building methods were employed. Hull shapes were improved and refined, rigs were made progressively more effective, without the actual sail area being changed. In 1950 the *planing dinghy* was born. Up until then planing was by no means an unknown condition, but with the conventional types of boat it was hardly ever achieved. Now hulls were actually designed as planing hulls. Eventu-

ally the fibreglass hull took over, which ensured complete watertightness and perfect uniformity of all boats of the same class.

In the 1924 Olympic Games, which were held in Paris, the first dinghy races were introduced, which were to be sailed single-handed. Due to lack of experience, the boat chosen for the purpose was much too large and also over-canvassed. It was about 19 ft (6 m) long and weighed nearly 1000 lb (450 kg) and should really have had a crew of three. The sail area on the wind was 215 sq ft (20 m²), added to which a spinnaker was set off the wind. The poor helmsman had no time for racing tactics, for he had his hands more than full trying to control such a large craft. He had nearly to resort to acrobatics looking after the tiller and the sheets, setting and lowering the spinnaker, and adjust-

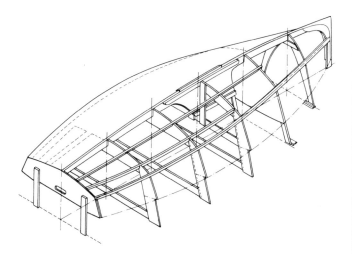

Fig. 147: Many dinghies have been specially designed for amateur construction like this Cherub dinghy designed by John Spencer. It is 12 ft long, has a beam of 5 ft and carries a sloop rig with a sail area of 88 sq ft.

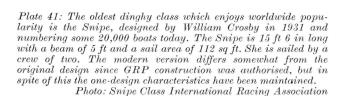

Plate 41: The oldest dinghy class which enjoys worldwide popularity is the Snipe, designed by William Crosby in 1931 and numbering some 20,000 boats today. The Snipe is 15 ft 6 in long with a beam of 5 ft and a sail area of 112 sq ft. She is sailed by a crew of two. The modern version differs somewhat from the original design since GRP construction was authorised, but in spite of this the one-design characteristics have been maintained.
Photo: Snipe Class International Racing Association

ing the centreplate.

At that time the gradual transition to the modern dinghy concept took place. The massive, clumsy hulls with their excessive sail areas and heavy rigging disappeared. Boats did not actually become shorter, on the contrary, they became longer but at the same time much lighter and narrower, so that much smaller sail areas were needed to drive them at comparable or even greater speeds.

The first one-design classes were introduced not long afterwards. To begin with, they had simple hulls intended for easy amateur construction. One of these early classes, the Snipe, achieved enormous popularity throughout the world. It was designed by William Crosby, then editor of the magazine *The Rudder*. The first boat was actually built by a 14-year-old amateur!

In Germany, a country which has always played an important part in dinghy sailing, the one-design dinghy was introduced later and never with the aim of making the boats suitable for amateur construction. The culmination of a long series of free classes were the long, narrow 10-, 15- and 20-square metre classes, which were masterpieces of the art of boatbuilding. The method of construction was extremely light-weight and also very complicated. Eventually, the 10-square metre class designed by the incomparable Reinhard Drewitz, was turned into a one-design, which shall be included in this survey because of its importance in the history of German dinghy classes.

If we look at the illustration in Fig. 149 we have to admit that by today's standards nearly every detail is unusual: there is the gaff rig, the very pronounced roach on the leech of the mainsail, the full-width battens, the wooden forestay spar, the extremely long, low and narrow hull, the short, forked tiller with its rope transmission to the rudder. The outer skin of the hull was frequently made of gaboon, a wood similar to mahogany but much lighter. The amazing thing was the method of construction. The 21 ft 8 in (6·6 m) long hull was planked up with planks only $\frac{1}{3}$ in (8 mm) thick and without the use of glue. The bent ash frames were $\frac{2}{5}$ in $\times$ $\frac{3}{5}$ in (10 mm $\times$ 15 mm) and set only 3 in (80 mm) apart to ensure watertightness even in heavy weather. The deck, too, was built of thin sheets of solid gaboon, all seams being backed by battens. Marine plywood was, of course, not available then. The heyday of the 10-square metre monotype, which was popular not only

198

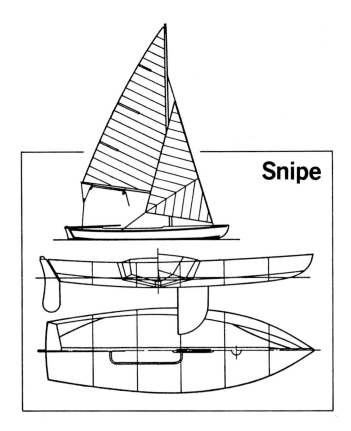

Fig. 148: The Snipe is one of the most popular dinghy classes in the world.

LOA	15 ft 6 in	Draft, plate down .	3 ft 5 in
LWL	13 ft 6 in	Weight without	
Beam	5 ft	crew	463 lb
Draft, plate up ..	6 in	Sail area	112 sq ft

in Germany but also in Switzerland and Austria, was between 1920 and 1938.

The years 1952 and 1953 were a milestone in the development of racing dinghy classes. Up till then, types and classes in different countries had evolved quite independently from each other. Now the idea of international collaboration began to take root. During an international competition organized in Holland in 1952 designers and yachtsmen were invited not to submit plans but to demonstrate their actual products. The boats were tested and compared in a series of races, at the end of which the Flying Dutchman was chosen as the International Two-Man Dinghy for inland waters. The design by the Dutchman U van Essen looks very much like a logical development of the classic German dinghy type, not quite so long but easier to plane. It met with enthusiastic acceptance in all those European countries which had always supported the classic racing dinghy. In 1960 the Flying Dutchman became an Olympic Class.

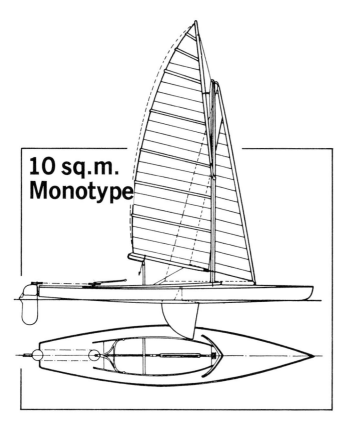

10 sq.m. Monotype

Fig. 149: The German 10 square metre Monotype is now only of historic interest. It was the end product of a long development of dinghy classes in which only the sail area was restricted.

LOA	21 ft 8 in	Draft, plate down	2 ft 11 in
LWL	19 ft 2 in	Weight without	
Beam	4 ft 7 in	crew	452 lb
Draft, plate up	3 in	Sail area	108 sq ft

While the Flying Dutchman was considered an excellent class for inland waters, the Small Boat Committee of the International Yacht Racing Union (IYRU) decided to hold another series of races off the rough Biscay coast to find a class suitable for coastal racing. This one-of-a-kind series took place off La Baule in France in 1953, and the winner was a dinghy called the Coronet designed by John Westell, which was 5·5 metres long. The French Caneton Association had for many years sponsored a dinghy class which was 5·05 metres in length. Impressed by the success of the Coronet at Le Baule, the association asked John Westell if he would be prepared to shorten his design to 5·05 metres, and in this way a new international class was born, which was given the simple name of '5-0-5'. It was introduced in France in 1954 and given international status in 1955.

The 5-0-5 was the first typical example of a dinghy designed for planing. Its entirely unorthodox shape combined a narrow waterline beam with ample beam

at deck level, an impression which is increased by the flared topsides. Another unusual feature was that after a capsize it could be righted in a moment and sailed on. The self-bailing cockpit was then a sensational innovation. Because of its built-in buoyancy compartments, the hull floats so high in the water that, even after capsizing, only very little water finds its way into the cockpit. Once the hull is righted, the water runs off by itself and the race can be continued without losing time with bailing.

*

THE CONTENDER CLASS: Now there were two successful, international two-man dinghy classes and the idea was put forward to find a modern, fast one-man dinghy by the same process. Once again the IYRU organized a series of one-of-a-kind races. In 1968 the third and last race in the series was held on the Ijsselmeer off Medemblik in Holland. Fourteen boats took part, all of them top of their class, and competition was exceptionally fierce. The final choice was the Australian-designed Contender, which was subsequently given international status.

Bob Miller of Sydney, the designer of the Contender, was both an experienced dinghy sailor and a sailmaker. Since then, his career as designer has been so spectacular that he has been appointed head of the design staff for the Australian America's Cup challenger.

Miller's original Contender, designed in 1967, was a hard-chine boat with very low freeboard. For the final eliminations in 1968 he built a new version with a slightly higher freeboard and rounded chine, and it was this new version that was the winning one. The unconventional design process is apparent from the lines drawing in Fig. 152.

Compared with all previous one-man classes the Contender differs by using a trapeze. Yet the hull in itself has good inherent stability and planes easily on the wind. Its rapid acceleration in the puffs is remarkable. The boat is cat-rigged, and the sail is characterized by the very pronounced roach on the leech. Sailing on a trapeze is very demanding on a one-man crew, for he has continuously to adjust the mainsheet, the tiller extension and his own body position all at the same time. Other boats in the design elimination were equipped with wooden sliding or folding seats. Meanwhile, the Contender is being built in fibreglass.

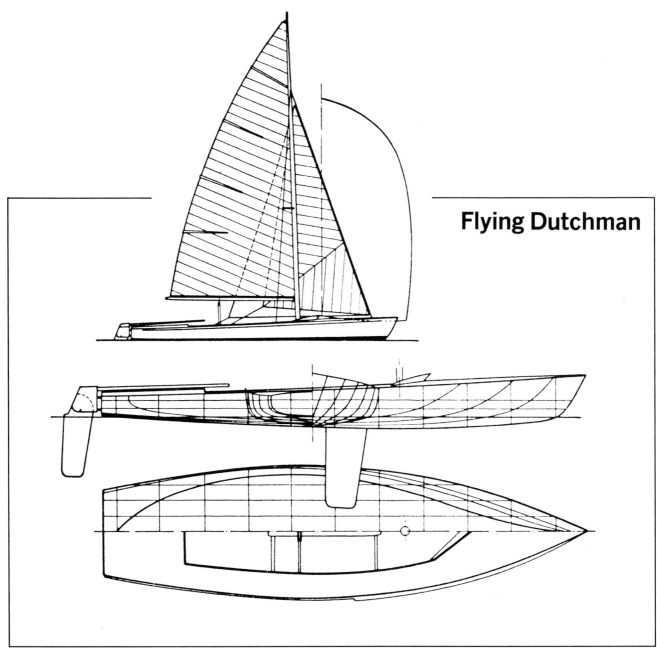

Fig. 150: The Flying Dutchman is a very fast and popular boat.

LOA	19 ft 10 in	Draft, plate down	3 ft 7 in
LWL	18 ft	Weight without	
Beam	5 ft 7 in	crew	352 lb
Draft, plate up	6 in	Sail area	161 sq ft

Flying Dutchman

THE O.K. DINGHY: This class illustrates that international single-handed dinghy racing is possible in much simpler boats. The class was formed with the aim of providing young sailors with a cheap yet high-performance boat, which would lead them onto the Finn class, which was then still in its heyday. The design was so successful, however, that the O.K. became an international class in its own right. Designed in 1957 by the Danish designer Knud Olsen, it became enormously popular in a very short time, not least because of its simple method of construction, which lent itself admirably to amateur building. In many countries the boat can be bought quite cheaply in kit-form, so that amateur completion is not a daunting undertaking.

One look at the rig immediately reveals its kinship

with the Finn. The mast is unstayed and can be bent simply by pulling on the mainsheet, and the boom is merely slotted into the mast without any fitting whatsoever. The watertight compartments on either side of the cockpit, which is quite small, keep the boat relatively dry during a capsize. Large fleets regularly assemble for racing in this class, and on a windy day one can see dozens of them capsize in the puffs, right themselves in a moment and sail on.

The full bending capacity of the mast is used only when sailing close-hauled in strong winds in order to flatten the sail. In light winds and on courses off the wind the mast is kept straight so that the sail can take up its full curvature.

THE MIRROR DINGHY: This is a decidedly unusual design which is, yet again, based on the advantages of amateur construction. It is, undoubtedly, this aspect which has made the Mirror Dinghy a very large class in the world, with numbers running into 50,000. The inspiration for the Mirror Dinghy came from the British national newspaper the *Daily Mirror*, who got together a group of experts, among them Barry Bucknell, of do-it-yourself fame, who thought up a novel way of 'welding' the seams of the hull, and Jack Holt, well-known designer of many British dinghy classes, who drew up the plans. The British magazine *Yachting World* undertook to popularize the boat in sailing circles and to organize the class association. The hull is built in $\frac{1}{4}$ in (6 mm) marine plywood and can be bought in kit form.

The seams in the hull are secured as follows: any two parts, say bottom and one side, have pairs of small holes drilled along their adjoining edges. A short piece of copper wire is then passed through each pair of holes and the ends twisted securely with pliers on the outside of the hull. Then a strip of fibreglass tape is glued with resin over the seam from the inside. When this has hardened, the twisted ends of the copper wire are snipped off and a similar fibreglass tape applied to the outside of the seam. The rest of the copper wire remains in the boat, well covered by glass and resin, but has no longer a function to fulfil. This method of construction has proved highly successful. To build a Mirror Dinghy, ready to sail, from a kit takes not much more than 100 working hours.

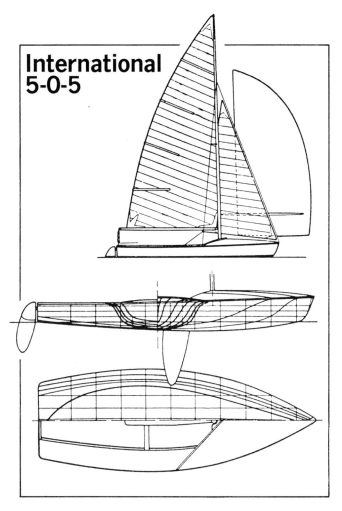

International 5-0-5

Fig. 151: The flared topsides of International 5-0-5 characterize the most up-to-date design feature in planing dinghy hulls.

LOA	16 ft 7 in	Draft, plate down .	3 ft 9 in
LWL	15 ft 3 in	Weight without	
Beam	6 ft 2 in	crew	308 lb
Draft, plate up ..	6 in	Sail area	150 sq ft

Of course, the Mirror Dinghy is not a high-performance racing machine, but it is quite a nippy little boat, which all children love and in which even adults can sail the occasional race. The gunter rig was chosen for practical purposes. The spars are relatively short and do not extend beyond the length of the hull when the boat is carried on the roof rack of a car, as is common practice.

Plate 42: The OK dinghy is simpler and cheaper than the Finn, but still possesses the same sailing qualities. See drawing, Fig. 153. Designed by a Dane, Knud Olsen, the OK is 13 ft 2 in long with a beam of 4 ft 8 in and quickly achieved worldwide importance. The mast can be bent by application of tension to the mainsheet enabling the sail to be flattened in stronger winds.
Photo: OK Dinghy International Association

Contender International Singlehander

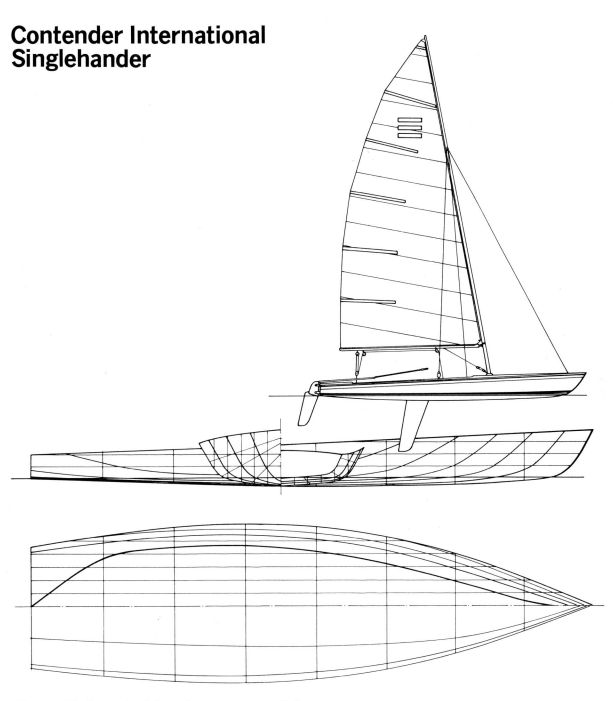

Fig. 152: The International Contender represents an entirely new concept in dinghy racing: a one-man boat with trapeze.

LOA	16 ft	Draft, plate down .	3 ft 4 in
LWL	14 ft 9 in	Weight without	
Beam	4 ft 8 in	crew	150 lb
Draft, plate up ..	3 in	Sail area	118 sq ft

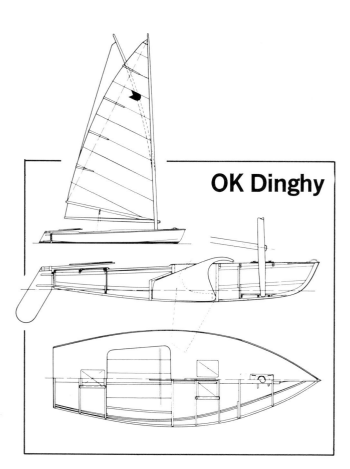

OK Dinghy

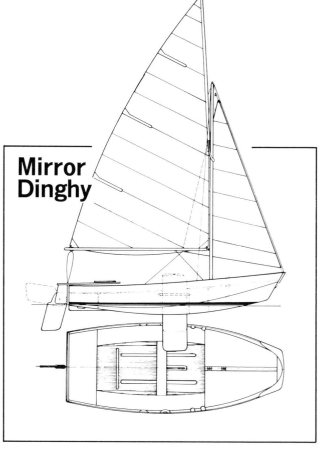

Mirror Dinghy

Fig. 153: The OK-Dinghy is basically a simple design, which also *lends* itself to amateur construction, but nevertheless retains all the characteristics of the Finn-Dinghy, on which it is modelled.

LOA	13 ft 2 in	Draft, plate up	6 in
LWL	12 ft 4 in	Draft, plate down	3 ft
Beam	4 ft 8 in	Sail area	89 sq ft

Fig. 154: The Mirror Dinghy was specially designed for amateur construction and is equally good for racing, family sailing or as a junior class.

LOA	10 ft 10 in	Draft, plate down	2 ft 3 in
LWL	9 ft 2 in	Weight without	
Beam	4 ft 7 in	crew	134 lb
Draft, plate up	5 in	Sail area	70 sq ft

THE LASER: The basic idea behind the Laser was to produce a fast one-man, one-design boat of the utmost simplicity yet with thoroughbred racing characteristics. To turn the idea into practice no less than three experts got together: Bruce Kirby designed the hull and sail plan, Ian Bruce the cockpit and deck layout, the rigging and the fittings, and Hans Fogh concentrated on the cut and production of the sail, which has a luff pocket for the mast.

The lines of the Laser in Fig. 155 reveal its striking similarity with the Contender. The small, narrow boat looks decidedly fast. The most important aspects, though, is the strict adherence to simplicity and uniformity. The prototype was first seen in 1971 in a one-of-a-kind race for low-priced planing dinghies. It attracted so much interest that it went into series production in a big way, with builders first in Canada and soon afterwards in England and the USA. Two years later there were already 10,000 boats in many countries, and it was not long before the well-organized class was given international status.

Success was not automatic, of course, because in practice things always work out differently to what they look like on paper. Thus, three different outlines of sail, all with the same area of 76 sq ft (7·07 m²) were experimented with. The original aluminium mast proved too soft and had to be made stronger, the optimum position being established by sailing trials in various winds. The spar is made in two parts to enable the whole boat to be carried on the roof rack of a medium-size car. There is no main halliard, since the sail slides over the mast. A Cunningham hole keeps the luff taut and, through being made fast on deck, prevents the mast from jumping out. The sail is loose-footed; a length of line serves as 'horse' for the mainsheet block. Simplicity everywhere. Nothing must be added to what is put on the boat by the builders.

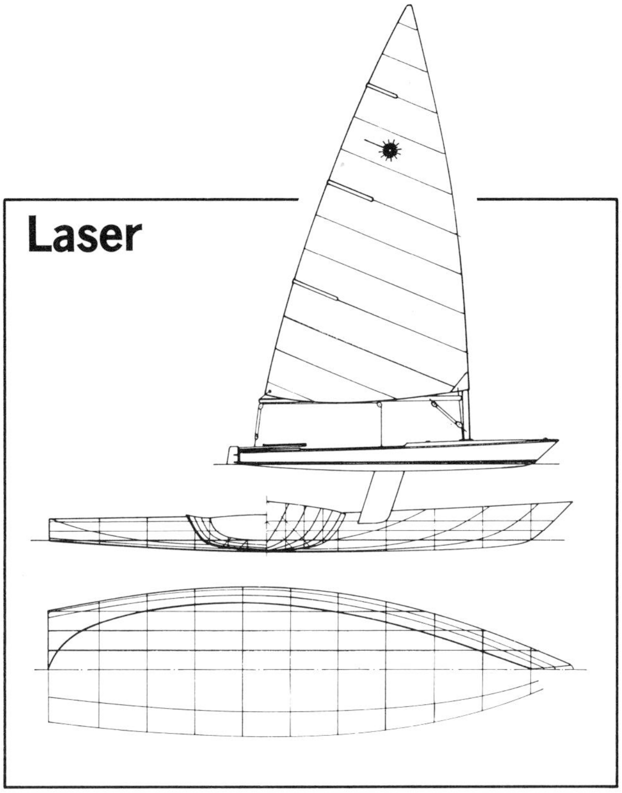

Fig. 155: The Laser quickly gained popularity because there was a widespread demand for a true one-design class. It is also a thoroughbred racing dinghy.

LOA	13 ft 10 in	Draft, plate down	2 ft 6 in
LWL	12 ft 6 in	Weight, equipped	125 lb
Beam	4 ft 6 in	Sail area	76 sq ft
Draft, plate up	4 in		

THE 420 AND 470: The 420 from France is a classic example of the suitability of fibreglass for the production of competitively priced one-design boats. The hull sections illustrated in Fig. 156 show quite clearly that construction in plastics was planned from the beginning and also that the advantages of moulding in plastic have been fully exploited.

The 420 was designed as early as 1958 by Christian Maury, and built on a large scale by Lanaverre at Bordeaux. It became so popular that it soon spread throughout the world and was given international status. Class rules are very strict to ensure uniformity. Equipped with spinnaker and trapeze, the boat has great appeal for the racing helmsman. It is particularly liked by young people and is, at present, one of the most popular junior classes in the world.

Some years later the French designer André Cornu designed a slightly bigger boat along the same principles, which was faster and therefore appealed even more to

Plate 43: You do not need a sailing club by the water here! A good many dinghies come on trailers from outlying districts. The same sailors probably meet up the following weekend at some other beach to compete in their Cherubs. This exciting dinghy is only 12 ft long with a beam of 5ft and has a sail area of 88 sq ft. Only the main dimensions of the hull are restricted and many of the boats are built by their owners. They are found mainly Zealand and Australia, but there are fleets in other countries.
Photo: John Felton

International 420

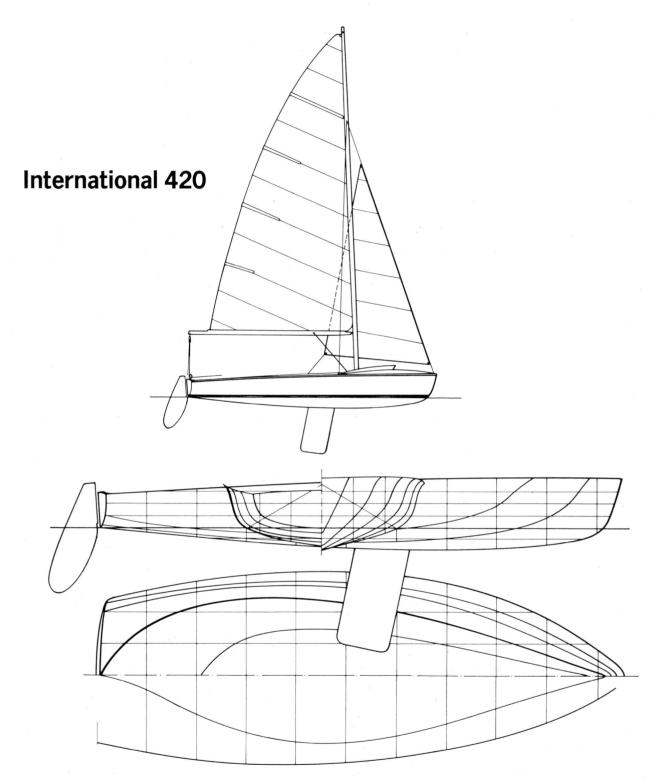

Fig. 156: Both the 420 and the 470 originated in France and are very similar in type and shape. Thus, the 420 shown here is representative of both.

	420	470
LOA	13 ft 9 in	15 ft 6 in
LWL	13 ft 2 in	14 ft 7 in
Beam	5 ft 4 in	5 ft 6 in
Draft, plate up	6 in	6 in
Draft, plate down	3 ft 2 in	3 ft 6 in
Weight, hull	176 lb	202 lb
Weight, fully equipped	215 lb	253 lb
Sail area	110 sq ft	137 sq ft

Korsar

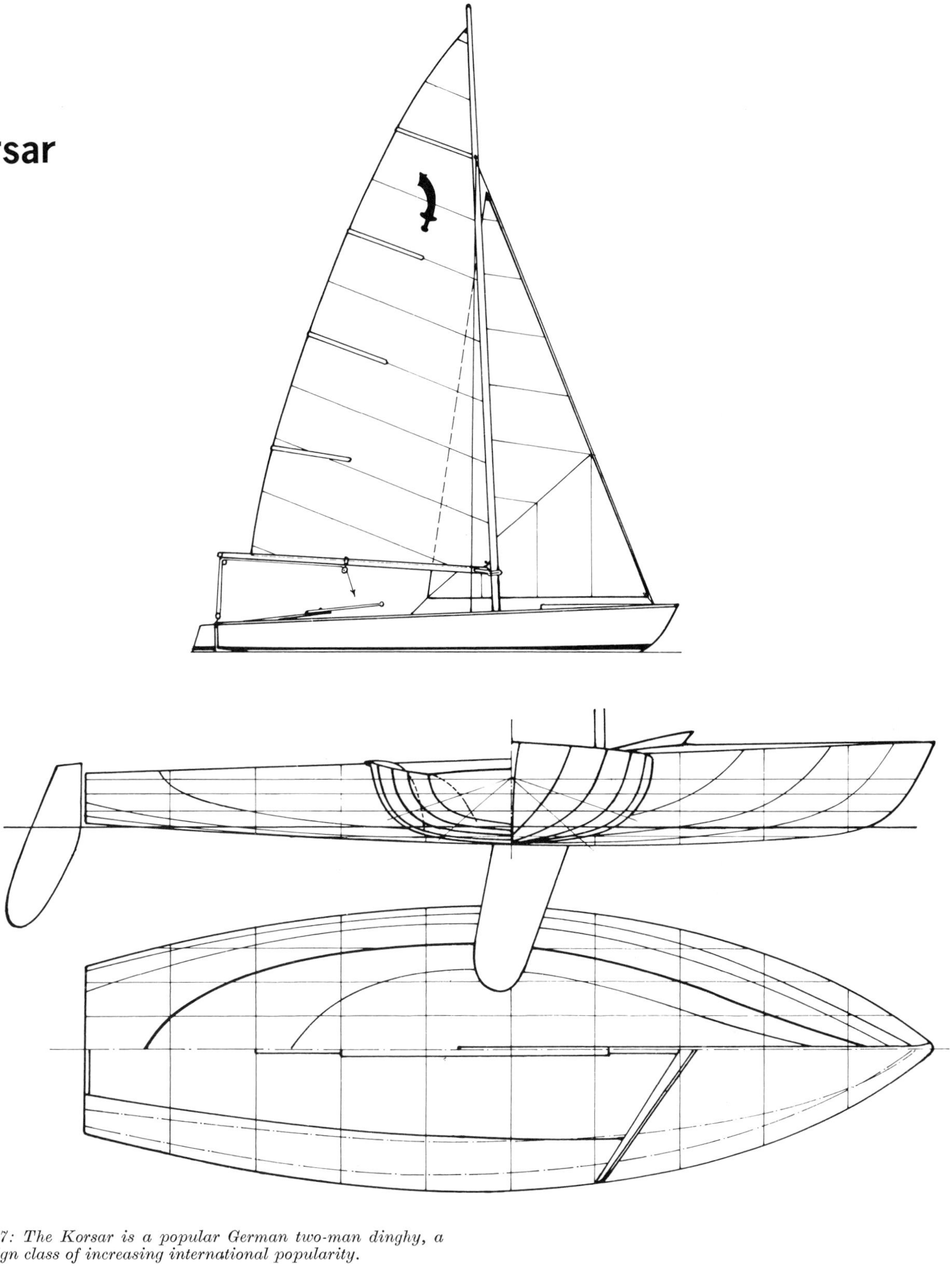

Fig. 157: The Korsar is a popular German two-man dinghy, a
one-design class of increasing international popularity.

LOA	16 ft 5 in	Draft, plate down .	3 ft 5 in
LWL	15 ft	Weight, hull	220 lb
Beam	5 ft 6 in	Weight, equipped .	275 lb
Draft, plate up ..	4 in	Sail area	158 sq ft

Plate 44: Close-up of a Laser. The dinghy is a cat or una rigged single-hander. The whole concept is aimed at uniformity, simplicity and good sailing qualities. In a very short space of time the Laser has achieved worldwide popularity. For plans see Fig. 155.

As you can see the mainsail is attached to the mast with a sleeve, thus doing away with a main halyard, and is only made fast at the tact by the Cunningham line.

Photo: Performance Sailcraft, Canada

racing owners. Called the 470, it soon became an international class and in 1976 was selected for the Olympics, in which there are now six types of boat. The class is increasing steadily; at present it numbers around 15,000 boats. Most of them are in France, but there are fleets in another 25 countries, notably Germany and Italy and also in Holland. The rules drawn up by the International 470-Association are very strict and forbid the slightest modification or improvement. In the important championship races only a single set of sails is allowed. The emphasis in competition is entirely on the skill of helmsman and crew. Figure 156 shows the 420, which the 470 resembles so closely that it is not illustrated separately.

THE KORSAR: This is a typical example of a classical, 'sound' German racing dinghy, very popular and often referred to as the small cousin to the Flying Dutchman. The Korsar has everything which might be expected of a dependable, conventional design without any extreme features: good stability, good speed, easy planing. The boat is equipped with spinnaker, spinnaker turtle, trapeze and mainsheet traveller. Originally built in moulded plywood, the Korsar is now also built in fibreglass.

The boat was designed by Ernst Lehfeld of Hamburg, the prototype being built in 1959; at the end of its trials it was given an enthusiastic reception by prominent dinghy sailors. Since then, its popularity has not waned and it now numbers around 4000 boats, being concentrated in Central Europe, mainly Germany, Austria and Switzerland. The class was made a national one-design in 1960, and since 1965 the German national youth championships are sailed in it. The design has proved not only successful but versatile, since it is lively and responsive as a racing boat but can be sailed with comfort and safety as a family boat.

The Korsar is the most popular boat in West Germany and as such has replaced the older Pirat. In order to discourage extremely light-weight construction, the minimum hull weight inclusive of all permanently attached fittings but exclusive of gear has been fixed at 100 kilos (220 lb). This forced some lighter boats to build in some ballast. Although the Korsar can just be carried on the roof of an average family car, it is better off on a trailer.

*

THE INTERNATIONAL MOTH: This unusual and imaginative class of lively little boats has been going now for over 40 years. The aim is exactly opposed to that of a strict one-design class, the principle being maximum freedom of hull shape and minimum restrictions. This makes the Moth the ideal boat for inventive do-it-yourself sailors, some of whom build a new boat every season. There are a large number of different standard plans, of which we are showing two. On the other hand, there are a number of one-design types even of this boat, one of them the Europe Moth, which gained popularity mainly in Germany and France.

There are very few restrictions in the class, the principal ones being: maximum length 3·355 m (11 ft), maximum beam 2·25 m (7·38 ft), sail area 8 m² (86·1 sq ft). Multihulls are not allowed, and hollow, concave bottom shapes are subject to certain restrictions. Weight and material of hull are entirely optional.

About 8000 of these very competitive one-man dinghies are at present sailing in about 20 countries. They are raced both in the international free class and, within narrower limits, in various restricted classes. The two plans in Figs. 158 and 159 are those of restricted classes which have been built in large numbers. The scow type was produced by the British designer Peter Milne and is sailed mainly in Australia, where it has proved its worth in the prevailing strong winds. The

Plate 45: The International 10 Square Metre Canoe with its narrow hull has a different kind of aid to stability. For details see Fig. 160. The helmsman of this 17 ft long dinghy, which has a beam of 3 ft 3 in, has to handle the mainsheet, jibsheets, tiller and centreplate and move in and out on the sliding seat Obviously, this is one of the most difficult boats to sail, but at the same time one of the fastest in the world. Photo: Redhead Studios

second plan is that of a more normal dinghy with a straight stem, and this was designed by the New Zealander Bruce Farr. Both types have proved fast in the wind conditions for which they were designed.

Using light plywood it is nowadays possible to build a Moth hull weighing little more than 20 kilos (44 lb), but 30 kilos (66 lb) is probably a normal average. In general, the boat with all gear, ready to sail, weighs 45 kilos (100 lb). The Moth has been recognized by the IYRU as a restricted high-performance class in Group A, and as such even fulfils the requirements for the Olympics.

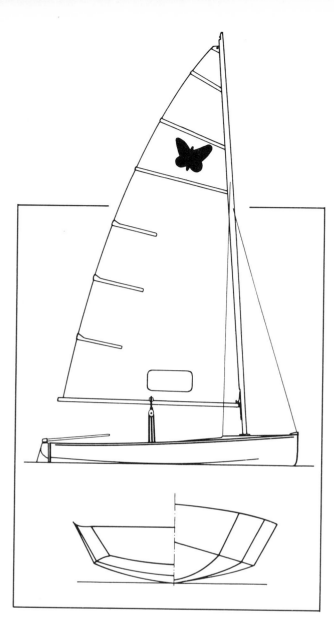

Fig. 158: International Moth: hard chine skiff design.
LOA .... 11 ft   Sail area .... 85 sq ft
Beam .... 4 ft 9 in   Weight, rigged ... 90 lb

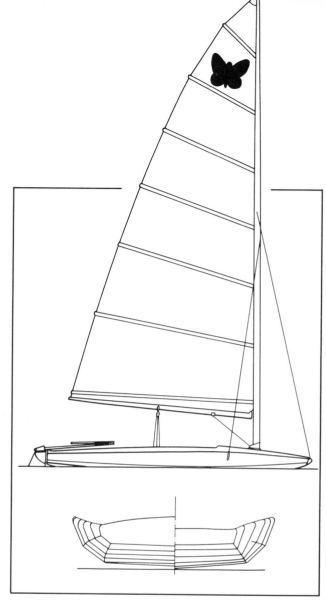

Fig. 159: International Moth, Scow design.
LOA .... 11 ft   Sail area .... 85 sq ft
Beam .... 4 ft   Weight, equipped . 80 lb

THE INTERNATIONAL 10 m² CANOE: Long before the introduction of the trapeze, sailing canoes had sliding seats. To give a typical example of this, if only for technical interest, we are including here the plans of the International 10 m² Canoe. Its story lies somewhat outside normal yachting history, but its qualities as a sailing craft and, above all, the speeds it is capable of, make it worthy of a short comment.

Most of these narrow boats are double-ended and round-bilged, although the class rules provide for a

hard-chine hull as an alternative. Its length of 17 ft (5·2 m) makes the boat look very narrow, although the beam is as much as 3·2 ft (1 m). The rig always consists of mainsail and jib. The most striking feature of the design is the long sliding seat, which can be extended as much as 5 ft on each side, measured from the gunwale. This amounts to a distance of over 13 ft between the extreme point on one side to that on the other. With that amount of beam it would not be difficult to cope with the 10 m² (107·6 sq ft) sail area, if the wind

Fig. 160: One of the first boats to use a sliding seat was the International 10 square metre canoe, which was for many years the world's fastest one-man dinghy.

LOA .... 17 ft
LWL .... 16 ft 10 in
Beam .... 3 ft 3 in
Draft, plate up .. 4 in

Draft, plate down . 3 ft 8 in
Weight, equipped . 209 lb
Sail area .... 108 sq ft

Fig. 161: The German Zugvogel class is built in two versions, dinghy and keelboat. Both are equally suited to racing or family sailing.

LOA .... 19 ft
LWL .... 17 ft 5 in
Beam .... 6 ft 2 in
Draft, hull ...... 6 in
Draft,
    centreboarder .. 3 ft 7 in
Draft, keelboat ... 2 ft 10 in

Weight,
    centreboarder .. 616 lb
Weight, keelboat .. 836 lb
Sail area,
    centreboarder .. 161 sq ft
Sail area,
    keelboat .... 183 sq ft

pressure were steady. Instead, the solo helmsman has to shift his position constantly and at the same time attend to the tiller and the sheets, a performance which calls for no less than acrobatics. The sliding seat is designed to jam as weight is put on it, but it slides freely when unloaded and can quickly be shifted to the other side. The very long, double-ended tiller extension is an interesting feature.

Since the helmsman only has two hands for everything, it is usual to jam the foresheets and work the boat with mainsail and sliding seat only. American followers of the class even belay the mainsheet and cope with differences in wind pressure by working the tiller and sliding seat. They swear they can make the boat point higher that way. The 10 m² Canoe is the fastest singlehanded sailing dinghy class in the world.

*

THE ZUGVOGEL: This mainly Central European class is unique in that it is, to our knowledge, the only class which allows a free choice between a centreboard and a keelboat version. The Zugvogel, meaning 'bird of passage', was produced in 1960 by the well-known German designer of plywood boats, Ernst Lehfeld. Initially built in plywood, it soon became so popular that a fibreglass version was introduced. The boat was originally planned as a family day-sailer, but soon there were racing fleets, and this has greatly helped in keeping the class up to date. The excessively massive and stiff wooden mast was replaced by a bendy alloy spar, which allows the curvature of the mainsail to be adjusted to the wind conditions. This works so well that most keel-version boats sail un-reefed in heavy winds.

The difference between the centreboard and the keel version is basically very small. The ballast keel is suspended in a case which is similar to the centreboard trunk but lower. The keel consists of a steel plate with a lead cigar weighing 80 kilos (176 lb) along the bottom, the total keel weight being around 100 kilos (220 lb). For road transport, the keel can be detached without too much trouble with the help of a simple tripod wedge, which is also used to alter the longitudinal angle of the keel when sailing. The cockpit is very roomy in both versions but looks even bigger in the keel version, because of the absence of a high centreboard case. The hull without keel is fairly heavy, weighing 200 kilos (440 lb), but this allows a very solid construction and long life. The following comparison shows how the greater weight of the keel version is compensated by a larger sail area:

Centreboard Zugvogel:
    Sail area .... 15 m² (161 sq ft)
    Weight ready to sail .... 280 kilos (616 lb)
Keel Zugvogel:
    Sail area .... 17 m² (183 sq ft)
    Weight ready to sail .... 380 kilos (836 lb)

This compensation has been so successful that, in fact, both versions perform equally well and are equally suitable for either racing or day sailing. The class, at present, numbers approximately 3000, of which half are centreboard boats and half keelboats. Most of them are found in Germany, but there are sizeable fleets in Austria, Switzerland, Holland, Italy and Chile.

Plate 46: The few measurement rules of the International Moth Class allow plenty of room for imagination. Chelsea Morning is a type built by the Moth specialist J G Claridge, Lymington and has been successful in many races. It was designed a deep-V forward and a flatter run aft by Mervin Cook. A remarkable feature is the extended side deck 'wings' built into the hull to allow the helmsman to sit out further.
Photo: Claridge

Keelboat Racing Classes

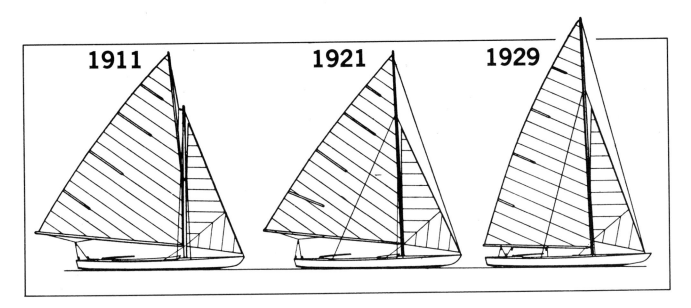

Fig. 162: The development of the Star rig since its inception in 1911. The current version is that of 1929, which has a very large sail area for the size and stability of the hull.

Developments in the fast keelboat field have been spectacular since 1960. This is best illustrated by a sentence from the first edition of this book, which said that 'no keelboat has yet been designed which is capable of planing'. Since then, light construction and aerodynamic improvements in hull shape and rig have resulted in a much less conventional concept: the light keelboat, which planes even in moderate winds.

Since a keelboat is, on the whole, a more costly acquisition than a dinghy, the tendency to experiment is kept within limits. Keelboat sailing is no less thrilling than dinghy sailing, and racing can be every bit as exciting, even though the risk of capsizing is absent and keelboats are not quite as lively as dinghies. The most important trophies on the yacht racing scene, among them the venerable yet always topical America's Cup and the coveted One Ton Cup, are competed for by keel yachts.

'Racing Classes' in this context, as compared to 'Cruiser Classes', means thoroughbred racing machines, some of which have no accommodation whatever. The fact that equally fierce races can be sailed in cruiser classes has been adequately illustrated in recent years. However, in this chapter we will deal with the open keelboats, starting with two illustrious veterans, the Star and the Dragon.

THE STAR: The Star was designed in 1911, or rather it was developed from its smaller predecessor, the Bug, designed in 1907. Her designer, William Gardner, had concentrated chiefly on large sailing yachts, among them the 187 ft (57 m) long ATLANTIC, who still holds the Transatlantic record. When he decided to lengthen the Bug by 5 ft (1·5 m) and called it Star, it caught on immediately, growing to a fleet of 22 in the first year. Its good design and attractive dimensions, the general need for a one-design keelboat and the fact that many experienced helmsmen were drawn to it, led to a steady rise in numbers and a reputation for the most passionately fought world championships.

If one looks at the simple lines of the hull it is difficult to understand why this class inspires yachtsmen to such fierce competition. One Star sailor recently called it 'a wonderful, exciting and terrifying box'. It has become known as a class in which there is constant hot rivalry for clever and intricate improvements within the tolerances, to a degree where there have been virtual 'designs' within the one-design, without, of course, violating the class rules. The Star has been the longest-running Olympic class, from 1932 to 1972.

The most successful world-class Star sailor, the Italian naval officer Augusto Straulino, sailed a boat built by Lippincot in the USA to win the 1956 European

213

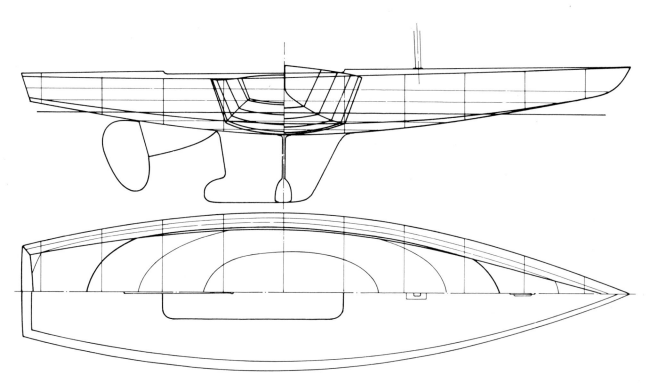

Fig. 163: The lines of a Star reveal its simplicity of shape. The drawing also shows the bulb keel and the rudder which is hung on a small skeg.

LOA	22 ft 7 in	Weight without
LWL	15 ft 6 in	crew .... 1654 lb
Beam	5 ft 8 in	Weight, ballast ... 880 lb
Draft	3 ft 6 in	Sail area .... 280 sq ft

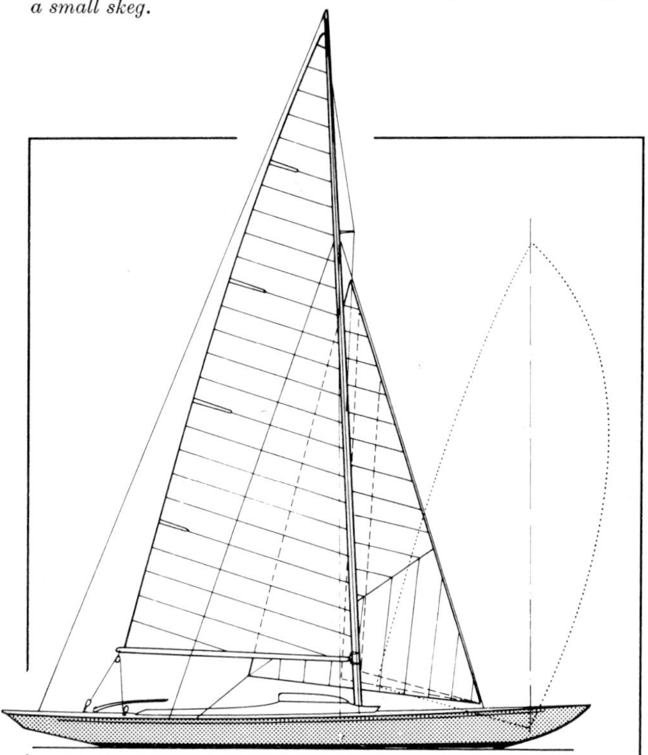

Championship in a fleet of 46 competitors from many countries. Immediately afterwards he shifted his proven rig onto an Etchell hull, also built in the States, and a week later won the World Championship against 60 competitors. The Russian Star crew, who won the Olympic Gold Medal at Naples in 1960, did not bring their own boat from Russia, as one might expect, but used an American boat with American sails, another 'design within the tolerances'.

The Star uses neither spinnaker nor genoa, but the 280 sq ft (26 m²) sail area keeps the two-man crew busy, especially since, in the interest of speed and balance, it is customary to lie along the weather rail, which complicates tiller and sheet handling.

*

Fig. 164: Sail plan of a Dragon. The dotted line indicates the spinnaker adopted in 1959 (half area).

LOA	29 ft 2 in	Weight without
LWL	19 ft 8 in	crew .... 3792 lb
Beam	6 ft 5 in	Weight, ballast ... 2205 lb
Draft	3 ft 11 in	Sail area .... 286 sq ft

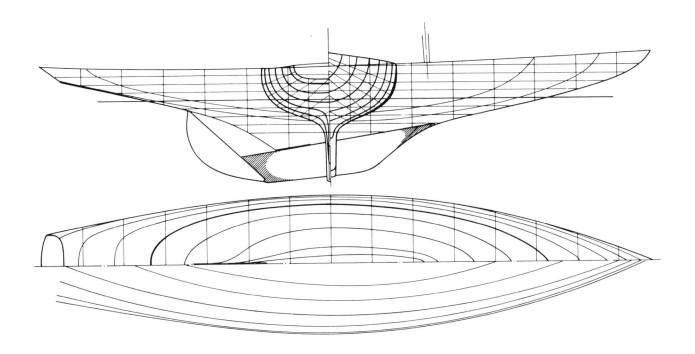

Fig. 165: Lines of a Dragon. Like the lines of the Swedish Skerry Cruiser, from which they were developed, they are characterized by harmony and simplicity.

The Swedish Skerry Cruiser class occupies a special position among keel racing yachts. These long, narrow boats are extraordinarily efficient and with a relatively small sail area reach amazing speeds in average winds; they are also very close-winded. These thoroughbreds with their high rigs and short booms still appeal by their pure, functional beauty. They were most popular between 1920 and 1930, but are still active now as a veteran class and have recently been given a new lease of life when the 30 m² class was made one-design in fibreglass.

*

THE DRAGON: Because the cost of building Skerry Cruisers was very high, a design competition was organized in 1927 with the aim of finding a simplified one-design class. The competition was won by the Norwegian Johann Anker, and the result was the Dragon class. Its international popularity increased steadily, and in 1948 it was first entered as an Olympic class, with 12 countries fighting for the laurel.

Originally, the Dragon was designed for cruising as well as racing. It had a proper cabin with two berths, hanging locker and small galley. Very soon, though, this accommodation was sacrificed to the improvement of racing performance. Only a short cuddy remains with no bulkhead separating the cabin from the cockpit, the accommodation being completely bare and used only for sail stowage.

The position of the mast was originally fixed in the plans and was retained for many years until, almost by chance, it was discovered that performance was noticeably improved by shifting the mast 10 in (25 cm) further forward. Today, Dragons have their masts stepped between 8 and 12 in (20–30 cm) forward of the position indicated in Anker's original plans. The same thing has happened to many other classes and individual yachts.

Dragons have such good stability that the mainsail

Tempest

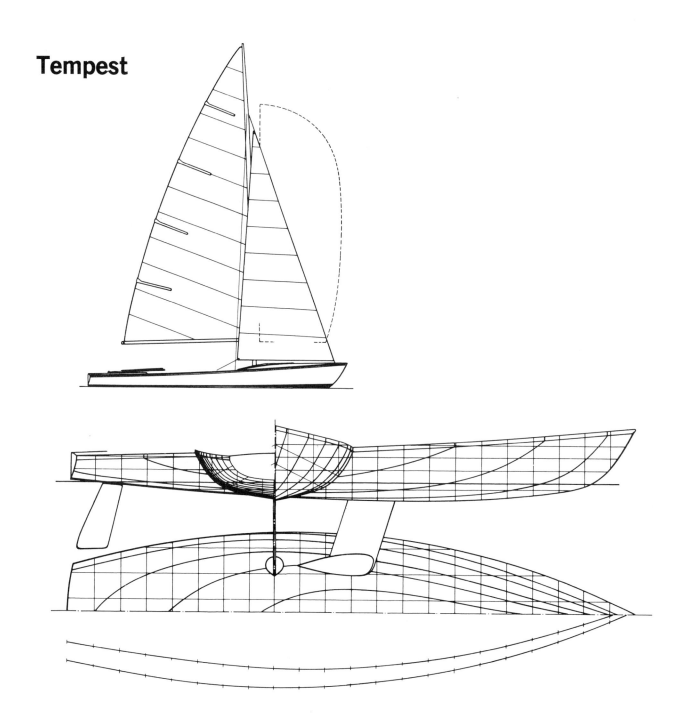

Fig. 166: The International Tempest two-man keelboat is really no more than a dinghy with a ballast keel. It was designed to replace the Star, which it equals approximately in speed.

LOA . . . . 22 ft
LWL . . . . 20 ft 4 in
Beam . . . . 6 ft 6 in
Draft, inc. keel . . . 3 ft 7 in

Weight, equipped . 1034 lb
Ballast weight . . . 495 lb
Sail area . . . . 248 sq ft

216

is never reefed in races. The large genoa can be set even in strong winds, and the working jib is only used for cruising. Many Dragons have done extensive cruising in open waters, which underlines their good seagoing qualities. It must never be forgotten, though, that like the Star the Dragon can fill up and sink if it heels excessively. Meanwhile, both the Star and the Dragon have been replaced as Olympic classes by smaller, more modern boats, i.e. the Tempest and Soling respectively.

*

THE TEMPEST: As can be seen from the lines in Fig. 166, the Tempest represents a completely new concept of keelboat. Its light-weight, dinghy-shaped hull combined with a modest amount of ballast at the end of a narrow fin make it a very up-to-date boat.

In 1963 efforts got under way to incorporate a modern, two-man keelboat in the IYRU class system, which culminated in elimination races at Medemblik, Holland, in May 1965. They were convincingly won by the Tempest designed by Ian Proctor. It won eight out of nine races in the series and only lost the ninth due to rudder damage. To establish its undisputed superiority, IYRU officials laid on another trial race in which the Tempest alone had to carry 40 kilos (97 lb) additional ballast in the shape of two sacks of sand. But even with this handicap she won by a convincing lead.

The Tempest was probably the first true planing keelboat. It is fast enough to beat an FD in the right wind conditions, and it is sailed like a dinghy, with the crew in a trapeze. On the occasion of one important championship a Tempest (a keelboat!) was sent per air freight via the polar route! Not surprisingly, it was chosen as successor to the Star to become the two-man Olympic class in 1972 and 1976.

The Tempest is by no means easy to sail because, for a keelboat, it is exceptionally lively. It is strictly one-design, which means that all existing fibreglass moulds, anywhere in the world, have originated from one and the same prototype; this gives a good guarantee for uniformity among hulls. The actual prototype, which won the elimination series, was made of cold-moulded laminated plywood. The keel fin with ballast cigar sits in a kind of centreboard case, and its position must not be altered during racing. When the boat is to be taken ashore or transported on a trailer the keel is easily detached. The rig is simple and the alloy mast sufficiently bendable to adjust the mainsail to the prevailing wind strength.

*

THREE-MAN KEELBOAT SOLING: The IYRU search for a modern three-man keelboat started in 1964 with an international design competition, from which emerged three relatively large keelboats of around 30 ft (9 m) length. Following that, elimination trials between actual boats were held at Kiel in September 1966. At the end of 11 races, two boats were recommended for the final choice; the Shillalah, which was the fastest, and a smaller, less expensive boat with very impressive characteristics, the Soling. In November 1967 the Soling was finally selected to become the new international three-man keelboat class.

By contrast with the other entrants in these trials, the Soling had not been specially designed and built for the occasion, but had already been around for some time and proved successful. Designed by the Norwegian Jan H Linge, the Soling is a sound, uncomplicated boat with excellent sailing qualities. Compared with the majority of entries it was about 1 ft 8 in (50 cm) shorter in the waterline, 3 ft 3 in (1 m) shorter overall and carried 7 per cent less sail area, yet it was only a fraction slower than the fastest of the larger boats. The Soling was obviously a wise choice, which has meanwhile been vindicated by its widespread success and popularity. There have been European Championships in the class since 1968, and in November of the same year it was chosen as the three-man keelboat for the 1972 Olympic Games. Since 1969 there have been North American Championships and World Championships.

The uniformity of boats is ensured by precise construction and measurement rules. Yards may only build from officially authorized moulds, and every hull has to undergo a control during which it is checked with a template; in addition, the centres of gravity of hull and keel are established with great accuracy. Uniformity of all sails, i.e. two mainsails, two foresails, two large spinnakers and two small spinnakers, is equally controlled.

The Soling has proved a fast, lively, easily handled and surprisingly seaworthy boat. On a reach it will easily surf and even plane in stronger winds.

Soling

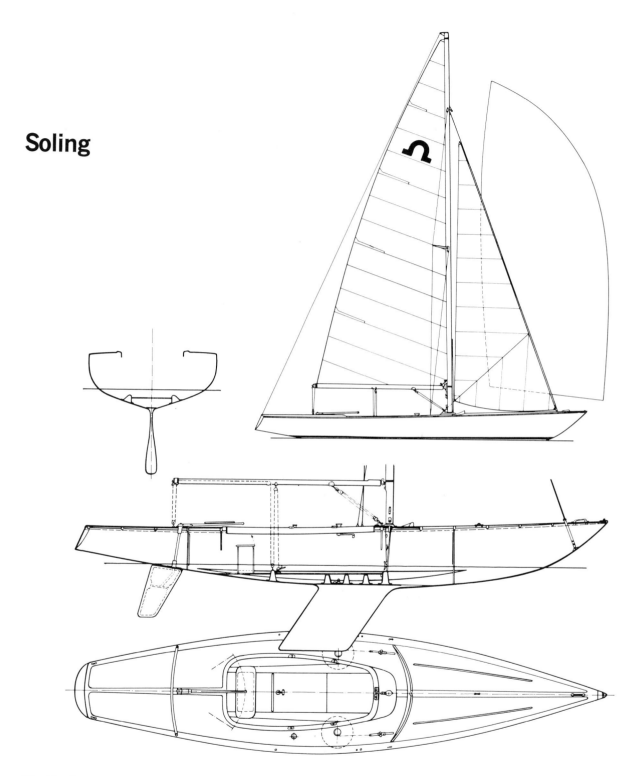

Fig. 167: The International Soling three-man keelboat has proved a particularly lucky choice and has quickly gained widespread popularity.

LOA	26 ft 9 in	Keel weight	1276 lb
LWL	20 ft	Ballast ratio	56%
Beam	6 ft 3 in	Minimum weight,	
Draft, hull	1 ft	hull	825 lb
Draft, keel	4 ft 3 in	Sail area	234 sq ft
Displacement ...	2277 lb		

International Formula Classes

The international keelboat classes described in the previous chapter, i.e. the Dragon, Star, Soling and Tempest, are typical one-design classes. Success in racing such classes depends, at least theoretically, entirely on the skill of the crew. However, within the wide spectrum of yacht racing, and especially in international racing, there is frequently a desire to put design and construction to the test. To offer scope in this direction the so-called Formula classes have been fostered for many years. Dimensions and hull shape of yachts of these classes are optional as long as they satisfy the rating of their particular class.

The International Yacht Racing Union introduced a class system as early as 1906, in which boats of different sizes were covered by an international measurement rule. But only after 1920, when certain factors were altered and a number of limits introduced, did the International Formula classes really start to blossom out.

Three classes in particular made an impact on international yacht racing: the 6-metre, 8-metre and 12-metre classes. These yachts which, in their latter days, had no accommodation whatever, were both expensive to build and to equip. Also, their displacement was considered excessive, especially with the advent of light construction methods. Besides, each new yacht carried with it the speculative risk of its design. It is not surprising, therefore, that in 1949 a new, smaller class was started, the 5·5-metre, for which a completely new formula was drawn up. It has survived the longest within these Formula Classes. The 6-metre has recently experienced a revival, whereas the 8-metre has long ceased to exist. The 12-metre, of course, has been the America's Cup class since 1958.

In the United States of America a different rating rule, the so-called Universal Rule, was introduced quite independently. This covered a number of classes, some of which achieved considerable importance. The only one to become internationally important was the very large J-class, with boats exceeding an overall length of 130 ft (40 m). These enormous racing machines fought for the America's Cup in 1930, 1934 and 1937. They had a rating of 76 ft and under the Second International Rule would have rated 23 metres. The most famous among these yachts built specially for the America's Cup Series were the British challengers SHAMROCK V, ENDEAVOUR I and ENDEAVOUR II, and the

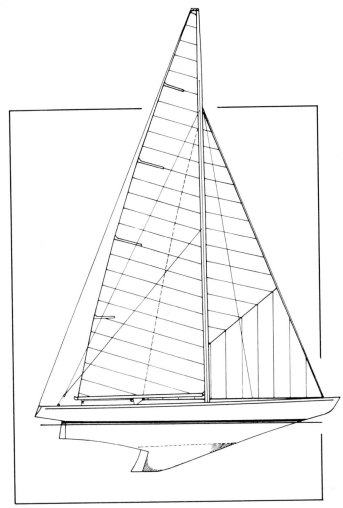

Fig. 168: INTREPID, *twice America's Cup defender. The original design by Olin Stephens won the 1967 series, the modified version by Britton Chance, which is shown here, won the 1970 series.*

LOA	64 ft	Displacement	59,850 lb
LWL	48 ft 9 in	Ballast weight	43,550 lb
Beam	12 ft	Ballast ratio	72%
Draft	9 ft	Sail area	1850 sq ft

victorious American defenders ENTERPRISE, RAINBOW and RANGER.

Ever since there have been rating rules there have been attempts to 'cheat' them, or find loopholes in order to gain an advantage. But very seldom, perhaps never, has an extreme, undesirable design gained notable success by exploiting loopholes. On the contrary, most attempts have been costly and disappointing. In 1958, four new America's Cup defenders were built, but none of them proved significantly superior to a fifth yacht, which was 20 years old. There was practically no difference between the pre-war VIM

219

and the new 12-metre COLUMBIA, which was finally selected. Only one of the four had a slightly unusual shape, and it was precisely this one which proved inferior to all the others. Both VIM and COLUMBIA had what might be called the ideal shape encouraged by the formula, free from any extremes. Both combined speed with excellent windward qualities and impeccable seakindliness.

All yachts built to the International Formulas are designed for racing. Their specifications contain practically nothing which would be necessary or desirable for cruising. However, when such a yacht has finished her racing career, it can be converted very satisfactorily into a cruiser with the necessary accommodation.

The table below was drawn up using the dimensions of representative yachts in each of the different classes. Naturally, since dimensions are not fixed they vary from yacht to yacht within one class. The modern tendency is for rather shorter lengths, mainly to save weight, but the table gives a good idea of the dimensions of the classical formula classes.

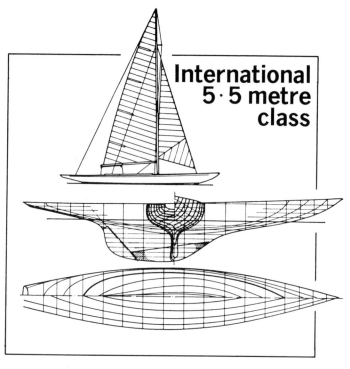

International 5·5 metre class

Fig. 169: The smallest of the IYRU classes still in use distinguishes itself by its exceptional simplicity. Originally, it did not even have a spinnaker, but one was later introduced.

APPROXIMATE DIMENSIONS OF YACHTS OF INTERNATIONAL FORMULA CLASSES

	5·5-metre	6-metre	8-metre	12-metre	J-class
LOA	9·80 m	11·25 m	14·75 m	21·00 m	41·30 m
LWL	6·60 m	6·85 m	9·15 m	13·75 m	26·50 m
Beam	1·90 m	1·98 m	2·65 m	3·65 m	6·55 m
Draught	1·34 m	1·60 m	1·95 m	2·72 m	4·58 m
Displacement	1·85 t	3·50 t	8·10 t	26·00 t	160·00 t
Weight of ballast	1·15 t	2·45 t	4·80 t	16·20 t	98·00 t
Sail area	28·00 m²	43·00 m²	74·00 m²	180·00 m²	702·00 m²
Crew	3	5	6	11	24

Ocean Racers Built to IOR

The object of the introduction of the International Offshore Rule was to formulate a handicap system common to those countries which followed the RORC Rule and those which used the CCA formulae. As such, one of its aims is to produce boats which are seaworthy and not extremes. But the rulemakers can never shut all loopholes and, in this case, they failed to predict the advent of the light displacement planing offshore hull. This has led to some hasty legislation in an attempt to outlaw these boats, but they offer exciting and fast rides, so they are here to stay; not everybody wants a heavy boat, with plenty of freeboard and a long deep keel. Experience shows that public demand usually has its way in the end, and the planing Half- and Quarter-Tonners will flourish, inside or outside the rule.

Nevertheless, a certain uniform tendency is recognizable in design to the IOR. If one compares the plans illustrated in this chapter with those of the International 8-metre designed to the 1950 IYRU Formula, one notices a recurring tendency towards strictly functional design. While at one time long overhangs provided the necessary anchorage points for wide, low sail plans, modern racing yachts have high-aspect ratio sail plans to go with today's short overhangs, which furthermore save weight.

One feature which is immediately apparent from the plans of all IOR yachts illustrated here is the ample beam concentrated in the mid-section. The fore section is slim and pointed to promote speed, especially on the wind. The price for higher speed is, of course, a wetter boat. The beam is equally reduced aft, so that the vessel sails on her 'mid-section bulge' so to speak. The transom is frequently inclined forwards, purely in the interest of weight reduction. The most striking difference, however, we find in the keel profile. Long keels with attached rudder have completely disappeared in ocean racers. The keel fin is as narrow and as low as possible and the ballast at the end streamlined for efficiency. Rudders have moved far aft near the stern or are even hung, dinghy-fashion, on the transom. In most designs there is a skeg, which covers most of the leading edge of the rudder. Helmsmen were quickly convinced of the advantages of this arrangement, and even in pure cruising boats there is now a tendency to move the rudder near the transom.

The division of IOR rated yachts into eight classes does not in any way impose narrow limitations. The handicap principle, whether for older, existing boats or new designs, is intended to give everyone an equal chance of winning. It involves a system of time allowance, to which we will get back later. The principle is that ocean racers of all sizes can race together, the winner being the one that wins on *corrected time*, not on elapsed time. In the case of ton-yachts, for example, a quarter-tonner, a half-tonner, a one-tonner and a two-tonner can sail a race together and each, on corrected time, has the same chances of winning. This is particularly important in Class I, which comprises boats with ratings varying between 33 to 70 ft (10·05–21·34 m). In the smaller classes the ton-yachts have a noticeably large number of adherents because, within one and the same ton-class, all boats have the same rating so that no time allowance needs to be applied. This means that they can race boat for boat, the winner being the one who finishes first. After this short introduction we will take a look at some typical IOR yachts.

In 1973 Class VIII was added to the IOR classification, which covers ocean racers considerably smaller than the quarter-tonner, and the Mini Tonner, which has the minimum IOR rating of 16 ft (4·9 m) had its first world championship in 1976. However the class is still in its formative stages, so we pass on to the well-established quarter-tonner.

The *quarter-tonner* is particularly well suited for illustrating the generous scope for variety offered by the IOR rating system. The quarter-tonner North Star 500 shown in Fig. 171, which in Europe goes under the name of Blue Bird 25, probably has the maximum dimensions possible in this class. The overall lengths vary between 21·6 ft and 25 ft (6·6 m and 7·6 m) and the beams between 6·9 ft and 9 ft (2·1 m and 2·75 m). Many of these boats have centreboards or drop-keels, which may give them a draft of less than 1·5 ft (45 cm), whereas true keel versions have a draft that varies between 3·6 ft and 5 ft (1·1 m and 1·5 m). The displacements range from 0·8 to 2 tons, the ballast ratio from 30 to 50 per cent and the sail areas from 215 sq ft to 290 sq ft (20 m² to 27 m²). There is, so far, no printed definition of working sail area, but it might best be formulated as 'true mainsail area plus 100 per cent foretriangle'.

The sail plan of the North Star 500 shows how many different headsails can be set within the foretriangle,

Ranger
One Tonner

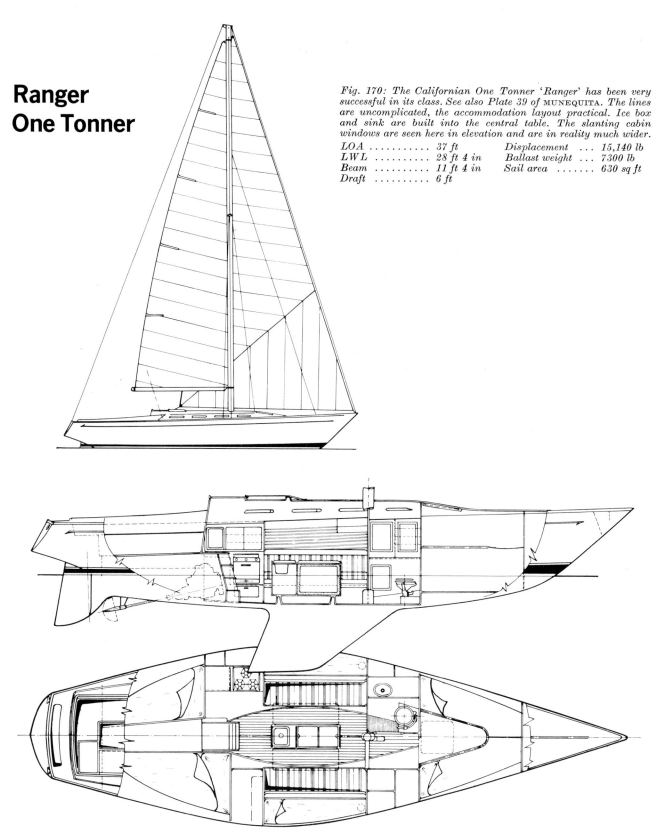

Fig. 170: The Californian One Tonner 'Ranger' has been very successful in its class. See also Plate 39 of MUNEQUITA. The lines are uncomplicated, the accommodation layout practical. Ice box and sink are built into the central table. The slanting cabin windows are seen here in elevation and are in reality much wider.

LOA	37 ft	Displacement	15,140 lb
LWL	28 ft 4 in	Ballast weight	7300 lb
Beam	11 ft 4 in	Sail area	630 sq ft
Draft	6 ft		

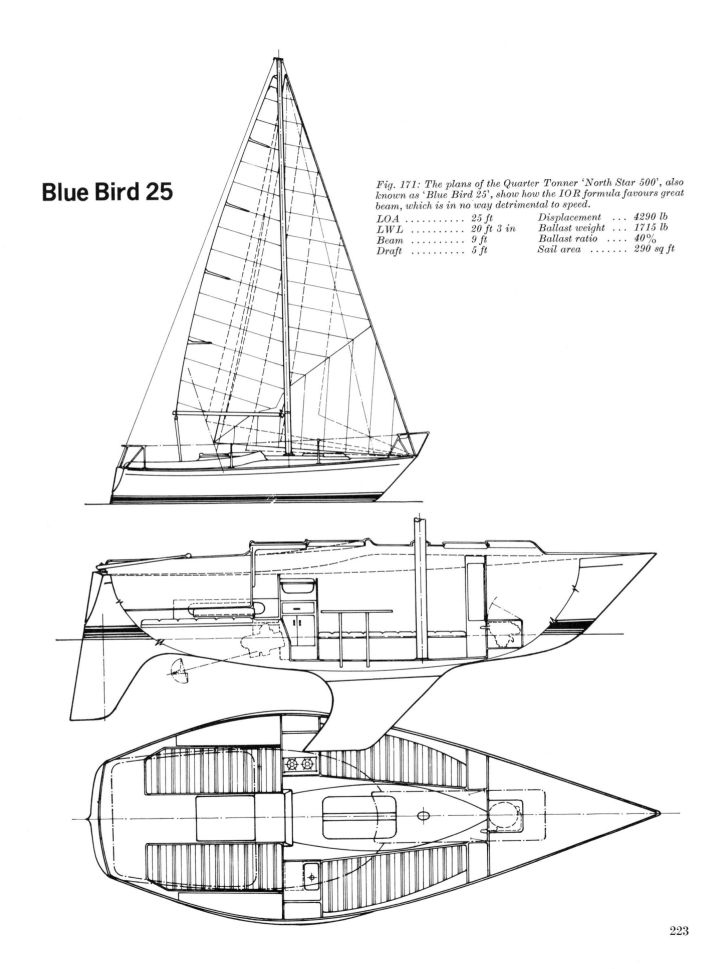

Blue Bird 25

Fig. 171: The plans of the Quarter Tonner 'North Star 500', also known as 'Blue Bird 25', show how the IOR formula favours great beam, which is in no way detrimental to speed.

LOA	25 ft	Displacement ...	4290 lb
LWL	20 ft 3 in	Ballast weight ...	1715 lb
Beam	9 ft	Ballast ratio	40%
Draft	5 ft	Sail area	290 sq ft

Scampi 30

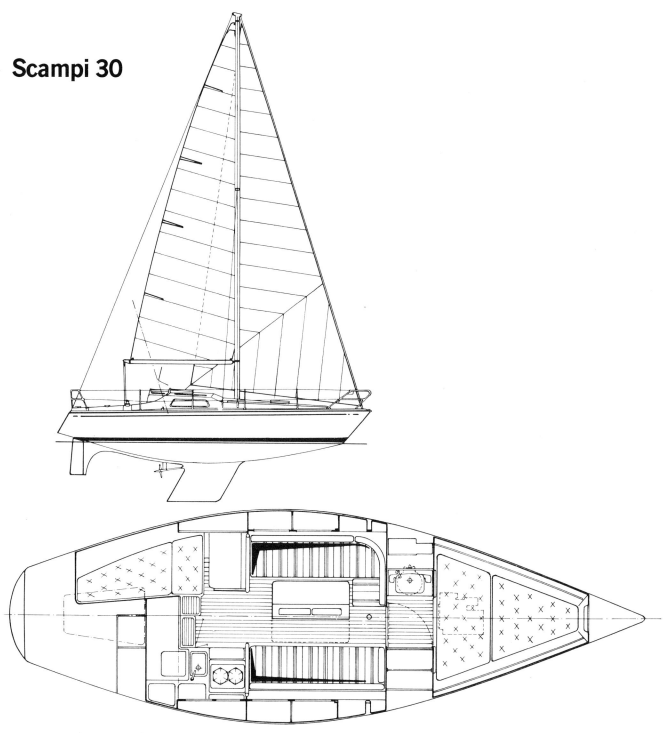

Fig. 172: The 'Scampi 30' is a successful and well-tried Half
Tonner. She is a fast boat with an attractive accommodation layout.

LOA	29 ft 9 in	Displacement	6600 lb
LWL	23 ft	Ballast weight	2530 lb
Beam	9 ft 11 in	Ballast ratio	38%
Draft	5 ft 2 in	Sail area	388 sq ft

though the spinnaker had been omitted. A spinnaker slotsail (tallboy) is indicated, set on a separate stay slightly aft of the forestay. The boat has a flush deck and an accommodation amounting to four berths, galley and heads; there is an auxiliary motor. The mast is stepped on the keel, whose profile illustrates the narrow, deep keel, the unusually large skeg and equally large rudder; their obvious function is to provide the yacht with stability on course when sailing before the wind.

The *half-tonner* is probably the most popular class of medium-size ocean racer at the moment. The rating of 21·7 ft (6·6 m) allows for quite a roomy ship, which makes it a popular choice even for cruising men. One successful, series-built half-tonner, which was illustrated in Fig. 143, is the Arpège designed by Michel Dufour. Although still designed under the RORC rule, when it was built in large numbers and won many races, it has maintained a good position under the new IOR rating.

The perspective lines drawing shows clearly the shape of the fin keel with its ballast bulb. The skeg and rudder are narrow and keep while the lines are sweet and flowing and make for a fast boat. Stability is provided by the ample beam in conjunction with the low ballast. The list of successes of boats of this type, particularly in European waters, is impressive.

Equally successful in Europe, but also very popular on the other side of the Atlantic, is the Scampi 30, designed by the Swedish designer Peter Norlin. The plan shown in Fig. 172 is that of the latest version. Compared with the Arpège, the Scampi is somewhat lighter but only a little smaller. She is different in many respects, be it the underwater profile, the shape of the superstructure, the sail plan or the accommodation. But basically the two boats are similar, and might be said to represent the quintessence of what is typical in today's half-tonner.

One unusual feature about the Scampi is the auxiliary motor, which is installed not aft but far forward in the forepeak, near the heads. There is sufficient room at that point for a small 12 hp diesel to be installed without affecting the weight distribution adversely. This arrangement makes for a more spacious cabin, especially more room in the galley.

Much thought has gone into the accommodation. The galley, near the companionway, is generously laid out and must be a sheer pleasure to the cook. To port there is a roomy chart table with stowage for navigation instruments.

Scampi has chalked up a remarkable list of successes: she won the half-ton world championships three times, in 1969, 1970 and 1971. In 1972 she won the North American half-ton championship, quite apart from many other races in Europe and America. To add to her virtues, she is a good family cruising boat and as such epitomizes the basic aim of the IOR formula, which is to encourage the design of sound, fast offshore yachts.

Compared with the Arpège and the Scampi, TITUS CANBY, another half-ton yacht illustrated in Fig. 144, is shortest overall, has the longest waterline length, the narrowest beam, the least weight and the smallest sail area. Which illustrates once again the great scope for variety which the IOR formula offers.

This brings us to the one-ton class, which is the one that initiated the whole ton-system in the first place. It is, therefore, not surprising that for many years now the most important races have been competed for in this class and that the famous One Ton Cup represents the *ne plus ultra* in ocean racing. We meet here the ideas of the world's top yacht designers, among them Olin Stephens and Dick Carter, whose rivalry has been watched with great interest for many years.

We have chosen an outstandingly successful one-tonner to represent the class, the American yacht LIGHTNING. As we study the plan in Fig. 173 we notice at once the trim tab on the trailing edge of the keel, which indicates that LIGHTNING was built before the introduction of the MAF (Movable Appendage Factor). In order to avoid the MAF penalty, the trim tab was permanently fixed in position, but this did not rob the boat of her position as best American one-ton yacht in 1972 and 1973. Had she not been so successful one might doubt whether the very small keel would be sufficient to counteract leeway. It has proved itself, though, and one cannot but admire the elegant underwater profile of this Olin Stephens design. The skeg and rudder, on the other hand, are generously proportioned, and one is tempted to ask whether they could not be cut down in the interest of reduced friction, considering the proven efficacy of the small keel.

The sail plan shows the typical modern racing rig, in which the foretriangle is larger than the mainsail. In this case it is larger by 45 per cent. The reason for this

226

Lightning
One Tonner

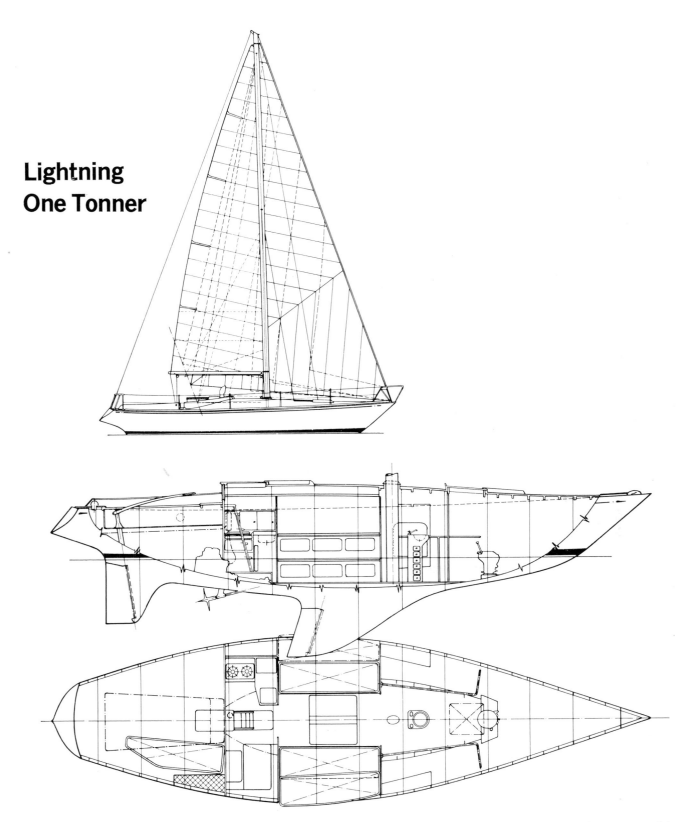

Plate 47: An excellent shot of a One Tonner designed by Sparkman & Stephens under construction in light alloy. Here you can see the pared-down shape of the modern ocean racer with its minimum hull resistance. There is no comparison with the early, heavy and bulky ocean-going yachts The modern type is not only superior in speed but has better handling qualities and points higher.

Photo: Sea Spray, Auckland

Fig. 173: The One Tonner LIGHTNING is one of the most successful American yachts in this class. The trim tab on the keel is no longer used to avoid the small penalty it entails.

LOA	38 ft	Displacement	15,365 lb
LWL	28 ft 9 in	Ballast weight	7300 lb
Beam	11 ft 9 in	Ballast ratio	48%
Draft	6 ft 3 in	Sail area	622 sq ft

Standfast

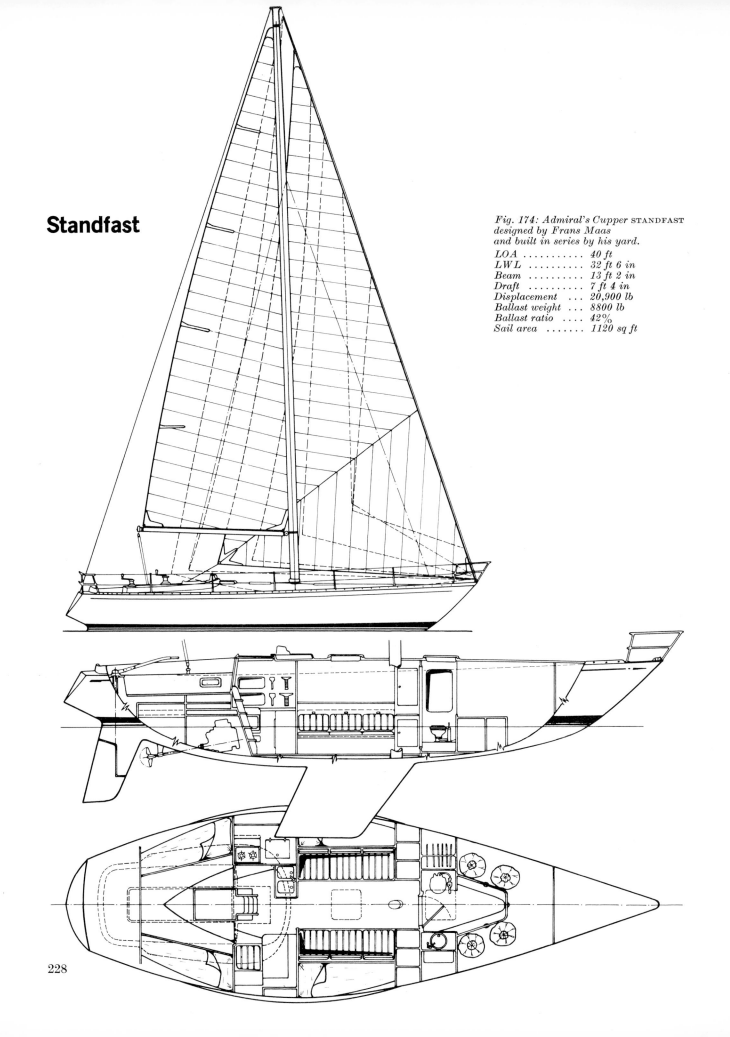

Fig. 174: Admiral's Cupper STANDFAST
designed by Frans Maas
and built in series by his yard.
LOA .... *40 ft*
LWL .... *32 ft 6 in*
Beam .... *13 ft 2 in*
Draft .... *7 ft 4 in*
Displacement ... *20,900 lb*
Ballast weight .. *8800 lb*
Ballast ratio *42%*
Sail area .... *1120 sq ft*

preference, as explained previously, lies in the great variety of headsails which can be set within the foretriangle, whereas the mainsail offers very little scope for variation. The diagonal line cutting the boom near the end is the LP-line, which is the limit for headsail clews; within this limit any triangular sail may be set without penalty. It can be seen from all the foresails indicated in the sail plan that this freedom is used liberally. In addition, there will be at least two spinnakers and, set on the stay aft of the forestay, the very effective spinnaker slotsail.

Instead of the conventional superstructure the boat has a curved flush deck, which is now very common and serves to reduce air friction. One effect of this arrangement is that the foot of the foretriangle comes below the deck, i.e. in the cabin, which ensures an almost wind-tight joint between foresail and deck, another is the great spaciousness of the cabin.

As with all competitive boats, the accommodation is severely curtailed and tailored purely for racing. Although there are five berths, a serviceable galley and a large chart table, the wash basin and heads stand free in space, and what looks like two more berths forward are actually sail bins.

The following yacht, STANDFAST, designed by the Dutch designer and builder Frans Maas, exceeds the normal one-ton size and belongs in the category of so-called Admiral's Cuppers. While she can compete in all Class I IOR races, her number one interest is the Admiral's Cup Series. The minimum rating for Admiral's Cup yachts is, at the moment, 29 ft, the maximum 45 ft IOR.

STANDFAST has many features which have become characteristic of modern ocean racers, among them the flush deck, the large foretriangle, the relatively small, narrow keel and the short overhangs. The comparatively large skeg and rudder for course stability illustrate another modern trend. The accommodation

is, once again, purely functional for racing purposes. Anything which is not strictly necessary in the way of comforts or berths has been dispensed with. There are six fixed berths, a well-equipped galley, good chart table, accessible auxiliary motor and bins for sail stowage forward.

The last example in this chapter is RECLUTA III designed by the young Argentinian German Frers, which is illustrated in Fig. 236. With a LOA of 48·4 ft (14·75 m) and an IOR rating of 35 ft she is still far below the upper limit of Class I, which is a rating of 70 ft (21·34 m). But since Class I starts with a rating of 33 ft (10·05 m) she can, nevertheless, be taken as representing the largest class. She is, besides, a successful boat having come second in the 1973 Fastnet Race out of 200 boats. She was also second on individual rating in the 1973 Admiral's Cup Series, and winner of the New York Yacht Club Cup, which was competed for in the Solent by over 100 yachts.

The success of RECLUTA III is all the more remarkable when one considers that she was designed and built in Argentina in only three months, and transported to Europe without having undergone trials. Once in Europe, her crew had one week in which to tune her before entering her in the Admiral's Cup Series. Her hull is made of laminated, epoxy-glued wood.

A peculiarity of RECLUTA III's layout is the second cockpit for the crew, which is forward of the helmsman's and navigator's cockpit and which has proved most successful. She is flush-decked, which is by now fairly normal for racing yachts of her size.

It may be interesting to note that RECLUTA III's rating of 37 ft comes exactly in the middle between the upper and lower limits for Admiral's Cup boats in 1973, i.e. 29 ft (8·84 m) and 45 ft (13·64 m). This shows that, in her case, the system of time allowance worked out fairly both upwards and downwards.

Some Successful Cruising Yachts

In the following pages a number of cruising boats are described which, individually or as a class, have had an ontstandingly successful career. The range from which one can choose is, of course, enormous and we have had to concentrate on just a few, each representing a notable design idea or having a remarkable cruising record. All of them have these things in common: they are uncapsizable, they have adequate living accommodation, and they have gained above average popularity in their home waters.

A considerable number of cruising yachts, in the hands of experienced crews, have completed noteworthy voyages. A number of Folkboats have crossed the Atlantic. One intrepid seafarer sailed a Folkboat from England to New Zealand via Tahiti, part of the way single-handed. The small yacht SOPRANINO triggered off the formation of the Junior Offshore Group with her Atlantic crossing in 1952. Another successful yacht was FINISTERRE which, helmed by Carleton Mitchell, won the Bermuda Race three times running, an extraordinary record.

In 1942 a class was launched in Sweden which, meanwhile, has become well known all over the world: the Nordic Folkboat. Initially the Swedes, used to the long overhangs of their Skerry Cruisers, did not take to this 'chopped-off' boat, the design of which was the outcome of a competition held by the Swedish Sailing Association. Nor were they attracted to the clinker construction, which, they said, did not make it look like a yacht. Then the Swedish shipowner and yachtsman Sven Salén decided to have 60 of these boats built on his own account. Thanks to this bold gesture it could be proved that the new class had everything a yachtsman could wish for: it was reasonably priced, outstandingly seaworthy, and suitable for both racing and cruising. The Folkboat is now represented in many countries, and it is built both in wood and fibreglass.

Two fearless British yachtsmen astounded the sailing world in 1952 by crossing the Atlantic in a very small, light yacht. SOPRANINO, designed by Laurent Giles, represented the then heretical idea of lightweight construction for offshore cruisers. When SOPRANINO proved the validity of the concept by completing the 10,000-mile Atlantic crossing and arriving in New York without a single mishap, she became famous overnight.

As a result of this successful crossing by Patrick Ellam and Colin Mudie, a large number of yachtsmen

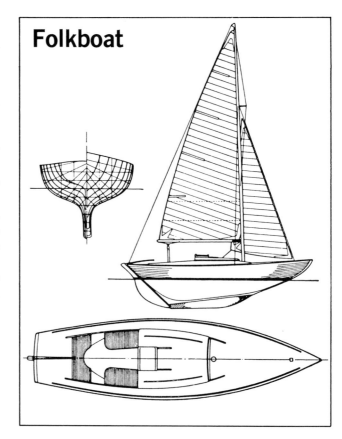

Folkboat

Fig. 175: The popular and well-tried Folkboat is now built in a number of different versions, all of which have the same dimensions.

LOA	25 ft 2 in	Displacement	4730 lb
LWL	19 ft 8 in	Ballast weight	2310 lb
Beam	7 ft 3 in	Ballast ratio	49%
Draft	3 ft 11 in	Sail area	262 sq ft

began to take an interest in offshore racing in small boats. Soon afterwards, the Junior Offshore Group was founded for this purpose, followed by a similar organization in America called the Midget Ocean Racing Club.

The clinker hull of SOPRANINO was so carefully designed that despite its strength it weighed only 430 lb (200 kg). The keel was a steel sheet with a cigar-shaped bulb of lead at the end; the total keel weight of 600 lb (272 kg) gave the boat all the necessary stability and made it uncapsizable. Moreover, the boat was so designed that, in the event of being turned completely upside down, it would be self-righting. Positive buoyancy even with the boat full of water was guaranteed by blocks of foam.

The British yacht MYTH OF MALHAM, designed by Laurent Giles in 1946, is included in this group because she is considered the pioneer of the short underwater plan and virtual absence of overhangs for ocean racers. She was built for one of the most experienced offshore yachtsmen, Captain John Illingworth. Both her design and the method of her construction attracted much attention at the time. In those days it was still thought that light-weight construction and a narrow keel were unsuitable for offshore work, but MYTH OF MALHAM proved very successful. By today's standards her keel is, if anything, too long.

John Illingworth was the originator of the masthead rig, which he first put into practice on his yacht MAID OF MALHAM in 1936. In the sail plan two foresails, a jib and staysail, are set simultaneously, which makes MYTH OF MALHAM a cutter. Since the foretriangle is so high, the mast and mainsail can be shorter and placed further aft than in the normal sloop rig.

The rig in conjunction with the short underwater profile made for a well-balanced boat. Her owner explained that she could be left to sail herself to windward quite confidently and for lengthy periods. He added that for extended voyages a rather longer keel would have been preferable to give her better stability on course in heavy seas. This could probably have been achieved by hanging the rudder on the transom, preferably with its own skeg, an arrangement which was not yet customary then.

Although no new yachts are built to the German KR-Formula, we thought it justifiable to include a representative here, since a large number of these KR-yachts are still very active and will be so for many years to come.

The 6·5 KR-yacht illustrated was designed by W Ohlendorf and built by Abeking & Rasmussen. This class, as well as the 6 KR, enjoyed particular popularity because it was reasonably priced, seaworthy, and could be handled by a crew of two while offering accommodation for four or five.

The KR-Formula allowed great scope of choice as to type, length–beam ratio, draft and sail plan, but the factors of the formula were such that they did not encourage extreme designs. This design illustrates well the whole Abeking & Rasmussen tradition, which is

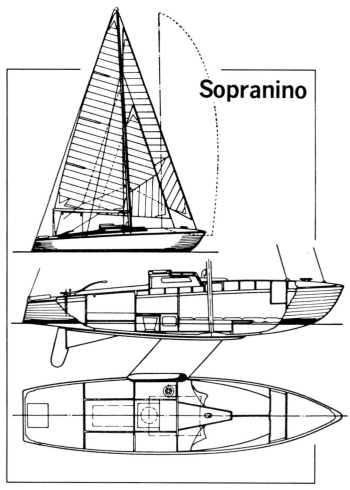

Sopranino

Fig. 176: When she crossed the Atlantic, the small yacht SOPRANINO pioneered a new era of ocean cruising and racing in small, light yachts.

LOA	19 ft 8 in	Displacement	1430 lb
LWL	17 ft 6 in	Ballast weight	598 lb
Beam	5 ft 4 in	Sail area	215 sq ft
Draft	3 ft 8 in		

biased towards fast and relatively slim boats with long overhangs. Although the interior layout was designed for naval use, it would satisfy many a private owner. Situated next to the companionway, the galley is light and well ventilated and the toilet compartment forward sensibly spacious; four permanent berths are generally acceptable. This particular yacht was built in mahogany, but numerous KR-cruisers were built in steel.

In striking contrast to this conventional type is the C & C 27 illustrated in Fig. 179, which has a small, narrow keel and separately hung rudder. With a very much shorter LOA she offers almost the same accommodation and represents a completely different type of

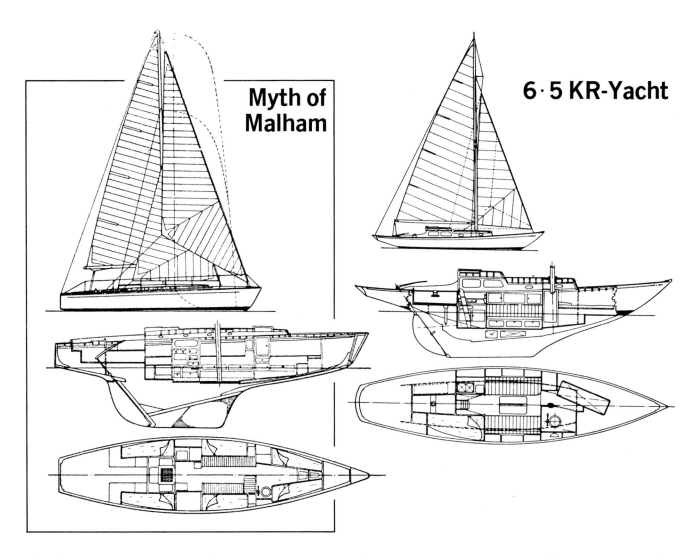

Myth of Malham

6·5 KR-Yacht

Fig. 177: MYTH OF MALHAM *was the first ocean racer with very short overhangs and a pared-down keel profile.*

LOA	37 ft 9 in	Displacement	17,600 lb
LWL	33 ft 6 in	Ballast weight	8800 lb
Beam	9 ft 4 in	Sail area	818 sq ft
Draft	7 ft		

Fig. 178: *Memories of the German KR-Formula: a 6·5 KR Cruiser designed and built by Abeking & Rasmussen.*

LOA	34 ft 11 in	Draft	4 ft 11 in
LWL	23 ft 7 in	Displacement	11,600 lb
Beam	9 ft 2 in	Sail area	449 sq ft

seagoing cruising yacht; her displacement is less than half that of the 6·5 KR. With a shorter mast but a much larger foretriangle, her light hull is driven by much the same sail area as the heavier KR-yacht. In fact, she illustrates convincingly the basic differences between the conventional, long-keeled type and its short-keeled, modern counterpart.

The C & C 27 was designed by the Canadian team of Cuthbertson & Cassian and it is built by numerous European and non-European yards. The four- to five-berth accommodation, which is self-explanatory from

the plans, offers standing headroom as far as the WC compartment. The sail plan only shows the large genoa, but her wardrobe naturally includes all the normal headsails including a large spinnaker. The standard auxiliary is a 10 hp Faryman Diesel, but alternatives are possible. When, in 1973, a group of European sailing magazines ran a yacht test on ten small cruisers of similar size, one report commented as follows on the C & C 27: 'She recorded the fastest speeds and was hardly stopped by the seas. All the test crews were impressed by her performance.'

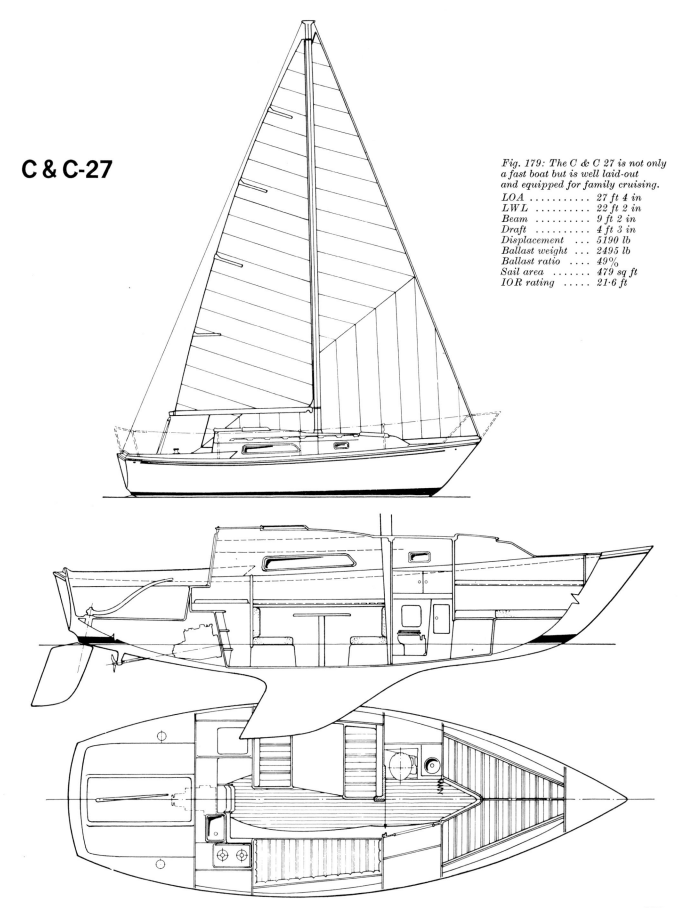

C & C-27

Fig. 179: The C & C 27 is not only
a fast boat but is well laid-out
and equipped for family cruising.

LOA .... 27 ft 4 in
LWL .... 22 ft 2 in
Beam .... 9 ft 2 in
Draft .... 4 ft 3 in
Displacement ... 5190 lb
Ballast weight ... 2495 lb
Ballast ratio 49%
Sail area .... 479 sq ft
IOR rating ..... 21·6 ft

Plate 48: The C & C 27, designed by the Canadian firm of Cuthbertson & Cassian, is a well-proven small boat which is surprisingly big for its length. In masterly fashion the IOR Rules have been used to create a fast racer and family cruiser at the same time The yacht rates IOR 21·6 ft, almost exactly a Half Tonner. Sail plan and accommodation layout are shown in Fig 179 The transom stern gives the boat a long waterline and allows it to have a large cockpit.
Photo: Schiffswerft Korneuburg

The unique record of having won the Bermuda Race three times running has made FINISTERRE one of the best-known racing yachts of our times. Her owner, Carleton Mitchell, an experienced offshore sailor, played a large part in her design. He wanted a boat with good stability but shallow draft to by-pass the difficulties which deep keeled yachts habitually have in river estuaries. He also wanted roomy accommodation and a fast hull with which he could win ocean races.

FINISTERRE, designed by Olin Stephens, had an unusually ample, even excessive beam by accepted standards. Her fixed draft was, indeed, moderate to the point where it seemed inadequate for an ocean racer, but good windward performance was ensured by

a large, deep drop-plate. The yawl rig, though not without inherent merit, was doubtlessly chosen because it was favourably rated under the current measurement rules. FINISTERRE proved that heavy weight need not be detrimental to speed and seaworthiness. She was originally designed to have a displacement of 8·3 tons on a LWD of 27 ft 6 in (8·4 m). The extensive equipment and accommodation specified by the owner raised the displacement to 10 tons and increased the LWL to almost 29 ft (9 m). But her performance did not suffer, on the contrary, she delighted everybody by her outstanding qualities in a seaway, and she made a great name for herself as a successful ocean racer. Although she can hardly be compared with a modern

Plate 49: A glance in the main cabin of the C & C 27. Right forward there are two berths, then there is a toilet compartment before the main saloon is reached The dinette to port converts to a double berth There is a spacious galley aft by the companionway.
Photo: YPS-Hamburg

IOR design, her dimensions are surprisingly similar to those of the larger One-Tonners which have, if anything, an even ampler beam and, of course, a deeper permanent draft.

It might be interesting to mention that the owner went into great detail in designing the accommodation. In a shed he built a model of the available hull space out of wooden battens, and within it he experimented with the berth; galley, heads and fore-cabin layout in order to determine accurately the space and headroom needed.

As a result of the amazing popularization of sailing, boat builders have produced a spate of new types of all shapes and sizes, many in search of a gap in the market.

Almost every prospective owner can now find among the standard models a boat to suit his purpose and taste without having to have it specially designed. It goes without saying that a series model is cheaper than a one-off.

Nor does the do-it-yourself enthusiast have to have his boat designed specially for him. Many designers specialize in plans for amateur construction, and many boats can be bought in kit form. Amateur construction is particularly popular in Britain and other English-speaking countries, where many sea-going yachts of considerable dimensions have been successfully completed.

Finisterre

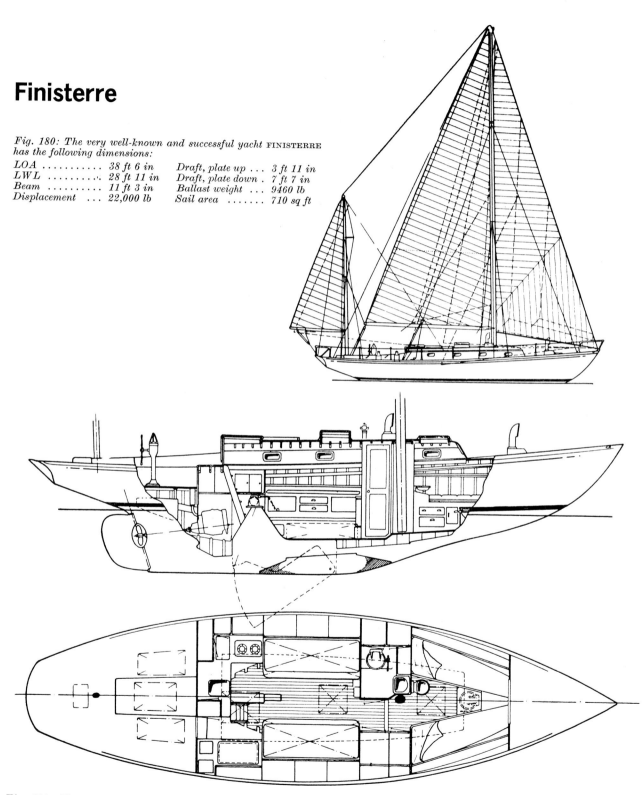

Fig. 180: The very well-known and successful yacht FINISTERRE has the following dimensions:

LOA	38 ft 6 in	Draft, plate up	3 ft 11 in
LWL	28 ft 11 in	Draft, plate down	7 ft 7 in
Beam	11 ft 3 in	Ballast weight	9460 lb
Displacement	22,000 lb	Sail area	710 sq ft

Fig. 181: The comprehensive and spacious accommodation of FINISTERRE proved itself in many long ocean races. Her beam was considered excessive at the time.

Some Large Sailing Yachts

Swan-65

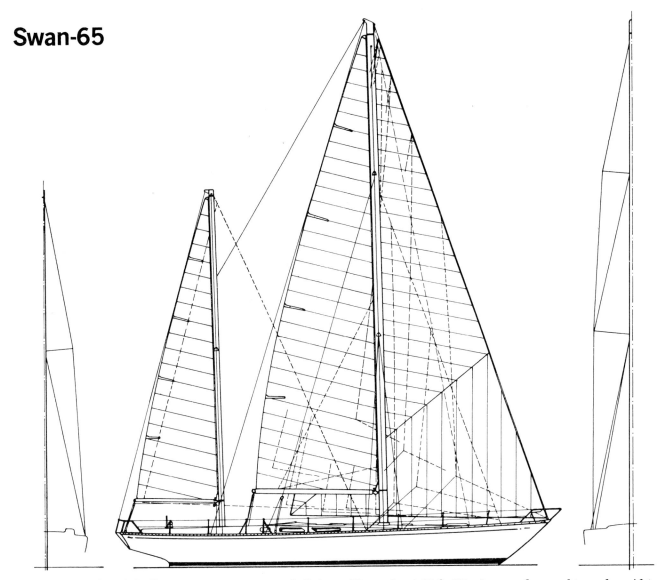

Fig. 182: Sail plan of the Swan 65, a true ocean racer built in series in Finland. The rig is characterized by outstanding efficiency, very thorough staying and a large number of auxiliary sails. The normal suit of sails comprises the following sails:

Mainsail	*619 sq ft*	*Large jib*	*778 sq ft*
Mizzen	*272 sq ft*	*Medium jib*	*520 sq ft*
Heavy genoa	*1367 sq ft*	*Small jib*	*264 sq ft*
Medium genoa	*1378 sq ft*	*Staysail*	*329 sq ft*
Drifter	*1378 sq ft*	*Main trysail*	*189 sq ft*
Reaching genoa	*1378 sq ft*	*Storm jib*	*140 sq ft*
Small genoa	*850 sq ft*	*Mizzen staysail*	*716 sq ft*
Tallboy	*460 sq ft*		

3 large spinnakers: light, medium and heavy
1 storm spinnaker

From about 65 ft (20 m) upwards a yacht can be said to belong to the category of really large yachts. Not only do yachts become more seaworthy as they increase in size, they also become faster and the accommodation on board improves enormously. Following the trend of recent years, even such large vessels are now produced in series in fibreglass. Their production presents no technical problems, although it may present a cost problem. To make the original mould for hull and deck is so expensive that the building of one-offs by this method is out of the question.

We begin this chapter with the well-established

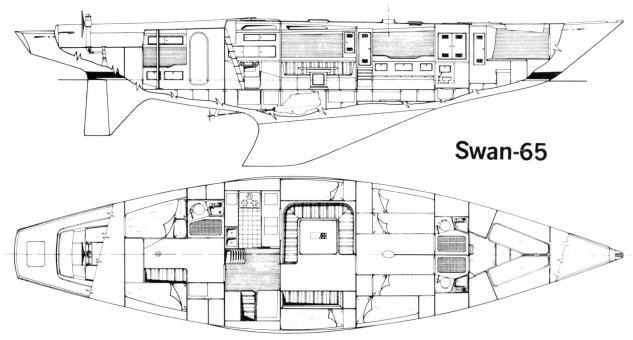

Swan-65

Fig. 183: Accommodation plan of the Swan 65 designed by Sparkman & Stephens and built in series by Nautor in Finland. She is flush-decked, which is normal for her size and gives her not only good deck working space but also greater spaciousness below.

LOA	65 ft	Displacement	57,200 lb
LWL	47 ft	Ballast weight	25,520 lb
Beam	16 ft 4 in	Ballast ratio	45%
Beam WL	14 ft 6 in	Sail area, ketch	904 sq ft
Draft	9 ft 3 in	Sail area, sloop	925 sq ft

Swan 65, which is a true ocean racer despite her size of 64·8 ft (20 m), and is a continuation of the smaller models in the Swan series. It was designed to the IOR and has proved a very fast ship. Like all of the 'Swans' she is a Sparkman & Stephens design.

A look at the sail plan shows that a well-balanced yawl rig is possible under the IOR measurement. The rig is well inboard so that the mizzen or jigger mast, too, has a permanent backstay. The ample beam ensures secure athwartships staying of both spars.

The accommodation is very comfortable and not tailored to pure racing needs. There is a separate owner's cabin aft with its own WC and washroom, both the galley and the navigator's corner are spacious, and the main cabin has a dinette arrangement. Adjoining, there is a guest cabin both to port and starboard, each with its own WC and shower. The two additional pipe cots in the fo'c'sle can be occupied by two extra crew members. The engine is a six-cylinder Penta Diesel with 106 hp max. and 75 hp continuous rating. It drives a

very efficient propeller with a 2·1:1 reduction.

*

WINDWARD PASSAGE: There is a category of ocean racers which are hurried madly across the world's oceans by their speed-conscious owners in order to prove to a spell-bound audience that theirs is the fastest yacht in existence. For a long time the American yacht TICONDEROGA was considered the fastest, then the Dutch–South African STORMVOGEL took that title off her. Next in the running was the large yawl ONDINE, illustrated in Fig. 256, which had as illustrious a career as STORMVOGEL before her.

For some years now the honour of being the world's fastest yacht has been held by the superlative WINDWARD PASSAGE, which put up spectacular performances in SORC (Southern Ocean Racing Conference) races in the Caribbean. She was the result of a commission to an unusually young British designer working in New

Windward Passage

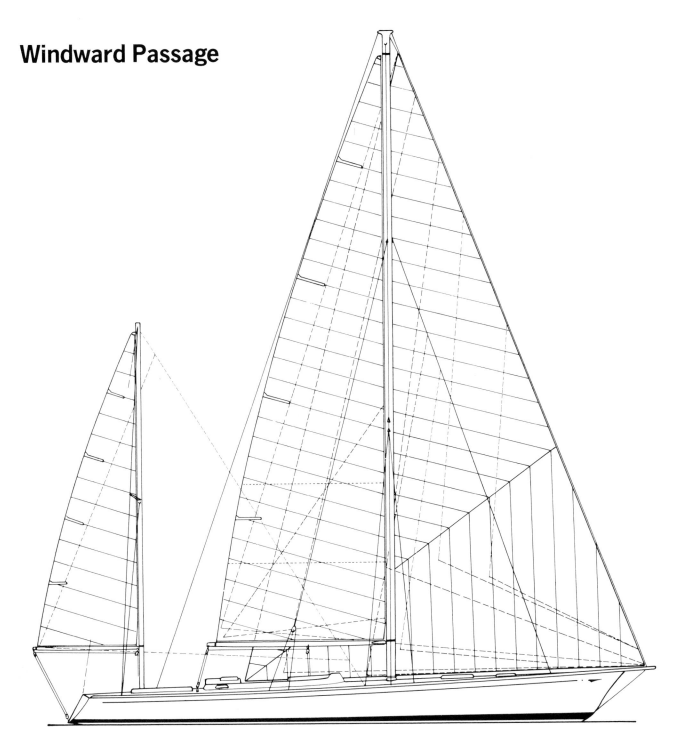

Fig. 184: Sail plan of the exceptionally fast yacht WINDWARD PASSAGE. This respected 'greyhound of the seas' has the maximum length which still permits her to compete in the Bermuda Race. She, too, has a flush deck. The small bowsprit, which is an unusual feature, benefits the many large headsails. The function of the mizzen mast is mainly to support the useful mizzen staysail, which is nearly three times as large as the mizzen itself. The masts are high and the booms short, all of which points to a very efficient rig.

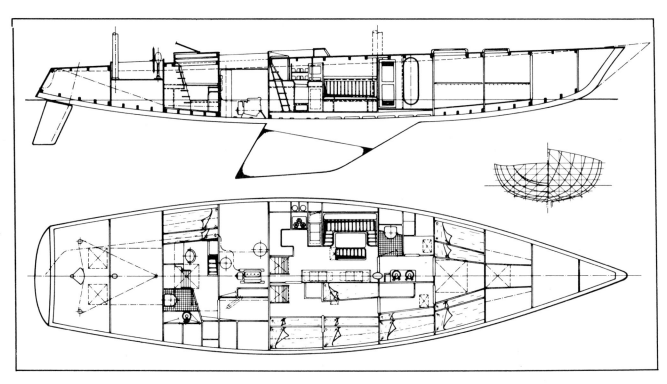

Fig. 185: Sections and accommodation plan of WINDWARD PASSAGE. *Her hull is positively dinghy-shaped. Even the keel looks more like a centreplate. Her accommodation has been designed primarily to suit the requirements of ocean racing: a large number of berths in several, very simple cabins, a pleasant central sitting area, a spacious galley and a surprisingly modest* owner's cabin. *The 40 hp diesel engine drives a retractable propeller via a Fairy hydraulic drive.*

LOA	72 ft 10 in	Displacement ...	80,000 lb
LWL	65 ft 10 in	Ballast weight ...	33,900 lb
Beam	19 ft 4 in	Ballast ratio	42·5%
Draft	9 ft 8 in	Sail area	2432 sq ft

York, Alan Gurney. Bob Johnson, former owner of TICONDEROGA, formulated his specification something like this: 'Draw me the fastest possible yacht, and to hell with rating rules!' Her construction was as unusual as her inception. She was built under a large tarpaulin at a small yard, which Bob Johnson owned at Freeport in the Bahama Islands. Standing keel-up, she was planked with very light spruce in three diagonal layers over the top of a great number of stringers, and subsequently covered with a synthetic cloth which, applied with epoxy glue, became permanently fused with the timber. Probably never before has a hull of this size been built so light. The lines in Fig. 185 show it to be pure dinghy shape. The finished hull had a total weight of only just over 30,000 lb (13,700 kg) inclusive of accommodation and engine installation. In addition, there are nearly 34,000 lb (15,400 kg) of lead ballast and 16,000 lb (7300 kg) of rigging, sails and racing gear,

which amounts to a total displacement of 80,000 lb (36,400 kg), which is incredibly low for an ocean racer of 72·85 ft (22·2 m) LOA.

The auxiliary installed is a 40 hp Westerbeke (Mercedes-Benz) Diesel with a hydraulic drive. The propeller is retractable, and the opening in the hull can be closed with a plate. Hence there is no propeller factor allowance, but the flush bottom is conducive to maximum speed.

*

CARITA: The design of *very* large sailing yachts, by which we mean lengths of 150 ft (50 m) and over, involves one technical problem: the subdivision of the sail plan in the interest of safe and simple handling. It was for this reason that CARITA, the largest yacht built since the war, was rigged as a three-masted

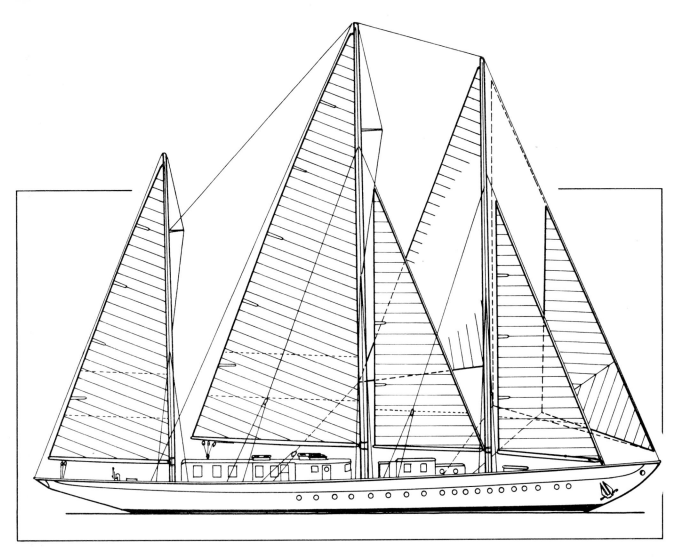

Fig. 186: Probably the largest of all the pre-war ocean racing yachts: the three-masted schooner CARITA. *She has two diesel engines with an output of 587 hp each, which means nearly 5 hp per sq ft of basic sail area and would classify her as a motor sailer, if her hull shape and rig were not those of a pure sailing yacht.*

schooner. Designed by Robert Clark, she was built in steel in Holland and has the following amazing dimensions:

LOA	....	170·56 ft (52·10 m)
LWL	....	121·60 ft (37·05 m)
Beam	....	28 ft (8·55 m)
Draft	....	15 ft (4·58 m)
Basic sail area	....	6727 sq ft (625 m²)
Sail area incl. staysails ...		9149 sq ft (850 m²)

The reason for the three-masted rig becomes quite plain when we examine what would happen if this sail area were put on a single-masted cutter rig: the main mast would have to have a height of 312 ft (95 m), whereas with the three-masted rig it had to be only 140 ft (42·7 m) high.

With vessels of this size the sail area need no longer be proportional because, due to their long waterline length, they reach much higher speeds than yachts of normal size. Nevertheless, the sail areas have to be carefully planned for feasibility of handling, which is demonstrated by CARITA's sail inventory:

Flying jib	....	947 sq ft (88 m²)
Boomed staysail	....	893 sq ft (83 m²)
Large jib	....	1927 sq ft (179 m²)
Mainsail on foremast	....	1378 sq ft (128 m²)
Boomed staysail on mainmast	....	1055 sq ft (98 m²)
Mainsail	....	2508 sq ft (233 m²)
Mizzen	....	1324 sq ft (123 m²)
Total basic sail area	.....	6727 sq ft (625 m²)

CARITA's displacement is somewhere between 500 and 600 tons. The hull has such smooth lines and produces so little resistance that a speed of 9½ to 10 knots is reached in even a moderate breeze.

*

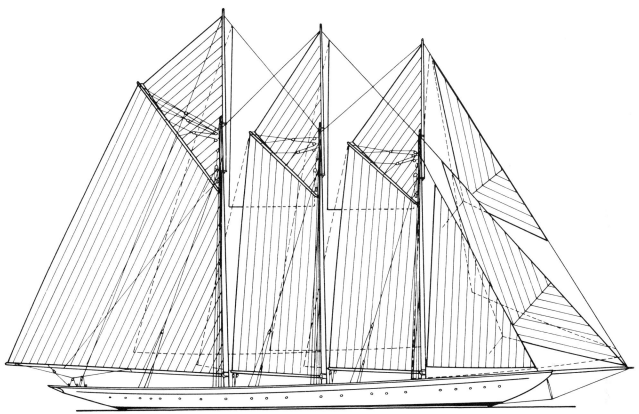

Fig. 187: Sail plan of the famous three-masted schooner ATLANTIC *designed by William Gardner, designer of the Star. Originally she carried internal ballast only but was subsequently converted for* *external ballast. Soon afterwards she competed for the Kaiser Cup in the 1905 Transatlantic Race, which she won in record time.*

ATLANTIC: The famous three-masted schooner ATLANTIC built in 1903 has even larger dimensions than CARITA. She comes from the board of William Gardner, who designed her for high speeds at sea. He could scarcely have dreamt, though, that her Transatlantic record would still be unbeaten some 70 years later. It was in the 1905 Transatlantic Race from New York to the Lizard on the south coast of England that ATLANTIC set the record time of 12 days, 4 hours, 1 minute and 16 seconds, which amounts to an average speed of 10·4 knots! Her dimensions were:

LOA	....	187 ft (57·00 m)
LWL	....	137 ft (41·80 m)
Beam	....	29 ft (8·85 m)
Basic sail area	....	18,514 sq ft (1720 m²)
Draft	....	15 ft (4·57 m)

The sail plan of ATLANTIC is shown in Fig. 187, and it is by no means the most efficient by modern standards. In fact, a number of modern ocean racers have come fairly close to her time, but that 1905 race for the Kaiser's Cup saw some really tough competition.

One small detail deserves to be mentioned as part of her history. Originally, following the trend of the day, ATLANTIC was built with movable internal ballast only. Before she entered for the 1905 Transatlantic Race, William Gardner decided to convert her and put all the ballast in an external keel, which was an audacious decision in those days. This conversion resulted in a complete change in the schooner's characteristics and

Plate 50: Up till now the fastest crossing of the Atlantic has been made by the three-masted schooner ATLANTIC *designed by William Garden in 1903. In 1905 she won the Kaiser's Trophy in the Transatlantic Race in the record time of 12 days 4 hours, which has never since been beaten She was 187 ft long with a beam of 29 ft and a working sail area of 18,514 sq ft. The sail plan is shown in Fig 187.*   *Photo: Rosenfeld*

243

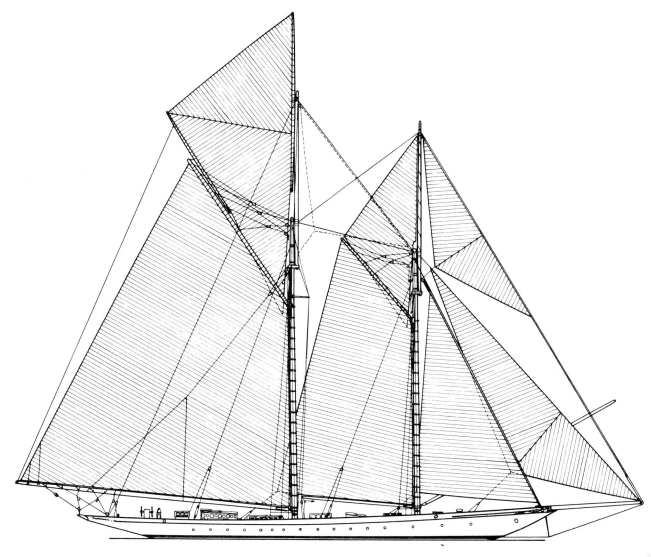

Fig. 188: Sail plan of the schooner METEOR *designed by Max Oertz for the German Emperor Wilhelm II and built in steel at the Germaniawerft in Kiel between 1908 and 1909. This was the first time that the Emperor had a yacht designed and built in Germany, having bought all his previous yachts abroad.*

LOA	154 ft 9 in	Lead ballast	105 ton
LWL	108 ft 6 in	Sail area	14,757 sq ft
Beam	27 ft 2 in	Highest point	
Draft	18 ft	above WL	166 ft
Displacement	266 ton		

Many of the details typical of yachts of those days can be distinguished in this drawing. The sails are bent to the masts by wooden mast hoops, to the topmasts by rope lashings. The peak halyards are rove through three or four-part peak tackles. The highest point of the main topsail gaff is 166 ft above the waterline. The main topsail gaff itself is 56 ft 9 in long, longer than the mast of a modern One Tonner.

Both masts have a topmast, which used to be lowered and lashed

on deck in a storm. The long overhangs are fully functional: they are needed to accommodate the enormous sail plan, the length of which, from the bowsprit end to the main boom end is no less than 200 ft. The spinnaker boom is 72 ft long. The spinnaker itself is of asymmetrical cut and is set to one side of the forestay only.

The fore topsail does not have a gaff, because it has to be lowered when going about and re-set on the other side. The main topping lift, which ends in lazy jacks, not only serves to support the heavy, 90 ft long main boom but also ensures that the acres of cloth of the mainsail come down neatly when lowered and can be lashed down together with the gaff. The mainsail and foresail are not taken off their booms but left bent on and protected by sail covers. The foot of the foresail is longer than its boom which means that two sheets, one on the boom end and one on the clew, had to be handled. Yachts in those days did not, of course, have lifelines, but the bulwarks in this case were about 1 ft 3 in high, which gave the guests on board an adequate feeling of safety. The crew, of course, was a paid, professional crew.

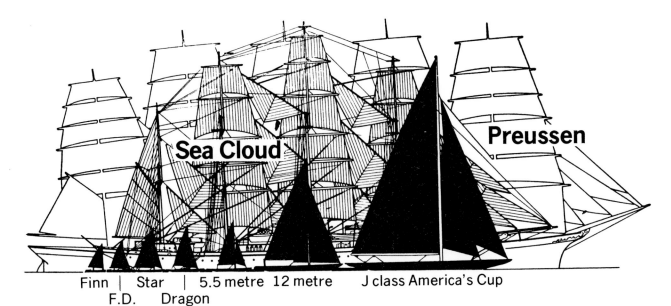

Finn | Star | 5.5 metre 12 metre | J class America's Cup
F.D. Dragon

Fig. 189: This drawing, in which a number of well-known sailing boat classes have been superimposed on two of the largest sailing vessels, gives an idea of their relative size. In the background we can see the outlines of the five-masted, fully-rigged ship PREUSSEN, the largest cargo-carrying sailing vessel of all times. In front of her is SEA CLOUD, the largest sailing yacht ever built, which was built to an American design by the Germaniawerft in Kiel and started life under the name of HUSSAR. The black silhouettes in the foreground represent, from left to right, the five Olympic classes as they stood in 1960, and finally the two classes which are associated with the America's Cup. All have been drawn to scale.

doubtlessly led to her ultimate victory.

Among the competitors in the same Transatlantic Race there was another large vessel with an unusual rig, called VALHALLA. She was spectacular not only by her size but also by her rig, which was that of a three-masted, full-rigged ship. Her dimensions appear enormous to modern yachtsmen. She was 245 ft (74·7 m) overall and 208 ft (63·5 m) in the waterline, with a beam of 36·8 ft (11·2 m) and a draft of 21 ft (6·4 m). Her speed, however, was disappointing, and she could get nowhere near ATLANTIC. For many years, though, she had the honour of being the largest sailing yacht afloat. Even up to the present she is the only yacht ever to have been rigged as a full-rigged ship. Her interesting sail plan is reproduced in Fig. 231. The classic beauty of her hull is evident, with its graceful yacht stern and typical clipper bow.

The largest of all sailing yachts was built in 1931 at the Germania yard in Kiel. Originally called HUSSAR she was later re-named SEA CLOUD and finally, as ANGELITA, became the State Yacht of the Dominican Republic. After a revolution her name was changed to PATRIA and now, as the last stage in her chequered career, she is offered for charter under the name of

ANTARNA. Figure 189 illustrates her enormous size in comparison with other large and small yachts. Her dimensions are:

LOA	316 ft (96·30 m)
LWL	254 ft (77·40 m)
Beam	49 ft (14·96 m)
Draft	16·8 ft (5·13 m)
Displacement	3390 tons
Sail area	35,521 sq ft (3300 m²)
Auxiliary power	2700 hp
Speed under power	14 knots

The enormous sail area is split up into 30 sails, 16 of them square sails, ·with the longest yard being 90 ft (27·4 m) long and having a diameter of 19 in (48 cm). The total weight of all the spars comes to 110 tons. The centre of effort of the sail area lies about 82 ft (25 m) above the waterline.

A few more figures might complete the picture of yachting in those days. SEA CLOUD had a crew which consisted of captain, 4 officers, 4 engineers, 6 mechanics, an electrician, a purser, a chief cook, a chief steward, 12 stewards, 4 cabin stewards and 31 other crew members, a total of 66; as Dominican State Yacht she also had a band of 12 musicians. Her monthly running costs were reckoned to be $15,000!

A comparison between these large yachts and some merchant sailing vessels of the last century might interest many readers. Many of the clippers were about 180 ft (55 m) in length and had a beam of about 30 ft (9 m). One of the largest clippers, which became famous under the name of FLYING CLOUD, had a length of 225 ft (68·6 m) and a beam of 41 ft (12·5 m). But all the sailing ships built as cargo carriers were surpassed in size by the five-masted, full-rigged ship PREUSSEN. This splendid ship was built for the Hamburg shipowner Laeisz in 1902 and was nearly 408 ft (124·3 m) long with a beam of just over 53 ft (16·3 m). Unfortunately her life was short, for one night in 1909 a small freighter crossed her path in the Channel without observing her right of way; the resulting collision caused serious but not fatal damage. Her total loss was caused by further unfortunate circumstances: in a sudden squall the anchor chain broke, leaving the disabled ship to be driven ashore, where she eventually broke up. The PREUSSEN had a deadweight of 8000 tons and a sail area of around 60,000 sq ft (5560 m²). Her crew consisted of captain, 3 officers and 42 men, a total of 46, which is 20 less than on board the very much smaller SEA CLOUD.

PREUSSEN's speed under sail was carefully measured, and also complemented by model tests, in an effort to assess the viability of these sailing vessels compared with the steadily growing fleet of steamers. Under favourable conditions PREUSSEN may have reached a speed of $17\frac{1}{2}$ knots, but her regular average speed on runs between Hamburg and the ports of Chile on the west coast of South America was only $7\frac{1}{2}$ knots. This may sound modest, but as an average for a sailing ship it is admirable and says much for the calibre of Laeisz's captains.

Yachts in the Single-Handed Transatlantic Race

During the first half of the twentieth century a number of solo sailors had proved that a small sailing yacht can be sailed single-handed over long distances, basically without very great risk. The time had obviously come for somebody to initiate the idea of a single-handed ocean race. As it happened, the first move in this direction was made in England, by Colonel Blondie Hasler, subsequently supported by Sir Francis Chichester. The editor of the Sunday newspaper *The Observer* also pledged support, and eventually the Royal Western Yacht Club took on the organization. In June 1960 everything was ready for the first Singlehanded Transatlantic Race. The course was from Plymouth to the Ambrose Light Vessel off New York, which was a great-circle distance of a little under 3000 sea miles; on the Azores route, which is warmer and safer, the distance was 3600 miles. However, the course being westward against the prevailing winds, a lot of tacking had to be done, which brought the true distances covered to as much as 5000 miles in some cases.

There were five entries, among which Francis Chichester stood out for being the only one to enter a boat of over 39 ft (12 m) in length. The four other yachts were all around 25 ft (7·5 m), among them two slightly modified Folkboats. In the light of what we know today it is not surprising that Francis Chichester in his GIPSY MOTH III won the race with a time of 40 days, which was then considered very good. Second was the small, modified Folkboat JESTER, whose helmsman Blondie Hasler commented casually that he had been on the helm for a total of one hour only, the rest had been done by his self-steering gear; his time was 48 days.

After an interval of four years, which has now established itself as the regular pattern, the second OSTAR (Observer Singlehanded Transatlantic Race) took place in 1964 with considerably increased support. One yacht, PEN DUICK II, sailed by the French naval lieutenant Eric Tabarly, had been specially designed and built for the race. She was an extreme light-weight plywood construction and the largest yacht competing. This time there was a fibreglass boat among the entries and a number of multi-hulls: two catamarans and a trimaran. Three of the entries were over 40 ft (12 m) in length, led by PEN DUICK II with 44·3 ft (13·5 m). This very light, fast boat, helmed by an outstanding offshore yachtsman, improved substantially on the winning

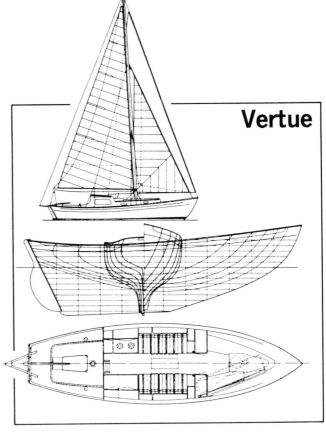

Fig. 190: The Vertue class was built in large numbers after 1936 and to this day has retained a reputation for safety and seaworthiness.

LOA	25 ft 6 in	Draft	4 ft 6 in
LWL	21 ft 6 in	Displacement	9415 lb
Beam	7 ft 2 in	Sail area	277 sq ft

time of the 1960 race by finishing in 27 days, 4 hours. Second was GIPSY MOTH III with a time of 30 days. The multi-hulls put up a disappointing performance; the fastest of them took 38½ days.

Four years later, in 1968, the scene had changed yet again: out of 35 starters 13 were multi-hulls, among them Tabarly's enormous aluminium trimaran PEN DUICK IV and the small flying proa CHEERS, a most unusual boat with a long, narrow main hull and an outrigger on the leeward side. CHEERS was admirably sailed by Tom Follett and turned out the sensation of the race. Of the 13 multi-hulls only 5 finished the race, but 3 of those finished 3rd, 5th and 7th respectively. Tabarly's big trimaran was involved in a collision shortly after the start and had to retire.

Winner of the 1968 race was SIR THOMAS LIPTON, a 56 ft (17·1 m) GRP-ketch of conventional design, sailed by the 25-year-old Geoffrey Williams. She carried a basic sail area of about 1184 sq ft (110 m²) and

Pen Duick IV

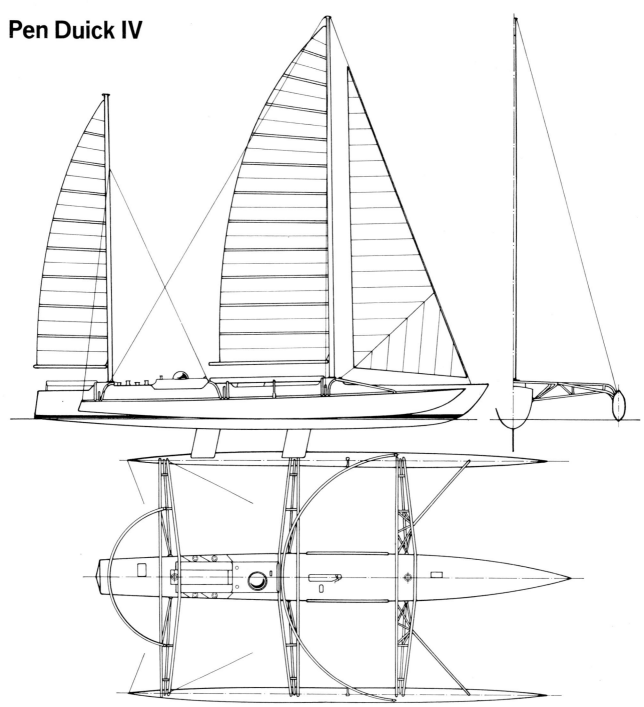

Fig. 191: The trimaran PEN DUICK IV, winner of the 1972 Trans-atlantic Race, sailed single-handed by Alain Colas. This tough young yachtsman managed to beat the 'monster' VENDREDI TREIZE convincingly. PEN DUICK IV, built in 1968, had by then already had a successful career of ocean cruising.

LOA	70 ft	Beam, central hull	6 ft 2 in
LWL	65 ft 8 in	Beam, floats	1 ft 10 in
Beam OA	35 ft	Displacement ...	15,400 lb
Draft	6 ft 6 in	Sail area	1205 sq ft

numerous headsails. The South African yacht VOOR-TREKKER finished 17 hours later. She was 49 ft (15 m) long with a basic sail area of 883 sq ft (82 m²) and was helmed by Bruce Dalling, one of South Africa's most eminent racing yachtsmen. Only another 11 hours later the first of the multi-hulls finished: the flying proa CHEERS, very bravely sailed by Tom Follett. Her main hull, though being all of 39·5 ft (12 m) long, was only 2·5 ft (75 cm) wide, and the necessarily limited accommodation made life on board extremely spartan. On the other hand, she had been infinitely cheaper to build than the two boats that beat her.

One thing which was fairly apparent from the beginning was proved convincingly by the results of the 1968 race: only very large, lightly constructed boats stood a chance of winning. The conventional belief that only heavy boats with a large amount of ballast could cross the Atlantic was finally thrown overboard. Proof was provided by the five unballasted multi-hulls, which had finished the race and which promised exciting prospects for the future. They had been disappointing only in so far as they had *not been faster* than the fastest mono-hulls. Another surprising fact emerged from this race: it was obvious that even 56 ft (17·1 m) LOA was not in excess of what one man could handle by himself. In the first race 39 ft (12 m) was thought amazing, in the second race the longest boat was over 44 ft (13·5 m) long, in the third race 56 ft (17 m) . . . Where was it going to end?

The 1972 OSTAR dawned with a number of surprises: there were as many as 54 entries from 7 countries. There were still some wooden boats, but the majority was now built of fibreglass, plus two of steel and two of light alloy. Speculation on optimum length had produced one spectacular result: the Frenchman Terlain turned up with an enormous plastic vessel, called VENDREDI TREIZE, which was all of 128 ft (39 m) long. She was designed by Dick Carter and rigged as a simple three-masted staysail schooner, as shown in Fig. 103. Would one man be able to handle a hull of this size? Would he be able to cope with the three large boomed staysails, each with a sail area of nearly 1000 sq ft (90 m²), even in strong winds?

Terlain's closest opponent was another Frenchman, Eric Tabarly's experienced crewman Alain Colas, who was now the owner of the alloy trimaran MANUREVA ex PEN DUICK IV.

She had been built purely as a racing machine, and originally she had pivoting profiled masts, but they had been replaced by normal spars. Designed by André Allegre and J Ruillard her central hull was 70 ft (21·3 m) long with a beam of only 6·1 ft (1·88 m). Her total beam, however, was as much as 35 ft (10·7 m). She did, in the event, win the race with a time of 20 days, 13 hours, which was an improvement of over 5 days on the previous winning time. VENDREDI TREIZE, the favourite, finished 16 hours later in second place. This is by no means proof, though, of the trimaran's superiority over the mono-hull. Alain Colas' grimly determined attitude makes one wonder whether he would not have won in VENDREDI TREIZE, too, although there is no way of proving this.

Third to finish was another French trimaran, CAP 33, sailed by Jean-Marie Vidal, with a time of 24 days, 5½ hours. Although not nearly as extreme as PEN DUICK IV she was designed along the same principles. Built in GRP, CAP 33 had a length of 52·5 ft (16 m) overall, a beam of 31·1 ft (9·5 m) and a well-balanced ketch rig. Hence the three fastest yachts were French-built and sailed to victory by Frenchmen.

Fourth to finish was the modern steel yacht BRITISH STEEL, 62·3 ft (19 m) long and 12·1 ft (3·7 m) in beam, which had already been sailed single-handed round the world. Fifth would have been the catamaran TAHITI BILL, which had taken part in the previous race under the name of GOLDEN COCKEREL but, through no fault of her own, she was involved in a collision shortly before the finish and had to retire. In the event it was another trimaran which came fifth, the successor to CHEERS, which had been aptly christened THREE CHEERS. She was once again sailed by Tom Follett, and her time was 27 days, 11 hours. Trimaran supporters rejoiced when the sixth yacht to finish was also a trimaran, ARCHITEUTHIS, with a length of 55 ft (16·75 m) and a beam of 27·8 ft (8·5 m).

The seventh boat, STRONGBOW, had been expected to do rather better, for she was very light with racy lines. On an overall length of 65 ft (20 m) she had beam of merely 10 ft (3·5 m), and her weight of 8 tons was nothing short of sensational. But luck and coincidence obviously play an important part, too, for only 8 minutes later the small mono-hulled yacht TOUCAN arrived, 34·4 ft (10·5 m) long and a mere 6·5 ft (2 m) in beam, which was sailed by Alain Glicksman. Both

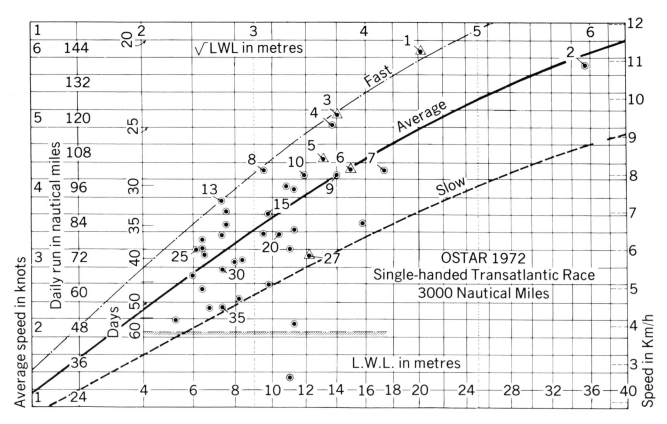

Fig. 192: This graph examines the results of the 1972 Single-Handed Transatlantic Race, based on the waterline lengths of the competing yachts. The figures alongside the curves are the order of arrival at the Ambrose Light Vessel off New York. The curves represent relative speed, or speed/length ratio, which is speed related to the square root of the waterline length. Relatively the fastest yachts were Nos. 1, 3, 4, 8 and 13. The largest of all competing yachts, VENDREDI TREIZE, which is No. 2 in the upper, right-hand corner, does not even reach the 'average' curve.

finished in 28 days and a little under 13 hours.

The results of the 1972 OSTAR have been summarized in a graph, from which many different conclusions can be drawn. Along the lower edge is a scale for LWL's of yachts. Along the left vertical edge we find, from left to right, the average speed in knots, the daily run in nautical miles and the number of days at sea. Sixty days, indicated by a shaded zone, was the time limit. Anyone exceeding this time limit was out of the race.

The potential speed of a yacht, as long as it is a non-planing type, is inherent in her LWL. The three curves are for relative speed, i.e. speed/length ratio. The upper curve is for yachts which proved particularly

fast in relation to their LWL, the middle curve is for a good average, and the lower curve for particularly slow yachts. The curves must not be taken, though, as a verdict on inherent quality, for speeds were naturally affected by broken masts and rigging as well as periods of calm.

One must not forget that speed potential does not increase indefinitely as length increases. If that were the case we would get straight lines instead of curves. All yachts are, in principle, exposed to the *same* wind strengths, which means that the wind strength does not increase proportionately to the square root of LWL. It is assumed that 90 per cent of technically possible speed is reached with a LWL of around 165 ft (50 m), 99 per

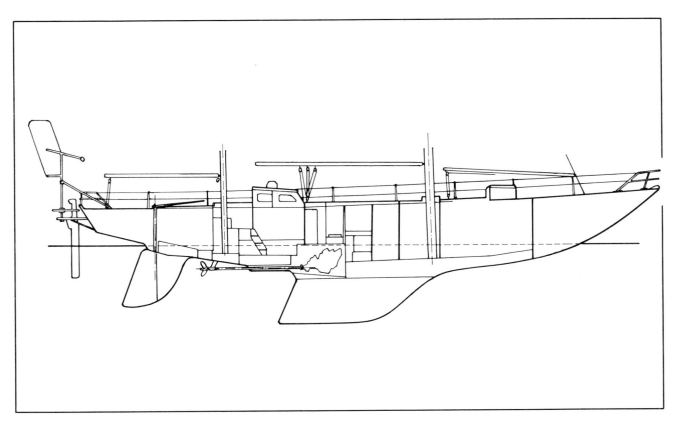

Fig. 193: Single-hander BRITISH STEEL, *in which Chay Blyth sailed round the world from East to West, following in the wake of Magellan, Drake and several others. Her very shape suggests that she is fast and close-winded, while the large rudder and skeg help to keep her on course. On the transom we can see the Hasler–Gibb self-steering gear. Chay Blyth completed his circumnavigation in 292 days.*

LOA	59 ft	Displacement ...	17 ton
LWL	46 ft	Lead ballast	5 ton
Beam	12 ft 10 in	Sail area	1507 sq ft
Draft	8 ft	Designer: Robert Clark	

cent with a LWL of around 245 ft (75 m). The construction of the curves was based on this assumption.

Viewed on this basis, the winning trimaran PEN DUICK IV was definitely the fastest boat, both for relative speed and absolute speed. Boats No. 3, 4, 8 and 13 were also very fast, 3 being the French trimaran CAP 33, 4 the surprisingly successful, heavy yacht BRITISH STEEL, 8 the small mono-hull TOUCAN and 13 the even smaller BINKIE. All of them, and many others too, reached a much higher relative speed than the super-yacht VENDREDI TREIZE, which is No. 2 in the graph.

If, however, we look at average absolute speed we are disappointed to find that only PEN DUICK IV reached a little more than 6 knots; the majority of yachts averaged 3 to 4 knots. But these figures are based on an assumed distance of 3000 nautical miles, which lay between the start and the finish. Not a single yacht, however, was able to maintain a direct course to the finish, and the true distances covered were probably about 50 per cent longer, which would make the true average speeds sailed 50 per cent faster.

In the graph, all the dots in circles represent mono-hulls, all the dots in triangles multi-hulls. The graph is of interest also to the cruising man who wants to know what average speed can be expected from a given LWL.

Small Circumnavigators

The performance of many small yachts and the innumerable accounts of adventurous voyages have shown that a small sailing boat is well capable of cruising the seven seas. Unfortunately, in many of the accounts the technical description of the boat in question is sparse or missing altogether. For this reason we will look here primarily at the design aspects of the various yachts rather than the feats they performed.

Ocean racing and cruising as a sport is a feature of the twentieth century, and even before 1920 it was only the occasional small boat which, in exceptional cases, crossed large stretches of open sea.

We begin with the famous SPRAY, which was the very first yacht to circumnavigate the world single-handed, sailed by her owner Joshua Slocum. Second, there are the plans of ISLANDER, which was twice sailed round the world single-handed before World War II, which may be said to mark the end of the 'antiquity' of yachting. It was after the end of the war, and after the post-war period of austerity had been overcome, that ocean racing and cruising embarked on its career of ever-increasing popularity. The double-ender LEHG II has been included in this chapter because she was sailed single-handed round the world in what was then the shortest time ever, moreover on an 'impossible' route.

*

The first solo circumnavigation of the world was accomplished by a boat which was not built as a yacht. Nor was her owner a yachtsman in the accepted sense of the word. One day when Joshua Slocum, a sea captain, found himself without a commission, a friend gave him a boat originally built for oyster fishing and almost 100 years old. Slocum set to work rebuilding it completely with his own hands, leaving practically none of the original timbers in place. He did, however, retain the original shape of the vessel. After one year's labour and 553 dollars poorer, he had a seaworthy little ship. He sailed her across the Atlantic twice under a sloop rig but later, in South America, he fitted a mizzen mast and turned her into a yawl.

In 1909 the American yachting magazine *The Rudder* published the re-constructed plans of SPRAY, which happened to be the same year in which boat and owner disappeared at sea without trace.

Slocum started his circumnavigation in Boston,

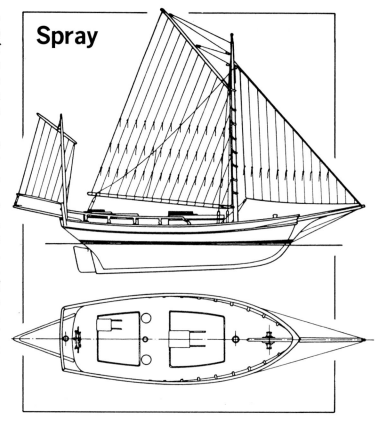

Fig. 194: SPRAY's outstanding seakindliness lead to numerous copies being built. Among them, PANDORA deserves to be mentioned, because she was the first small yacht to round Cape Horn. She was built in Australia in 1910.

LOA .... 41 ft		Draft .... 4 ft
Length along deck . 36 ft 6 in		Displacement ... 16·2 ton
LWL .... 32 ft 2 in		Ballast .. only interior ballast
Beam .... 14 ft 2 in		Sail area .... 1162 sq ft

USA in April 1895 and returned in June 1898. During the 46,000 sea miles he covered, he fully exploited SPRAY's remarkable ability to sail herself once he had found the correct rudder and sail trim. On one occasion she sailed herself for 23 days over a distance of 2700 sea miles without her owner spending more than an hour at the helm. Slocum was not only an experienced sailing ship captain, who understood how to get the best from his boat, he had also been careful in choosing his route in such a way that he benefited from quartering trade winds over long stretches.

SPRAY's dimensions and the way in which she was built show her to be a strong, dependable vessel with

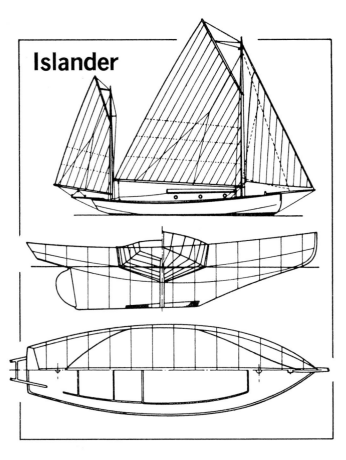

Islander

Fig. 195: ISLANDER *was built by her owner, Harry Pidgeon, entirely single-handed. He sailed her round the world twice, without any fuss and quite unsung.*

LOA	34 ft	Displacement	10 ton
LWL	27 ft 6 in	Ballast weight	1243 lb
Beam	10 ft 9 in	Sail area	635 sq ft
Draft	5 ft		

Thomas Fleming Day, offshore sailor *par excellence* and editor of *The Rudder*, crossed the Atlantic in 1911 in a yacht called SEA BIRD, 26 ft 3 in (7·8 m) in length. He sailed her into the Mediterranean and finally to Rome. This was probably the first Transatlantic crossing in a really small, genuine yacht. SEA BIRD was designed by Fred W Goeller, who was on the editorial staff of *The Rudder*. She had the following dimensions: LOA 26 ft 3 in (7·8 m), LWL 19 ft 6 in (5·8 m), beam 8 ft 6 in (2·55 m). The hull was of simple hard-chine section, making her suitable for amateur construction. Her successful Transatlantic voyage aroused such enthusiasm for offshore sailing, as well as amateur construction, that within a short space of time *hundreds* of Sea Birds were built. One of these, by the name of SEA QUEEN, became very well known, because she turned turtle in a typhoon and righted herself again. Her owner was the famous single-handed sailor, Captain Voss. The boat survived this misfortune, which occurred in the Sea of Japan near Yokohama, without any ill effect and proved once more just how seaworthy a small, well-found vessel can be.

The popularity of the Sea Bird type surpassed that of any other design at that time. Some time later, encouraged by this success, her designer drew up the plans for a somewhat larger yacht along the same principles, which he named SEAGOER. She came to the notice of a certain Harry Pidgeon, who had spent most of life farming and knew nothing whatever about sailing. Still, he had interested himself in sailing matters for some years, and later he showed himself to be a born sailor. He obtained a set of plans and, without the slightest knowledge of boat building or sailing, decided to build a Seagoer himself.

He set to work with admirable energy and began to build his boat, without any help, on the beach near Los Angeles under the kindly Californian sky. His persistence was rewarded, and in 1918, eighteen months later, this clear-thinking and hard-working man was able to launch his own boat, which he named ISLANDER. His savings of 2000 dollars had just been enough to pay for the building materials.

He spent the first four years learning to sail and gaining experience on longer sea crossings. Then, in 1922, he started on his first circumnavigation, which he completed successfully in 1925. In 1932 he decided to do it all over again, although by then he was already

good initial stability. Although, judging from the stability curve, she would seem uncapsizable, the absence of fixed external ballast makes this extremely doubtful. Be that as it may, her successful circumnavigation resulted in many copies being built, one of which sailed round the world under the name of IGDRASIL.

After his return in 1898 Slocum remained true to SPRAY and sailed to many places along the American coast, still single-handed until, one day in 1909, he left New York and was never seen again. Since no storms were reported at that time, it may be supposed that SPRAY was run down by a steamer at night . . .

64. His advancing years did not prevent him from trying a third time, this time with his wife, since he had married meanwhile. But the two of them were unlucky. Their ISLANDER, tried and tested in all weathers, was driven ashore in a gale on the rock-bound coast of the New Hebrides and completely wrecked. Harry Pidgeon and his wife were rescued and never stopped to mourn the loss of their wonderful boat. This occurred 27 years after ISLANDER had been launched and her owner had reached the age of 77.

The surprisingly simple lines of the boat, especially the hard-chine sections with straight sides and floors, were chosen for the sole purpose of simplifying building by amateurs with limited wood-working skill. The long-term aim was to make offshore sailing accessible to more people. Her suitability for offshore work is best attested by Harry Pidgeon's own words when he said, after his second circumnavigation, that he would probably have made his voyage in any other solidly built yacht but in none other would it have been as effortless. He had never reached port hungry or short of water, and never had gale-force winds, either on the high seas or near the coast, given him any cause for concern.

*

The most adventurous of the earlier circumnavigations was made by the Argentinian Vito Dumas in his boat LEHG II. He left Buenos Aires on 27th June 1942 and returned to his home port on 7th September 1943, taking only a little over one year to round the world. He chose the loneliest, stormiest and most inhospitable route of all, following approximately the 40th Parallel South, where the ocean is scarcely interrupted by land. The frequency of gales in this zone have earned it the name of the Roaring Forties. Dumas broke several records on his voyage: he was the first single-hander to round Cape Horn successfully; he made the first circumnavigation in the 'wrong' direction, i.e. from west to east; he was the first single-hander to round three capes, and finally he covered the longest distances at sea between stops, calling only at three ports: Cape Town, Wellington and Valparaiso. He never lay to a sea anchor nor under bare poles, nor did he ever trail hawsers to slow him down.

LEHG II's time was considered exceptionally fast in those days, but she was not in a race or out to win a

254

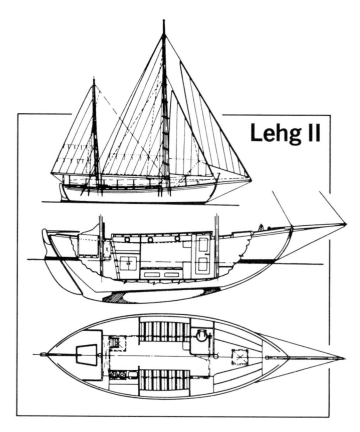

Fig. 196: LEHG II is a Colin Archer-type double-ender. She proved her worth during her lone circumnavigation from 1942 to 1943.

LOA	31 ft 4 in	Displacement	8·5 ton
LWL	27 ft 6 in	Ballast weight	3 ton
Beam	10 ft 10 in	Sail area	452 sq ft
Draft	5 ft 7 in		

prize. Twenty-six years later, in 1968, the British Merchant Navy officer Robin Knox-Johnston won the single-handed 'Round the World' race, and the interesting thing is that his SUHAILI was almost the spitten image of LEHG II. There were a few inches difference in the hull dimensions, but the shape was the same and she, too, was ketch-rigged with a little more sail area. But since she was sailed in a race, and non-stop at that, her time was very much shorter.

SUHAILI rounded all three capes, like LEHG II, but since both start and finish were at Falmouth on the south coast of England, the total distance she covered was about 10,000 sea miles more; yet she only took 10 months and 9 days. She was probably the slowest of the nine starters, but all the others had to give up for various reasons. Francis Chichester in his GIPSY MOTH, 53 ft (16·2 m) long and very fast, only took 9 months, although he had spent quite some time in Sydney to make certain alterations.

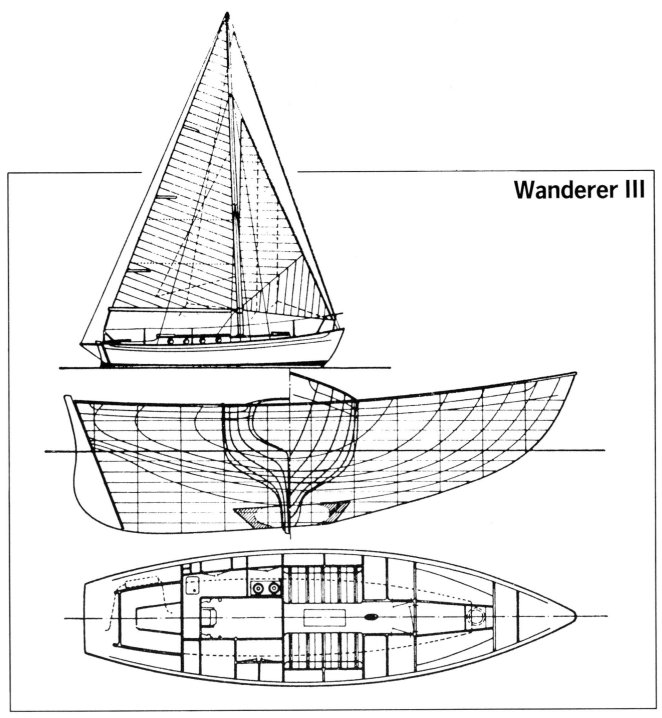

Wanderer III

Fig. 197: The successful circumnavigator WANDERER III was sailed round the world twice by Eric and Susan Hiscock.

LOA	30 ft 6 in	Displacement	9 ton
LWL	26 ft 5 in	Ballast weight	3·1 ton
Beam	8 ft 5 in	Sail area	420 sq ft
Draft	5 ft		

The above plans are of WANDERER III, another small yacht which sailed round the world twice. Her owner Eric Hiscock and his wife Susan both had considerable practical sailing experience and saw in this great adventure the culmination of many years of cruising. In this respect they differ from the three already described, who were not yachtsmen in the strict meaning of the world, but who might be said to have had an obsession to sail round the world. The Hiscocks' world voyages might be regarded as a model of how an experienced yachtsman, having spent much time on careful planning and selection of gear, can achieve such a feat in an exemplary way. As this book goes to print the Hiscocks are on their third voyage round the world in the much larger WANDERER IV.

When the Hiscocks asked Laurent Giles to design

255

Kairos

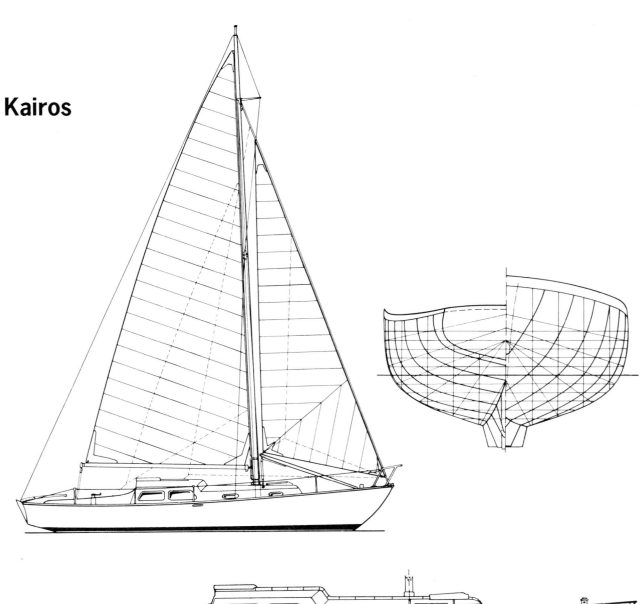

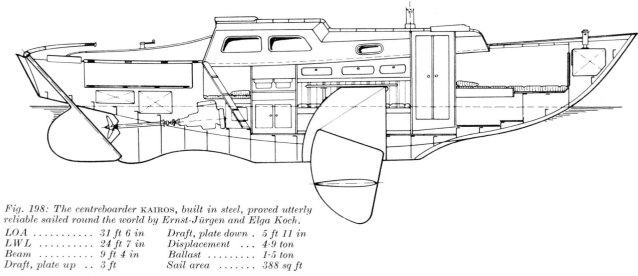

Fig. 198: The centreboarder KAIROS, *built in steel, proved utterly
reliable sailed round the world by Ernst-Jürgen and Elga Koch.*

LOA	31 ft 6 in	Draft, plate down .	5 ft 11 in
LWL	24 ft 7 in	Displacement . . .	4·9 ton
Beam	9 ft 4 in	Ballast	1·5 ton
Draft, plate up . .	3 ft	Sail area	388 sq ft

WANDERER III for them, they already had a great deal of experience in offshore cruising in a boat which was only slightly smaller. WANDERER III was a *happy ship* from the beginning. Launched early in 1952 she started on her first circumnavigation in July of the same year, returning to her home port exactly three years later, in July 1955.

If we look at WANDERER III's sail plan we notice that the sail area is generous for a hull of this size, the reason obviously being to obtain adequate driving power even in light winds. The jib is taken only three-quarters of the way up the mast, whereas the genoa goes to the masthead. The various sail areas have been carefully calculated to give a balanced ship at all times, with a maximum sail area on the wind of 603 sq ft (56 m²), as much as with a minimum of 117 sq ft (11 m²) under trysail and storm jib. On long stretches before the wind twin spinnakers were used. These were tri-angular, each with an area of 161 sq ft (15 m²), and enabled the boat to steer herself even before the wind. If we compare WANDERER III's sail plan with those of the three preceding boats, we notice that she is the first with an all-inboard rig and without a bowsprit. This was only possible because designer and owner had the courage to settle for a comparatively high mast.

Eric Hiscock said about WANDERER III: 'She never gave us a moments anxiety, even in difficult wind and weather conditions. She always did what we asked of her. She has served us well and has returned in perfect condition.'

*

The four yachts we have looked at so far have all had a fixed deep keel and ample draft. KAIROS, on the other hand, in which the German couple Jürgen and Elga Koch sailed round the world, had a drop plate. She too has similar dimensions to the preceding yachts (with the exception of SPRAY, which was much bigger). An overall length of between 30 ft and 35 ft (9–10 m) has proved to be the most satisfactory size for ocean cruising and also provide the necessary space for comfortable accommodation and for stowage.

The plan shows how the drop plate is arranged. Since it serves as support to the cabin table, it is not in the way nor does it take up space which might be needed in other ways. With the plate up the draft can be halved. Since the righting moment of the shallow ballast keel is, of course, less than that of a deep ballast keel, KAIROS was given the ample beam of 9 ft 4 in (2·85 m), which is almost 1 ft (30 cm) more than WANDERER III. She was designed by Theodor Stölken of Hamburg and built entirely in steel, including deck and superstructure. Steel has proved an excellent material for long voyages and in this type of boat ensures an absolutely watertight plate case together with reliable operation of the drop plate. Nothing is more troublesome than a plate that sticks because the wood has swollen, or which bangs about because there is too much play.

The Kochs sailed round the world in KAIROS between 1964 and 1967 and covered 33,300 sea miles. She, too, did not use self-steering gear, but she was so well balanced that she would steer herself on practically all points. On the wind this is comparatively easy, and before the wind it was accomplished by setting twin spinnakers. In very heavy weather KAIROS was hove-to, and Jürgen Koch writes in his book: 'We learned to trust completely in our ship drifting hove-to.' To date KAIROS is still the only steel yacht with a drop plate to have circumnavigated the world.

*

The Transatlantic crossing of the small yacht SOPRANINO aroused in John Guzzwell, an experienced offshore yachtsman, the desire to round the world in a very small yacht built by himself. He asked Laurent Giles to design her for him, and he built TREKKA single-handed in 1955 in British Columbia, Canada.

Hardly anyone before had contemplated the possi-bility of an offshore yacht of such small dimensions. Nor would anyone have trusted in such a short under-water profile or in such lightweight construction. TREKKA was a decidedly unusual design, yet the fact that she rounded the world successfully proves the validity of the design concept.

In yachts of such small size the accommodation is usually very limited, because stowage space has to be found for a large amount of gear. Thus, the designer stipulated a very high freeboard but softened this impression by giving the top plank tumble-home (which can be seen at the bow) over the entire length of the boat. The deck is made of plywood and covered with

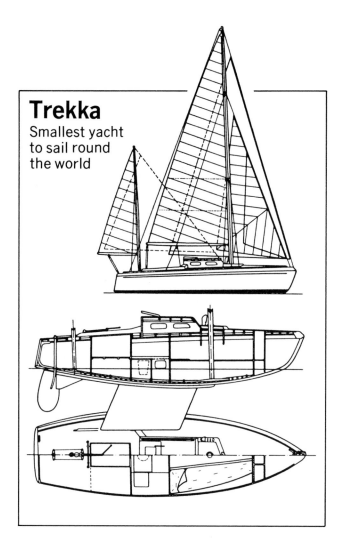

Trekka
Smallest yacht
to sail round
the world

Fig. 199: TREKKA *was one of the first really small, light circumnavigators. She was built and sailed round the world single-handed by John Guzzwell.*

LOA	*20 ft 10 in*
LWL	*18 ft 6 in*
Beam	*6 ft 8 in*
Draft	*4 ft 6 in*
Displacement ...	*3125 lb*
Ballast weight ...	*1300 lb*
Sail area	*197 sq ft*

fibreglass. The hull skin is surprisingly thin, only just over $\frac{1}{2}$ in (14 mm); seams are glued. The dinghy-type hull is built over a laminated keel, which has a fin keel of $\frac{3}{8}$ in (9·5 mm) galvanized steel fixed to it.

The yawl rig has the modest sail area of 197 sq ft (18·3 m²). However, a staysail can be set from the mizzen mast and a large genoa is provided for light airs, which together increase the sail area to 338 sq ft (32 m²). Twin jibs were set before the wind.

*

A GRP CIRCUMNAVIGATOR: In his 30 ft (9·2 m) fibreglass yacht APOGEE Alan Eddy successfully rounded the world in five years. APOGEE is ketch-rigged and has a transom stern with a hung rudder. Her voyage began in June 1963 and ended in January 1969, after having covered 39,000 sea miles. Her owner tells his story in a small book, which makes interesting reading. His opinion on the use of GRP for the construction of ocean cruising yachts is that he can wholly recommend it.

Eddy experienced really heavy weather on only four occasions. Each time, he says, life on board was *extremely uncomfortable*. His final summary is worth quoting: 'After all that I have said about safety and dangers at sea, I certainly do not want to give the impression that long voyages at sea are something unpleasant. On the contrary, about 50 per cent of the time I had splendid sailing weather, and another 40 per cent could still be described as reasonably good. Only less than 10 per cent could be rated as unpleasant. During periods of fine weather fantastic distances can be covered in a day. Between the Galapagos Islands and the Marquesas, for example, APOGEE covered 1285 sea miles in 8 days, during "flying fish weather", which is an average of 160 sea miles a day. Whenever possible I sailed in the Trade Wind belt. But I must say that I genuinely admire anybody who rounds the three capes, Cape of Good Hope, Cape Leeuwin and Cape Horn, in a small yacht.'

ROUND THE WORLD IN A HOME-BUILT TRIMARAN: Bernhard Rhodes, a young English ship's carpenter, was determined to build with his own hands, and very little money, the cheapest possible offshore yacht which could be sailed round the world. He designed the trimaran KLIS himself and built her in his free time in two years; total cost around £400. The hull skin was made of $\frac{1}{4}$ in (6 mm) marine plywood, the deck of $\frac{3}{8}$ in (10 mm) marine plywood, frames, girders and spars of Columbia pine. The hull was fibreglass-covered as far as the waterline, but during his stay in St Croix in the West Indies Rhodes covered the whole boat with nylon and resin.

Here is another example of what a determined amateur can do: Bernhard Rhodes not only drew up his own sail plan but actually made his own sails, as well as his self-steering gear.

Any catamaran or trimaran sailor occasionally wonders what would happen if his vessel capsized and whether he could right it. Rhodes did a practical experiment in a quiet Tahitian lagoon. He removed anything valuable on board and replaced the weight with ballast. Then, with the help of seven men, he capsized KLIS, mast downwards. He then tried to right her on his own by letting one of the side hulls fill with water and using the spinnaker boom as a lever. In this way he finally managed to submerse that hull completely, raising the opposite hull out of the water in doing so. After two hours' work KLIS was righted and could be bailed out. Whether the same operation could be successfully undertaken by one man actually *at sea* is another question.

The author met KLIS in New Zealand having already rounded half the world, partly single-handed, partly with a crew of two. He never found out whether she completed the round trip. Anyone wanting to cover large distances of open sea in a vessel as small and as light as KLIS not only needs to be an exceedingly good sailor, but he needs a great deal of luck.

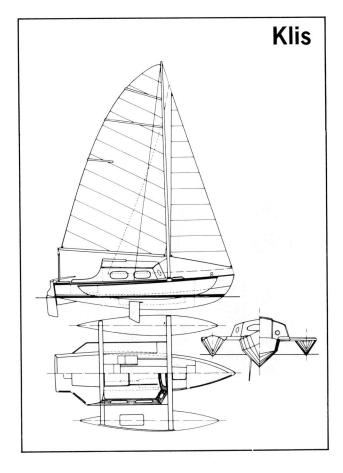

Klis

Fig. 200: The small and surprisingly light trimaran KLIS was sailed by her enterprising owner and builder Bernard Rhodes from England to New Zealand and since then, probably, round the world.

LOA	22 ft	Weight, fully	
LWL	20 ft 4 in	equipped	2200 lb
Beam OA	14 ft	Sail area	258 sq ft
Draft, plate up	1 ft 8 in		
Draft, plate down	3 ft		
Weight, empty	1100 lb		

Trailable Yachts and Dinghy Cruisers

There are two reasons why anyone should want to trail a sailing boat, or a motorboat for that matter. In Europe it is common for boat owners to take their boats away in the holidays to explore waters further away from home. In large, spacious countries like Australia and New Zealand, and to a lesser extent in the USA where, in contrast to Europe, practically everyone lives in his own house with garden and garage, people do not keep their boats in the club grounds or the club anchorage, where space is nearly always restricted, but at home, in the garden, the garage or under the car port.

The author was introduced to one yacht club in New Zealand, which is exclusively a 'Trailer' Yacht Club. It occupies a fairly large plot of land, but the stretch of water in front of it is very small. There are three launching ramps, but there is not a single boat in sight. On Saturday morning a steady stream of boats on

trailers starts to arrive. They are launched in seconds and the owners take their cars and trailers to the large car park, where they remain for the day, or even till the next day. As each boat returns from its weekend out, it is equally quickly hauled out of the water on its trailer. Nearby is a wash bay, where owner and crew hose the remains of salt water off the boat. Then the boat is trailed back home again. One only has to count the trailers in the car park to know at any time how many boats are out sailing. This kind of set-up obviously keeps club subscriptions very low. It must be added here that the small, protected stretch of water in front of the club has access to the sea. There is another aspect to this popularity of trailer-boats: amateur construction. People who have the necessary space in their houses or gardens like to build their own boats, especially in Australia and New Zealand.

The first boat featured here is a typical New Zealand

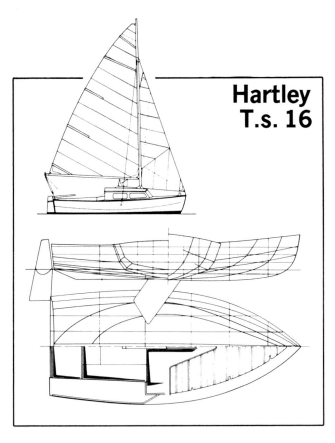

Hartley T.s. 16

Fig. 201: Trailer-sailers are particularly popular in Australia and New Zealand, where they are trailed from home and back again and kept in the garden or garage.

LOA	16 ft 5 in	Draft, plate down	3 ft 7 in
LWL	15 ft 7 in	Displacement	1100 lb
Beam	7 ft 2 in	Interior ballast	100 lb
Draft, plate up	8 in	Sail area	180 sq ft

'trailer-sailer' from the board of *the* designer of amateur-construction plans, Richard Hartley. We see here a solid, stable boat of double-chine shape, about 16 ft (5 m) long, called the Hartley Trailer Sailer 16. We chose this boat because it has been built in large numbers, more than three-quarters of them by amateurs. Hundreds of these boats are sailing in New Zealand and Australia, and a few other countries, too. Far from being particularly smart or modern, they have proved themselves in practice. There are several sizes in the series: 12 ft, 14 ft, 16 ft, 18 ft and 21 ft.

Since they carry comparatively little ballast, these boats can, of course, capsize, but this happens very rarely. If it does, they do not fill up, because the cockpit seats and side decks are sufficiently buoyant to keep the boat afloat above the line where water would get inside. After a capsize they are easily righted. The 16-footer has 100 lb (45 kg) of ballast stowed just forward of the centreplate case. The 18-footer carries 285 lb (130 kg) of internal ballast, the 21-footer as much as 495 lb (225 kg).

There are quite a number of other boats which have either been designed specifically for trailing or, due to their size and underwater shape, are especially suited to being trailed. The next one we look at is a drop-keel boat designed by the French designer Charles Chaveau; it is quite a bit bigger and has a good deal more accommodation.

The most unusual aspect about this French design is the shape and arrangement of the drop keel, which runs on rollers inside a curved casing. This scarcely intrudes in the main cabin, and it does not seem to be inconveniently placed in the forecabin either. Chaveau has been concentrating on this type for years, and it reflects his extensive experience. The drop keel has a 495 lb (225 kg) streamlined ballast keel at its lower end. When the keel is fully lowered, the ballast is at a useful depth, when it is fully raised the ballast remains just below the hull. At the foot of the mast, in the cabin, we can make out the winding handle which raises and lowers the keel. A drop keel of this type certainly provides better stability than the internal ballast of the Hartley Trailer Sailer and, even more so than the latter, this boat can be considered virtually uncapsizable. Relying on greater stability, the sails are cut rather higher. A pulpit and lifelines, though rather low, provide a useful safety factor. Since the boat is intended mainly for inland waters, the mast can be lowered.

*

Our American representative in this series is once again slightly bigger and described as a 'trailer yacht'. This type does not have a centreplate or drop keel but a permanent ballast keel of very modest draft. The Coronado 23, built by Coronado Yachts of California in fibreglass, was designed by the Australian designer Alan Paine, off whose board came the America's Cup challengers GRETEL and GRETEL II.

The Coronado 23 is intended primarily as a family boat for holidaying and weekending. For its length it has a modest sail area, which also takes into account the shallow ballast keel, which gives the boat a draft of only 2 ft (60 cm). This does make the boat uncapsizable,

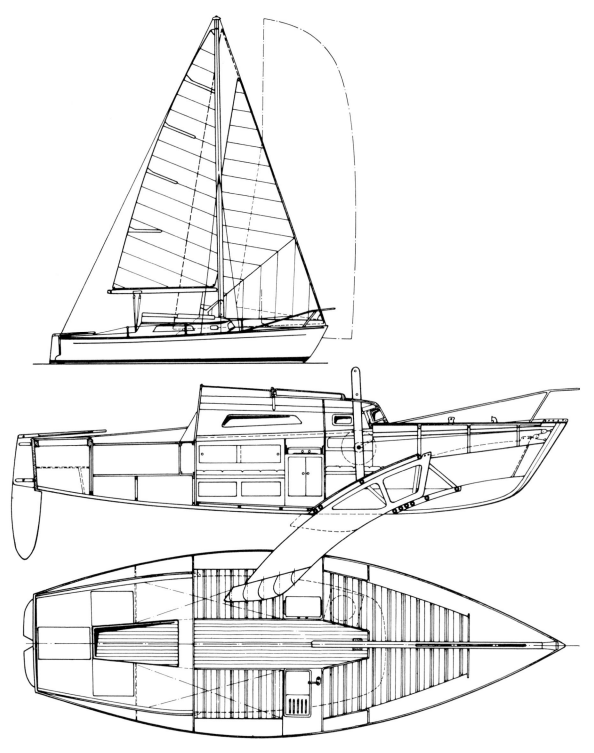

Fig. 202: Dinghy cruiser with drop keel. In the fully retracted position only the lead bulb remains outside the hull. This makes the boat very suitable for trailing and for use in shallow waters.

LOA .... 21 ft 8 in Draft, plate down . 4 ft 7 in
LWL .... 19 ft 5 in Displacement ... 2420 lb
Beam .... 7 ft 6 in Ballast on keel .. 495 lb
Draft, plate up .. 1 ft 8 in Sail area .... 180 sq ft

262

but gives her only a modest performance on the wind. On the other hand, the long keel gives good longitudinal stability and makes launching easy.

In the perspective drawing of the Coronado 23 on its trailer we can see part of the accommodation, which consists of a dinette to port, a single berth to starboard, a galley further forward and two berths in the fore-cabin, with the possibility of a WC in between. The auxiliary is a 6·5 hp outboard, which is stowed in the port cockpit locker, together with a separate petrol tank.

The fibreglass hull is unusual in that all the fore-and-aft and sectional stiffeners are incorporated in the lining moulding, which is carefully matched up to the outer hull to make a light yet strong construction. The

mast is stepped on deck, exactly over the main bulkhead and its two supports. Columbia Boatyards of California produce the same boat with a slightly different accommodation layout.

*

The true dinghy cruiser (JOLLENKREUZER in German) originated on the lower Elbe in Germany shortly before World War I. Starting life as a dinghy with a small cabin, it quickly gained popularity, especially on the lakes and rivers round Berlin. Its heyday is now definitely over, but there are still classes of the 15 m², 20 m² and 30 m² types around. Genuine dinghy cruisers have no ballast at all and are capsizable. Whether or not a dinghy cruiser suffers a capsize at some time

263

Coronado 23

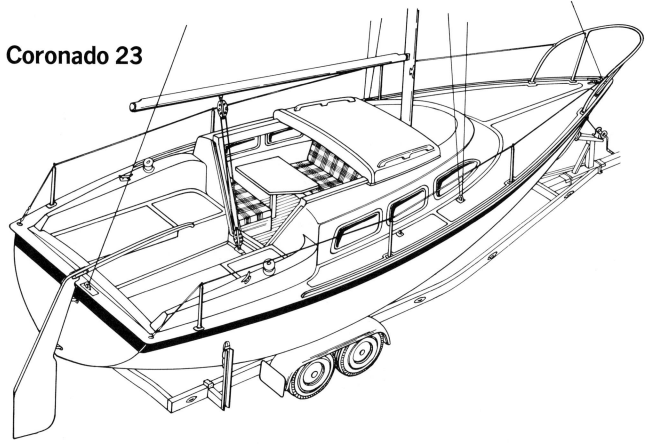

Fig. 203: The American trailer cruiser Coronado 23 on its twin-axle trailer. She is a small but surprisingly seaworthy cruiser with a shallow ballast keel, large cockpit and comfortable accommodation.

LOA	*22 ft 8 in*	*Displacement* ...	*2310 lb*
LWL	*20 ft*	*Exterior ballast* ..	*814 lb*
Beam	*8 ft*	*Sail area*	*218 sq ft*
Draft	*2 ft*	*Outboard motor* ..	*6½ hp*

during its career depends entirely on the seamanship of those who sail it. If it does capsize, it is almost imposs-ible to right it without outside help. On the other hand, because of its extremely shallow draft, a dinghy cruiser has access to all the secluded, secretive corners on lakes and rivers and can even be run up on the bank or shore. It can, of course, be trailed, but this is not very often done.

The plans in Fig. 204 show one of the most successful 20 m² dinghy cruiser, BIELEKEN. She was built with about 8 in (20 cm) more beam than laid down in the class rules, and her many successes in racing vindicated that modification. BIELEKEN was designed by G Brandt, who foresaw the increased beam as a speed-promoting factor from the beginning. BIELEKEN's hull is excep-tionally long for her sail area of 20 m², and this is another factor in favour of speed.

The smaller 15 m² dinghy cruiser has a length of 21 ft 4 in (6·5 m) and a beam of 6 ft 10 in (2·1 m), while the largest in the series, with a sail area of 30 m², is 29 ft 6 in (9 m) long and has a beam of 9 ft 2 in (2·8 m). Many dinghy cruisers have made lengthy passages in the open sea, but the risk cannot be justified. As soon as the weather deteriorates markedly, a boat like this, which is capsizable, finds herself in grave danger and this did, indeed, happen in a number of cases.

*

The Bélouga, which is similar to the German dinghy cruiser, enjoys great popularity in French waters. It has been built in large numbers and illustrates the popular demand for a light, shallow-draft cabin boat.

The Bélouga class was designed in 1943 by E Cornu

264

20 sq.m.
Dinghy Cruiser

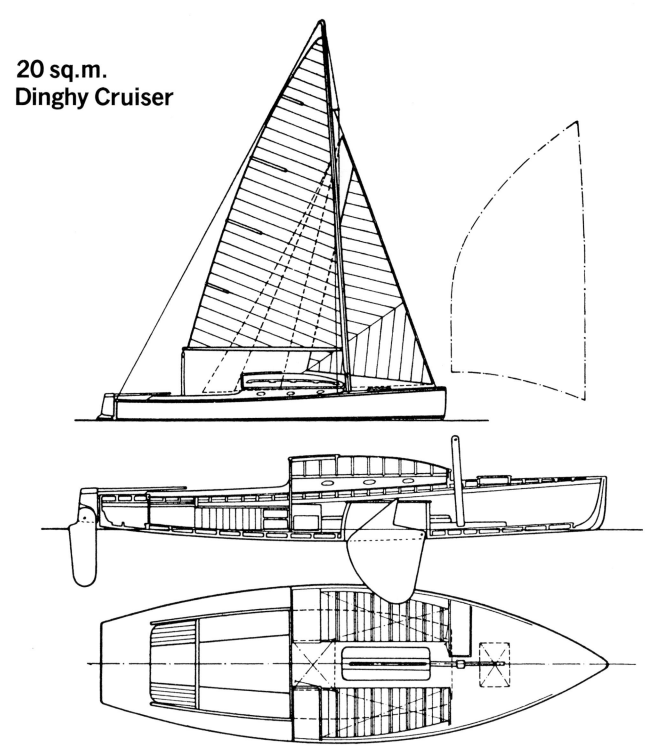

*Fig. 204: This typically German dinghy cruiser for inland waters
is a very fast boat with extremely shallow draft.*

LOA	25 ft 5 in	Draft, plate down	3 ft 10 in
LWL	24 ft 7 in	Displacement	2200 lb
Beam	8 ft	Sail area	215 sq ft
Draft, plate up	7 in		

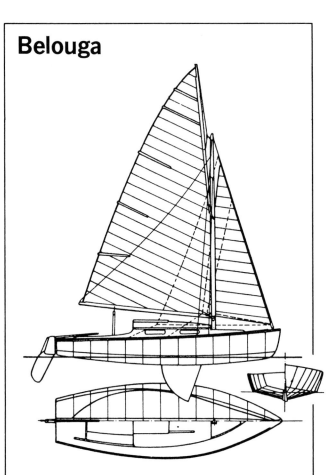

Belouga

Fig. 205: The French version of the dinghy cruiser, the popular Bélouga, is a hard-chine boat of lively performance on inland waters.

LOA	21 ft 4 in	Draft, plate down	3 ft 9 in
LWL	19 ft 4 in	Displacement	1540 lb
Beam	7 ft 4 in	Sail area	213 sq ft
Draft, plate up	9 in		

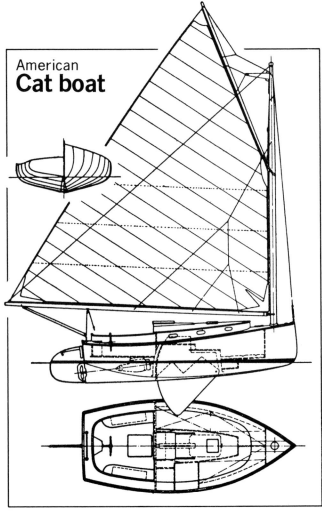

American Cat boat

Fig. 206: Many of the typical features of the American Cat Boat are those of a dinghy cruiser. It has gone through decades of development and by its origins could indeed be called the grandfather of the dinghy cruiser. It is a very beamy, comfortable family boat.

LOA	23 ft 11 in	Draft, plate down	6 ft
LWL	23 ft 3 in	Displacement	4400 lb
Beam	10 ft 9 in	Exterior ballast	none
Draft, plate up	2 ft 4 in	Sail area	581 sq ft

in co-operation with the successful racing helmsman Jaques Lebrun. To keep building costs low and facilitate amateur construction, the hull has a simple hard-chine shape, but it is normally planked with solid timber rather than plywood.

The Bélouga is gunter-rigged, probably because this gives the sail plan a lower centre of effort, but also on account of the ease with which the shorter mast can be

lowered and stowed when the boat is cruised on inland waterways. As long as all boats of one class are the same, it is of no importance that they could all be slightly faster if they had a high-aspect ratio rig. The accommodation of the Bélouga consists of two berths, hanging locker, table and small galley, a layout which is fairly usual in boats of this size. It is easily trailed. The large centreplate gives it a good performance on the wind. With the plate raised, the draft is minimal, so that the boat can be run straight onto any gently shelving shore.

*

Quite a different type is the American Catboat, which has been exceptionally popular in the United States for over a hundred years. Figure 206 shows one of the most commonly built types as regards dimensions, rig and accommodation. This boat was designed and built by the Crosby Boatyard, which was building such craft as early as 1860. Since then, and until recent times, there have been numerous builders of catboats, and types differ considerably from each other. What they all have in common is the short, beamy hull with the mast stepped very far forward near the stemhead. Thanks to their exceptionally ample beam these boats can carry an abnormally large sail area, all in a single sail. During its early history the catboat was always gaff-rigged, but more recently Bermudan sails are equally common.

Nowadays these boats are hardly ever built in wood, but the modern plastic hulls look every bit as good as the wooden ones used to, and they are equally sturdy. Most of these boats have no external ballast. Owners of catboats find the spacious cockpit particularly convenient and appreciate the respectable turn of speed these boats can develop, especially in light winds. Their wide beam gives them good initial stability, and they can be sailed unreefed up to considerable wind strengths. The long keel provides directional stability, while the large centreplate makes the boat quick in stays and close-winded.

The position of the mast so far forward might fill the critical observer with some anxiety, but over the years all the potential problems have been very satisfactorily solved, like the optimum mast diameter, the arrangement of the hog and what strengthening is necessary for the deck. While some people might find the lack of a foresail a disadvantage, this is offset by the unusual roominess of the cabin uninterrupted by a mast. In the plan shown the mast is supported by a single forestay only, but many catboats also have a pair of shrouds. It obviously took a lot of experimenting to establish the correct relationship between the sail area, the short, beamy hull and the position of the centreplate so that

Plate 53: The German trailer-sailer, the Traveller, designed by Uwe Mares and built in fibreglass by Klepper. By carrying the cabin sides out to the gunwale the designer has put an unusual amount of accommodation in 19 ft 8 in, there being no less than four full length berths. The boat has a beam of 8 ft and a sail area of 193 sq ft. The cockpit is very roomy and there is a lifting keel operated by a winch.   Photo: Klepper-Werke

the boat would be reasonably balanced in all weathers. The particular boat we have shown has a proper steering wheel, which is unusual for such a small vessel, but many others have a conventional tiller.

*

A completely different type of shallow-draft centreplate boat enjoys great popularity on the River Plate.

267

Whaleboat
Juana Maria

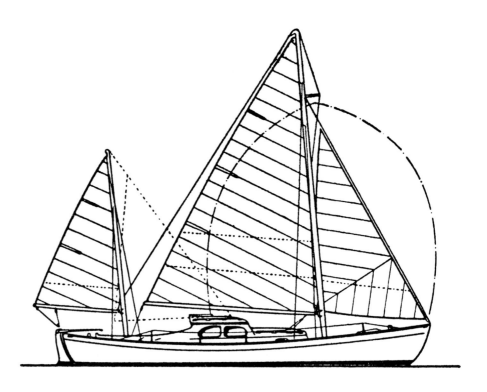

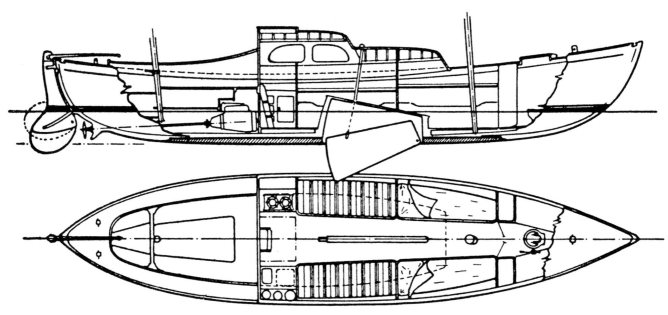

Fig. 207: The Argentinian Whaleboat is, strictly speaking, a
centreplate keelboat, for it has a certain amount of built-in ballast.
In the shallow estuaries of the River Plate it is very popular.

LOA	*34 ft 1 in*	*Draft, plate down*	*4 ft 1 in*
LWL	*30 ft 8 in*	*Displacement*	*9460 lb*
Beam	*7 ft 10 in*	*Ballast*	*1452 lb*
Draft, plate up	*2 ft*	*Sail area*	*350 sq ft*

The whaleboat, being long and narrow, is the direct opposite to the American catboat. It further differs from all the preceding types in that it is double-ended and has an external ballast keel with a weight of 0·6 tons. JUANA MARIA, shown in Fig. 207, is off the board of Manuel M Campos, who has great experience with this kind of craft.

The very wide, shallow River Plate has a number of small, attractive tributaries, particularly on the Uruguayan side, which Argentinian sailors like to visit. Since the whaleboat has a draft of only 2 ft (60 cm) it can easily negotiate the usual sandbank off the confluence and proceed up these delightful little rivers. Under sail it is essential to lower the plate. The long, slim hull with its fine lines makes this a very fast boat, despite the modest sail area. There is room for a spacious cockpit and four permanent berths below. Under the doghouse, which does not in any way impair the boat's attractive appearance, the headroom is 5 ft 6 in (1·65 m).

The low ketch rig makes for a low centre of effort of the sail area, which is essential with such a shallow hull. In very light winds the sail area can be considerably increased by using a number of extra sails, including a staysail between the masts and a large spinnaker.

The ratio of the ballast keel to the total weight is only a little over 15 per cent, which is a minimum necessary to safeguard against capsizing. In practice, though, stability has proved adequate, although the modest ballast weight is at a very shallow depth. The boat probably has just enough excess stability to be uncapsizable. Similar types of whaleboat are found in other parts of the world, particularly in the estuaries of large rivers, where sandbanks and shallow harbour entrances favour shallow-draft vessels.

Junior Classes

Plate 54: Optimist dinghies.   Photo: Yacht-Archives

The term 'Junior class' describes mainly boats which offer good, competitive racing for youngsters from about 14 years onwards. But children can learn to sail at a much earlier age, and so we will start this chapter with the smallest of small dinghies, the Optimist.

INTERNATIONAL OPTIMIST: It was the thought that children could learn to sail their own dinghies, long before they are old enough to join one of the rather more sophisticated junior classes, which gave rise to the inception of the Optimist dinghy. The designer and boat-builder Clark Mills from Florida, USA, was asked by his yacht club to suggest a design which would be suitable for children from eight years onwards. It had to be built in marine plywood and so easy to assemble that the children themselves, with some help from parents or older sailing friends, could have a go at building it. In this way the Optimist was born in 1947, and it did, indeed, become a dream boat for

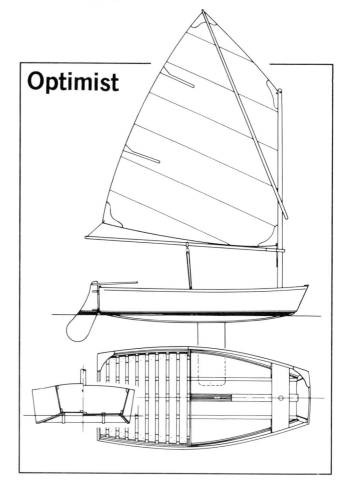

Fig. 208: The Optimist is an international class boat for children from about 8 years onwards. Despite its simple form it is a good performer.

LOA	7 ft 8 in	*Draft, plate down*	2 ft 7 in
LWL	6 ft 10 in	*Weight, hull*	66 lb
Beam	3 ft 8 in	*Weight, equipped*	88 lb
Draft, plate up	3 in	*Sail area*	35 sq ft

children. It was cheap to build, good to sail and every boy and girl felt at home in it.

Anyone who thinks that this simple, box-shaped hull could not possibly make much of a sailing dinghy is soon disabused of this prejudice when he sees an enthusiastic group of youngsters in training or sailing a race. The boat is exactly what it set out to be: sturdy and stable in bad weather, beamy for safety, yet at the same time smart and lively. It had an enthusiastic welcome in many countries, and one is probably not far wrong in estimating that the total number built so far must be around 30,000.

In Scandinavia one sees large fleets of Optimists with conspicuous advertising on their sails, which means that at least the sails, in many cases even the complete hull kits, were donated by the respective firms, so that the children built and painted the boats with very little expense to themselves. The upper age limit is usually fixed at 15, when the now experienced youngsters graduate to a bigger and more competitive dinghy.

Like other boats, the Optimist has been brought up to date since its early days. It is now made of lighter plywood, even in plastic, it has Terylene or Dacron sails and an alloy mast. The status of the class is now such that even world championships are held.

*

INTERNATIONAL CADET: Once children have outgrown an Optimist or some other small sailing tender, the Cadet is the logical choice. It was designed for rather more serious racing, and its larger size makes it eminently suitable for use as a two-man junior class. The design by Jack Holt was sponsored by the magazine *Yachting World* and was so favourably received, that the IYRU selected it as an International Junior Class quite early on.

The Cadet's rig is calculated to appeal to racing-minded youngsters, for it not only includes a jib but even a small spinnaker. The bow is not pointed but has a small transom, which simplifies construction and makes the hull slightly more roomy. The floor is no longer flat, as in the Optimist, but V-shaped. The hull is decked all round, so that it looks more like a fully-fledged racing dinghy than a tender. Thousands of these boats are sailed in many countries. In racing, they must have a crew of two, the upper age limit being 18.

*

It must always be remembered that all junior classes are capsizable, but this fact is neither considered a drawback nor particularly dangerous. It is conditional, though, that every young sailor can swim (*every* yachtsman should be able to swim) and that life-jackets are worn at all times. If a boat does capsize on occasions, the only consequence is laughter by the others, who will usually assist in getting the victims back to the shore where they can bail the boat out. If the water is very cold, though, it is advisable not to run the risk of a capsize.

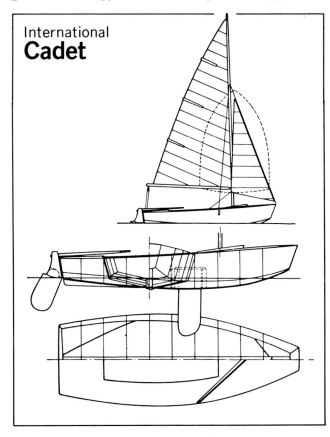

International **Cadet**

Fig. 209: The International Cadet is a junior class for older children who have some experience and want to race rather more seriously.

LOA	10 ft 6 in	Weight without	
LWL	9 ft 3 in	crew	154 lb
Beam	4 ft 2 in	Sail area	56 sq ft

Pirat

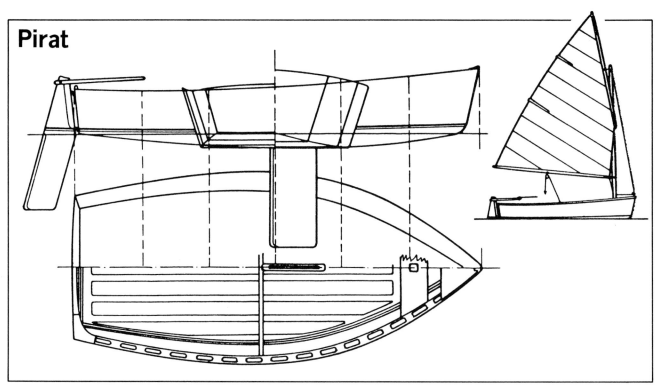

Fig. 210: The Dutch Pirat is a junior class as suitable for small beginners as the International Optimist. Its shape is rather more pleasing, but amateur construction is not quite as simple.

LOA	. . . . 7 ft 10 in	Weight without	
LWL	. . . . 7 ft 4 in	crew	. . . . 66 lb
Beam	. . . . 3 ft 9 in	Sail area	. . . . 35 sq ft

It would be impossible to mention every junior class in existence. Junior classes can be produced almost *ad lib* by taking any proven racing class boat and reducing its sail area, which makes it at once safer and simpler to handle. The American Penguin class, for example, has too little stability to be safe for youngsters. The author, when his two sons were small, had the mast of a Penguin shortened and the 80 sq ft (7·2 m²) Bermudan rig replaced by a 40 sq ft (3·6 m²) lugsail; thus modified, the rather narrow dinghy was suitable even for a ten-year old.

*

It is entirely possible to design a small dinghy, like the Optimist, with a pointed bow instead of a transom and this has, indeed, been done in the Dutch Pirat dinghy. Dimensions and lines of this boat are very similar to those of the Optimist, but at the same time

272

the Pirat represents a rather more sophisticated development of the same idea. As in the Optimist, the bottom is flat athwartships. The Pirat is less than 2 in (5 cm) longer and beamier by only 1 in (2·5 cm) with the sail area exactly the same, yet the boat looks completely different. It was designed by J Kraaier, who skilfully chose the dimensions to coincide with the standard size of sheets of marine plywood.

The Pirat, too, has only a mainsail, which is a lugsail. In this way the mast can be kept short and the sail simple. There are no fittings to the rigging, and a single halliard hoists and lowers the sail. There are no floor stringers; the bottom is simply reinforced by glued-on strips of plywood. Centreboard and rudder are also made of plywood. The simple hull design encourages amateur construction, and indeed Pirats have been built by whole forms of schoolchildren.

*

The world-wide popularity of the Lightning class inspired the inception of a similar, smaller boat for young people: the American Blue Jay junior class, designed, like the Lightning, by Sparkman & Stephens. With a LOA of 13 ft 6 in (4·12 m) the Blue Jay is quite a large boat. Its beam is 5 ft 2 in (1·58 m) and its weight, ready to sail without crew, is 275 lb (125 kg). It has a normal Bermudan sloop rig of 90 sq ft (8·4 m²) plus a large spinnaker.

Australia fosters a junior class, which is completely different in that it has a long bowsprit. Called Vee-Jay, it has a LOA of 11 ft 6 in (3·5 m) and a beam of 4 ft 3 in (1·3 m); it is almost completely decked with only a small opening for the cockpit. If the boat capsizes, it can happen that not a single drop of water gets into the hull, because it floats so high. As indicated by the bowsprit, the boat carries an unusually large sail area: 118 sq ft (11 m²). The young Australians rig the boat ashore and put it in the water with all sails up.

The largest of all junior-class boats is probably the German Pirat (not to be confused with the Dutch Pirat). This thoroughbred racing dinghy was designed by Carl Martens and enjoys great popularity in Ger-many and neighbouring countries. Its dimensions are LOA 16 ft 4 in (5 m), beam 5 ft 3 in (1·61 m), weight with all gear 375 lb (170 kg). The sloop rig has a measured sail area of 108 sq ft (10 m²).

In recent years many young people have taken to the 420, which has already been described in the chapter on racing dinghies. It has all the characteristics of a highly competitive racing dinghy, yet its size makes it suitable for young people who already have a good grounding in junior sailing and want to graduate to rather more serious racing.

Since 1953 the so-called Junior Gold Cup keelboat championships have been held in Europe. Originally the competing countries were Denmark, Norway, Ireland, Finland and Sweden, later to be joined by Britain and Portugal. The competing boats are not dinghies but junior keelboats, a small version of the Folkboat, clinker-built and made unsinkable by built-in buoyancy. The boat was designed by the Swedish designer A Salander and has the following dimensions: LOA 16 ft 8 in (5·7 m), LWL 14 ft 9 in (4·5 m), beam 5 ft 8 in (1·75 m), draft 2 ft 11 in (0·9 m), sail area 161 sq ft (15 m²), ballast 606 lb (275 kg).

Motor Sailers

The nature and purpose of the motor sailer allow for many different interpretations, which give rise to endless discussion. Supporters of the type maintain, for example, that it is considerably more seaworthy than a pure motor cruiser and at the same time has better accommodation than a pure sailing yacht. Older yachtsmen tend to turn towards motor sailers because, although they have not lost their enthusiasm for sailing, they are rather more demanding when it comes to comfort below decks. They also like the modest sail area, which makes handling easier, and the extra engine power which makes them independent of the sails in bad weather, in calms or during difficult conditions.

Today's sailing yachts, with their compact shape and their fairly powerful auxiliary engines, make it more and more difficult to draw a genuine borderline between an auxiliary sailing yacht and a motor sailer. In general one can say that if a boat is faster under sail than under power it is undoubtedly a sailing yacht. If it is faster under power than under sail it is better described as a motor sailer. However, this criterion of speed can be misleading since it has been possible to get higher and higher engine performance out of smaller and lighter auxiliary engines. It might, therefore, be more useful in practice to categorize motor sailers as follows:

1. The pure sailing yacht by shape, equipped with a powerful engine. It retains the appearance and the characteristics of the sailing yacht, i.e. large sail area, moderate freeboard and good windward performance.
2. The true motor sailer, normally called a 'Fifty-Fifty'. This has a more modest sail area, shorter overhangs and a higher freeboard than the true sailing yacht. Its windward performance is reduced but still acceptable.
3. The motor cruiser with auxiliary sails. It looks more like a pure motor yacht with a still higher freeboard and a wide transom stern. The sail area is just sufficient to sail well on a broad reach in a fresh breeze, but the underwater profile of the hull no longer permits sailing to windward, except under power.

It has been said that the ideal motor sailer should be a 'Ninety-Ninety', i.e. it should have 90 per cent of the characteristics of a true sailing yacht and 90 per cent of

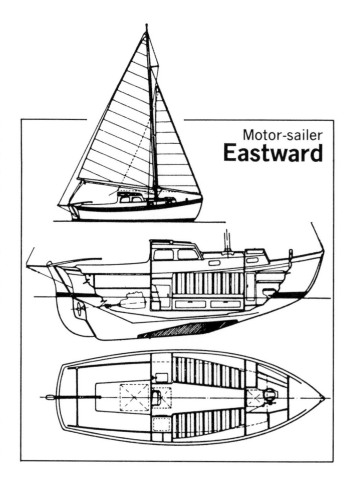

Fig. 211: The 'Eastward' motor sailer is a sturdy cruising boat with good sailing performance and a large cockpit.

LOA	23 ft 4 in	Draft	3 ft 10 in
LWL	20 ft	Ballast in keel	2200 lb
Beam	8 ft 8 in	Sail area	250 sq ft

the speed and accommodation of a pure motor yacht. Undoubtedly, this goal can be closely approached, but such a design must be a true motor sailer as a type in its own right, rather than being based on a pure sailing yacht or a pure motor yacht design.

The smallest motor sailer illustrated here is EASTWARD, a good-looking and balanced little ship. The underwater profile is that of a sailing yacht with deep draft and a proper ballast keel. The superstructure, on the other hand, is definitely that of a motor sailer.

EASTWARD was designed by the American designers

Plate 55: *A fine shot of the successful Barbary Class motor sailer. This ketch-rigged yacht is 32 ft 6 in long with a beam of 10ft 4 in and a working sail area of 480 sq ft. She is designed by Walter Rayner and built in fibreglass by F C Mitchell & Sons of Parkstone The accommodation is well thought out and attractive Power is provided by a 4 cylinder 42 hp Mercedes diesel.*
Photo: Mitchell & Sons, England

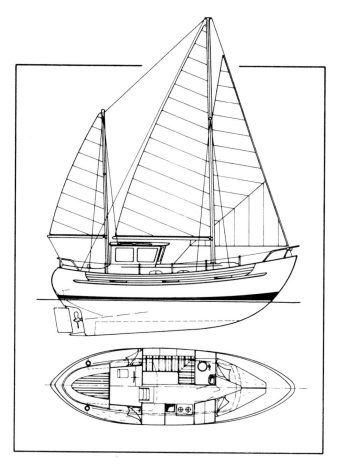

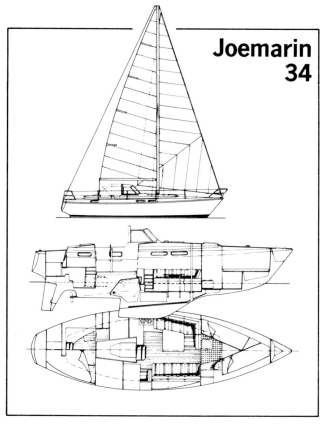

Joemarin
34

Fig. 212: The British motor sailer 'Fairways Fisher 30' is of a completely different character, being modelled on a Baltic fishing boat.

LOA .... 30 ft
LWL .... 25 ft 2 in
Beam .... 9 ft 6 in
Draft .... 4 ft 7 in
Displacement ... 14,300 lb
Thames
  Measurement .. 9·5 ton
Sail area .... 330 sq ft

Fig. 213: The hull lines of the 'Joemarin 34' motor sailer come very close to those of a pure sailing boat hull. She is series-built in Finland and has gained a reputation for good sailing performance.

LOA .... 34 ft 2 in
LWL .... 28 ft 8 in
Beam .... 10 ft 4 in
Draft .... 4 ft 7 in
Displacement ... 11,000 lb
Sail area .... 506 sq ft

Eldredge–McInnis, who succeeded in making her a handy, spacious and pleasant-to-sail little boat. The engine output of 25 hp seems scarcely adequate, but a higher speed under power was neither required nor would it seem advantageous. For higher speeds the underwater sections at the stern would have to be those of a motor-boat hull, and this would impair the sailing qualities.

The sail area is ample but still easy to handle. There is a permanent backstay and a jib boom, which means that tacking can be done without bothering about runners or foresheets. A large sail area calls for a hull with ample stability, and for this reason the lead keel weighs nearly 1 ton. The accommodation is simple and roomy, and the cockpit is unusually large. The generous

headroom in the cabin allows for two additional berths to be rigged by folding the back-rests of the saloon berths upwards.

The following type, the Fairways Fisher 30, is quite obviously modelled on a Baltic fishing ketch. The main aim here is reliability and seaworthiness. Although the type as such suggests timber construction, the hull is, in fact, moulded in plastic. All woodwork above is in teak, below in teak-veneered plywood; even the deck and the bulwark strip on the outside are teak.

The very deep draft makes it possible to place the cabin sole rather low and keep the superstructure, except for the wheelhouse, reasonably low. The accommodation comprises an L-shaped dinette, which can be converted into a double-berth, faced by the chart table and galley on the starboard side. There are two quarter-berths aft and in the small fore-cabin, separated from the saloon by the WC compartment and two hanging lockers, there are two further berths.

The engine is usually a 36 hp Volvo Diesel with a 2:1 reduction gear. The engine compartment is big enough, if need be, to house two engines. A number of other diesel engines are optional.

If we look at the overall appearance of the Fisher 30, we notice above all the inclined front of the wheelhouse. This design feature has proved useful among professional fishermen. The ketch rig can easily be adapted to different wind conditions. The boat will sail either under mainsail alone or under foresail and mizzen when the wind is too strong for her to carry full sail. The canoe stern will appeal to many people, although it makes for a less roomy cockpit.

*

The motor sailer Joemarin 34, which follows next, is a completely different concept: she is virtually a true sailing yacht equipped with a powerful engine. Designed by Hans Groop, the Joemarin 34 is built in Finland in plastic. The underwater profile is no different from that of an outright sailing yacht, being characterized by a deep, midships ballast keel and a separate skeg and rudder aft. The Finnish builders, Joemarin O.Y., do not advertise her as a motor sailer but as a sailing yacht with generous auxiliary power. She does, however, incorporate features which are not those of a thorough-bred sailing yacht, like the centre cockpit with its effective shelter, the generous freeboard and the after cabin.

In keeping with the motor sailer concept she has spacious and comfortable accommodation. In the fore-cabin we find two berths, a WC and a hand-basin. In the saloon there is an L-shaped dinette, which converts to a double berth, and a single berth facing it. There is a galley to port and a generous chart table to starboard. Under the cockpit sole there is plenty of room for the 47 hp Perkins Diesel.

The after cabin, in this case, is the owner's accommodation. A large double berth takes up all the space on the starboard side, the hanging locker being to port. An ingenious, sliding WC disappears under the cockpit sole when not in use. Access to the after cabin is via a

Plate 56: The Fisher 30 is just one of the many types and sizes of fibreglass motor sailer built by Fairways Marine at Southampton. Seaworthiness is the main consideration The boat can also be supplied as a sloop. Power is provided by a diesel engine of between 20 and 45 hp. Photo: Eileen Ramsay

small stern cockpit. All-round lifelines give a feeling of safety.

The rig, a modern sloop rig with large foretriangle, is once again that of an outright sailing yacht, which changes foresails to adapt to changing wind conditions, and sets anything from a large genoa to a small storm jib without initially reefing the mainsail. The Joemarin 34 fits well into group 1 of our previous categorization.

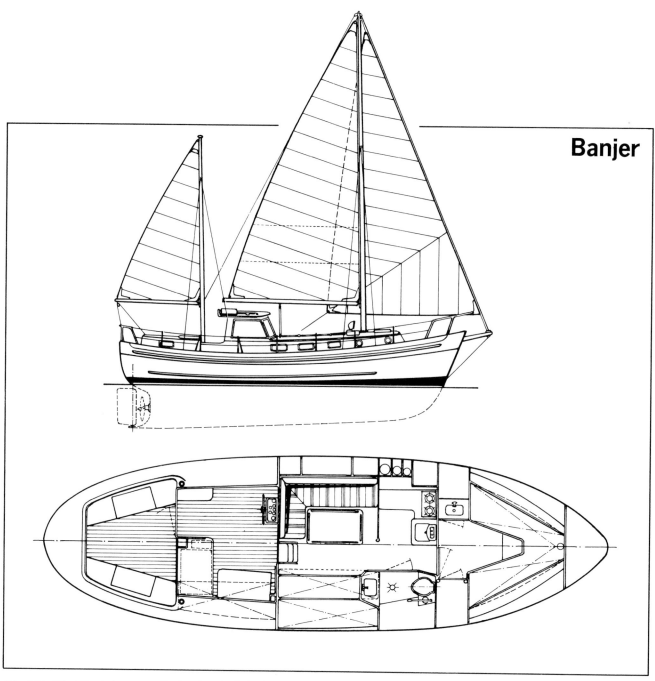

Fig. 214: The 'Banjer' motor sailer has been built in large numbers and has proved itself as a reliable, seaworthy vessel.

LOA .... *36 ft 6 in*	*LWL* .... *33 ft 6 in*		
Beam .... *11 ft 5 in*	*Sail area,*		
Draft .... *4 ft 7 in*	*gaff-rig* .... *301 sq ft*		
Ballast .... *8800 lb*	*Sail area,*		
Displacement ... *26,400 lb*	*bermudan rig* . *452 sq ft*		

The well-known motor sailer Banjer is, once again, a complete contrast. While the Joemarin 34 has the underwater profile of a true sailing yacht, the Banjer has the exceptionally long keel of a true motor sailer. While her performance under sail is not nearly comparable, the engine output is better used through appropriate gearing and a large-diameter propeller.

Besides, the accommodation below deck is considerably improved.

The Banjer is built in a number of different versions, two of which are illustrated in Fig. 214. At the top we can see the centre-cockpit version, with a small wheelhouse, whereas the accommodation plan shows the after-cockpit layout with a larger wheelhouse, which is

278

Plate 57: The well-known motor sailer Banjer has proved a fine vessel in heavy weather. A little over 36 ft long with a beam of 11 ft 5 in she is built in fibreglass in Holland For details see diagram, Fig 214. In the photograph the boat has a large wheelhouse and small cockpit aft, but there are two other versions with after cabins.   Photo: Eista Werft, Holland

also shown in Plate 57. The rig, too, is optional. Besides the Bermudan ketch rig illustrated, a gaff-ketch rig with a shorter mainmast is offered, which may look old-fashioned but has its admirers. In all versions the accent is on the seaworthy motor sailer rather than the sailing yacht. The hull as such has seaworthiness written all over it, in its lines, its long keel and its

bow shape. With an overall length of 36 ft 6 in (11 m) she is an attractive little ship with some similarity to a North Sea crabber. There is plenty of headroom everywhere, and sail handling has been made easy. The short bowsprit is not there for its romantic looks, but helps to diminish weather helm by shifting the centre of effort of the sail area further forward. To damp down

279

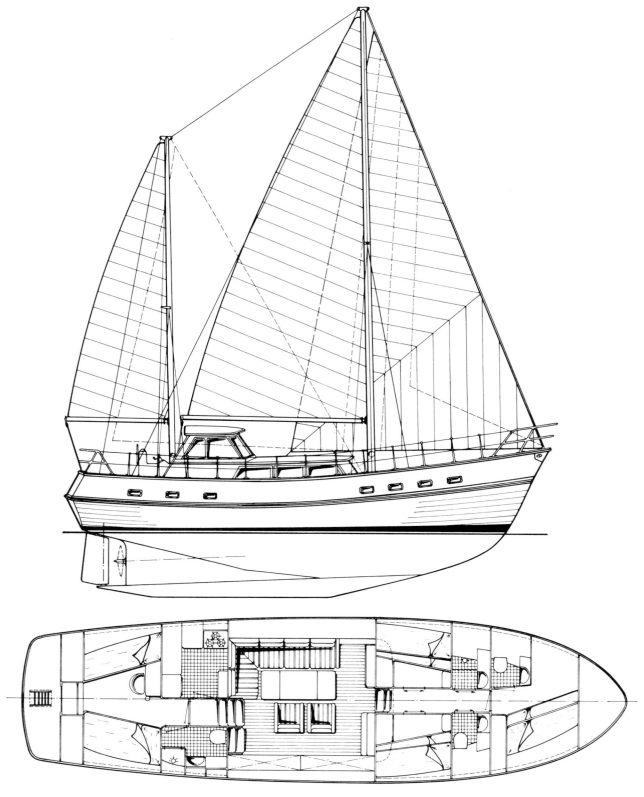

Fig. 215: The largest of the motor sailers shown in this chapter comes from Norway, where it is series-built in GRP. It is modelled on a Norwegian fishing boat; even the clinker construction has been imitated.

LOA .... 56 ft
LWL .... 48 ft 5 in
Beam .... 14 ft 9 in
Draft .... 7 ft 4 in

Displacement,
  approx. ...... 35 ton
Sail area .... 1185 sq ft

Plate 58: The Columbia 41 is a motor sailer with the shape of a normal sailing yacht. The hull shape and the rig ensure good sailing qualities. The raised centre cockpit has a good deal of useful space underneath, used in this case as a galley and spacious toilet with shower. She is 40 ft 8 in long with a beam of 11 ft 2 in and rigged as a sloop has a working sail area of 645 sq ft, though she can also be rigged as a ketch.
Photo: Columbia Yachts, Costa Mesa, California

the eternal rolling in a seaway part of the sail area, i.e. the jib and jigger can be set. This steadies the boat considerably and needs hardly any attention as long as a steady course is steered.

The accommodation, as shown in the plan, is self-explanatory. There is a total of five berths in the saloon and fore-cabin, and in the centre-cockpit version there are two more in the after cabin. At a pinch, someone can sleep on the bench seat in the wheelhouse.

The standard engine installed is a four-cylinder Perkins Diesel with an output of 72 hp at 2250 rpm. The rather large propeller is driven via a 3:1 reduction gear. Maximum speed is in excess of 8 knots, cruising speed 7 knots. The large number of Banjers so far built have given an excellent account of themselves during cruises at sea.

*

It will by now be apparent that motor sailers come in any number of different shapes and types. In conclusion, we feature a very 'modern' design which, in its lines, closely resembles a Norwegian trawler. This very large boat, almost 55 ft (17 m) long, does in fact look like a wooden boat, although it is series-built in plastic. Even the planking has been imitated, and this together with the pronounced sheer and the high bulwarks makes the type look very authentic. The Norwegian yard that builds it, Batservice Verft, did previously build wooden trawlers and has many years of experience in producing this type of vessel. This motor sailer does, of course, make full use of modern technology and has alloy masts, stainless steel rigging and all the latest fittings. It is built to Lloyd's 100 A1 and a certificate is issued to any owner who wants it.

The very beamy, deep-draft hull gives a convincing impression of seaworthiness, and this is enhanced by the builders' specification which states that the ballast is situated in the lowest part of the keel, whereas trawlers of this type do not normally have external ballast. The propeller is exceptionally large and, since it is slow-turning, very efficient. The balanced rudder is of generous proportions which, indeed, it needs to be to make any impression on a keel of this length, which is specifically aimed at directional stability.

The helmsman has his own open position just aft of the mizzen mast, where we can see the wheel; there is a second wheel in the shelter of the wheelhouse. All-round lifelines together with high bulwarks give a feeling of absolute safety at sea, even in bad weather.

The rig is once again a ketch rig, which has proved most suitable for vessels of this size. Following the current trend, the foretriangle is fairly large. In fact, the whole sail area is ample, from the mizzen which is by no means negligible in size, to the large mizzen staysail which will certainly make itself felt on a reach. A number of foresails have been indicated by dotted lines. A spinnaker is hardly ever set on this kind of boat. After all, a motor sailer has so much reserve power that its owner will hardly ever apply himself to the finer points of sailing.

The accommodation plan in Fig. 215 is largely self-explanatory. In the saloon, apart from the dinette and easy chairs, there are two folding berths to starboard. The two guest cabins forward have two berths each as well as a washroom, one with WC and the other with shower. The two berths and WC compartment in the fo'c'sle are intended for a two-man permanent crew. The owner's cabin with its two berths is aft, the owner's washroom is opposite the large galley.

The five motor sailers we have featured represent five different types, yet they do not by any means exhaust the scope of possible variations. When it comes to motor sailer design, the possibilities are virtually unlimited.

Open Racing Catamarans

If one considers that the conventional keel-yacht has to have more ballast the larger its sail area, one must admit that it is a paradoxical compromise. The increased sail area ought to produce higher speed, but the hoped-for increase in speed is largely consumed by the increase in the ballast weight. Any fixed ballast not only provides stability but has a braking effect. The modern dinghy, on the other hand, shows that it is possible to sail very fast without any ballast at all. It fulfils the speed ideal without any dead ballast through combining light weight with power to carry sail.

It was an obvious idea to experiment with another type of boat which would have good stability without using permanent ballast. Of course, improved stability must not be bought at the expense of increased beam, as this in itself would be speed-reducing.

However, if two narrow hulls are connected by a bridge structure to form a unit, high initial stability can be obtained without losing speed potential. A twin-hulled boat of this type is called a catamaran although, as a matter of interest, this Polynesian word does not mean 'twin-hulled' but 'a raft made of several logs'.

The idea of twin hulls certainly originated in Polynesia, but its introduction into Europe goes rather further back than one might think. Even in the days of King Charles II people were experimenting with twin-hulled sailing vessels. Nat Herreshoff, in 1875, was probably the first to demonstrate high speeds with a light-weight catamaran. But none of these early efforts attracted sufficient interest to win the catamaran as much as one supporter.

For a long time experimenters with catamarans were puzzled by the inexplicable (?) fact that, despite the use of extremely narrow hulls, catamarans failed to reach really high speeds. In fact, as late as 1940 the enormous effect of surface friction was not understood.

The breakthrough came with the advent of two new materials, which we now take for granted: reliable, water-resistant marine plywood and synthetic, waterproof glues. Even now, some 20 years later, they have already been replaced as building materials by GRP and polystyrene. It was also realized that thin, deep hulls develop too much frictional resistance, and shallow hulls with more or less semicircular section were adopted.

The first modern, fast catamaran appeared in Hawaii. Shortly after World War II, the talented catamaran enthusiast Woodridge Brown designed his famous MANU KAI. Brown was an experienced aircraft pilot and also had considerable knowledge of aircraft construction. In Alfred Kumalai, a native Hawaiian boat-builder, he found a clever co-operator. Together they

Plate 59: The international single-handed catamaran AUSTRALIS was designed by Australian, Kevin Johnston and was chosen as the best of all the participants in the IYRU Trials in 1967. This very fast single-hander is probably the best that has been achieved in A Class. It is built in England under strict control by Sailcraft Ltd, Brightlingsea. The boat is 18 ft long with a beam of 7 ft 6 in and has a single sail of 150 sq ft.   Photo: Theo Kampa, Holland

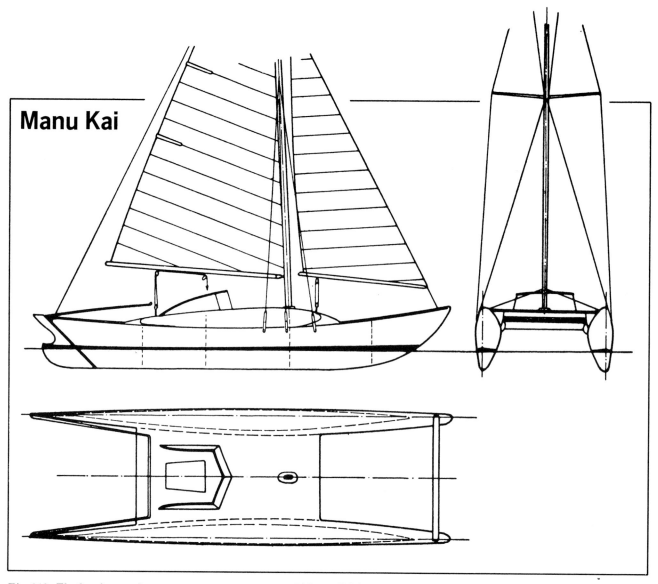

Manu Kai

Fig. 216: The first fast, modern catamaran was MANU KAI, *which was built in Hawai. She was extremely light and caused a sensation with her speed.*

LOA	40 ft	Beam WL	1 ft 10 in
LWL	34 ft 2 in	Draft	1 ft 10 in
Beam OA	13 ft 1 in	Displacement	3300 lb
Beam, each hull	2 ft 7 in	Sail area	506 sq ft

built an extremely light catamaran, which relied largely on methods used in aircraft construction. MANU KAI, despite her length of 40 ft (12·2 m), was built entirely of very light, thin, water-proof marine plywood.

We can see in Fig. 216 the so-called Hawaiian school of catamaran design: the two hulls are asymmetrical, their rather more curved side turned inwards, and they have no centreplates.

In favourable wind conditions these craft are reported to have reached speeds of up to 20 knots, but if one watches them sailed by holidaymakers off the beaches of Hawaii, they are no faster than conventional boats. They have proved very suitable for this purpose, though,

284

because they can be run up on the beach without difficulty.

The long keel profile of this type of catamaran gives considerable steadiness on course at the expense of handiness. For long passages in the Pacific Ocean this lack of quick response is relatively unimportant, but it is a great disadvantage when racing on a triangular course. It is, in fact, frequently necessary to back the jib to go through stays.

*

The real acceptance of the catamaran as a class boat in its own right began in 1957, when the British Prout

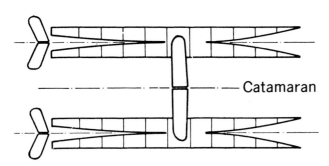

Fig. 217: The early catamarans gave a disappointing performance, because in their design the effect of surface friction had been underestimated or even ignored. The illustration shows the wetted surface of a modern racing catamaran.

brothers produced a type of catamaran which differed essentially from the Hawaiian design. For the first time small fleets of class catamarans competed against each other in organized races.

The Prout brothers' revolutionary catamaran was, of course, the now-famous Shearwater. Their first experiments consisted in joining two canoe hulls, but their Mark III type already had the most important characteristics of the modern racing catamaran: symmetrical hulls with semicircular section and a centreplate. More recent designs normally have a plate in each hull.

Soon after the successful début of the Shearwater, other catamarans appeared on the scene, some of them designed by talented amateurs. Meanwhile, the argument continues among yachtsmen whether a twin hull planes or not. Many catamaran experts insist that it does not, even though it sails extraordinarily fast. In practice, it is hardly possible to establish by observation whether a catamaran is in a planing position or not, but it is fairly obvious that it does, because in no

Shearwater

Fig. 218: The first modern, open racing catamaran was the Shearwater designed by the Prout brothers in 1957.

LOA	16 ft 6 in	Draft, plate up . .	6 in
LWL	15 ft 7 in	Draft, plate down .	2 ft 7 in
Beam OA	7 ft 6 in	Weight without	
Beam, each hull . .	1 ft 6 in	crew	308 lb
Beam WL	1 ft 2 in	Sail area	160 sq ft

other way could it sail so fast. However, the sensation of incipient planing is less pronounced in a catamaran than in a mono-hull, because the simultaneous pressure on the lee hull and the formation of large amounts of spray tend to eclipse it.

Since those early days, catamarans have proliferated enormously, and racing catamarans have been classified as follows:

Class	A	B	C	D
No. of crew	1	2	2	3
LOA	18 ft (5·49 m)	20 ft (6·10 m)	25 ft (7·62 m)	optional
Maximum beam	7 ft 6 in (2·30 m)	10 ft (3·05 m)	14 ft (4·27 m)	optional
Sail area	150 sq ft (13·94 m²)	235 sq ft (21·84 m²)	300 sq ft (27·88 m²)	500 sq ft (46·46 m²)
Spinnaker	—	—	—	800 sq ft (74·32 m²)
Trapeze	for helmsman		for crew only	

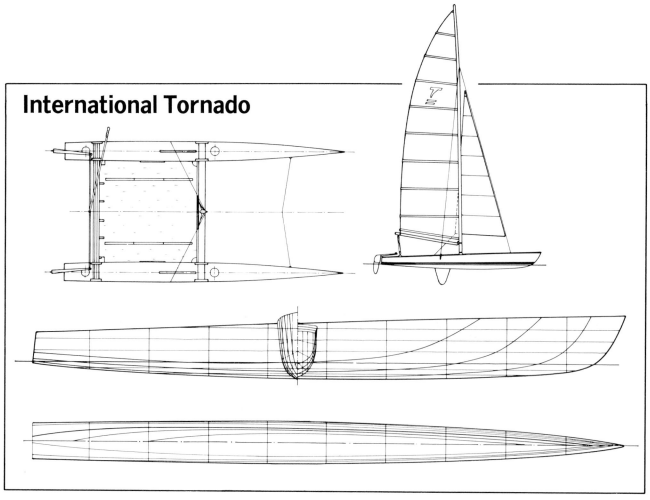

International Tornado

LOA	20 ft	Draft, plate down .	2 ft 6 in
LWL	19 ft	Weight, equipped .	280 lb
Beam OA	10 ft	Sail area	235 sq ft
Draft, plate up ..	7 in		

There are a number of additional regulations, e.g. all classes are permitted to have hydrofoils and instead of a trapeze may use sliding or folding seats. Class C is officially termed the 'International C-Class'. All dimensions for length, beam and sail area are the maximum permitted dimensions, which means that it is optional to fall short of them. It also means that, for example, a B-Class catamaran may race with the C-Class.

One particular B-Class catamaran, the Tornado, attained international status and was made an Olympic Class. Its sail area, length and beam conform exactly to the maximum B-Class measurements. The Tornado emerged victorious from an IYRU one-of-a-kind race off the Isle of Sheppey. Designed by Rodney March. an electrical engineer and amateur designer, the prototype was planned by the well-known catamaran helms-

man and boatbuilder Reg White.

Figure 219 shows the rounded shape of the rather slim, symmetrical hulls, which apparently emerged quite simply from the way $\frac{3}{16}$ in (4·5 mm) plywood allowed itself to be bent. The bow lines are unusually fine, and it is only the relatively high freeboard and the lightness of the hull which prevent undercutting. The after sections are comparatively flat and semicircular, and each hull has its own centreplate. There is no solid deck structure between the two hulls, only a canvas platform. Rigid connection of the two hulls is ensured by two alloy girders, the thicker one slightly forward of amidships, on which the mast is stepped, and a lighter one aft. Unlike many other catamaran designs, the Tornado has no girder right forward, which means that the pull of the fore halliard comes straight on the hulls,

Plate 60: A similar type but rigged as a sloop is the Tornado Catamaran, which has achieved Olympic status. Designed by Rodney March to the B-Class formula it was also chosen after the keenest competition. The Tornado is built by Sailcraft Ltd, *Brightlingsea and is 20 ft long with a beam of 10 ft and a sail area of 235 sq ft. See diagram, Fig 219.*
Photo: Evecom Multihulls, Amsterdam

see Plate 60, which have to resist the pull inwards.

The fact that even this fastest of all B-Class catamarans sets a foresail is symptomatic of how much slower catamarans are, after all, than sand- or ice-yachts. The foresail is kept so small because here it is the sail itself, rather than the foretriangle, which is measured. The Tornado is a strict one-design class, in which all measurements are binding.

The international success of the Tornado is illustrated by the fact that so far over 1500 of them sail in more than 20 countries, and this figure will probably rise as the next Olympic Games draw near. It is built in fibreglass by 30 accredited yards, but wooden construction and even amateur building are equally permitted. It is said that the Tornado has brought a new dimension to sailing, that of 'flying on the water'.

*

It was the need to negotiate the breakers on the American Pacific Coast which inspired the design of Hobie Alter's 14 ft Hobie Cat. Born on the coast of California, this exciting, fast little boat has quickly become popular. The designer was originally a surfboard manufacturer and as such was well acquainted with the problems of negotiating rolling, breaking seas. His idea was that if he could produce a boat which could safely get through the breakers and out into the relatively calm, open sea, there would be a demand for it on so many beaches that it could be built in large series. He was right, for the Hobie Cat has turned up on all the surf-bound beaches.

Plate 61: The Hobie Cat is fully described in the diagram, Fig 220. It is particularly suitable for sailing through surf and offers splendid sport on exposed coasts. Here a Hobie Cat leaps in the air as it sails through surf.

Photo: Coast Catamarans, California

Plate 62: After the leap in the air the Hobie 14 falls into the trough of a wave, but the nylon platform remains relatively dry. You can see the long, sharp bow of the port hull, while the other three hull ends are under water. An attractive sport for young sailors at the beach. Photo: Coast Catamarans, California

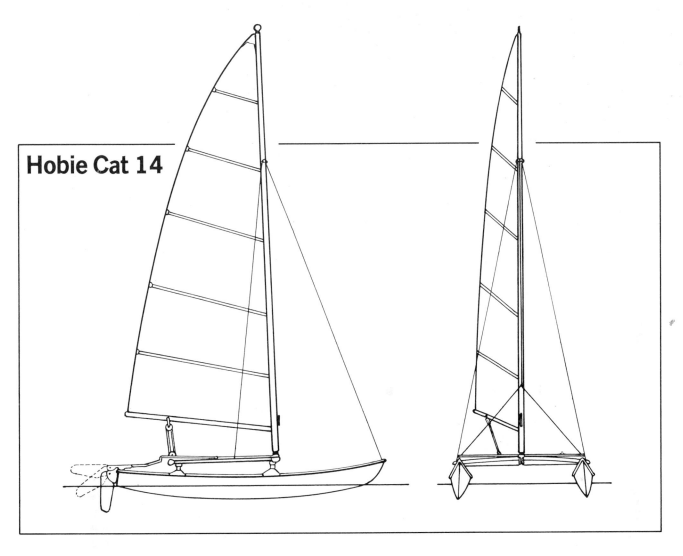

Hobie Cat 14

Fig. 220: The small surf-catamaran 'Hobie 14' has found many enthusiastic supporters on exposed beaches where breakers have to be negotiated before the open sea can be reached.

LOA	14 ft	Draft	8 in
LWL	13 ft 1 in	Weight, equipped	215 lb
Beam OA	7 ft 8 in	Sail area	118 sq ft

It was, of course, essential for this small catamaran to have no centreboard, because this would inevitably be battered to pieces in no time at all. To ensure, nevertheless, the necessary windward performance, the hulls are asymmetrical, with the flatter side on the outside. It is thus the outside of the lee hull, which is normally lower in the water, which counteracts leeway. Both hulls are filled with synthetic foam and are completely sealed, so that no water can enter. Even the alloy mast is sealed to prevent it being weighed down if the boat should capsize. Anyone who watches a fleet of Hobie Cats, on a Hawaiian shore for example, being got ready in minutes and sailed through the surf to race in the open sea, cannot fail to be impressed by the idea.

The platform between the two hulls, which is made of coated nylon cloth, is raised exceptionally high to keep it as dry as possible. The boat is essentially a one-man

boat, but there is room for two or three people. The rudder can be raised and lowered via the tiller, and this is essential when launching and running up on the beach, or when sailing in very shallow water, the draft as such being only 8 in (20 cm). The total weight, with the sail up, is a mere 215 lb (98 kg). The boat can be transported on a trailer, but it can also be dismantled and put on the roof-rack of a car. No individual part, i.e. hulls, platform, mast, boom and rudders, weighs more than 55 lb (25 kg).

Even in a modest breeze these small catamarans are lively, and racing them off the warm Pacific beaches is great fun. Following the enthusiastic response to the Hobie 14, Alter designed a 16-footer along the same lines and equally a one-design boat. There is also now a smaller model, 12 ft in length, which cannot be dismantled and calls itself a 'Mono-Cat'.

Cruising Catamarans

Plate 63: The main cabin of a modern cruising cat. This cosy scene is on a Cherokee catamaran built in fibreglass by Sailcraft, Brightlingsea. The boat is 35 ft long with a beam of 16 ft 5 in and a sail area of 614 sq ft.   *Photo: Helen Simpson*

All catamarans discussed so far have been open, dinghy-type vessels. In this chapter we will look at a number of cruising catamarans, some of them with generous accommodation, as shown by the following plans. The Hirondelle, designed by Chris Hammond and built by BCA Marine Development in England, is only 23 ft (7 m) long. Cruising catamarans of such modest size, but with comparatively ample accommodation, have a particularly great following in Britain. The type is inevitably a compromise, for either one settles for a boat with a moderate sail area, which is slower but reasonably proof against capsizing, or one sets a larger

sail area to get a faster boat, which, in a sudden gale, can only be prevented from capsizing by concentrated attention on the part of helmsman and crew.

Although the Hirondelle does not quite fall into the second category, it comes close to it, which means that those who sail her must at no time forget that she can flip. If she does go over, she can only be righted with massive outside help because, with her mast pointing perpendicularly downwards, she is at least as stable as in an upright position. Hence it takes a tremendous effort to turn her back again. There are certain precautions one can take to prevent a complete capsize:

Plate 64: *The Iroquois is a popular cat in British waters. It was designed by J MacAlpine-Downie and the Mark II version is seen here under sail. Both hulls are equipped with a dagger board. Built by Sailcraft, Brightlingsea in fibreglass. The boat is 30 ft long with a beam of 13 ft 6 in. See also Fig. 222.*
Photo: Fred & Joan Armes

Plate 65: *This Apache catamaran has a float at the masthead. Its purpose is to prevent the boat turning turtle should it capsize. The Apache is built by Sailcraft, Brightlingsea and can be rigged as a cutter, sloop or ketch. Length 41 ft, beam 19 ft, sail area 780 sq ft.*
Photo: Sailcraft, Brightlingsea

one is to settle for a smaller sail area, on principle; another is to fit an automatic mainsheet release; and finally a float can be fitted to the masthead which stops the complete capsize once the mast is horizontal.

The Hirondelle has a great deal of accommodation for its size: there are wide, comfortable berths aft in both hulls, another berth forward, and an immense double-berth in the main cabin, where we also find the galley and dinette, while the WC is forward in the port hull. The perspective lines drawing shows the rounded hull sections and the shape of the bridge deck. The two centreboards, one in each hull, have not been indicated,

but they can be seen in the accommodation plan, exactly amidships, in each hull. As usual there is a rudder to each hull, operated jointly by a connecting bar. In the middle of the after bridge deck we can see an opening, which takes the outboard motor.

*

Quite similar in shape but considerably larger is the popular Iroquois, designed by J R Macalpine-Downie. She is series-built by Sail Craft Ltd at Brightlingsea, England, and has proved fast and seaworthy. As with

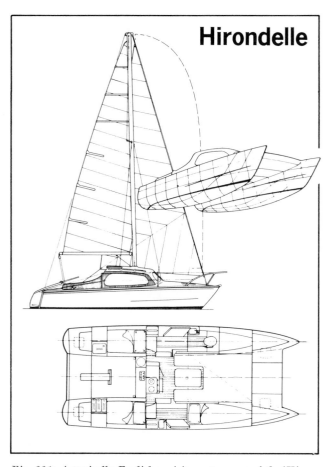

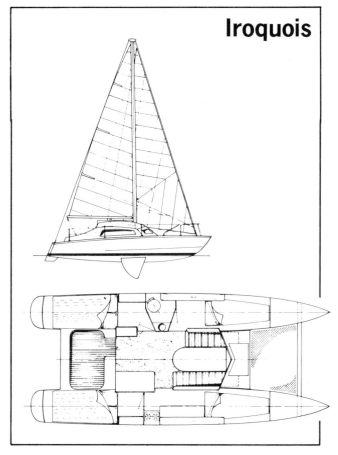

Fig. 221: A typically English cruising catamaran of the 'Hirondelle' type. For its modest length it has generous accommodation, while the hull shape suggest good sailing qualities.

LOA	22 ft 8 in	Draft, plates down	4 ft
LWL	20 ft	Displacement	2310 lb
Beam OA	10 ft	Sail area	270 sq ft
Draft, plates up	1 ft 3 in		

Fig. 222: The 'Iroquois' catamaran has been built in considerable numbers and several versions.

LOA	30 ft	Draft, plates down	4 ft 5 in
LWL	26 ft 9 in	Displacement	5500 lb
Beam OA	13 ft 6 in	Sail area	410 sq ft
Draft, plates up	1 ft 4 in		

all catamarans, it must be said that she is potentially capsizable, depending on the amount of sail set and the way in which she is sailed.

The Iroquois was originally built in wood, but we show here the latest model, which is moulded in fibreglass. The two hulls and the bottom of the bridge deck form one moulding, the upper deck, cabin top and cockpit another, the two being joined at the gunwale. The Iroquois, too, has round-section hulls with moulded spray strakes. There is sufficient built-in buoyancy to keep her afloat after a capsize.

The sail plan reproduced in Fig. 222 is the one for the

cruising version. The racing version has a slightly higher mast with a larger sail area, which makes her a very competitive boat. This is born out by the fact that she has won the Crystal Trophy three times in succession. Each of the hulls has its own retractable plate, which is indicated in the accommodation plan at the extreme outer edge of each hull. The good shape of the hulls, the ratio between individual hull beam and overall beam, and the ratio between plate size and sail area, all combine to make the Iroquois a fast and easily handled boat, which goes through stays without difficulty.

As is fairly normal in this size, the main cabin does

Plate 66: *This picture shows clearly the typical twin-hull configuration of the catamaran, as well as the spray strakes, which many English catamarans have. An unusual feature is the pivoting centreplate, while the majority of cruising cats have a dagger plate in each hull. This is a Cherokee built by Sailcraft, Brightlingsea (see also Plate 63).*

not have standing headroom, whereas the side cabins in the hulls do. There we find the galley, the WC compartment and the berths: two double berths aft and two single berths forward. The dinnette amidships converts to another double berth. The cabin top is kept low to reduce windage and hence improve the sailing qualities.

No provision is made for a permanently installed auxiliary engine, but a 20–30 hp outboard with long shaft will provide good performance under power.

*

The Spindrift 45 by the Australian designer Lock Crowther is already a large catamaran. It is described as an ocean-cruiser and hence is considered, at least by the audacious Australians, as very seaworthy. As the name suggests, it is 45 ft (13·75 m) in length with an individual hull beam of only 3 ft 3 in (1 m), which is very narrow for that length. The boat is obviously very fast, and daily runs of up to 300 miles when cruising should be well within reach.

The hulls are moulded in fibreglass with built-in polystyrene, and according to the designer this sandwich construction method can be followed even by

293

amateurs. The bridge deck and superstructure are made of marine plywood. This combination had already been successfully applied to previous Spindrift designs, 37 ft (11·25 m) and 51 ft (15·5 m) in length, and is simpler than the laminated, glued construction which is usual in lightweight wooden hulls.

In keeping with a widespread practice of secrecy among catamaran designers, the size and location of drop plates and rudders is not indicated in the plans, but we can say that the Spindrift 45 has a plate at the outer edge of each hull and that it is a dagger plate, which means it moves vertically up and down.

The accommodation has only been indicated for the central portion, where we find the galley, chart table and dinnette. A catamaran of this size can easily accommodate 8 berths, possibly even 10.

An interesting feature about the sail plan is the two forestays. The inner one is removable and only used on long sea passages for setting an additional foresail. Even without this, the foretriangle is very large, with an area in excess of the mainsail. The total sail area including the foretriangle is 932 sq ft (86·6 m²), with the large genoa set even as much as 1302 sq ft (121 m²).

If one looks at the beam of the boat one notices that with 23 ft (7 m) it is exceptionally large. Catamarans of this length usually have a beam of around 19 ft (5·8 m); the extra beam improves stability and reduces the risk of capsize.

*

It might be of interest to hear what Lock Crowther, the designer, has to say about the seaworthiness of his type of catamaran. He thinks that their safety depends on the good seamanship of those who sail them. Having said that, an offshore multi-hull can be so designed that it remains habitable even if turned upside down. For this purpose, watertight hatches are incorporated in the floor of the main cabin, which can be opened from inside. For long sea passages there must, of course, be plenty of reserve buoyancy. In addition an inflatable life-raft and a radio buoy must be carried on board.

In spite of sombre warnings, long sea passages in multi-hulls frequently turn out lucky, as was proved recently by the Swales, a young British couple with two small children, who even rounded the Horn with a high sea running. Their catamaran ANNELIESE was an

294

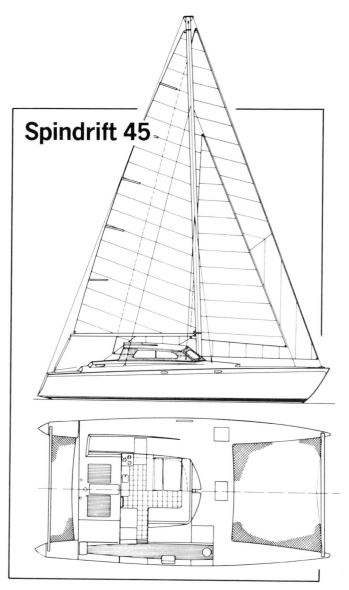

Spindrift 45

Fig. 223: The fast cruising catamaran has many adherents in Australia. The 'Spindrift 45' is one example.

LOA	45 ft 2 in	Displacement ..	11,440 lb
LWL	39 ft 6 in	Weight, empty ..	7920 lb
Beam OA	23 ft	Load capacity	
Draft, plates up ..	1 ft 3 in	max.	5060 lb
		Sail area	932 sq ft

Oceanic, 30 ft (9·15 m) long and with a beam of 14 ft 9 in (4·5 m), by Bill O'Brien, one of Britain's best-known catamaran designers. It was, as is usual, completely unballasted and hence capsizable. The fact that a trimaran, too, has rounded Cape Horn must not, however, be taken as proof of the seaworthiness of unballasted multi-hulls. It would be more realistic to say: yes, it can be done, but the risk is tremendous and the average sailor cannot be expected to take it.

Trimarans

We have already mentioned and illustrated two trimarans in previous chapters without considering in detail the characteristic shape and behaviour of the type. The first was the long, light alloy trimaran PEN DUICK IV, winner of the 1972 Single-Handed Transatlantic Race, Fig. 191, and the other the very small plywood trimaran KLIS, Fig. 200, which sailed round the world. Between these two there exists a wide range of cruising tris, whereas those which race are few in number.

The questions which are usually asked are: Which type is faster, the catamaran or the trimaran? Which type is safer at sea? And finally: How does the accommodation compare?

The answer to all three questions depends on whether one wants to live in the central cabin, which is inevitable in the trimaran, or whether one wants to spread out into the side hulls while the main cabin is kept on a platform *above* the water. If one ignores this question, the catamaran is doubtless the faster of the two, and so it is if we are talking about boats of dinghy size and without any accommodation. As soon as we compare boats with accommodation, the speed depends on the individual design. A pure racing machine like Eric Tabarly's PEN DUICK IV is unlikely to be surpassed in speed by any catamaran. But when it comes to pure cruising types, a catamaran will normally be superior to a trimaran with comparable accommodation. The main reason for this is the smaller wetted surface of the catamaran as compared with the trimaran. However, the difference is so small, especially for cruising, that the question of safety at sea must take priority.

In recent years, say since 1960, a lot more cruising has been done in trimarans than in catamarans, and we are talking here about the modern, light type of multihull. One might even go so far as to say that the trimaran shape has been specially developed for cruising purposes, because the deep central cabin provides better living comfort. The difference is not significant, though, and quite a large number of cruising catamarans, too, have completed extensive sea passages, like the Swale family mentioned earlier, who rounded the Horn. The safety angle, emphasized at the end of the chapter on catamarans, is no more favourable for trimarans, either. Safety essentially depends on the experience and wariness of the crew. Two well-known trimaran designers are missing at sea on board their

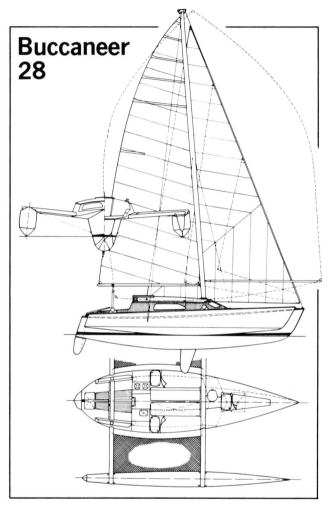

Fig. 224: The fast trimaran 'Buccaneer 28' is an Australian design. It can be seen that the floats only just touch the water.

LOA	28 ft 3 in	Draft, plate down	4 ft 11 in
LWL	26 ft 3 in	Weight, empty	1980 lb
Beam OA	21 ft 6 in	Displacement,	
Beam, central hull	4 ft 2 in	total	3960 lb
Beam, cabin	8 ft	Sail area	613 sq ft
Draft, plate up	2 ft 1 in		

own products: Arthur Piver from California, who pioneered offshore cruising in unballasted trimarans, and the Australian designer Hedley Nicol, whose designs were particularly aimed at speed. Capsizes have happened frequently with both trimarans and catamarans. Only very small boats stand a chance of being righted again, larger models need massive outside assistance.

Many amateur boatbuilders are drawn towards

multi-hulls, partly because there are good do-it-yourself plans available, and partly because they are of the erroneous belief that these boats are not only fast but very stable. True, their speed exceeds *fractionally* that of a conventional cruising yacht, but when it comes to great stability, this only applies to the vessel in an upright, virtually unheeled position. This can be most misleading, for the angle of heel will remain quite insignificant even as the wind increases, so that the wind strength cannot be assessed from the attitude of the boat. Then, suddenly, there is a hard puff, and unless someone is at hand to release the sheets immediately the boat can capsize with spectacular suddenness.

The question of simplicity of construction for the amateur builder with limited skill has to be approached with caution. Many amateur builders have proved themselves capable of completing such boats in a reliable manner, but there are equally many cases of appalling incompetence where amateur-built multi-hulls have fallen apart at sea. The fact that this has happened more often to trimarans than to catamarans must probably be attributed to the preference of amateur-builders for trimarans, rather than to the type of boat.

One important aspect about multi-hulls is the large deck area, which is always virtually level. This, combined with the total absence of rolling, obviously contributes to attracting people to multi-hulls. Of course, one must not make the mistake of expecting to build such a boat 'cheaply, from a few sheets of plywood'. A well-designed, properly built and equipped multi-hull costs the same as a comparable mono-hull.

The small trimaran KLIS has already been described. With a length of 22 ft (6·7 m) and a beam of 14 ft (4·25 m), she has an exceptionally large deck area formed largely by the solid platforms between the main

hull and the floats. In the larger Buccaneer 28, Fig. 224, a different principle is employed. Instead of solid platforms, nylon nets are stretched between the main hull and the floats. This allows it to be dismantled for trailer transport or winter storage in a restricted space. Also, the amateur builder does not need so much space for building, since the main hull and everything that goes with it is only just over 9 ft (3 m) wide, whereas the total beam of the Buccaneer 28 is 21 ft 6 in (6·55 m). The floats are connected to the main hull by strong tubular alloy girders. There is one centreplate, which is in the main hull. It should be added that most trimarans do not have a centreplate at all but instead a small, wooden fin on the underside of each float to counteract leeway.

In spite of the very low appearance of the superstructure of the Buccaneer 28 the headroom in the central hull is 5 ft 7 in (1·7 m) from the galley to the WC compartment. There are four berths, one of them being the bench seat in the saloon. The plans show what good use has been made of the restricted space in the narrow central hull. The whole design obviously reflects years of experience. Speed has been a prime consideration, for this is what is required off the extensive Australian coasts. It can be seen that the floats only just touch the water when the boat is completely upright. As she heels slightly, the lee float is immersed according to wind pressure, while the windward float lifts completely out of the water.

The sail plan shows a generous sail area, which can, of course, be adapted to the prevailing wind conditions. As is usual in multi-hulls, the roach on the mainsail leach is quite pronounced in the upper part and is supported by four full-width battens. Although the foretriangle is quite large, the length of the spinnaker boom actually exceeds the base of the foretriangle, a feature which is not normally found in European designs, even if a boat is not restricted by class rules.

*

Figure 225 shows an even faster type, described as an ocean racer: the Kraken 33 Mark IV designed by Lock Crowther. With a length of nearly 33 ft (10 m) and the enormous beam of 23 ft (7 m), it can carry an unusually large sail area. The design was aimed primarily at reducing skin friction by keeping the wetted surface as

Plate 67: An unusually lively picture of a fast cruising trimaran. The small amount by which the leeward float is submerged shows that the high speed is reached in only a modest wind strength with the help of a large genoa. The windward float is quite clear of the water indicating the lightweight construction of this trimaran as well as the fact that it is designed to have both floats just above the waterline of the main hull when on an even keel. MANTA II *is a Kraken 33 designed by the Australian, Lock Crowther and has a length of 33 ft, a beam of 23 ft and a sail area of 592 sq ft. See perspective drawing, Fig. 225.*

Photo: Courier Mail Printing Services

Kraken 33 Mk IV

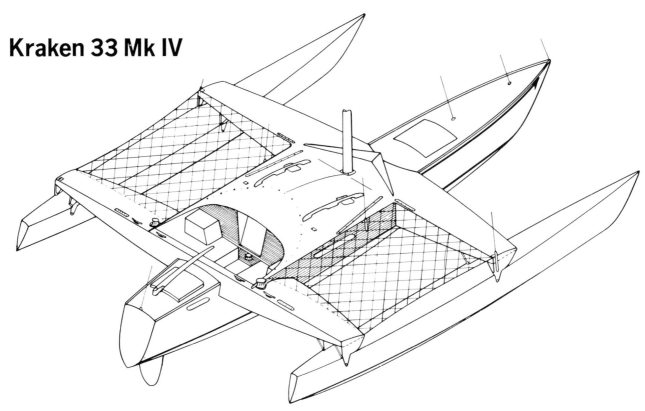

Fig. 225: Perspective drawing of the Australian fast trimaran 'Kraken 33', which is described as 'ocean racer'. It is the end product of a long design series.

LOA	32 ft 10 in	Draft, plate down .	4 ft 2 in
LWL	30 ft	Displacement ...	4000 lb
Beam OA	23 ft	Headroom	6 ft
Draft, plate up ..	1 ft 7 in	Sail area	592 sq ft

small as possible. For example, the centreplate is not pivoting as in the Buccaneer, but it is an obliquely retractable daggerplate. The wetted surface of the Kraken 33 is claimed to be 30 per cent less than in previous designs. The connections between main hull and floats in this trimaran are by plywood box girders, which are an integral part of the hull. Where they join the floats they are raised to prevent them from being dragged through the water as one float is submersed. We can see from the plans that the cockpit is small and well sheltered. The rudder can be seen just forward of the central transom. The nylon netting is taken right up to the cabin top so that the narrow cabin side windows are actually below the netting.

*

To conclude this chapter we will look at a trimaran of the type that Arthur Piver pioneered, in which the

wings between central hull and floats are in the shape of wide side decks, which are an integral part of the whole hull structure. Arthur Piver was probably the one designer who did most to make the trimaran popular in its early days, especially by producing plans which could be used for amateur construction. His transatlantic crossing to England in 1960 and his transpacific voyage to New Zealand in 1961 also did much to popularize this type of multi-hull.

The Cross 37 shown here has been developed from the Piver-type and is typical of a moderately fast cruising trimaran. The sectional view shows how the wings between central hull and floats have been utilized for accommodation: the two pilot berths are actually outboard of the central hull. The fact that the Cross 37 was designed with stability rather than speed in mind is born out by the main hull and the floats being much beamier than in the previously discussed types. Also,

Plate 68: Ocean Bird is one of the most unusual trimarans. The centre hull is almost that of a normal, mono-hull yacht, and the floats are adjustable. being swung out when the boat is sailing and housed alongside the main hull when moored. Over 25 of this ingenious design by John Westell have been built, one of which sailed from England to the West Indies. The boat is 30 ft long and has a beam of 13 ft with the floats housed, of 23 ft with them extended, and a sail area of 463 sq ft.
Photo: Honnor Marine Ltd, England

with the boat on an even keel, both floats are slightly immersed. To reduce leeway on the wind, the central hull is fitted with a wooden keel, which is about half as long as the hull overall. Arthur Piver's own designs have two small keels, one on the underside of each float.

The Cross 37 is shown here ketch-rigged, but she can equally be supplied as a sloop; the enormous beam greatly facilitates the secure staying of the mast. An interesting factor about the foresail is the boom. As the jib is sheeted in on the wind the boom, which pivots on deck some distance inboard of the forestay, stretches the foot of the sail to the full, whereas it allows it more and more flow as the sheets are eased and the boom pivots further outboard.

One problem which has not been given much popular attention is being much discussed recently: should the floats be designed to be fully supporting, i.e. should the lee float support the weight of the hull as it heels, or should they be fully submersible? The Australian designer Lock Crowther strongly advocates the latter case. If we look at his Kraken 33 we see that his floats are fairly small, but he points out that adequate stability is nevertheless ensured by the very great beam. According to Crowther, the helmsman can judge the amount of stability left in reserve by the degree of immersion of the lee float which, in his designs, must be fully submersed before the main hull can be lifted by the wind. Before this happens, the observant helmsman takes action to prevent a possible capsize. If, on the other hand, the float is weight-bearing and non-submersible, there are no such early-warning symptoms and the hull, in a gale, can suddenly be lifted and capsized through 180°. The designer concludes that his type of design can weather *any storm* at sea and always remain under full control.

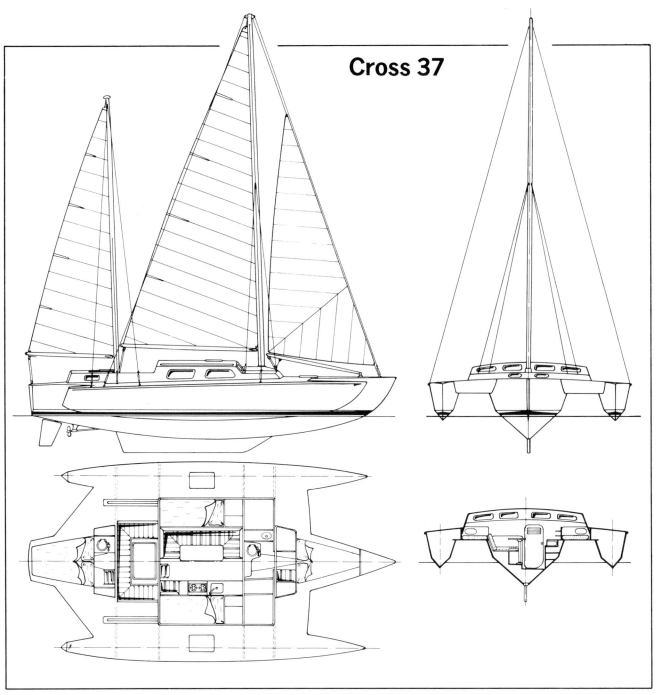

Cross 37

One ought to add, though, that this requires a high degree of seamanship and constant vigilance, as has been demonstrated by the many instances in which cruising catamarans and cruising trimarans have actually capsized. And after all, no amount of good design will make up for a lack of good seamanship.

Fig. 226: Californian cruising catamaran, which is a development of the Arthur Piver type. The 'Cross 37' was designed for amateur construction and distinguishes itself by very simple hull lines and solid wing decks.

LOA	*37 ft 3 in*	*Displacement*	*. . . 9000 lb*
LWL	*34 ft 2 in*	*Ballast*	*none*
Beam OA	*20 ft 9 in*	*Sail area*	*495 sq ft*
Draft incl. keel . .	*3 ft 2 in*	*Auxiliary motor* .	*15–20 hp*

Faster than the Wind

Many catamaran sailors are convinced that they sail faster than the wind and, under favourable conditions, this is absolutely true. These conditions are: a fast, light racing catamaran, an apparent wind from slightly forward of abeam, and a constant, moderate breeze blowing over a smooth water surface. It is quite wrong to think that a catamaran can sail relatively faster in a strong wind of, say, 25 knots than in a constant good breeze of 10 knots. The emphasis is on *relative*, which means relative to the wind speed. The boat's *absolute* speed will, of course, be faster but not proportionate to the increase in wind speed. At a wind speed of 25 knots a catamaran will hardly ever go as fast as 25 knots, but in a wind speed of 10 knots it can easily reach and even exceed 10 knots.

While a light racing catamaran can *exceptionally* sail faster than the wind, there are sailing craft which do so *regularly*. These are the sand- and ice-yachts. Both have one thing in common: they do not sail on the water. A hundred, even two hundred, years ago boats sailing on the ice on long runners were the fastest craft in existence. On the Hudson River near New York, where the railway track ran alongside the river, it was a favourite sport for ice-yachts in those days to race the fast steam trains. In favourable winds the ice-yachts won.

Once the resistance of water is eliminated, exceptionally high speeds can be reached under sail. How high depends entirely on the skilful way in which the energy of the wind can be converted into forward thrust. The author has designed, built and sailed a number of sand-yachts, which easily reached speeds of 35 knots in a true wind speed of only half that. Ice-yachts can go very much faster than that; up to 55 knots is quite normal for the average, small ice-yacht. Even 100 knots have been reported, reached in wind speeds of only a quarter that.

Ice yachting has a long history, especially in Nordic countries. In Frederik af Chapman's interesting work *Architectura Navalis Mercatoria*, published in 1768, and reprinted by Adlard Coles Ltd in the 1970s, there is a reproduction of an ice-sleigh, which worked on the same principle as a modern ice-yacht.

Figure 227 shows a 12 m² ice-yacht designed by Erik von Holst. This is a well-proven one-design, whose excellent characteristics and simple construction have won it great popularity. It is characteristic of the

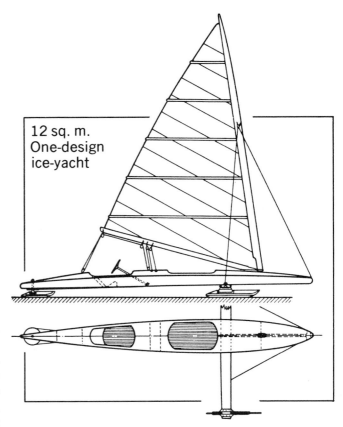

Fig. 227: An ice yacht is in its element as soon as its speed significantly exceeds that of the wind speed. All it needs is a smooth surface of ice.
LOA .... 23 ft 6 in   Sail area .... 130 sq ft
Beam OA ...... 7 ft 6 in

standard European type with a hollow, flexible axle beam, to which the two front runners are attached. A third, pivoting runner, which is the rudder, is situated at the stern and is usually steered by a wheel, sometimes by a tiller. The hull, or fuselage, consists of two longitudinal plywood bearers, which are boxed in with a deck and bottom. There is one cockpit for the helmsman aft and another for the crew further forward.

The American type is similar to the European type, but the layout is in the reverse order; the mast and axle beam are at the after end, the steering runner at the bow.

Most ice-yachts are cat-rigged without any headsail. The mainsail has full-width battens and is semi-rigid. In the 12 m² one-design the mast is hollow and pivoting, with an elongated pear-shaped section. Since high speeds call for quick and precise handling of the sails, the mainsheet is double-ended, one end being led into each of the two cockpits, so that both helmsman and crew can attend to the mainsail.

The principles of ice yachting are entirely different

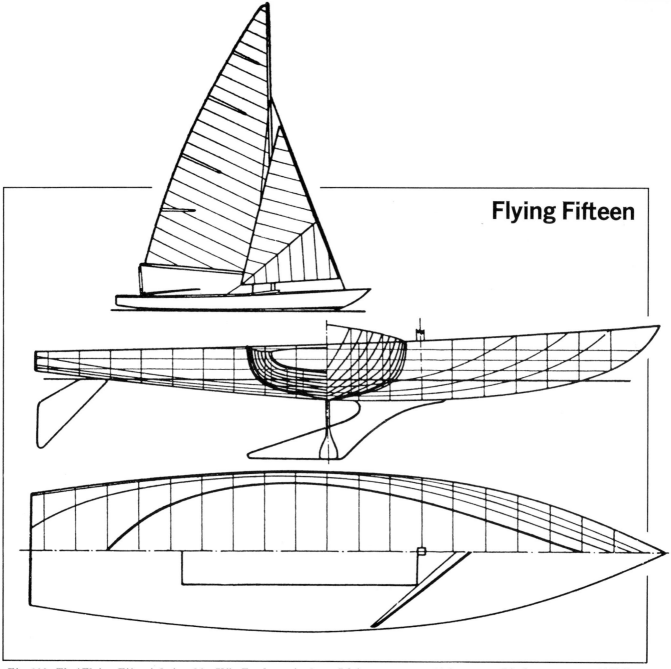

Flying Fifteen

Fig. 228: The 'Flying Fifteen' designed by Uffa Fox has gained particular popularity in Britain. It is fast but hardly ever reaches wind speed.

LOA	20 ft	Displacement ...	1000 lb
LWL	15 ft	Ballast weight ...	400 lb
Beam	6 ft 1 in	Sail area	150 sq ft
Draft	2 ft 6 in		

from those of sailing on the water. An ice-yacht will never sail close to the wind, because on that point of sailing it would not go particularly fast; only off the wind does it unfold its spectacular speed potential. Its slowest point of sailing is before the wind, and its fastest point of sailing is with the wind on the beam, when it can reach several times the wind speed. If we refer back to Fig. 89, we see that the angle of incidence of the apparent wind for an ice-yacht on this point of sailing is similar to that which occurs with a normal yacht sailing close on the wind, so that the ice-yacht will actually be close-hauled. This is the reason why

302

courses for ice-yacht racing must be laid out at 90° to the true wind to allow the craft to develop their full speed potential.

When an ice- or sand-yacht has to lay a mark dead to windward, it is sailed much freer than a conventional yacht, which would naturally be made to point as high as possible. If a sand- or ice-yacht is made to point that high, it is disappointingly slow. A conventional yacht close-hauled sails approximately 4 points = 45° off the true wind. A catamaran, because of its higher speed, will get to the mark faster if it tacks towards it no closer than 5 points = 56° off the true wind, and an ice-yacht

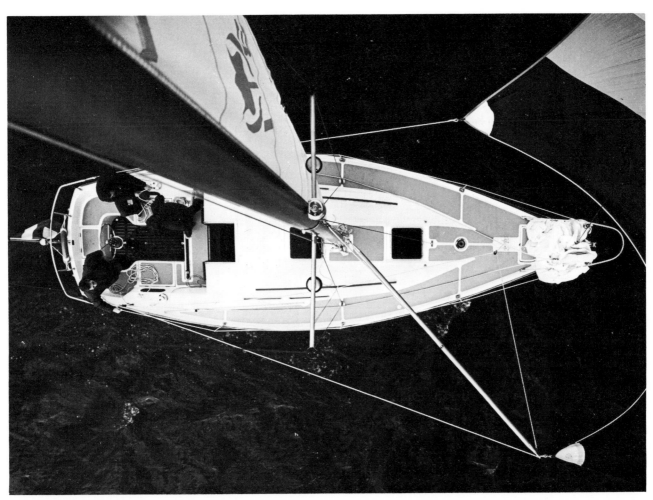

Plate 69: A view of the deck of a modern, fast cruising yacht. This is a Contest 31HT, built by Conyplex in Holland, which is the size of a Half Tonner. The view from the masthead shows the very pleasing hull shape and the roomy cockpit with wheel steering, Her dimensions are LOA 31 ft, LWL 24 ft 7 in, beam 10 ft 4 in, draft 4 ft 9 in or 5 ft 9 in.   Photo: Theo Kampa

should go no closer than 6 points = 67°.

The difference between the conventional yacht and the ice-yacht becomes most obvious before the wind. An ice-yacht will never sail dead before the wind, because its speed would necessarily be slower than the wind speed. Instead, it will go on a broad reach and *tack downwind*, which is exactly the equivalent to tacking upwind, except that when going about the yacht *gybes*. This explains why spinnakers are never used on ice-yachts. An ice-yacht sailing downwind under spinnaker would be very much *slower* than one tacking downwind.

Sand-yachts are built on the same principles as ice-yachts. Instead of runners they use proper pneumatic tyres of the type used by small sports aeroplanes, with a small diameter and wide track. As is to be expected, sand-yachts are not as fast as ice-yachts, but sailing in them is equally exhilarating. A good, hard, sandy beach is needed, such as is usually found on sea-coasts with a considerable tidal range, where one can enjoy several hours of very smooth, hard sand.

In several parts of Britain and also along the coast of Belgium and Friesland sand yachting is a popular sport. The hulls vary in shape and material, some being built in plywood like ice-yachts, others having only an open tubular steel framework. The strains on the structure are greater than on the hull of a water-borne yacht, as any careless amateur-builder of such a craft will quickly find out.

By comparison with ice-yachting, sand-yachting has the advantage that it can be done during the warm season and in parts of the world where waters never freeze. On the Atlantic coast of South America, for example, there are long stretches of firm sand where sand-yachts can sail for hundreds of miles at low water and where the prevalent wind direction is at right angles to the beach.

Hulls and Rigs of the Future

Can the attainable speed of sailing craft be significantly increased by radical changes in hull shape? Up until now, most of the progress in this direction has been made not through changes in hull shape but through light-weight construction. Most dinghies, as well as some keelboats, plane because they are so light. True, radically new hull-shapes have made some headway in this direction, we only have to think of the catamaran and the trimaran. Is it possible that in future even more unconventional hull-shapes might be devised which will further increase the speed of vessels under sail?

It can safely be said that most of the attempts to improve the speed of sailing craft failed through ignorance of aerodynamics and hydrodynamics. Any number of wing sails or aerofoils have been condemned to failure from the outset by being rigged on ridiculous rowing boat or tender hulls. What contribution to speed improvement can aerofoils or hydrofoils make? The problem is perfectly accessible to mathematical calculation, but the fact is that all over the world amateur designers and inventors try to hit on something entirely new and sensational.

The fastest water-borne sailing boat in 1974 was not a catamaran, not a trimaran, but a mono-hull, which was not even designed for planing. It was not propelled by a wing sail or an aerofoil but by an ordinary sloop rig consisting of mainsail and foresail. We are thinking of CROSSBOW, which has already been mentioned in an earlier chapter. The features which are responsible for its high speed potential are the length and light weight of the hull (LOA 59 ft (18 m), beam 1 ft 10 in (56 cm)) and the stabilizing outrigger for helmsman and crew, which must not touch the water. Over a measured distance of 500 metres CROSSBOW, after several attempts and under optimum wind and water conditions, reached the spectacular speed of 33·5 mph = 29 knots. Second came an International Tornado catamaran with hydrofoils fitted to the hull, which reached a speed of 21·5 knots. Both boats are not usable for normal sailing. The Tornado's hydrofoils, for example, act as brakes as soon as the wind speed drops. CROSSBOW is an even more extreme design, devised purely for the 500 metre trial run. It scarcely responds to the tiller and can only be sailed on the port tack. It cannot go about and it cannot be sailed before the wind. During the trials it was constantly accompanied by a motorboat which had to tow it back to the start at the end of each run.

The British aerodynamics expert Hugh Barkla has frequently aroused attention by his ingenious ideas. We have tried to reproduce one of them in Fig. 229, based on Barkla's sketches. In this completely revolutionary design of a sailing vessel both the hull and the rig are radically unconventional. Extremely light construction allows the hull to lift out of the water and be supported only by its hydrofoils, while its shape above the water is aimed at eliminating air resistance.

Even more striking is Barkla's futuristic rig, which in its basic principle looks very tempting on paper. In practice, the problem is much more difficult to solve, if indeed it admits resolution. Assuming that it were possible to build the structure very light, aerodynamically efficient and technically reliable, how could the sail area be reduced in a gale? How could it be increased before the wind, when it would obviously be too small? So far it is nothing but a tantalizing idea. Although attempts were made to build the rig, no one was seriously interested in using it in practice, and hence the project was never pursued.

Hydrofoils seem to hold out rather more promising prospects. Nevertheless, their practical application is so limited that they will hardly interest the average sailor. Their history goes some way back. In the early fifties the shipyard of Gordon Baker, in conjunction with the US Navy, carried out experiments with different types of hydrofoils fitted to light dinghies to establish whether wind force alone was sufficient to provide the necessary dynamic lift. As seen in Fig. 230, the experiments were successful. Under optimum conditions of wind strength and direction the boat sailed with so-called total dynamic lift. Sitting only on its foils without actually displacing any water, it is reported to have reached speeds up to 23 knots.

Since then, numerous experiments have been made with hydrofoils, especially fitted to catamarans. The Tornado in the speed trials which we mentioned before was fitted with hydrofoils and came second with an average speed of 21·5 knots over the 500 metre distance. This makes us suspect that Baker's boat reached its 23 knots only momentarily. It must also be remembered that speedometers are hardly ever completely reliable. The problems of hydrofoil sailing have meanwhile started to be mastered, but the conditions remain the same. It can only be done with a suitable wind strength,

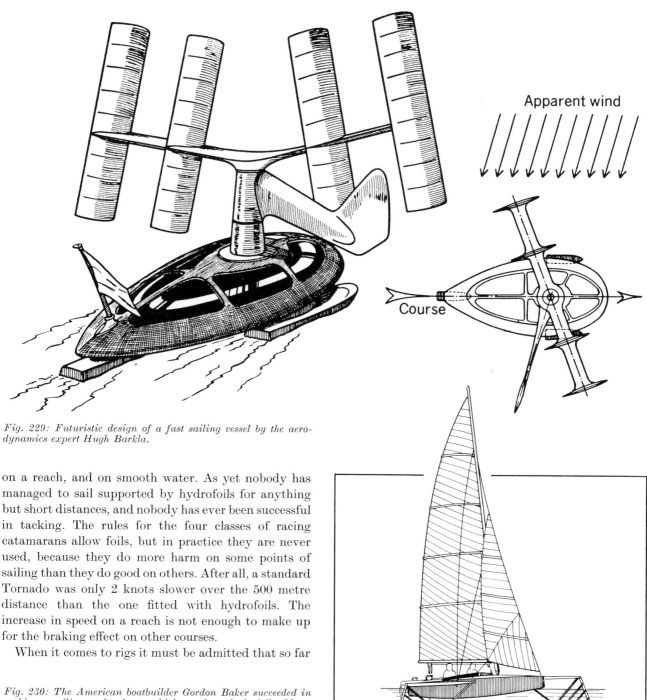

Apparent wind

Course

Fig. 229: Futuristic design of a fast sailing vessel by the aero-dynamics expert Hugh Barkla.

on a reach, and on smooth water. As yet nobody has managed to sail supported by hydrofoils for anything but short distances, and nobody has ever been successful in tacking. The rules for the four classes of racing catamarans allow foils, but in practice they are never used, because they do more harm on some points of sailing than they do good on others. After all, a standard Tornado was only 2 knots slower over the 500 metre distance than the one fitted with hydrofoils. The increase in speed on a reach is not enough to make up for the braking effect on other courses.

When it comes to rigs it must be admitted that so far

Fig. 230: The American boatbuilder Gordon Baker succeeded in making a sailing yacht plane at high speeds on hydrofoils. Many similar attempts have been made since then, most of them successful providing wind and course were favourable. The speed record for sailing yachts, however, is held by a very long, slim displacement boat (1977).

Plate 70: This experimental rig was developed with the object of reducing the heeling effect of the wind by obtaining a thrust component directed upwards. This so-called kite rig was designed and built by S Neppert, Bremen.　　　　　Photo: Schröder

nothing better or more efficient has been found than the conventional Bermudan rig consisting of mainsail and several different foresails. It is the variety of possible foresails which makes this rig so adaptable to changes in wind and course. Nobody doubts that a *rigid sail* is slightly more efficient on the wind, but it poses many practical problems: how can the asymmetry of the sail profile be applied to both tacks? How can the sail be hoisted, reefed, stowed and trimmed to different points of sailing? Even a symmetrical profile lacks adaptability, how much more so an asymmetrical one, which offers improved dynamic efficiency. The ordinary cloth sail, on the other hand, automatically and on all points of sailing adopts the correct asymmetrical shape and

admirably fulfils all the other requirements as well, with the only exception that on the wind it is minimally slower than a rigid sail.

A great number of experiments have been carried out with the aim of finding a means of wind propulsion which does not cause heeling. Many a budding inventor thought he had found the answer when an unsuspected squall capsized his boat and demonstrated very convincingly that he was on the wrong tack!

If it were possible to obtain propulsion from the wind without the secondary effect of heeling, this would be a revolutionary step forward, which would change the face of yachting. If heeling could be totally eliminated, sail areas could grow to enormous dimensions, producing fantastic driving force and uncanny speeds without ever having to be reefed.

On second thoughts one must come to the conclusion that all this is a fallacy. The wind cannot produce any driving force unless it is diverted from its course. If a sail or any other device deflects the wind from its course, the effect takes place *above the water*, no matter what shape or arrangement one might devise for a rig. The resistance of the hull, on the other hand, occurs *in the water*. Consequently, any force which attacks at any height above the water must necessarily cause the hull to heel.

Many aerodynamic research centres have tested aerofoils in wind tunnels, usually at small angles of incidence such as those applicable to aeroplane wings.

Many inventors have allowed themselves to be misled by these tests. Numerous aerofoils have been tried out on sailing boats, but nothing usable has as yet come from these experiments. It is probably true to say that most yachtsmen, including the author, are not keen on depriving the sport of yachting of its own particular charm by introducing some strange, complicated, futuristic rig, even if it is aerodynamically more efficient.

We can take it for granted, though, that the existing conventional cloth sail will be gradually further improved by modifying its shape, making it simpler to handle and by reducing the weight of the rig as a whole, and that this, in turn, will result in improved speeds.

The Beginnings of Ocean Racing

Until the end of the last century, yachtsmen rarely ventured offshore. It was thought that offshore sailing was safe only for boats of at least 100 ft (30 m) in length.

Just as Columbus is considered the initiator of deep-sea navigation, so the little yacht SPRAY is acclaimed as having demonstrated to the world the possibilities of offshore sailing. Before Captain Joshua Slocum, between 1895 and 1898, sailed his SPRAY over all the oceans of the world, only three isolated ocean races had taken place. The yachts competing in them were all of appreciable size and had large paid crews. The dimensions of the smallest of them, the schooner VESTA, were

Plate 71: A bird's eye view of the motor sailer Columbia 41 shown on Plate 58. You can see the sailing yacht hull, giving good windward performance under sail.

Photo: Columbia Yachts, California

LOA 105 ft (32 m), LWL 99 ft (30·2 m), beam 25 ft (7·6 m).

The owner of such a large vessel considered himself rather like a racehorse owner, not like the jockey, whose job it is to ride the horse to victory. Hence many of these yachts sailed under the command of a paid captain, while the owner was not necessarily on board.

The first real ocean race took place in 1866 as a result of a bet for 90,000 dollars. It was complicated by the fact that it was sailed at what is the worst time in the North Atlantic. The start was on 11th December, the destination the Isle of Wight. Three vessels competed in this race, but only one of the owners took part in it on board his yacht; at 25 he was the youngest of the three. His courage was much admired, and he was loudly cheered at the start. To appreciate his daring one must remember that yachts in those days did not have a deep ballast keel and by our standards were not particularly seaworthy.

All three competitors, HENRIETTA, FLEETWING and VESTA, finished on Christmas Day in 1866 with only nine hours difference between them. A tragic accident overshadowed the great feat. One stormy night at sea an enormous wave broke over the deck of FLEETWING and washed six men overboard. For five hours the yacht stayed in the vicinity searching for the missing men, but none of them could be found.

Four years later a second transatlantic race was organized, this time in the opposite direction. In July 1870 the British yacht CAMBRIA and the American yacht DAUNTLESS started on a race from Ireland to Sandy Hook near New York. Both vessels were about 130 ft (36 m) long, which was then considered normal. Theirs was the first *international* ocean race, from which CAMBRIA emerged as the winner. Shortly afterwards, CAMBRIA tried to win the America's Cup back for England, but this attempt was as unsuccessful as all the successive ones made by England, Canada, Australia, France and Sweden right up to the present day.

The spars and rigging of yachts in those days were enormously heavy. Hollow masts and winches to ease the handling of sheets and halliards were unknown. Halliards were not made of flexible steel wire but of heavy hemp, rove through countless clumsy blocks, and it took many hands to hoist a mainsail. The masts were only 55 to 60 ft (18–20 m) long, but they carried additional topmasts up to 30 ft (10 m) in length. In bad

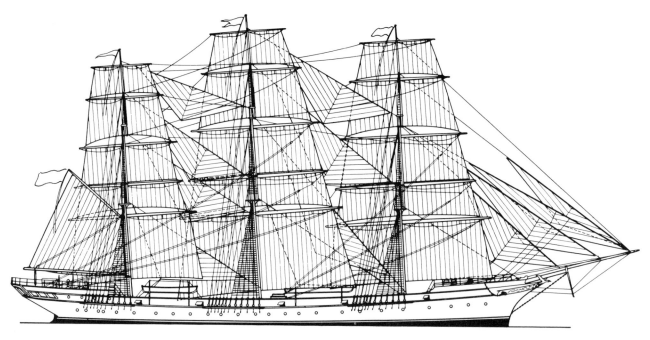

Fig. 231: The large yacht VALHALLA, *rigged as a fully-rigged ship, took part in the 1905 Transatlantic Race, when she was the largest but by no means the fastest boat. She is the only yacht ever rigged in this way and was, indeed, a stirring sight. Her LOA was 245 ft, her beam 36 ft 9 in.*

weather the topmast was taken down and lashed on deck.

After the third ocean race in 1887, which was sailed from New York to Cork in Ireland, the fourth took place in 1905 and was won by the first *modern* yacht, the famous three-masted schooner ATLANTIC (Plate 50 and Fig. 187). She was under the command of the ablest, most experienced and most intrepid of all professional yacht skippers, the unforgettable Charley Barr. ATLANTIC was of much more modern concept than any of the yachts competing in previous ocean races, and the beauty of her design was much admired. Although she was originally built with internal ballast only, she was modified shortly before the race and given a ballast keel. She had a basic sail area of 18,514 sq ft (1720 m²) and the impressive dimensions of 187 ft (57 m) LOA, 137 ft (41·8 m) LWL, 29 ft (8·25 m) beam and 15 ft (4·57 m) draft.

Charley Barr, her indefatigable captain and helmsman, gave her not a minute's rest. Although the wind

increased to gale force and the owner and his six guests on board entreated him to shorten sail or heave to, he pressed on under full canvas. At no time during the night or day did ATLANTIC shorten sail, and never did Barr lose a second in making a decision or in giving orders for a manoeuvre to be carried out. Her best day's run was 341 sea miles, and even her worst, which was on a calm day, was 112 miles. Relentlessly driven on, she established a record for transatlantic crossings under sail which, right up to the day that this is written (early 1974), has never been beaten. She took

12 days, 4 hours, 1 minute, 19 seconds

to cover the 3014 miles from Sandy Hook to the Lizard.

The immediate reaction to this transatlantic race was an increasing interest in ocean racing. In the following year, Thomas Fleming Day, then editor of the American magazine *The Rudder* and an experienced ocean sailor, organized a race to the Bermudas, which he won himself in his yacht TAMERLANE. In doing so, he initiated the oldest of the regular ocean races, the

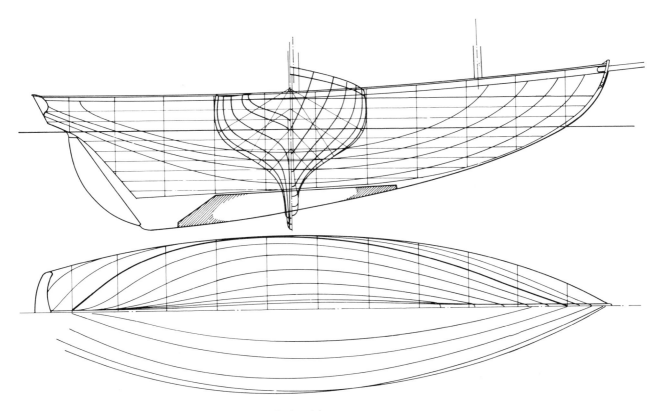

Fig. 232: Lines of the famous staysail schooner NINA *designed in 1928 by W Starling Burgess and Henry Gruber. She was the first ocean racing yacht designed for a Transatlantic race specifically to fit a rating rule, and she won the race convincingly.* NINA's *sail plan is reproduced in Fig. 117.*

Bermuda Race, which for many yachtsmen is the crowning event of their racing career.

Many years later, in 1928, the first transatlantic race for smaller yachts was organized. The competitors were divided into two classes, one for vessels over 55 ft (16·75 m) LWL and the other for those between 35 ft (10·65 m) and 55 ft (16·75 m) LWL. The participation of these 'small' yachts was considered a great risk and quite revolutionary for a transatlantic race. This was the last ocean race in which yachts were allowed to have a paid skipper and crew, and at the same time the first in which small boats were crewed and helmed exclusively by amateurs. It was also the first time that a handicap formula was applied to the smaller yachts and this, equally for the first time, led to a yacht being designed and built especially for an ocean race with this formula in mind.

At the suggestion of King Alfonso XIII of Spain, the 1928 race was sailed between New York and Santander. It was won by the famous NIÑA, which had been speci-

ally built for this race. She beat all those in the group of larger yachts, even on elapsed time, although she was in the smaller group. It was this race which proved, beyond doubt, that amateur yachtsmen are capable of sailing their vessels across vast expanses of ocean with the greatest confidence and efficiency.

The interest in ocean racing increased steadily. When, in 1931, a race was organized between Newport, USA and Plymouth, England, ten yachts entered, of which eight had been specially built for the race. One of the smallest, DORADE, won a surprise victory, beating the favourites HIGHLAND LIGHT and LANDFALL, also built for the race. Her victory was mainly attributed to the fact that she chose a northerly course, but also to the untiring efforts and attention of her helmsman and crew, the then twenty-three-year old Olin Stephens, his younger brother Roderick, their father and three other crewmen.

Plate 72: The Argentine yacht GAUCHO is an example of a Colin
Archer type. For several years she cruised round the world with
her Argentinian crew, particularly the North Atlantic, which
earned her the Blue Ribbon for Ocean Sailers. Designed by
Manuel M Campos, Buenos Aires, she is very like LEHG II in
Fig. 196, in which Vito Dumas circumnavigated the world, and
also the British boat SUHAILI, in which Robin Knox-Johnston won
the first single-handed race round the world.

Photo: Roberto Uriburu

The Ocean Racing Scene Today

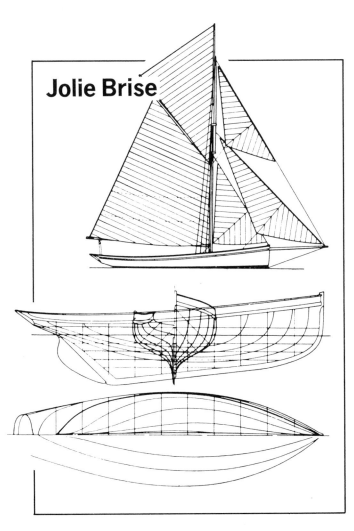

Jolie Brise

Fig. 233: The cutter-rigged ocean-racing yacht JOLIE BRISE *started life as a pilot cutter at Le Havre. She had a spectacular career as a yacht, taking part in many ocean races and winning the Fastnet Race three times: in 1925, 1929 and 1930.*

When the first race from the Isle of Wight to the Fastnet Rock Lighthouse off the southern tip of Ireland took place in 1925, the entry of small yachts with amateur crews in such an *extremely dangerous* race was called 'sheer lunacy'. Experts prophesied scores of shipwrecks off England's rocky coast or at least heavy damage to hulls and rigging. Despite their fears and premonitions, the organizers stood fast, and the Fastnet Race has now become Europe's most important ocean race, being incorporated in the Admiral's Cup Series.

It is generally believed that it was the Bermuda Race in 1906 which initiated ocean races as a regular event. But the same year saw the start of the very important race in the Pacific, which starts in a Californian port, usually San Francisco or Los Angeles and finishes at Honolulu on the island of Hawaii. One could go even further back, to the Chicago–Mackinnac Race, which has been held annually on the Great Lakes in the United States ever since 1898. Although this is sailed on Lake Michigan, which is a fresh-water lake, it is justifiably classified as an ocean race, since the lake is nearly 350 miles long and over 100 miles wide.

When the Fastnet Race was first started in 1925 it was a purely British affair, and it was scheduled as an annual event without consideration for other important ocean races. But it was not long before American yachtsmen wanted to try their hand in European races, while British yachtsmen equally wanted to take part in American races. Thus, after 1931, the Fastnet Race was held every other year, ending in uneven numbers, while the Bermuda Race was held every other year ending in even numbers. This mutual arrangement led to a lively interchange of experience and ideas, and eventually culminated in the internationally recognized IOR rating for ocean racers.

In the southern hemisphere interest in ocean racing was gradually aroused by all this activity 'up north', and in 1945 the Australians initiated the annual Sydney–Hobart Race. This great South Pacific event always gets international participation, not only from New Zealand nearby but also from Britain and the USA.

Another regular event of the southern hemisphere was started in 1947 with the Buenos Aires–Rio de Janeiro Race. This, too, became a great success, for both Argentina and Brazil are very much engaged in yachting, and it gets regular international support, chiefly from Britain, Germany and the United States of America.

The finish in Rio is always timed to coincide with the spectacular Carnival of Rio so that, after a 1200-mile Southern Atlantic crossing, the intrepid seafarers are treated to an extravagant spectacle which is unique in the world. The attraction of the Rio Carnival is so great that in recent years even the South Africans have held a race to Rio. Named the Cape Town–Rio de Janeiro Race, it was first held in 1971 and repeated in 1973 due to popular demand. International support was unexpectedly great, despite the enormous distance of

3800 miles. Both Cape Town as the start and Rio with its February carnival and the picturesque Bay of Guanabara, proved powerful attractions for blue water racing men from all corners of the globe.

The distances for ocean races get greater and greater. The now regular Cape Town–Rio Race is already longer than the irregularly held Transatlantic Race of the northern hemisphere and, when the first Round the World Race was announced, the response was stunning. The distance involved is 26,700 miles, the start being in Portsmouth, England, and the first lap finishing in Cape Town, South Africa, the second in Sydney, Australia and the third in Rio de Janeiro; the finish was back again in Portsmouth.

The first Whitbread Round the World Race started on 8th September 1973 and there were no less than 17 starters, all in Class I with IOR ratings ranging from 33 ft to 70 ft, the three largest being rated 69·2 ft, 64·4 ft and 61·9 ft respectively. In overall length they ranged from the 81 ft 6 in (nearly 25 m) BURTON CUTTER, skippered by the experienced Atlantic sailor Leslie Williams, to the two smallest entries with 45 ft (13·7 m) each. The entries were made up as follows: 5 from Great Britain, 4 from France, 3 from Italy, 1 from West Germany, 2 from Poland, 1 from Mexico and 1 from South Africa. Ten were ketch-rigged, three yawl-rigged, three sloop-rigged and one schooner-rigged.

Building materials covered the whole spectrum of possibilities: six yachts were built in fibreglass, three in steel, three in alloy, two in sandwiched fibreglass, two in solid timber and one in moulded plywood. Time allowance was by time on distance. Scratch boat and hot favourite at the start was the large yacht GREAT BRITAIN II designed by Alan Gurney and sailed by Chay Blyth and his paratrooper crew. On the first lap alone he had to give the smallest participating yacht a time allowance of nearly 10 days. Eric Tabarly with his new PEN DUICK VI was also given very good chances, but had his hopes dashed by a broken mast right at the

Great Britain II

Fig. 234: When it comes to racing round the world, even if it means rounding Cape Horn, the conventional heavy-displacement ocean-going yacht is no longer competitive. GREAT BRITAIN II, *whose sail plan is shown here, has a lightweight hull built on the GRP-sandwich principle and carries a great number of auxiliary light-weather sails. She was designed by Alan Gurney and is very similar to his successful* WINDWARD PASSAGE, *Figs. 184 and 185.* GREAT BRITAIN II *rates 69·2 ft and her principle dimensions are:*

LOA	77 ft 3 in	Displacement	73,000 lb
LWL	68 ft 3 in	Ballast	34,320 lb
Beam	18 ft 5 in	Ballast ratio	47%
Draft	9 ft 9 in	Sail area	2530 sq ft

The yacht is fitted with a 72 hp Ford diesel engine. Her skipper Chay Blyth had sailed the same course, single-handed, once before in BRITISH STEEL, *but in the opposite direction. His crew of paratroopers, although trained in hard discipline, had no experience in sailing. The accommodation of* GREAT BRITAIN II *differs very little from that of* WINDWARD PASSAGE, *see Fig. 185.*

Plate 73: A successful Admiral's Cup contender designed by German Frers Jnr in Argentina and built of cold-moulded laminations in record time. RECLUTA III *is 48 ft 5 in long, has a beam of 14 ft and a working sail area of 1060 sq ft. Forward of the after cockpit for the helmsman and navigator she has a long narrow cockpit for the rest of the crew. See diagram, Fig. 236.*
Photo: Beken, Cowes

beginning. After motoring to Rio de Janeiro and having a new spar fitted, which was sent by air, he suffered the same accident again later in the race, after which he retired.

Without commenting on which particular aspects, i.e. hull design, type of rig, human factors, rating system, etc. had the greatest bearing on performance, we give overleaf a summary of results in the 1973/74 Round the World Race:

RESULTS OF THE FIRST ROUND-THE-WORLD YACHT RACE 1973-1974

Name of Yacht	Rig	Material	LOA	Nationality	Designer	Skipper	Remarks
1. Sayula	Ketch	GRP	64 ft	Mexico	Sp & Stephens	Ramon Carlin	Standard Swan 65, rolled over once
2. Adventure	Cutter	GRP	54 ft 8 in	Britain	C & Nicholson	Pat Bryans	Standard Nicholson 55, rudder damage
3. Grand Louis	Schooner	GRP	61 ft	France	D Presles	André Viant	The only schooner
4. Kriter	Ketch	Moulded Plywood	68 ft 3 in	France	Auzepy Breneur	Alain Glicksman	Rolled over once
5. Guia	Sloop	Wood	45 ft 2 in	Italy	Sp & Stephens	Giorgio Falck	Conventional solid timber constr.
6. Great Britain II	Ketch	GRP Sandwich	72 ft 3 in	Britain	Alan Gurney	Chay Blyth	Scratch boat. Lost 1 man
7. Second Life	Ketch	GRP	71 ft 3 in	Britain	v d Stadt	Roddy Ainslie	Standard Ocean 71
8. CSeRB Koala	Ketch	GRP	50 ft 3 in	Italy	Robt Clark	Doi Malingri	
9. Tauranga	Yawl	GRP	55 ft 2 in	Italy	Sp & Stephens	Eric Pascoli	Standard Swan 55. Lost 1 man
10. Brit. Soldier	Ketch	Steel	59 ft	Britain	Robt Clark	John Day	Previously sailed single-handed round world by Chay Blyth
11. P von Danzig	Yawl	Steel	59 ft	W Germany	Henry Gruber	Meyer-Laucht	Built 1936 in Gdansk (Danzig)
12. Otago	Ketch	Steel	55 ft 2 in	Poland	H Kujawa	Z Pienkawa	Built 1960 in Gdansk
13. Copernicus	Ketch	Wood	45 ft 2 in	Poland	L Rejewski	Z Perlicki	Conventional solid timber constr.
14. 33 Export	Yawl	Alloy	57 ft 5 in	France	André Mauric	Jean-P Millet	Lost 1 man
RETIRED							
Burton Cutter	Ketch	Alloy	81 ft 5 in	Britain	John Sharp	Leslie Williams	Structural damage
Pen Duick VI	Ketch	Alloy	74 ft 2 in	France	André Mauric	Eric Tabarly	Dismasted twice
Jakaranda	Sloop	GRP Sandwich	57 ft 1 in	S Africa	Sp & Stephens	Rich Bongert	Retired first lap

In 1957 Britain introduced a novel racing event for ocean racers: a four-race series, which was also an international team event. From hesitant beginnings this Admiral's Cup Series soon met with firm international response, and now similar multi-race series, most of them for international teams of three yachts, are held in many yachting centres of the world.

The Admiral's Cup Series comprises the following races: originally two, but, since 1977, three 30-mile inshore races over a triangular course in the Solent, counting for single points. The Channel Race, laid out over a 225-mile triangular course in the English Channel, which counts for double points. Finally, the 605-mile Fastnet Race, which counts for treble points and hence is the decisive race.

Any skipper who sets out to win the Admiral's Cup for his country has to forego personal ambitions in favour of furthering the performance of his national team of three yachts. In the 1973 Admiral's Cup Series, when competing yachts had to have an IOR rating of between 29 ft and 45 ft, 16 nations entered 16 teams of three yachts each, which means that 48 yachts in all had to be selected in national eliminations. The following countries were represented: Argentina, Australia, Belgium, Bermuda, Brazil, Denmark, Finland, France, Great Britain, Holland, Ireland, Italy, Portugal, South Africa, United States and West Germany.

Since the start of the Admiral's Cup Series in 1957 and up to 1977 the Cup has been won seven times by Great Britain, twice by the USA, once by Australia and

IMPORTANT OCEAN RACES

Venue	Name of Race	Distance N Miles	First Race	Remarks
North Atlantic USA	Bermuda Race	635	1906	Every other year, on even numbers. Most important ocean racing event.
North Atlantic England	Fastnet Race	605	1925	Every other year, on uneven numbers, alternating with Bermuda Race. Most important European ocean-racing event.
South Atlantic	Buenos Aires– Rio de Janeiro	1,200	1947	Every three years. Most important event in South American ocean racing.
South Atlantic	Capetown–Rio	3,800	1971	Longest of the regular ocean races, with strong international support.
Pacific	California– Honolulu	2,225	1906	Every other year on even numbers. Fastest ocean race with exceptional daily runs.
Australia	Sydney–Hobart	680	1945	Annually. International event of great importance to yachting in Australia and New Zealand.
Caribbean	St Petersburg– Ft Lauderdale	284	1930	Annually, originally to Havana. The salt-water race which has been held most often.
Great Lakes USA	Chicago– Mackinnac	333	1898	Annual fresh-water race. Oldest of all regular long-distance races.
North Atlantic	Transatlantic Race	3,000	1866	Irregular, but of significant influence on international ocean-racing.
Seven Oceans	Round-the-World Race	26,700	1973– 1974	Longest of all ocean-races with only three stops. Regularity of event uncertain but possibly 4-yearly.

once by West Germany.

At the end of the 1973 series it was decided to fix the rating limits at 30 ft–44 ft, and for the 1977 series they were further reduced to 30 ft–42 ft IOR.

The Admiral's Cup has inspired many yacht clubs the world over to introduce similar series, either as international team events or for individual yachts. One of them is the Onion Patch Trophy, which is contested over four races, one of them being the Bermuda Race. Then there is the SORC series which ends with the long race round Florida between Fort Lauderdale and St Petersburg.

Australia has incorporated its Sydney–Hobart Race in the Southern Cross Series. This is sailed around Christmas which is, of course, the middle of the Aus-tralian summer, while the northern hemisphere is in the grip of winter, and hence international support is considerable. The series is held every other year, over the Christmas following an Admiral's Cup Series, and comprises two short 30-mile races, a medium-distance race of 180 miles and the 680-mile Sydney–Hobart Race.

To have successfully participated in the Admiral's Cup Series is considered the crowning event of every ocean-racing man's career. It is not inconceivable that at some time in the future it will yield its role as the recurring highlight of the ocean racing scene to the Round the World Race.

The table above lists the most important ocean races.

Recluta III

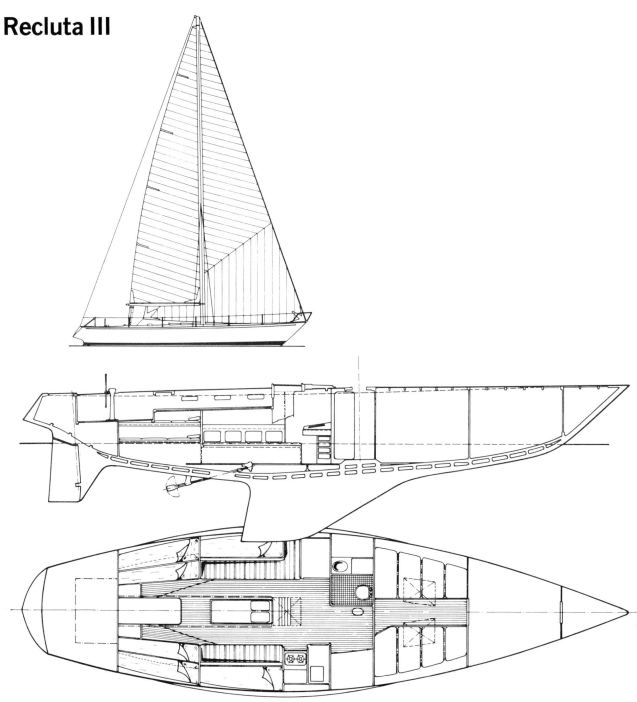

Fig. 235: The large IOR yacht RECLUTA III was designed especially for the 1973 Admiral's Cup Series by the young Argentinian designer German Frers. She finished second on points in the series and second in the Fastnet Race out of more than 200 entries.

LOA	48 ft 5 in	Ballast	7·4 ton
LWL	39 ft 5 in	Ballast ratio	52%
Beam	14 ft	Sail area	1060 sq ft
Draft	7 ft	IOR rating	37 ft
Displacement	14·2 ton		

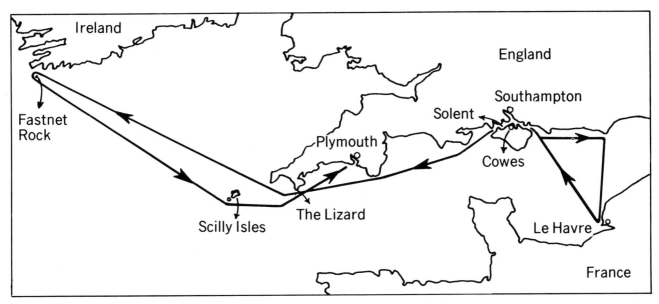

Fig. 236: The series for the coveted Admiral's Cup consists of the 225-mile Channel Race, which covers a triangular course seen on the right, three 30-mile races in the Solent, and the series is concluded by the 605-mile Fastnet Race, which finishes in Plymouth.

The America's Cup

For over 120 years a heated battle has raged over a racing trophy, which is not even made of gold. It was presented in 1851 by a group of British yachtsmen, and was won the same year by the American schooner AMERICA in a memorable race round the Isle of Wight. The superiority of the American schooner was by no means as obvious as is often claimed, but the notable differences in hull shape and rig compared with the British yachts of that period provoked interminable comment and discussion.

AMERICA was designed by a young naval architect by the name of George Steers and built by William H Brown. In the contract her building price had been fixed at 30,000 dollars, but since Brown could not finish her by the agreed date, the sum was eventually reduced to 20,000 dollars. The America's Cup was worth 100 guineas, about 300 dollars. To try to regain or defend it, more and more costly yachts have been built, and it is estimated that so far some 50 million dollars have been spent in the pursuit of this elusive trophy.

The dimensions of the AMERICA are representative of that period: LOA 101 ft (31 m), LWL 90 ft 3 in (27·5 m), beam 23 ft (6·7 m) and draft 11 ft (3·35 m). She had very fine bow lines, and the striking feature about her sails was that they were made of cotton and cut particularly flat. British yachts in those days used sails made of heavy hand-woven flax and cut much fuller.

Only the Scottish yacht TIARA had similarly fine waterlines. Unfortunately she was delayed by bad weather on passage and did not reach the start in time to take part in this memorable race. In later races she beat all the yachts which had been beaten by the American schooner. If TIARA had been in time for the start, maybe the '100-guinea prize', as it was then called, would have become the 'Tiara Cup' and remained in Britain.

AMERICA's victory spelt the death of full-bowed hulls of the 'cod's head and mackerel tail' type; from then onwards the lines of yachts became finer and finer. Schooner-rigged vessels competed for the last time in 1876, after which all competitors for the America's Cup have been single-masted, either cutters or sloops. The winners of the 1885 and 1887 races, PURITAN and VOLUNTEER, had flat, beamy, dinghy-like hulls with enormous centreboards and internal ballast only.

In the following years the ingenious designer Nathaniel G Herreshoff led the field in America's Cup

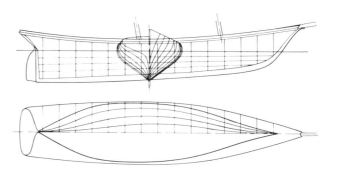

Fig. 237: Lines of the schooner AMERICA. She has extremely fine lines forward and aft and a deep mid-section, which enabled the loose internal ballast to be placed as low as possible.

designs. His bold designs, often ahead of their time, were built with impeccable precision at his own yard. The largest of his cup defenders, RELIANCE of 1903, had the following dimensions: LOA 143 ft (43·8 m), LWL 84 ft 6 in (27·35 m), beam 25 ft 10 in (7·85 m) and the considerable draft of 19 ft 9 in (6·1 m). She was a gaff cutter and had a sail area of 15,780 sq ft (1500 m²), the largest sail area ever set on one mast. The outer skin of the hull was made of a $\frac{1}{4}$ in (6·3 mm) thick corrosion-resistant bronze alloy, called Tobin Bronze, on nickel steel frames. The deck was made of aluminium plates of the same thickness and covered with a layer of cork to give better grip.

RELIANCE must go down in history as the first 'racing machine'. Every detail of her hull and rigging was designed with an eye to speed. Her halliards, for example, were made of steel wire, and the halliard winches were below decks, as were the main and foresheet winches.

The rating rules in use after 1883 encouraged the design of fast yachts, but it was soon realized that a rather less extreme and less costly type of vessel was called for. The Universal Rule of America of 1903 produced the J-class, which competed for the cup in 1930, 1934 and 1937. The average sail area of the J-class was more or less fixed at 7590 sq ft (705 m²), but the LWL could vary between 74 ft (22·9 m) and 87 ft (26·6 m), with a displacement of between 105 tons and 162 tons.

ENTERPRISE, winner of the 1930 race, was the shortest and lightest of all the J-class. In 1934 Britain entered Sir Thomas Sopwith's ENDEAVOUR I, which

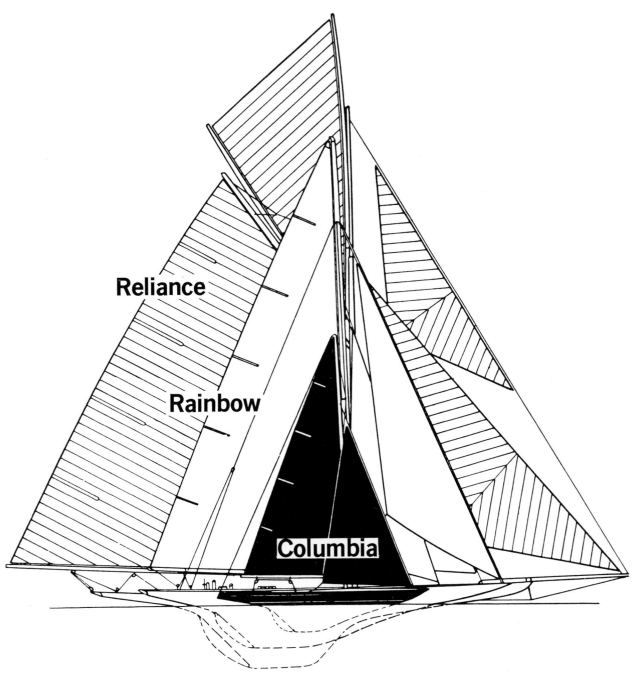

Fig. 238: Comparative sizes of important yachts which have competed in the races for the America's Cup. In the background the largest of all cup defenders, RELIANCE, in the middle the J-class yacht RAINBOW, and in the foreground COLUMBIA representing the still current 12-metre class.

RELIANCE
LOA	144 ft	Draft	20 ft
LWL	89 ft 7 in	Sail area	16,150 sq ft
Beam	25 ft 9 in		

RAINBOW
LOA	128 ft	Draft	14 ft 7 in
LWL	82 ft	Sail area	7556 sq ft
Beam	21 ft		

COLUMBIA
LOA	69 ft 5 in	Draft	9 ft
LWL	46 ft 3 in	Sail area	1820 sq ft
Beam	11 ft 10 in		

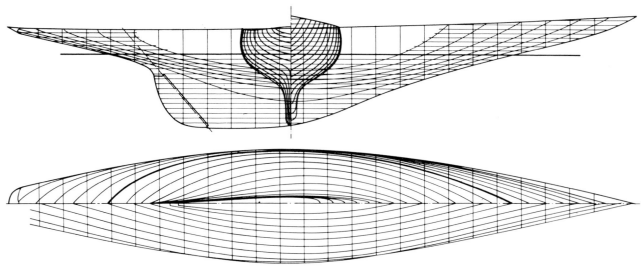

Fig. 239: The 1934 America's Cup series saw for the last time a
yacht which had been designed entirely without model tests.
ENDEAVOUR I, whose lines are shown here, was designed by
Charles E Nicholson. She was faster than RAINBOW, her opponent,
but did not win the Cup. Her design is a masterpiece, and her
lines are of classical beauty.

LOA	130 ft	Draft	15 ft
LWL	84 ft	Displacement	143 ton
Beam	22 ft	Sail area	7450 sq ft
Beam WL	21 ft		

came closer to victory than any challenger since. She
came from the board of Charles E Nicholson and, at the
time, was undoubtedly the most perfect yacht ever
designed without resorting to tank tests.

In 1937 America stole the show with the 'super yacht'
RANGER, whose speed and windward performance
baffled everybody who saw her. She was designed
jointly by Starling Burgess and Olin Stephens, after
extensive tank tests carried out by the model-test
expert K S M Davidson.

After World War II, considering the enormous cost
involved in building these huge machines, which were of
no particular use after the races, a much smaller type of
yacht was chosen for the America's Cup. This was the
12-metre class built to the IYRU Rule. This could not
be done, however, until the charter had been changed
by a court of law, since it stipulated a minimum LWL
of 65 ft (19·8 m). This was reduced to 44 ft (13·4 m),
and at the same time the condition was lifted which
stipulated that challengers had to get to the races
on their own keel and under sail.

Before 1920 the crews, including the helmsman, were
almost exclusively paid professionals. RELIANCE, in
1903, was skippered by the same Charley Barr who, in
1905, sailed the three-masted schooner ATLANTIC across

the North Atlantic in record time and won the Kaiser's
Cup. From 1920 onwards the helmsmen and part of the
crews were amateurs. Since the 1930 race between
SHAMROCK V and ENTERPRISE, the America's Cup races
have finally passed into the hands of amateurs.

Since its inception in 1851 the America's Cup has
been competed for in 22 series. All without exception
were won by the American defenders, even if they did
not always have the faster yacht, as in 1934 when the
British challenger ENDEAVOUR I came so close to
victory. The Australian GRETEL II was equally superior
to the American defender INTREPID in speed, but the
Americans won on superior racing tactics.

As the J-class before them, the 12-metre yachts sail
without handicap, boat for boat. Their dimensions
differ slightly from boat to boat, which is in the nature
of the formula. On average they are:

LOA	69 ft (21 m)
LWL	46 ft 6 in (14·2 m)
Beam	11 ft 6 in (3·5 m)
Draft	9 ft (2·75 m)
Displacement	29 tons
Sail area	1830 sq ft (170 m²)

The following is a short summary of the 12-metre challenges, all of which were won by the American defenders:

Sept 1958   COLUMBIA beat SCEPTRE (Britain).
Sept 1962   WEATHERLY beat GRETEL I (Australia).
Sept 1964   CONSTELLATION beat SOVEREIGN (Britain).
Sept 1967   INTREPID beat DAME PATTIE (Australia), the first yacht to be fitted with a trim-tab on the keel and the rudder hung aft on a skeg.
Sept 1970   INTREPID beat GRETEL II (Australia). There had, initially, been an elimination series between the French yacht FRANCE, owned by Baron Marcel Bich, and the Australian yacht GRETEL II, since both were challenging. GRETEL II won convincingly. INTREPID, designed by Olin Stephens for the 1967 race, had her hull and rigging modified for the 1970 race by the young designer Britton Chance.

Sept 1974   COURAGEOUS beat SOUTHERN CROSS (Australia). Aluminium hulls were permitted for the first time, and three new aluminium boats competed in the defender trials with the old wooden INTREPID. There was little to choose between INTREPID and COURAGEOUS. SOUTHERN CROSS beat FRANCE in the challenger trials, but lost in straight races to INTREPID.
Sept 1977   COURAGEOUS beat AUSTRALIA. The defender trials were hotly contested by two new boats, INDEPENDENCE and ENTERPRISE, but the revamped Sparkman and Stephens COURAGEOUS stayed ahead. Four boats challenged: FRANCE yet again, SVERIGE mounting the first Swedish challenge, and AUSTRALIA and GRETEL II, both from Australia.

The Conquest of the Sea

Fig. 240: The caravelle SANTA MARIA, *in which Christopher Columbus set out to find the sea route to India. This intrepid sailor was the first to venture out on a long, uninterrupted sea voyage far away from any coast. With a relatively modest length of 85 ft.* SANTA MARIA *had a crew of 45.*

Not so many centuries ago most people believed that they lived on a flat island surrounded by an equally flat sea; the idea that the earth is round being unknown 500 years ago. When the first Portuguese seamen sailed down the coast of Africa, they noticed with astonishment that the midday sun stood at the zenith, and when they sailed further, they made the unbelievable observation that it even bore north at noon. Since prehistoric times no European had ever before seen the midday sun other than in the South.

The first European to have trodden on American soil *may* have been the Irish monk St Brendan, who is reported to have sailed there in the fourth century, although this has not been proved. Several centuries later the Vikings certainly succeeded in reaching the American mainland. These fair-haired Norsemen had developed a particularly seaworthy but extremely light vessel, a double-ender, in which the bow and the stern were alike. The construction of the Viking ship was a tremendous technological advance and was made in complete isolation.

True blue water navigation, that is sailing across open stretches of sea without following the coastline, began with the boldest of navigators of his time, Christopher Columbus. He already believed that the earth was round, although he underestimated its true diameter. He had obtained his knowledge from the

Arabs, who had calculated the earth's diameter with extraordinary accuracy but expressed it in Arabic miles. Since Columbus based his calculations on the shorter Italian mile, he arrived at a much shorter distance to India than was in fact the case. His error was the cause of a scarcely suppressed mutiny of his crew, as well as the confusion of the continent of America, which he finally reached, with the legendary land of India. For this reason the islands in the Caribbean are called the West Indies and the natives of America became known as Red Indians.

Prince Henry of Portugal, known today as Henry the Navigator, founded the first school of navigation. His star pupil, Captain Gil Enneas, had already boldly explored a large part of the African coast without ever reaching the southern tip of the African continent. It was not until after Henry's death that Table Mountain, the Cape of Good Hope, was discovered and rounded by a clever Portuguese sailor by the name of Bartholomew Diaz. In doing so he prepared the way for the intrepid Ferdinand de Magellan, who set off on the first circumnavigation of the earth. Unfortunately, Magellan never succeeded in completing it, because he was killed by the natives of an island after having covered the larger part of his voyage. His daring route took him over unknown seas, of which no charts existed, without nautical almanacs and with no other help but his seaman's instinct to show him the way. Nobody had as yet discovered a way of establishing longitude.

Vasco da Gama, Bartholomew Diaz's successor, was the first captain actually to take his ships to the legendary India which, until then, had only been reached overland. He got there in 1498, six years after Columbus had mistaken the Caribbean islands for part of India. How far it was from there to the true India Columbus never discovered, because there was no way of measuring longitude. Vasco da Gama made his voyage unaccompanied by the experienced Diaz, but Diaz had supervised the design and building of the ships. They were no longer caravels like those in which Columbus sailed, but a larger, more seaworthy type, which the Portuguese called *nao*. It had to be capable of weathering all the storms it might encounter in rounding Africa and also carry a large, profitable cargo.

Columbus was the first of the captains who fearlessly ventured out into the open sea without following the

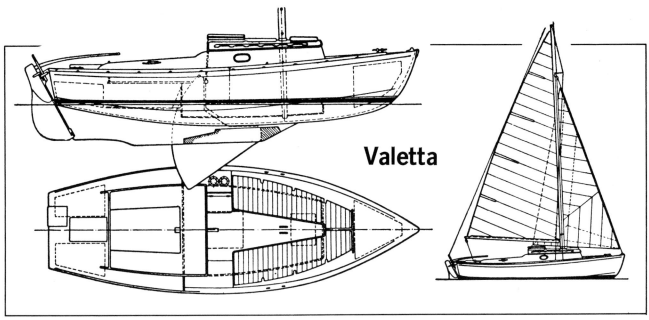

Valetta

Fig. 241: A small, undemanding centreboard keel-yacht like the 'Valetta' class designed by A Chiggiato, is likely to find many friends in sailing circles.

LOA	19 ft	Draft, plate down .	4 ft 3 in
LWL	17 ft 6 in	Displacement ...	1500 lb
Beam	6 ft 9 in	Ballast	485 lb
Draft, plate up ..	2 ft 2 in	Sail area	200 sq ft

coast. Vasco da Gama also did so when he sailed in an arc from Cape Verde directly to the southern tip of Africa, the latitude of which could be established. As time went by the knowledge spread that well-built ships had nothing to fear from the open sea but that dangers threatened on the coasts. It was not at sea but along the shoreline that most shipwrecks were found.

Alan Villiers calls Columbus, da Gama, Magellan and Cook the greatest discoverers, who sailed out in small ships across the open sea and changed the face of the world.

Magellan set out in 1519 with a fleet of five small ships. He found the passage through the southern tip of South America which bears his name and which, even today, is difficult to negotiate. He felt his way carefully through the narrows of the dangerous Straits of Magellan, between threatening cliffs and unknown reefs. It was a difficult undertaking with ships which were far from being as manoeuvrable as a modern yacht. Besides, there were the variable and constantly changing winds, so that it is not surprising that one of his ships mutinied at this point and turned back. Unfortunately it was the best ship and the one which had the reserve food rations on board. Nevertheless, this intrepid man did not give up but continued on his way,

which led him and his companions over the endless expanse of the world's largest ocean. He did not allow himself to be put off by the dilapidated condition of his ships nor by the barely suppressed opposition of his crews. With four ships he sailed for 98 days without sight of land. His men suffered unspeakable torments, since the drinking water had deteriorated so far that it was necessary to hold one's nose to be able to drink it. Food supplies had become so short that they ripped the pig-skin protection off the rigging and made it palatable by soaking it in sea water. Magellan finally lost his life on the Philippine island of Mactan, when he tried to settle a quarrel between the natives. A similar fate was also met by another famous discoverer, Captain Cook.

One of Magellan's men, Lieutenant Sebastian el Cano, managed to sail the last remaining ship back to Spain. When the VICTORIA arrived at her Spanish home port, she was the first vessel to have sailed round the world. This adventurous voyage took place between 1519 and 1522. One hundred and seventy lives and three ships were lost. Only thirty-one men of the crews of Magellan's original fleet reached home.

Sixty years later the second circumnavigation was completed by a wonderful little ship called the GOLDEN

325

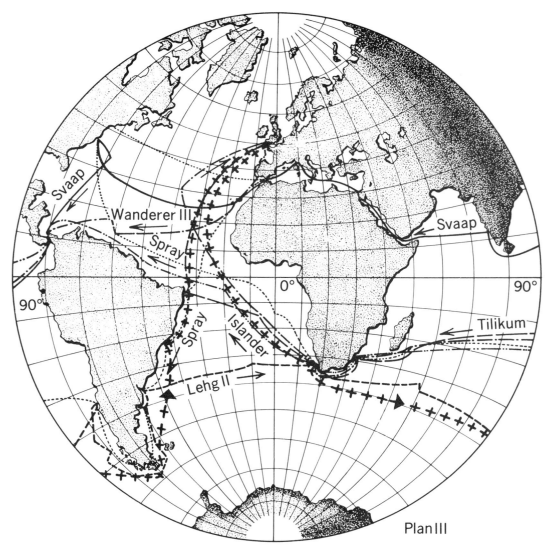

Plan III

Svaap
Wanderer III
Spray
Svaap
90°
0°
90°
Spray
Islander
Tilikum
Lehg II

Plan III: ATLANTIC HEMISPHERE
The majority of today's round-the-world yachtsmen set out from some European port and set course across the Atlantic, past the Azores to the Panama Canal. The routes of the most famous of the earlier circumnavigators have been entered here. The first of them, SPRAY, sailed through the Magellan Straits. Columbus' voyage across the Atlantic, which is marked by a dotted line, was positively insignificant compared to the feats of some modern yachts, which were very much smaller. Columbus' route has become the classic route for the Transatlantic Single-Handed Race, which was started in 1960 and is held every four years, starting in England and finishing in the USA. Some of the competing yachts, though handled by only one man, are longer than Columbus' SANTA MARIA.

HIND. She was commanded by an outstanding young captain, Francis Drake, who is better known as a pirate than a seaman. He had been licensed as a privateer by Queen Elizabeth of England. He, too, met difficulties similar to those which beset Magellan, and only one of his original fleet of five ships returned. His circumnavigation took place between 1577 and 1580.

It was two hundred years later that the English seaman and humanitarian Captain James Cook made two voyages round the world. He was an explorer as well as a navigator, and he was also very concerned about the welfare of his crew. It is said that his men signed on with him freely, which was quite contrary to the custom of the day, when seamen were recruited by force or trickery or found themselves aboard ships as a punishment.

Cook's first world voyage took place between 1768 and 1771 in a Whitby collier named ENDEAVOUR. His

326

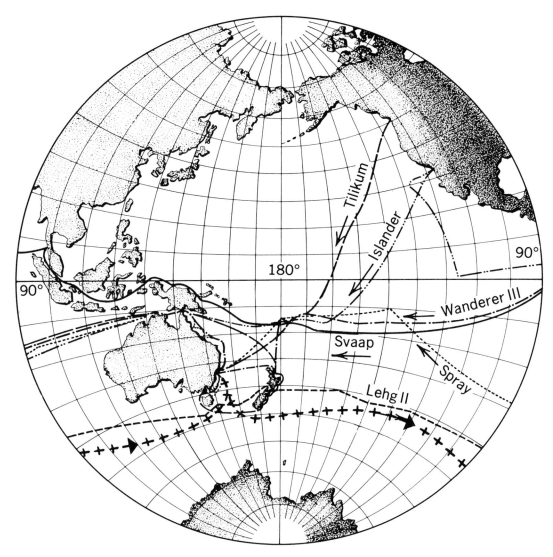

PACIFIC HEMISPHERE
The Pacific hemisphere is characterized by vast, uninterrupted
expanses of ocean. Nearly all the routes entered here led via the
Polynesian Islands south of the Equator. Even TILIKUM *and*
ISLANDER, *who set out from a North Pacific coast, made straight*
for this southern paradise.
*   Only* LEHG II *on her lonely voyage ignored these tempting*
latitudes, as did entrants in the Round the World Race, which was
held for the first time in 1973–74 and again in 1977–78 for fully-
crewed yachts and took the most difficult of all routes round three
capes, marked here by bold crosses.

second journey was made between 1772 and 1775 in
two ships, ADVENTURE and RESOLUTION which were,
once again, sturdy colliers from Whitby.

Cook's second voyage is particularly important, for
he sailed round the Antarctic polar circle and proved
that there is no land connection with the Antarctic
sub-continent. It is believed that he took with him,
for the first time, one of those amazing new instruments
with which longitude can be determined. This was a
ship's chronometer, designed and built by Harrison
shortly before. It must be emphasized that Cook was
probably the first to take effective measures towards
keeping his crew in good health. Thanks to his efforts
not one of his men died of scurvy.

During his third voyage, after having at last been
made Captain, this outstanding navigator and explorer
of foreign shores was killed on one of the Hawaiian
islands.

Sailing Round the World in Yachts

The first person to sail round the world in a yacht, and at the same time a sovereign conqueror of the sea, was in fact a sea captain and shipowner, Joshua Slocum, who was born in Canada in 1844. He made his single-handed circumnavigation in the small yacht SPRAY between 1895 and 1898. SPRAY has already been illustrated in Fig. 194 in the chapter on small circumnavigators, and Fig. 242 gives an artist's impression of her. She began her great voyage rigged as a sloop, but was later fitted with a mizzen mast and changed into a yawl.

Slocum completed his lonely voyage in three years, which means he took about the same time as Magellan, Drake and Cook. His voyage and the perfection with which it was executed astonished the world and made a great impression in seafaring circles, where this exceptional feat could be truly appreciated. Ocean-crossing yachtsmen have always considered Slocum their forebear, overlooking the fact that he was really a professional seaman.

The next sporting circumnavigation of the world was made by Harry Pidgeon, whose yacht ISLANDER is illustrated in Fig. 195. He was so pleased with his solo-voyage on the high seas that he sailed round again in the same yacht. His first voyage took place between 1921 and 1925, the second between 1932 and 1937.

While Pidgeon was on his first voyage, an equally exceptional blue-water yachtsman set off on a similar single-handed journey: the Frenchman Alain Gerbault set sail in FIRECREST in 1923 and completed his voyage in 1929.

Before 1930 only three circumnavigations were made altogether by small yachts. The feats of SPRAY, FIRECREST and ISLANDER aroused great enthusiasm for ocean cruising among sailing men. Their skippers published their experiences in book form, providing would-be imitators with valuable hints and information and contributing greatly to making blue-water sailing extremely popular. The number of yachts which have sailed round the world with a crew of no more than two must by now have reached a hundred, while there had been no more than three before 1930!

The majority of these vessels have been over 30 ft (9 m) long but there have been a few exceptions, for example the small yacht TREKKA, which was only 20 ft 10 in (6·35 m) long. Most have been single-masted, either sloop or cutter rigged; the rest have been ketch,

Fig. 242: The yawl SPRAY was the first small boat to sail round the world. Her voyage covered the years 1895–8, and her skipper was Captain Joshua Slocum

yawl or, exceptionally, schooner rigged. Most were equipped with auxiliary engines, but there have been some which used sails exclusively, even in dangerous situations or in restricted waters.

The outstanding sailor Irving Johnson, in his German-built schooner YANKEE, sailed round the world seven times in such astonishing safety that he changed adventure to tourism. Eventually he sold the very large YANKEE and had himself a smaller vessel with shallower draft built, in which he could explore the inland waters of Europe and the Mediterranean.

An almost classic route has emerged from the many circumnavigations. It begins in the country of origin, usually on a North Atlantic coast, and goes initially to

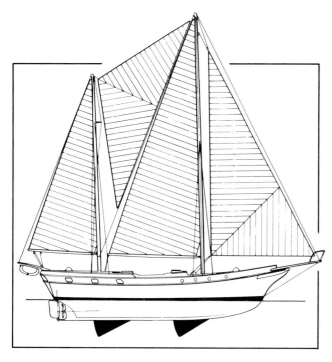

Fig. 243: The American Irving Johnson, an experienced sailor, circumnavigated the world four times in his 95 ft yacht YANKEE I, *which was built in Germany in 1912. For rather more leisurely sailing projects he then had the ketch* YANKEE II *built, which was designed by Sparkman & Stephens without reference to any class or rating rules. Her shallow draft is to enable her to negotiate the inland waterways of Europe, while the two plates in tandem give her the necessary draft in open waters. An interesting feature of her rig is the fisherman staysail set between the masts.*

the Panama Canal. This way the troublesome and dangerous rounding of storm-ridden Cape Horn or the passage of the inhospitable and narrow Straits of Magellan can be avoided. Then follows the longest stretch across the open sea; approximately 3000 miles to the Marquesas. It then continues across the Pacific to the Polynesian Islands and eventually along the north coast of Australia into the Indian Ocean. The classic return voyage goes by way of the Cape of Good Hope into the Atlantic again, the whole extent of which has to be traversed to return to the northern point of departure.

To sail round the world has become an almost casual affair, and even a single-handed race round the world has been held. There were nine starters, five of which retired in the early stages. Two sank, and of the two who remained one decided to withdraw to his Polynesian paradise without finishing the race, which was eventually won by Robin Knox-Johnston in the slowest of all competing yachts, exceptionally well

prepared and superbly sailed. The striking thing about the race was that it had to be sailed non-stop and that all three Capes had to be rounded. SUHAILI covered a little more than 30,000 miles and took 313 days. Nigel Tetley in his trimaran VICTRESS would have finished in a very much shorter time, about 260 days, if his light multi-hull had not fallen apart and sunk in the North Atlantic when he had already covered 28,000 miles and only had another 1000 or so to go.

VICTRESS was the first multi-hull without a ballast keel to round Cape Horn. Lieutenant Commander Tetley was of the opinion that the rounding of the Horn as such was not at all too bad and that people are in the habit of exaggerating this. Far worse, he said, are the 12,000 miles through the Roaring Forties.

This first single-handed, non-stop race round the world, started in 1968 and was won in April 1969 by the heavy double-ender SUHAILI. Nowadays sailing round the world is considered no more than a 'civilized personal adventure', which is no longer sensational and causes hardly any comment. Whoever wants to do it, providing he has the necessary knowledge of seamanship, can do so with very little risk. There is now an ever-increasing procession of sailing yachts making their way along the classical route round the world. You meet them in the Caribbean and then again at the Galapagos, in Tahiti, in Australia or New Zealand, and for the last time in Durban or Cape Town. In the end, at the end of three years and after the final long and tiring trek through the shipping lanes from Cape Town back to Europe, one is glad to be home again. Anyone who is looking for an exceptional feat to perform will soon be at a loss, especially after Chay Blyth's performance going round 'the wrong way'.

As a young paratrooper Chay Blyth had been in the news when he crossed the North Atlantic in an open rowing boat together with a comrade from his regiment, John Ridgeway. In 1970 he had another gripping idea, which was soon turned into practice when the British Steel Corporation agreed to finance the building of a large steel yacht. She was put on the stocks in March 1970 and already in October 1970 Chay was able to start on the most enterprising of all circumnavigations so far: single-handed, non-stop and in the 'wrong' direction, i.e. from East to West. The yacht was appropriately called BRITISH STEEL and had the following dimensions: LOA 59 ft (18 m), beam 12 ft 9 in

(3·9 m), draft 8 ft (2·45 m), displacement 17 tons, working sail area 1507 sq ft (140 m²). She was designed by the very experienced naval architect Robert Clark and is illustrated in Fig. 193.

Chay Blyth's great voyage started on 18th October 1970 off Southampton and took him straight down down through the tropics to Cape Horn. Exactly on Christmas Eve of 1970 he rounded the Horn, where he met some calm weather at first but later increasing winds and high seas. Although at this time of year it is summer in the southern hemisphere, it was bitterly cold. In the Roaring Forties, where the prevailing winds are westerly, Chay's westerly progress was, of course, *against* the wind and current, which was hard work and very tiring. But the modern and strongly built BRITISH STEEL proved herself exceptionally capable. On 21st May she rounded the Cape of Good Hope, and on 6th August 1971, 292 days after her departure, she arrived back where she had started. Both skipper and boat were in excellent condition and proved that there is hardly anything in the way of long-distance sailing feats that cannot be done.

We must, however, mention the case of a very young solo circumnavigator, the 16-year-old Robin Lee Graham, who set out to round the world in his 24 ft (7·35 m) sloop DOVE in July 1965. His father had taught him to sail at an early age, and he had a good knowledge of astro-navigation. Five years and 33,000 miles later, married, he arrived back at his Californian home after having spent time on the Pacific islands, in Australia and South Africa. On his return voyage he sailed across the South Atlantic, through the Panama Canal and via the Galapagos Islands.

We cannot conclude this chapter without having mentioned the unforgettable adventurer at sea, Captain Voss, who demonstrated that successful ocean crossings can be made in very primitive craft. One must add to this, however, that Captain Voss, who originally came from Elmshorn near Hamburg, was an exceptionally capable seaman. In 1901 an Indian in British Columbia had sold him a dugout canoe, 38 ft (11·6 m) long and only 5 ft 6 in (1·68 m) in beam. He rebuilt it to his own ideas, put a cabin on it and rigged it as a three-masted schooner. For three years Captain Voss sailed his TILIKUM, which did not even have a proper keel, across virtually all the oceans of the world and very nearly completed a round trip. He was an unusually talented sailor, and his remarks about the types and uses of sea anchors still hold good today, and are an important contribution to safety and comfort in ocean sailing. TILIKUM can today be seen as a museum piece in Vancouver.

Not only men have conquered the North Atlantic. In 1952 a small yacht, FELICITY ANN, only 23 ft (7 m) long and similar to a Vertue sloop, set out from England. It was not only her small dimensions which aroused comment but the fact that she was sailed single-handed by a courageous woman, Ann Davison. Since then notably Clare Francis has staked a claim to a place in the history books as a female blue-water sailor.

Special Sails for Extended Ocean Cruising

Synthetic fibres are now universally used in the making of sails, and even cruising sails are no longer made of cotton. Very soon there will not be a sailmaker left who has the necessary know-how to cut a cotton sail, which stretches about ten times as much as one made of polyester and this has to be taken into account in the cutting. Other arguments against the use of cotton sails for long-distance cruising are shrinkage when wet, formation of mildew and lower durability. On average, one suit of synthetic sails will outlast two of cotton sails.

There are ways in which the long-distance sailor can lengthen the life of his sails. He can dispense altogether with sail battens and with wooden or metal headboards. The panels of the mainsail can be cut parallel to the leach instead of at right angles to it, and this will prevent a possible tear from extending over the whole width of the sail and thus put it out of action. Normal working headsails should have no overlap to stop chafing on the shrouds; in light winds any of several light-weather headsails may be set, which have a considerable overlap. In a two-masted rig a mizzen staysail is a very useful addition.

The theory that long-distance cruisers should be, if anything, undercanvassed has long been recognized as an error. There must, of course, be a storm jib and trysail for heavy weather, the latter also being useful as a possible jury mainsail, but the basic sail area should be that of a normal fast cruising yacht, plus several large light-weather sails. The days of heavy weather encountered at sea are normally much fewer than the days of fine weather or complete calm. Wallowing about in the calms of equatorial waters is more demoralizing than having to cope with storm conditions.

Long ocean passages are usually so planned that they make good use of steady trade winds. Under these conditions, with the wind mainly from aft, the disadvantages of the modern fore-and-aft rig become apparent. The helmsman is forced to constant vigilance, because the wave motion and the rolling of the boat bring her constantly to within inches of gybing. An accidental gybe entails serious risk of the boom or one of the backstays breaking, and at the very least it causes the crew some very anxious moments.

Twin spinnakers or twin jibs make this dreaded course before the wind safe and comfortable by steadying the yacht on her course and cancelling out completely the risk of an accidental gybe. There is a subtle difference between twin spinnakers and twin jibs, which is not in the cut but in the way they are set. If their luffs are hanked to a forestay each, they are twin jibs; if their luffs are loose between deck and masthead, they are twin spinnakers.

Once it was customary to set a reaching foresail on long ocean passages off the wind. This was very similar to an ordinary square sail and was set on a yard before the mast. Since the introduction of modern twin headsails it has fallen into disuse.

The first time twin headsails were used was in 1930 when the Irish sailor Otway Waller sailed single-handed to the Canary Isles in his 26 ft (8 m) yawl. He used two triangular headsails designed by himself, which were boomed out by short spinnaker poles. Their sail area could be reduced by a Wykeham Martin roller reefing gear.

At first sight twin headsails seem simple enough to use, but in practice there can be unexpected difficulties, which are illustrated in an account by Marin Marie. While crossing the North Atlantic in his new yacht WINNIBELLE, which he had had delivered from the yard virtually at the last minute and had had no time to try out in advance, he struggled for two hours to set his twin jibs, and when he had finally got them up and drawing all the sheets and halliards were in a frightful tangle. With much patience and by making many small alterations he finally sorted everything out and got his twin jibs into working order. It then became obvious that the sail area of both sails was much too small to drive the boat adequately in normal winds, so he decided to set his ordinary spinnaker as well. But the stabilizing effect of the twin jibs was excellent, especially after he had lashed the sheets to the tiller, and WINNIBELLE sailed herself safely for 26 days, in which she covered 2600 miles.

Waller's idea aroused the interest of the American designer Frederik A Fenger, who consequently spent much time and effort on the improvement of twin running sails. Another experienced deep-sea yachtsman by the name of Gill recognized the advantages of having twins cut so that the clew was high above the deck. This facilitates enormously their setting, and enables the booms to swing out and down without catching on the railing. Figure 244 summarizes the outcome of all the improvements made to twin-spinnakers, especially by Fenger, and also illustrates twin-jibs (bottom right).

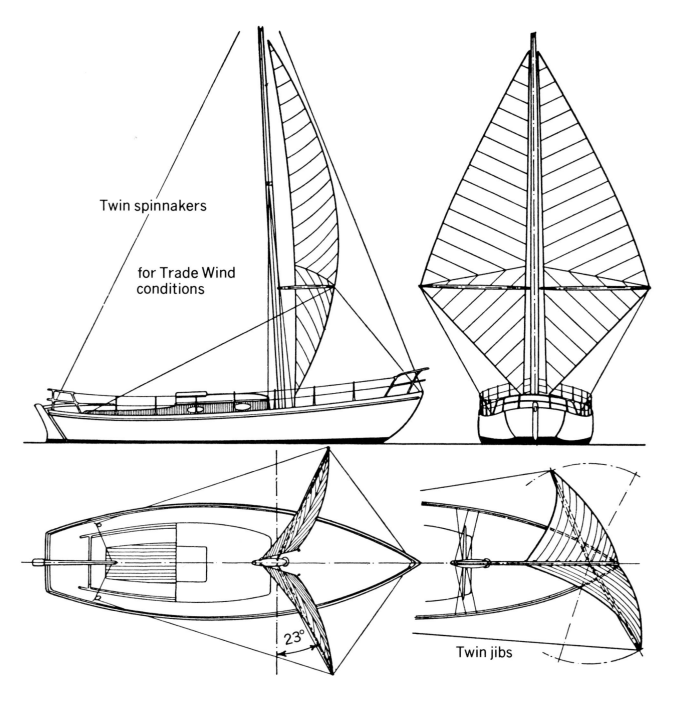

Twin spinnakers

for Trade Wind
conditions

23°

Twin jibs

Fig. 244: Long-distance ocean passages with following trade winds have only become really enjoyable since the introduction of twin headsails. Twin spinnakers are set flying; twin jibs, lower right-hand corner, are hanked to twin forestays. Twin headsails are very effective in keeping the yacht on course and enable her to sail herself over long distances.

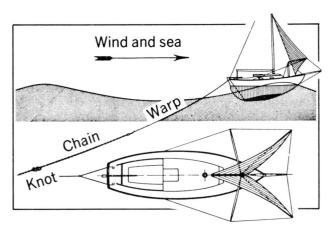

Fig. 245: Marcel Bardiaux set his twin jibs on a short mast stepped on the foredeck. With the help of no less than four booms he got this type of head-rig, which is reputedly difficult to adjust, to set very effectively. He also towed a warp and chain with knots tied in it to help keep the boat on course.

Fenger recommends that twin spinnakers be set close to the mast rather than forward, in order to leave a slot between the two through which the air can escape. The eye-bolts on either side of the mast ought to be at a distance from the centreline equivalent to 3–4 per cent of the luff, and the same distance forward of the mast. Fenger also advises that twin spinnakers should be boomed out at an angle of 23° forward of the beam, since this angle gives the best stabilizing effect.

It should be noted that the spinnaker tack is not made fast directly to the eye-bolt on deck but to a strop, which raises it approximately 20 in (50 cm) above the deck. This makes for improved visibility and stops water, which might be shipped, from getting caught in the sails.

The sail area of the twin spinnakers shown here is comparatively modest. To find the best dimensions in practice it is recommended to determine first the maximum possible lengths the booms can have without interfering with the rail as the sails are set and lowered. If the height of the clew is at 30 per cent of the total sail height, the booms can be of convenient length. Since the luffs are loose and not hanked to stays, the sails must have a wire luff. The booms are kept rigidly in place by adjusting the length of the sheets leading aft and the guys leading forward.

Most yachts can steer themselves with this arrange-

ment without the sheets having to be lashed to the tiller. The stabilizing effect of twin spinnakers is easily understood if one examines the way the wind acts on them. As soon as the yacht goes off course, the sail which is now to weather offers a greater sail area to the wind, while the leeward sail is left almost without any wind. The combined effect immediately forces the boat to fall off and return to her proper course. The angle of 23° seems to be particularly favourable and encourages this behaviour quite automatically, so that it is practically impossible for the vessel to wander off-course unless an especially bad sea and a very short keel combine to make adverse conditions.

The alternative of twin jibs is characterized by the fact that the two jibs are hanked to twin forestays. Many yachtsmen prefer this arrangement, because they can use two normal jibs. The main problem here is to find a suitable pivoting point for the booms. If it is on the mast, the angle at which the jibs can be set is seriously restricted. Since the luffs of the sails pivot round their forestays, the booms, too, ought to be attached to the forestays in order to have the same freedom of movement as is characteristic of twin spinnakers.

One solution is to provide an 'artificial' pivoting point near the forestays, as has been illustrated in Fig. 245. The round-the-world sailor Marcel Bardiaux erected a short mast on the foredeck of his yacht LES QUATRE VENTS with the sole purpose of providing an efficient pivoting point for his jib booms; he had to use *four* booms to get a satisfactory angle of pull. The arrangement shown here proved very efficient and enabled him to set his twin jibs at any desired angle. The only disadvantage was that the mast stump, the four booms and all the necessary rigging cluttered the foredeck and impeded his free movement at this strategic point.

In spite of their obvious disadvantages four booms are decidedly useful, because they make it possible to let the twin jibs out at an extreme angle, see Fig. 245, without too much pull coming on the sheets.

Twin headsails have improved the fore-and-aft rig in its only weak point: its unstable behaviour before the wind. They are a great improvement on the former reaching foresail, which they have replaced for the deep sea cruising man once and for all.

Self-Steering Devices for Sailing Yachts

All keelboats and many dinghies can steer themselves for shorter or longer distances on the wind with the helm lashed. The shorter the underwater profile, i.e. the keel, the less she will be inclined to steer herself satisfactorily. As a rule, the jib has to be sheeted in hard, the mainsail eased and the tiller lashed in such a way that the boat has a tendency to pay off. Obviously, this is a precarious state of balance. On a reach or before the wind, self-steering is hardly ever possible without mechanical aids, except by using symmetrical headsails before the wind, as discussed in the previous chapter. Slocum was delighted with his SPRAY, because she did actually sail herself on a broad reach for long distances. But Slocum had to sacrifice a good part of the potential drive to balance her. He, too, had the jib sheeted in hard, the mainsail let right out and the tiller, presumably, lashed slightly to weather. Only boats with a very long keel could be expected to sail themselves in this way on a reach.

Most boats, on the other hand, will steer themselves in this natural way on the wind, and with the help of twin headsails before the wind. If the sheets are made fast to the tiller, this gives even greater scope. In connection with twin running sails the arrangement is shown in Fig. 244, bottom left. On the wind, the mainsheet is led to the tiller via a block on the weather deck. On the leeward side the tiller is restrained by a strop which is either completely elastic, e.g. shock-cord, or has a piece of elastic inserted in it. As pressure on the mainsail increases, the mainsheet pulls the tiller up and thereby counters the boat's natural tendency to come up into the wind. As pressure on the mainsail eases the shock-cord retrieves the tiller.

Mechanical self-steering devices are a relatively recent invention. Some experiments were made before 1960, e.g. the British yacht BUTTERCUP was fitted with self-steering gear, and so was MICK THE MILLER in 1955. When the first single-handed Transatlantic Race was sailed in 1960, all of the five competing yachts were equipped with some sort of automatic device. Francis Chichester, who won the race in 40 days, had fitted a home-made device which he called 'Miranda'. Since it acted directly on the yacht's normal rudder, its vane area was fairly large and could even be reefed. Through winning the race, Francis Chichester contributed greatly towards popularizing the idea of vane steering.

The most commonly used kind of self-steering mechanism is directly activated by the wind, which means that it steers a course *relative to the wind*; if the wind direction changes, so does the heading of the boat. This can go unnoticed unless the compass is checked frequently. Apart from this type there are self-steering devices which work quite independently from the wind direction and which can be used on sailing yachts. These we will discuss later.

A number of self-steering devices do not act on the rudder but incorporate a small rudder or paddle of their

Plate 75: 300 Nicholson 32's have been built over the years. The owner of this one has had a Hasler steering vane fitted. The wind vane of this is angled exactly along the direction of the wind even if it appears on first sight to be otherwise. This is a first-class sea-going boat, 33 ft long with a beam of 9 ft 2 in and 600 sq ft sail area, built in fibreglass by Camper & Nicholson, Gosport.
Photo: John Etches, Bournemouth

335

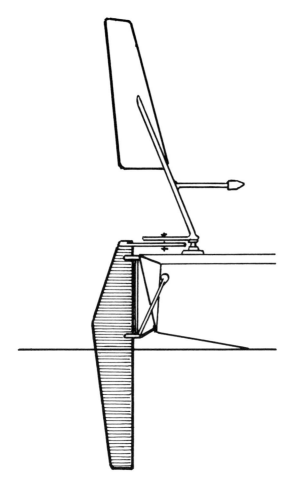

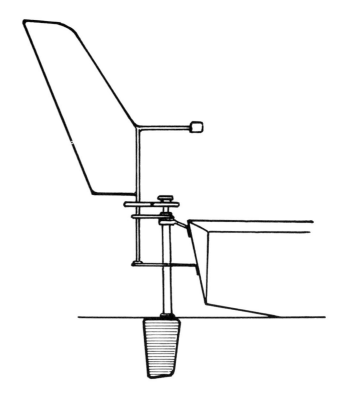

Fig. 246: The type of vane self-steering shown here was originally used on model boats. On the left a Michael Henderson design of 1955, on the right a more recent model by John Adams. Both gears operate a small auxiliary rudder, and both incorporate a reversing mechanism between vane and rudder, because they have to move in opposite directions.

own, which is either hung freely on the transom or is mounted on the main rudder. In either case there is a wind vane at a certain height above deck level, which activates this small paddle via some mechanism. It is a well-known shortcoming of wind vanes that they develop insufficient steering power in light winds. Some devices, with this in mind, incorporate a number of interchangeable vanes of different size. A larger vane area is also required before the wind, because the apparent wind is less, and because more steering power is needed to cope with the boat's tendency to yaw.

A great deal of a steering mechanism's effectiveness depends on the ability of the owner to balance the boat properly to start with. If she has excessive weather helm, for example, the sails have to be modified or even the mast shifted. Many modern yachts are naturally

steady on course with very little rudder pressure, and they are particularly suited to the installation of a wind-operated self-steering device. To operate any one of the different systems, the wind vane is initially disengaged so that it swings freely in the wind. The yacht is then steered on the required course and the sheets are so trimmed that there is as little pressure as possible on the rudder. Then the vane is engaged. If it takes over the steering accurately, no further adjustments are needed. If not, the vane has to be trimmed, perhaps repeatedly, until it keeps the yacht on course.

If this ideal state can be achieved, the vane can steer better than even a conscientious helmsman. This has been proved during trials over set courses, when all relevant data concerning apparent wind, deviation from course etc. were recorded. There can be no doubt that

336

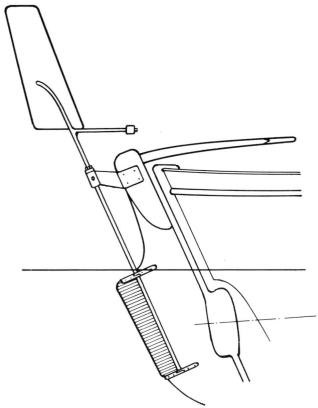

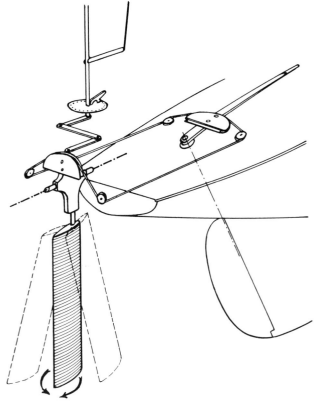

Fig. 247: Boats with their rudder hung on the transom can use this particularly simple self-steering system, in which a tab is attached to the after edge of the main rudder. It was known as the Flettner rudder in the Twenties. As the tab turns to one side, so the main rudder turns to the other and steers the boat. No reversing mechanism is needed, but there has to be a gearwheel and clutch for setting the vane.

Fig. 248: The Hasler–Gibb pendulum-servo gear developed by Colonel 'Blondie' Hasler is very popular among yachtsmen. The wind vane pivots the auxiliary rudder, which, in turn, is swung to one side by the water pressure and thereby operates the main rudder. Since the power obtained from the water pressure is much greater than that of the original wind pressure on the vane, the operation can be called servo-assisted.

on long passages, when the crew is tired, a self-steering device is a godsend.

Due to the natural properties of flowing air and water, steering vanes are normally installed at the stern, they have a near-vertical pivoting axis, and they activate the yacht's rudder or a small auxiliary rudder. Figure 246 illustrates two such types with auxiliary rudder, the one on the left being a 1955 version by Michael Henderson, the one on the right a more recent design by John Adams; in both, only the small auxiliary rudder is used for steering. Under working conditions the wind vane, which is shown here amidships, would be aligned to the wind. For example, if the yacht were sailing on the starboard tack, the vane would point aft over the port quarter. If the yacht tries to luff up in a puff, the wind comes onto the port side of the vane and pushes its

trailing edge to starboard. However, to make the yacht pay off, the trailing edge of the *rudder* needs to be pushed to *port*, and this is the reason why there has to be a reversing mechanism incorporated between the vane and the rudder. In the model on the left this is a set of levers, on the John Adams design on the right a number of gear-wheels.

If a yacht has the rudder hung on the transom, the self-steering arrangement can be very simple, see Fig. 247. A trim tab is mounted on the trailing edge of the yacht's rudder, which turns this into a Flettner-rudder of the type which was used experimentally on cargo steamers in the twenties. In this arrangement no reversing mechanism is needed, because the rudder automatically turns in the opposite direction to the trim tab, and very little force is needed. There has to

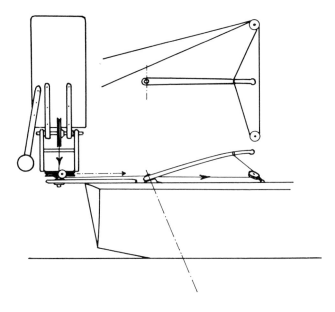

Fig. 249: As opposed to the other wind vanes featured in this chapter, which pivot round a vertical axis, the vane in the QME gear illustrated here swings round a horizontal axis. As the boat goes off course and the wind strikes the vane on one side, the vane goes over and pulls on a line led over a drum, which activates the tiller. A second drum lower down carries the line with which the vane is set.

be a gear-wheel and clutch to set the vane.

The so-called Hasler–Gibb self-steering system is particularly popular with British yachtsmen. It was developed over the years by the great enthusiast of single-handed transatlantic sailing, Colonel H G Hasler. Its method of operation is altogether original. It uses the wind vane only as a sensor while the actual steering is done by water pressure. In this 'pendulum-servo-gear' the wind vane once again operates an auxiliary rudder. This is pivoted by the vane as indicated by the arrow in Fig. 248, and it is also free to swing round a horizontal axis. As soon as the auxiliary rudder is at an angle to the flow of water it swings to one side or the other, as indicated in the drawing. A semi-circular segment with a line led over it to the tiller is mounted above the auxiliary rudder on the shaft. As the rudder swings so it activates the tiller via the line. Hence it is the *swinging rudder* which operates the main rudder, and since this is achieved by water pressure, which is much greater than the air pressure

which initially operates the vane, the gear can be said to be servo-assisted.

Although the Hasler–Gibb gear looks cumbersome and complicated on the stern of a yacht, it has proved itself many times on long ocean passages. In the 1972 Single-handed Transatlantic Race 10 different types of self-steering were recorded on 40 competing yachts. Among them the Hasler–Gibb type just led the field.

In all the systems we have discussed so far the wind vane pivots round a vertical axis. But it can be done differently, as shown in Fig. 249, where the vane swings round a horizontal axis, balanced by a counterweight. As the wind strikes one side of the vane, it goes over to the opposite side. As the wind eases, it returns to the vertical. Under the vane is mounted a drum over which passes a line, and this is activated as the vane goes over. The line is led down, round a block and then to the tiller, which means that the vane operates the main rudder directly. A second drum lower down carries the line (shown by the dotted line) by which the vane is set to the required angle. This unusual system, too, has been successful in practice. It is manufactured in Britain under the name of QME.

Motor cruisers have long used automatic pilots, which are electronically operated. They take their instructions from the compass and pass them onto the rudder either electrically or electro-hydraulically. This type of automatic pilot steers relative to the compass course, not relative to the wind. It has, however, proved successful on sailing yachts, above all during long trade wind passages. Jürgen Wagner, for example, used one on his catamaran WORLD CAT, in which he sailed virtually round the world. As the wind direction changes, the yacht does *not* follow this change but continues on her set course, which means that either the sails have to be re-trimmed or the compass heading changed. An experienced skipper will nearly always notice a change in wind direction, even if he is asleep in his bunk. Since these auto-pilots use electric current, one condition for their use is that a yacht has a plentiful power supply, i.e. has a powerful engine or generator with which to charge the batteries.

Automatic pilots can, alternatively, take their instructions from an optional wind vane, which is very small and devoid of all the cumbersome appendages which are typical of mechanical wind-vane steering systems.

Prior to the 1972 Single-handed Transatlantic Race the rules concerning the use of self-steering installations were changed. Previously only mechanical wind-vane systems were allowed, but now electrically operated systems were admissible. With one qualification, though: the required electric current had to be produced *naturally*, not by a motorized or chemical generator. Ten yachts made use of this new possibility, but none of them was able to produce enough current *naturally* to keep the system operative during the whole of the race. Some of them harnessed the yacht's permanently revolving propeller into generating electricity, others used a wind generator.

Wind-vane self-steering has been described as an *ever willing and undemanding crew*, or as the *third man on board* who requires neither food nor berth. The advantages of vane self-steering are so outstanding that no yacht will do without it on long ocean passages. It is essential, though, to make sure that the chosen model is *strong and reliable* to avoid unpleasant accidents underway.

Four Ways to Weather a Storm

If wind and sea conditions become excessive for a small boat she can take action in various ways without getting into a dangerous situation. It is even possible to get a relatively comfortable ride in a heaving sea, so that the crew can rest while they wait for a change in the weather. Depending on circumstances, any of the following methods can be adopted:

> Running under bare poles and towing hawsers.
> Heaving-to.
> Leaving the yacht to itself under bare poles.
> Lying to a sea anchor and putting out oil bags.

The choice of the most suitable method does not only depend on the crew's preference for one or the other or the size and shape of the vessel. One can only run before the wind, for example, if there is sufficient searoom to leeward. Yachts with a long underwater profile prefer to heave-to, because this gives most control over the boat while speed and leeway are kept to a minimum. The relative position of the yacht to the seas can even be determined and maintained within limits. However, if there is a dangerous coast to leeward, the skipper must try by all possible means to gain searoom to windward. If no headway can be made under severely reduced sail, the engine should be started to help the boat get clear of the lee shore. To run for the nearest harbour is a dangerous course of action, especially if visibility is reduced by spray. Many yachts have been lost in this way. *The safest place to be is on the high seas!*

If a yacht is far out at sea with a small crew, the easiest of all methods is frequently employed, namely that of leaving the yacht to itself under bare poles, or 'a-hull'. Those who advocate this method are of the opinion that, although it is uncomfortable for the crew, the hull suffers the least strain because it is left to choose for itself the most suitable position between wind and waves.

HEAVING-TO

Any sailing boat with a reasonably long underwater profile can be made to heave-to. For this purpose it is best to set a trysail and storm jib as shown in Fig. 250. The yacht is brought broadside onto the wind with the jib backed. Backing the jib, i.e. sheeting it into weather, serves a double purpose: it prevents the boat from coming up into the wind and acts as a brake to forward

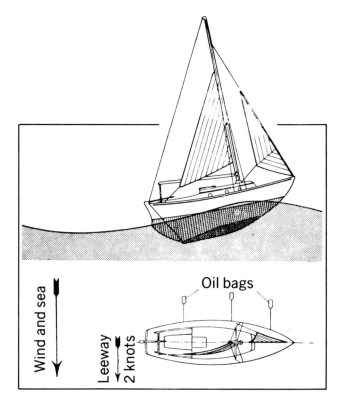

Fig. 250: *When hove-to the normal sails are replaced by a trysail and storm jib. The jib is backed, i.e. sheeted into weather, so that the yacht makes practically no headway. The boat then lies broadside onto wind and seas and makes slight leeway. The rolling movement is diminished by the pressure of the wind on the sails. Note the way the oil bags are towed.*

motion. The trysail is sheeted to leeward more or less hard, depending on the behaviour of the yacht.

If well balanced, the boat will not make any headway and will take up a stable position with the wind coming from 6 to 7 points from the bow, i.e. slightly ahead of the beam. Usually the tiller is lashed for further security.

A vessel hove-to under storm sails will slowly drift to leeward. The trysail will impart some drive, but the jib sheeted to weather will prevent the boat from making headway or coming up into the wind. The tiller is usually lashed slightly to leeward to reduce the luffing tendency even further. The balance thus established only leaves a resultant to leeward, which causes a small amount of leeway.

The seas will now hit the boat on the weather beam, which seems anything but desirable. But in drifting to leeward the yacht leaves a broad wake, which smooths the water surface to windward and lessens the impact of approaching seas. With storm sails sheeted in the hove-to position the yacht will not roll excessively, so that altogether a fairly comfortable ride can be expected.

The wake can be further smoothed by trailing oil bags as shown in Fig. 250.

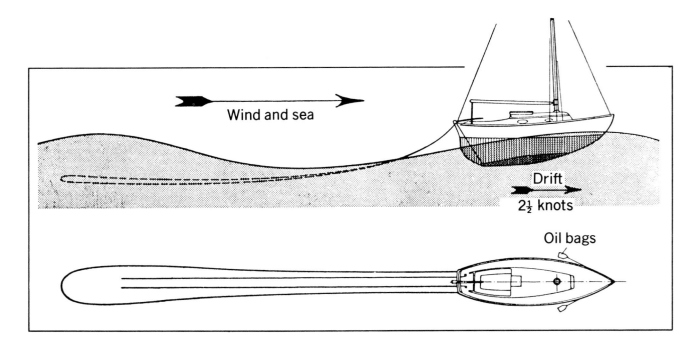

Fig. 251: When running before a storm no sails are set. To slow the boat down and to hold her steady on course several long warps are towed.

RUNNING UNDER BARE POLES

If the seas are so heavy that heaving-to seems no longer safe, or if there are no obstacles to leeward and one wishes to run as comfortably as possible downwind, the vessel can be allowed to run before the wind under bare poles. This means taking in all sail and letting the wind act on the spars and rigging only. The ride will be relatively comfortable, and there is no longer any need to change or reef sails. The biggest drawback lies in the fact that constant attention on the helm is needed to prevent the boat from coming up into the wind. With a following heavy sea this could be extremely dangerous, because the boat is likely to be swamped and even have hatches and superstructure stove in.

When a boat runs before the wind under bare poles, its speed is less than that of the following waves. Every time the boat is overtaken by a wave crest, it receives a powerful push forwards, which can only be countered by concentrated attention to the helm. As soon as the bow touches the trough of the wave, where the particles of water are receding, the acceleration at the stern is met with a strong deceleration at the bow. This upsets the balance of the boat and can easily lead to her

broaching to, unless the helm is constantly kept under control.

In order to reduce speed before the following seas it is advisable to pay out ropes or lines over the stern as shown in Fig. 251. The heavier and longer these are, the stronger their braking effect will be. Marcel Bardiaux, on his long trade wind passage, used a line of synthetic fibre some 80 ft (25 m) long to which he attached a chain, between 50 and 100 ft (15–30 m) long, with a thick knot tied in the end, see Fig. 245. At the same time he set his twin jibs, described in an earlier chapter, which kept him on course without difficulty; by angling them far ahead he could reduce headway to a minimum.

A small sea anchor such as a spar or some other object tied to a rope and paid out astern can be used with equal success. Whichever method is used, particular attention must be paid to the danger of chafe and possible breaking of the ropes at points where they pass through hawse pipes or fairleads. Where lines are exposed to chafe they should be protected by wrapping strips of sailcloth round them.

The major inconvenience of this kind of riding out a storm is the necessity for constant and undivided attention to the helm, except with Bardiaux's twin jib system, which provided very good steadiness on course.

LYING A-HULL, i.e. LEAVING THE YACHT TO LOOK AFTER ITSELF

When, shortly before the war, the small German sloop ZUGVOGEL arrived at Buenos Aires after a successful Atlantic crossing, the precarious state of her sails and rigging caused amazement among experienced yachtsmen. In reply, her skipper explained that during the crossing they had met with very little really heavy weather. On a few occasions, when he had considered the strain of wind and seas too much for the old hull and its rigging, he had taken in all sail and left the yacht to look after herself. He had not used a riding sail or a sea anchor, nor had he run before the wind under bare poles or trailed hawsers. He and his crew had simply sat in the cabin and waited for better weather.

The idea is certainly tempting. It makes sense that without the wind pressure on the sails and without the braking effect of a sea anchor or warps, the strain on the hull and rigging must be less than with any of the other methods. But the boat's movements are usually irregular and unpredictable, and this does nothing for the comfort of the crew aboard. In very strong winds seas tend to break over the deck with increasing frequency. Most yachtsmen will not approve of this passive strategy. It is, nevertheless, a good idea to leave a yacht at least once to herself so that her behaviour can be studied. The occasion might easily arise when unforeseen circumstances such as illness, injury or exhaustion leave no other choice.

The irksome and violent movement can be alleviated by dropping the bow anchor and chain. Their braking effect will stabilize the vessel and possibly even give her a tendency to keep head to wind; at least it will stop her from being constantly pooped.

LYING TO A SEA ANCHOR

The use of a sea anchor in weathering a storm is not generally accepted, although it offers one special advantage: of all methods mentioned it causes the least drift to leeward. It may therefore be tried when there is not enough searoom to make any other method safe. In principle, a boat lying to a sea anchor is attached to a relatively fixed, immovable point, or at least the most immovable point the sea has to offer. It would, there-

fore, be logical to assume that a vessel lying to a sea anchor would safely remain head to wind. Strangely, this is not so. Most yachts take up the most unexpected positions, usually with the stern diagonally to wind and sea. The mast, which in most yachts is situated in the forward third of the boat, is probably to blame for this strange attitude.

There are various ways of improving the position. If there are two masts, a riding sail can be set on the jigger and sheeted amidships. This usually prevents the boat from lying broadside onto the wind and sea. The same can be achieved in a one-masted rig by setting a small jib back to front, i.e. with the luff facing aft, on the permanent backstay, on the end of the boom or even flying. If it is set on the boom end, the boom must be hauled in amidships and so must the sheet of the sail. Thus rigged, even a sloop can lie to a sea anchor head to wind.

Some yachts ride more comfortably if the sea anchor is put out over the stern. The mast, the relative position of which has been reversed, has then a stabilizing effect. The seas now roll up against the stern, but unless this is particularly wide and low there is little risk of the yacht getting pooped except on rare occasions.

The anchor warp should be equal in length to the length of the waves, from crest to crest, or a multiple thereof. In this way the boat and the sea anchor are at the crest or in the trough of a wave at the same time and move in the same direction.

A sea anchor is a very efficient aid, especially for small craft which can use a sea anchor of modest dimensions. Beyond a waterline length of about 30 ft (9 m) the sea anchor would have to be of impractical size, and it would be difficult to handle it safely in a storm. It is probably for this reason that it has not been generally adopted for small yachts either, despite its many advantages.

THE USE OF OIL AT SEA

Oil, any oil, has two properties which make it useful at sea: it spreads quickly over the surface and it changes the natural surface tension of the water.

Even a small amount of thin oil will quickly cover a fairly large area and have a damping effect on disturbed seas. Once a certain amount of oil has spread to weather of the yacht, the surface of the water will become noticeably calmer. The oncoming waves thus

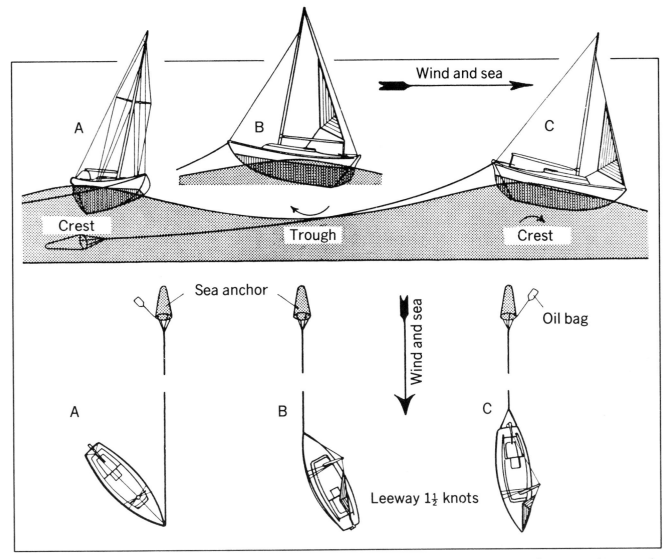

Fig. 252: When lying to a sea anchor most boats adopt an altogether unexpected position relative to the wind and only rarely lie head to wind. Setting a small steadying sail as in B improves the situation, as does paying the sea anchor out over the stern as in C. Of all the ways of weathering a storm, lying to a sea anchor causes the least drift.

meet a relatively calm zone over which they cannot continue in their natural rhythm. They break prematurely and at a safe distance.

The best way to disperse the oil slowly is by using bags made of ordinary sailcloth and holding about half a gallon; they are usually filled with oakum or woollen rags. To make them more porous, several small holes should be made with a sailmaker's needle just before lowering them into the water.

If one carries oil on board especially for this purpose, it should preferably be crude linseed oil. If no vegetable oil is available, mineral oil is suitable, as long as it is not too thin. In the absence of bags the oil can be dispersed by any other suitable method, like pumping it through the WC, as long as it is done slowly. It is important to use the oil sparingly to make it last as long as possible.

The three illustrations in this chapter show how the bags should be put out. When hove-to, they are trailed over the beam, when running before the wind over either side of the bow, and when lying to a sea anchor they are made fast to the anchor itself.

Heavy-Weather Experiences

Nautical literature contains a great number of subjective descriptions of the behaviour of small boats in heavy weather at sea. Anyone who wants to prepare himself and his yacht for an ocean voyage will find much valuable information in these accounts.

The so-called Pilot Charts are a valuable aid in planning a voyage, and so is the publication *Ocean Passages for the World*. With their help it is possible to plan a voyage round the world in such a way, time- and route-wise, that the risk of encountering really bad weather can be largely eliminated. But although nobody will intentionally run into the arms of a storm, boat and crew must always be prepared and equipped to face

Plate 76: A highly original ocean-going yacht designed by Colin Mudie as a cathedral-hull ketch-rigged motor sailer. GREEN LADY *has excellent stability and scarcely rolls. Built by W A Souter & Son, she is 80 ft long with a beam of 32 ft 10 in and a working sail area of 1615 sq ft, but this can be increased to 2950 sq ft.*
Photo: Roger M Smith, Cowes

one. Most people discover in these circumstances that they act with more courage and determination than they themselves had thought possible. As far as the safety of the vessel is concerned, it depends largely on how strongly it is built and how effectively water can be kept out.

In exceptional circumstances it can happen that a boat turns turtle, i.e. rolls over through 360°. Quite a number of cases are known in which this happened, but the case of TZU HANG, to which it happened twice, is probably unique. The incident deserves closer study, because on both occasions, in spite of serious damage and thanks to the courage and determination of her crew, the yacht reached safety under a jury rig.

TZU HANG is ketch-rigged with a length of 46 ft (13·6 m), a beam of 11 ft 6 in (3·15 m) and a draft of 7 ft (2·15 m). In February she was underway from Australia through the Pacific Ocean towards Cape Horn, planning to reach England via the Atlantic. She had a crew of three on board: the owner Miles Smeeton, his wife Beryl, and John Guzzwell, an experienced yachtsmen, who had interrupted his voyage round the world in his small yacht TREKKA. TZU HANG met with her first accident about 900 miles off the Magellan Straits after having covered 5000 miles of the Pacific Ocean. Continuous storms had set a heavy sea running in the Roaring Forties, and large waves of enormous height continuously overtook the yacht, which was running before the wind under bare poles and trailing several big lines.

The crew had taken all necessary precautions. All hatches had been tightly closed, all movable objects had been securely stowed, and there was no feeling of anxiety on board. On the contrary, John Guzzwell was just preparing to film the sea in all its terrible beauty. Smeeton's wife Beryl was at the helm secured by a life-line, when suddenly an enormous, almost vertical wall of water approached the boat from aft and buried it. Beryl Smeeton's life-line parted, and she was torn from the cockpit and swept into the sea. The two men were below in the cabin at the time and did not get an accurate impression of what had happened. A few moments later TZU HANG righted herself again, still afloat but with an alarming amount of water inside her and both masts broken. The brave helmswoman was found swimming alongside in the midst of wreckage which surrounded the yacht.

Plate 77: In this picture you can see very clearly the cathedral-hull shape of Colin Mudie's GREEN LADY *(see Plate 76). The tops of the tunnels are some way over the waterline. The greater part of the displacement obviously comes from the centre hull, while the side hulls simply provide stability. There is a light Danforth anchor to be seen forward.* Photo: Brian Manby, Lymington

Reconstructing the incident and judging from the way things had been thrown about in the cabin, the crew came to the conclusion that the boat had been completely turned over by the seas, although it was not quite clear whether she had pitch-poled in a complete somersault or whether she had righted herself on the same side. A gigantic wave must have lifted her stern and pushed her bow down almost vertically. For a few moments she was completely submerged until she managed to right herself diagonally and return to the surface.

Despite the damage done to the deck and the loss of both masts, TZU HANG's crew managed to reach the coast of Chile under a jury rig. As soon as the damage had been repaired, they resumed their voyage. Smeeton had been advised not to go through the Panama Canal but to be sure not to miss the wonderful, snow-covered chains of the southern Andes, and so TZU HANG set course once again for Cape Horn.

The first accident had happened while running before the wind under bare poles. Miles Smeeton, therefore, decided to employ different tactics if they should again run into bad weather. He was convinced that the strain on the boat would be less if she was left to herself lying a-hull, so this is what he did when TZU HANG once again ran into very heavy weather. This time there were only two on board, the owner and his wife. For many hours the yacht looked after herself extremely well, and then the incredible thing happened a second time: a wave of tremendous height and force enveloped her and turned her over. Again she was dismasted, and again she righted herself, and thanks to the admirable determination of the Smeetons she managed to reach Valparaiso under a jury rig.

Is there any other action Smeeton could have taken to survive such exceptionally heavy weather in the South Pacific? One thing he did not do in either incident was to use oil to calm the seas. Possibly the worst could have been prevented that way, but it is doubtful whether the oil would have lasted him through 16 hours of storm. In any case, the experience of TZU HANG points to some useful conclusions:

1. A strongly built yacht, sailed by an experienced and determined crew, can survive the worst storms at sea, including being pitch-poled.
2. Small yachts should, if possible, avoid such dangerous sea areas where long storms over unlimited expanses of water can be expected to build up enormous seas, the size of which continues to increase as long as the storm lasts.
3. Although most deep-sea yachtsmen do not agree with the use of oil, it continues to be an efficient means of calming the sea if it is employed correctly and if there is sufficient oil to last out the storm.

Many sailing yachts, including unballasted multihulls, have crossed vast stretches of ocean without

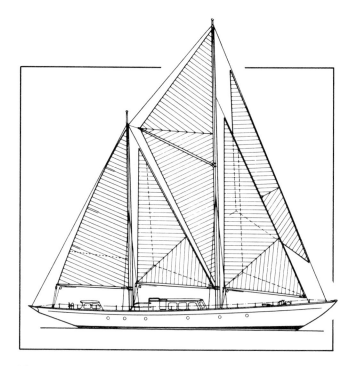

Fig. 253: An ocean cruiser like this one is at home on all the oceans of the world and need fear no heavy weather. This wishbone ketch was designed and built by Abeking & Rasmussen in 1959. Note how the space between the masts has been fully used.

LOA	*94 ft 6 in*	*Draft*	*9 ft 8 in*
LWL	*65 ft 2 in*	*Sail area*	*3025 sq ft*
Beam	*20 ft 8 in*		

running into any danger. Patrick Ellam, the skipper of the tiny SOPRANINO, which was the first small boat of modern construction to cross the North Atlantic, says about his voyage that they never used the trysail, although it was a comfort to have it on board. They also had oil bags and a sea anchor on board but never saw the necessity to put them to use.

Safety Equipment for Extended Ocean Cruising

LIFELINES: The life and well-being of the crew are the most valuable assets on board, and absolutely *everything* must be subordinated to them. It is scarcely imaginable that only a few decades ago most yachts went to sea without the protection of lifelines round the hull, let alone a bow or stern pulpit.

Today all sea-going yachts are fitted with lifelines, including a bow and stern pulpit, both of which were not actually introduced until after World War II. Continuous lifelines all the way round the hull not only give a sense of safety but make for more working space on deck. The upper line in smaller yachts should be no less than 20 in (50 cm) from the deck, better still 24 in (60 cm), and in larger yachts 30 in (75 cm) would be advisable. If the vertical gap between deck and lifeline exceeds 18 in (45 cm), a second lifeline must be fitted, in larger yachts two might be necessary. The lower line should be removable to make it easier to recover a man overboard.

The RORC in Britain and the equivalent national yachting authorities in other countries publish safety regulations for racing yachts, in conformity with overall recommendations laid down by the Offshore Racing Council.

SEA ANCHOR: The use of a sea anchor has been explained in a previous chapter. Figure 254 illustrates the two classic types which Captain Voss made the subject of thorough study during his many ocean voyages in small boats.

The necessary dimensions of a sea anchor depend on the wind resistance of the yacht. The mouth of the bag is usually one-tenth of the yacht's LWL or one-third of her beam. The bag should be one and a half to two times the diameter of the mouth and made of strong Terylene or Dacron sailcloth. To enable the water to flow through smoothly, a small opening of one-tenth the mouth is made at the pointed end of the bag. A small buoy or float is frequently attached to the mouth ring on a line approximately 15 ft (5 m) long to regulate the depth of the anchor in the water.

The length of the sea anchor's line should be as near as possible the length of the waves from crest to crest, which can be calculated with some accuracy from the graph in Fig. 259. A watchful eye must be kept on protection of the line, for any number of sea anchors have been lost during storms at sea through chafe.

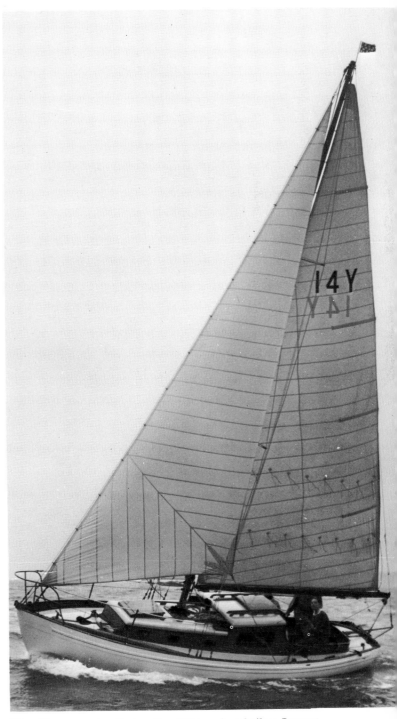

Plate 78: HUSSAR *is a Vertue. Over 100 have been built to Laurent Giles' design, first introduced in 1936. This sea-kindly boat has made a lot of friends. LOA 25 ft 3 in.*   *Photo: Beken & Sons*

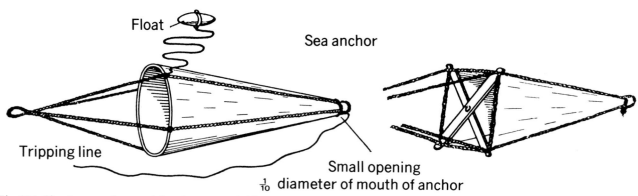

Float

Sea anchor

Tripping line

Small opening
$\frac{1}{10}$ diameter of mouth of anchor

Fig. 254: Classic sea anchor as tried and recommended by Captain Voss. On the left the normal version, on the right an emergency solution.

Where the lead is through a hawse pipe or fairlead it should be wrapped with sailcloth.

If no sea anchor is available, it is easy enough to improvise. A piece of sailcloth stretched between two short lengths of spar rather like a square sail is said to be effective. If everything fails, anything should be paid out overboard which can in any way slow the yacht: anchors and chains, all available lines with bailers and buckets tied to their ends, even a door, or anything which the inspiration of the moment might suggest.

INFLATABLE DINGHY AND LIFERAFT: The inflatable rubber dinghy was originally designed for use by aircraft. It combines maximum buoyancy with minimum weight and stowage space needed. A tender built of wood, fibreglass or metal loses much of its stability and buoyancy when it is full of water, but an inflatable dinghy retains most of its flotation even when it is completely filled with water. An inflatable which carries four persons can be folded into a small parcel 18 in (45 cm) by 30 in (75 cm). There are self-inflatable models, which incorporate a capsule of compressed carbon dioxide. When they are thrown into the water, after having been secured on deck with a line, the capsule breaks and the boat automatically inflates itself in 10 to 12 seconds.

There is the case of a small, plywood-built New Zealand boat which had competed in an Australian series of races and was getting ready to sail back home across 1500 miles of open sea. A friend offered the three-man

crew the loan of an inflatable dinghy, which they initially refused, because they were convinced of the seaworthiness of their vessel and had had no problems on the crossing from New Zealand. Eventually though they accepted it and, lo and behold, in the Tasman Sea they were rammed by a whale and sank within minutes. The three spent several days in the inflatable before they were picked up by a passing cargo ship. If they had not accepted the loan of the inflatable . . .

Inflatable liferafts as opposed to dinghies are becoming increasingly popular. By comparison with the normal inflatable dinghy they are round and incorporate a canopy, which gives shelter from wind, water and intensive sun radiation. Liferafts are obligatory equipment for ocean-racing yachts as prescribed by the IOR and the relevant national racing authorities, and they must be big enough to hold the entire crew of the yacht. They come in sizes for 4, 6 or 8 persons, and they are inflated, including the canopy support, in 30 to 40 seconds by a carbon dioxide capsule.

A liferaft must have packed in it emergency rations and water as well as a sea anchor or drogue, bellows or pump, hand flares, signalling lamp, repair kit, knife, bailer and two paddles. The drogue is to help keep the raft in the same position, as far as this is possible. The anchor line is made fast on the side opposite to the entrance, which in this way faces away from the wind. The canopy is bright orange to facilitate detection during rescue operations.

LIFEJACKETS AND LIFEBUOYS: No yacht

348

Fig. 255: TINKERBELLE, *one of the smallest sailing boats to cross the Atlantic in recent years, has the following dimensions:*

LOA . . . . 13 ft 8 in   Beam . . . . 5 ft 3 in
LWL . . . . 12 ft 9 in   Sail area . . . . 102 sq ft

Robert Manry bought TINKERBELLE *as an open rowing and sailing boat for family sailing when he was 30. Only later he added a small cabin, made the cockpit self-draining and installed a new, ballasted centreboard, which weighed 100 lb. Several polystyrene blocks, which have been indicated in the plan, made the boat unsinkable. His single-handed voyage from Falmouth, Massachusetts, to Falmouth on the south coast of England took 78 days during June, July and August of 1965, when the boat was already 37 years old and her owner 47.*

In order to have enough room for drinking water, food and gear, Manry made do without a berth and simply slept curled up on top of his provisions. He took 110 litres of drinking water in 25 plastic bottles but only used half, which amounts to a daily ration of only ⅞ pint (½ litre). He practised proper astro-navigation but had no experience of ocean sailing before he set out. Fortunately he was never sea-sick but admits that one of his biggest problems was sinking morale and repeated hallucinations, which is common with most single-handed sailors. He found the crossing ideal for losing weight – he lost nearly 40 lb. He rarely sailed at night but lay to a sea anchor with only a small steadying sail set aft. In very heavy weather he lay hove-to and felt relatively safe. Once he was thrown overboard when TINKERBELLE *nearly capsized and only managed to get back on board after a tremendous struggle.*

Incredible as it appears, TINKERBELLE *had neither pulpit nor lifelines. In his fascinating book* TINKEREBELLE, *published by Collins, Robert Manry gives a never-ending list of all the things he took with him, among them 20 books (half of them on navigation), lots of tools, spare parts, a very complete medicine chest, an emergency survival kit in the case of shipwreck, an inflatable life-raft with gas bottle and radio transmitter, two cameras and many more items of gear, quite apart from food and drink. And all that in an old, wooden, 13 ft clinker-boat.*

Tinkerbelle

should leave her mooring without having at least as many lifejackets as there are people on board. The official recommendations are that they must be of the type which keeps the wearer's nose and mouth above water if he is unconscious. Self-inflating types must not be stowed under berths or in closed lockers because the damp may cause them to inflate. Each lifejacket should have a twin-tone whistle attached to it.

Every seagoing yacht must have two horseshoe life-buoys, which are rigged within reach of the helmsman and ready for immediate use. One must be equipped with a whistle, a high-intensity water light, and a drogue. The other must have, in addition, a dye marker and pole with a yellow or orange flag on it, which will fly at least 8 ft (2·5 m) off the water. The lifebuoys themselves should also be yellow or orange.

BILGE PUMP: Making a really reliable bilge pump has always been one of the most difficult problems. Metal parts necessarily corrode under the influence of

salt water, moving parts fail, and filters and pipes get clogged. Safety rules for ocean-racing yachts specify at least two bilge pumps, to be operated independently, and accessible even in heavy weather. One must be of the diaphragm type.

In emergencies bilge pumps installed on solidly built, dry yachts are the ones most likely to fail, because they are never used. For this reason every bilge pump should be checked at regular intervals, its working parts greased and all pipes cleaned. In emergencies, of course, the good old bailer, now made of plastic, will still come into its own.

FIRE-EXTINGUISHER: Fire on board a yacht is a greater danger than the worst storm imaginable. Every skipper has to take the utmost care to ensure that no flammable gases, either fuel vapour or gas from the cooker, penetrate below decks. Quite a few sensible boat owners refuse to contemplate bottled gas for cooking; in USA the Coastguard regulations governing

Plate 79: DELANTA, *designed by E G van der Stadt, is built in series production by Dehler Bootsbau. She can be had in a keel and is supplied with a stub keel and centreplate or with a narrow, deep fin keel. There is a small overhang aft, which gives room for* two comfortable quarter berths; there are two more berths forward. *The superstructure extends almost to the topsides, and there is a lot of room below.* DELANTA *is 25 ft long with a beam of 8 ft 2 in and a sail area of 323 sq ft.*
Photo: Dehler Bootsbau

installation are very strict. In Argentina an unpleasant smelling additive to the gas makes leaks easy to detect, but the author has known people who objected to the smell so much that they preferred to use 'clean' gas, even though the risk of explosion is much greater.

The need to guard against gas escaping from the cooker cannot be over-emphasized. Even if the bottle is tight and the pipes expertly installed, a gust of wind down the companionway can blow out the flames without anybody noticing. And all the while gas continues to escape. Every member of the crew has to be alerted to this possibility and urged to keep his eyes open. Under no circumstances must the cooker be re-lit without ensuring complete dispersal of the escaped gas through adequate ventilation; do not forget that it is heavier than air and will lie in the lowest part of the bilge.

There should be at least two fire-extinguishers on board, of the type and number required by the country of registry; one of them should preferably be accessible from on deck.

What applies to bilge pumps, applies equally to fire-extinguishers, although it sounds absurd: if they are never used, they are liable to fail in an emergency, except that the consequences are probably very much more serious in the case of the fire-extinguisher. If the fire-extinguisher is of the type that specifies servicing, this should be done by the manufacturers without fail once a year.

RADIO RECEIVERS, TRANSMITTERS, RADAR: The advent and general adoption of radio telephony has considerably simplified navigation. Formerly, a ship at sea was isolated from the world, now it is in close and constant contact with the shore and with other ships. The possibility of listening to weather forecasts and time signals has greatly increased safety at sea. Time signals are particularly important for determining position, and they dispense with the need for a chronometer on a yacht. Since the hot, current-consuming valve has been replaced by the cold, economical transistor, radios on board have become a much simpler affair. A small, portable transistor radio can work for months on its batteries, independent of the ship's supply or generator. No boat should be without one, even if it is only to listen to the weather forecast.

For long ocean passages away from coasts, when isolation is for long periods, a radio transmitter and receiver with a minimum output of 25 watts is needed.

Nowadays, any commercial vessel, from the big ocean liner right down to the coastal fisherman, is equipped with radar, which enables it to remain fully operative even at night and in fog. Commercial vessels fear small sailing yachts, which frequently cannot be made out clearly on the radar screen. Sailing yachts, for their part, fear commercial traffic. The *International Regulations for Preventing Collisions at Sea* give basic

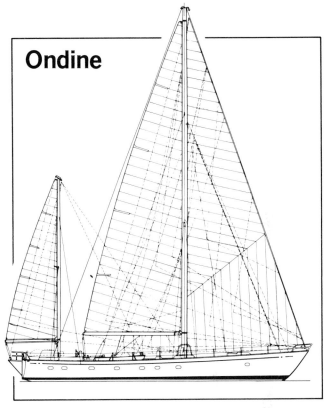

Ondine

Fig. 256: Sail plan of the ketch ONDINE, *a fast and successful ocean racer built in aluminium alloy by Abeking & Rasmussen in 1967. She was designed by the late William H Tripp, whose premature death was a great loss to yacht design, and built for the American racing skipper Sumner Long.*

LOA .... 73 ft 2 in	Draft, plate down . 14 ft 9 in
LWL .... 65 ft	Displacement ... 55 ton
Beam .... 16 ft 5 in	Ballast .... 25 ton
Draft, plate up .. 10 ft 8 in	Sail area .... 2700 sq ft

Note the large number of headsails indicated, as well as two possible mizzen staysails. There are, in addition, four spinnakers. ONDINE *is the third yacht by that name.*

instructions for the conduct of vessels in restricted visibility concerning sound signals, readiness of engine, need for safe speed, etc. Beyond that, the sensible thing to do for the crew of a sailing yacht in poor visibility (which also includes hail, snow or heavy rain) is to put on lifejackets and, if the draft of the vessel permits, stand into shallow water, where they will be safe from commercial traffic. The danger of being run down is particularly great in shipping lanes and off busy seaports.

What can the skipper of a yacht do to increase the chance of being seen on a radar screen? Radar detects any solid object, which means not only ships, buoys

coastlines and floating objects, but also the wave motion all round the yacht. The sensible thing to do is to mount a radar reflector *as high above deck as possible*, which will give the boat a fair chance of being detected at a distance of 4 to 6 miles (7–10 km). It is important that the reflector should be mounted permanently and immovably and that it should be mounted correctly, i.e. side up, not corner up. What one should not do is to anchor near to navigation buoys, since one's own radar reflection might be mistaken for a reflection from the buoy. Audible fog signals, as specified by Rule 35 of the *International Regulations for Preventing Collisions at Sea*, should, of course, be given.

Safety at sea also includes all the measures necessary to ensure the crew's health and well-being. There must be sufficient drinking water on board, preferably in several small containers, also suitable, sustaining food including fresh fruit and vegetables and additional vitamin preparations. A small first-aid box must contain everything necessary for the immediate treatment of injuries and illness, including all the minor ailments and irregularities which are typical of life on board.

Plate 80: A large boat on a perfect spinnaker run. If she was racing she would carry a spinnaker staysail to fill the gap between the spinnaker and the main. The Nicholson 55 is 54 ft 6 in long. She is built in fibreglass by Camper & Nicholson at Gosport. She can be supplied in a cruising version with centre cockpit and after cabin. Photo: Eileen Ramsay

The Sea and the Winds

In the far-off days of the early sailing ships, the apparent dimensions of the earth expanded before the eyes of mankind as adventurous explorers strove to push out into the unknown. The history of the exploration of the open sea, however, is no more than 500 years old.

The predominantly land-bound life which most people are forced to lead in pursuit of their living makes them go in search of the sea whenever they seek solitude, spiritual relaxation and wide horizons. Only the sea offers man the possibility of reaching all five continents with his very own means of transport. Indeed, his means of transport becomes his home, which gives him shelter and security. The times are long gone when a sea voyage was an exhausing and highly dangerous undertaking, not so much due to wind and weather but because people were ignorant of the principles of healthy nutrition. The terrible scourge of scurvy often caused the death of half of a ship's crew. If the cause of the disease had been known, it would have been easy to prevent it. It has been estimated that in the first twenty years of the seventeenth century over 10,000 European sailors lost their lives through scurvy.

Scurvy occurred probably for the last time in 1915 on board the fast German cruiser KRONPRINZ WILHELM. During World War I she captured and sank one cargo ship after another, after first taking over the best of the other ship's food supplies. Her store rooms were bursting at the seams with frozen meat and venison, tinned meat, eggs, ham, sausages, cheese, white flour, biscuits, sugar, coffee and large amounts of tinned vegetables. But after a short time at sea, in the midst of all this plenty, 50 sailors could no longer stand up. After two more weeks their number had risen to 110. In the end, the ship was not beaten by the enemy but by scurvy when she gave herself up to internment in the American port of Newport Mews in April 1915. Neither the ship's doctor nor the American medical commission which came on board could diagnose or cure this long-forgotten illness: scurvy. It was an American nutritional expert who hit on the answer and cured every sufferer on board with vegetable soup and wheat germ within three weeks.

The earth has a surface of 196,500,000 square miles, of which 55,500,000 square miles are land and 141,000,000 square miles are made up of the seven oceans of the world. These are really one single ocean with the continents scattered in it like islands. If one assumes that two sailing boats are unable to see each other if they are 10 miles apart, the oceans of the world would hold one million craft which, if they were evenly spaced out, could not see each other.

Sea water, on average, contains 35 parts per thousand by weight of salts, mainly chlorine and sodium; the salt content makes sea water heavier than fresh water. Thirty-four cubic feet of sea water have an average weight of 2240 lb = 1 long ton, compared with 2216 lb for fresh water. A Dragon lying in sea water displaces no less than 132 lb (60 kg) of pure salt, a modern One Tonner as much as 440 lb (200 kg)!

When sailing in a small boat on the open sea, a person is forced by circumstances to lead a fundamentally different life from the one he is used to on land. The wind, which changes in direction and strength, influences course and route, and causes wave motion, heeling, rolling, pitching and leeway. Currents accompany or oppose the boat, cold and heat interfere, clouds obscure the sun and the stars, which are the sailor's guides. Near coasts the tidal flow causes high and low water and ever-changing currents, which affect the boat on its journey.

The constantly changing conditions ensure that long ocean voyages, far from being monotonous, often turn into adventures, which put the courage, initiative and skill of skipper and crew to the test. The wind provides cheap and never-ending propulsion. If a motor yacht were used for long voyages, the quantity of fuel needed would be enormous and take up so much space that there would be no room for accommodation.

Irregular as winds may seem in most parts of the world, they nevertheless follow a certain regular and known pattern. On the basis of this knowledge the so-called Pilot Books are prepared, which contain all the information necessary for planning long ocean passages.

In the equatorial zone the calms or doldrums prevail, but on either side of this zone we find belts of constant trade winds. In the northern hemisphere their main direction is from the north-east, whereas in the southern hemisphere they blow from the south-east. These wide belts of trade winds are the mainstay for ocean voyages under sail, and their average speed varies between 5 and 11 knots (Force 2–4) in the North Atlantic and between 11 and 13 knots (Force 4) in the South Atlantic; in the

Indian and Pacific Oceans their average speed is slightly lower.

Further towards the poles, between 40 and 65 degrees latitude, there are again wide zones of constant winds in both hemispheres, this time from a predominantly western direction. Among them are the Roaring Forties, which have made the 40th Parallel South so notorious.

Wind forces are still measured by a table drawn up in 1806 by the British hydrographer Admiral Beaufort and therefore called the Beaufort Scale. It was recognized internationally in 1874, and during World War II was extended by the US Navy from its original maximum value of 12 to 17. This extended scale was adopted by the International Meteorological Committee in 1946 and is in current use today.

The frequency of different wind forces in different sea areas can be found in appropriate nautical handbooks. A gale frequency of 10 per cent would mean that on 10 per cent of occasions on which the wind force was measured it was above 8 Beaufort. Such a high gale frequency does not normally occur in waters frequented by yachtsmen.

The possible force of the wind is of twofold interest for the blue-water sailor: it determines the amount of wind pressing on the sails and also the magnitude of the waves. Pressure depends mainly on the prevailing wind force, but the shape of the object it strikes is also relevant. As mentioned in a previous chapter, a flat disc has a coefficient of resistance of 1·16, a cylinder of 1·2 and an open hemisphere of 1·42. In the following table the pressures have been indicated which would be exerted on one square foot (one square metre) of surface, assuming a coefficient of 1·2 as being a good average for all existing shapes.

As can be seen, the pressure remains below 2 lb/sq ft

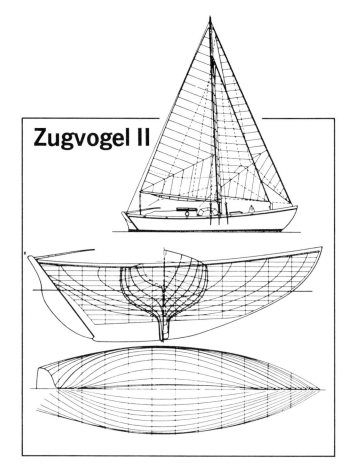

Zugvogel II

Fig. 257: The heavy-displacement yacht ZUGVOGEL II has proved very seaworthy and easily handled by a small crew. She was designed by the author and built by her owner on the edge of the Brazilian jungle.

LOA	30 ft 4 in	Displacement	8·6 ton
LWL	24 ft 7 in	Ballast	2·5 ton
Beam	9 ft 4 in	Sail area	415 sq ft
Draft	5 ft 6 in		

(10 kg/m²) in wind conditions suitable for normal, unreefed sailing. In a hurricane, on the other hand, the pressure may rise to and even exceed 40 lb/sq ft (190 kg/m²).

WIND PRESSURES AT VARIOUS WIND SPEEDS

	Wind Speed	Wind Pressure with C = 1·2
Pleasant sailing breeze	10 knots	0·4 lb/sq ft (1·9 kg/m²)
Limit of unreefed sailing	20 knots	1·6 lb/sq ft (7·6 kg/m²)
Storm	60 knots	14·0 lb/sq ft (68 kg/m²)
Hurricane	100 knots	40·0 lb/sq ft (190 kg/m²)

BEAUFORT WIND SCALE

Official Values of the 1946 International Meteorological Committee in Paris
Mean Speeds at 10m. height

Beaufort Number	Mean Speed km/h	Mean Speed knots	Speed Range. km/h	Speed Range. knots	Speed Range. m/sec.
0	0	0	0–1	0–1	0–0·2
1	3	2	1–5	1–3	0·3–1·5
2	9	5	6–11	4–6	1·6–3·3
3	16	9	12–19	7–10	3·4–5·4
4	24	13	20–28	11–16	5·5–7·9
5	34	18	29–38	17–21	8·0–10·7
6	44	24	39–49	22–27	10·8–13·8
7	55	30	50–61	28–33	13·9–17·1
8	68	37	62–74	34–40	17·2–20·7
9	82	44	75–88	41–47	20·8–24·4
10	96	52	89–102	48–55	24·5–28·4
11	110	60	103–117	56–63	28·5–32·6
12	125	68	118–133	64–71	32·7–36·9
13	141	76	134–149	72–80	37·0–41·4
14	158	85	150–166	81–89	41·5–46·1
15	175	94	167–183	90–99	46·2–50·9
16	193	104	184–201	100–108	51·0–56·0
17	211	114	202–220	109–118	56·1–61·2

The Size of Ocean Waves

Every wind, however light it may be, disturbs the surface of the water, even in a small lake or pond. But only at sea, with its almost unlimited range and great depth, can waves develop to large dimensions, which depend merely on the strength of the wind and its duration.

Anyone who knows the sea will appreciate the difficulties involved in estimating the size of waves or even measuring them. Any strong sea motion is characterized by a disconcerting irregularity. No wave is the same as another, and there seems to be no regular pattern; even the height of waves alters constantly. If the sideways extension of a wave is examined, it will be found to be surprisingly short. If two or more different wave systems from different directions meet and overlap, the picture becomes even more confusing.

There has never been more attention given to the study of ocean waves than during and after World War II. A lot of data have been computed to give a clearer picture of the seemingly irregular pattern. The Norwegian oceanographer Sverdrup did a great deal of meticulous, detailed work analysing and computing measurements, which he methodically took at sea. He published his findings in the form of two interesting diagrams which contain curves indicating the height and wave period of ocean waves depending on the intensity and duration of the wind. The wave period is the time lapse between two wave crests travelling past a fixed point.

The two diagrams reproduced here are based on Sverdrup's work, except that 'wave period' has been substituted by the more practical measurement of 'wave length'. They show how the height and length of

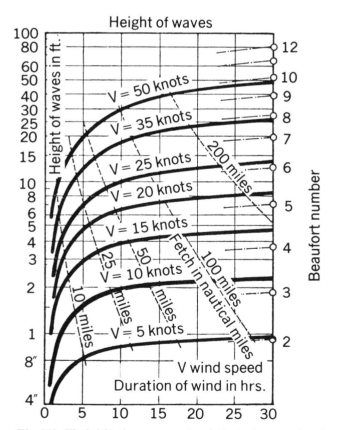

Fig. 258: The height of ocean waves in relation to the strength and duration of the wind. The wind strength (V) is indicated in knots along the curves and also in Beaufort numbers along the right edge.

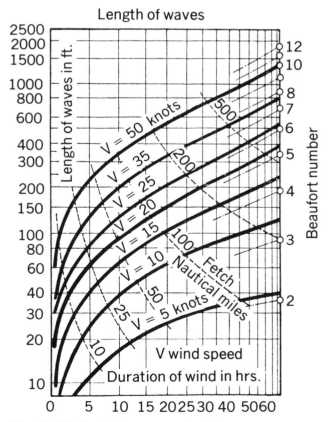

Fig. 259: The length of ocean waves in relation to the strength and duration of the wind. In both graphs, the curves are crossed by dotted curves, which indicate the 'fetch', i.e. searoom to windward, which limits these wave sizes.

ocean waves increase in proportion to the strength and duration of the wind and the fetch, i.e. the distance of the water surface over which the wind travels. 'Wave height' means the vertical distance from wave crest to wave trough. The relationship of wave period to wave length and wave speed is expressed as follows:

Wave speed ...... $v = 2 \cdot 27 \times \sqrt{\text{wave length}}$

Wave period ...... $t = 0 \cdot 44 \times \sqrt{\text{wave length}}$

where wave length is in feet, wave period in sec and wave speed in ft/sec.

An example will best explain the use of both diagrams. We shall assume a gale of force 8, i.e. 41 knots, which blows over a water surface more than 50 nautical miles in extent. After a duration of 5 hours an average wave height of 14 ft 6 in can be expected; the wave length will now be 160 ft. Both values can be taken directly from the graphs. Once the wave length is known, the wave speed is arrived at by the following equation:

$$v = 2 \cdot 27 \times \sqrt{160} = 28 \cdot 7 \text{ ft/sec} = 17 \text{ knots}$$

the wave period being

$$t = 0 \cdot 44 \times \sqrt{160} = 5 \cdot 6 \text{ sec.}$$

This means that under these conditions an anchored yacht would be lifted by a wave crest every 5·6 seconds. This has, indeed, been confirmed in practice.

The type of wave most frequently encountered in coastal navigation during strong winds is 6 ft 6 in (2 m)

high and about 80 ft (24 m) long. In these conditions sailing in a small yacht can still be enjoyable if the crew are not affected by seasickness. If they are, it can be most unpleasant, and for a novice even unbearable. From the two graphs it can be deduced that in order to produce such waves a wind of 22 knots = Force 6 must have blown across the water surface for about 7 hours.

Strong gales lasting many hours can produce waves of up to 26 ft (8 m) high. Greater heights have rarely been recorded, except in the Roaring Forties, where waves of over 50 ft (16 m) in height seem possible during hurricanes of exceptional duration; the wave length would then be 650 ft (200 m).

A knowledge of the wave length to be expected under certain conditions helps to choose the correct length of line for a sea anchor. If the boat is in a trough at the same time as the anchor is on a crest, they will be moved in opposite directions, which puts unnecessary strain on both line and boat. Ideally, they should each be on a crest or in a trough at the same time, which means that the length of line should be equal to the wave length.

Most people think that wave motion is always an unpleasant experience and that anyone sailing at sea is in constant danger of his life. But it is true that on this restless sea a small boat and her crew can have an enjoyable, happy time. If a vessel is strongly built, well equipped and helmed by an experienced skipper, she can cross the seven oceans of the world without being exposed to undue danger.

Dangers at Sea

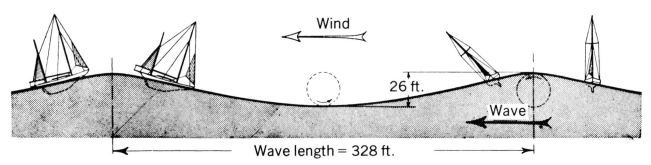

Wind

26 ft.

Wave

Wave length = 328 ft.

Fig. 260: Scale drawing to illustrate a boat's behaviour in a gale and heavy seas, the average wave height being 26 ft, the wave length 328 ft. The two circles show the orbital movement of the water particles on the crest and in the trough of the wave.

Long ocean crossings have been successfully completed by many vessels, some of them very small and some frankly inadequate like, for example, an amphibious Jeep. The first prerequisite for safe ocean navigation is an absolutely seaworthy craft. Most ocean cruisers are built to be non-capsizable as well as unsinkable, but the latter condition is hardly ever completely fulfilled. Today's cruising boats are unsinkable only as long as the hull remains intact and no large amounts of water get inside. It would be perfectly possible, however, to build a truly unsinkable vessel, which remains afloat even when full of water.

We know of a number of cases in which perfectly seaworthy yachts between 30 and 45 ft (9–14 m) in length have capsized and turned turtle, so that their keels were uppermost. In none of the known cases did this lead to the sinking of the boat concerned, but the mysterious disappearance of the modern ocean-cruising yacht REVONOC gives food for thought. It is feared that she overturned in a similar way and, due to damage to her decks or hull, filled up and sank, taking every member of her experienced crew with her. Other yachts which have turned turtle or pitch poled are TYPHOON, LEHG II, SILVER QUEEN and TZU HANG, but all of them righted themselves and remained afloat.

The exceptional case of TZU HANG, which met with this accident twice in succession, deserves closer study. Both times she was in the South Pacific bound for Cape Horn. From the owners' report one can assume that a gale of Force 8 to 9 had been blowing over the limitless expanses of the Pacific for about 16 hours when each of the accidents happened. From the graphs in Figs. 258 and 259 one can assume that at a mean wind speed of 40 knots (75 km/h) the waves must have had an average height of 27 ft (8 m), a length of about 320 ft (100 m) and a speed of advance of 40 ft/sec = 24 knots (44 km/h).

These conditions are illustrated in Fig. 260, which also shows a ketch in a heavy sea with mizzen reefed and storm jib set. The ketch is drawn to scale and corresponds in size to the four yachts previously mentioned, which overturned completely. The sketch indicates the orbital movement of the water particles in the wave crest (forward) and in the wave trough (backward). This, together with the constantly changing direction of the wave inclination, causes a never-ending switch between acceleration and deceleration. Sailing as such involves no great risk under these conditions, even if the boat is continuously rolling and pitching.

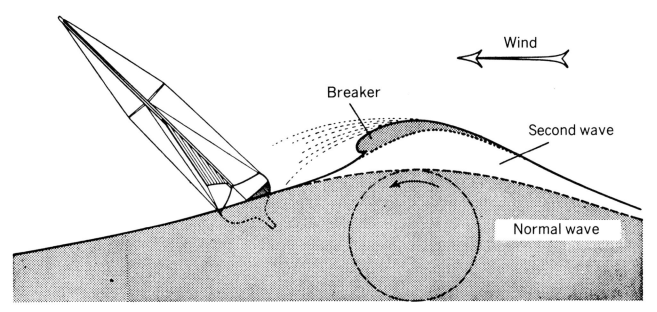

Fig. 261: An abnormally high crest is formed if two different wave systems meet and two crests coincide. Frequently the combined crest loses its stability and becomes a dangerous breaker.

The bad-weather conditions just described could be called typical, but they do not usually last for long. The wave motion does not remain orderly and from time to time two different wave systems meet and the water masses unite in one crest. The normal wave, which is perfectly stable, cannot support the weight and height of the second wave so that it becomes unstable and breaks. This means that the actual wave pushes a great mass of water in front of itself, which advances at high speed and in violent disorder to break over anything which happens to be in its path.

A boat intended for transatlantic crossings must be built, equipped and helmed in a way which enables her to survive such occurrences in perfect safety. Every owner who has plans for blue-water sailing must keep his boat in top condition all the time and carry out necessary repairs to the hull, deck or rigging as soon as any wear or damage becomes apparent. Particular danger points are the foot of the mast, and the deck area between the mast and the shroud chainplates, where enormous forces concentrate. Metal parts must be protected against corrosion, especially in places where copper or bronze fittings are in the proximity of iron or steel. Points to be watched are water intakes, keelbolts, propeller-shaft, etc.

All openings on deck must be capable of being securely fastened. All hatches must have additional fastenings, which can be operated from inside. All scuppers and drains must be of reasonable diameter to ensure quick drainage. There must be storm blinds which can be fitted to the larger windows.

Every sailor knows how important a watertight deck is, especially if he has ever made the acquaintance of leaking decks and their unpleasant effects. Before the advent of fibreglass yacht construction it was almost impossible to build a wooden deck that never leaked, even under the onslaught of heat, cold, persistent drought and sudden rain.

All-round lifelines are now fitted to every ocean-going yacht as a matter of course, but many small cruisers performed great feats without this protection. ISLANDER was sailed single-handed round the world twice without lifelines. The bow pulpit was first introduced in 1937 and did not become commonplace until after World War II; the stern pulpit is even more recent.

The size of a yacht is of no fundamental importance in relation to its sea-going qualities. Both Slocum and Voss expressed the opinion that, in their experience, a small boat of solid construction can be safer at sea than

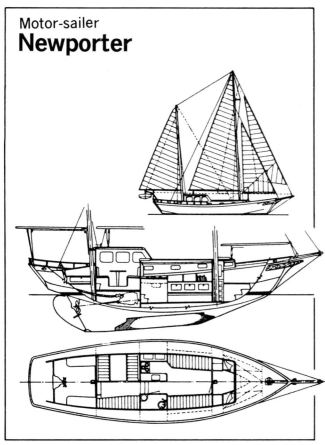

Motor-sailer
Newporter

Fig. 262: This ketch-rigged motor sailer would make the ideal vessel with which to explore the islands of the Pacific. Designed by C E Ackerman she is sturdily built, stable, seaworthy and roomy below.

LOA	40 ft	Draft	6 ft
LWL	32 ft	Displacement	11·4 ton
Beam	13 ft	Sail area	765 sq ft

a large ship, and the skipper of the small sloop SOPRANINO called her 'one of the safest boats that ever sailed the sea', although she was only 19 ft 8 in (6 m) long, 5 ft 4 in (1·63 m) in the beam and weighed 0·65 tons.

There is another aspect, however. The smaller the boat, the more difficult it becomes to find the space to stow the extensive gear which is needed for long voyages at sea. There must also be sufficient living space left for the crew. The amount of drinking water and food needed can be dictated only by the number of persons on board and the length of the voyage, not by the size

of the hull. And since a smaller boat will normally take longer to reach her destination than a larger one, the water and food ration per head must be even larger.

Some summers ago an ocean race in the English Channel was overtaken by a severe storm. Only a very few competitors were able to finish, and the majority decided to give up and either heave-to or lie a-hull. None of them suffered serious hull damage, but many had masses of water break in through leaking hatches and skylights, companionway doors and ventilators. Those with a low freeboard had their cockpits constantly full of water, since the drain pipes were not big enough to cope. In many cases it was found that the bilge pumps did not function and bailers, buckets and saucepans had to be used. Fortunately all of the people involved in this incident were experienced and energetic seamen, who were perfectly capable of coping with the sudden if not quite unexpected dangers.

Masts and riggings suffered surprisingly little damage on that occasion, because they were generally well built and maintained. But a large number of stanchions were broken at the base, where they were welded, or had their screws torn out of the deck. One yacht was laid over with such violence that her mast came level with the water and two men went overboard; fortunately, both were got back on board very quickly. Another yacht had to retire because her stem-head fitting broke and the staying of the mast was endangered.

In a storm any experienced sailor will feel safer out in the open sea than he would inshore. He can then weather the storm in various different ways without much risk, either by heaving-to, lying to a sea anchor or running before the wind trailing hawsers. It is only by staying out at sea that he can avoid the greatest of all dangers, that of being wrecked ashore.

The desire to run for shelter has frequently led to the total loss of a yacht. Since it is practically impossible to study a chart in a storm, it is easy to misread a leading mark or overlook a warning. Very often the disturbed sea inshore makes steering difficult and foils any attempt to tack or gybe. Many a boat has been wrecked in this way on the rocks of a harbour entrance, only yards from safety. Not infrequently the auxiliary engine stops at such a critical moment, usually as a direct consequence of the weather. The violent movements of the boat can loosen rust and dirt in the tank, which then clog the filters and pipes. Frequently sea

water enters the engine through the exhaust pipe. A well-planned engine installation, carried out by an experienced mechanic, helps to avoid such accidents. A small, neglected detail, such as a loose bolt, a leaking pipe or a fault in one of the many parts that make up the engine can lead to the total loss of a boat and endanger the lives of her crew.

Plate 81: Modern yachts are also built in Asia as, for example, at Cheoy Lee's yard in Hong Kong. This yard used to specialize in traditional teak building, but today fibreglass is used. Shown here is a Clipper 33, a ketch-rigged cruiser. LOA 32 ft 10 in (without bowsprit), beam 10 ft 2 in, sail area 522 sq ft and a minimum draft of 3 ft 8 in. Many other designs are built, mostly for American customers. Photo: Cheoy Lee, Hong Kong

Ship's Compass and Sextant

Navigation instruments on a ship serve to solve the two basic problems of what is the position of the ship, and which course is she steering? The exact position at sea is best determined by an astronomical fix, for which a sextant is used. The course, on yachts, is determined with the help of a marine magnetic compass.

Undoubtedly the magnetic compass is the most important instrument on board a yacht; it cannot be replaced by any other instrument. It may not be generally known that the compass needle neither indicates geographic north nor magnetic north. The magnetic needle simply aligns itself to the local magnetic field or *magnetic meridian*. Since the magnetic lines of force cover the earth's surface in apparently irregular fashion, their deflection from geographic north, called *variation*, is different from place to place. The local variation is shown on the chart for the particular zone, which also indicates the yearly increase or decrease in variation caused by the magnetic pole revolving slowly round the geographic pole. Some places have practically no variation, like the River Plate, for example, while others suffer from 'unreliable variation'; there is one such area off the east coast of Sweden, which is best avoided altogether or only crossed in very good visibility.

The compass reacts not only to the earth's magnetic field but also to magnetic influences of the ship itself. Nearly every vessel has a certain magnetic line of force, either caused by its steel hull, by iron parts in the rigging and in the engine, or even by electrical apparatus and cables. A compass should, therefore, be installed as far away as possible from such disturbing local influences. The angle by which the magnetism of the vessel deflects the compass needle from the magnetic meridian is called *deviation*. It must not be forgotten that the magnetic field of a yacht shifts sideways when she heels and thus the deviation changes. This is so because any iron parts, which may lie vertically below the compass, such as the engine, then no longer do so.

The deviation caused by the magnetism of the vessel can be corrected almost completely by an experienced compass adjuster. The usual procedure on yachts, however, is to measure and record the deviation on various headings in a table, which can be consulted by the navigator. When covering long distances at sea, the deviation must be checked and the table corrected, because the earth's horizontal magnetic force increases

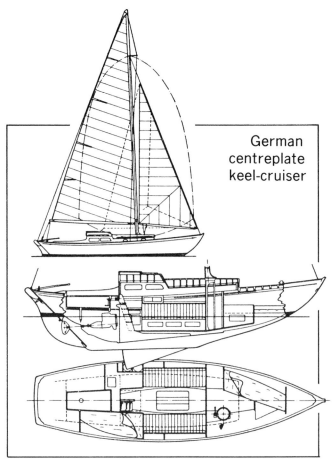

German centreplate keel-cruiser

Fig. 263: This successful German centreplate keelboat with transom stern is particularly suitable for coastal cruising in tidal waters. It must not be forgotten that the centreplate may affect the compass deviation and that the amount of deviation may differ depending on whether the plate is up or down. This boat was designed by Abeking & Rasmussen and has the following dimensions:

LOA	28 ft	Draft, plate up	3 ft 2 in
LWL	22 ft	Draft, plate down	5 ft 6 in
Beam	8 ft 3 in	Sail area	390 sq ft

towards the equator and decreases towards the poles. When, some years ago, we shipped our cruiser from Argentina to Rotterdam in order to sail her from there to Finland, we noticed in the Kiel Canal, where a compass check is easy, that there were drastic changes in our deviation table, which we had carefully compiled in Buenos Aires. The change from latitude 35 degrees South to 54 degrees North involves a considerable reduction in the horizontal component of the earth's magnetism and an increase in the vertical component. The latter affected the compass through a part of the engine nearby and greatly magnified the deviation.

Such problems can be avoided by using a hand-bearing compass, which is read in an elevated position on deck, sufficiently far removed from the vessel's magnetic influences almost to eliminate deviation. It is

Plate 82: SCAMPI, *designed by the Swede Peter Norlin, has been very successful. A further development is the Norlin 37 shown here. You can see how the IOR Rating Rule not only allows, but positively encourages the design of attractive boats. The Norlin 37 is 36 ft 2 in long with a beam of 11 ft 10 in and a sail area of 645 sq ft.* *Photo: Solna Marin AB, Sweden*

possible to put the boat on course by using the hand-bearing compass, read off the course as indicated by the steering compass and maintain it. A hand-bearing compass is also used to take bearings to fix a yacht's position in coastal navigation.

If a vessel is out of sight of the coast, her position must be established by different means. Before the ship's chronometer was introduced, European seamen navigated by the 'Three L's': *latitude, lead* and *lookout.* Thanks to the fixed position of the Pole Star, indicating the celestial North Pole, it was possible to fix latitude fairly accurately even in the earliest days of navigation. Longitude was merely estimated on the basis of time sailed, and hence became more and more unreliable the further away a ship got from her home port.

Many yachtsmen dream of the day when all they will

need is a type of small receiver to get an accurate fix. They call it electronic navigation and argue that it will do away with all the complicated formulas and terms used in astro-navigation. But even today a ship's captain at sea uses a sextant every day to get an astronomical fix, because it is the most reliable of all known methods.

Anyone who goes to the trouble of acquainting himself with astro-navigation will be surprised how simple it really is, and how the precise knowledge of one's position at sea increases self-confidence. The most difficult part, which is spherical trigonometry, is supplied in ready-made tables. Any talented boy or girl of 15 can learn, in no more than 20 hours, how to take sun sights with a sextant and do the necessary calculations. After a few hours' routine practice the moon,

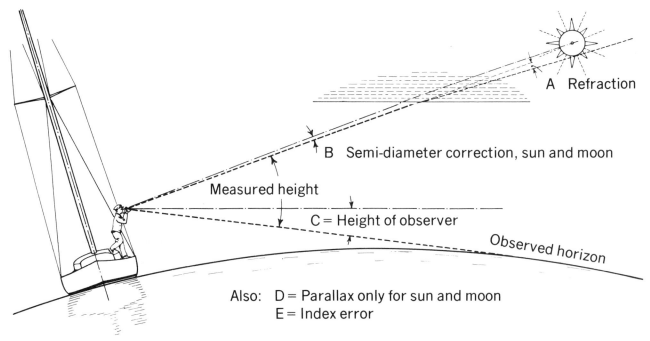

A Refraction

B Semi-diameter correction, sun and moon

Measured height

C = Height of observer

Observed horizon

Also: D = Parallax only for sun and moon
       E = Index error

Fig. 264: A sextant measures very accurately the angle between a heavenly body and the horizon. The result must subsequently be corrected for a number of variations, which have been illustrated here. The end result is the true angle between the centre of earth, centre of heavenly body and true horizon.

planets and stars can be embarked on. The tables required fall into two groups: the current edition of the annual Nautical Almanac, and secondly the Tables of Computed Altitude and Azimuth. The Nautical Almanac lists for each of 24 hours, on the hour, the position of sun, moon, planets and Aries. As with geographical positions, these positions are given in latitude and longitude, except that longitude is expressed by the Greenwich Hour Angle (GHA), which is the angle at the pole measured from the Greenwich meridian westerly round to 360°. Thus, the German island of Bornholm, which is latitude 15°E, would be GHA 345°. Celestial latitudes are expressed in degrees North and South. Time is, of course, GMT = Greenwich Mean Time. For each 15 degrees East the time is one hour earlier than Greenwich, every 15 degrees West is one hour later. Once the altitude of the heavenly body observed has been established by a sextant sight, and the approximate (dead reckoning) position of the yacht is known, the true altitude and eventually the latitude of the observer are calculated with the help of tables. The result is not, however, an exact position but a

position line, somewhere on which the ship must be situated.

The following tables are available: HO 249 of the US Hydrographic Office (English equivalent AP 3270), which lists, in two volumes, the most important latitudes and declinations up to 29 degrees, and in a third volume the computed calculations for the dawn and dusk observations of selected stars. These tables, which are published for Air Navigation, are much used by yachtsmen because of their compactness. Secondly, there is the slightly more extensive and more accurate publication called HO 214 (English equivalent HD 486), which lists all declinations applicable in practice. Each volume covers 10 degrees latitude, which means that the long-distance sailor needs 6 volumes. Finally, there is the most recent publication, HO 229, in which each volume covers 15 degrees of latitude, so that 4 volumes are needed for long-distance cruising. These tables are extremely accurate, much more accurate than is appropriate to a sextant sight.

Once, when we met Eric Hiscock in WANDERER IV in the South Pacific, during his third circumnavigation,

Plate 83: A pushpit gives good protection for the crew as can be seen here. This is the cockpit of the Contest 31HT. The roomy cockpit is well laid out with steering wheel, winches and mainsheet traveller.
Photo: Theo Kampa

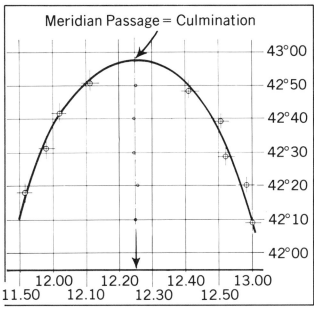

Fig. 265: A reasonably accurate fix, probably the simplest of all astronomical fixes, can be obtained by constructing a curve of the meridian passage of the sun. With practice and care it should be possible to determine the moment of culmination almost to the second. With the help of a nautical almanac the exact geographical position of the sun for that moment is found, and this, in turn, establishes the longitude of the ship's position. Latitude is found by applying a number of corrections plus the sun's declination to the observed meridian altitude. Many round-the-world sailors have relied solely on this simplified method. However, sextant sights are only accurate in reasonably calm weather.

he told us that he found his very old, small, English volume of tables more than adequate and that he needed none of these large, modern publications.

The sextant is simply an instrument for measuring angles, usually between the sea horizon and a heavenly body. Its use, too, would be very simple if the constant rolling and pitching of the yacht did not interfere with the taking of sights. A further problem is finding the actual horizon and not being misled by a higher ridge of waves in front of it. The sextant can measure angles up to 120 degrees, which are read straight off the arc, the minutes off the micrometer drum or, in older models, off the vernier with the help of a microscope.

It is by no means necessary to acquire a very expensive sextant. One of the many plastic sextants and octants on the market will give perfectly satisfactory results, especially for the beginner who wants to practise. An octant measures angles up to 90° and as such is quite adequate. At sea one should always carry two sextants on board. If the main instrument should be damaged or even go overboard, a relatively cheap plastic replacement kept as a spare will see one through.

Fred Rebell, this amazing and little known vagabond of the oceans, used the most primitive sextant which he had constructed himself; the arc was made of a toothed saw-blade!

Every measurement of the altitude of a heavenly body has to be accompanied by a *simultaneous* time check. There is no need for an expensive and delicate ship's chronometer; a good ship's clock or even a wrist watch is sufficient, as long as its accuracy is checked against a radio time signal every time before a sight is taken.

In conclusion I want to say a few words about electronic navigation instruments.

D/F SET (RADIO DIRECTION FINDER): This simple instrument is useful above all at night or in fog, as long as the boat is within range of a transmitter and no large land masses are in the path of the signal. Over a range in excess of about 100 miles the accuracy of the bearing can no longer be relied on. A D/F set suffers from errors in the same way as the compass; any metal fitting, such as the mast or the shrouds, can deflect the signal. The existence of errors on certain headings must be tabulated and allowed for in plotting bearings.

LORAN: This stands for 'long range navigation' and is an ocean radio aid, which requires a special, expensive receiver. Most Loran transmitting stations are sited on the American coasts, and they come in pairs, one being the 'master', the other the 'slave'. The difference in time of arrival of the pulses from each station is measured electronically, and the information is used to plot a position line on a special chart.

DECCA: This is a similar system to Loran but of British origin and with stations chiefly round the coasts of the British Isles, the North Sea and the Channel, but also in a growing number of localities abroad. It, too, requires a special receiver and chart.

CONSOLAN: This needs no special receiver other than a D/F set. Consolan stations send out a pattern of dots and dashes, the relative number and sequence of which will provide a line of position. This has to be crossed with another position line obtained from another station, or perhaps from a sextant sun sight, to get a fix.

A very simple method of position fixing, which has taken many a sailor right round the world, is to take a sun sight at the moment of the sun's meridian passage, i.e. a noon sight. One starts taking sights at regular intervals about half an hour prior to the sun's transit, and continues for half an hour after; from the sights taken a curve is constructed which gives the moment of transit with great accuracy. With the help of information taken from the Nautical Almanac latitude can then be calculated.

Plate 84: The Westerly Chieftain is a bilge keeler with an after cabin. She has comfortable accommodation in 26 ft 3 in with a beam of 8 ft 6 in, without unduly restricting the centre cockpit. It looks as though no one is steering because the wheel is mounted on the aft bulkhead. Designed by Laurent Giles & Partners. A sail area of 345 sq ft gives the boat a good performance. Builder: Westerly Marine, Portsmouth.

Photo: J A Harvey, Portsmouth

Electronic Instruments for Improved Performance

The previous chapter deals with *navigation* instruments, above all the compass and the sextant, which are used by the yachtsman to determine his course and find his position at sea. The present chapter will give a short survey of *electronic* instruments, whose function it is to improve sailing performance and safety. As such, they are of interest to the racing as well as the cruising fraternity.

Some of these instruments are capable of improving the precision of a helmsman's sailing technique to an amazing degree. Others scan the bottom of the sea and tell him how much water he has under the keel. In their entirety they are a kind of sixth sense, which complements the helmsman's natural intuition.

The classic wooden chip log and the improved patent log, both of them towed, have fallen more or less into dis-use. There are now electronic speedometers which do away with the need of towing a long line and which record distance as well as speed sailed. The 'feeler' is usually a small shaft projecting through the bottom of the hull at the end of which a small propeller is sited. As the vessel moves through the water, this rotates and the rotation is transmitted electronically to the recording instrument. The helmsman can read straight off a dial how the easing or sheeting in of the genoa, for example, affects the boat's speed. A number of speedometers record distance sailed at the same time, and this is particularly useful to the crusing navigator for establishing his daily run.

The instrument for measuring depth of water is known as the *depth sounder* or *echo sounder*. Echo sounders for yacht use normally have two scales, one for deep water (which, in British instruments is normally calibrated in fathoms), and one for shallow water, which gives accurate readings down to 2 feet or so. In the more sophisticated, recorder type of depth sounder a stylus traces a permanent record of the echos on paper. This is useful if one wants an overall picture of the seabed over which the boat has passed. This type of instrument is not much used on yachts, but it is normal equipment on larger fishing vessels.

Another very useful instrument is the compass repeater. Anyone who has steered a compass course knows how tiring it is to focus continually on the compass rose. A magnified compass course indicator can be the answer to this problem. The installation is simple: the steering compass drives a repeater, which is

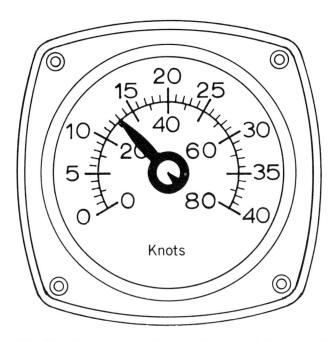

Fig. 266: The anemometer indicates the speed of the apparent wind. The instrument shown here has two scales, an outer one for normal wind strengths, and an inner one for gale and storm force winds.

a simple dial with a large pointer. As long as the yacht sails on the course set on the steering compass, the pointer of the repeater is at zero. Any deviation from course is clearly indicated by a swing of the pointer to port or starboard. In fine weather a scale is used which is graduated to 20° each to port and starboard, while the heavy-weather scale is graduated from 0° to 40° on either side. Such a repeater can be installed anywhere on board, and more than one repeater can be operated off the same master compass.

Next, we will consider briefly three instruments which measure aspects of the wind. When the yacht is underway, they measure, of course, the apparent wind.

To start with, there is the *anomometer* or *wind-speed indicator*. It consists of a rotor with conical cups attached at the ends of spokes, mounted at the masthead, which turns at a speed proportional to the speed of the wind. The indicator, mounted below, has either a single or a dual scale, one for moderate wind speeds, which goes up to say 25 knots, and another for gale force winds, which may go up to 90 knots. Once the helmsman knows the apparent wind speed and the

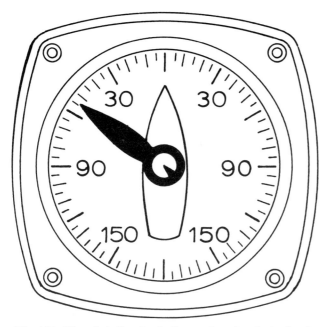

Fig. 267: The wind direction indicator gives the relative bearing between the yacht's heading and the apparent wind.

Fig. 268: The close-hauled apparent wind indicator is an instrument supplementary to the wind direction indicator, and no-one who has ever used one will want to do without it. It magnifies the scale from 0 to 40 or 45 degrees and thus gives a more accurate reading when sailing close-hauled. Some of these instruments reverse to read out downwind angles, in which case 0 degrees is dead astern.

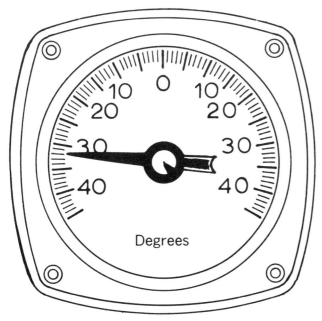

boat's speed, he can come to an intelligent guess as to the true wind. Such knowledge helps him to determine when to change No. 2 genoa for No. 1 genoa or working jib, when to reef the mainsail and when to hand the spinnaker.

The *wind direction indicator*, which measures the angle between the apparent wind and the boat's centre-line, uses a small wind vane, which is mounted at the masthead above the wind speed rotor. Only when the yacht is anchored or motoring can the indication be zero. On the wind, the indication is normally around 30°, port or starboard. The dial is graduated to 180° on either side, 180° being dead aft.

Since the graduation is necessarily small, having to cover a full 360 degrees, it is difficult to read it accurately on the wind, when the optimum angle is absolutely critical. And it is true to say that once a helmsman has got used to sailing by instruments he often loses his natural 'delicate touch'. Hence, for angles of incidence (of the apparent wind) of between 20° and 30° a special instrument with an expanded scale for that sector is needed. This is the so-called *close-hauled apparent wind indicator*, which is graduated from 0° to 40° or 50° off the bow on each side. This instrument is coupled to the main wind direction indicator.

Until not so long ago it was normal simply to watch for the mainsail and foresail luffs to lift, and meanwhile have nagging doubts about the correct position of the sheet leads. Nowadays helmsmen and crews of ocean-racing yachts will concentrate entirely on the readings of their instruments. The sheet leads are gradually moved, while the yacht maintains a steady, close-hauled course, until the speedometer indicates maximum speed. The angle of the apparent wind is then read off the wind direction indicator and recorded for future use under similar conditions.

It is not surprising to hear that the speedometer, too, can have an indicator with an expanded scale coupled to it. The expansion can be up to five times, so that even minimal changes in speed are recorded.

Larger racing yachts, above all IOR ocean racers, are now equipped with most or all of these instruments without exception. When COLUMBIA defended the America's Cup successfully in 1958 she caused something of a sensation by being the first yacht to have such instruments on board. Some time later, the 'black

Plate 85: A small British cruiser with the cabin carried out to the topsides. This is the Vivacity 650, which, for her size, has very good accommodation. The cockpit extends right aft to the transom. She is a twin bilge keeler, but can also be supplied with a fin keel. The good deck space is a useful working area and is surrounded by guard rails. A comfortable boat for a small family and especially suitable for the British market. LOA 21 ft 3 in, beam 7 ft 2 in, sail area 215 sq ft.

Builders: Russell Marine Ltd, Southend-on-Sea

box' came into use, which was a sort of electronic computer to convert speed sailed into speed made good to windward; this enabled the helmsman to decide instantaneously whether it paid to pinch the boat, or whether it would be profitable to sail freer but faster. These small computers were eventually banned from most races, not only because of their expense but also because they threatened to kill the helmsman's natural touch for good.

Many racing skippers make a habit of working out an 'operations manual', which can be drawn up with the help of the recording instruments just mentioned. It contains tabulated data on, say

(a) scale of true wind speeds
(b) the optimum sail combination for each wind speed
(c) the optimum sheet lead for each sail
(d) changes over the whole range of courses

Since a yacht on the wind is nearly always heeled, it is not uncommon for the larger ocean racers where cost is of little account, to install two sets of electronic instruments, one to port and one to starboard, usually in a vertical line. In this way the helmsman always has one set near him on the windward side. If there is only one set, it is normally arranged horizontally across the cabin top above the companionway.

It is somewhat surprising that repeater compasses coupled to the main steering compass are so rarely used. One or more can be installed at various strategic points like, for example, over the skipper's bunk. It is also possible in this way to install the main steering compass at a spot where it is far removed from all deviating influences. Another tempting possibility is to insert a corrector between main steering compass and repeater which compensates for both variation and deviation, so that the repeater compass actually indicates the true course.

Electronics is a fascinating and ever-expanding field, and we can expect that many new developments will find application in sailing.

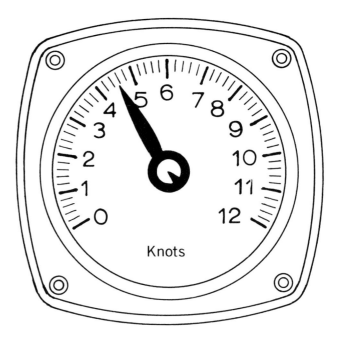

Fig. 269: The speedometer, an instrument of great value on any larger yacht, is usually operated by a small impeller installed in the bottom of the boat and projecting slightly. There are models which also indicate distance run and others which have an expanded scale for showing momentary changes in speed. These are particularly useful on racing yachts.

Synthetic Sail Cloths

When, a hundred years ago, the first cotton sails were made for large yachts, they aroused great admiration because of their flexibility, smoothness and light weight compared with the heavy flax sails hitherto used. One century has seen the advent, the predominance and the decline of King Cotton; it is so rare now to come across a cotton sail that many of the younger generation do not even know what one looks like.

When sails were still made from cotton, the panels were often cut straight and sewn together with parallel seams. The curvature was added by a roach along the foot and the luff, the fullness of which shifted quite naturally towards the middle of the sail, because the material stretches. By comparison polyester sailcloth (Terylene or Dacron) has no or very little give, and the curvature has to be built into the cut of each panel. The shape of the sail is predetermined, as though it were made of thin metal.

When a Terylene or Dacron sail is hoisted for the first time, it does not have to be put through the tiresome process of breaking in but can be used to the full from the first moment. Even then it is not advisable to put excessive strain on it to start with, not on account of the cloth itself but for the sake of the stitching, which is not embedded in the cloth as it used to be in cotton sails but sits on the surface and should be allowed to 'set' gradually.

The advantages of synthetics have long convinced every yachtsman. Many hours, which once had to be spent drying cotton sails, can now be spent actually sailing. Nobody worries any more about getting back to the mooring and having the sails down in a hurry before the evening damp gets into them. A cotton sail must on no account be put into the sail bag wet, because it would get stained by mildew in no time; besides, a wet cotton sail is liable to lose its shape for good. Cotton sails can absorb over 50 per cent of their own weight in moisture, polyester sails only 2 per cent. Nevertheless, Terylene and Dacron should not be stowed away in sail bags wet, either. But if they are left to dry loosely spread out in the fore cabin, they will not normally develop mildew. Mildew, contrary to common belief, can grow anywhere, even on glass, and it is therefore wise to let even polyester sails dry out thoroughly.

On any other account, though, synthetics will scarcely be affected by wet, nor will they lose their

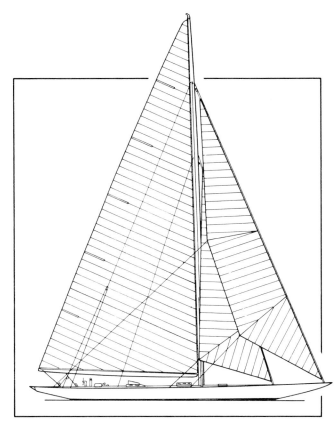

Fig. 270: Sail plan of the J-class yacht RAINBOW, *an America's Cup defender. These yachts were over 130 ft long and had a sail area of about 7550 sq ft.* RAINBOW *was designed by W Starling Burgess in 1934. She had a quadrilateral jib with two sheets and a very slightly overlapping staysail. Running backstays make up for the lack of a permanent backstay, which would be rather more common today.*

shape, and this in itself was enough reason for their rapid and general adoption. On long ocean races and in extended ocean cruising this advantage is of inestimable value. On top of that, yachts with Terylene and Dacron sails are also *faster*, so much so that during the transition period, boats with cotton sails were at a considerable disadvantage. In compiling the Portsmouth Yardstick it was found that Terylene or Dacron sails resulted in a 3 to 4 per cent increase in speed, which is equal to an increase in driving force of 7 to 10 per cent, which can mainly be attributed to reduced air friction on the sail surface.

The strength of the individual fibres from which a sail cloth is made determines the durability of the material. For some 50 years Egyptian cotton was considered best for sails, although the cotton fibre itself is only short. Polyester fibre can be extruded in endless lengths and is also stronger. The tensile strength of a thread is expressed by its 'breaking length', which indicates what length of thread would break under its own weight. The following table gives the breaking lengths in miles of some commonly used fibres:

Egyptian cotton	12·4 miles
Polyester fibre	28 miles
Nylon fibre	31 miles

Nylon has several disadvantages which makes it unsuitable for working sails. It is excessively elastic and is badly affected by ultra-violet radiation, so that every time it is exposed to sunlight it loses some of its strength. However, its elasticity and great strength make it very suitable for spinnakers. Over the years increasingly thinner and lighter nylon cloths for spinnakers have been made, right down to half-ounce. This would be used for an extremely light, ghosting spinnaker commonly called a floater. These very light-weight nylon cloths are not, of course, used for normal and heavy-weather sails.

A frequently discussed and never resolved point is the question of fillers and finishes applied to synthetic cloth. Fillers, which are pressed into the weave, are used to stabilize the cloth, i.e. eliminate any kind of stretch, while finishes or coatings are surface-applied and reduce the porosity of the material, making it smooth, shiny and water-repellent. The fact that both have been used from time to time to improve tem-porarily the appearance of poor-quality cloth has not enhanced their reputation.

Without a doubt, tightly woven polyester cloth without any filler or finish is far superior to anything ever previously used for making sails. The manufacture of such a cloth is expensive, and a great deal of research has gone into it, particularly on the part of ambitious sailmakers like the American Ted Hood. When, after long and painstaking experiments, he finally suc-ceeded in producing his own, super-tightly woven polyester cloth in narrow widths, it proved superior to any other sailcloth on the market. Meanwhile, other firms, too, are producing this type of cloth. As yacht designers are striving for constant improvement of hull design, so sailmakers aim to improve not only the cut of sails but also the materials from which they are made. Some very high-quality cloths are treated lightly with resin fillers; the important point here is that the filler must be sparingly applied and pressed very thoroughly into the weave.

Plate 86: *The motor sailer* TAHITIAN, *designed by New Zealander Richard Hartley, has a ferro-cement hull. Though the boat appears to have a motor sailer hull, the underwater sections are those of a true sailing boat. LOA 45 ft 3 in, beam 13 ft 6 in and a ketch rig of 1055 sq ft sail area.* Photo: Richard Hartley, NZ

Jeremy Howard-Williams, in his book *Dinghy Sails*, suggests the following procedure for testing the quality of sail cloth: 'Crumple a sample of cloth and then rub it back and forth between your hands as though washing it. You will soon see if there is a lot of loose filling in the material, for it will craze and possibly even flake off if it is bad.'

Finally, I must say a word about the compatibility of mast and mainsail, forestay and foresail. Since con-trollable mast bend is becoming more and more widespread and has even crept into the America's Cup races, every mainsail has to be cut so as to match exactly the amount of mast bend. This means that the mast bend has to be measured accurately and the sailmaker given the details when a new mainsail is ordered. He must also be told type and size of fitting at the tack and the type of mast groove, to make sure that the sail fits at those critical points, which is by no means always the case.

When cutting a foresail, every sailmaker allows for a certain slackness in the forestay. If a mast is so rigidly stayed that no slack occurs in the stay, the sailmaker must be told so. Conversely, if the slack in the forestay is more than average, he must equally be acquainted of that fact so that he can allow for it when cutting the sail.

The invention of synthetic fibres has been a boon to yachting. No longer is it necessary, when making a long passage, to cram a spare suit of sails into a ship already overloaded with gear, food and drinking water. The life of polyester sails is approximately three to four times that of cotton, so that spare sails for long voyages are needed only in exceptional cases. The fact that this makes polyester sails less costly in the long run is another welcome aspect.

Conventional and Modern Building Materials

Industry in general and boatbuilding in particular are currently at a stage of development where synthetic building materials are starting to outweigh natural ones to a considerable extent. Natural timber is only used for the sake of its warm feel and appearance. The fibres used for sailcloth, upholstery and floor covering are all synthetic. But when we look back over the history of ship and boatbuilding we find that wood has probably played the most important role. True, the first iron ship was built over 150 years ago, but even in the period from 1940 to 1945 a large number of surprisingly large naval vessels were built of wood, not counting the ultra-light, fast torpedo boats. The largest wooden ship ever built was the VICTORIA of the Royal Navy, which was built in 1859 and had a displacement of 6000 tons.

As a material for ship and boatbuilding, wood has a number of outstanding advantages, although it has a few drawbacks as well. If it is well looked after it can have a surprisingly long life. All over the world wooden yachts, which were built before the turn of the century, are still in commission. A fairly large wooden yacht, well built and maintained, should have a life of at least 40 years; this means an annual depreciation of only $2\frac{1}{2}$ per cent. The first of the larger yachts built at my own yard, all of them between 50 ft and 60 ft (15·5–18 m), are still in such good condition after 30 years that they will certainly outlast the average 40 years.

In this chapter I want to give a short survey of five different materials, all of which will have a part in boatbuilding in the future:

> Natural solid timber
> Composite woods like marine plywood and moulded laminates
> Metals, chiefly steel and aluminium alloys
> Synthetic resins, i.e. glassfibre reinforced polyester
> Ferro-concrete, also called ferro-cement

SOLID TIMBER

Solid timber, which has been an admirable material for boatbuilding for so long, is as imperfect as it is natural. Many different species of trees yield an impressive variety of timbers, but on the whole, and especially in tropical countries, not nearly as many trees are planted as are felled. Different types of wood differ in structure, weight, colour, strength, flexibility, durability, resistance to rot, shrinkage and warping. There are differences within the same species and even within wood off

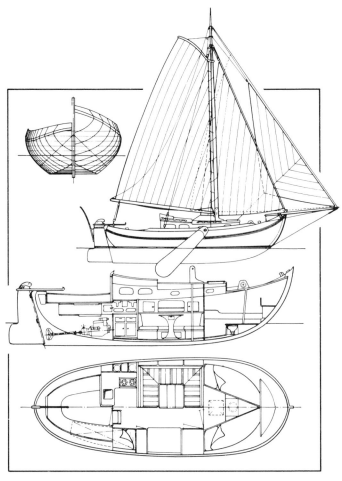

Fig. 271: Like all Dutch yachts, the botter was originally built in wood, later in steel. All botters have flat bottoms to enable them to take the ground in tidal waters. For sailing on the wind they have leeboards. As the name suggests, the leeward one is lowered when sailing to windward.

LOA	26 ft 6 in	Draft,	
LWL	23 ft	boards down	4 ft 2 in
Beam	10 ft	Displacement,	
Draft,		approx.	4·8 ton
boards up	2 ft 3 in	Sail area	450 sq ft

the same tree.

Wood is the only building material which is buoyant in itself. Unfortunately it also absorbs water, and hence changes shape between being wet and being dry.

Before being used for boatbuilding, timber has to be stored for many years to allow it to dry and become seasoned. It is then carefully selected, piece by piece; faulty material is rejected and different runs of grain selected for particular purposes. It takes trained craftsmen to make a perfect job of timber in boatbuilding, but simplified methods can be tackled by the skilful amateur builder.

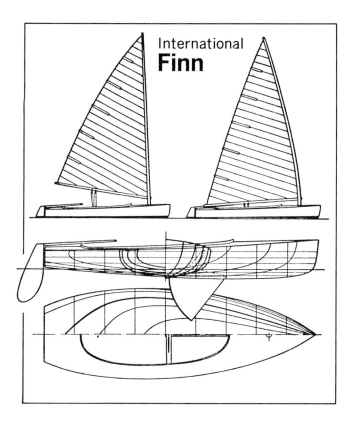

Fig. 272: When the Finn became the Olympic one-man class in 1952, fibreglass was not yet an established building material. Like the Firefly, which was the Olympic one-man class in 1948, the Finn originally had a hot-moulded, laminated wooden hull, which is very light. This building method is very sound, but the life expectancy of the hull, especially if the shell is rather thin, does not match that of the GRP hulls now available.

LOA	14 ft 9 in	Draft, plate up	7 in
LWL	13 ft 3 in	Draft, plate down	2 ft 9 in
Beam	5 ft	Sail area	108 sq ft

Plate 87: A small ferro-cement motor sailer designed by Richard Hartley. She is only 27 ft 3 in long with a beam of 9 ft and a draft of 3 ft 9 in. Even when the boats are built by amateurs, experts are called in to lay-up the hull.   Photo: Richard Hartley, NZ

COMPOSITE WOODS

Shrinkage and swelling can be eliminated if thin layers of wood are glued on top of each other across the grain. The invention of synthetic resin glues shortly before World War II has led to the production of marine plywood for boatbuilding, and has also made it possible to mould complete round-bilge hulls from several thin laminations of wood.

Marine plywood, which is usually made with phenol formaldehyde glue, has a number of useful characteristics. It is much stronger than solid timber and neither warps nor shrinks. High-grade marine plywood should have no flaws or unevennesses. Since it comes in standard sheet sizes it can be used with hardly any waste. The simplicity of using it when building large areas like decks, floors and bulkheads considerably reduces labour costs.

Techniques of building in plywood have been steadily improved over the years. While at one time plywood boats could only be built with flat bottoms and sides, it is now possible, by means of the so-called 'conical projection', to produce shapes of amazing perfection.

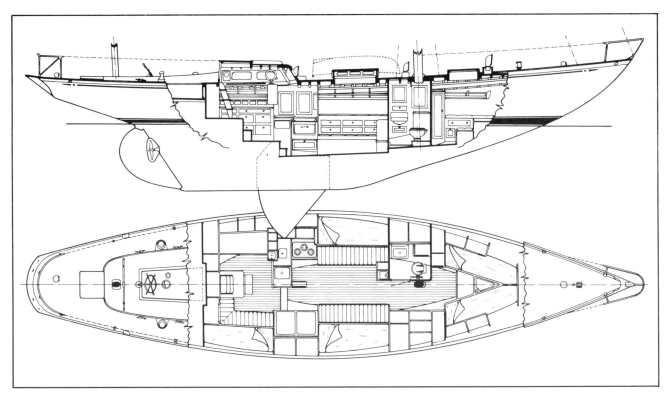

Fig. 273: Accommodation plan of the well-known ocean-racer CARINA, whose sail plan is reproduced in Fig. 76. Large ocean racers are nowadays built in any of a number of materials: solid timber, laminated wood, rarely steel, more frequently aluminium alloy, fibreglass sandwich or simply fibreglass. Ferro-cement has been used for yachts of up to 65 ft and even above, but it is suitable only for pure cruising yachts, because it results in heavy, relatively slow hulls.

Even rounded shapes to any specification can be turned out since techniques of cold-moulding-and-glueing have been perfected. One method is to cover one skin of narrow plywood panels, laid either fore-and-aft or up-and-down, with another one in which the panels overlap the seams in the first skin. Clinker-building with plywood panels is also common.

The lightness of plywood makes it very suitable for planing dinghies and fast, planing motorboats. Even sailing yachts of considerable size have been built in plywood.

Another way in which a wooden hull of practically any desired shape can be produced is to laminate it. In this process panels of $\frac{1}{8}$ in (3 mm) wood veneer are laid diagonally over a mould, which can be solid or skeletal. On top of this another layer of veneer is glued diagonally across the first layer. Sometimes a third and fourth layer is applied, depending on the size of hull. Larger hulls are frequently sheathed with fibreglass. Un-

fortunately this method is often referred to as cold-moulded plywood, which is wrong, because the material used is not plywood but veneers of solid timber.

METAL

In some countries, especially Holland and Germany, the building of even small yachts in steel has been developed to some perfection. Steel, like other materials, has advantages and drawbacks, but in practice it has been shown that hulls as small as 20 ft (6 m) and if necessary even down to 12 or 13 ft (3·5 or 4 m) can be built in steel. But the building of small hulls, say up to 65 ft (20 m), in steel requires specialized skill and craftsmanship, and cannot be compared with what goes on in shipyards which turn out large iron ships.

The tendency of steel to rust can be countered in two ways. Firstly, there are now types of steel for boat-building with a much reduced tendency to rusting, and secondly there are epoxy-tar paints, which are ex-

Plate 88: Two hulls in the yard of a builder specializing in ferro-cement, Ferro Craft Marine, Greenhithe. Designed by Larry Davidson they are 40 ft long with a beam of 13 ft and a draft of 6 ft 6 in. The steel framework is built with the keel uppermost, then turned over to be coated with concrete. The boat on the right has its initial outer coating of concrete.

Photo: National Publicity Studios, NZ

ceptionally adhesive. Before application, the hull must be sand-blasted. Zinc-spraying, by comparison, has proved less satisfactory. But even before the advent of any of these protective paints and processes a 2 to 3 mm ($\frac{1}{8}$ in) steel hull could have a life of 30 years or longer, if it was well looked after.

Small steel hulls are heavier than equivalent wooden hulls. Aluminium alloy, on the other hand, is about as light as plywood and has all the advantages of metal: it does not swell or shrink and it does not open up if it dries out ashore. The greatest drawback of aluminium alloys is their tendency to corrode through galvanic action, and also the higher costs, which are between 20 and 30 per cent above those for a steel hull.

GRP = GLASSFIBRE REINFORCED POLYESTER

During the last war a synthetic resin was invented in the United States, which has had a revolutionary effect on boatbuilding. This material, which has become known as polyester, was used for making radar housings for bomber planes, after metal housings had caused excessive interference.

Polyester resin possesses the valuable property of hardening spontaneously without the application of heat or pressure. The amount of heat generated by the chemical reaction is so small that it is hardly noticeable in practice.

The hardened resin by itself is brittle and has no tensile strength, but if it is reinforced with glassfibre it results in a material which is strong, resilient and flexible and has a very long life. It is known in the USA as FRP, short for fibreglass (or fiberglass) reinforced polyester.

GRP hulls are not built but moulded, which means that initially a mould has to be produced. For this reason fibreglass can only compete in price with conventional building materials if the cost of one mould

377

can be spread over a large number of hulls. But the material has a number of outstanding qualities, which have made it universally popular in a very short time. By contrast with wood, plywood or metal it can be moulded into absolutely any shape. Hulls can be made in one piece, without seams and joints that could leak. Heat, cold, drought or damp cannot affect it in any way. It is completely impermeable to water, cannot be corroded in sea water and is not attacked by teredo. Decks and superstructure, too, can be moulded in one piece and thus be completely watertight.

Fibreglass has proved very resilient. If it is involved in accidents, the damage is usually very much lighter than it would have been to a wooden hull in comparable circumstances. It is important, though, that a fibreglass hull be made of an adequate thickness and that the glass content is *as large as possible*. It is the fibres of glass which take the strain, the function of the polyester resin being to hold them together. As ever, top quality hulls can be built to Lloyd's specification.

It should be mentioned that one-offs can be built in fibreglass without the cost of making first a male and then a female mould. I am thinking of the hand-lamination method, in which a wooden structure, which forms the outline of the hull and is positioned keel up, is first covered with sheets of polyurethane foam and then with an outer skin of fibreglass amounting to 60 per cent of the total specified thickness of the hull. The hardened shell is lifted off the wooden structure and the remaining 40 per cent of GRP thickness applied to the inside. At my own yard we have built boats in this 60/40 method by using a thin, cold-moulded plywood hull, which was GRP-covered inside and out. The method has proved unexpectedly successful, and it has also been established that sound wood embedded in fibreglass remains sound for a very long time.

FERRO-CEMENT

Seen through the eyes of the conventional boatbuilder, ferro-cement is an alien material. The now-current thin-wall method of building ferro hulls, which has nothing to do with the World War I concept of concrete shipbuilding, was pioneered by Professor Luigi Nervi, an Italian architect and yachtsman, who built himself a much-acclaimed 47-ft (15-m) sailing yacht in 1947. However, Nervi's idea was not widely taken up until around 1960, when interest revived in New Zealand due to a temporary shortage of good boatbuilding timber. The New Zealand Forestry Commission at that time prohibited the felling of Kauri trees in order to protect the dwindling stock of this valuable timber. Consequently, there was a reversion to Nervi's method, and the New Zealanders, who are traditionally do-it-yourself enthusiasts, started building their cruising boats in ferro-cement. The method involves making a frame of iron pipe, reinforced with closely-spaced lengths of welding rod. This is covered inside and out with anything up to four layers of chicken wire mesh, wired together and moulded into shape. This carefully prepared framework is then covered on both sides with concrete aggregate, usually by a skilled labour force. The normal hull thickness is about $\frac{3}{4}$ in (19 mm). It is easy to make hulls of greater thickness but almost impossible to get below $\frac{3}{4}$ in (19 mm) and still finish up with a reliable skin. Australian boatbuilders have succeeded in building ferro-cement dinghy hulls only $\frac{1}{4}$ in (6 mm) thick, but their strength and durability are questionable. It has happened that such 'eggshell hulls' have simply broken up in a seaway.

Ferro-cement can be considered a useful boatbuilding material in places where there is a shortage of timber and where other materials and methods are inaccessible. One must not be misled, however, into thinking that this method is either particularly cheap or particularly simple. Many amateur efforts have been abandoned in the face of excessive problems and excessive cost. The hull itself represents only 20 per cent of the total cost of a boat, and very little of this is saved by the method. If a professional labour force is used, nothing at all is saved, because the manual labour involved is considerable.

There are advantages to ferro-cement, which make it attractive: it is fire-proof, it does not corrode and it does not rot. But there are drawbacks too, quite apart from the increased weight. It is impossible to check, once the hull is completed, whether the aggregate was the best, whether the sand was salt-free and of good quality, and whether there are no voids in the concrete. Anyone who wants to sell a used ferro-cement boat will be shocked, for the second-hand price is unexpectedly low and bears no relation to the actual cost of the boat. Anyone who does decide on ferro-cement construction, for whatever reason, is strongly advised not to try and do his own thing but to get plans and instructions from

Plate 89: A special layer of fine concrete is laid over the outside of a carefully prepared steel reinforcement consisting of frames, stringers and inner and outer layers of wire netting. Two weeks later an inner layer of concrete is put on. For medium-sized boats a hull thickness of ¾ in (20 mm) is built up. Other manufacturers perform the laying-up operation in one with equal numbers of workers inside and outside the hull. Only experienced craftsmen can achieve a bubble-free outer skin.

Photo: NZ Ferro-Cement Marine Assoc.

experts in this field, most of whom are probably to be found in New Zealand.

The following table compares the different materials used in boatbuilding. The thicknesses quoted are average, and ferro-cement was included only for weight-comparison. The given thickness of ⅜ in is purely academic and does not really occur in practice.

	Specific weight	Comparative thickness	Weight per sq ft
Solid timber	0·7	½ in	1·72 lb
Plywood	0·6	⅓ in	0·98 lb
Fibreglass	1·6	⅙ in	1·31 lb
Aluminium alloy	2·7	⅛ in	1·25 lb
Steel	7·8	1/16 in	2·40 lb
Ferro-cement	2·6	⅜ in	5·32 lb

Auxiliary Engines in Sailing Yachts

The use of an auxiliary engine distinguishes the large number of cruising boats from the pure racing machines. Although the purist resents the use of mechanical propulsion, the advantages of an auxiliary are undeniable. With it, one can get home in a calm, the batteries can be charged, and not infrequently its timely use can prevent a collision or even save the boat from running aground and breaking up in a storm.

The modern marine engine, expertly installed, needs little care and maintenance to ensure efficient operation. It is of small consequence whether one chooses a petrol or a diesel engine; both can be equally reliable. The diesel engine has the advantage of using a fuel which does not make an explosive mixture. Its disadvantages, which are steadily being diminished by design developments, are greater weight, larger size, more noise and more vibration.

The petrol engine has really only one disadvantage: the fuel it uses is explosive. If such an engine is installed, great care has to be taken to ensure that no fuel should leak into the boat. Unfortunately, there is still no such thing as a properly marinized carburettor, and the dangers of a dripping fuel feed can only be minimized by fitting a fireproof drip container underneath it. On the whole, whenever possible, a modern small diesel engine should be installed.

Boats of less than 23 ft (7 m) in length can be adequately driven by an outboard motor. Although, in theory, even larger craft could use one, their higher freeboard and the greater weight of the motor make installation and handling difficult.

In most boats the engine is fitted below the waterline, so that careful attention has to be given to the installation of the exhaust pipe, through which water might get into the engine; if the silencer is sufficiently high, it can be made to act as a trap. But condensation can run back and enter the engine through an open exhaust valve even after the motor has been stopped. The exhaust exit itself must be so situated that toxic fumes cannot find their way into the cabin; a number of tragic accidents have occurred in this way. If water is injected into the silencer, it cools the exhaust gases and at the same time reduces the noise; the pipe between the engine and the silencer should be cooled by a water-jacket.

The fuel tank has to be made and installed with great care, especially if it holds petrol. Where the filler spout comes through the deck the joint has to be gas-tight, preferably by a short length of butyl rubber pipe. A breather pipe or air vent must be fitted to the tank, for without it the fuel would not flow. Its exit should be at a suitably elevated position on deck so that, even if the boat heels violently, fuel cannot escape and water cannot get in.

Salt water attacks not only all the metal parts of the engine but also destroys electrical insulation in the engine and other electrical installations on board. High humidity combined with salt in the air often causes the battery to leak its charge away.

The propeller-shaft should only be made of high-grade material. On sailing yachts it is usually very short and not a particularly expensive item; stainless steel or monel metal are best. So-called sea water-resistant bronze alloys are often attacked by galvanic action, despite their name, and quickly shows signs of corrosion near the stern gland.

How can the output needed from an auxiliary engine be calculated? It is not usual to work out detailed mathematical resistance/propulsion computations, because the premises on which these have to be based are rather feeble. To help the owner in his deliberations the graph in Fig. 274 and the table at the end of this chapter have been drawn up.

In many cases the speed under power is not expected to match the speed which can be reached under sail in a good breeze. On the other hand one must not forget that a modest engine output will not be sufficient in a gale or heavy sea. A Dragon needs an engine output of 10 to 12 hp to reach the same speed under power as it reaches, on average, under sail. But even with an output of only 2 hp it would reach the appreciable speed of $2\frac{1}{2}$ knots in calm weather.

Any simplified engine-output computation does not allow for the degree of propeller efficiency. If the shaft turns at high revolutions, even the best propeller will be inefficient. It is not possible here to go into this question of optimum revolutions without embarking in great detail on the whole subject of propeller computation. Hence, the graph refers to 'medium propeller revolution'.

The graph in Fig. 274 is a very good guide to required engine output. It is graded into three curves: on the right is the curve for minimum engine output, on the left the curve for maximum effective engine output,

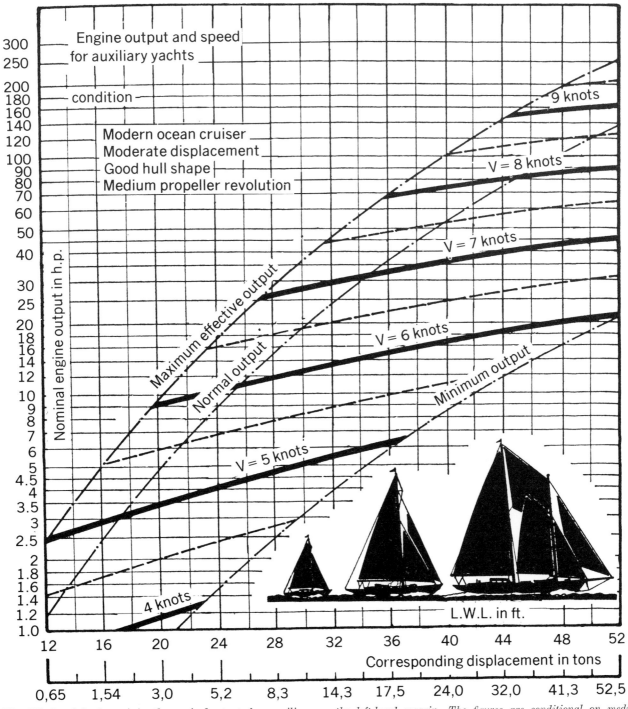

Engine output and speed for auxiliary yachts

condition

Modern ocean cruiser
Moderate displacement
Good hull shape
Medium propeller revolution

9 knots

V = 8 knots

V = 7 knots

V = 6 knots

Maximum effective output

Normal output

Minimum output

V = 5 knots

4 knots

Nominal engine output in h.p.

L.W.L. in ft.

Corresponding displacement in tons

| 12 | 16 | 20 | 24 | 28 | 32 | 36 | 40 | 44 | 48 | 52 |

| 0,65 | 1,54 | 3,0 | 5,2 | 8,3 | 14,3 | 17,5 | 24,0 | 32,0 | 41,3 | 52,5 |

Fig. 274: Graph for determining the required output of an auxiliary engine, valid for medium-displacement cruising boats. For any given LWL, see lower edge of graph, the required speed is found on one of the curves and the necessary engine output read off along the left-hand margin. The figures are conditional on medium propeller revolutions, possibly achieved by a reduction gear, and optimum propeller efficiency.

Plate 90: A true cruising boat sailing to windward. She is technically rigged as a ketch, but the sail area of the mizzen is scarcely larger than on a yawl. The jib is rigged on a boom so that it needs no attention when the yacht is tacked. SYLTU was designed by John Atkin, Darien, with a transom-hung rudder and has the following dimensions: LOA 35 ft 6 in, LWL 31 ft, beam 10 ft 6 in, draft 4 ft 7 in, sail area 484 sq ft. Photo: Morris Rosenfeld

---

REQUIRED OUTPUT OF AUXILIARY ENGINE
in relation to working sail area

To reach half the normal speed under sail

1 hp per 110 sq ft (10 m²)

To reach three-quarters of the normal speed under sail

1 hp per 55 sq ft (5 m²)

To reach the same average speed as under sail

1 hp per 27 sq ft (2·5 m²)

To have ample power reserve, and for motor sailers

1 hp per 10 sq ft (1 m²)

and between them the curve for normal engine output. The term *maximum effective output* means that a normal yacht then reaches the limits of her inherent speed potential and will not go faster even with increased drive. Any engine output in excess of this will only result in increased wavemaking.

If the LWL of the yacht in question does not correspond to the displacement as given in the graph, it is nevertheless the yacht's LWL on which the reading of the graph has to be based and the output, as read off the left-hand margin, has to be proportionally increased or decreased. For example, a yacht with a LWL of 28 ft (8 m) needs a normal engine output of 15 hp if her displacement is 8·3 tons. A lighter built vessel with the same LWL but a displacement of only 7 tons would need an engine with an output of $15 \times \dfrac{7}{8·3} = 12·6$ hp and reach the same speed of about $6\frac{1}{4}$ knots.

The table in the left hand column looks at the question from a different angle. Since every square foot of sail area produces a certain amount of drive, which depends on the wind and which can be calculated, the required engine output can be determined in relation to the sail area. This makes the table valid for any kind of sailing boat, from the ocean racer to the pocket cruiser.

An engine requires the same loving care and maintenance as the hull and the sails; it should be kept clean, free of rust and well ventilated; it should be so installed that it is easy to check the oil level and change the oil; the stern gland of the propeller shaft should also be reasonably accessible so that the packing can be renewed when necessary; it must also be possible to make adjustments to the gears without resorting to acrobatics. If every part of the engine is easily accessible, maintenance is made easier and the engine is better looked after. Fuel filters must be cleaned or changed from time to time, batteries must be checked and topped up. Trouble taken with an engine is repaid by it many times over. Not only does its smooth running constitute a safety factor but it provides a number of amenities on board which rely on the availability of electricity. There is hardly a cruising boat nowadays which does not have an engine.

Propellers for Sailing Yachts

On the whole, a sailing yacht uses her engines only when wind and sails do not provide sufficient or sufficiently adaptable propulsion: when entering or leaving congested harbours and anchorages, when manoeuvring in narrow channels, or when becalmed. For the rest of the time, when the engine is not in use, the propeller merely causes additional resistance. This can be quite appreciable or it can be almost imperceptible, depending on the type and size of the propeller and the way it is installed.

FIXED OR MOVING PROPELLER BLADES: A propeller with fixed blades will normally cause more resistance under sail than one in which the blades can be set at different angles or folded back. In the *feathering propeller* the blades can be angled for forward, reverse and neutral drive, and also for a sailing position, which causes the least possible resistance. A further advantage of the feathering propeller is the fact that it requires no reverse gear to the engine, but under power it is inferior to the normal, fixed-bladed propeller. It also requires a hollow shaft, which takes the blade adjusting mechanism, and for the same reason it has a very thick hub. In rivers and estuaries sand or other small particles in suspension sometimes get into the boss and jams the mechanism. On the whole, the *folding propeller* has proved most satisfactory on sailing yachts. In the sailing position, the blades fold back almost by themselves, aided only by the flow of water, and they open as soon as the engine starts to turn the shaft.

CENTRE OR QUARTER INSTALLATION: If the fitting of an auxiliary engine is planned from the beginning, it is undoubtedly advisable to install the propeller on the centreline rather than through the quarter. In the centre it will cause the least resistance, while on the quarter the current is stronger and hence the resistance greater; installation through the quarter is thus only recommended if, for some reason, the deadwood cannot be drilled to accommodate the shaft. To minimize resistance, propeller, shaft diameter and shaft bracket have to be kept as small as possible. The effect of one-sided propulsion can be compensated by installing a clockwise propeller on the port side and an anti-clockwise propeller on the starboard side.

In the case of a centre installation the aperture for the propeller should encroach as little as possible on the rudder but be cut largely out of the deadwood.

TWO- OR THREE-BLADED PROPELLER: Nearly all folding or feathering propellers installed in sailing boats are two-bladed. Motor vessels generally use three-bladed screws with fixed blades because of their superior performance. The aim in a sailing boat is normally to incur the least resistance under sail. Unfortunately a two-bladed propeller, whether fixed or adjustable, often gives rise to unpleasant vibration under power, which is caused by both blades passing simultaneously through the dead water behind the stern post. For this reason a three-bladed screw is installed in all cases where power is considered more important than sail, and where maximum drive is required for working off dangerous coasts.

FIXED OR FREE-ROTATING PROPELLER: If, under sail, the propeller rotates freely at the same revolutions that would be necessary to drive the vessel under power at the same speed, there should, in theory, be no resistance. For this ideal to be approached, the propeller and its shaft would have to be extremely free-rotating. In practice, this is prevented by friction in the stern gland, in the bearings and through partial contact of the clutch plates inside the gear box. If the engine is fitted with a reduction gear, which cannot be driven from the propeller end since the reduction would become reversed, the propeller has to be fixed in the least damaging position or the shaft must be fitted with its own clutch, by which it can be disengaged.

Since, in practice, free rotation is doubtful, a propeller will always turn more slowly than it should. In fact, it might cause as much resistance as a fixed propeller. On the whole, the following combinations are recommended:

two-bladed propeller, central . . . . . fixed
three-bladed propeller, central . . . . free-rotating
two-bladed propeller, off-centre . . . free-rotating
three-bladed propeller, off-centre . . free-rotating

If a rotating propeller is very stiff, there is no point in letting it rotate. So that the propeller can be fixed with the blades in the optimum position, a mark should be applied to the propeller shaft inboard at the appropriate point. Better still would be a device for automatically blocking the shaft in the correct position, but

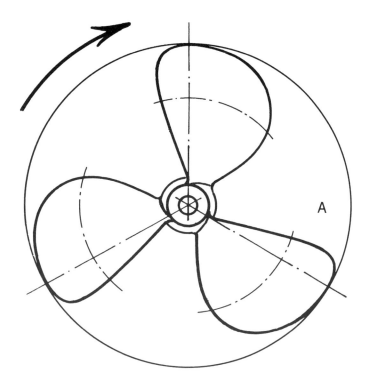

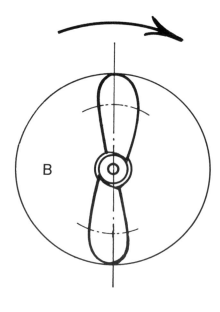

Fig. 275: Both propellers shown here take the same engine output but do not give the same speed under power. The large, three-bladed propeller A runs at 1000 rpm. It pushes the boat faster but causes considerable resistance under sail. The small, two-bladed propeller B turns at 2500 rpm, is much less efficient but causes practically no resistance under sail.

this would, of course, have to be released before the engine is started.

LOWER EFFICIENCY, LESS RESISTANCE: In a sailing yacht it is not normally imperative to install a propeller with a view to optimum efficiency, because the engine is only used occasionally and for short periods. It is, therefore, of advantage to install a propeller of lower efficiency, if it causes less resistance under sail.

Both propellers illustrated in Fig. 275 can take up the same engine output, but at different revolutions. While the large propeller is designed to run at 1000

rpm, the smaller has to run at 2500 rpm to give the same output. In a case like this the owner has to decide whether he prefers improved performance under sail even though the small, high-revving propeller will give him about 10 per cent less power when motoring.

But even a relatively low-revving propeller can be made to suit the special requirements of a sailing yacht. If, for example, the optimum diameter is reduced by 15 per cent, the pitch has to be increased by 20 per cent for the screw to take up the same output from the engine. This results in a 2 per cent loss of speed under power, but both the reduced diameter and the increased pitch will lead to improved performance under sail.

Plate 91: A modern offshore boat sailing perfectly on a calm sea with an ideal breeze. D'ARTAGNAN, a Dufour 35, was built in France. She is 35 ft 3 in long, with a beam of 11 ft 6 in and a working sail area of 614 sq ft.   Photo: Erwan Quemere-Marina

Appendix I
Normal Ground Tackle for Racing and Cruising Yachts

NORMAL GROUND TACKLE FOR AVERAGE CRUISERS AND RACERS

The following figures are a general guide in cases where neither class rules nor local experience suggest otherwise.

LWL

Heavy Yacht	16	19	23	26	29	32	36	39 ft
Light Yacht	19	23	26	29	34	39	42	46 ft

ANCHOR AND CHAIN

Fisherman's Anchor	26	33	40	46	55	66	83	105 lb
Danforth Anchor	11	13	15	18	22	28	35	44 lb
Length of Chain	11	14	17	20	23	26	30	33 fath
Diameter of Chain Links	$\frac{1}{4}$	$\frac{5}{16}$	$\frac{5}{16}$	$\frac{3}{8}$	$\frac{3}{8}$	$\frac{7}{16}$	$\frac{7}{16}$	$\frac{1}{2}$ in

    Light kedge anchor for short mooring periods in fine weather: 50 per cent of above weights.

    Heavy anchor for bad weather: 50 per cent heavier than above.

    If an anchor line or steel wire rope is used, the weight of the anchor should be increased by 25 per cent.

ANCHOR WARP

Synthetic Fibre (dia)	$\frac{7}{16}$	$\frac{1}{2}$	$\frac{9}{16}$	$\frac{5}{16}$	$\frac{11}{16}$	$\frac{3}{4}$	$\frac{7}{8}$	$\frac{7}{8}$ in
Length	14	17	22	25	28	33	38	43 fath

    A similar line should be kept on board for towing.

MOORING LINES

    2 mooring lines whose length should be the same as the yacht's LOA and whose diameter is 25 per cent less than the anchor line.

    2 further mooring lines whose length should be three-quarters of the yacht's LOA and whose diameter is 40 per cent less than the anchor warp.

WIRE ROPE FOR KEDGE ANCHOR

Length: same as the length of anchor line.

Diameter: same as the diameter of chain links.

Material: stainless steel, if possible.

Appendix II
Conversion Table for Weights and Measures

CUBIC MEASURE

1 cubic inch	16·387 cm³
1 cubic foot	28·316 cm³
1 imperial gallon	4·546 dm³
1 US gallon	3·785 dm³
1 pint = $\frac{1}{8}$ US gallon	0·473 dm³
1 registered ton	2·832 m³

WEIGHTS

1 ounce	28·35 g
1 pound	453·60 g
1 short ton	907·20 kg
1 long ton	1016·00 kg

COMPOSITE

1 ounce/sq yd	33·907 g/m²
1 ounce/sq ft	305 g/m²
1 pound/sq in	0·0703 kg/m²

TEMPERATURE

0° C	32° Fahrenheit
10° C	50° F
20° C	68° F
50° C	122° F
100° C	212° F

LINEAR MEASURE

1 inch	25·4 mm
1 foot	304·8 mm
1 yard	914·4 mm
1 fathom	1·829 m
1 statute mile	1609·3 m
1 nautical mile	1852·0 m

SQUARE MEASURE

1 square inch	6·452 cm²
1 square foot	0·093 m²
1 square yard	0·836 m²

SPEEDS

1 ft/sec	1·097 km/h
1 mph	1·609 km/h
1 knot = 1 nautical mile/h	1·852 km/h
1 knot = 0·514 m/sec	1·686 ft/sec

OUTPUT

1 PS = 736 Watt

1 HP = 746 Watt

1 HP = 1·4% more than 1 PS

PHYSICAL PROPERTIES OF WATER AND AIR

Density ρ of water, normal	1·94 lb sec²/ft⁴
Density ρ of air, normal	0·0024 lb sec²/ft⁴
Kinematic viscosity γ of water, normal	0·0000125 ft²/sec
Kinematic viscosity γ of air, normal	0·000157 ft²/sec
Average specific gravity of sea water	64·0 lb/cu ft

35 cubic feet of sea water weigh 1 long ton = 2240 lb

36 cubic feet of fresh water weigh 1 long ton = 2240 lb

VARIOUS FIGURES

1 nautical mile is the length of a minute of arc of a circle of the earth, measured at the equator = 6080 feet.

The earth in its rotation passes through one degree of longitude every 4 minutes or through one minute of arc every 4 seconds.

The polar axis is 27 miles shorter than the equatorial axis.

The spacing of knots on a traditional log line for measuring the speed of a boat should be 48 ft 3 in for use with a 30 second sand glass, or 23 ft 7 in for use with a 14 second sand glass.

Index